Social Work Practice

A CANADIAN PERSPECTIVE

Second Edition

Edited by
Francis J. Turner

Prentice
Hall

Toronto

*To my sisters and brothers, whose support and
interest over the years have been unflagging.*

National Library of Canada Cataloguing in Publication Data

Main entry under title:
  Social work practice : a Canadian perspective

2nd ed.
Includes index.
ISBN 0-13-041394-1

1. Social service — Canada. I. Turner, Francis, J. (Francis Joseph), 1929– .

HV40.S67 2002   361.3'2'0971   C2001-901331-0

ISBN 0-13-041394-1

Vice-President, Editorial Director: Michael Young
Editor-in-Chief: David Stover
Acquisitions Editor: Jessica Mosher
Marketing Manager: Judith Allen
Associate Editor: John Polanszky
Production Editor: Joe Zingrone
Copy Editor: Tara K. Tovell
Production Manager: Wendy Moran
Page Layout: Heidi Palfrey
Art Director: Mary Opper
Cover Design: Alex Li
Cover Image: Copyright © Digital Vision Ltd.

1 2 3 4 5   05 04 03 02

Printed and bound in Canada.

Contents

Preface

It is only a very few years since the first edition of this volume was published. Indeed so short did this time seem that we wondered at the publisher's suggestion that it was time for a new edition. However, as we deliberated about this, three factors emerged in support of the decision.

First, since the initial writing much has changed in our world, change that has made an impact on the nature and practice of social work in Canada. These changes have not been dramatic but they have been of sufficient import to require some editorial updating of most of the chapters.

Second, the reaction by our colleagues to the first edition, — although very positive — has not been without criticism. I have been appreciative of such comments, criticisms, and suggestions received both from a formal evaluation of the texts done by Pearson Education Canada, and also from the informal comments of colleagues from all over the country.

I have considered all such comments and have asked the various authors to do the same. These criticisms were not always consistent, but they have been seriously considered. There is no doubt that, although the text was aimed at having a multi-theoretical and multi-method scope, more emphasis was given in the first edition to the micro and mezzo components of social work practice (particularly in Part 4) than to the critically important component of macro practice. The third factor that favoured a new edition was our wish to add important topics that were lacking in the first edition. In this regard we have included chapters on spirituality, mediation, and international issues — all topics suggested by colleagues as needed to give a clearer picture of social work practice as it exists in Canada now.

My colleagues and I have been pleased with the interest shown in the text to date. We are aware that, since our profession is a dynamic, changing entity — reflecting a range of perspectives and challenges in the diversity of our country —the last word on what constitutes social work practice in Canada will never be contained between the covers of a single book. Our conviction that there is something unique about social work practice in Canada remains even more strongly than when we first began this venture.

Out of respect for my francophone colleagues, I should mention that a criticism one could make of *Social Work Practice: A Canadian Perspective* is that — as with so many other textbooks in social work — it exists only in English. The irony of this predicament has long bothered me. To write about social work practice from a Canadian perspective and only afford space to the English perspective is a distortion of the true picture of social work practice in Canada. I have long struggled with his issue, but to date without success. I will be looking for ways to address *Social Work Practice*'s missing French link in the future.

I am grateful to the following people for their recommendations on the second edition of *Social Work Practice*: Dr. Emily Katherine Drzymala, Elizabeth Radian of Red Deer College, Leigh MacEwan of Laurentian University, and Edward Kruk of the University of British Columbia. I'd also like to thank the staff at Pearson Education Canada, including acquisitions editor Jessica Mosher, associate editor John Polanszky, and production editor Joe Zingrone. The fine eye of copy editor Tara Tovell was also much appreciated.

As well, I want especially to express my appreciation to the various contributors of chapters to the text. It is their wisdom and knowledge of our profession as it exists in Canada that has made it possible to produce a truly Canadian picture of social work practice.

—*F.J.T.*

Contributors

Dan Andreae
Dr. Dan Andreae, PhD, RSW is past president of the Ontario Association of Social Workers, first elected in 1993. Previous positions include the first executive director of the Alzheimer Society for Metropolitan Toronto. He has recently completed his Doctorate at the Ontario Institute for Studies in Education, and has authored several publications on social and health care policy issues. In 1994, Dan was awarded a Governor General's Commemorative Medal for his contribution to social services.

Ken Banks
Dr. Ken Banks is a professional social worker and sociologist. He is director of the Family Service Institute and has taught community development and research methods in the Faculty of Social Work at Wilfrid Laurier University. He is co-author, with Marshall Mangan, of *The Company of Neighbours: Community Development, Action Research*, published by the University of Toronto Press, 1988.

Cathryn Bradshaw
Cathryn Bradshaw holds an MSW from the University of Calgary and is currently in a private clinical practice. She practises in the areas of counselling and mediation, and research, development, and dissemination.

Catherine Mary Brothers
Catherine Mary Brothers received her MSW from Waterloo Lutheran University in 1969. Currently the Executive Director of Catholic Family Counselling Centre in Waterloo, Ontario Cathy has served on the Boards of Directors for Family Service Ontario and the Ontario Association of Credit Counselling Services. She continues to serve on the Board of St. Mary's General Hospital, Kitchener, where she has just completed a term as Board Chair.

Barbara A. Chisholm
Barbara A. Chisholm is a qualified professional social worker who received her MSW from the Simmons College School of Social Work in Boston, Massachusetts. Her professional career has included work with Children's Aid Societies in New Hampshire and Ontario, in mental health and day care, and in teaching, consulting, writing, and advocating for children and families. Since 1978, she has been in private practice as a child and family consultant, specializing in issues of separation and divorce as they affect children.

Dr. Nick Coady
Dr. Nick Coady holds a PhD from the University of Toronto and an MSW from Wilfred Laurier University. He is currently with the Faculty of Social Work at Wilfred Laurier

University. Nick's practice background includes residential child welfare work, individual and family work with adolescents, group work with male batterers, and general family service agency counselling. His areas of teaching span individual, family, and group work. His areas of publication and research include the therapeutic relationship, the integration of theory and practice, and family support programs.

John Cossom

John Cossom, professor emeritus at the School of Social Work, University of Victoria, recently retired after teaching in four schools of social work in Ontario, Saskatchewan, and British Columbia. He also practised in child welfare, family services, and corrections.

Hugh A. Drouin

Dr. Hugh A. Drouin holds a Master's Degree from the University of Windsor and a Doctorate from Laval University. In addition he has done post-graduate clinical studies at Adelphi University. He is currently the CEO for Family Service Ontario. As well, he has had a rich and varied practice profile as a clinician, academic, author, administrator, and consultant. He has extensive experience as a seminar leader for a variety of professional government and industrial groups. His most recent publications focus on the role of spirituality in practice. As a part-time faculty member at McMaster University School of social work he recently received a teaching award for excellence.

Glenn Drover

Dr. Glenn Drover is an adjunct professor at the Maritime School of Social Work, Dalhousie University. He also taught at McGill University, Carleton University, the University of British Columbia, and City University of Hong Kong. He has written on many aspects of social work and social welfare and also on globalization and free trade.

Peter Dunn

Professor Peter Dunn holds a PhD from Brandeis University and is currently with the Faculty of Social Work at Wilfred Laurier University. His research interests include: disability policy, issues related to poverty, gender concerns, social housing, program evaluation, and alternative interventions.

Julie M. Foley

Julie M. Foley is currently vice-president for North America for the International Federation of Social Workers and is the recent past president of the Canadian Association of Social Workers. She is currently the executive director of the Scarborough Community Care Access Centre.

Donald M. Fuchs

Dr. Donald M. Fuchs holds a PhD degree in Social Work from the University of Toronto and is currently professor and dean of the Faculty of Social Work, University of Manitoba. He has practised, taught, and conducted research in the area of child abuse prevention through strengthening neighbourhood social networks ties, program development, and evaluation.

Luke J. Fusco

Luke J. Fusco holds an MA in social work from the University of Chicago and is currently dean and associate professor in the Faculty of Social Work, Wilfrid Laurier University, Waterloo, Ontario. He has thirty years of practice in individual, family, couple, and group counselling, and ten years experience in family mediation and dispute resolution.

Nora Gold

Dr. Nora Gold is a research associate at the Faculty of Social Work, University of Toronto and a visiting scholar at the Centre for Women's Studies in Education, Ontario Institute for Studies in Education at the University of Toronto (OISE/UT).

Sheila Hardy

Sheila Hardy is an associate professor and former coordinator in the Native Human Services program at Laurentian University. She is a member of WUNSKA and has also been involved in research and teaching with Aboriginal communities locally and nationally.

Rose Marie Jaco

Dr. Rose Marie Jaco is a professor emerita at the School of Social Work, King's College London. She has taught in the areas of individual and family social work, and has a particular interest in communication and interviewing theory. Dr. Jaco teaches, conducts a private practice, and serves as a board member in several community agencies.

Kathy Jones

Kathy Jones holds an MSW from Wilfred Laurier University and is currently director of Community Services with Southern Kings Health and Community Services. She is a past vice-president of the Canadian Association of Social Workers and chaired the committee that completed the 1994 CASW *Social Work Code of Ethics.*

Jan B. Lackstrom

Jan B. Lackstrom is a social worker. She is the coordinator of Family Services in the Ambulatory Program for Eating Disorders at the Toronto Hospital, and a sessional instructor at the School of Social Work, York University.

Grant Macdonald

Dr. Grant Macdonald completed both his MSW and PhD at the University of Toronto's Faculty of Social Work. He is currently the director of the Graduate Program in Social Work at York University.

Gail MacDougall

Gail MacDougall is an assistant professor at the Maritime School of Social Work, Dalhousie University. Her practice areas have included family medicine, child welfare and mental health. In addition, she has served the profession through extensive involvement with the Nova Scotia Association the Canadian Association and the International Federation of Social Workers.

Rob MacFadden

Dr. Robert MacFadden is a professor at the Faculty of Social Work, University of Toronto who has been teaching, writing, and researching in the area of information technology (IT) and social work practice since the early 1980s. He has been active nationally and internationally in IT development and is currently exploring Web-based training in social work and higher education.

Mary MacKenzie

Mary MacKenzie holds an MSW from Dalhousie University and is employed as the coordinator of adult protection in Prince Edward Island. She also has a small private practice and serves as registrar for the Prince Edward Island Social Work Registration Board.

Colin Maloney

Colin Maloney holds a masters degree in philosophy from the University of Toronto and a doctorate in theology from the Georgian University in Rome, Italy. He has practised in the child welfare field for the last twenty years and has served on a variety of government task forces.

Jannah Mather

Professor Jannah Mather is former dean of the Faculty of Social Work at Wilfred Laurier University, Waterloo, Ontario. She holds an MSW from the University of Michigan and a PhD from the University of Illinois. She has practised in the fields of child welfare and mental health.

Anne-Marie Mawhiney

Dr. Anne Marie Mawhiney holds a PhD from York University and is a professor of social work at Laurentian University, where she teaches in the BSW and MSW programs. She was a former coordinator of the Native Human Services program and former director of (NORD).

Glenda E. McDonald

Glenda E. McDonald, MSW, CSW, is currently the registrar of the Ontario College of Social Workers and Social Service. She has extensive experience in social work administration and has taught at several social work faculties. She has practised in the fields of mental health and geriatrics and served on the boards of several provincial and national organizations.

Sharon McKay

Sharon McKay holds an MSW from Smith College and is currently Dean of the Faculty of Social Work, University of Regina. She has practiced in the fields of child welfare and psychiatric social work and was appointed to the Department of Social Work, Lakehead University for fifteen years prior to her move to Regina in 1990. She has served as President of the Ontario Association of Social Workers (1985–87) and has served on the CASW and CASSW boards of directors.

Ellen Sue Mesbur

Dr. Ellen Sue Mesbur received her MSW from the Faculty of Social Work, University of Toronto, where she also earned her MEd and EdD. She has been a faculty member of the

School of Social Work, Ryerson Polytechnic University since 1969, and was director of the school for ten years. Her areas of teaching and scholarly interest are group work practice, gerontological social work practice, and field education.

Cheryl Regehr

Dr. Cheryl Regehr is an associate professor in the Faculty of Social Work at the University of Toronto. She is also the academic coordinator of the Centre for Applied Social Research at the university. Her practice background includes direct service in mental health, sexual assault recovery programs and sex offender treatment programs. Ms. Regehr has also been involved in the administration of community and emergency mental health programs and sexual assault care centres. Currently she is the clinical director of the Critical Incident Stress Team at Pearson International Airport. She remains involved in the practice of forensic social work specializing in civil litigation and criminal court assessments of trauma victims and violent offenders. Dr. Regehr's program of research involves examining aspects of recovery from trauma in such diverse populations as victims of rape and firefighters witnessing traumatic events. Her publications address both issues of trauma and the interface between the law and mental health.

Elizabeth Ridgely

Elizabeth Ridgely, MSW, RSW, is the executive director of The George Hull Centre for Children and Families and director of The George Hull Centre Family Therapy Training Program, Toronto, Ontario. She is adjunct professor of Social Work Practice, Faculty of Social Work, and lecturer, Department of Psychiatry, University of Toronto.

Roberta M. Roberts

Dr. Roberta M. Roberts holds an MSW degree from the University of Pennsylvania and EdD and research diploma in social work from the University of Toronto. She is currently a sessional lecturer at the Faculty of Social Work at the University of Toronto. She is co-chair of the OASW Professional Development Committee and an active member in continuing education programs. She has practiced in the fields of child welfare, forensic psychiatry, young offenders and children's mental health and currently teaches in the areas of family violence with research interests in professional identity and field education.

Dr. Michael Rothery

Michael Rothery holds an MSW degree from the University of British Columbia, and a PhD from the University of Toronto. He is currently with the Faculty of Social Work at the University of Calgary. His practice has been in the fields of child welfare and mental health, and his current research interests are in the family violence area.

William Rowe

Dr. William Rowe is the director of the School of Social Work and Centre for Applied Family Studies at McGill University. He is also an adjunct professor at the School of Social Work at Memorial University of Newfoundland. He contributes to the social work and medical literature in HIV and the sexuality of disabled persons. His doctorate is from Adelphi University. He is the current editor of *The Social Worker* and has authored and edited numerous materials on a range of subjects including client-centered theory and child sexual abuse.

Carol A. Stalker

Dr. Carol A. Stalker holds a PhD in Social Work from Smith College, Northhampton, MA, and an MSW from Wilfrid Laurier University, Waterloo, Ontario. She is an Associate Professor, Faculty of Social Work, Wilfrid Laurier University and a registered social worker in Ontario. She has practised for over twenty years in the fields of mental health and child welfare, and currently does research evaluating treatment of adults abused as children, and examining factors that contribute to maintenance of treatment gains. Her teaching includes courses in the treatment of victims of violence and abuse and on social work practice with individuals and groups.

Malcolm J. Stewart

Dr. Malcolm J. Stewart holds an MSW from Wilfred Laurier University and has recently completed his PhD in social work at the University of Toronto. He is past executive director of the Ontario Association of Social Workers, and teaches social work and social policy at York University and the University of Toronto.

Barbara Thomlison

Barbara Thomlison, PhD, is a former professor of Social Work at the University of Calgary, Canada and now a professor at Florida International University School of Social Work. She is interested in the area of child welfare and mental health, and is also in private practice. Much of her research has concerned children's mental health and child maltreatment and ways to improve practice by strengthening families.

Ray J. Thomlinson

Dr. Ray J. Thomlison is professor and Dean of the School of Social Work, at Florida International University and former Dean of the Faculty of Social Work at the University of Calgary. He is the author of numerous articles and book chapters with particular emphasis on the impact of behavioural therapy techniques and outcome research on social work practice.

Glenn Thompson

Glenn Thompson has an extensive background in a variety of non-profit and governmental organizations in Canada and Britain, dealing with individual and social problems. Between 1975 and 1991 he served as deputy minister in six Ontario government ministries including Correctional Services, Labour and Housing. Following his retirement from the Ontario Public Service in 1991 after 31 years, Mr. Thompson joined the Canadian Mental Health Association, Ontario division, as executive director. In the fall of 2000, he joined the new territorial government of Nunavut in Canada's Arctic and is active in the redevelopment of health and social services as executive director, Baffin region.

David Turner

Dr. David Turner, (LLB Dip, SW, RSW) is associate professor in the School of Social Work at the University of Victoria, Victoria, British Columbia. He teaches law and legal skills for social work and child and youth care work students. His major interests are in children's rights, advocacy, and conflict resolution techniques as they apply to professional practice. He is a registered social worker and has developed several community crime prevention and cross cultural programs. He has been Mayor of Victoria, Chair of the Police Board, and a school board trustee. His latest publication is *A Legal Handbook for the Helping Professional*, Second Edition with Max Zuhleman, 1998, School of Social Work, University of Victoria.

Francis J. Turner

Dr. Francis Turner is professor emeritus at Wilfrid Laurier University, Faculty of Social Work. His current interests are use of theory in practice, international social work and cultural and ethnic differences with particular interests in the use of interpreters in practice. He is currently the editor of *International Social Work*.

Leslie M. Tutty

Dr. Leslie M. Tutty received her doctorate of social work from Wilfrid Laurier University. She has been a member of the Faculty of Social Work at the University of Calgary since 1989 teaching clinical and research courses. Her research has focused on abused women, sexual abuse prevention, and group treatment for women and children survivors of sexual abuse.

Anne Westhues

Dr. Anne Westhues holds a DSW from Columbia University and is a professor at Wilfrid Laurier University in Waterloo, Ontario. She teaches social policy, community interventions, and evaluation research. Her research and publications are in the areas of policy, program development, and evaluation, adoption, and social work education.

Michael Kim Zapf

Dr. Michael Kim Zapf is a full professor at the University of Calgary, Faculty of Social Work. Following years of practice in the Canadian North, his writing and teaching concentrate on the issues of geography and remote practice. As head of the BSW Access Division he works with a cross-cultural team on the design and delivery of a new collaborative Learning Circle model of undergraduate social work education in rural, remote and Aboriginal communities across Alberta.

CANADIAN SOCIAL WORK PRACTICE: AN OVERVIEW

Francis J. Turner

This book begins from the perspective that there is something unique in the way social work is practised in Canada. Over the last several years, as I have consulted and discussed, pondered, analyzed, and speculated about this, and as I have examined the material of the individual chapters as they emerged, I have sought to identify the variables that contribute to this uniqueness.

From my perspective, six Canadian realities appear to have influenced the way the profession has developed and how it is practised. These are not the conclusions of a historian of the profession who would examine the influencing variables in a more rigorous manner, but observations made over the last forty years as the profession has emerged and developed. I will identify these realities and then follow with a further listing of the qualities of Canadian social work that appear to have emerged from these Canadian features.

The first of these comes from our history. The fact that Canada emerged first from a blending of our First Nations peoples, our French ancestors, and our English ancestors, and the fact that we have had a virtually open border of information-sharing between the United States and ourselves has meant that our profession's development has been multi-influenced.

In addition to these roots of diversity, Canada has long had a relatively open policy of immigration. Thus, over the decades, millions of people from many parts of the world have come here to become Canadians. A part of this reality is our long proclaimed tradition that has attempted to minimize assimilation and support respect for and encouragement of a cultural mosaic. This has also influenced the way social work is practised, inasmuch as legislation, policies, and services have emerged in ways that attempt to respect these differences. We are not suggesting here that these responses have been ideal or as sensitive as they might have been, only that there has been a long tradition of attempting to respect difference.

A further Canadian factor that appears to have marked the development of practice has been the reality of a relatively small population, the majority of whom are located along a narrow band in the south, with a very small segment spread over the remaining huge geographic expanse that makes up this country. As several of the following chapters will discuss, the reality of social work in Canada is that much of it is practised in small communities in remote, highly separated areas.

A particular facet of our geography is our weather which, in its extremes, has markedly influenced not only the need for and availability of resources, but also the day-to-day psychosocial functioning of persons. The impact of this factor on our practice is more subtle, but nevertheless real.

A further factor that needs to be taken into account is our several-tiered governance system with its complex sharing of powers and resources among the federal, provincial, and municipal governments, further complicated by a vast difference in the size and economic strength of the provinces. This results in a highly complex, interconnected network of federal, provincial, municipal, private, and voluntary services.

A final Canadian reality that appears to have influenced the development of social work practice in Canada is our unique value set that makes Canada "Canadian." Dan Andreae discusses this factor in more detail in his chapter on Canadian values. The fact of the existence of a distinct and unique Canadian value set is the point to be made here. This value set in turn has influenced the development of the profession and has coloured the way that the profession is practised.

The foregoing has only identified some factors unique to Canada that appear to have shaped our profession as it exists. What is of greater importance is how these factors have influenced the development and practice of social work. To date there appear to be at least twelve attributes that distinguish the practice of social work in Canada and which make it distinct from the way social work is practised in at least some other countries.

I will present a brief overview of these factors here and then let the chapters that make up the body of this volume demonstrate more clearly and thoroughly how they are translated into a body of social work practice we can and should call Canadian.

1. *Diversity.* One of the attributes of Canadian social work practice that becomes quickly evident to someone wanting to look over the profession's shoulder is the fact that practice in Canada is highly diverse. It is difficult to imagine any form, theory, strategy, technique, or method of social work activity that is not used. There clearly is no one sanctioned method or theory.

2. *Comfort with diversity.* Related to diversity is a comfort with diversity that is sufficiently widespread to make it a distinguishing mark in itself. Certainly tensions still exist about such things as perceived emphasis, whether too great or too little, on the micro-macro dichotomy. However, these seem to belong more to the halls of academe than to the reality of the front-line worker. Although individual practitioners may have preferred positions on various professional topics, this is much different than holding that one theory, method, or practice focus is inherently better than another.

   Certainly it would be naive to suggest that within this diversity there are not intra-familial squabbles about what particular method, strategy, or theory is to be preferred in particular situations. These differences, however, tend not to be holy wars and disciple-driven cults, but rather preferences based on adaptations of knowledge to the idiosyncrasies of practice in different areas of the country and to the different demands of practice within such areas.

3. *High flexibility.* A significant aspect of the diversity and the existing comfort with it is a high degree of flexibility among methods, theories, fields of practice, and techniques. Clearly, individual practitioners develop their own unique styles of practice and build their

practice around preferred theories, but rarely does this occur with a rigid "I have the only truth" approach. As one meets practitioners from different parts of the country, one discovers that most of our colleagues have practiced in highly diverse situations and settings and have made use of a range of methodologies. Certainly, there are well-known colleagues who have developed high levels of skill and knowledge in particular areas of practice, or in the use of a particular theoretical focus. They indeed are specialists and, in some instances, superstars in the field. But such persons are the exceptions and are rightly looked upon as teachers, monitors, leaders, consultants, role models, exemplars, etc., and are not the persons on whom I should model my practice exclusively.

While it may be that in schools and faculties of social work students frequently select particular streams of practice, areas of concentration, or specialties, nevertheless the areas of practice into which a person goes after graduation often bear little resemblance to students' professional school curricular concentration, whether mandated or selected. Certainly, for the most part, new graduates are hired on the basis of their educational profile. However, within two or three years of graduation we see a high level of diversity in the positions that individuals seek and accept. What is of interest is that there is a comfort with this flexibility among practitioners and employers in the profession. This same comfort with flexibility is apparent in most of the licensing, certification, and registration procedures across the country, inasmuch as one is admitted to colleges or their equivalent on the basis of being a social worker, not a particular kind of social worker.

4. *A paucity of holy wars.* Having served on many heated and rhetorically rich curriculum committees in many schools both here and in other countries, I need to be careful in suggesting that strong conceptual differences do not exist as to what constitutes "correct" social work practice in Canada. Clearly some such conceptual differences about practice exist. As well, we have persons of stature who are strongly attached to particular positions about practice. But these are the exception. We do not have, nor have we had in our professional history, theoretical or practice-related differences that have split the profession, or divided large cadres of colleagues into recognizable rival groups as has taken place in other countries.

Differences between and among schools and faculties do of course exist, although at times it appears that sometimes they are more imagined than real. But never have they been of the nature of some of the intense struggles that have taken place among our colleagues in the United States. And even when we have alleged differences between persons or groups of practitioners apart from the coffee room scuttlebutt, such differences about practice are not of the intensity that causes serious divisions among persons and groups.

5. *Comfort with plurality.* Another characteristic that seems to differentiate Canadian social work practice from that in some other parts of the world is the comfort with plurality among social work practitioners. Although there are similarities in the terms, plurality is different from diversity. Diversity was alluded to earlier. Here I am talking about that quality or characteristic, which appears to be observed frequently enough to mark it as a central tendency, that involves the expectation that contemporary Canadian social work practitioners be multi-skilled and multi-theoretically informed. Even when a person has become highly specialized, there is a comfort with other specializations among other people.

Here we are talking about the expectation and acceptance and understanding that a Canadian social work practitioner needs to be a person able to work from a highly pluralistic position in terms of theory, method, techniques, and client target groups. This concept is frequently translated into the term "generalist."

6. *Use of technology.* Earlier in this chapter Canada's unique size, geography and weather and the way our population is dispersed were identified as factors that have marked Canadian social work practice. How so? One particular way in which this has occurred is in the extent to which the profession has integrated various components of technology into practice. Although more taken for granted than proclaimed, it appears that, because of our geographic realities, a great deal of social work is practised through the media of telephones, video hook-ups, and more and more by way of computers.

   With Canada as the world's leader in per capita number of telephones, it is not surprising that the telephone is a major medium of communication with the profession. Unfortunately, the telephone is so much a part of our daily lives that as a profession we have as yet underrated the potential of other technical communication resources for the delivery of even the most sensitive and intimate types of service. A later chapter in this book addresses this topic.

7. *The profession's size.* A further distinguishing feature of Canadian practice relates to the size of the profession. Using university trained professionals as the criterion, and keeping in mind the challenge of accuracy, there appear to be about 18,000 to 20,000 university-trained social workers currently practising in Canada. This is not a large group compared to some other professions. One consequence of this is that the profession is a rather close-knit group. One does not have to be a Canadian social worker very long before one knows colleagues in all parts of the country. It would be difficult to find two Canadian social workers from different parts of the country who could get together and be unable to name a mutual acquaintance in the profession. This reality appears to account at least partially for the comfort with plurality and diversity mentioned earlier.

8. *Our bilingual reality.* A further important factor that marks Canadian social work practice is that of the official bilingual structure of the country. There are few countries in which social work practice has developed in a milieu where there were two different societies, languages, and traditions, each of which brings not only to the history of the country but to the development of the profession two value systems and traditions that strongly influence the way the profession has emerged. Clearly this reality has influenced practice. Although it is difficult to be precise about the nature and extent of such influences, the previously mentioned comfort with diversity and plurality is clearly one result.

   Thus as a profession we appear to be more culturally sensitive and aware of the reality of other cultural, ethnic, and racial differences with which we interact than colleagues in other countries. Although the traditional political position has been one of biculturalism, in recent years we have become increasingly aware of the cultural richness that our First Nations peoples have to contribute to the development of a caring society and the social network that emerges from such a value. With several schools of social work giving special attention to both training and services for First Nations people, it is clear that these projects are influencing practice. In a more general way, the profession's understanding of the sensitivity, skills, and mutual respect required when there are differences among people is expanding

9. *Our common identity.* A facet of our size which influences social work's identity in Canada is the strong common identity that exists within the profession. To this point

we have been stressing that the distinguishing feature of social work practice in Canada has been its diversity. A paradox arising from this diversity is that within it, or over and above it, there can also be found a commonality of values, concerns, and commitments. These, like many other aspects of the "Canadian Persona," are strengthened because we are different and respect differences. This reality enables us to continue to formulate and to change, test, and reshape on an ongoing basis that profile of theory and knowledge and skills that uniquely combine to make up social work practice in Canada.

10. *Pragmatism.* Flowing from the challenges of size, diversity, and geography there is a unique quality of Canadian social work practice that makes it highly pragmatic and open to new ideas. A reverse side of this attribute appears to be a lessened or a less prominent interest in research, especially practice research. Without further data, I need to be careful not to overstate this and would ask that it be viewed more as a speculation than as an assertion. It may well be that much Canadian practice research by social workers is published in American journals. Also, some excellent texts, including research texts, have been published by Canadian colleagues. Nevertheless, after decades of attempting to expand the amount of research concerning front-line practice, it appears that we are still less committed to the formal testing of knowledge and more pragmatically committed to a position that says "let's try it and see if it works."

11. *Canadian diffidence.* Implied in the previous topic, but separate from it, is another quality of social work in Canada that appears to set it apart from practice in other countries. Here I refer to either a reluctance or a shyness about our own successes and professional competencies. For some reasons not yet fully understood, Canadian social workers have not been strong in sharing our practice wisdom with each other. Certainly there are national conferences of various bodies, such as Family Services Canada, but these are few in number. There are some excellent journals, again few in number. For some time now social work has been one of the disciplines taking part in the annual Learned Societies conference. This has been an important venue for the presentation of professional material and is not to be minimized. However, compared to other countries we do appear to do much less of our own publishing. The number of journals and the number of texts written and published in Canada is not extensive and hence greatly underrepresents what is unique about our own practice. What I believe is even more serious is a tendency to accord work, ideas, and practice advances in other countries more status than our own home-grown material. Certainly we need to be aware of what is happening elsewhere, but in not having strong ongoing assessments of our own practice there is a real risk that material from elsewhere will be inappropriately applied here. As well, I suggest that when we do not loudly proclaim it, material developed here may be overlooked or undervalued in comparison to that which has crossed borders, especially from our south.

12. *Undue American influence.* This typically Canadian lack of confidence in our abilities is particularly reflected in the textbooks and journals on which we rely for much of our teaching. Many of the texts and reading lists used in the teaching of social work, especially the micro-mezzo components, come from other countries, especially the U.S. As members of a worldwide profession committed to the idea that knowledge from any source is relevant, it would be a mistake to become overcommitted to a "made in Canada" position. However at this time in our history, we are overly reliant on American texts and journals. This has particular impact on teaching, as there are clear differences in the ter-

minology used in the two countries. For example, having taught in both countries, I have observed clear differences in their use of such terms as *culture*, *race* and *ethnicity*, all issues of great importance within contemporary practice. As well, American texts tend to represent the profession as one principally practised in large urban settings, which is clearly not the reality of much of our situation in Canada, where practice tends to take place in small, often isolated communities.

SUMMARY

The preceding pages suggest that, for a variety of historical, political value, and geographic reasons, there is a distinct body of Canadian social work practice that can and needs to be identified. The following chapters analyze and discuss practice across the broad spectrum of these variables. The challenge to the reader is to decide whether the picture of quality social work practice that emerges is one that could apply equally well anywhere in the world, or whether it reveals a unique form of quality practice that is properly called *Canadian* social work.

CANADIAN VALUES
AND IDEOLOGIES
AND SOCIAL WORK
PRACTICE
Dan Andreae

Social workers, whether practising as clinicians, policy makers, community organizers, or administrators, are influenced directly and/or indirectly by certain values that are endemic to the Canadian experience. To be a social worker in Canada is to be subject to a complex and different social milieu than, let us say, that in the United States, Australia, or Germany, to cite a few examples. At first glance, it may appear that the subject of Canadian values has minimal, if any, relevance to everyday social work practice and should be placed more appropriately in the domain of philosophy, political science, economics, history, psychology, or sociology. Yet the unique constellation of principles and values that underlie and frame the Canadian reality determine, in part, how we treat each other as human beings, the priorities that we hold supreme, the resources available to clients, and the policies that are enacted and pursued by agencies, institutions, and governments. Therefore it is important for social workers in Canada, whether new to the field or longstanding practitioners, to have an understanding of the core values that have been attributed to Canadian society and how these are particularly different from those of the United States, as well as to have an appreciation of how these shape social policy development and influence the parameters of social work practice.

HISTORICAL CONTEXT

First, it may be asked, are there certain commonly agreed upon values shared by most Canadians that help to define the character of the nation? Is Canada a fundamentally different country than our neighbours to the south and, if so, how? Canadians may instinctively "know" that they are dissimilar yet many may not be able to articulate these idiosyncrasies in a cogent manner. One quintessential difference is that Canada as a nation has evolved evolutionarily, unlike the United States, which gained independence from Britain through a bloody revolution. Many colonial Americans in the latter eighteenth century quarrelled with their mother country over issues such as taxation and representation and were prepared to take up arms for their cause against Britain. These Americans were largely influenced by the philosophy of John Locke, who postulated the theory of natural rights in which people were entitled to be free, equal, rational, and moral. His philosophical exhortations served as a galvanizing force for democratic revolution around the world, including the French and American Revolutions, and his theories formed the cornerstone for liberal democratic political theory and action. Woven into the American fabric, emanating from its revolutionary roots, is the belief in the concepts of life, liberty, and the pursuit of happiness, which serve as the American credo. A strongly individualistic culture emerged that placed paramount emphasis on individual initiative and responsibility, the valour associated with the conquering of the American frontier, and a profound distrust of government and state intervention. Indeed George Washington, who became America's first president in 1789, eschewed the suggestion that he should be crowned king of the nascent nation because it ran contrary to the populist sentiment on which the country was founded following the War of Independence. The framers of the American Constitution, wary of power being concentrated in any one person or sector, instigated the system of checks and balances which essentially divided power among the executive, legislative, and judicial branches of government, virtually ensuring that none would become predominant. This apparently democratic arrangement of power relationships did place greater power in the hands of citizens who directly elected the president and the members of Congress in the House and Senate, but it also sowed the seeds of stalemate and paralysis in the system of government.

This reality has great importance in the arena of social policy, as it has often proven difficult for a president or block in Congress to secure the necessary cooperation among branches essential to successfully implement social and health care legislation. This balkanization of power, combined with a visceral suspicion of activist government and a strong individualistic skein in the American character has made it, in essence, impossible to enact comprehensive, universal government-initiated programs, as has been possible in Canada. As the two parties that make up the American party system, the Democratic and Republican parties, are loosely-based coalitions of interests that do not exert strict party discipline, members of Congress have considerable liberty to vote their own constituents' interests ahead of their overall party concerns. This also makes it considerably more difficult to achieve a necessary consensus to put forth fundamental social reforms. In addition, the American system relies heavily on political donations from corporations and special interest groups such as the National Rifle Association, tobacco companies, or organized labour, several of which are adamantly opposed to "socialistic" measures, which are perceived as detrimental and antithetical to free enterprise interests. By contrast, Canadian campaign finance laws are structured so as to minimize the domination of special interest groups, although certain corporate interests do wield considerable clout.

By comparison, the Canadian parliamentary system, based on the British model, champions party discipline, and members of Parliament are expected to vote in accordance with party dictates. Constitutionally, governments can fall if they lose a vote of nonconfidence or a vote on a key piece of legislation such as a budget. In the United States, governments are not forced to resign if defeated on legislation. There are very few free votes in the parliamentary system although this does occur on rare occasions. On the federal level, whether a Liberal, Conservative, New Democrat, Reformer, or Bloc Québécois, a member of Parliament is expected to adhere to party directives, and discipline can be swift and punishing for those who voluntarily deviate from party orthodoxy. While the federal Canadian system may, on one level, appear to be less democratic and more draconian than its American counterpart, it is extremely efficient in marshalling forces to pass social and health care legislation such as unemployment insurance, Medicare, and social, health, and educational transfer payments to the provinces. In effect, a majority government in Canada has a virtual carte blanche during its mandate to enact whatever legislation it chooses, which gives it enormous power, latitude, and influence.

Occasionally in the United States a president has succeeded in passing major social legislation reforms, as did Franklin Roosevelt, who enacted his New Deal following the 1932 election, and Lyndon Johnson, who implemented the Great Society programs following his 1964 election triumph. However, it must be remembered that both of these landmark developments in American history occurred following crises that paved the way for government intervention: Roosevelt as a result of the Great Depression of the 1930s that almost destroyed the capitalist system and which created untold human misery and hardship, and Johnson following the assassination of John F. Kennedy, when public sympathy was high for the new president and his initiatives such as the War on Poverty. However, neither of these agendas went so far as to institute a government-sponsored universal welfare state, and the resulting programs can be considered remedial rather than truly transformative. For example, America still lacks universal health care coverage such as exists and is taken for granted in Canada. The latest concerted foray to implement such coverage by President Clinton in 1993 met with resounding defeat by the cacophony of powerful special interests wary of perceived massive government intervention into health care delivery.

Unlike the United States, Canada did not experience a traumatic "war of independence," and continued to be governed by the British and its colonial laws and customs. Canada engaged in what historian Seymour Lipsett has termed a "counter-revolutionary past" (Selman, 30). Indeed, during and especially following the American Revolution, loyalist immigrants from the United States laid the foundation for a distinctly Canadian society. For their part, Loyalists were committed to entrenching a way of life manifestly different from that developing in the republic to the south. In terms of a political philosophy, they held views about humans and society that contrasted sharply with those of the American Revolution. The Loyalists believed that only a strong central government would ensure an orderly society. Their experiences during the revolution helped to confirm their perspectives. British political leaders ensured in the Canadian Constitution Act of 1791 that the system of government implemented in the surviving British North America (BNA) colonies was consistent with the idea of a conservative society, checking democracy with revitalized monarchical and autocratic institutions. In order to preserve a society distinct from the United States, the BNA colonies joined the War of 1812, somewhat reluctantly, to fight the Americans. These influential Loyalists, who were deeply conservative, believed that human nature was fundamentally base and that government and other institutions were needed to exert control in order to check what they saw as the inherently undisciplined character of human beings (Avery, 103). According to Canadian political philosopher George Grant, in his seminal work *Lament for a Nation*, the early leaders of BNA identified a lack of public restraint in the democratic republic to the south. Their conservatism was essentially a social doctrine that public order and tradition, in contrast to freedom and experiment, were central virtues. Indeed conservatism in Canada traditionally strove to assert the rights of the community to restrain freedom in the name of the common good. In its earliest expression, this conservative nationalism expressed itself in the use of public control in the political and economic spheres. An example of the differences between Canada and the United States can be seen in the contrasting approaches to the opening of their respective frontiers. In Canada, the law of the central government was used more extensively and less reliance was placed on the free settler than occurred in the "wild" American West (Grant, 71).

Historically Canada has been more willing than America to use governmental control over economic life to protect the common good against public freedom. George Grant notes interestingly that several key public initiatives have been by Conservative governments at the federal and provincial levels, including Ontario Hydro, the Canadian National Railway (CNR), and the CBC, among others (Grant, 71). This conservative ethos was also found in Quebec, although in a different way. Quebec was essentially a rural, church dominated, agrarian society. The English and French did not have much in common except the fact that both recognized that they could only be preserved outside of the United States. The French went along fundamentally because they had no alternative but to accept the endurable arrangements proposed by the ruling English. The French and English had limited common ground in their sense of social order, a belief that society required a high degree of law, and respect for a public conception of virtue. Both would grant the state much wider rights to control the individual than was recognized in the libertine ideas of the American Revolution. However, according to George Grant, their different visions of conservatism never crystallized into a consensual bond, thus leading to friction and discord, vestiges of which reverberate today (Grant, 68).

It may appear peculiar and even surprising to the reader to associate a concern with the public good over individual freedom with the Conservative party. However, although the Tories initially championed Canadian sovereignty and nationalism, the party has increasingly become identified with corporate interests, free enterprise and, in the latter 1990s, with following the ideology of minimal government intervention, a quintessentially American approach similar to that advocated by the current Republican party. It can be argued that John Diefenbaker, who served as Conservative Prime Minister from 1957 to 1963, and lost an election in 1963 in large part because of his adamant public opposition to U.S. missiles on Canadian soil, was the last truly nationalist prime minister, without question the last such Conservative leader (Grant, 26). The last two Conservative prime ministers, Kim Campbell and most notably Brian Mulroney, led a party which has strayed far from its historical origins, with Mulroney defending free trade and unabashed continentalism. The Liberal party, which had originally promoted a continentalist approach to trade and commerce, became increasingly nationalistic during the Pearson regime (1963–1968), led by individuals such as Finance Minister Walter Gordon, and especially so under Pierre Trudeau (1968–1979/1980–1984), who implemented such measures as the National Energy Program (NEP) and the Foreign Investment Review Agency (FIRA) to protect Canadian ownership. However, the present day Liberal government under Jean Chrétien, elected in 1993, has largely followed the economic and trade policies of Brian Mulroney, even signing into law the North American Free Trade Agreement (NAFTA), making it difficult to distinguish between the philosophies of the two parties. It may appear paradoxical given Canada's conservative historical origins that universal social programs would find fertile soil, thrive, and receive widespread public support. This is in part a result of the reliance on strong central government combined with a realization that for a sparse population to survive in a harsh and often inhospitable climate, people must band together and support each other for mutual survival.

CANADIAN VALUES

Certainly it is a challenging exercise to define and articulate certain shared value clusters that define Canada and its people. Indeed, Hannah Arendt has stated that what unites the citizens of a republic is that they inhabit the same public space, share its common concerns, acknowledge its rules, and are committed to its continuance to achieving a working compromise when they differ (Welton). As has already been indicated in this chapter, Canada is considerably different from the United States historically, politically, culturally, economically, and socially. It is also different than it was 20 years ago and, in many ways, is barely recognizable from 50 or 100 years ago. Canada is a complex nation and society, constantly in a state of flux. It is divided into six major regions: the Maritimes, Ontario, Quebec, the Prairies, British Columbia, and the North, each distinct from the others (Selman, 29). Some provinces tend to associate themselves with their particular region such as occurs with several Maritime provinces in eastern Canada, while others such as British Columbia, it has been said, tend to have a greater affinity with the northwestern United States than with fellow provinces east of the Rocky Mountains. Some provinces such as Alberta, British Columbia, and to a lesser extent Ontario are considered "have provinces," rich in natural resources and human capital. Others such as Newfoundland or Nova Scotia have historically been less well off financially and have consequently experienced serious dislocations resulting in high unemployment and economic uncertainty.

Quebec represents a unique situation within the Canadian federation. It is overwhelmingly French-speaking and its continued participation in Canada is questionable as of this writing. Quebec has its own legal system, based in part on the Napoleonic Code, and a distinct culture. Historically a conservative and rural church-based society, Quebec began to industrialize and modernize during the Quiet Revolution of the 1960s, during which it developed increasing self-confidence and established its own intellectual elite. The movement toward sovereignty, always present, gained political legitimacy and momentum upon the election as Premier, in 1976, of René Lévesque, a popular and charismatic politician and leader of the separatist Parti Québécois (PQ). In his campaign platform, Lévesque promised to hold a province-wide referendum on the question of separation, which then occurred in 1980. Although the separatist forces were defeated by a margin of 60 percent to 40 percent, the seeds of fervent patriotism were sown for continued separatist activity. After subsequently losing to the Liberal party led by Robert Bourassa, the PQ once again regained power in 1993 and initiated a second referendum campaign in 1995. For a variety of intricate reasons beyond the scope of this chapter, PQ Premier Jacques Parizeau and federal Bloc Québécois leader Lucien Bouchard, who spearheaded the campaign, barely lost, shocking many Canadians across the country, who realized how close they had come to losing Canada. Bernard Landry was recently elected as Premier of Quebec and is committed to pursuing the separatist option.

For contextual reasons, it is important to remember that Quebec entered somewhat reluctantly into a partnership with English Canada to form a new country following its defeat by the English at the Plains of Abraham in 1759, and has always viewed itself as a founding or charter member of Canada. This reality has led some theorists to refer to English and French Canada as the "two solitudes." Serious constitutional difficulties have been encountered because Quebec considers itself to be a distinct society and Quebec leaders insist that this term be entrenched in the repatriated Constitution of 1982. However, other provinces also view themselves as equally distinct and do not want to give this status solely to Quebec. They are also concerned that entrenching this clause into the constitution might confer special legal status on Quebec. This protracted constitutional battle has created, and is creating, tremendous strain within the Canadian federation and has galvanized many Canadians to identify and cherish uniquely communal values and to define what it means to be a Canadian.

Historically a nation of French, English, and Aboriginal roots, Canada has, since World War II, become increasingly multicultural and is now considered one of the most pluralistic and diverse countries in the world. The component of the population from the British Isles, which made up 61 percent of the population in 1871, had fallen to about 40 percent in 1981. The French element fell from 31 percent to 27 percent during the same period. The rest of the population in 1981 could be categorized into 70 small but clearly defined ethnic groups, the most significant of which, seen in a national perspective, were German (5 percent), Italian (3 percent), and Ukrainian (2 percent); Native people constituted the next largest group. Since that survey, immigration in Canada has accelerated, including many people from Southeast Asia, Hong Kong, and other Pacific Rim countries, among others (Selman, 27). Canadians have, on the whole, taken pride in a policy that encourages integration rather than assimilation into the society, which has been labelled a "cultural mosaic" as opposed to the "melting pot" that exists in the United States. Canadian author Peter Newman has asserted that the policy of social mosaic or multiculturalism "remains our most single important national characteristic." The Canadian policy "takes as its starting point the assumption that many groups that make up a multi-ethnic or pluralistic society have unique cultural characteristics that can often enhance and strengthen the national political community." The policy of multiculturalism was formally proclaimed in 1971, was entrenched in the repatriated constitution and charter of rights and freedoms in 1982, and was the subject of legislation in 1988. The value of tolerance toward other groups and their acceptance has been considered a hallmark of the Canadian experience (Selman, 27).

Another value that has been attributed to Canadians is an adherence to law and order. Leslie Armour has noted the Canadian attitude towards the law "which derives its force from the ideal of community and not from the arbitrary decision of any one individual" (Selman, 31). R.B. Elder stresses a Canadian tendency to feel that the social gospel should have primacy over individual rights (Selman, 31). Dominique Clift stresses some of the same features of the Canadian psychology, tracing it in part to Canada's "peaceful and evolutionary development" from its colonial past and its ingrained tendency to "get along" and seek compromise. She states, "Canadian politics knows very little of competing ideologies. Its primary concern is not so much to convey the will of the majority as a basis for government policy but to point out the way towards fruitful accommodations between competing groups ... and to satisfy sectional claims without weakening the foundations of national unity" (Selman, 31).

The conservative tendencies in Canada, referred to in the previous historical context section, have led to an acceptance of communitarianism, which has been aided by people trying to get along in a forbidding and rugged territory. R.B. Elder has stated that, from its beginnings, Canadian social thought has had a communitarian basis. He states that Canadians have a much stronger "idea of community" than have Americans and that there is a conviction in Canada "that there are values to which the individual must submit" (Selman, 32). Leslie Armour, in *The Idea of Canada*, gives particular stress to communitarianism as a Canadian attribute. He states, "This book argues that the idea of an organic society, one in which the individual has not traditionally been pitted against his society but in which the individual and his society have been seen as a continuity in which neither is intelligible without the other, was deeply embedded in our beginnings, and has never been eradicated" (Selman, 32).

A number of writers have pointed out that Canadian society has a high regard for policies that protect the disadvantaged members of society. Peter Newman refers to our "relatively gentle society" (Selman, 32); Robin Matthews states that out of that cultural attribute came a more "humane" outlook than exists in the United States. Matthews broadens this idea in his book *Canadian Identity*, in identifying many characteristics of Canadians which have flowed from "the Liberal view of society" which "has shaped the very air Canadians breathe." He points out, as does Elder, that the ideas inherited in the Social Gospel, which were such a force in the development of Canadian thought and policy, further strengthened the readiness of the Canadian community to support a number of welfare measures, especially in the post World War II period (Selman, 33). Clift, in her analysis of Canadian society, relates this support for social welfare in Canada to our tendency to stress "cooperation and solidarity" in our policies (Selman, 33).

The Social Gospel message provided a profound philosophical rationale and frame-work for the Cooperative Commonwealth Federation (CCF, later the NDP) and served to influence the social policies of the other political parties. A number of other authors, both scholarly and popular, have pointed out support in Canada, compared to the U.S., for social security and welfare state measures. An example of this is provided by author Richard Gwynn who, in his book *The 49th Paradox*, discusses at some length what he terms the liberalism of Canadian thought compared to American. By way of summary, he quotes an American leader: "You have a quality of civility that is precious and you have an immensely superior social system" (Selman, 33).

Canadians have traditionally turned to the use of public agencies to solve social, polit-ical, and economic problems. Gwynn states, "Canadians trust their government in a way that Americans find quite incomprehensible," and further, "Canadians believe in their state" (Selman, 33). The fact that Canadians have been willing to use government and its agencies in this way was, in part, a response to the need that existed for certain services before there was a sufficiently large economy in place to make it possible to rely wholly on the private sector. Hershel Harden (1974) has described Canada as "a public enterprise culture with an aptitude for managing government owned commercial enterprises" (Selman, 33).

Certainly Canadians have also wished to assert their independence in economic and cultural spheres and did not want to be American. In the case of culture, Canadians were first strongly alerted to the issue by the report issued in 1951 of the Royal Commission on National Development of the Arts, Letters and Science, the "Massey Commission." The Commission spoke out strongly about the dangers posed by an "alien culture" and proposed a series of measures to strengthen Canadian culture and to ward off what was termed "relentless American cultural penetration" into Canada. This has been an ongoing concern for Canadians, with particular attention paid to policy that conserves the means of the distribution of culture, broadcasting, the press, and book and periodical publishing (Selman, 33). The level of concern about these issues, which dominated the policies of the Liberal government in the 1970s and 1980s, was not renewed by the Conservatives under Brian Mulroney after 1984, nor to any great extent by the Chrétien Liberals. Topics surrounding Canadian culture were a prominent feature of the free trade debates that dom-inated the federal election of 1988.

There has always been a great fear of economic domination. Prime Minister Trudeau often referred to these problems with the analogy of a mouse living next to an elephant and all the difficulties entailed by such a reality. Beginning in the 1950s, Walter Gordon and other prominent Canadian figures worried about the extent and possible harmful effects of American ownership of Canadian institutions and resources. The preliminary report of the Royal Commission on Canada's Economic Prospects came out in 1957 and described American investments in Canada as "large and getting larger" (Selman, 34). Gwynn states that economic nationalists dominated the political scene during the 1960s and 1970s and adds that this was "the first time that ideology had played a major role in Canadian politics" (Selman, 34). Fear of American hegemony in economic affairs has many causes, but S.D. Clark notes that resistance to U.S. influence in Canada "is very largely the concern of a bureaucratically oriented Canadian community" (Selman, 34). As D. Stains has stated, "the United States has been a powerful continental presence, friendly and supportive, but also threatening and ominous" (Selman, 34). This ambivalent attitude toward the United States has characterized the Canadian relationship since the inception of this country and has had an indelible effect on the Canadian character. Although Canada is a multi-layered and labyrinthine society with cleavages among regions (e.g., east versus west; federal versus provincial jurisdictions; rich versus poor; English versus French; among different religious denominations; between genders; among Liberals, Conservatives, and Socialists; and among ethnic groups) there appear to be core values that cut across individuals, groups, and ideologies, which paint a portrait of a distinct Canadian society and ethos.

Often Canadians know what they are not—mainly American—but this represents a reactive rather than a proactive definition of national identity and character. Canadians often refer to such facts and features as a lower crime rate than in the United States, less civil strife (in part due to the fact that Canada has never experienced a violent civil rights struggle such as occurred in the United States during the 1950s and 1960s), more tolerant and accepting of different cultures and viewpoints, more consensual as opposed to individualistically-oriented, and more caring and compassionate as exemplified by programs such as Medicare, unemployment insurance, or government-subsidized higher education. Naegel in a 1961 essay pointed out that any nationality requires what he terms "principles of coherence." These may be positive values or they may be negative—for instance, that we are not like "the British or Americans." He continues, "the positive principles of coherence involves ... the elaboration of a range of cultural accomplishments .... Such accomplishments proceed within a consensus. The general consensus of a society—its dominant value system—in turn is recognized to the accomplishments that can be attributed to members of society" (Selman, 35). Leslie Armour asserts that Canadians, for all their worrying about lack of shared national goals, have over time demonstrated a strong sense of national identity. He defines national identity as "those ideas which, whether anyone consciously attends to them or not, are dispositional states which large numbers of Canadians have in common and which shape, to one degree or another, our communal life." He insists that a national identity exists in Canada and has been "strongly influential." He finds that identity in Canada's sense of community. Although there have been "flirtations with continentalism," which he terms "lapses," but nevertheless a result of conscious policy, they have always been stopped "by a deeper sense of the community's convictions." He sums up the abiding ideas of the Canadian identity as communitarianism, pluralism, and a "sense of history" (Selman, 35). It may therefore by postulated that Canadians do indeed possess value systems that incorporate a strong sense of communitarianism, collectivity, pluralism, tolerance, and caring due to several factors encompassing history, geography, culture, economics, politics, and circumstance. These underlying values become operationalized in approaches to government policy-making including that of the modern welfare state.

CANADIAN SOCIAL PROGRAMS—PAST, PRESENT, AND FUTURE

Currently, Canadian social and health care programs are under assault, leaving many Canadians worried and confused about future directions and their ramifications. Most Canadians still cherish the values of caring, tolerance, and sharing, which have undergirded Canada's approach to social policies. According to the federal government, asked what they want, Canadians overwhelmingly (78 percent) stated that our social programs are essential (Social Planning, 9). This endorsement is contrasted by an edginess that calls into question the financial support of these programs every time their reform or review is mentioned. The confusion of Canadians has been caused in part by political leaders at every level of government, who have convinced the public that burgeoning levels of deficit and debt leave no options but to streamline, slash, or abolish social programs. They have argued persuasively that because of the exorbitant costs of paying interest on these debts, Canada can no longer afford to support longstanding universal programs. The political and corporate elite, worshipping at the altar of deficit reduction, can be found in all political parties and have framed contemporary debates in such a way that to challenge this prevailing orthodoxy is to risk marginalization. The actual causes of our current financial woes are issues such as the high cost of interest on the debt and lack of taxation on corporations—in short the cause is not social programs, which account for only a small portion of government expenditure.

Indeed the process of convincing people that debt reduction remains the most important policy goal of government largely began under the leadership of Brian Mulroney but has been continued and even accelerated under Liberal Prime Minister Jean Chrétien. During Mulroney's tenure, between 1984 and 1993, his government enacted cutbacks either overtly or by stealth, a process that relies mainly on technical amendments to taxes and transfers that are as complicated to explain as they are to comprehend and thus largely evade media examination and public scrutiny. The prime vehicle employed for this procedure is the Department of Finance which has control over tax policy, intergovernmental fiscal transfers, and expenditure restraint measures. The stealth approach was used for the partial de-indexing of tax credits, and certain transfers to individuals, cuts in federal social transfers to the provinces, change in the financing of unemployment insurance, and the clawback of family allowances and old age security benefits. Another technique of the Mulroney government was to cut the share of social expenditures to provinces and payments to Crown corporations, for example the CBC. These policy trends were rationalized at the time as being the result of fiscal restraint and program reform designed to respond to the needs of an aging population, an economic recession, and unemployment. However, these policy directions have resulted in the end of universality of social programs as Canadians have come to know them, whereby every citizen in society is entitled to the same benefits regardless of present economic circumstances. These policy decisions are critical, as they determine who is protected by society, the conditions under which protection is available, and the level of benefits provided. The federal Liberals, within weeks of returning to power in 1993, directed then Human Resources Minister Lloyd Axworthy to conduct a far-reaching review of Canada's social security system with the unstated aim of transforming its structure, ultimately leading to reduced benefits (Metro Network, 9). Finance Minister Paul Martin's 1994 budget saw massive cuts to unemployment insurance and his 1995 budget saw, among other things, the elimination of the Canada Assistance Plan (CAP), established in 1965, and its replacement by the unconditional and greatly reduced block funding ($7 billion over two years) of Canada's Health and Social Transfer (CHST). Across Canada, citizens are particularly concerned about any possible changes to Medicare, a social program considered by many to be the centerpiece of Canada's civility and a hallmark of Canada's unique value system (Rachlis, 31). Values of Medicare are incorporated in Table 2.1.

An in-depth discussion and analysis of the current restructuring and re-engineering of Canada's welfare state is beyond the mandate of this chapter except to state that, in the author's opinion, people appear increasingly worried and perplexed because changes to social policy, including potential alterations to Medicare, are in conflict with, and antithetical to, traditionally held and accepted Canadian morals, ethics, and principles. These changes may be symptomatic of Canada's becoming a harsher and less caring society and at the same time are in danger of hastening this process. Indeed, the values long held by Canadians are in the process of reevaluation and transformation, with a newly formed consensus yet to emerge. These changes are reflective of a worldwide phenomenon that is in large part beyond the direct control of Canada or any other sole country. Factors include globalization of markets and trade, which weaken national sovereignty as capital moves with mercurial speed across national boarders. The North American Free Trade Agreement (NAFTA) erodes Canada's control over jobs and economic development, as corporate interests are encouraged to move operations to a jurisdiction that allows them to minimize costs while max-

---

TABLE 2.1   Canadian Values for Health and Health Care

Essential Values

1. Equity
   - Canadians should have equal opportunity to achieve health and well-being.
   - Canadians should have equal opportunity to receive health services according to their needs.

2. Quality
   - Canadians should enjoy as high a quality of life as possible.
   - Canadians deserve high-quality health care.

3. Informed Choice
   - Canadians should be encouraged to make informed choices about their health care.

Instrumental Values

1. Health Environments
   - Public policy should focus on ensuring that all Canadians live in social, economic, human-built, and natural environments that enhance health and encourage healthy choices.

2. Accountability
   - Health care providers should be accountable for the public money they receive, including being accountable for the quality of care patients receive.
   - Citizens should be accountable for their choice of primary care provider.

3. Efficiency
   - Because resources are finite, it is important that health care services are delivered in the most efficient fashion possible.

4. Citizen Participation
   - Canadians should be encouraged to participate fully in their own care and in the care of their families.
   - Canadians should be able to participate meaningfully in decisions about their health care system.

imizing profits. Dr. Michael Welton, in his paper "Civil Society as Theory and Project, Adult Education and the Renewal of Global Citizenship," addresses the calamitous implications to Canada of such a policy:

> The most devastating illustration of Canada's new situation within the global market is the way the North American Free Trade Agreement (NAFTA) was forced upon a largely unwilling populace. Our political elites, led by Brian Mulroney, attempted to engineer public opinion, telling us that jobs would flow north once the agreement was put in place. Hundreds of thousands of Canadians didn't agree with the Prime Minister, and a mobilized civil society was engaged in an intense learning process over a several month period. Mulroney attempted to demobilize civil society; he did not succeed. But he did manage to block any kind of deep influence that was being generated within civil society. NAFTA passed. Between June 1989 and October 1991, Canada lost 461,000 factory jobs. In an impassioned critique of the Roman Catholic leadership, *Behind the Mitre*, Tony Clarke observed: "The country lost 23.1 per cent of its manufacturing jobs after the FTA was enacted, the worst drop since the Depression. Over 150,000 of these jobs had disappeared before the formal onset of the recession in 1990. In the same period the U.S. yielded only 6.3 per cent of its manufacturing jobs, roughly one-quarter of the Canadian loss. At the same time, the Mulroney government began the process of harmonizing Canada's social programs with those of the U.S. as required under the FTA, including the withdrawal of federal funding from our unemployment insurance program and the reduction of federal funding for health care, social assistance, regional development, and post-secondary education" (1995, p.1 51). Civil Society was under seige in Canada, and the System was driving "straight through our heart" to the unjust society (Barlow and Campbell, 1995) (Welton, 1996).

Corporate interests often accuse countries that offer generous social benefits of increasing the cost of business through social welfare provisions and threaten to leave unless these are curtailed, or use this as a rationalization for downsizing or moving locations. Governments across the western world appear to have abandoned their customary protective role as the custodians of indigenous values. In Canada, the provinces have been clamouring for greater powers from the federal government and, given the current economic climate, the federal government appears willing to accede to their demands in order to download costs onto the provinces and ultimately the local community. The precarious situation in Quebec, which is a key province demanding increased formal powers, has led other provinces to do likewise, and Ottawa, wishing to accommodate Quebec, seems to believe it has little choice but to capitulate. This leads to a gradual devolution of powers and a concomitant erosion of central government authority. This has serious implications for the setting of national standards, which is of great importance to the future of social and health care programs across the country.

Another key influence has been the accelerated continentalization, or Americanization, of Canada on political, economic, social, and cultural levels. Canada is increasingly influenced by the hegemony of the United States, exacerbated by measures such as the previously mentioned Free Trade Agreement. Canadian business is increasingly controlled by Americans as well as other foreign interests who are more likely to close a branch plant in Canada in order to locate in another jurisdiction, for example the southern United States, Mexico, the Philippines, or India, thus costing jobs in Canada. In addition, technology and lightning-fast communication networks mean that information can be transferred almost instantaneously anywhere around the world, thus accelerating the trend toward globalization and unwalled nations. Some of these radical changes will continue into the next millennium, and Canadians will have to learn to adjust and cope with this tumultuous postmodern world while, at the same time, protecting core values that have contributed to our civility.

IMPLICATIONS FOR SOCIAL WORK PRACTICE

Social workers deal each day with the impacts of funding cutbacks and shifting value structures, whether counselling a recently unemployed parent or a family struggling to make ends meet on reduced welfare payments; or dealing with domestic violence situations due to increased stress in the workplace and society in general or seniors straining to survive with curtailed services. The programs to which social workers have access across the country for their clients, the resources which are available, and the policies adopted and pursued by agencies, institutions, and government are largely built upon, and are outgrowths of, prevailing societal value structures. Should these value clusters and orientations erode or change, then it is quite likely that the services representative of these convictions will essentially change to reflect a new, emerging consensus. Canada's traditional values of caring, sharing, communitarianism, and tolerance have provided an ethical paradigm upon which Canadians have built a humane approach to the provision of social welfare. However, these programs, long accepted and even taken for granted by Canadians, are not inevitable or secure. As values and ideologies change, so will the institutions and programs that manifest those values. If Canadians continue to integrate and embrace a more Americanized approach to problem-solving, then our caring world view will give way to a more individualized, rugged and harsh way of perceiving the world. This may lead to further decreases in funding for social services, an erosion of Medicare, the implementation of user fees, privatization, and a deterioration of national standards.

Shared values form the core and soul of a nation and its people. Therefore, it is imperative for social workers at every stage of their career and in all fields to become aware of the important role that Canadian values have played in formulating a unique approach to social policy, to understand this historical context, and to understand the relevance of Canada's values to every day social work practice, whether working in a counselling office or hospital, working with groups in communities, designing policies, or administering programs. For by becoming aware of Canada's legacy and approach to social welfare, social workers can be in a position to protect and champion compassionate values, which serve as models not only for social work practice but for interacting with fellow human beings in a humane manner. At this time in Canadian history, debates are occurring around the new relationship between the state and civil society; Canadians are in the process of re-engineering the social accord that has been in place since the end of World War II when the modern welfare state was instituted. Canadian values, which were paramount at that time, are being challenged, and social workers must act individually and collectively to defend these values as well as what they represent and what they have accomplished. Social workers must not only do this for themselves, but for the clients they serve and ultimately for the future well-being of the Canadian nation.

REFERENCES

Andreae, D. (1995). A discussion of the current state of Canada's social welfare system and the adult educator's potential contribution to redefining public policy debate to affect societal transformation. Toronto, Ontario: Graduate paper prepared for the Ontario Institute For Studies In Education.

Avery, D.H., Kirbyson, D.C., Goodman, D.M., Young, R.J. (1989). *Canada in a North American perspective,* Scarborough, Ontario: Prentice Hall Canada Inc.

Clark, G. (1965). *The uneasy neighbour.* New York, New York: David McKay Company Inc.

Cockerton, C. & Hanna, W. (1996). *The human project: readings on the individual, society and culture.* Scarborough, Ontario: Prentice Hall Canada Inc.

Fraser, B. (1967). *The search for identity: Canada postwar to present 1945–1967.* Garden City, New York: Doubleday and Company.

Grant, G. (1965). *Lament for a nation.* Toronto, Ontario: McClelland and Stewart Limited.

Lapierre, L. (1992). *Canada, my Canada: what happened?* Toronto, Ontario: McClelland and Stewart Limited.

Matthews, R. (1988). *Canadian identity: major forces shaping the life of a people.* Ottawa, Ontario: Steel Pail Publishing with assistance of the Canadian Council and the Ontario Arts Council.

McClellan, G.S. (1977). *Canada in transition.* New York, New York: The H.W. Wilson Company.

Rachlis, M.P. & Kushner, C. (1995). *Strong medicine: how to save Canada's health care system.* Toronto, Ontario: Harper Collins Publishing Limited.

The Metro Network for Social Justice, Economic and Political Literacy Working Group (1996). *An economic and political literacy primer. A training manual for Metro Network for Social Justice Economic and Political Training.* Toronto, Ontario: The Metro Network for Social Justice.

Selman, G. (1991). *Citizenship and the adult education movement in Canada.* Vancouver, British Columbia: The Center For Continuing Education. The University of British Columbia.

Social Planning Council of Metropolitan Toronto (May 16, 1995). *Rewriting the contract with Canada.* Submission to The Standing Committee on Finance Regarding Bill C-76, The Budget Implementation Act. Toronto, Ontario: Social Planning Council of Metropolitan Toronto.

Social Planning Council of Metropolitan Toronto (1994). *Paying for Canada: perspectives on public finance and national programs.* A joint statement by: Child Poverty Action Group, Citizens For Public Justice, Social Planning Council of Metropolitan Toronto. Toronto, Ontario: Social Planning Council of Metropolitan Toronto, Special Collection (C.I.).

Smith, G. (1971). *Canada and the Canadian question.* Toronto, Ontario: University of Toronto Press.

Taras, D. (Ed). (1993). *A passion for identity: an instruction to Canadian studies.* Scarborough, Ontario: Nelson Canada, a division of Thomson Canada.

Welton, M. (1996*). Civil society as theory and project, adult education and the renewal of global citizenship.* From a paper presented to the Reconciling the Irreconcilable Conference: Leuwen, Belgium, May 1996.

POSTMODERNISM, SOCIAL WELL-BEING, AND THE MAINSTREAM/PROGRESSIVE DEBATE

Sharon McKay

The 1995 *Concise Oxford Dictionary* defines *intervention* as the practice of "interfering" for reasons determined by a state "so as to prevent or modify the result or course of events." This definition calls attention to the moral essence of interventive acts, for interfering can be for reasons that are good and those that are not, regardless of whether these are decided by the state, the community, or some other body such as a profession. Practitioners express social work's fundamental beliefs and values, commitments, and priorities through their interventions. Yet the goals of intervention and the means by which they are met have been the subject of intense debate throughout social work's history (Siporin, 1975; Reid & Popple, 1992). Frequently, these revolve around the extent to which the profession serves as an arm of the state, and the degree of influence that the state exerts over the uses to which social work puts its knowledge and expertise.

All professions exist to some degree by virtue of community or state sanction (Greenwood, 1957). Public recognition of a profession's knowledge and expertise and support of its value stance is essential if members are to carry out their practice with a reasonable degree of autonomy. Social work, however, is primarily located in agencies managed by the state or heavily dependent upon state funding. The extent to which intervention accommodates the state has been a core professional concern during most of social work's history. Critics claim that the profession's values, ethics, and knowledge base derive from dominant ideologies and assumptions, and the frame of reference, including intervention options, is limited to those acceptable to the state, causing social work to compromise its social change mission.

In the past two decades, Canadian social work scholars have made significant contributions to this debate, and to the development of theoretical perspectives that challenge traditional approaches to practice often referred to as *conventional* or *mainstream* social work.[1] This

---

[1] The terms *mainstream*, *conventional*, and *progressive* social work are troubling to me, primarily because they appear to divide practitioners into two camps. It appears in the *progressive* literature that practitioners can be categorized this way and most are believed to be in the "wrong" camp. The exclusiveness of self-acclaimed "progressives" is somewhat ironic at best, and at worst has the potential of undermining and debilitating the spirit of large numbers of front-line practitioners carrying out solid good work, albeit on an individual, small-group, or family basis. Although the terms have become part of today's professional parlance, they are placed in italics to indicate the unease with which they are used in this chapter.

chapter explores some of these contributions, placing particular emphasis on conflicting world views. These perspectives have challenged the profession and helped it grow, yet I would argue that at this point strong differences of opinion threaten to deeply divide our practice community and severely weaken social work's voice in matters of urgent social concern. To a large extent, we are "talking past one another" in counter-productive ways.[2] All too frequently the significance of various points of view is lost or dismissed, and efforts to enhance and strengthen our professional mission are seriously undermined.

At the beginning of this new century, new ideas emerge that challenge conventional and progressive ideologies. This chapter draws upon interpretations of postmodernism and the potential mediating perspectives of new approaches to welfare theory, to formulate a tripartite statement of purpose that may assist in building a stronger, less divisive sense of professional mission. Practice principles are posed for strengthening unity of purpose and respect for diverse approaches to intervention. A questioning attitude and critical self-evaluation are deemed essential for intervention work.

CONFLICT OVER PURPOSE:
THE PROGRESSIVE/MAINSTREAM DEBATE

Social work's identifying characteristic is its dual focus on person and environment. However, professional education and practice tend to emphasize the "personal" over environmental pressures and concerns. Critics allege that a major consequence of this tendency has been the "privatizing" of personal troubles. Social work has not challenged the social order, thus serving a conservatizing function, acting as the "social control" arm of the state.

In response to this criticism of traditional practice, Canadian scholars have led the way in articulating models of *progressive* social work, primarily through work built upon a structural approach to practice. Originating with the work of the late Maurice Moreau, the structural approach "aims to bring a radical critique to the central core of social work, namely its practice intervention" (Carniol, 1992). This critique focuses on identifying and addressing oppressive features of the environment: ageism, sexism, racism, ableism, heterosexism, etc. Drawing from Marxist and feminist theory, attention is paid to ways and means in which various forms of inequality are reproduced in society. Interventive practices aim to address "personal and political change" with clients (1–22).

Mullaly (1993) and Carniol (1984) believe that *mainstream* practice views the existing social world as legitimate and socially responsible whereas *progressive* practitioners assume that the social order and attendant inequities in societal structures and institutions are the cause of people's social problems. They strive to alleviate the painful effects of inequality and change the form of predominant systems and ideologies.

Mainstream practitioners do not refute the emphasis on social action, as the importance of attempting to change the social environment is implicit in their emphasis on person-environment transactions. Virtually all practice texts published since the early part of this century draw attention to environmental work. However, the assumption that *all* social problems stem from features of the dominant social order is not accepted. Moreover, terms used by *progressives* such as "oppositional" work, "unmasking" agency structures, and "exposing unde-

---

[2] I am grateful for the observation of Dr. Dan Salhani of the University of Regina Faculty of Social Work in this regard, and for his extremely helpful editorial assistance.

mocratic structures" (Carniol, 1984, 1987 and 1992) are seriously problematic both because of their emotional and political overtones and because they fit at best precariously with prevailing ethical codes.[3]

Popple (1992) outlines a brief history of the dualistic nature of the profession, noting that social work's emphasis on both person and environment produces conflict that can be boiled down to basic questions: "These questions involve, on one side, whether social work should concentrate on social or on individual change and on the other, whether social workers should be objective professionals more or less dispassionately carrying out a technical social function or partisan, selfless crusaders for various social causes" (141).

Mainstream or *conventional* and *transformative* or *progressive* social work perspectives on practice express different ideological viewpoints in relation to the questions Popple has framed. These viewpoints significantly influence the practitioner's assessment of the situation faced and the choice of interventive activities. Hence, it is essential that practitioners have a clear understanding of their own ideological leanings, and how these influence their values, thoughts, and actions, and the impact they have on their approaches to intervention. Likewise, it is imperative that the profession move beyond what appears to be an ideological impasse. In a society increasingly recognized as complex and diverse, how does social work ensure the best use of its collective knowledge and skills? How do we better address complex questions having to do with fundamental fairness in the distribution of individual and collective choices and opportunities, rights and responsibilities, especially in a resource limited environment? What new ideas and frameworks exist that can help us in the immensely difficult task of acting in the service of both justice and charity?

If social work is to play a significant role in contributing to human betterment in this new century, it is fundamentally important that a way be found to advance beyond the "ideological clash" (Carniol, 1984) that plagues the profession and work together on issues of much greater import than internecine conflict.

THE CHALLENGE OF POSTMODERNISM

Current ideas of postmodernism challenge both mainstream and progressive perspectives and approaches to practice. These are frequently difficult to understand and can seem bleak and despairing. However, the key concepts are relevant for social work, especially in relation to debates about mission and purpose.

Postmodernists' primary claim is that modernity, defined as "a period of time lasting from the Enlightenment of the eighteenth century and the rise of liberal/capitalist society" has come to an end (Irving, 1994, 20). Modernity is generally characterized as an age of growing belief in the scientific ideal; that is, that through new developments in the biological, physical, and social sciences, the problems and concerns of people over the ages would be reduced, and possibly eliminated. That is, solutions would be found for most of what

---

[3] In the Moreau et al. report, at least one illustration of structural practice raises serious ethical questions about the worker's conduct. This is a situation where the social worker speaks to her client about an upcoming court case concerning the client's attempt to gain full, unsupervised custody of her children, currently wards of the Children's Aid Society. The client has a history of depression and alcohol addiction. In the excerpt illustrated, the social worker repeatedly criticizes the Children's Aid social worker, John, e.g., "When John said that, I thought I would punch him.... He was basically saying if we threaten you enough, then you'd go straight." When the client comments that the last time John phoned he was nice to her, the worker replies, "Maybe he has had his little knuckles rapped." The illustration is viewed as an example of defense of the client, and no comments are made about the ethics of the worker's approach (Moreau et al. 1993, 169–176).

plagues humankind: disease, pestilence, poverty and other forms of social misery. Postmodernists argue that the promise of modernity has not been met, that science may have found its limits, and that the social ills of the ages are not resolved, and indeed may have been exacerbated by the scientific and technological accomplishments associated with modernistic thinking. Many postmodernists refer to the Holocaust as a phenomenon that exemplifies in a chilling way the inexorable march of modern technology.[4]

The postmodern critique of traditional theories offers social work a way of thinking about the "world views" that we generally refer to in speaking about social work purpose. It has been suggested that these views arise from dominant metanarratives or grand theories, and these in turn "serve to legitimate dominant political, scientific, and professional discourses" (Leonard, 1994, 14). Accordingly, metanarratives have been characterized as serving an oppressive function in society, perpetuating the capitalist/liberal social order to the advantage of the few over the many. Universal acceptance of dominant ideas and ways of doing things is assumed and diversity is ignored. It is often suggested that submerged in these metanarratives are the voices of the marginalized, e.g. the poor, the aged, the disabled, persons of colour, women, etc. The submerging of voices can result in social injustice. Therefore, it is necessary to deconstruct these narratives in order that all voices be heard and accepted as having validity. The discourse needs to be broad and emancipatory.

A number of social work scholars have recently called attention to postmodernism and its relevance for social work . It is their view that theory, concepts, language, values, and ethics central to practice are heavily influenced by dominant power groups, and must be challenged (Epstein, 1994; Chambon, 1994). This would seem to support *progressive* social workers' charges that *mainstream* social work acts as an agent of social control in the service of the capitalist enterprise. A closer look, however, suggests that many of the assumptions related to *progressive* practice must also be challenged. For the message of postmodernity is that the root of dominance lies in claims to general truth. These must be abandoned "in favour of a theory of difference of the diverse concrete social experiences of specific populations" (Leonard, 1995,7). To the extent that *progressive* theories make such claims to general truth, there is no reason to suggest that *progressives* should be any more exempt from criticism than the *mainstream* theorists that not infrequently have been pilloried by individuals holding strong *progressive* points of view.

Leonard states that this notion of difference, and the need to respect diverse claims, is "a painful renunciation which strikes at the impulse to generalization which often lies at the heart of *progressive* approaches to social welfare" (7). He and Brown (1994) speak, for example, of the uneasy relationship of feminism to postmodernity because feminist theory points to the centrality of women's experience, which in turn may lead to "the creation of a universalized, essentialized, uniform and immutable notion of 'the woman" as a category" (39).

From a social work perspective, the postmodern emphasis on difference poses a troubling image, that of a potential cacophony of voices, each speaking to their own uniqueness and personal claims to the resources of the state, and none able to identify with the other. If this is the postmodern future, what hope is there for working together toward transformative social change? Acknowledging this dilemma, Leonard calls for a way of recognizing some

---

[4] Observation personally conveyed by Dr. Ken McGovern, Dean, Campion College, University of Regina. I am deeply indebted to Ken McGovern for his astute comments on my explication of the challenge postmodernism poses to the *mainstream/progressive* debate. His assistance has been invaluable in expanding my understanding of postmodernist theory, including the process of revising the first edition of this chapter.

degree of commonality across diverse claims. Commonality is necessary to build the solidarity essential to such change.

Has the emergence of postmodernism and its implications for both mainstream and progressive practice created yet another theoretical and interventionist impasse? Commenting that "...dogmas of the Left can be pernicious as those of the Right...," Leonard (1995, 13) calls for adopting a primary critical attitude of skepticism. He urges a "dialogical" form of practice based on "critical pluralism," or recognition of the different paths to follow toward transformative social change and economic and social justice. In this regard, new ideas about the ways that people seek to have their needs met may be of assistance.

SOCIAL WELL-BEING AND THE CONCEPT OF CLAIMSMAKING

Emerging alongside the Canadian postmodernist literature, Drover and Kerans and others have been developing ideas about welfare theory, questioning how people attain a state of social well-being. They point to the idea of claimsmaking as a way of describing the actions that people take to have their voices heard and their needs recognized by society and its institutions. The process is that of "a contesting of cultural norms and assertion of new claims (against the state)" (Kerans & Drover, 1993, 52). The claimsmaking process raises several moral issues and questions and has implications for social work ideological stances and for the role of social work in assisting marginalized and oppressed people to effectively position themselves so that their claims will be recognized.

What is social well-being, and how does the claimsmaking process "fit" into ideas about social work intervention? Rioux and Hay define well-being as "the pursuit and fulfillment of personal aspirations and the development and exercise of human capabilities, within a context of mutual recognition, equality, and interdependence" (1993, 5).

In their edited book, Drover and Kerans (1993) and others explore ideas relevant to the defining of human need and the process of claiming rights to well-being. One of the central themes is how needs are defined; who defines these and what is the nature of the definition? In a 1993 article, the same editors observed that in the claimsmaking process, various groups struggle for "standing" or recognition for the legitimacy of their claims (Kerans & Drover, 1993, 50). Political decision-making will inevitably determine what needs will be recognized; hence the importance of being recognized as having a legitimate claim to the resources of the state and/or its institutions.

Drover and Kerans are interested in the dynamics of claimsmaking, including responses to various claims. As claimsmaking is an action process, they propose that ideas about welfare can be approached from the perspective of social action. This proposal "landed us in the middle of one of the central philosophical disputes of our time" having to do with universalist versus difference approaches to welfare (1993, x). How are questions of distributive justice determined? In what ways are basic needs defined? Can there be universal standards of the necessary ingredients for social well-being? What is a "fair share" of society's resources? What are the obligations of the state? How are questions of resource allocation to be made in the context of scarce resources? How are "natural endowments" and "handicaps" to be recognized and factored into questions of distributional equality? What about the needs of future generations—how can today's decisions be made in an ecologically responsible manner?

Responding to these questions leads back to issues related to the social order raised by progressives and postmodernists. Associated with these are fundamental questions connected to the nature of the social contract between governments and their citizens, debated since the time of Aristotle. What is the nature of the state's responsibility for the welfare or well-being of all of its citizens? What is the nature of the contract between each and every member of a community or society? Ideological debates within social work reflect the complexity of these questions. Progressives argue that the state concerns itself with the well-being of dominant power groups and systematically excludes certain groups from obtaining their rightful share of the state's resources. From a progressive point of view, mainstream practitioners tend to concentrate more on responsibilities of individuals and groups toward each other as family and community members. In this way, progressives believe that mainstream practitioners "privatize" issues, absolving the state from its share of responsibility. To some extent, the debates between progressives and mainstream practitioners have to do with differing ideas about who social work represents—the state or the community? Progressives appear to believe that social work always represents the state, whereas mainstream practitioners might well argue that this is the case only for imposed services, such as in child welfare, juvenile corrections and psychiatric institutions. Proffered or sought services are more representative of a community caring for its members.[5] From either viewpoint, the claimsmaking concept accentuates the necessity of strengthening individual and collective political skills if social work interventions are to be effective in the larger task of building a fairer and more equitable society.

The social well-being framework supports a reconceptualization of the role of government to that of empowering groups and communities to determine their own needs, and to design and regulate their services to meet these needs. The key elements of well-being (self-determination, mutual recognition and interdependence, equality, security, citizenship rights, democratization) can be exercised by decentralizing decision-making processes and supporting development of locally-based resources for addressing local issues and concerns (Rioux and Hay, 1993; The Roeher Institute, 1993).

In this regard, Drover and Kerans point to the importance of community. The re-emergence of social movements in Canada and elsewhere suggests that people are seeking groups and organizations that can adequately represent their diverse needs. From an inteventionist point of view, Wharf (1990) argues that social work needs to strengthen its grounding in community. Wharf views social reform as the primary objective of community work, noting that "the community [is] the meeting ground between social problems and social policies" (20 & 22).

Finally, "wellness" as a concept has been foremost in recent policy formulations of several provinces and territories, suggesting that ideas of social well-being may be influential in the task of reconfiguring governments and institutions to be more responsive to people's needs. New initiatives in the Northwest Territories and in Saskatchewan point to wellness as an idea that brings people together to work toward improving their communities and personal lifestyles (McKay, 1996). Underlying motives for governments' re-emphasis on community are questioned, coming as they do in a time of serious budget restraint. Nevertheless, if social work is to play a relevant role in the restructuring process, re-emphasis on community practice is essential.

---

[5] Germain and Gitterman (1980) conceptualize entry to service as being sought, proffered, or imposed. Practitioners must take service entry into account as this affects the nature of the relationship between practitioner and client and will heavily influence assessment and intervention processes.

THE INTERVENTION CHALLENGE

The foregoing discussion draws attention to the implications of debates about purpose and new and emerging schools of thought on social work interventive practices. Intervention activities go by many names: counselling, family therapy, behaviour modification, group work, community organizing, and so on. The choice of interventive activity, as has been mentioned, flows from assessment of the person-environment-situation complex. There is another element underlying this choice, however, and that is the element of moral purpose. What is the end goal of the interventive work and will this end goal contribute to the betterment of the human beings involved and to the larger society? Notions of the "end goal," as we have seen, may differ in accordance with the practitioner's own ideological point of view and where one fits in the mainstream/progressive debate.

Drawing upon the extensive work of mainstream and progressive scholars, I suggest that the mainstream/progressive/postmodern conundrum be resolved by reconceptualizing social work purpose, placing emphasis on three goals: *to support and strengthen people's natural abilities and capacities for handling their own affairs; to improve environments to ensure the conditions are present to maximize social well-being and provide care where needed; and to work toward transforming the conditions and social structures that create an inequitable social order.*

This tripartite formulation of purpose intends to strengthen social work's mission in relation to the commitment to social change. It is this commitment that is questioned by progressive social workers and others. As has been pointed out by social work scholars who have been influenced by the postmodern critique, progressive approaches can be equally problematic (Chambon, 1994, 1999; Leonard, 1994, 1997). By incorporating social work's responsibility to work toward transformative change, the statement calls attention to the importance of both recognizing diversity and working towards social justice, principles that seem to drive the postmodern enterprise. At the same time, it incorporates a strengths-oriented perspective, assisting people to draw upon their own personal and collective capacities and the resources in the environment to effect needed change. The statement acknowledges the interdependence of individuals, groups, society at large, and eco-systems by emphasizing that environmental improvement is for the purpose of maximizing social well-being.

Practice principles drawn from both the mainstream and progressive literature intend to mediate, if not resolve, the fervor of the debate respecting social work purpose:

1. *Critical Self-Awareness.* This is the recognition, as far as possible, of one's personal history, emotions, idiosyncrasies and ideological stance, motives, capabilities, and limitations, and how these factors influence the way one works with others. Critical self-awareness is purposeful, intended to strengthen the practitioner's ability to reflect on the practice process and to take corrective steps in the use of self where appropriate (Rossiter, 1995). In this regard, one must be cognizant that mainstream and progressive practitioners can each be blinded by the strength of their personal needs. The charges that mainstream practitioners fail to put energy toward social change because the therapeutic enterprise is personally satisfying can also be cast toward progressive practitioners, where the personal need to confront and challenge authority figures may cloud judgment and override considerations for the client's personal and/or collective welfare. In this regard, Rossiter (1995) writes: "the problem with [structural approaches] is that success depends on the client taking the proper political perspective—in fact the

social worker's definition of oppression....the belief that the social worker has a whole, rather than a partial perspective reinvokes paternalism and reinstates traditional power relations between worker and client" (14—see note 6).

2. *Augmented anticipatory empathy.* In their discussion of steps to be taken preparatory to contact with the client system, Germain and Gitterman (1980) refer to the process of anticipatory empathy, first conceptualized by Theodore Reik (1948). This process consists of four steps: identification (identifying with the client system's cognitive and emotional state); incorporation (taking on the client system's thoughts and feelings as though they are one's own); reverberation (recalling experiences of one's own that will assist in understanding the client system); and detachment (removing oneself from the preceding three steps in order to draw upon one's knowledge base for concepts, ideas, and other information that may be helpful to understanding the client system's situation). Carniol (1992) speaks of the idea of social empathy, described as a process of consciousness-raising, different from "the individualistic version which characterizes conventional social work" (13). In this process, the practitioner links the client's experiences with those of others in similar situations and shares information about groups that seek collective solutions. The worker encourages the client to participate in such groups, and assists in linking the client to them. As a means of enhancing the practitioner's preparation for contact with the client system, and ensuring that awareness of public issues is integral to this process, I suggest that the anticipatory empathy construct be augmented by including social empathy as a fourth step, followed by detachment. The steps in order of implementation would then be: identification, incorporation, reverberation, social empathy, detachment.[6]

3. *Attention to communicative ethics.* This involves paying particular attention to communication processes in order to ensure that the dialogue is compassionate and just. That is, that the dialogue emphasizes the active participation of the client system, and the "listening" capacities of the worker. Rossiter (1995) proposes that "such an approach demands from the worker the capacity to hold one's theories and perspectives in abeyance in order to take the perspective of the other. It requires the ability to give feedback from one's perspective in ways that do not annihilate the voice of the other. It requires the ability to tolerate and incorporate feedback that puts one's theories at risk. The principle is that the process of speaking and listening is the practical ground for justice and compassion" (18).

She claims that unrecognized "disempowering" practices, wherein the practitioner reproduces traditional power relations between worker and client, limit both the mainstream and progressive approaches to practice. Rossiter describes her experiences as a social work educator teaching communications courses that traditionally have been based on "saying the right thing" in various forms of simulated situations. She claims that the effect of this approach on students is to inhibit their ability to hold a meaningful dialogue with a client because of the pressure to respond in the "right way." In her view, this approach is technologically driven and tends to "oppose reflection and critical thinking."

Rossiter urges that social work educators reorient teaching to encompass a reflective mode of learning. The goal of such learning would be for students to develop two basic capacities: "i) the ability to take the perspective of another and ii) the ability to reflect critically on the ways one interprets the stories of others" (18). She draws from mainstream and progressive social work to enhance the communication process, and proposes that students be taught three communicative steps: i) empathic listening ii) reflection on one's own capacities and constraints, and iii) advancing the process toward the "bigger picture."

4. *Skepticism.* This refers to adopting a questioning attitude toward theories and explanations of truth of any kind. Practitioners should bear in mind that there are always other
ways of explaining observed behaviours and that understanding why and how things
happen must be based, as far as possible, on meaningful dialogue between the practitioner
and the other, whether this be the client(s) or some other person or persons relevant to
the assessment and intervention process. Recognizing that explanations can be emotionally charged because of one's personal values and beliefs or ideological world view
is important here. Distinguishing between what we know and what we value is critical
to appropriate intervention activities (Gordon, 1965).

Leonard (1995) speaks of the influence of postmodernism on social policy and
social work intervention, education, and research. He stresses that the postmodernist critique of foundation beliefs calls attention to the concepts of difference and diversity and
that these ideas have particular implications for those who attempt to practice progressive social work, which he describes as a socialist approach to social welfare. He
cautions that claiming "a status of absolute Truth" of any kind is questionable. Leonard
urges the adoption of skepticism as a critical attitude necessary to develop new forms
of practice based on a different form of dialogue between those who provide social
welfare services and those who are predominantly seen and acted upon as "targets of
intervention" (11): "Skepticism is the primary critical attitude we must adopt towards
all classification, remembering their frequent use as the means with which to 'discipline
and punish' subordinate populations."

5. *Partnership.* This refers to working collaboratively at all times with the client or client system. In essence, the work is shared and the partners are recognized as equals, although different. The client system has expertise in relation to the issues that bring practitioner and
client together. The practitioner possesses a different kind of knowledge, which includes
theories, resources, research, and policies affecting the issues. Where services are imposed,
there will be limits on the partnership relationship, but the essential principle of working
collaboratively still holds, as far as is possible within regulatory boundaries.

6. *Empowerment.* Overuse of this term has weakened the significance of its meaning,
which is, "having access to power" (Miley, O'Melia, DuBois, 1995, 68). The interventive challenge here is to determine how to gain access to power. Prior to this, however,
it is important to understand empowerment in its various dimensions—personal, interpersonal, and structural. Having power means having access to resources at each of
these levels. Personal resources include having a good sense of one's abilities and competence, and a strong sense of one's self-worth. Interpersonal resources include having
confidence in one's interactions with others, experiencing others' regard for one's abilities and opinions, and the ability to be influential in one's interpersonal relationships.
Structural empowerment refers to having access to information, resources, and opportunities at the level of the larger society. To operationalize this principle, practitioners can
adopt a strengths-focused and competence-promotion perspective, drawing upon and/or
creating needed resources in the social and physical environments (Miley, et al., 61–79).

7. *Strengthening Community.* Infused throughout the progressive and social well-being literature is recognition of and support and respect for collective interests and needs.
"Community" represents the spaces wherein people share their values, interests, concerns,
experiences, and resources. It is a connecting space that can be geographical or based

upon other diverse features of people's lives, such as sharing common identities and/or organizational loyalty. Yet globalization, competing interests, oppressive forces, dominant ideologies, and historical and current conflict of various kinds can weaken and fracture communities and impair their ability to work together in a meaningful way to meet the needs of their members. There is an urgent sense that community well-being is seriously at risk.

The current re-emphasis in Canadian social work literature supports the principle of strengthening community. Development of Aboriginal, northern, and feminist models of social work practice provides important frameworks for intervention (Wharf, 1992; Morrissette, V., McKenzie, B. and Morrissette, L., 1993; Delaney, R. and Brownlee, K., 1995; Delaney, R., Brownlee, K. and Zapf, K., 1996; Baines, C.T., Evans, P.M. and Neysmith, S.M., 1991; Taylor, S., 1992). Moreover, the political climate is ripe for strengthening social work's expertise in community. Ideas of democratization, citizens' rights, citizen participation, and community self-determination have gained considerable public attention in Canada over the past two decades and are reflected daily in local, provincial, and national politics and other institutions. To some degree, these ideas also reflect a growing public acceptance of, and respect for, diverse populations. Social work can play a strong role in facilitating community connectedness, self-direction and development, influencing social policy development toward more just and caring communities, and joining with others to "advance a vision of an inclusive and egalitarian public good" (Fisher and Karger, 1997, 180).

8. *Professional influencing, political action.* "Professionalization" is frequently viewed as the primary driving force behind social work's perceived unwillingness to adopt a *transformative* ideology and agenda. However, concerns about a weakening social justice mission have been expressed by both progressive and mainstream thinkers. These concerns have been linked to the profession's efforts to be recognized. Claiming that professionalism creates a climate wherein practitioners tend to drift toward forms of intervention that are most satisfactory to their own sense of themselves, some critics propose that social work abandon its professional credentials altogether. Proposing unionization as an alternative, Reeser (1996) comments: "As long as social work responds to the predominant values and assumptions of professionalism, it will react to the demands of the marketplace, emphasize individual status aspirations, and focus on providing those services that are most satisfying to the egos and class interests of social workers" (248).

Leonard (1994) believes that the postmodern critique represents a powerful indictment of professionalism because dominant grand theories have been articulated within professional practices. But the criticisms flow from the critics' ideological stances. How much do the critics know about professional social action activities in Canada? Across the country, over 10,000 social workers belong to their provincial bodies. Most are employed by agencies that to some degree limit their ability to speak out on matters of great concern. Political influencing is a key mandate of all provincial associations and of our national body, CASW. The professional associations offer a collective means of addressing issues that cannot be dealt with in many workplaces because of organizational restrictions or because the accumulated knowledge is not available. Not all members are active but their fees do support the associations' efforts to make the "voice" of social work heard on matters of significant importance to provincial and national social policy-making and implementation. This voice is frequently expressed in collaboration with or alongside representatives of many other diverse groups sharing similar interests and concerns.

Speaking out with a strong voice requires resources, including sufficient funding, a critical mass of volunteers, and solid research. Regrettably, resources are in limited supply, in part because of the debilitating effects of intraprofessional conflict that hamper the profession's "best efforts." From a claimsmaking perspective, social work's internal differences have weakened the profession's "positioning" as a legitimate voice in the country's policy debates. From an intervention perspective, I argue that active commitment to the work of our professional associations is a necessary and essential ingredient of the reformist enterprise.

CONCLUSION

Many would agree that social work is currently "under siege." The global economy, federal and provincial deficits, and declining government and agency funding heighten concerns about the profession's viability. Yet never before in recent history has there been such an urgent need for a strong profession. An alarming number of Canadians experience severe economic hardship in today's "jobless" economy. These are the young, the middle-aged and elderly, high school and university graduates, and well-educated professionals. Economic difficulties relate to and intensify all too familiar social ills: family breakdown, addictions, violence, illness, and despair. The profession is positioned at the front lines of social misery. No other discipline is as well suited to act in partnership with, and on behalf of, a growing social underclass. But the profession's voice is weak, and its influence on a macro scale is indeed minimal.

The challenge for social work in this new century is to ground its interventive practices in a clearly articulated, revitalized expression of identity and purpose. Seeking commonality among diverse opinions and knowledge and value bases can be the hallmark of a profession founded on a commitment to both charity and social justice. The postmodernist critique affords an opportunity to put mainstream and progressive debates to rest. Adopting a tripartite statement of purpose and principles and a social well-being framework can assist in strengthening the profession's leadership and interventive effectiveness in an increasingly complex world.

REFERENCES

Baines, C.T., Evans, P.M., and Neysmith, S. M. (Eds.). (1991). *Women's caring: feminist perspectives on social welfare.* Toronto: McLelland & Stewart.

Brown, C. (1994). Feminist postmodernism and the challenge of diversity. In A.S. Chambon and A. Irving (Eds.). *Postmodernism and social work* (pp. 35–48). Toronto: Canadian Scholars' Press.

Carniol, B. (1984). Clash of ideologies in social work education. *Canadian Social Work Review.* Canadian Association of Schools of Social Work, 184–199.

Carniol, B. (1987). *Case critical: the dilemma of social work in Canada.* Toronto: Between the lines.

Carniol, B. (1992). Structural social work: Maurice Moreau's challenge to social work practice. *Journal of Progressive Human Services*, Vol. 3(1), 1–20.

Chambon, A.S. (1994). Postmodernity and social work discourse(s): notes on the changing language of a profession. In A.S. Chambon and A. Irving (Eds.). *Postmodernism and social work* (pp. 63–72). Toronto: Canadian Scholars Press.

Chambon, A.S., Irving, A., and Epstein, L. (1999). *Reading Foucault for Social Work*. New York: Columbia University Press.

The Concise Oxford Dictionary (1995). (9th ed.). Clarendon Press, Oxford.

Delaney, R. and Brownlee, K. (Eds.). (1995). *Northern social work practice*. Thunder Bay: Centre for Northern Studies, Lakehead University.

Delaney, R., Brownlee, K., and Zapf, K. (Eds.). (1996). *Northern social work practice: issues and strategies*. Thunder Bay: Centre for Northern Studies, Lakehead University.

Drover, G. and Kerans, P. (Eds.). (1993). *New approaches to welfare theory*. Aldershot, Hants.: Edward Elgar Publishing.

Epstein, L. (1994). The therapeutic idea in contemporary society. In A.S. Chambon and A. Irving (Eds.). *Postmodernism and social work* (pp. 21–34). Toronto: Canadian Scholars' Press.

Fisher, R. and Karger, H.J. (1997). *Social work and community in a private world: getting out in public*. New York: Longman.

Germain, C. and Gitterman, A. (1980). *The life model of social work practice*. New York: Columbia University Press.

Gordon, W.E. (1965). Knowledge and value: their distinction and relationship in clarifying social work practice. *Social Work*, 1965, 10 (3): 32–35.

Greenwood, E. (1957). Attributes of a profession. *Social Work*, 2 (3): 45–55.

Irving, A. (1994). From image to simulacra: the modern/postmodern divide and social work. In A.S. Chambon and A. Irving (Eds.). *Postmodernism and social work* (pp. 35–48). Toronto: Canadian Scholars' Press.

Kerans, P. and Drover, G. (1993). Well-being & social movements. In M. Rioux & D. Hay (Eds.). *Well-Being: a conceptual framework and three literature reviews*. Vancouver: Social Planning and Research Council of B.C.

Leonard, P. (1994). Knowledge/power and postmodernism: implications for the practice of a critical social work education. *Canadian Social Work Review*, 11(1): 11–25.

Leonard, P. (1995). Postmodernism, socialism and social welfare. *Journal of Progressive Human Services*, 6(2) 3–19.

Leonard, P. (1997). *Postmodern Welfare: Reconstructing an Emancipatory Project*. London: SAGE Publications.

McKay, S. (1996). Rural and northern strategies in support of community-based change: implementing a social well-being framework. In Delaney, R., Brownlee, K., and Zapf, K. (Eds.). *Northern social work practice: issues and strategies*. Thunder Bay: Centre for Northern Studies, Lakehead University.

Miley, K.K., O'Melia, M., and DuBois, B.I. (1995). *Generalist social work practice: an empowering approach*. Boston: Allyn and Bacon.

Moreau, M., Frosst, S., Frayne, G., Hlywa, M., Leonard, L., and Rowell, M. (1993). *Empowerment 11: snapshots of the structural approach in action*. Ottawa: National Library of Canada.

Morrissette, V., McKenzie, B., and Morrissette, L. (1993). Towards an aboriginal model of social work practice: cultural knowledge and traditional proctices. *Canadian Social Work Review*, Vol. 10, No. 1: 91–108.

Mullaly, R. (1993). *Structural social work: ideology, theory, and practice.* Toronto: McClelland & Stewart.

Popple, P.R. (1992). Social work: social function and moral purpose. In R.R. Nelson, & P.R. Popple (Eds.). *The moral purposes of social work* (141–154.). Chicago: Nelson-Hall.

Reeser, L. (1996). The future of professionalism and activism in social work. In Raffoul, P.R. and McNeece, C.A. (Eds.). *Future issues for social work practice*, (240–253). Needham Heights, Mass.: Allyn & Bacon.

Reik, T. (1948). *Listening with the third ear.* New York: Farrar, Straus.

Rioux, M. and Hay, D.I. (Eds.). (1993). Well-being: a conceptual framework. In M. Rioux and D.I. Hay, (Eds.). *Well-Being: a conceptual framework and three literature reviews.* Vancouver: Social Planning and Research Council of B.C.

The Roeher Institute (1993). *Social well-being: a paradigm for reform.* Toronto.

Rossiter, A. (1995). Teaching social work skills from a critical perspective. *Canadian Social Work Review*, Vol. 12, No. 1: 9–27.

Siporin, M. (1975). *Introduction to social work practice.* New York: Macmillan Publishing Co., Inc.

Taylor, S. (1992). Gender in development: a feminist process for transforming university and society. In *Social work discussion papers: oval works: feminist social work scholarship* (25–40). St. Johns: School of Social Work, Memorial University of Newfoundland.

Wharf, B. (1990). Lessons from the social movements, in Wharf, B. (Ed.). *Social work and social change in Canada.* Toronto: McClelland & Stewart Inc..

Wharf, B. (Ed.). (1992). *Communities and social policy in Canada.* Toronto: McLelland & Stewart Inc.

C h a p t e r

SPIRITUALITY IN

SOCIAL WORK

PRACTICE
Hugh A. Drouin

Spirituality is as much a part of the human search for fulfillment as any other aspect of humanity.
(Early, 1998)

WHY THE RECENT LONGING FOR SPIRITUALITY?

In his book *The Road Less Traveled*, Scott Peck began with the words "Life is difficult." In his sequel, entitled *Further Along the Road Less Traveled*, he began by adding the words "Life is complex" (Peck, 1995, 13). Life certainly is increasingly more difficult and more complex in our fast-paced world. Social workers, as front-line professionals, are perhaps more sensitive to the increasing difficulties and complexities in their own lives and those of their clients. "Unprecedented changes brought about by globalization, the telecommunication explosion, and rapid advances in all types of technology, will make life even more fast paced and unpredictable as we move forward into the 21st century" (Drouin, 1999, 11). Faced with this contemporary unpredictability, people are searching for life anchors that will secure them through these turbulent times. Traditional life anchors such as church, family, and work have become increasingly less reliable.

In Canada, people are turning away from the church as their primary spiritual resource. Dr. Reginald Bibby, a leading Canadian expert on the sociology of religion writes, "The spiritual, personal, and social needs of an increasing number of people are not being met by churches—and often by no other institution or source either. Those empty pews become a symbol of fragmented, empty lives"(1995, 11).

The family, which has traditionally been a shelter from life's storms, is being undermined by government social policies that do not actively support it. Canada is in the disgraceful position of having the second highest poverty rate—after the United States—in the developed world (Drouin, 1999, 11). Global mobility of workers also means that extended family members do not often live in close proximity to one another. It is not uncommon for grandparents and grandchildren to be living in different time zones. "Spirituality holds much allure for a society facing widespread economic hardship, political uncertainty and family breakdown" (Stackhouse, quoted by Chamberlain, 28). The family is also facing the strain of unprecedented workplace stress.

Work, which had become a god for many in the last decades of the twentieth century, has turned out to be very much a false god. In many ways, workplaces have turned on their workers. They have become impersonal, harsh, and dehumanizing, ravaging people's very souls. Many of our workplaces are requiring more and more from their employees while at the same time doing less and less to support employees' psychological, emotional, family, and spiritual lives. Many workers feel they can't run any faster. More and more are describing themselves as "being stressed out and on the edge of burnout." They want to know if there is a greater purpose and meaning to their lives. They are tired of having to suppress the spiritual longings of their souls.

Massive corporate downsizing has caused fear and pain in those who have been let go and those who have been left behind. Many companies speak of people as their greatest resource and then turn around and lay off a third of their workforce. "Corporations throughout North America have fallen victim to willful neglect of their employees. The age of the downsizing frenzy continues to produce far too many victims. While some will argue that this is necessary to increase profits, accountability and productivity, this process of change has many dark valleys in terms of its human costs" (Drouin and Rivard, 1997, 1). People no longer feel safe at work; they no longer experience loyalty and a sense of belonging. People are no longer feeling the same level of connection or commitment to the company. They must search elsewhere for this connection, and for many this is the beginning of their spiritual search (Chamberlain, 29). Rutte writes that "The security we thought we got from the corporation is a myth. Real security comes from a connection to that which is truly secure—the spirit" (Quoted in Canfield and Miller 1996, 2).

Western society's overemphasis on individualism and materialism is showing cracks. The breakdown in community is resulting in a longing for more profound and meaningful connections to each other, to ourselves, and to something greater than ourselves. Two recent books address this issue in very insightful ways. The first is Robert Putnam's book, entitled *Bowling Alone*. This groundbreaking work by the Harvard professor of public policy shows the importance of rebuilding social capital and social networks in order to construct a more compassionate and civil society. He writes, "In 1992, three quarters of the U.S. workforce said that "the breakdown of community" and "selfishness" were "serious" or "extremely serious" problems....Those of us who said that people had become less civil over the preceding ten years outnumbered those who thought people had become more civil, 80 percent to 12 percent....More than 80 percent said there should be more emphasis on community, even if that put more demands on individuals" (2000, 25). The second work is a book entitled *Connecting,* by Larry Crabb, a licenced psychotherapist for over twenty-five years and professor of graduate biblical counselling at Colorado Christian University. He writes, "There's something about togetherness, at any level, that affects the heart. I have come to believe that the root of all personal and emotional difficulties is a lack of togetherness, a failure to connect that keeps us from receiving life and prevents the life in us from spilling over onto others (1997, 32). The longing for deeper connectedness has now become a pressing psychological, emotional, and spiritual need for an increasing number of us.

Demographic factors are also contributing to the current interest in spirituality. The children of the baby boom generation are now entering their 50s and they are asking the usual mid-life questions. Is there a bigger purpose for my life? What is really important for me to do or to become in the last half of my life? What mark do I want to leave on the world? These are spiritual questions and they are having a huge impact on our culture because they are being asked by a generation that comprises one-third of the population. People are beginning to question whether work has a place in our spiritual destiny because it takes up such a large part of our physical, social, and spiritual energies. "We are slowly awakening," writes Chamberlain, "to the fact that we are not simply human doings but human beings"(1997, 25).

Popular culture, always a mirror to what is taking place in the wider society, is exploding with spiritual themes. On the bestseller list have been books such as *Caring for the Soul, The Cloister Walk, The Seven Spiritual Laws of Success, Working on God, How to Know God, Reclaiming Higher Ground, Inspirational Leadership*, and many others. The Dalai Lama recently appeared before hundreds of thousands in Central Park. Magazine cover stories on spiritual subjects abound: *Time* featured "Jesus on the Web" one year, and the next year asked, "Does Heaven Exist?" A recent *Life* issue asks, "When You Think of God, What Do You See?" *Newsweek* ran a story entitled "The Mystery of Prayer: Does God Play Favorites?" and *U.S. News and World Report* asks, "The Bible: Is It Real?" and "Why Did Jesus Die?" Television and movies abound with spiritual themes. TV productions such as *Touched by an Angel* and *Providence*, and movies such as *Ghost, City of Angels, Meet Joe Black*, and *The Sixth Sense* all reflect a spiritual renaissance in our culture (Wolman, 2001, 16–17). In Canada, a recent edition of *Maclean's Magazine* titled its cover story "Soul Searchers." The feature article explored the growing number of Canadians who are seeking spiritual renewal by accessing retreat centres. The author, Sharon Doyle Driedger, writes, "It is a silent revolution. Quietly, privately, more and more Canadians are slipping away from hectic lives, claiming time for inner reflection in solitude" (April 16, 2001, 42). Wolman comments further on the current spiritual explosion when he writes:

> College campuses, always an important barometer of the current concerns and interests of the next generation, are also experiencing their own resurrection of interest in questions of morality, the spirit, religion, and the meaning of life. The most popular undergraduate course at Harvard University last year was a lecture course titled "The Bible and Its Interpreters," with an enrolment of 853 students....
>
> Medical education also reflects the demand for spiritual awareness on the part of students, in this case those who will be part of the healing profession. Harvard Medical School, like medical schools at Stanford, Duke, John Hopkins, Columbia, and others, have introduced courses on spirituality and healing, which tend to be some of the most popular in the curriculum; and undergraduate and graduate programs in psychology are now beginning to include discussions in their classes on the usefulness of spirituality in psychology. (26)

Wolman concludes that "the need for spiritual enlightenment to combat chaos and violence and provide some sort of inner peace has never been more profound" (22).

Yet another factor influencing the growing interest in spirituality is the increased body of research into workplace spirituality (Marcic, 1997; Mitroff and Denton, 1999). Much research activity is also going on in medicine, in the fields of body mind communication and the effects of spirituality and religion on healing (Wolch, 2000). An increasing body of research in the area of "SQ" or spiritual intelligence is also emerging (Zohar and Marshall, 2000; Wolman, 2001), from the increasing discoveries of brain research. SQ research is attempting to show "how we are biologically equipped by our brains to be spiritual creatures" (Zohar and Marshall, 2000, 36). Research into spirituality is also going on in the field of marriage and family therapy. "According to the *Family Journal*, over the past 15 years at least seven studies have directly assessed the relationship between marital satisfaction and spirituality. The results: higher scores on marital satisfaction are associated with higher levels of spirituality" (Chamberlain, 1997, 27). Spirituality is now out in the open and impacting the business, medical, research, and therapeutic communities.

HOW IS THE SOCIAL WORK PROFESSION RESPONDING?

The social work profession itself is undergoing a time of profound changes and challenges. A recent landmark comprehensive study of the profession, entitled *In Critical Demand: The Occupation of Social Work in Canada* (2000), began by identifying the context of the study with these words: "Social work finds itself in a time of dramatic change that seems at times to be tearing at the very fabric that comprises its raison d'etre"(p.1). The study identifies the growing need for social work services. Yet, it also identifies a growing devaluation of the profession by policy makers and the general public. This, combined with funding cuts, and more intense and complex cases, contributes to high stress and burnout in the profession. In light of these dramatic changes many social workers are asking spiritual questions about their own lives and practice—questions such as: How can I have a real impact on my clients when I am limited by funding, heavy caseloads, and my own high stress? Can I justify this stress long term? What will give? Will it be my family life, my sense of self, my hopes, my dreams?

What is this saying to the social work profession? I believe it is alerting us to the need to pay increased attention to how the profession is addressing the growing spiritual longings of its practitioners, of its clients, and of society in general. At this time in its history, the social work profession is being forced to navigate in very rough seas. It will need many anchors to keep it secure, but at its very core it will need to discover strong spiritual anchors to thrive in the new millennium.

Some evidence indicates that the profession is responding, albeit more slowly in Canada than in the U.S. In the U.S., the importance of spirituality in the lives of clients has been acknowledged in the curriculum policy statement of the Council on Social Work Education and in the *Diagnostic and Statistical Manual* of the American Psychiatric Association (Cascio, 1998, 523). Thus far in Canada, the *CASSW Board of Accreditation Manual* does not specifically address spirituality. Standard 5.10 H, reads: "the curriculum shall insure that the student will have awareness of self in terms of values, beliefs and experiences as those impact on social work practice" (*Accreditation Manual*—July 2000 version). This is as close as it comes to addressing spiritual issues in practice. More than eighteen American social work programs already offer specialized courses on the topic of spirituality and that number is increasing rapidly (Canda and Furman, 1999, 72). Separate courses on spirituality and/or religion are a recent phenomenon even in the U.S. All but four of these courses were first developed within the last five years. (Russel in Canda, 1998, 21). In Canada, only a handful of courses are being offered in spirituality in social work practice. There is some evidence in this country of a growing interest, as evidenced by the more frequent inclusion of spiritual themes at social work conferences, seminars, and workshops.

Generally, the last five years have seen an increasing interest in spirituality in the social work profession. Furman and Canda report that "five hundred articles, book chapters, or books related to social work on religion and spirituality" have already been published (1999, 71). They further report that "two social work practice texts and a human behavior theory text focusing on spirituality were recently published by Bullis, 1996, Canda, 1998, and Robbins, Chatterjee, and Canda, 1998. In general, recent social work textbooks now commonly refer, at least briefly, to spirituality and religion." (90). The Society for Spirituality and Social Work, headed by Robin Russel from the School of Social Work at the University of Nebraska—Omaha, sponsors conferences, seminars, and publications on "spiritually sensitive social work theory, practice, education, research, and policy"(163). The Society is receiving many requests from social work programs across the United States, for advice and information on curriculum development. A recent Society-sponsored conference in St. Paul Minnesota "opened with a panel of presentations about ways that we can nurture the soul of social work. A common theme was that we need to cultivate and support the spiritual development of ourselves, colleagues, students, and clients in all aspects of the helping experience" (Furman and Canda, 183). With the growing interest in spirituality in social work practice, it is important to attempt to define spirituality while recognizing that the definitions will continue to need refining as research and knowledge grows in the area.

WHAT IS SPIRITUALITY?

Spirituality is not easy to define. It is deeply felt but not easily articulated. Some have done an honourable job of describing their spiritual journeys. In *Markings*, the memoirs of Dag Hammarskjold, the very much revered former secretary general of the United Nations writes:

> I don't know Who—or what—put the question, I don't know when it was put. But at some moment I did answer Yes to Someone—or Something—and from that hour I was certain that existence is meaningful and that, therefore, my life, in self-surrender, had a goal. From that moment I have known what it means "not to look back" and "to take no thought for the morrow." (Quoted in Gallagher, 1999, 138.)

In attempting to further define spirituality, Winifred Gallagher, in her book *Working on God* (1999), relates the story of a man called Jeff who was concerned about someone going through a painful divorce. Jeff says, "In a crisis, we focus on the difficulty, ...but there's always something else that's going on too, something invisible that has to do with holding on to what's important and letting go of what's not" (139).

Social work scholars and others writing on the theme of spirituality like to distinguish between spirituality and religion. In their book, *Spiritual Diversity in Social Work Practice, The Heart of Helping*, Canda and Furman make the distinction in this way:

> Spirituality relates to a universal and fundamental aspect of what it is to be human—to search for a sense of meaning, purpose, and moral frameworks for relating with self, others, and the ultimate reality. Spirituality may be expressed through religious forms, or it may be independent of them. Religion is an institutionalized pattern of beliefs, behaviors, and experiences, oriented toward spiritual concerns, and shared by a community and transmitted over time in traditions. (37)

Canda and Furman further stress that "a definition of spirituality that will be acceptable for the common base of the profession needs to be inclusive of diverse religious and non-religious expressions" (38).

Spirituality has many other definitions and components. Below are other ways of understanding spirituality which may be helpful to social workers on their own journeys and in helping clients on theirs. Spirituality can be understood as:

1. Finding Our Place in the World

Martin Rutte, one of the authors of *Chicken Soup at Work*, defined spirituality in this way at a recent conference: "Spirituality in not a specific answer but rather a series of questions. A question allows you to look more deeply. It allows you to search for what's true for you, and in so doing deepen your own experience" (Spirituality at Work Conference, Toronto, Canada, 1998).

As we discover what is true for us, and that our spiritual experiences provide a deeper meaning in our lives, we begin to discover that we do have a unique and special place in the world.

2. A Longing for the Transcendent

Wayne Dyer, in his book *Wisdom of the Ages,* quotes the Zen proverb which says that "when the student is ready, the teacher will appear"(19). In the same vein, he quotes from Goethe, who says that "man is not born to solve all the problems of the universe, but to find out what he has to do" (19). Innate in us is the longing to connect to someone or something that is bigger than we are. We long to discover the path that will lead us to answer the questions: Who are we to be and what are we to do in this world? We desire as helpers to leave a legacy. Zohar and Marshall, in their groundbreaking book *Spiritual Intelligence, The Ultimate Intelligence*, express the longing for the transcendent in this way:

> Human beings are essentially spiritual creatures because we are driven by a need to ask fundamental or ultimate questions. Why was I born? What is the meaning of my life? Why should I go on when I am tired, or depressed, or feel beaten? What makes it all worth while? We are driven, indeed we are defined, by a specifically human longing to find meaning and value in what we do and experience. We have a longing to see our lives in some larger, meaning-giving context, whether this is the family, the community, a football club, our life's work, our religious framework or the universe itself. (4)

3. Searching for Inspiration from Within

Spirituality is the search to find more inward balance. Spirituality always begins by exploring one's interior life. It is about transformation in the deepest recesses of the self as we respond to life's more difficult questions. The richer our inner lives become, the more we will have to offer the world. Spirituality is about transforming our internal world so we can transform our external world. "Our behaviors are an outward manifestation of our inner life. If others cannot discern indications of our spirituality in our behavior, then it is not likely to be evident within ourselves either" (Marcic, 1997, 9). Michael Stephens, the president of one of the largest insurance companies in North America described inner inspiration in this way: "Transform yourself, you transform your family. Transform yourself, you transform your workplace. Transform yourself, you transform the nation. Transform yourself, you transform the world" (Spirituality at Work Conference, Toronto, Canada, 1998).

4. Developing Gratitude as a Way of Life

Many of us go to bed at night with the news and arise with it in the morning. The last thing we do at night and the first thing we do in the morning is to fill our minds with what's wrong with the world. It is any wonder that depression is the leading mental illness in our society?

Gratitude is part of spirituality because it helps us to embrace life more fully. It helps us to think about what's good in our lives and in the world. What would happen to our mindset if our evening and morning rituals consisted of thinking of ten things we are thankful for in our lives instead of listening to the news or to our fears and anxieties? We might just get healthier emotionally and physically. It has been demonstrated that gratitude "releases positive endorphins throughout the body, creating increased health. Gratitude not only heals, it rejuvenates the body" (Huffman, quoted in Hay, 115). James Eubanks offers this advice:

> Acknowledge the people in your life: those you love and those you may not love. In a true sense, they are all the same. They are your teachers. Be grateful for them. While doing so, realize how powerful you are, how moving your life is, and to what extent you are blessed in just being here. And then watch what happens. (quoted in Hay, 80)

Meister Eckhart, an early Christian mystic, stated that the most important prayer is just two words: "Thank You" (quoted in Hay, 128). The great German philosopher Goethe, toward the end of his life, said "that there would be very little left of him if he were to discard all that he owed to others" (quoted in Hay, 238).

In summary, I define spirituality in this way:

> Spirituality is becoming more human, by being more deeply connected to the God of our understanding and to others, so that we can offer fresh hope, faith, love and new life to the world. Spirituality is what enables us to grow greater compassion and community in our families, in our workplaces and ultimately in the world. Spirituality is the life force which unifies our lives.

OPPOSING AND SUPPORTIVE POSITIONS TO INCLUDING SPIRITUALITY IN THE MAINSTREAM OF SOCIAL WORK PRACTICE

Now that we have presented some definitions of spirituality, it is important to acknowledge that spirituality in social work practice remains controversial. Although there is increasing support in social work education and practice for including spirituality, it continues to be debated and many in the profession would object or be very cautious. This caution is to be welcomed, as it will assist in further defining and researching this important human experience and its implications for future practice.

In the recent *Spirituality in Social Work, New Directions* (Canda, ed., 1998), Early summarizes some of the objections to the integration of spirituality in social work practice. Some of the objections include "that the spiritual is unobservable and that introduction of spirituality threatens the imposition of the social worker's religious or spiritual frame of reference on the client problem" (68). Although this is not a new argument, it remains a valid one. The introduction of spirituality in practice necessitates spiritual self-awareness on the worker's part and spiritual sensitivity to the client by recognizing and accepting the client's spiritual and religious diversity. Cascio (1998) relates that practitioners often avoid spiritual issues because of the confusion between spirituality and religion.

> Religion in particular often holds negative connotations for some practitioners. First it is frequently equated with rigidity and dogmatism. In addition, some have expressed a fear of pathological consequences that religion can foster, such as excessive guilt, a view of God as punitive rather than healing and reinforcement of passivity by waiting for God to intervene. Other difficulties cited in regard to organized religion are the unequal treatment of women and the perpetuation of gender stereotypes....[T]here is [also] misconception that religion and spirituality are concerned solely with "other-worldly" matters rather than the here and now. (524)

The most comprehensive examination of the spirituality debate in social work is found in the 1999 text *Spiritual Diversity in Social Work Practice, The Heart of Helping,* by Edward Canda and Leola Furman. The authors conduct an analysis of thirty articles, book chapters, or books published from 1988–1998, examining statements of opposition or support for dealing with spirituality or religion in social work education. The results of Canda and Furman's analysis are presented below. Table 4.1 presents the opposing and supportive articles analyzed (Canda and Furman, 1999, 61), and Table 4.2 provides the opposing and supportive statements that they contain (63–4).

Table 4.1	Thirty Selected Publications Debating Inclusion of Spirituality and Religion in Social Work Education, 1988–1998
Opposing Positions	**Supporting Positions**
Clark, 1994	Canda, 1988b
Sullivan, 1994	Canda, 1988c
Weisman, 1997	Joseph, 1988
	Loewenberg, 19988
	Canda, 1989a
	Canda, 1990a
	Constable, 1990
	Denton, 1990
	Dudley & Helfgott, 1990
	Krill, 1990
	Logan, 1990
	Netting, Thibault & Ellor, 1990
	Siporin, 1990
	Marshall, 1991
	Ortiz, 1991
	Sheridan & Bullis, 1991
	Sheridan et al., 1992
	Amato-von Hemert, 1994
	Canda & Chambers, 1994
	Cowley & Derezotes, 1994
	Furman, 1994
	Derezotes & Evans, 1995
	Krill, 1995
	Bullis, 1996
	Van Soest, 1996
	Canda, 1997a
	Russel, 1998

Table 4.2	Resolving the Debate about Studying Religion and Spirituality in Social Work	

OPPOSING POSITIONS	SUPPORTING POSITIONS
Institutional Defects	**Institutional Challenges and Strengths**
Sectarian views are too limiting or biased for the profession.	Use an inclusive view of spirituality.
Rigidity, dogmatism, and judgmentalism of religion is worrisome.	Engage diverse ideological and spiritual perspectives.
Religions are basically status quo maintaining.	Address the role of religions in both restricting and promoting justice.
Spiritual concerns are overly focused on micro rather than macro justice.	Identify both micro and macro implications of spiritual and religious perspectives.
Personal Defects	**Personal Challenges and Strengths**
Religion is an expression of psychopathology.	Identify the role of religions in both restricting and promoting mental health.
Spirituality is inherently personal and idiosyncratic.	Link micro and macro issues of spirituality.
Domain Concerns	**Domain Implications**
Religion and social work are separate and mutually exclusive domains.	Religion, spirituality, and social work are interrelated and complementary.
Religion and spirituality are not very important for understanding clients.	Religion and spirituality are crucial for understanding clients.
Addressing religion and spirituality would undermine the status of the profession.	Addressing religion and spirituality competently would enhance the status of the profession.
Value Conflicts	**Value Dilemmas**
Involving religion increases the danger of proselytization and violation of clients' self-determination.	Address spirituality in a manner consistent with professional values.
Social work should be value-free or objective.	Social work is inherently value-based and spiritual.
Religion and spirituality are inconsistent with a scientific professional base for practice.	Addressing spirituality is consistent with the contemporary philosophy of science in social work.
Social workers tend to be irreligious or uninterested.	Social workers are often religious and always spiritual; ethical and moral reflection in practice are necessary.
Inadequate State of the Art	**Emerging State of the Art**
Concept of spirituality is too vague for use.	Refine definitions.
Efforts to combine religion and social work are not adequately developed.	Utilize extensive available knowledge and skill for linking spirituality to service; continue development.

Table 4.2	Resolving the Debate about Studying Religion and Spirituality in Social Work (continued)
Workers are unprepared to address, so better to ignore or refer.	Enhance education of workers.
Curriculum Concerns	**Curriculum Opportunities and Responsibilities**
Curriculum is already too crowded.	Implement both infusion and specialization in curriculum.
Educators are unprepared to teach, so better to ignore.	Have continuing education and curriculum development for teachers.

The opposing positions decribed here are not comfortable with mixing spirituality and religion with social work practice. They see many practical and logical difficulties and do not feel that it is appropriate to include it in education and practice. They see basic defects in religious institutions and individuals and see these defects being amplified in education and practice if spirituality is introduced in the curriculum and practice. They also are suspicious that religion and spirituality cause more harm than good in people (Furman and Canda, 1999). They see spirituality as potentially too rigid, judgmental and narrow: "Since the profession of social work has a purpose to promote individual well-being and social justice for all people, opponents argue it is not appropriate to use sectarian, judgmental, status-quo-maintaining, micro focused, fantasy-based frameworks to guide our profession" (Furman and Canda, 66).

We must keep the opposing views to the integration of spirituality in social work constantly in mind as they will inform us of potential difficulties. However, it is clear from the growing literature, research, and broad spiritual renaissance in society, that social work as a profession will need to keep responding to what has become a very prevalent social phenomenon. Again, Furman and Canda address the spiritual debate in the profession in a constructive fashion.

> Supporters generally agree that there are legitimate concerns about using competitive and rigid ideological, judgmental, or oppression-maintaining frameworks to guide social work practice. But this applies to both religious and nonreligious forms of belief and behavior. Political ideologies, human behavior theories, practice models, and agency policies and procedures all can reflect rigid, punitive, judgmental, or oppressive assumptions. We need to face these biases and obstacles to human well-being and justice whenever they are found, in religious settings and elsewhere. Avoiding the topics of religion and spirituality because of these problems only allows them to continue without open examination. (66)

Supporters view spirituality and religion in social work practice as possible resources and strengths that both clients and communities can access. They see a well-developed, wise, and professional application of spirituality as a force for good and for positive change in students, social worker, and clients. Supporters are cognizant of the potential pitfalls and tensions but see these as opportunities for knowledge growth in the profession through continuous dialogue, study, and research, leading to the appropriate integration of spirituality in social work education and practice. "The contrast between the lack of opposing publications and the plethora of supporting publications is quite remarkable. It belies the impression among many social workers that this topic is taboo" (Furman and Canda, 1999, 62).

Spiritually Sensitive Social Work Practice

It is only in the place of healing that we dare show our wounds. One of the most worthy aspirations of spiritually sensitive social work practice is to create this place of healing in our work with individual clients, couples, and families. Given the stress and strains that social workers are under at the beginning of the twentieth century, social workers in positions of leadership will also be called upon more often to create these places of healing in their own organizations. Such developments will be based on the leadership wisdom and compassion that understand that carers need caring.

This place of healing is most often created when the helping relationship is immersed in caritas. Caritas is a form of transformational spiritual love. Max Siporin, in his book *Introduction to Social Work Practice,* writes that "love is a basic value for social workers" (70). Of the many forms of love, that called caritas ... is considered to be the highest (C.S. Lewis, quoted in Siporin, 1975, 70). Gordon Allport writes that "the motive behind social work always has been and will continue to be caritas, and this motive is infinitely valid" (Quoted in Siporin, 70). Paul Tillich, the famous theologian, defined love in social work practice in this way: "Fundamental in the philosophy of social work is a listening love, or caritas—the love which descends to misery and ugliness and guilt in order to elevate. This love is critical as well as accepting and is able to transform what it loves" (Quoted in Siporin, 70). It is this caritas or transformational love that empowers the social worker. Without caritas, the essence of the human person would be lost to the social worker. Even if given the best technology and skills at his or her disposal, the social worker without caritas would be unable to perform his or her art, that of transforming human lives. But where does this caritas come from? I believe that this transformational love can only come from our deep connection with our spiritual selves. This is why it is critical for social workers to be opened to spirituality if they want to be able to participate more fully and more deeply in the transformation of lives.

The mission of social work, as defined in our code of ethics, implies a commitment to service, to social justice, to upholding the dignity and worth of the person, to integrity, to competence and to the importance of human relationships (Canda and Furman, 1999). "All of these commitments imply a stance of compassion with a transpersonal, that is, ego-transcending, orientation, a profound and challenging spiritual ideal" (6). Canda and Furman argue further that

> To the extent that we remain alert to his continuing call to service as a spiritual journey, we retain a sense of purpose, excitement, and vitality. This is a very personal and compelling reason to keep the connection between spirituality and social work alive and well within our practice as students, practioners, educators, and researchers. (12)

Spiritually Sensitive Social Work Leadership

Spiritual leaders are servant leaders. That is, they see service to others in their organizations as a privilege, honour, and spiritual calling. Spiritual leaders are people-centred. When they look at their staff, they don't see human resources. They see people with lives full of potential. Abraham Maslow said, "The unhappiness, unease and unrest in the world today are caused by people living far below their capacity"(Quoted in Percy, 1997, 12). Spiritual leaders are people-miners. They see their place and calling in the world as a mining expedition to discover all that is good in others and to help them release their gifts so they can increase their capacity for their own and others' benefit in the organization. Spiritually sensitive servant leadership aims to raise an organization to higher ground by treating everyone in the organization, regardless of position, as a precious human being. As Percy, a prominent organizational consultant, notes in his book, *Going Deep* (1997), the spiritually sensitive social work leader recognizes "that the workplace is also a human place. A place where human beings seek connection, fulfilment, meaning" (4). Percy writes further that "We are not just human resources and head count, meant only to be re-engineered and deconstructed. We are the sacred handiwork of God" (11). Spiritually sensitive leaders deeply respect the sacredness in others.

CONCLUSION

In the next few years of the twenty-first century, social work will continue to be challenged to remain open to the growing and expanding spiritual developments in the world. It will need to embrace these new developments in order to build further knowledge and research that can potentially enrich the lives of its members and that of its clients. Spirituality also has the potential to transform social service organizations into nurturing, respectful, healing, and sacred places of work for social workers. Social workers in such healing organizations will have more to give to their clients as they themselves will be the recipients of respect, nurturing, and healing.

The integration of spirituality into social work practice presents an unprecedented opportunity for the profession to deepen its impact on society.

REFERENCES

Bibby, R.W. (1995). *There's got to be more! Connecting churches and Canadians*. Kelowna, B.C.: Wood Lakes Books.

Canadian Association of Schools of Social Work, Canadian Committee of Deans and Directors of Schools of Social Work, Canadian Association of Social Workers, and Regroupement des Unite de formation universitaire en travail social (2000*). In critical demand: the occupation of social work in Canada.*

Canda, E.R. and Furman, L.D. (1999). *Spiritual diversity in social work practice. The heart of helping*. New York: The Free Press.

Canda, E.R. (Ed.) (1998). *Spirituality in social work, new directions*. New York: The Haworth Press.

Canfield, J. and Miller J. (1996). *Heart at work*. Toronto: McGraw Hill.

Cascio, T. (1998). Incorporating spirituality into social work practice: a review of what to do. *Families in Society: The Journal of Contemporary Human Services*. Families International, Inc. September/October.

CASSW. (2000). *Board of accreditation manual*. July.

Chamberlain, P. (1997). The quest for spirituality. *Faith Today*, September/October.

Crabb, L. (1997). *Connecting, a radical new vision*. London: Word Publishing.

Denton, E.A. and Mitroff, I.I. (1999). *A spiritual audit of corporate America. A hard look at spirituality, religion, and values in the workplace*. San Francisco: Jossey-Bass.

Driedger, S.D. (2001). Soul searchers. *Maclean's*, April 16.

Drouin, H.A. (1999). Some reflections on family on the eve of the 21ˢᵗ Century. *OASW Newsmagazine, The Journal of the Ontario Association of Social Workers, 26*(3), 11–12.

Drouin, H.A. and Rivard, D.B. (1997). *No stone unturned. Building compassion, community and spirituality in the workplace.* Toronto: Family Service Institute.

Dyer, W.W. (1998). *Wisdom of the ages. A modern master brings eternal truths into everyday life.* New York: Harper Collins.

Gallagher, W. (1999). *Working on god.* New York: Random House.

Hay, L.L. (1996). *Gratitude: a way of life.* Carlsbad, CA: Hay House, Inc.

Marcic, D. (1997). *Managing with the wisdom of the heart. Uncovering virtue in people and organizations.* San Francisco: Jossey-Bass.

Peck, S.M. (1995). *The road less traveled.* Toronto: Simon and Schuster.

Percy, I. (1997). *Going deep in life and leadership.* Toronto: MacMillan Canada.

Putnam, R. (2000). *Bowling alone. The collapse and revival of American community.* New York: Simon and Schuster.

Rutte, M. (1998). Keynote Address, Spirituality at Work Conference, University of Toronto, Canada.

Siporin, M. (1975). *Introduction to social work practice.* New York: MacMillan Publishing Co.

Stephens, M. (1998). Keynote Address, Spirituality at Work Conference, University of Toronto, Canada.

Wolch, S. (2000). Rethinking medicine: health and healing in the 21ˢᵗ century, *CBC Ideas.* Toronto: Produced by Canadian Broadcasting Corporation.

Wolman, R.N. (2001). *Thinking with soul. Spiritual intelligence and why it matters.* New York: Harmony Books.

Zohar, D. and Marshall, I. (2000). *SQ, spiritual intelligence, the ultimate intelligence.* London: Bloomsbury.

THE THEORETICAL BASES OF PRACTICE

Francis J. Turner

If there is any single term that best describes the theoretical bases of contemporary Canadian social work practice it would be that of diversity. Thus, if one examined the methods courses of Canadian faculties and schools of social work, or questioned practitioners from a sample of agencies as to the theoretical base from which courses were being taught or upon which practice is based, a myriad of responses would be found. These would cover the broad spectrum of social work practice theories currently extant in social work literature. Indeed one of the challenges facing professors and practitioners, and one of the quandaries facing students, is what theories to teach and what theories to follow (Turner, 1996).

That one needs to build practice on a theoretical base is a given of any profession prepared to be accountable for the actions it takes with, and on behalf of, clients. It would be understandable to imagine that we should be able to talk of a general theory of social work practice. However, as knowledge of the human person in interaction with societal systems expands, so too does the awareness that, at this point in our history, there is no one theory that helps us to understand the entirety of the broad range of societal situations, issues, personal reactions, and problems encountered by today's practitioners. Over the years, as social workers' sphere of influence has expanded, so too have the bodies of theory that have emerged to aid us in understanding phenomena in a way that gives us direction as to how to proceed (Lewis, 1982).

To fully understand the varying perceptions of theory that a beginning practitioner will meet in practice it is important to understand something of how practice theory developed in social work. The earliest small-system or micro-practitioners, then called "caseworkers," practised from what might be called an "atheoretical" base. They acted from a deeply-felt concern for the mammoth social problems of the day and their terrible impact on persons. Their perception of human functioning was based on a moralistic view of humans, but one greatly tempered by an awareness of the debilitating effects on human potential of the social realities in which they lived. But there was also an awareness of the complexity of the causes of these social realities and the range of individual responses to them, as well as of the inadequacies of any then existing perceptions of human or societal functioning to explain them.

Thus when psychoanalysis emerged in the early decades of this century with a rich theoretical explanation of many of the day-to-day realities social workers met in the persons and situations of their clients, it was seized upon as "the theory"— and not only by social workers but by many in other human service professions, especially in North America. Since it was a theory so rich in its conceptual base, and since it filled a much needed gap for practitioners, the enthusiasm with which it was adopted is understandable. For many it became all-explaining and was an important cause of the complex division in the profession between emphasis on social change and work with individuals, groups, and families. The risk of this kind of over-zealous adherence is that at times situations and persons are made to fit the theory rather than the reverse. Along with this enthusiasm came a tendency in some social work circles to view this theory in an almost dogma-like fashion. A corollary of this was to consider those who did not subscribe to it to be non-believers. Indeed at times the theory was used to counter those who challenged it, diagnosing such challenges as a form of "clinical resistance" requiring treatment by those of the faith.

However, early in the development of Freudian theory some of the very gifted and highly intelligent first students of the "master" did challenge aspects of the theory and several new schools of thought began to emerge. Among these questioners were many who had quickly realized that psychoanalytic theory could not explain aspects of reality that were systemic and societally-based rather than intra-psychic. Further, colleagues had long recognized and understood that there were many more healthy aspects of personalities than first understood by psychoanalysis. Thus some social workers began to look to other emerging schools of psychoanalytic thinking and beyond. For micro-focused social work the most important of these emerged from the thinking of Otto Rank, whose theory of social work practice came to be called functional theory. By the mid-1940s a large segment of caseworkers, especially in the United States, found this a much more compatible theory, closer to the realities of practice than psychoanalytic thinking. This theory began to be taught in several high profile schools of social work, most notably the University of Pennsylvania. However, many practitioners and teachers still remained very identified with more traditional Freudian theory. Thus there quickly emerged in our profession the first major theoretical split between what came to be called the "diagnostic school" and the "functional school." What is important to understand about this division in the profession is that the advocates of each were strongly of the opinion that there could be only one theory, or one truth, and thus those who held a contrary opinion were viewed to be in error and indeed, depending on the intensity of one's adherence to one school or another, as heretics (Dunlap 1996).

Although for the most part this division occurred in the United States, elements of this division were present in Canadian practice since many Canadian social work practitioners and academics received their professional training south of the border. Even though this diagnostic-functional schism is no longer an issue of importance in contemporary practice, the fall out from it is still a reality. This shows itself in the strong tendency in some parts of the profession to continue to view theories as quasi belief systems. When this happens, persons who become strongly attached to a particular body of theory will frequently argue its importance by discrediting or ignoring other theories.

At times these inter-theoretical differences are at the level of friendly rivalries and healthy challenges between the various advocates. However, at other times such differences have become strongly entrenched and acrimonious. Thus at times schools have become strongly identified with particular theories and have overlooked others. Similarly, some agencies structure their services along a particular and frequently highly restricted theoretical base, as do some practitioners.

Clearly there is an important place in social work for persons and services to become expert in any one particular theoretical orientation. What is of concern is this being done in a manner that holds that there is no other valid theory.

THE PRESENT SITUATION

Thankfully, the tendency to view theory dogmatically has not been as intense in Canada as in other places. Even though it has existed here, the tendency has abated considerably since the late 1970s. There are several reasons for this. The first was the growing understanding that rightfully to be designated as a theory a body of thought had to be capable of being tested, and tested on an ongoing basis. Unlike a belief system, a theory is a set of concepts in a constant process of being translated into testable procedures and thus in a constant state of development. The second factor, related to the first, was the dramatically increased commitment to an understanding of research as an essential function of a profession that dared to intervene in the lives of clients and the intricacies of social systems and conditions.

The third factor was the growing awareness of the limitations of our theoretical base of practice, and concomitantly an excitement and respect for the emerging richness of knowledge about the human condition, societal structures, and their interaction, which other theories presented.

A fourth influencing factor—one still not universally accepted but which is having a strong impact on practice—is the growing understanding that the many theories available to us are rarely mutually contradictory but rather are interlocked in a way that enhances our understanding and the effectiveness of practice by giving us a broader range of alternatives with which to function.

From the interaction of these variables, accompanied by a growing awareness of the immensities of practice demands and challenges, and the necessity of a greatly expanded research base, the 1980s and 1990s have been marked by a growing acceptance and welcoming of the fact that a pluralistic theoretical base is a requirement for contemporary social work practice in any part of the profession.

This acceptance of a pluralistic theoretical base seems to have taken place more rapidly in Canada than elsewhere. Although we do not have adequate data at present, it may be that Canada's long tradition of multiculturalism has been a factor in this. Whatever the cause, there has been a much quicker acceptance of theoretical diversity, a much lesser degree of inter-theoretical acrimony, and a greater ability to deal with diversity than in many other parts of the world (Goldstein, 1990).

THEORY IN PRACTICE

But what is the relationship between theory and practice? Let us begin with a brief understanding of theory. Theory is the term that describes those efforts that have marked the history of the human race to explain various aspects of the reality around us in a special way. Such explanations are not based on authority, belief systems, the alignment of the planets, or on the charismatic qualities of the author; they are provided in a manner that can be tested and verified by others. That is, explanations stemming from a theory are deductions based on observation and reason. Such observations and predictions, if accurate, will be verified by others. Theory is not a closed system, but, as mentioned earlier, a very dynamic one that expands and develops as more and more is found about aspects of the human condition in interaction with society and its systems. Thus a particular theory is *never* the last word on a topic but an ongoing effort to explain some aspects of reality based on the accumulation of knowledge at that point in time. Hence an important component of theory is that it is always changing as new observations are made, as new techniques emerge, and as new hypotheses are formulated about some aspect of reality.

Because of the complexity of the social work endeavour in Canada, as in other parts of the world no theory attempts to explain all the reality with which we deal. Rather, to an increasing extent theory focuses on specific components of that reality.

The purpose of theory for a social worker is of course to make practice as effective, safe, and efficient as possible with the greatest degree of certainty that is available. Thus for the practitioner, theory helps us to answer important questions: Who is the client, what is the reality in which he or she is living, what is it that he or she seeks, what kinds of resources, skills, knowledge, theories, strategies and techniques do I or others have available that would seem most useful in this situation? What are the kinds of risks for the client, for others in the client's life, and for me, if I proceed in a specific way based on my understanding of the situation and the persons and systems involved? What are the various possibilities open to me to achieve a particular goal and, among these, which ones appear to be most appropriate in this situation? What is the level of my understanding here? That is, with what degree of confidence am I functioning? What are the aspects of this situation that I do not understand, that do not appear to fit into my theoretical repertoire? Are there others who might better understand? When am I comfortable and confident to act on my own? When should I involve my colleagues? When should I seek other resources and other competencies? We always need to keep in mind the potential risk to clients and the potential, when dealing with larger systems, to create more systemic problems than one is solving.

In summary, theory gives us the conceptual legitimacy to function responsibly in our practice. Of course, because we are dealing with fellow humans and complex social systems, rarely do we act with total certainty. Thus we need to be aware of the awesome responsibly we have in practice to be constantly in a searching, learning, testing mode (Imre-Wells, 1984).

OUR THEORETICAL REPERTOIRE

In earlier times there was a hope that a unified body of thought would emerge that could be called "social work theory." It was presumed that for social work to stand alone as one of the major professions in the human services it should have a distinguishing body of theory. This concept emerged from a mis-perception that each profession had its own unique and unified body of theory, and that somehow the concept of diversity in our profession weakened our identity. However, as the body of knowledge of the human professions developed over the past several decades, it soon became clear that no one profession has a single body of theory. All are aware that to fully address the range of situations within the scope of each profession a range of theories is necessary. Thus, theoretical diversity is a distinguishing feature of all the human professions. Certainly in one sense one can talk about psychological theory, or social work theory, or psychiatric theory, but this needs to be understood in a generic or abstract way that encompasses a wide range of differing models of theory.

In contemporary social work practice in Canada there can be identified close to thirty different theoretical bodies that drive practice. Since there are a variety of ways in which theories can be classified, and since some theories are very similar, it is important that this figure of thirty not be seen as an absolute. Different authors would come up with a different count. What is important to know is that the range is broad and highly diverse—a very long way from the turn of the century when the profession was without theory. One possible listing of these theories is as follows (Turner, 1996):

Aboriginal theory	Life model theory
Behaviour theory	Materialist or structuralist theory
Client-centered theory	Meditation
Cognitive theory	Narrative theory
Communication theory	Neurolinguistic programming theory
Constructivism	Postmodernist theory
Crisis theory	Problem-solving theory
Ego psychology theory	Psychoanalytic theory
Empowerment theory	Psychosocial theory
Existential theory	Role theory
Feminist theory	Systems theory
Functional theory	Task-centred theory
Gestalt theory	Transactional analysis theory
Hypnosis	Transpersonal theory

All of these theories can be found within the practice of at least some Canadian social workers. Some might add others, few would delete any from the above list. Again it is to be stressed that this is not to be seen as a definitive list. Since we know that theories are dynamic systems, within the current spectrum of existing theories some are moving closer together, some farther apart, and new systems are emerging.

SOME COMMON THREADS

But are these systems totally separate from one another, or do they have similar qualities that would justify their being included in a listing of social work theories?

Indeed there is much in common among these theories. Each of these systems attempts to address some aspect of the person-in-situation, the uniting thrust of social work practice. Each asks the same types of questions about individuals, their value set, the structure of personality, their significant environments, and their interaction with significant others and the impinging systemic factors. Each addresses the nature of the helping relationship and the nature of the helping process, the goals of the helping process, and the requisite qualities of the helping person or persons. Each views practice from a multi-method perspective. They differ from the viewpoint of emphasis and importance given to each method. Each identifies its own cluster of helping skills, and techniques for intervention. And most importantly, each examines and speaks to the issues of what kinds of situations it is best suited for, what the limitations of its use are, and in particular, for what kinds of persons and situations there are known risks in its application. Finally, each seeks to measure the extent and strength of its empirical base to help give a level of confidence or a warning to be careful in the application of the theory (Siporin, 1989).

In summary, each is a social work theory. Each attempts to address some aspects of the person-in-situation paradigm in a manner that gives a particular focus that can be of differential assistance to some persons in some type of need in some situations. Each then must be seen as a part of the continuum of practice theories (Turner, 1997).

DEALING WITH DIVERSITY

Obviously one of the great challenges to the beginning Canadian social worker is how to come to terms with this rich diversity in a manner that ensures that one's practice is as rich, diverse, and effective as is possible within a practitioner's capabilities at any point in his or her career. If all one had to do was to learn about each theory and its potential and draw upon it as appropriate, the situation would not be overly daunting. We all have learned to deal with diversity in our lives. Our clients deal with considerable diversity on a day-to-day basis.

However, there are two factors that make this challenge of theoretical plurality more difficult. Earlier it was pointed out that one of the ways in which theories differ is in their value perspectives on several critical human bases. Since we are all human, it is understandable that we will find that some theories fit our personal value profile more readily than others. We will like some theories more than others. They will suit our view of the world, and in so doing, often make it difficult to understand or be sympathetic to other theories that are less appealing to us because of their different value bases.

For example, one of the ways in which theories differ is in the value orientation of "time." As human beings, we all have to come to terms with our perception of time. For some of us the present is most important, for others, the past, and for still others the future. No one of these preferences is better than the others. However, people who differ in these preferences can be quite different in the way they address certain life situations and quite uncomfortable with others who view the world differently. But theories also have to come to terms with the question of time. Thus some theories stress that one needs to understand the past in order to understand and deal with the present. Others view the past as less important than the present and consider the therapeutic challenge to be dealing with the present. Still others view human activity as aimed at preparation for the future and therefore believe that in providing help the stress should be on the future. The present is to be used to prepare for the future.

What is important about this is that a practitioner may select a particular theory or set of theories because they fit his or her value set, not understanding that the selected theories may not fit the client. A client may want very much to review her past history in order to understand her current functioning. We may view this as unimportant and say that what she should do is deal with the present and solve problems in the here and now. This could well result in a situation where from the very beginning client and social worker view the helping process very differently, with the possibility that it indeed will not be helpful. What we may view as client resistance may in fact be the client's bewilderment about our view of the world (Latting, 1990).

As mentioned above, time is a value that influences some of our life preferences including theory. It appears that many Canadian social workers are either present- or future-oriented and that few seem to be past-oriented. If this is so then traditional or older theories will not be as popular as those that are the latest fashion. This does appear to be the case.

An example of this is the question of functional theory which, as mentioned earlier, was once a major social work theory but is now scarcely mentioned except for historical interest. Some recent writings (Dunlap, 1996) show that this theory is still very relevant to some aspects of practice and thus we ignore it to the possible detriment of some of our clients.

There are other values besides time that differentiate persons. These may also result in significant differences between the theories to which the social worker is attracted and the client's view of the helping process. Some of these involve our view of human activity, our relationship to nature, our relationship to each other, and the nature of human action (Kluckhohn & Murray, 1953).

This question of differing perceptions of which theories are important and are thus to be used is not only a matter for individual practitioners but also can influence which theories agencies, services, or policies support or do not support.

In addition to the fact that some theories will be more attractive to some practitioners than to others, as dynamic systems they have both sociological and political characteristics. Thus at different times in the history of the profession and in different places some theories have been "in" and other theories "out." If these decisions were based on the proven efficacy of a theory or lack thereof this would not be a serious matter. Indeed it would be a question of service quality. However, it appears that trends that affect the rise and fall of a theory's popularity are often fueled by other factors, such as the reputation of the proponents, rivalries between agencies and schools, even government policies as to what is supported and what isn't (Turner, 1995). At this time in Canada there is considerable policy thrust toward short-term, problem-solving forms of theory and practice. In such circumstances it is imperative that we attempt to value a theory on its credentials and potency for helping particular presenting situations, not on our or someone else's untested preferences. The challenge is to view each body of theory in a neutral way and to judge it for its ability to respond helpfully to particular clients or situations. But of course we are all human and will have our preferences. Our challenge is to attempt to include in our ongoing process of self-awareness the possibility that we are theory-biased and thus may restrict our repertoire of theories. In so doing we limit our effectiveness and utility to some clients or groups of clients or presenting situations (Specht, 1990).

THE BASIC FIVE

But assuming that as students and beginning practitioners we are committed to a position that welcomes with excitement that richness that flows from a thirty-theory base, where do we start? Surely we cannot be expected to know them all before we graduate! And even more anxiety-provoking, surely we cannot be expected to make use of them all!

This question is an ongoing challenge to the designers and implementers of curricula in our schools. For this author it has been a long-standing query and challenge. At this point I have come to the conclusion that, before graduating, an aspiring social worker should have a beginning competence in at least one theory from each of the five types of theories. Note that I refer to types of theories, not specific theories, bearing in mind that there are similarities between and among theories.

1. A Developmentally-Based Theory

I suggest that it is important that a student be well grounded in one theory that looks at present functioning from the perspective of a person's bio-psychosocial history. There are several in our range of theories that do this. Many of the clients we meet, and many of the situations we meet, can only be understood from the perspective of earlier history and the impact and interaction of significant others, significant events, and significant sociopolitical systems in their lives and current functioning. At one time this type of approach was seen as the essence of social work practice at the micro level. However, for reasons related to history and sociopolitical factors, this type of theory fell out of fashion in many parts of our country. There is a swing back to stressing their importance again, but whatever the fashion the evidence is strong that the type of intervention to which these theories give rise is effective and is sought by many of the persons with whom we will interact professionally (Mishne, 1993).

2. A Cognitively-Based Theory

The second type of theory needed by all practitioners in today's society is one based on the ability of people to learn and unlearn about themselves, their behaviours, their values, their impact on others, and the impact of other persons and systems on them. These types of theories have some relationship to the first cluster but are not as focused on the dynamic understanding of early histories or developmental factors. Rather they focus on patterns of learning and, in particular, on helping persons use their cognition to alter behaviours and to take critical decisions in their lives based on reasoning. Unfortunately for some colleagues, because of the very different perspectives of these two types of theory, either-or positions have been taken, so students can get led into either-or perspectives. Again there is a very strong research base that shows that many, but not all, persons can be helped in a wide variety of situations by skilful use of the techniques that have emerged from the various cognitive therapies. Thus it is irresponsible for someone to set him or herself up as a practitioner without knowledge of the nature and potency of this type of theory.

3. An Emergency or Crisis-Oriented Theory

One of the important emerging roles of social workers, not only in Canada but throughout the world, is dealing with persons who have undergone a real or perceived traumatic situation such that their regular problem-solving processes have been critically upset. As well, we are learning that it is not only the persons who have experienced these events but also the people who are close to them and indeed people who are the helpers who often find themselves in need of crisis- and trauma-related intervention. In the past we used the term "crisis work" to cover this type of situation but with growing experience we now know that persons not only need therapeutic assistance at the time of the event but often for some time after. The bodies of theoretical knowledge in this area are growing, and society is increasingly expecting social workers to be the experts and leaders in this area of practice. Thus all social workers, regardless of their regular professional foci of practice, need to have basic therapeutic theory-based skills in this type of trauma and post-trauma work and should have these by the time they graduate. In this strange and often violent world in which we live we just do not know when we are going to be called upon to function in this role.

4. A Problem-Solving and Task Theory

The fourth area where all social workers in this country need to be competent at graduation is in dealing with here-and-now issues on a short-term issue and problem-solving basis.

Again several of our theories address this type of work. All have strong research bases. Thus it is incumbent on all to have knowledge and skills in at least one of these. Many persons coming to social workers want, need, and are able to deal with very concrete issues in their lives. Solutions, outcomes, and action-oriented activity are what is wanted and needed. Again, as with all of our theories, this is not for everyone. But as with the other four theoretical positions, the mere fact that a theory does not help everyone or is not appropriate for everyone does not take away its importance. For many, for a variety of resource and political reasons, this type of theory and the practice stemming from it is seen as the *sine qua non* of micro social work practice. Regardless of the political issues related to the reduction of funding, there is abundant evidence that many persons approaching social workers want and can make use of intervention formats that deal with concrete problem-producing issues. Hence it is important that practitioners be competent in such strategies—but for the good of the clients, not because of the agenda of funders (Reid, 1984).

5. A Systems-Based Theory

Because of the essential commitment of social work to a "person-in-situation perspective," which implies an understanding of the interface of a broad spectrum of factors, it is essential that all social workers have a strong foundation in a systems theory. Although social work from its earliest days understood the power of various external influencing factors on individuals and families and communities, it was only with the emergence of systems-based theories that we had available to us a conceptual base that helped us fully appreciate the complexity, diversity, and inter-influencing component of inter-systemic factors. As these theories have developed, new vocabulary has emerged of use to all practitioners, even those not particularly systems-oriented. Although at one time it was thought that systems theory in its original presentation would emerge as the basis of a general social work theory, we now know that it, and related theories, are not sufficient in themselves but do serve as powerful conceptual tools to help us better understand the many facets of the situations with which we deal in practice.

In summary, we are positing that these five types of theory appear to be essential to a basic practice repertoire for a beginning social worker in a Canadian setting. It will be noted that in the above discussion specific theories under each of the five types of practice skill were not identified. This reflects the fact that under each of the five types of competencies there are several theories that would achieve the same goal. All are important; it will be up to the school or faculty and the practicum settings to ensure that each student is knowledgeable about the strengths and limitations of at least one theory in each category. It may be that as we gain more experience in this it will clarify that there is a core theory for each cluster that has the best pedagogical and practice payoff. At this time it would be best to view all as having equal value.

Before closing it needs to be underscored that in suggesting these five areas as core areas for the beginning practitioner this in no way takes away from the importance of theories that address other aspects of the human condition. Each is important; each must be available to the persons and system we serve and seek to influence. For example, none of the five theoretical clusters suggested above is a macro-oriented theory as such. This was deliberate, as it is a given that all theories rightly called social work theories have to address all elements of the macro-micro spectrum. Each functions from the position that social work operates from the interaction of person-in-situation and thus seeks to bring about change in all relevant systems.

THE CHALLENGE

Obviously the challenge for the beginning Canadian social worker to be theoretically equipped is huge. In the past, students were exposed to at most one or two theories, and if this was expanded it was only to show how the other theories were deficient (Shulman, 1984). For a long time we longed for a richer theoretical base, as we were aware of the many persons we were not helping or for whom we seemed to have little to offer and of the enormity of systemic flaws that needed to be addressed. We now have the conceptual riches which we sought. Our task is how to deal with the richness. Research of recent years has shown that we help most persons with whom we come in contact and that there are strategies of social action that bring about sought change. What we don't know yet is how we can do more. Nor do we have a clear picture of those patterns of person and situation where we are least effective. Certainly in matters of large resource deficits we are often at a loss, especially in view of changing government policy toward the safety net. However, it may be that the challenge of these drastic budget cuts will help us to devise both theoretical and action strategies that will permit us to do an even better job (Rubin, 1985; Thomlison,1984).

What we need to do is humbly acknowledge what we do not know while applauding the richness of our knowledge base. Even though as individuals we cannot be and never will be fully proficient in the application of all of our thirty theories, to say nothing of the new ones that will emerge in the years ahead, by the time we leave school we should know at least the range of these theories, something of their known application, and most importantly, something of their known deficits and risks. Most particularly, we will know that our theoretical knowledge acquisition only begins with our professional training (Curnock & Hardicker, 1979). One of the great satisfactions of being a professional in today's world is this process of ongoing learning to ensure that our practice is sound and ethical and based on an ever-expanding, ever-diversifying theoretical foundation.

REFERENCES

Curnock, L. & Hardicker, S.P. (1974). *Towards Practice Theory.* London: Routledge and Keagan.

Dunlap, K. (1996). Functional theory and social work practice. *Social work treatment,* (4th ed.). F. Turner (Ed.). New York: Free Press, 319–340.

Goldstein, H. (1990). The knowledge base of social work practice: theory, wisdom, analogue, craft? *Families in Society,* (1), 32–43.

Imre-Wells, R. (1984). The nature of knowledge in social work. *Social Work, 29* (1), 51–56.

Kendall, P.C. & Butcher, J.N. (Eds.). (1982). *Handbook of Research Methods in Clinical Psychology.* New York: J. Wiley.

Kluckhohn, C. & Murray, H.A. (Eds.). (1953). *Personality in nature society and culture.* New York: Knopf.

Latting, J.K. (1990). Identifying the "Isms": enabling social work students to confront their biases. *Journal of Social Work Education,* (1), 36–44.

Lewis H. (1982). *The intellectual base of social work practice.* New York: Haworth Press.

Merton, R.K. (1957). *Social theory and social structure.* Glencoe Ill.: The Free Press.

Mishne, J.M. (1993). *The evolution and application of clinical theory.* New York: Free Press.

Reid, W.J. (1984) . Treatment of choice or choice of treatment: an essay review. *Social Work Research and Abstracts*, (2), 33–38.

Rubin, A. (1985). Practice effectiveness: more grounds for optimism. *Social Work,* (6), 469–476.

Shulman, L. (1993). Developing and testing a practice theory: an interactional perspective. *Social Work,* (1), Jan. 91–93.

Siporin, M. (1989). Metamodels, models and basics: an essay review. *Social Service Review, 63*(3), 474–480.

Specht, H. (1990). Social work and popular psychotherapies. *Social Service Review, 64*(3), 345–357.

Thomlison, R.J. (1984). Something works: evidence from practice effectiveness studies. *Social Work,* (Jan.–Feb.), 51–56.

Turner, F.J. (1996). *Social work treatment,* (4th ed.). New York: Free Press.

Turner, F.J. (1995). Social work practice: theoretical base. *Encyclopedia of Social Work,* (19th ed.). R. Edwards, (Ed.). Washington D.C.: NASW, (Vol. III). 2258–2265.

Turner, F.J. (1997). *Social work theories and models.* A chart comparing 27 theories by fifty variables, Toronto Ont: F.J. Turner.

DIVERSITY IN CANADIAN SOCIAL WORK PRACTICE

Sheila Hardy and
Anne-Marie Mawhiney[1]

INTRODUCTION

Everyone views situations and events through their own lenses, which are influenced by upbringing, personal and family values, and significant experiences. When we have not had experience with a particular situation, we acquire it vicariously through what others tell us, the media, what we read in books, or learn in school. Although we tend to think of all Canadians as having a common socialization process, our ways of thinking and living are diverse because of geographic location, dominant political ideology, language, culture and race, gender, class, and relative power and prestige. Even in cases where a group of people have the same experience, each individual in the group may perceive that experience in different ways. Likewise, others outside the group may interpret the experience in ways that are very different from those who have actually lived the experience. The philosophical term for this is egocentrism—where something only exists as viewed by an individual.

As social workers, we need to understand experiences that people have and the situations in which they find themselves through their own lenses, and then provide the kinds of support that is necessary to improve their situation in ways that *they* find meaningful. This is indeed a challenge because for many of us our natural tendency is egocentric; in social work practice, being egocentric risks limiting the extent to which we can be helpful and, even more importantly, also risks doing more harm than good (Deegan, 1990, 302). It is also a challenge because we must be accepting of the fact that we can never fully understand the experience of others through their own lenses. We can strive to do so but must also acknowledge our limitations in this regard. However, we need to understand the others' experiences to the extent that we can empathize with their situation. Empathy allows us to move beyond our own egocentric views in order to help other people.

---

[1] The authors have made equal contributions to this paper and have put authorship in alphabetical order.

In this chapter, we look at diversity—the ways that people are different from one another and how these differences shape various ways of living and thinking, different assumptions, values, and beliefs. Diversity is an important issue for Canadian social workers because we work on a daily basis with people who are different from ourselves; people of different social classes and material conditions, ages, races, cultures, ethnicities, genders, abilities, and sexual preferences. In this chapter, we discuss diversity as it relates to ethnicity, race, culture, and gender, in the hope of broadening your understanding of social work practice. We also discuss the ways that issues related to diversity can influence how we work with people who ask for our help. We call social work practice that incorporates concepts related to diversity *inclusive social work practice* (Nakanishi and Rittner, 1992).

INCLUSIVE SOCIAL WORK

From the Second World War until very recently, social work practice has stemmed from the dominant, traditional ideology, formulated from a Euro-Canadian, middle-class, white, heterosexual perspective. We call this viewpoint *Eurocentric*—thinking that the only reality is that experienced by Euro-Canadians. The assumptions and ways of seeing things with this dominant perspective have not successfully prepared social workers to work effectively with populations from outside the dominant group. Inclusive social practice acknowledges the fact that we as social workers need to draw upon a range of knowledge, skills, and methods to achieve an understanding of others' situations.

Social work knowledge, skills, and methods evolve, and beliefs, assumptions, values, and techniques shift because of new information, the impact of certain social movements, and new experiences. This can add to our ability to understand others and help in more appropriate and meaningful ways. For example, Aboriginal social work practice is only very recently becoming visible to those who have not grown up in a First Nations community. Each First Nations culture has its own assumptions, values, beliefs, ways of thinking and living. As teachings about traditional healing methods become more widely known among Aboriginal workers, different perspectives on Aboriginal helping are also evolving. This in turn shapes not only the practice of those working directly with First Nations people but it also provides opportunities for other social workers, as well as the profession itself, to consider the ways that social work practice has been historically limited by its Eurocentric assumptions and values, and to become more inclusive in its orientation.

Inclusive social work gives us a way to think about our practice critically. Inclusive social work practice requires us to consider how our own assumptions and ways of thinking about people can facilitate or impede our work with others; when our assumptions and ways of thinking are inclusive then we can work effectively with people whose realities and experiences differ from our own. Inclusive social work practice means that we promote practices that are respectful of peoples' relationships to the world around them and the ways that their relative power and prestige shapes their ability to realize their own goals. Thus, inclusive social work practice, or "anti-discriminatory" (Thompson, 1993) practice acknowledges and respects diversity. Each diverse group, as well as individuals in these groups, makes an important contribution to our day-to-day lives in Canada, each adding different experiences and world views. In the ideal, people from diverse backgrounds and experiences would live together in mutual respect and harmony. However, as most social work practitioners recognize, discrimination exists across genders, across cultures, races and ethnic groups, across abilities and social classes, and across sexual preferences: "...we understand that what is truly disabling to us are the barriers in our environment preventing us from living out the full range of our human interests and gifts and preventing us from living, loving, worshipping, and working in the community of our choice" (Deegan, 309).

While as social workers we may believe that we do not discriminate against people we probably can think of times when we were in the company of friends, family, or coworkers when jokes and innuendoes were made. What did you do? Did you laugh with the group? Did you sit silently and wonder what to do? Part of social work's mission is to change discriminatory practices to inclusive and supportive ones, which recognize the important and unique contributions of each person in Canada. Discrimination occurs at the personal level, between individuals; at the social level, between social groups; and at the institutional and policy levels, where certain widespread practices exclude or discriminate against certain groups or individuals.

Inclusive social work practice incorporates a comprehensive understanding of the dynamics associated with discrimination, power, and oppression, and seeks to minimize or eradicate these in all relationships between people, and between people and institutions. The main difference between many social workers and inclusive practitioners is the extent to which the latter have moved beyond mere recognition of the dynamics associated with discrimination to take action—action not only in terms of promoting social change but also in terms of developing within themselves the knowledge and skills and the self-awareness needed to work across diverse situations.

What is viewed from a dominant perspective as discriminatory practice shifts from one particular historical, social, political, and economic context to another. For example, consider the acceptance of same-sex benefits by the federal government; this finally happened in the late 1990s. Previous practices that excluded the partners of homosexuals from receiving extended benefits were discriminatory on the basis of sexual orientation. In this example and as well as others it is evident that the context for the shaping of policies has an important influence on their development. Thus, it is important for inclusive social workers to watch for commonly held beliefs and assumptions about any individual or social group and to advocate changes in these and the practices associated with them when they are discriminatory. It is important not only to consider the ways our practice may be discriminatory but also to be critical about policies, research, and administrative practices that may seem to the dominant group to be inclusive but which are experienced by others as excluding them or treating them differently.

Within each multicultural, Aboriginal, or gender grouping there are different ways of interpreting experiences, based on factors related to, among others, gender, class, age, and sexual orientation. The concept of multiple world views is important here because it moves us away from the idea that social work practice is based on uniform and generic practices or "interventions" that are effective regardless of the person's situation. In fact, our ways of helping are never "pure" or "objective"; they are always informed by the unique situation of the person asking for our help and our own perceptions and knowledge. The concept of world view suggests that we enter into the ways of thinking and living of those asking for our help, so that we can understand their unique experience through their own lenses to the best of our ability. In order to accomplish this we need to engage in a process of connecting with their assumptions, beliefs, values, and experiences.

There are several dimensions influencing our personal and professional relationships with others. These dimensions shape how we see others and how we interact with them, include or exclude them, and ways that we oppress or discriminate against them. These dimensions include the degree to which we have or don't have power; since most social workers do have a certain degree of power in our relationships with people seeking our help it is important that we acknowledge to ourselves and those asking for help the ways that this power can impede our inclusive practice. The dimensions also include diversity within particular groups as well as the idea that people within one group are also diverse. Internalized oppression is another dimension that helps us each understand the extent to which we are, ourselves, oppressed by the stereotypes of others and not able to act in a non-discriminatory way because of our own socialization processes.

Power and Oppression

In many respects the notion of social equality is an illusion. From a values perspective we, as social workers, say that people from all groups are equal and worthy of equal treatment. However, in the Canadian context as well as elsewhere, the day-to-day realities for many is very different; discrimination and oppression exist and limit the extent to which many people are able to achieve their goals. Some people hold more power than others and most of them act on this power. People are excluded on a regular basis because of the colour of their skin, because of their accent or the language that they speak, because of their gender, because of their sexual preferences, or because of their lack of privilege. It is important also to consider that people may experience multiple reasons for exclusion and as a result experience multiple oppressions. For example a woman born in India who immigrates to Canada may experience oppression because she is a woman, because she is an immigrant, because of the colour of her skin, because she speaks with an accent, because she may not understand the dominant language very well, or because she may have come from a lower class or caste. Most people outside of those with the most power have had experiences where they have been treated in ways to reinforce the idea that they are not equal to those with relative power. When such treatment results in the limiting of opportunities to achieve our goals, then we are being oppressed.

Many—if not most—of our clients do not have power or privilege, and they are most often oppressed because of their age, their material conditions, gender, culture, race, ethnicity, or sexual preference. While working with people who are asking for help on a specific issue we need to consider the ways that ageism, racism, sexism, ableism, heterosexism, and classism oppress them. For example, many heterosexual social workers may not be sensitive to how difficult it is for many homosexuals or lesbians to have to hide significant and intimate relationships from their families, friends, or colleagues. Deegan also speaks of spirit breaking, in which people who have a disability are dehumanized to the extent that their spirit is broken: "...these wounds 'numb' or at times 'break' our will to live, rob us of hope, and instill a deep sense of apathy, despair, personal worthlessness, and self hatred. Many of us experience these wounds as more disabling than the mental illness or physical injury/syndrome we may have been diagnosed with. It is these wounds that take a long, long time to heal" (1990, 130).

Diversity within Groups

Another dimension to consider is diversity within each group. Each situation is distinct and while we may be able to come up with some points that are common we will also be coming up with a lot of individual and group differences. Diversity also implies other things. Within each group there is wide diversity, so we cannot assume to understand everyone from that group based on a limited amount of knowledge. We need to exercise caution in looking at areas or behaviours that we may perceive as common to a group. The danger in doing this is contributing to stereotyping which becomes discriminatory. Balancing the knowledge of similarities and maintaining respect for individual differences and the uniqueness of each situation may seem a simple task but requires a great deal of personal awareness and skill as a social worker. For example, in Canada there are many Aboriginal linguistic groupings. While the language grouping may be similar in one, two, or more First Nations, cultural practices may differ from one First Nation to another. As well, we must also consider the individual differences within each First Nation. Understanding diversity means moving beyond recognition that this dynamic exists, and toward appropriate action. In this dimension it requires stepping back and examining how we view groups of individuals. What do we perceive, individually and as a society, various groups having in common? How does this affect the way in which individuals talk and behave with them? Or, at a more personal, self-critical level, do I see how my preconceived perceptions are affecting how I behave and act? What areas of personal development do I need to work on?

Respecting diversity does not mean imposing one way of thinking or working; in fact at times it means working in parallel or even in isolation rather than together. It also means understanding when it is time to join together and when it is time to support from a distance others' struggles, recognizing their own unique paths to empowerment.

Internalized Oppression

It is important that inclusive social workers understand that people can be oppressed in many different ways. For example, many may think it is relatively easy to identify the ways in which oppression occurs as the result of one's age, gender, race, and physical ability, whereas it may be more difficult to identify consequences of oppressions for those qualities that are less visible such as learning, hearing, or visual challenges. Internalized oppression also takes other forms. An example of internalized oppression is the discrimination among some Afro-Americans within their own social group against those with darker skin. The oppression is internalized from dominant society's messages through the media, schools, religious institutions, and other forms of socialization.

We also have to keep in mind that certain abilities are often hidden from our view. By putting our own expectations upon people, we run the risk of further marginalizing or excluding them inadvertently. As social workers we must be aware of our preconceived ideas and the ways that these may be limited by our experiences, or lack of them, with groups different from our own. We need also to be aware of some of the ways that we have internalized stereotypes that are presented in the media, in school, in religious institutions, by our family members and friends, and elsewhere. It is important that we, as social workers, become aware of our own prejudices and limitations, and overcome these so that we can work in a non-discriminatory fashion with those asking for our help.

RACE, ETHNICITY, AND CULTURE

While Canada prides itself on being a multicultural mosaic where diversity, equality, and harmony are valued, the truth of the matter is that despite attempts to address inequities related to race, ethnicity, and culture, many people have been and continue to be oppressed, marginalized, and excluded either overtly or covertly from full meaningful participation in

Canadian society. For example, in the 1960s, Canadian child welfare policies resulted in the apprehension of large numbers of First Nations children. Social workers at that time believed that they were acting in the best interests of these children. Today, most social workers recognize that these past practices were discriminatory and are now supporting First Nations autonomy in establishing child welfare policies and services.

Models of anti-discriminatory (Thompson, 1993) and ethnic-sensitive practice (Devore & Schlesinger, 1991) have emerged to address issues in social work practice related to, among others, race, ethnicity, and culture. These models have contributed to social work practice in that they critically examine past practice and provide sound ways in which we can become more inclusive social workers. Models that address the issues related to race, ethnicity, and culture also recognize the need to understand history an as important component in understanding a people's experience. Armitage (1995) provides an excellent synopsis of the difference between the historical experiences of minority immigrants and new settlers to Canada and the Aboriginal people. He documents these differences as the following:

- As Aboriginal peoples were owners, occupiers, and users of the land before European settlement, the natural environment is relevant to their religions, cultures, and social lives in ways which it could not possibly be for any immigrant group.

- Aboriginal peoples were, and in many cases still are, rural peoples, while immigrants are typically urban dwellers.

- Aboriginal peoples did not choose to live as a minority within an alien culture, while immigrant groups came to new countries either through choice or to escape more serious difficulties in their countries of origin.

- In each country there are some laws that only apply to Aboriginal peoples (9).

Social work practice needs to forge beyond mere intellectual understanding of race, culture, and ethnicity and move toward practice that is centred on the values, beliefs, assumptions, and ways of living and thinking of those with whom we are working. What this means then is that social workers need to strive toward developing skills and in-depth knowledge of other groups. In striving to do this we are acknowledging the diversity that exists and can then move to a form of practice that is meaningful to the people we work with. Naturally, we may find it easier to work with those of our own racial, ethnic, or cultural group just as it is easier to work with those who speak the same language as we do. It means that we need to put considerable time and energy into gaining an understanding of people who are different than we are. Even those who may have an advantage of speaking the same language as the people with whom they are working, or come from the same or similar cultural and ethnic background, need to consider the likelihood that they have been affected by dominant ideology through their work, home, media communications, and the educational system. We need to acknowledge that most of us have been affected in varying degrees by dominant ideology.

The challenge for social workers is to be respectful by valuing diversity of race, ethnicity, and culture by striving for a true and meaningful understanding of others' experiences rather than merely acknowledging superficially the differences in diversity. There are many social workers who understand at an intellectual level concepts that relate to inclusive social work but who are unable to act on this understanding in their lives and in their professional practice. In addition, in attempting to be correct when we work with another culture, race, class, or the other gender, we at times may ask questions that could be experienced by others as offensive. For example, by questioning which form of address is correct, social workers often show their lack of understanding of the context and experiences of those they may be working with. Social workers need to question what their underlying values, beliefs, and assumptions are about people who are of a different race, ethnic group, or culture. In gaining an understanding of our own biases we move one step closer in understanding another frame of reference. So rather than being concerned with what is "correct," the challenge is to look at our own use of language and question whether the intent to understand is in fact coming from a deep, genuine, and respectful need to understand another group's context and experience. Showing respect, rather than trying to be "correct," means understanding and responding appropriately to each unique situation and its political, historical, and social context: "If one would approach others more often on nonsocially related issues—areas of commonality— he or she would eventually learn about the social differences as well. In doing this one is not being blind to social differences between people; one is placing those differences in a larger context that allows the richness and variation of all people to be seen, legitimated, and respected. In doing so, people speak as visible men and women" (Burghardt, 1982, 116).

GENDER AND SOCIAL WORK PRACTICE

Women's struggles for voice, equality, and even the right to vote have been documented since the latter half of the nineteenth century. Victorian pioneers such as Frances Power Cobbe, Josephine Butler, and Millicent Garrett Fawcett were strong advocates for improved living conditions for women (Caine 1992). In the last two decades, within Canadian society support for women's choice in the productive roles that they will take on, whether in paid or unpaid work or a combination of both, has increased. Images of the family from the media in the 1950s showed married women as happy homemakers sending their husbands off to work and their children to school. These images, and the realities that shape them in real-life situations, have changed. Our mothers and grandmothers tell us that we and our children have many more choices than they did concerning unpaid and paid work, inside and outside the home—choices that have been fought for and hard won by pioneers in the women's movement. It is important to understand this history and the gains that have been made. Otherwise we risk becoming complacent and losing these gains (Pierson and Cohen, 1993; Caine, 1992; Meyers, Chandler, in Van den Bergh and Cooper, 1986).

As social workers, professional ethical standards support our advocacy for improved material conditions and the eradication of all discrimination on the basis of gender, age, ability, sexual preference, class, race, or ethnicity (Turner and Turner, 1995, 629). Many women social workers have made important contributions to our social work practice— both direct and indirect—to the ways that we deliver social work services, the ways that we understand power and oppression, and the ways that policies have excluded and still exclude women from the same privileges and opportunities that men enjoy. These leaders in social work, many feminists, made visible and gave voice to the many ways in which patriarchy shaped social work practice and policies, and oppressed and silenced women. Such oppressive practices and policies have, at times, been implemented by women social workers, and this has often set up a dissonance between what these women social workers would see as "good practice" and what policies tell them to do (Callahan and Attridge, 1990). Feminist social work practice encourages us to work in ways that are consistent with our selves as women, our beliefs, and our ways of thinking, communicating, and relating to others

(Valentich, 1996). While feminist social workers do not speak with one voice or use only one approach, there are some points in common. One feminist vision of Canadian society is one where women have equal say and power, and where a shift in interactions and relationships across genders is realized so that the various women-centred values, ways of thinking and organizing are heard and included in the process by which Canadians make decisions, formulate policies, and provide services. Activism is an integral part of feminist practice because structural change is needed to strive toward the eradication of oppression.

Alice Home points out two important contributions of the women's movement to social change: "The first is feminists' assertion that personal experience is at the very root of social/political change, while the second is the choice to use the small group as the primary tool for effecting change on all fronts" (Home, 1991). Feminist social workers often work collectively with those asking for help. This is not to say that the personal struggle is ignored; rather it is addressed in ways that connect personal change to political and social action, and to join individuals in a common struggle together. Thus, in contrast to the isolated, "specialized," social work methods of casework, group work and community work, the feminist approach is integrative, which is consistent with social work's origins in any case (Elliott, 1993). Whether we start with an individual or group, feminist social workers address personal *and* collective struggles.

Feminists have also helped us to understand power in different ways from the traditional concept. For feminists, power "is viewed as infinite; as energy, strength, and effectiveness; and therefore distributed throughout all organizational members..." (Hooyman and Cunningham in Van den Bergh and Cooper, 1986, 169). Whether we are working with others within formal organizations or in small, informal groups, all members are viewed as having power and knowledge, and as making valued contributions. Empowerment, then, becomes a process of drawing upon all the unique and important abilities of each member of the group, so that their own power, knowledge, and authority is recognized and valued. Some suggest that any feminist social work should be inclusive: "any woman's experience could be expressed and heard" (Cohen in Pierson and Cohen, 1995, 263).

Another contribution made by feminist social work practice is by restructuring organizations and managing them so they also become more inclusive. A feminist model of administration shifts from a hierarchical, bureaucratic organizational structure to one where democratic and collective decision-making practices are encouraged so that all members of the organization are involved (Home, 1991, 159), and process and product are emphasized over content and procedure (Hooyman and Cunningham in Van den Bergh and Cooper, 1986, 167, 170).

Feminism must also become inclusive of the voices of all women who are resisting oppression and not only those voices from Eurocentric groups of women in Canada. Recently women of colour, First Nations, and working class and poor women's experiences of multiple oppressions have become more evident to others (Gutierrez, 1990). In their analyses of feminism and First Nations, Brown, Jamieson, and Kovach (1995) suggest that "by controlling the feminist agenda, White women can manipulate the issues of minority women by considering only those which do not threaten the sisterhood myth. The universalizing concept of sisterhood, that all women experience the same oppression, negates minority women's unique experience" (73). Feminism needs to strive toward ensuring that the voices of women who do not necessarily see their situation as the same or even as similar, are included. We, as women, have multiple social identities, which need to be acknowledged and respected. For example, if an Afro-Canadian woman chose to become a member of an activist group, it may be with the intent of ensuring that the voices of Afro-Canadians including women are heard, acknowledged, and respected as worthy and valid of inclusion. It does not mean any one Afro-Canadian woman speaks for all Afro-Canadian women, nor does it mean that she aligns herself necessarily with the feminist agenda nor with the anti-racist agenda; rather, she speaks as one Afro-Canadian woman.

KNOWLEDGE AND EXPERIENCE WITH ANOTHER GROUP

For most people from one of the dominant groups in Canada, it is relatively easy to function within their own social group with little experience or personal exposure to other groups. Caucasian, English-speaking people in Canada, and French-speaking people in Quebec, have a range of choices about the ways in which they want to live, and they are relatively free to act in their day-to-day interactions based on their own assumptions, beliefs, and values. However, the history of French-speaking people in Quebec makes analysis more complex than for English-speaking Caucasians. The historical social and economic domination by the English in Quebec has led to the oppression of the francophone group. To many currently living outside Quebec it may appear as though the francophones are the dominant group in Quebec, but the history of this oppression is still pervasive there in the ways that federal economic policies and practices have impacted on the ways of living and thinking among Québécois. Thus, while we can speak of the range of choices enjoyed by the two dominant groups in Canada, we need to understand that the hegemony of the francophone group in Quebec is still relatively recent in comparison to that of the anglophones in Canada.

In contrast to the situation in Quebec, throughout Canada most people from other groups, including francophones outside Quebec, experience a degree of immersion into the dominant group at some point. While they may be able to live within a neighbourhood that is consistent with their own origins and ways of living, most will be schooled in dominant institutions and many will work outside their own social group, within work settings where the dominant group is in the majority, and all will be inculcated with dominant values through the media. While it may not be impossible in Canada to live in complete isolation from one of the dominant groups, it is very unlikely. There are three possible interactive contexts between two groups or two people in different groups:

1. *Isolation*. Our lives are completely immersed within our own group; we only relate to those who share the same ways of living and thinking. For social workers, a possible mission may be to put all of our talents, skills, and energies into improving the lives of those in our own group.

2. *Interaction*. We basically live within our own group but relate regularly with another and over time start to understand more and more the standpoint of that group. For social workers, our mission may be to act as a bridge between the two; linking resources between groups with needs for these resources; translating where there are problems of understanding between two groups; mediating, promoting understanding (but not appropriating the voice of the other group).

3. *Immersion*. We are completely immersed in the other group and have either been excluded or have excluded ourselves from our own group, temporarily or permanently. For social workers, our missions may be to act as a resource to the other group in ways that they define as meaningful.

In contrast to many groups in Canada, a large number of people from the dominant society have little exposure to other groups unless they choose to immerse themselves to some degree. Thus, in many instances, those outside the dominant groups in Canada and Quebec are overwhelmed with the ways of one of the dominant groups, while few of those from the English-speaking dominant group have the same first-hand experience of being in the minority with another group. Even fewer have the experience of being in the minority in a context where they also have less power. They are limited in the extent to which they can understand the process of learning about other groups, unless they have spent extensive periods of time living in another culture or language, and in contexts where they have not assumed power and prestige in the others' situation.

CRITICAL REFLECTION

How do we learn to relate more effectively with other groups? Paulo Friere (1985) has suggested that a process of critical reflection can enable us to blend intuitive sense and intellectual rationality. This means that we need to go beyond an intuitive sense of what to do and move toward a more organized way of learning how to develop as inclusive social workers. It means being receptive to new ways of thinking and living as well as being open to concrete feedback, which may be painful at times, about our own limitations because of our own internalized oppression. It means putting ourselves into situations that are new to us where we are the learners, without power, and risking being treated in discriminatory ways. It means reflecting on these new experiences and extracting "lessons" which can be applied to other new situations. It means asking questions so that we can learn from others, and knowing when to remain silent. It means never speaking for another group but also concretely supporting their speaking. It means never "doing for" but rather "doing with," when invited, or leaving the space for them "to do themselves." According to Friere, critical reflection is a life-long process of learning and building our own behaviour based on what we have learned. It also means allowing us to expose ourselves to mistakes and to learn from them. It means ongoing self-awareness and an ability to analyze our own interactions with others as well as their interaction with us.

Learning a long list of behaviours or "recipes" does not help us relate to other groups. For instance, being told to look directly into the eyes of male colleagues and to speak in a strong voice as a recipe to become "more assertive" or more like men in the way that they communicate. Rather than following such "recipes" it is important to observe and respond in a reflective way to what we see. The following questions may assist in the process of observation:

- What is the history of the group from which this person or these people come? In what ways has this history influenced their ways of living and thinking? To what extent are they knowledgeable about their own history?

- What is this person saying that seems to fit with my own understanding? What is this person saying that seems to be different from the way I see things? What is this person saying that I am having difficulty understanding and how can I clarify this without imposing my own views? What are the values and belief systems that are influencing what this person is saying? Where can we find common ground and which parts do I respect and accept as being different from my own ideas? Is it appropriate or not to talk about these differences or should I just listen right now? Do I communicate differences while showing respect? If so, then in what ways? Do I suggest points in common? How can I do this without making inappropriate assumptions?

- What do I already know about this person's ways of thinking and living? What don't I know? What questions can I ask and how can I ask them so that I show my interest but don't impose my own ways of thinking and living?

- Is the other person's speed of speech fast or slow? How is silence used? Is there lots of silence or little? How long is the period of silence between listening to someone and responding? In a group situation, how do people signal that they want to speak? Who speaks first? What is the pace of the interaction between and among people? Is it rapid or slow, in comparison to my own group? Is a speaker ever interrupted? If so, when and under what circumstances? In what way is the person interrupted? If the speaker is never interrupted, how do others respond non-verbally to the speaker? Does it seem to depend on who the speaker is?

- In discussions, what is the organization of the process for thinking about things? Is it ordered and rational or is it intuitive and creative? Is a right-brain or left-brain thinking style most common? Are we looking at things holistically and then in parts or vice versa? What is the problem-solving process? To what extent are story-telling, personal examples, or metaphors used? Do we move from the personal outward or the external inward? Or is another process used? What cues am I given to explain what is going on? How do others let me know if I am on track?

This critical reflection requires us to engage in a life-long commitment to personal growth and change. In the past, much damage has been done by well-meaning social workers when they have not considered the diverse uniqueness of individuals, families, groups, and communities. Instead, everyone was treated from a dominant perspective of helping instead of acknowledging that differences exist and that there are many forms of helping. Our challenge as social workers is how to truly become inclusive practitioners, whether we are working with individuals, families, groups, or in policy research and administration. It requires each of us to look deeply into ourselves and to challenge our own beliefs, values, and assumptions. This self-reflection needs a life-long commitment to what can be a painful but very worthwhile process.

REFERENCES

Armitage, A. (1995). *Comparing the policy of Aboriginal assimilation: Australia, Canada and New Zealand.* Vancouver: University of British Columbia Press.

Belenky, M.F., Clinchy, B.M., Goldberger, N.R., & Tarule, J.M. (1986). *Women's ways of knowing: the development of self, voice, and mind.* Basic Books, Inc.

Brown, L., Jamieson, C., & Kovach, M. (1995). Feminism and First Nations: conflict or concert? *Issues and Debates, 35,* pp. 68–78.

Burghart, S. (1982). *The other side of organizing: resolving the personal dilemmas and political demands of daily practice.* Cambridge, MA: Schenkman Pub. Co.

Caine, B., *Victorian Feminists.* (1992). Oxford, U.K.: Oxford University Press.

Callahan, M. & Attridge, C. (1990). *Women in women's work: social workers talk about their work in child welfare.* Victoria, B.C., University of Victoria.

Cardinal, H. (1969) *The unjust society: the tragedy of Canada's Indians.* Edmonton: New Press.

Cardinal, H. (1977) *The rebirth of Canada's Indians*. Toronto: New Press Publishers.

Deegan, P.E. (1990). Spirit breaking: when the helping professions hurt. *The Humanist Psychologist, 18,* 301–313.

Devore, W. & Schlesinger, E. (1991). *Ethnic-sensitive social work practice*. New York: Macmillan Publishing Comapny.

Elliott, D. (1993). Social work and social development: toward an integrative model for social work practice. *International Social Work, 36,* 21–36.

Freire, P. (1985) *The politics of education: culture, power and liberation*. South Hadley, MA: Bergin & Garvey.

Gutierrez, L.M. (1990). Working with women of color: an empowerment perspective. *Social Work, 35,* 149–153.

Home, A.M. (1991). Mobilizing women's strengths for social change: the group connection. *Social Work with Groups, 14,* 3–4, 153–173.

Nakanishi, M. & Rittner, B. (1992). The inclusionary cultural model. *Journal of Social Work Education, 28,* 27–35.

Pennell, J., Flaherty, M., Gravel, N., Milliken, E., & Neuman, M. (1993). Feminist social work education in mainstream and nonmainstream classrooms. *Affilia, 8,* 317–338.

Pierson, R.R. & Cohen, M.G. (1995). *Canadian Women's Issues: volume II, bold visions*. Toronto: James Lorimer & Company.

Sefa Dei, G.J. (1993). The challenges of anti-racist education in Canada. *Canadian Ethnic Studies, XXV, 2,* 36–51.

Thompson, N. (1993). *Anti-disciminatory practice*. London, U.K.: British Association of Social Workers.

Turner, J. & Turner, F.J. (1995). *Canadian social welfare* (3rd ed.). Scarborough, Ontario: Allyn & Bacon Canada.

Valentich, M. (1996). Feminist theory and social work practice. In Turner, F. *Social work treatment.* (4th ed.). New York: The Free Press.

Van den Bergh, N. & Cooper, L.B. (1986). *Feminist visions for social work.* Washington D.C., National Association of Social Workers.

GEOGRAPHY AND CANADIAN SOCIAL WORK PRACTICE

Michael Kim Zapf

The overall purpose of this book is to examine the practice of social work from a Canadian perspective. The social work profession has long asserted a dual focus on persons and their environments, suggesting that any serious attempt to develop a Canadian perspective on practice must take into account the unique features of our northern environment. In contrast to our counterparts in other circumpolar regions, Canadians have been criticized for failing to recognize and give full expression to our geographic reality as a northern people in a northern country (Hamelin, 1988; Zaslow, 1971). Is this criticism valid for Canadian social work? To what extent have relevant geographic factors have been incorporated into the knowledge base for social work practice in Canada?

This chapter begins with a brief overview of efforts to incorporate Canada's northern geographic reality within the developing social work knowledge base. Attention is then focused on the American specialization of rural social work and the more recent Canadian interest in remote practice. The discipline of human geography offers a framework that allows examination of the Canadian practice environment from the perspective of five different geographic subsystems: demographic geography, political geography, economic geography, cultural geography, and phenomenological geography. Such geographic perspectives may be associated with an antagonistic stance evident in published accounts from the practice literature of northern Canada. The chapter concludes with a look forward to implications of geographic factors for Canadian social work practice in the new era of globalization.

A NORTHERN IDENTITY WITHIN CANADIAN SOCIAL WORK?

To what extent has Canadian social work identified and attempted to incorporate our northern reality? Until recently, it could be argued that we have engaged in northern window dressing while ignoring our geographic reality as urban theory and practice issues have dominated the agenda of the profession. For example, consider the summer of 1984, when Canada was privileged to host the Eighth International Symposium of the International Federation of Social Workers. A special issue of our Canadian Association of Social Workers' journal, *The Social Worker*, was published as background material for foreign delegates in an effort "to reflect Canadian realities" and "provide a state of the art summary of the profession" in this country (Torjman, 1984, 3). Following a brief description of our physical geography and settlement patterns, the first issue was identified:

> The geographic diversity and rural/urban "imbalance" in Canada have presented difficulties in many contexts including social welfare services.... (Drover, 1984, 6).

Northern Canadians may have been encouraged to find geographic factors highlighted for the world as the identifying issue of Canadian social work, but they would soon have been disappointed to discover that the theme did not appear again in the entire overview of Canadian practice.

The dominance of urban theory and practice issues was quite common in the Canadian social work literature at that time. For example, Armitage's (1975) *Social Welfare in Canada: Ideals and Realities* declared an intention to introduce students to "those factors in Canadian society that influenced the form and substance of social welfare" (v), yet our geography was not presented as one of those factors. Rural areas were dismissed as exhibiting "all the same problems as their larger metropolitan counterparts" (42); rural/urban disparities were not addressed in the discussion of redistribution. In the second edition, Armitage (1988) did recognize demographics as having a major impact on social welfare in Canada, but the issues put forward involved maturing baby boomers and immigration, with no specific mention of the demographic patterns whereby our population is scattered over our vast northern land mass.

The first edition of Turner and Turner's (1981) *Canadian Social Welfare* held great initial promise for the incorporation of northern issues. At the very beginning was a photograph of Commissioner Stu Hodgson of the Northwest Territories in a parka standing in front of an airplane on a snow-covered strip, with his arms around two young Inuit children. Similar to the CASW journal described previously, this romantic frontier image of northern practice was put up front to set the tone for a discussion of social welfare in this country, yet less than one percent of the content of the book actually addressed northern concerns.

Out of fairness to the writers selected here as examples, it must be acknowledged that a valuable service was done insofar as they worked to establish a knowledge base for Canadian social work. They also included a few pages on Native issues, as did other writers at the time who were publishing collections and critiques of social welfare in Canada (Yelaja, 1985, 1987; Carniol, 1987). There was some evidence in the later 1970s of Canadian interest in rural social work: the formation of the Canadian Rural Social Work Forum in 1976, and the inclusion by Wharf (1979) of a rural case study in his community work collection. Yet none of these Canadian initiatives addressed directly the geographic reality of our northern context and related practice issues.

No conspiracy or deliberate suppression of northern concerns is being implied here, but it could well be argued that there appears to be a pattern of oversight. Perhaps the lack of specific attention to northern issues continued because it was simply easier for us to accept the developing American specialization of rural social work than to grapple with our own distinctive northern context.

RURAL SOCIAL WORK

The social work profession in the United States has long been satisfied with a relatively simple distinction between urban and rural areas as practice settings. Rural social work became well established during the 1930s, given the context of the economic depression and the dust bowl conditions. Numerous articles on rural social welfare appeared at that time in the journal *Rural Sociology*. Josephine Brown (1933) published the first book on social casework in rural communities. Following the 1930s, however, rural social work disappeared from the literature for three decades! This curious phenomenon may have resulted from a combination of factors: the general post-war trend to urbanization, a move toward clinical practice, the addition of analytic psychology to our knowledge base, and the concentration of social work training in urban graduate schools.

Rural social work reappeared on the scene in the 1970s with an entry in the 16th edition of the *Encyclopedia of Social Work* (Ginsberg, 1971). Soon afterward, the American Council on Social Work Education established a Task Force on Rural Practice. An annual Institute on Social Work in Rural Areas was initiated in the United States, with collected papers published in the newly established *Journal of Human Services in the Rural Environment*. This flurry of activity in the 1970s led Martinez-Brawley (1981) to conclude that "rural social work had succeeded in gaining a place in the ranks of the profession" (201).

Most of the rural practice literature produced during the 1970s can be characterized as descriptive, subjective, and anecdotal. Rural workers described their experiences and identified differences from urban practice. Rural social workers in general were depicted as employed by public multi-purpose agencies to provide informal and personalized service under conditions of high visibility with few professional supports. The dominant theme in this new literature was the modification and adaptation of urban programs and services for non-urban areas—overcoming geographic obstacles and community resistance to ensure that rural peoples had access to all the services available in the cities. In this way, American rural social work developed as a specialty or field of practice within the urban-based social work profession.

REMOTE PRACTICE

In the mid 1980s, several Canadian authors began to identify major differences between rural social work and practice in remote northern communities. Presenting to the International Institute on Social Work in Rural Areas at the University of Maine in 1984, Brian Wharf began to suggest this distinction. His keynote address was subsequently published in a Canadian journal (Wharf, 1985). The major turning point, however, was the publication of the first edition of Collier's book *Social Work With Rural Peoples: Theory & Practice* (1984), which included a specific chapter on social work in remote communities. Collier connected the mission of northern social work with the state of underdevelopment and exploitation experienced by most northern regions. Zapf (1985, 1985b) then argued that American rural social work theory was not sufficient to guide practice in northern Canada where social workers encountered intense conflicts between the role for which they had been trained and the demands of northern communities. McKay (1987), building on the work of Hudson and McKenzie (1985), called for the inclusion of a conflict perspective as a necessary adjunct to ecosystems theory for practice in northern Canada.

The European Centre for Social Welfare Training and Research (Maclouf & Lion, 1984; Ribes, 1985) grappled with these same issues and proposed a new category of "remote" or "isolated" practice setting, calling attention

> to a nuanced perception of the rural world, remote or isolated rural areas being clearly opposed, from the spatial and qualitative points of view, to semi-rural areas and peri-rural areas (Maclouf and Lion, 1984, 8).

Lindholm (1988) examined the commonalities of social work practice in the five Nordic countries (Denmark, Norway, Finland, Sweden, Iceland). Recognizing that there were significant differences among the countries, she still concluded that there were enough common traits to justify a search for "a separate identity for Nordic social work and its training" (11).

The 1990s witnessed a proliferation of Canadian literature related to practice in the North. Building on the theoretical foundation from the mid-1980s that began to recognize and consider northern practice issues, these works are mostly collections of readings from northern practitioners, administrators, students, and academics. *The Northern Review* devoted an entire special issue to social work in northern Canada (Wharf, 1992). A compilation of readings from northern Manitoba was published that same year (Tobin and Walmsley, 1992). The following year, Grant MacEwan Community College in Edmonton published a collection of reflective essays from students and teachers involved with Aboriginal social work outreach education programs in northern Alberta (Feehan and Hannis, 1993). Also in 1993, Collier published a second edition of his influential book. During the last half of the decade, Lakehead University's Centre for Northern Studies initiated a Northern Social Work series that now includes volumes on northern practice (Delaney & Brownlee, 1995), northern issues (Delaney, Brownlee, & Zapf, 1996), northern strategies (Brownlee, Delaney, & Graham, 1997), northern community work (Delaney, Brownlee, & Sellick, 1999), and social work with northern organizations (Brownlee, Sellick, & Delaney, 2001).

The social work profession has a very eclectic knowledge base, drawing material from many other disciplines. We clearly recognize contributions from related social science disciplines such as psychology, sociology, economics, and anthropology. Yet there has been little interaction with the discipline of geography, a curious situation for a profession that professes concern with context and environment. The remainder of this chapter will explore elements of the Canadian northern reality from several geographic perspectives in an attempt to identify and understand the influence of geographic factors on the practice of social work in this country.

GEOGRAPHY AND SOCIAL WORK IN NORTHERN CANADA

Many of us last encountered academic geography in high school where we had to place names on intimidating blank maps and memorize long lists of capital cities, annual precipitation, landforms, and economic products. As expressed by Taaffe, Gauthier, and O'Kelly (1996):

> Unfortunately, the popular stereotype that geography is a discipline steadfastly devoted to long factual inventories and the rote memorization of place locations and the detailed characteristics of mountains, rivers, and other physical features still persists (3).

Most of the country names and borders we learned so many years ago are now hopelessly out of date. We may have actually understood little about why particular settlement patterns emerged, or how regions interact and affect one another. Many of us probably suffer from what de Blij (1996) has labelled "geographic illiteracy" (1).

Modern geography is a discipline that has been described as "synthesizing or integrative" (Taaffe, Gauthier, & O'Kelly, 1996, 41), and "multifaceted" in that it "uniquely straddles the divide between the social and the physical (natural) sciences" (de Blij & Muller, 1994, 40). Current geographic frameworks focus not only on physical geography (landforms, coastlines, climates, soils, vegetation, animals, etc.) but also on human geography (spatial patterns of human activities). Arguing that pure natural landscapes no longer exist, geography has turned much of its attention to "cultural landscapes" (de Blij & Muller, 1994; Fellmann, Getis, & Getis, 1997). This new human geography generally incorporates several subcategories or particular fields of analysis; for example, demographic geography, political geography, economic geography, cultural geography, and phenomenological geography. Perspectives derived from these geographic subsystems can be applied to the Canadian reality in an effort to better understand our social work practice context.

Demographic Geography

With regard to demographic geography, there is evidence in the recent literature to support a population figure of 10,000 as indicative of a qualitative difference between rural and urban settlements. In their study of towns and villages in Canada, Hodge and Qadeer (1983) found a "threshold distinction" which appeared as an "upper population limit of ten thousand persons...a definition slightly at odds with the Census, but a more realistic view in our opinion" (13–14). While any attempt to define rurality using a population threshold must ultimately be regarded as arbitrary and intuitive, this population threshold of 10,000 may reflect the point at which concerned and active natural helping systems are replaced by specialized social services. Support can be found in the Canadian literature (McVey, 1992; Norris & Johal, 1992; Trant & Brinkman, 1992; Wilkins, 1992; Zapf, 1992) for the utility of this 10,000 population figure as a meaningful threshold for distinguishing between rural and urban communities.

The overall population dispersion pattern in Canada reveals a startling reality: only one percent of the population occupies the northern 80 percent of the land mass (Beaujot & McQuillan, 1982). Nine out of ten Canadians live within 200 miles of the American border; six out of ten live in the narrow urban corridor between Quebec City and Windsor. In simple terms, the pattern is one of a narrow ribbon of population to the south and a vast hinterland to the north. The settlement pattern in northern Canada has been characterized as "nodal" (Birdsall & Florin, 1992, 466), featuring "only about 250 small communities scattered across a territory as large as Europe" (Hamelin, 1978, 68). Only a handful of these small settlements exceed or even approach the 10,000 population threshold. Social services have tended to be designed and delivered from centralized agencies in urban centres to the south.

Political Geography

From the perspective of political geography, the province has generally been accepted as the unit of analysis for all Canadian social policy discussions. Provincial residents are often assumed to share common values and vision, a common ideology, as we examine similarities and differences in programs across provinces. As Hodgetts (1966) observed, Canadians have never been very clear "about the existence of regions with identifiable interests separate from the interests historically contained in and expressed through provincial units" (100). Limitations imposed by using the province as the unit of analysis have caused us to consider our vast northern region as an awkward jumble of territories and provincial top-ends (Coates & Morrison, 1992; Hamelin, 1984). North-south issues have been tackled separately within the artificial confines of seven different provinces and two (soon to be at least three) federal territories.

Social policy and program planners have tended to view their own separate northern regions as variations of the south, posing service delivery problems. Northern Albertans are treated as disadvantaged southern Albertans, entitled to the services available in Calgary or Edmonton; Yukoners are seen similarly as disadvantaged southern Canadians entitled to the full range of services and resources available in the south. It is not inherent in our political geography that all federal and provincial policy-makers deliberately set out to exploit their northern hinterland regions. Rather,

> The key issue is that acceptance of the province as unit of analysis carries with it a mind set that can be damaging for northern people. A provincial perspective limits our ability to move beyond problems of service delivery towards appreciation of the very lifestyle and ideology that might serve as the foundation for relevant social policy in the North (Zapf, 1995, 69).

Economic Geography

Efforts to explore the economic geography of Canada have used labels such as "centre-periphery," "metropolis-hinterland," "core-periphery," "centre-margin," or "heartland-hinterland" (Bone, 1992; Collier, 1993; Curtis & Tepperman, 1990; Davis, 1990; de Blij & Muller, 1994; Dunk, 1991; Lockhart, 1991; Lotz, 1970; Southcott, 1993; Usher, 1987; Weller, 1993; Westfall, 1980). Power, control, and the ability to innovate are located in the heartland or core urban regions in southern Canada; the northern hinterland is dependent upon this southern heartland for investment capital, technical expertise, markets, information, and general well-being. Economic development has been imposed upon the northern region in powerful waves (gold rushes, military bases, mineral and oil extraction, hydroelectric megaprojects, forestry, recreation), episodic bursts of activity related to the needs of the south rather than the needs of the North. Such ongoing economic underdevelopment in the Canadian North has been depicted as a purposeful relationship designed to transfer value from the hinterland to the urban areas of the south (Coates & Powell, 1989; Collier, 1993). The intensity of the exploitative relationship of dependence between northern and southern Canada has prompted several authors to refer to areas of northern Canada as a domestic Third World (Carniol, 1987; Collier, 1993, Jull, 1986; Weller, 1984).

As a component of this economic exploitation process, social work has been accused of damage control, addressing only the most serious social disruptions caused by the heartland's ongoing exploitation of the hinterland (Collier, 1993). Liberal and benevolent intentions from a dominant southern heartland can result in decreased control and a sense of violation in the northern hinterland. Lipton (1977) referred to such strong urban bias as "more than simply mistaken, but less than dishonest" (63). Friere (1970) spoke of "cultural invasion, good intentions notwithstanding" (84). Using even stronger language, Castellano (1971) called attention to "a destructive kind of contract...a violence perpetuated against the person allegedly helped" (352). Other labels that have been applied to this process in the Canadian literature include: "welfare colonialism" (Paine, 1977), "benevolent colonialism" (Durst, 1996), "compassionate colonialism" (deMontigny, 1992), "cultural wounding" (Arges & Delaney, 1996), and "colonial dominion" (Abele, 1989).

Cultural Geography

Cultural geographers concentrate on cultural landscapes, or the spatial distribution of world views, values, and traditions (de Blij & Muller, 1994; McCann, 1987). A community of people tend to construct a common model or map of the world derived from their shared experiences and then use these categories as a background screen against which incoming experiences are interpreted. Without such a set of assumptions, the world would be experienced as chaotic and unpredictable. Cultural geography adds a spatial component or relevant context to this notion of culture. Differing cultures or world views pose no problem as long as they are located far enough apart so as not to interfere with each other. Conflict only occurs when they meet, when two or more groups have designs on the same physical environment and attempt to interpret events in that environment using different cultural screens (Zapf, 1995). Dominant groups may have the power to force their cultural patterns on minority groups. Problem definitions and solution strategies will likely be framed within the ideology of the dominant group.

Traditional world views in northern Canada have emphasized harmony with the environment as expressed through stewardship, sharing, cooperation, present orientation, and co-existence; this northern set of cultural traditions conflicts with the assumptions of individual autonomy, future orientation, private ownership, and manipulation of the environment for profit evident in the industrial south (Collier, 1993; Franks, 1984; Jull, 1985, 1986; Moore & Vanderhaden, 1984; Page, 1986). Yet social work developed as a specialized profession within industrial urban society, and most social work education in Canada is still concentrated in the southern population ribbon where the great majority of universities and graduate research centres are located. Social workers trained and comfortable within that southern cultural milieu might be expected to encounter difficulties when moving to a remote northern community to practise in the context of a different world view, values, and traditions.

> The newly located worker attempts to understand the community using frameworks from his or her own familiar culture and profession. Applying metaphors from the South leads to a limited view of the northern community as a pathological variation of the southern experience. During the settling-in period in a northern community, supports for the familiar professional role weaken, and a new social circle emerges as the worker must interact closely with community residents to meet most of his or her daily needs. Eventually the worker enters into the system of local meanings and priorities. This shift will probably be accompanied by a stressful period of frustration and disorientation, giving way eventually to regained confidence and a sense of well being as the worker learns to operate within the new system of meanings (Zapf, 1993, 701–702).

Phenomenological Geography

Places have meanings for people as they perceive and subjectively experience their environments. Phenomenological geographer Edward Relph (1976) concluded that

> The essence of place lies...in the experience of an "inside" that is distinct from an "outside"; more than anything else this is what sets places apart in space and defines a particular system of physical features, activities, and meaning. To be inside a place is to belong to it and to identify with it, and the more profoundly inside you are the stronger is the identity with the place (49).

Such a distinction between inside and outside identification is found frequently in the literature on rural areas in general and northern settlements in particular. Following a model from anthropology, Relph (1976) developed a continuum for levels of identification with place.

The new social worker may arrive in a northern community with a perspective of objective outsideness acquired through professional training in the south and supported by the government employer. At this level of Relph's continuum, the person separates consciously and deliberately from place for professional or academic reasons; places are considered theoretically according to some system of attributes rather than as places of immediate experience. This is the sense of professional distance, of assessing the community as a target system, a collection of resources and problems. The northern community, however, will not likely allow the new worker to maintain this objective, outside perspective offering only specialized technical skills. Cut off from the supportive professional social circle of the southern urban centre (professors, supervisors, professional association), the new social worker begins to experience the remote community in an immediate sense, becoming aware of the values and experiences of the people who live there. Eventually the worker may even enter into the meanings of the community; the community becomes less a target group and more a home (Zapf, 1985b).

Viewed from the perspective of Relph's (1976) continuum, the worker may come to identify with the community as an insider. Relative position within the community hierarchy is assigned based on performance and skills related to perceived community needs. Legitimacy derives from any proven results relative to the community's goals. The sense of duty perceived by the social worker as a community member reflects the intensity of the connection with the local place.

GEOGRAPHY, SOCIAL WORK, AND A "CULTURE OF OPPOSITION"

While Canadian social work has begun to acknowledge the uniqueness of northern/remote practice, northern issues remain largely outside the focus of the mainstream profession. Northern concerns are seldom addressed in the major publications, nor do they have prominence on the agendas of national conferences. The Canadian remote practice literature may now be where the American rural practice literature was in the early 1970s—arguments for differentiation plus scattered published collections of field experiences. A comprehensive model has yet to be developed from this literature. There even remains considerable lack of consensus about the definition of "North," an imprecise and relative term that often reveals more about the person using it than the region labelled (from Whitehorse, the community of Old Crow is north; Torontonians may consider Sudbury or even Orillia as north).

Coates (1994) offered a provocative critique of conceptualizations of "North" and academic attempts to define characteristics of northern regions. After considering many of the same spatial, economic, cultural, political, and phenomenological approaches that have been used in this chapter, Coates concluded that such efforts do not adequately respond to the need for "a North-centred and regionally-sensitive theoretical approach" (40). As the culmination of many years of northern research and publications, he advanced one simple "organizing pattern of behaviour that appears to get to the core of Northern life" (41). In his words:

> Northern/remote regions, I suggest, are characterized by a culture of opposition. This opposition originates with the fundamental non-indigenous struggle against the environment and against the indigenous inhabitants. From this base, the conflict expanded over time to include struggles with Southern governments, transients, corporate influences, and Southern/popular conceptions of Northern realities. Northerners, therefore, developed in relationship to others and in conflict with various natural, economic, and social forces. With the oppositional approach rooted in historical events and perpetuated by contemporary influences, Northern regions have maintained and internalized a culture of antagonism and struggle (Coates, 1994, 41).

Strong evidence of this pervasive "culture of opposition" can be seen in the published experiences of social workers in the Canadian North. Consider the following accounts selected from the literature on northern social work practice and administration:

caught between opposing forces, [workers] had to choose between following their consciences and ensuring a continuance of their paycheques (Lotz, 1982, 28);

the world view of the agency may be utterly opposed to that of the community. The agency may, in fact, be actively assisting to destroy that world. But that is the job (Collier, 1993, 44);

[workers] could not resolve the conflict between their ideals...and the realities of a colonial bureaucratic system that did not support them in the way...the situation warranted (Koster, 1977, 158);

the role conflict forced workers to make a choice between their community and their profession (Zapf, 1985b, 188);

factors which may encourage public servants to be cautious about or hostile to efforts to enhance community control may relate to the tensions and conflicts involved in weighing citizen needs and demands against those associated with professional norms, administrative standards and normal operating procedures (Cassidy, 1992, 29);

the work of these practitioners is normally governed by province-wide social policies which do not 'fit' with the needs of northern peoples...the practitioner frequently represents an organization or system which denies people access to needed services and resources (McKay, 1987, 266 & 268);

the immediate situation rather than standardized and established professional practice becomes the best judge of what must be done (Nelson, McPherson, & Kelley, 1987, 69);

when the southern administrative culture is transplanted, as it is into the North, the gap between reality and the means employed to deal with the reality is further increased...It is hard to see how the public service can truly adjust to the North unless ideological systems compatible with the regions are developed and accepted first (Hamelin, 1984, 172–173);

agency directors, who are often faced with having little discretion for the major elements of their programs, recognize that many of their programs are not suitably designed for northern settings (Delaney & Brownlee, 1996, 47);

the programs of government...all too often do not reinforce and strengthen the society and culture of native populations, but conflict with them...this pressure is all the more severe because of the large size of the government sector in the north (Franks, 1984, 238);

government programs were implemented according to metropolitan perceptions. Northern needs in health, education, shelter, and welfare were identified by the government and responded to by the Government. Though intentions were humanitarian, programs often proceeded in ignorance of how the Native people lived and therefore often did not solve fundamental problems (Usher, 1987, 503);

the response of social services in remote communities needs to be cooperative...Often southern paradigms only compound the existing problems and further aggravate cultural change and conflict (Kamin & Beatch, 1992, 92);

northern social workers live day to day with the enforced dependency upon the south. They are familiar with the problems of managing systems where the real power and authority remains in the south. They are used to seeing clients abused by decisions made by people who live far away (deMontigny, 1992, 81).

Just as Coates (1994) argued that an internalized "culture of opposition" has been an "internally destructive and ultimately self-defeating" (42) pattern for northern regions, a similar sense of grievance and antagonism amongst northern social work practitioners may be inhibiting the development of identifiable and useful models of remote practice.

GEOGRAPHY, SOCIAL WORK, AND GLOBALIZATION

As we enter a new millenium, the Canadian social work literature addresses new issues arising from the globalization of all human activity. We are encouraged to look beyond provincial and national boundaries, to make global connections using the new technologies, and to consider global forces in our assessments, interventions, and advocacy efforts. In this move to a global perspective, there is the potential for a more complete understanding of the impact of geographic factors on Canadian social work practice.

Although globalization is most often presented in economic terms, Midgley (2000) reminds us that there are also social, political, cultural, and demographic dimensions for social workers to consider. This multi-dimensional approach was confirmed in an international survey of social workers (Rowe, Hanley, Moreno, & Mould, 2000). Yet these very aspects of globalization identified as important in the social work literature are the same as the subsystems of human geography introduced earlier in this chapter. It would be ironic but welcome if Canadian social work came to a fuller understanding of our own geographic base through the development of a global perspective.

Drover (2000) examined issues of rights and active citizenship in the global era, exploring a sense of global citizenship that transcends the confines of national boundaries. One form of this global citizenship is defined by "geographic continuity" (34). Even within an expanded notion of being a global citizen, there remain persistent and strong aspects of region, territory, and place. In another discussion of the importance of geography to Canadian social welfare (Zapf, 2001), I have stressed the importance of recognizing and developing this *place* component of our profession's declared dual focus on *person/place*.

Perhaps the fundamental question was put most clearly by Haas & Nachtigal ((1998) when they asked "what it means to live well in a particular place" (Preface, vii). In their series of short but provocative bibliographic essays, the authors considered what it means: to live well ecologically (developing a sense of place); to live well politically (developing a sense of civic involvement); to live well economically (developing a sense of worth); to live well spiritually (developing a sense of connection); and to live well in community (developing a sense of belonging). The basic question underlying Canadian social work practice may be: What does it mean to live well in this place (this continent, this country, this region, this community)? Meaningful answers must involve a fuller understanding of our geographic reality.

REFERENCES

Abele, F. (1989). Canadian contradictions: forty years of northern political development. In K.S. Coates & W.R. Morrison. (Eds.). *Interpreting Canada's north: selected readings*. Toronto: Copp Clark Pitman.

Arges, S., & Delaney, R. (1996). Challenging the southern metaphor: from oppression to empowerment. In R. Delaney, K. Brownlee, & M.K. Zapf (Eds.). *Issues in northern social work practice* (pp. 1–22). Thunder Bay: Lakehead University Centre for Northern Studies.

Armitage, A. (1975). *Social welfare in Canada: ideals and realities*. Toronto: McClelland & Stewart.

Armitage, A. (1988). *Social welfare in Canada: ideals, realities, and future paths* (2nd ed.). Toronto: McClelland & Stewart.

Beaujot, R., & McQuillan, K. (1982). *Growth and dualism: the demographic development of Canadian society*. Toronto: Gage.

Birdsall, S.S., & Florin, J.W. (1992). *Regional landscapes of the United States and Canada* (4th ed.). New York: John Wiley & Sons.

Bone, R.M. (1992). *The geography of the Canadian North: issues and challenges*. Toronto: Oxford University Press.

Brown, J.C. (Ed.). (1933). *The rural community in social casework*. New York: Family Welfare Association of America.

Brownlee, K., Delaney, R., & Graham, J.R. (Eds.). (1997). *Strategies for northern social work practice*. Thunder Bay: Lakehead Centre for Northern Studies.

Brownlee, K., Sellick, M., & Delaney, R. (Eds.). (2001). *Social work with rural and northern organizations*. Thunder Bay: Lakehead Centre for Northern Studies.

Carniol, B. (1987). *Case critical: the dilemma of social work in Canada*. Toronto: Between the Lines.

Cassidy, F. (1992). Organizing for community control. *The Northern Review*, *7*, 17–34. (Special theme issue on social work in the North).

Castellano, M. (1971). Out of paternalism and into partnership: an exploration of alternatives in social service to Native people. In J.A. Draper (Ed.). *Citizen participation Canada: a book of readings*. Toronto: New Press.

Coates, K. (1994). The rediscovery of the North: towards a conceptual framework for the study of northern/remote regions. *The Northern Review*, *12/13*, 15–43.

Coates, K., & Morrison, W. (1992). *The forgotten North: a history of Canada's provincial Norths*. Toronto: James Lorimer.

Coates, K., & Powell, J. (1989). *The modern North: people, politics and the rejection of colonialism*. Toronto: Lorimer.

Collier, K. (1984). *Social work with rural people*. Vancouver: New Star.

Collier, K. (1993). *Social work with rural people* (2nd ed.). Vancouver: New Star.

Curtis, J., & Tepperman, L. (Eds.). (1990). *Images of Canada: the sociological tradition*. Scarborough: Prentice-Hall Canada.

Davis, A.K. (1990). Canada as hinterland versus metropolis. In J. Curtis & L. Tepperman (Eds.). *Images of Canada: the sociological tradition* (pp. 141–152). Scarborough: Prentice-Hall Canada.

de Blij, H.J. (1996). *Human geography: culture, society, and space* (5th ed.). New York: John Wiley & Sons.

de Blij, H.J., & Muller, P.O. (1994). *Geography: Realms, regions, and concepts* (7th ed.). New York: John Wiley & Sons.

Delaney, R., & Brownlee, K. (1996). Ethical dilemmas in northern social work practice. In R. Delaney, K. Brownlee, & M.K. Zapf (Eds.). *Issues in northern social work practice* (pp. 47–69). Thunder Bay: Lakehead University Centre for Northern Studies.

Delaney, R., & Brownlee, K. (Eds.). (1995). *Northern social work practice.* Thunder Bay: Lakehead University Centre for Northern Studies.

Delaney, R., Brownlee, K., & Sellick, M. (Eds.). (1999). *Social work with rural and northern communities.* Thunder Bay: Lakehead Centre for Northern Studies.

Delaney, R., Brownlee, K., & Zapf, M.K. (Eds.). (1996). *Issues in northern social work practice.* Thunder Bay: Lakehead University Centre for Northern Studies.

deMontigny, G. (1992). Compassionate colonialism: sowing the branch plant. In M. Tobin & C. Walmsley (Eds.). *Northern perspectives: practice and education in social work* (pp. 73–82). Winnipeg: Manitoba Association of Social Workers and The University of Manitoba Faculty of Social Work.

Drover, G. (1984). Policy and legislative perspectives. *The Social Worker, 52*(1), 6–10.

Drover, G. (2000). Redefining social citizenship in a global era. *Canadian Social Work Review, 17* (Special Issue: Social Work and Globalization), 29–49.

Dunk, T.W. (Ed.). (1991). *Social relations in resource hinterlands.* Thunder Bay: Lakehead University Centre for Northern Studies.

Durst, D. (1996). The circle of self-government: a guide to Aboriginal government of social services. In R. Delaney, K. Brownlee, & M.K. Zapf (Eds.). *Issues in northern social work practice* (pp. 104–125). Thunder Bay: Lakehead University Centre for Northern Studies.

Feehan, K., & Hannis, D. (Eds.). (1993). *From strength to strength: social work education and Aboriginal people.* Edmonton: Grant MacEwan Community College.

Fellmann, J., Getis, A., & Getis, J. (1997). *Human geography: landscapes of human activities* (5th ed.). Madison: Brown & Benchmark Publishers.

Franks, C.E.S. (1984). The public service in the north. In L.E. Hamelin (Ed.). *Managing Canada's North* (pp. 210–241). Toronto: Institute of Public Administration of Canada.

Friere, P. (1970). *Pedagogy of the oppressed* (M.B. Ramos, translator). New York: Seabury Press.

Ginsberg, L.H. (1971). Rural social work. In *Encyclopedia of social work* (sixteenth issue, volume 2). New York: NASW.

Haas, T., & Nachtigal, P. (1998). *Place value: an educator's guide to good literature on rural lifeways, environments, and purposes of education.* Charleston: Appalachia Educational Laboratory.

Hamelin, L.E. (1978). *Canadian nordicity: it's your North, too* (W. Barr, translator). Montreal: Harvest House.

Hamelin, L.E. (Ed.). (1984). *Managing Canada's North: challenges and opportunities.* Toronto: Institute of Public Administration of Canada.

Hamelin, L.E. (1988). *The Canadian North and its conceptual referents.* Ottawa: Canadian Studies Directorate, Department of the Secretary of State of Canada.

Hodge, G., & Qadeer, M.A. (1983). *Towns and villages in Canada: the importance of being unimportant.* Toronto: Butterworths.

Hodgetts, J.E. (1966). How applicable is regionalism in the Canadian federal system? In P. Fox (Ed.). *Politics in Canada* (2nd ed.). Toronto: McGraw-Hill.

Hudson, P., & McKenzie, B. (1985). Native children, child welfare, and the colonization of Native people. In B. Wharf & K. Lewitt (Eds.). *The challenge of child welfare.* Vancouver: UBC Press.

Jull, P. (1985). The aboriginal option: a radical critique of European values. *Northern Perspectives, 13*(2), 10–12.

Jull, P. (1986). Take the north seriously. *Policy Options* (September), 7–11.

Kamin, A., & Beatch, R. (1991). A community development approach to mental health services. *The Northern Review, 7*, 92–105.

Koster, D. (1977). Why is he here?: white gossip. In R. Paine (Ed.). *The white Arctic: anthropological essays on tutelage and ethnicity*. University of Toronto Press.

Lindholm, K. (1988). In search of an identity—social work training in the nordic countries. *Nordic Journal of Social Work, 8*, 4–14. (Special supplementary issue in English of *Nordisk Sosialt Arbeid* on the occasion of IFSW's World Conference in Stockholm 1988).

Lipton, M. (1977). *Why poor people stay poor: a study of urban bias in world development*. London: Temple Smith.

Lockhart, A. (1991). Northern development policy: hinterland communities and metropolitan academics. In T.W. Dunk (Ed.). *Social relations in resource hinterlands*. Thunder Bay: Lakehead University Centre for Northern Studies.

Lotz, J. (1970). *Northern realities: the future of northern development in Canada*. Toronto: New Press.

Lotz, J. (1982). The moral and ethical basis of community development: reflections on the Canadian experience. *Community Development Journal, 17*(1), 27–31.

Maclouf, P., & Lion, A. (1984). *Aging in remote rural areas: a challenge to social and medical service* (Eurosocial Reports #24). Vienna: European Centre for Social Welfare Training and Research.

Martinez-Brawley, E.E. (1981). Rural social and community work as political movements in the United States and United Kingdom. *Community Development Journal, 16*(3), 201–211.

McCann, L.D. (1987). Heartland and hinterland: a framework for regional analysis. In L.D. McCann (Ed.). *Heartland and hinterland: a geography of Canada* (2nd ed.) (pp. 2–37). Scarborough: Prentice-Hall Canada.

McKay, S. (1987). Social work in Canada's north: survival and development issues affecting aboriginal and industry-based economics. *International Social Work, 30*, 259–278.

McVey, J.S. (1992). Growth of small and medium size business: a rural-urban comparison. In R.D. Bollman (Ed.). *Rural and small town Canada* (pp. 45–67). Toronto: Thompson Educational Publishing.

Midgley, J. (2000). Globalization, capitalism, and social welfare: a social development perspective. *Canadian Social Work Review, 17* (Special Issue: Social Work and Globalization), 13–28.

Moore, M., & Vanderhaden, G. (1984). Northern problems or Canadian opportunities. In L.E. Hamelin (Ed.). *Managing Canada's North: challenges and opportunities* (pp. 182–187). Toronto: Institute of Public Administration of Canada.

Nelson, C., McPherson, D., & Kelley, M.L. (1987). Contextual patterning: a key to human service effectiveness in the North. In P. Adams & D. Parker (Eds.). *Canada's subarctic universities* (pp. 66–82). Ottawa: Association of Canadian Universities for Northern Studies.

Norris, D.A., & Johal, K. (1992). Social indicators from the General Social Survey: some urban-rural differences. In R.D. Bollman (Ed.). *Rural and small town Canada* (pp. 357–368). Toronto: Thompson Educational Publishing.

Paine, R. (Ed.). (1977). *The white Arctic: anthropological essays on tutelage and ethnicity*. University of Toronto Press.

Page, R. (1986). *Northern development: the Canadian dilemma*. Toronto: McClelland & Stewart.

Relph, E. (1976). *Place and placelessness*. London: Pion.

Ribes, B. (1985). *Youth and life in remote rural areas* (Eurosocial Reports #27). Vienna: European Centre for Social Welfare Training and Research.

Rowe, W., Hanley, J., Moreno, E.R., & Mould, J. (2000). Voices of social work practice: international reflections on the effects of globalization. *Canadian Social Work Review, 17* (Special Issue: Social Work and Globalization), 65–87.

Southcott, C. (Ed.). (1993). Provincial hinterland: social inequality in northwestern Ontario. Halifax: Fernwood Publishing.

Taaffe, E.J., Gauthier, H.L., O'Kelly, M.E. (1996). Geography of transportation. Upper Saddle River, New Jersey: Prentice-Hall.

Tobin, M., & Walmsley, C. (Eds.). (1992). *Northern perspectives: practice and education in social work*. Winnipeg: Manitoba Association of Social Workers and The University of Manitoba Faculty of Social Work.

Torjman, S.R. (1984). Editorial. *The Social Worker, 52*(1), p.3.

Trant, M., & Brinkman, G. (1992). Products and competitiveness of rural Canada. In R.D. Bollman (Ed.). *Rural and small town Canada* (pp. 69–90). Toronto: Thompson Educational Publishing.

Turner, J.C., & Turner, F.J. (Eds.). (1981). *Canadian social welfare*. Don Mills: Collier Macmillan.

Usher, P.J. (1987). The North: one land, two ways of life. In L.D. McCann (Ed.). *Heartland and hinterland: a geography of Canada* (2nd ed.). Scarborough: Prentice-Hall Canada.

Weller, G.R. (1984). Managing Canada's north: The case of the provincial north. In L.E. Hamelin (Ed.). *Managing Canada's North*. Toronto: Institute of Public Administration of Canada.

Weller, G.R. (1993). Hinterland politics: the case of northwestern Ontario. In C. Southcott (Ed.). *Provincial hinterland: social inequality in northwestern Ontario* (pp. 5–28). Halifax: Fernwood Publishing.

Westfall, W. (1980). On the concept of the region in Canadian history and literature. *Journal of Canadian Studies, 15*(2), 3–15.

Wharf, B. (Ed.). (1979). *Community work in Canada*. Toronto: McClelland & Stewart.

Wharf, B. (1985). Toward a leadership role in human services: the case for rural communities. *The Social Worker, 53*(1), 14–20.

Wharf, B. (Guest Ed.). (1992). *The Northern Review, 7*. (Special theme issue on social work in the North).

Wilkins, R. (1992). Health of the rural population: Selected indicators. In R.D. Bollman (Ed.). *Rural and small town Canada* (pp. 283–292). Toronto: Thompson Educational Publishing.

Yelaja, S.S. (Ed.). (1985). *An introduction to social work practice in Canada*. Scarborough: Prentice-Hall Canada.

Yelaja, S.S. (Ed.). (1987). *Canadian social policy* (rev. ed.). Waterloo: Wilfrid Laurier University Press.

Zapf, M.K. (1985). *Rural social work and its application to the Canadian North as a practice setting* (Working Papers on Social Welfare in Canada Publications Series, #15). University of Toronto Faculty of Social Work.

Zapf, M.K. (1985b). Home is where the target group is: an analysis of the role conflicts faced by an urban-trained social worker in a remote northern community. In W. Whitaker (Ed.). *Social work in rural areas: a celebration of rural people, place, and struggle* (pp. 187–203). Orono: University of Maine.

Zapf, M.K. (1992). Educating social work practitioners for the North: a challenge for conventional models and structures. *The Northern Review*, 7, 35–52. (Special theme issue on social work in the North).

Zapf, M.K. (1993). Remote practice and culture shock: social workers moving to isolated northern regions. *Social Work*, *38*(6), 694–704.

Zapf, M.K. (1995). Ideology and context: development and social welfare in Canada's North. In B. Kirwin (Ed.). *Ideology, development and social welfare: Canadian perspectives* (3rd ed.) (pp. 55–78). Toronto: Canadian Scholars' Press.

Zapf, M.K. (2001). The geographic base of Canadian social welfare. In J.C. Turner & F.J. Turner (Eds.), *Canadian social welfare (4ᵗʰ ed.),* (pp. 67–79). Toronto: Pearson Education Canada.

Zaslow, M. (1971). *The opening of the Canadian North, 1870–1914.* Toronto: McClelland & Stewart.

CANADIAN POLITICAL PROCESSES AND SOCIAL WORK PRACTICE

Ray J. Thomlison and
Cathryn Bradshaw

Social work practice is inextricably linked with political processes. These processes are both informal and formal and are often simply referred to as *politics*. Depending upon one's interests and experiences, the degree and intensity of participation in politics varies among social work practitioners. It is certain, however, that whether or not practitioners are direct participants in political processes, they are subject to the consequences of their political outcomes. It is the purpose of this chapter to examine some of these political processes within the Canadian context of social policies and programs. The emphasis here will not be on understanding the policies and their related programs but rather on highlighting some of the political processes by which policies and programs are developed in Canada. Within this brief overview, an argument is developed that the existing processes are subtly changing and social work practitioners are very well positioned to seize the opportunity to be more influential than ever before in these new political processes.

POLITICAL PROCESSES

Defining what is meant by the concept of politics and political processes is a subject of study in its own right. For the purposes of this review, *political processes* refers to formal and informal structures of human interaction that have the objective of guiding power, influence, and authority toward the formulation of policies and programs within the field of social welfare. The fundamental political process within a democratic society is operationalized through some form of representation of the citizenry by an election procedure. Although the procedures and structures may differ among jurisdictions, the objective of population representation in the formulation of legislation, programs, and accountability remains consistent.

In essence, this definition of political process speaks to any democratic system. It is, however, for many, a deceptively simple process. It is all too easy to assume that representation and participation in legislative governance is simply a matter of casting one's ballot at election time. Such a perception denies the complexity of the underlying attendant processes that lead to the ultimate presentation and decision-making in a legislative assembly. Metaphorically, the end of the process, in the public political gallery, is the tip of the iceberg. As with the iceberg, it is the most visible part, but probably represents the least amount of the totality of the political processes leading to the public presentation of the proposed legislation. In other words, the main part of the process is less visible and for many virtually unseen.

For the professional social worker, particularly those in direct practice, it is important to be informed about and participatory in the various political processes leading to policies and programs that have an impact on their practice potential. Participation does not necessarily need to occur at what might be termed the "macro" level or large governmental level. Political processes in the social agency, local community, or municipal level parallel those at the provincial or federal level. The strategies and mechanisms to participate in the process of influence remain the same.

In reality, for most social work practitioners, when you pause to think about it, political processes, while acknowledged as important, probably have a lower level of priority in terms of their day-to-day practice concerns. It may be that a reordering of priorities would lead to a stronger presence of the social work perspective in policy change. Such a reordering might be easier if an understanding of political processes and strategies (techniques) of participation were more clearly integrated as a legitimate component of practice knowledge and skills.

In order to provide a base for this perspective it is helpful to review the Canadian context within which social policy and social welfare programs are developed, critiqued, and modified.

THE CONTEXT

Canadians have a sense of pride in having created a social welfare system that guarantees a basic standard of living for all of its citizens. Although it has its critics and is certainly not a perfect system, Canada's post-World War II health, welfare, and education programs combine to ensure all Canadians universal health care, income security based on need, and free access to educational opportunities to the completion of high school. While there have always been ongoing debates about the cost of these programs, there has been a newly found public energy and support to reform the welfare system. This movement, often referred to as the "swing to the right," is not peculiar to Canada. It is a reality in most western societies including England, the United States, Australia, and New Zealand. The focus of these protests has been on government debt coupled with public opinion that taxes must be reduced. Since the bulk of public expenditure supports programs in health, education, and welfare, it is these program areas that are most often the subject of intense debate and, consequently, the target of fiscal cuts.

Canadians have on the whole supported some change, yet they remain ambivalent and somewhat confused as to how far government should go. For example, they have strongly resisted changes in the areas of health care and pensions for the aged. The federal government has, however, succeeded in terminating the universal family allowance, a guaranteed income benefit paid to mothers for each child. Further, the government served notice of its intention to restructure the welfare system, and conducted a Social Security Review of all program policies and services in 1994/95. The purpose of the review was to produce recommendations for changes that would challenge the foundations of the existing health, welfare, and educational systems in Canada. Such significant efforts in data gathering and consensus activities focusing on change are a major challenge in a federal system such as we have in Canada.

THE CANADIAN POLITICAL SYSTEM

Canada is geographically the second largest country in the world, second only to Russia. Relatively speaking, however, it is small in population, with less than 30 million people. In fact, it can be argued that this combination of large geography and small population provided the necessity for Canada to develop a unique system of governmentally "subsidized capitalism," setting the foundation for a more liberal welfare system than that of its southern neighbours in the United States. Immigration patterns in recent years have produced new consequences for policy makers and social work practitioners in delivering services to persons from a multiplicity of cultural groups.

British North America Act

Canada has a parliamentary system, is democratically governed, and has a constitution rooted in its dominant British heritage. The original constitution of 1867, known as the British North America (BNA) Act, remained under the control of the British parliament until 1982 when it was "repatriated" to Canada. The BNA Act, which provided the framework for the division of legislative and financial powers, did not clearly allocate social welfare responsibility to either the federal or provincial governments. Through judicial interpretation, social welfare was judged to reside within provincial jurisdiction. Provincial responsibilities, under the BNA Act, included the administration of social welfare, health care, and employment programs. As the need for health care and welfare increased nationwide, the responsibility for initiating and paying for these services by the provinces created a fiscal burden that the provinces were unable to meet (Guest, 1985). Most of the taxation powers remained within the domain of the federal government. Provinces could collect direct taxes (e.g., income tax, sales tax) but only the federal government could collect indirect taxes. Indirect taxes, such as the previous manufacturing tax, may be passed on to consumers of the goods or services so taxed. So in the realm of social and health care programs, provincial governments needed to consider how they would raise the revenue to pay for the programs.

Unable to adequately finance social welfare programs on their own, provinces would need to await either an amendment to the BNA Act granting federal jurisdiction over such matters or the development of strategies to secure federal monies without violating the federal-provincial jurisdiction as set out in the BNA Act. The federal government developed cost-shared programs as a means of providing financial assistance to the provinces and territories. These arrangements did not involve changing the constitutional distribution of powers, yet now the federal government had a "de facto" influence over the provincial jurisdiction of welfare and health services (Strain & Hum, 1987). These arrangements preserved Canadian federalism, while facilitating the delivery of significant social programs. The federal government now had "spending powers" in social welfare and health due to the inability of provincial governments to fund their own provincial programs. This spending power allowed the federal government to institute national standards in health care, education, and social welfare.

Constitution of Canada

Canada's Constitution sets out the fundamental structure of the Canadian federation and its most basic institutions. Since its repatriation in 1982, the Constitution has been the focus of a great deal of debate for change, particularly in relation to the relative powers of the federal and provincial governments. The close vote, during the Quebec referendum of 1995, for continued federalism has heightened the angst of most Canadians concerning the future of Canada. Among the issues this vote raised was that of a Canadian identity. Recent debates about what it means to be Canadian focus on the Canadian welfare state. Our social safety net, especially our universal health care program, seems to many Canadians to be at the heart of what it means to be Canadian. These programs are seen as features that distinguish Canadians from their neighbour to the south. With the move toward reduced funding for social services in Canada showing no signs of abating, many social workers may want to increase their involvement in the political process.

While the majority of legislation controlling social welfare programs is controlled and financed at the federal level of government, it does not mean that a significant degree of planning and action does not occur at the provincial and local levels. Indeed, with greater pressure coming from the provinces to develop and control their own programs, more responsibility is being turned over to the provinces. In turn, the provinces are showing every indication they want to divest more responsibility for services to the municipal levels.

The Participants

Policy-Makers   The policy-makers are the elected officials of each level of government. The federal power structure includes prime minister and Cabinet, administrative support mechanisms such as the Prime Minister's Office and the Privy Council Office as well as a host of committees, departments, and bureaucrats. Shaping social policy development and implementation actually involves five major groups of players: politicians, bureaucrats, the media, special interest groups, and all voters who participate in electing politicians (Sarpkaya, 1988). Each of these players makes decisions and expresses views that combine self-interest with influencing the various instruments of government policy.

Bureaucrats   Bureaucrats (public or civil servants) have played a larger role in policy development since the institution of such central administrative bodies as the Prime Minister's Office (PMO). Politicians rely on the information and advice of the bureaucrats at various levels of government. These bureaucrats work within competing yet cooperating departments, bureaus, and agencies. Their primary purpose is to advise the government as to the implications of various courses of policy action or inaction. However, the version of the "public good" that these bureaucrats present to the politicians will be coloured by other players who have the ability to influence their thinking and advance their own careers. In this way, the policies that they support are not always determined by the social problem on the table.

Media   The media plays a substantial but indirect role in influencing policy development. The media has the power to influence the flow of information between the major policy players. Because the media is in the business of providing services through which to seek advertising contracts, they need to have access to newsworthy items. This means that the media can be courted by those persons and groups who have information that could develop into a "breaking story." Thus, the media forms an important link in a reciprocating chain of give-and-take between policy players.

Special Interest Groups   Special interest groups are sometimes known as pressure groups because they have as their raison d'être the promotion of personal and group self-interest through influencing government policies. Indeed, "interest group" denotes a vague, non-polit-ical entity, while "pressure group" emphasizes the true nature of the activities performed by these groups. Interest or pressure groups have been defined as "organizations whose members act together to influence public policy in order to promote their common interest" (Pross, 1992, 3). Special interest groups may take several forms: issue-oriented groups, service groups, regional or community-oriented groups, and professional associations (Dobell & Mansbridge, 1986; Thorburn, 1985). Having a priority focus on one area of interest, within the broad spectrum of social policy, *issue-oriented groups* may include such issues as income for the poor, crime prevention, or social rights. An example of this type of interest group would be the AIDS Action Committee. *Service groups* tend to address a wide range of service areas of concern to their members. Groups representing the interests of seniors, the disabled, or women would be examples of this type of pressure group. *Regional or community-oriented groups* are geo-graphically and/or culturally primed. The group members would lobby on behalf of the con-stituents of the region or community and represent to governments the unique social needs of these people. Social planning councils or regional health boards would be typical of this type of interest group. An "expert" perspective is given voice in social policy planning through professional associations, professional schools, and research groups.

   Professional associations, such as those representing social workers, as well as for-malized *labour groups* are special interest groups who have a long history of participation in the political process. While they have the best interests of their memberships as their pri-mary objective, they often play a prominent role in advocating for social change and for the maintenance of social welfare programs.

   Special interest groups derive their power to influence policy from several sources: 1) they have influence on voters and have the ability to deliver a block of voters in support of a government position; 2) they provide information regarding public preferences either orally or through written briefs to government sources; and 3) they have time and money to contribute to favoured political parties. Pressure groups use the media and its influence on decision-makers through their ability to provide the media with stories and information favourable to elected officials who support and promote their special interests. This way interest groups can stimulate voter action for or against a particular policy change (Sarapkaya, 1988).

   Social policy advocates, no matter which type of interest group they represent, generally perceive themselves as concerned with the "human side" of the policy agenda (Dobell & Mansbridge, 1986). They generally consider government officials, whether elected or civil servants, to have a primarily administrative focus. These interest groups advocate for issues they consider to have been neglected for political reasons or dominated by economic con-siderations (Dobell & Mansbridge, 1986). Interest groups can maximize their pressure power when groups representing different levels of constituents (i.e., community, regional, provincial, national, and international) form coalitions or alliances around specific themes, policies, or programs. This collective group action has the power to mobilize a large num-ber of voters and raise public concern around the issues. Some of the pressure techniques available to interest groups include obtaining or using information from polls, providing professional or expert input, having personal contact with politicians and officials, and providing individual or group commentary through the media. Information dissemination, public awareness, and public relations play an increasingly important role in the social policy network by controlling the flow of information and providing contacts with bureaucrats and elected officials.

The purpose of lobbying governments is to influence legislative or administrative decisions. Policy formation draws upon input from interest groups and coalitions that advocate from cooperative or adversarial lobbying positions vis-a-vis the government's position on the issue. In order to achieve their purpose and influence government decisions, it is imperative for interest groups to be familiar with the complexities of the process of public decision-making (Sarpkaya, 1988).

The Stages of the Process

The basic process involved in policy development is that of conflict resolution among the competing interests of all five types of policy players (politicians, bureaucrats, media, special interest groups, and voters). The main interplay on policy issues is between politicians, bureaucrats, and special interest groups. Thus, the consultative process involves elected officials and public service or bureaucratic officials as well as advocates from non-governmental organizations or interest groups. The prime minister, in consultation with Cabinet ministers, ultimately controls the choice of policy direction (Sarapkaya, 1988). This represents a "monopoly of political authority" compared with the more diffuse authority structure in the United States (Thompson & Stanbury, 1979). A concentration of power within the Canadian federal executive accounts for the contention that interest groups exercise relatively less influence in Canada than they do in the United States. This concentration of policy power allows the Canadian government some latitude, in policy decisions, to do only that which is minimally required for re-election.

Pre-election periods may find governments more concerned with the influence of special interest groups and voters, whereas in mid-mandate times there may be an emphasis on promoting less popular policy positions. Behind the scenes, however, individual players continually operate to influence the prime minister and Cabinet. To understand the influence these players have on policy decisions, knowledge of the workings of social policy's legislative process is essential.

The Legislative Process

The legislative process involves three phases of development: pre-legislative, legislative, and post-legislative phases.

Pre-Legislative Phase This phase provides special interest groups with their greatest participation and influence. The outcome of this phase of policy development is the production of a document by bureaucrats for the Cabinet. This detailed outline of the proposed policy direction is the result of the distillation of information from various sources and represents the bureaucrats' "read" on the probable impact of taking this direction on the Canadian public and the political future of the politicians involved.

Policy initiation, feasibility testing, and proposal modification represent the policy formation steps that precede the presentation of the Cabinet document (Thompson & Stanbury, 1979). The first two steps in this phase represent the prime areas where special interest groups can pressure for their positions and interests to be considered. Policy proposals that represent the ideas and interests of pressure groups can initiate policy development. In considering the feasibility of a policy direction, bureaucrats test out their ideas through "trial balloons" in the media and with non-governmental groups.

Feedback received by the bureaucrats may generate a careful evaluation of the social policy initiative under consideration. Many interest groups have found that their greatest sphere of influence is at this policy formulation stage and is directed more at key bureaucratic players than at elected officials. Thus, developing access to and establishing credibility with these bureaucratic decision-makers is of crucial significance to special interest groups. Most of the action for interest groups in Canada is at this bureaucratic level, whereas in the United States lobbying efforts are primarily directed at elected representatives. However, many pressure groups have found that taking their issue to the forum of public opinion is a more effective lobbying strategy than directing efforts at influencing these centralized policy-making structures (Pross, 1992).

A "culture of consultation" has developed between government officials and non-governmental organizations that is particularly relevant at this phase of the legislative process. By the early 1970s, the "participation phenomenon," as part of a growing consumer-groups awareness, was having an impact on policy formulation as well as other life domains (Dobell & Mansbridge, 1986). Informed consumers expect to be involved in decision-making through participation in planning, impact analysis, policy review, and other organizational or political exercises. The consumer-oriented groups have challenged the established domains of professional and research interest groups in social policy networking. A relevant example of the consultation process at work was provided by the Social Security Review (SSR), 1994–95. Through a motion made in the House of Commons in January 1994, the SSR was mandated to recommend ways and means of "modernizing and restructuring of Canada's social security system, with particular reference to the needs of families with children, youth and working age adults." A standing committee would conduct a review of social programs with a view to charting a new course for Canadian social policy (Jennissen, 1996; Pulkingham & Ternowetsky, 1996). The committee was to consult broadly, to analyze and to make recommendations to Cabinet. The consultation took the form of public hearings, with over 200 submissions received in the initial round and further input in the form of a workbook directed at soliciting feasibility information.

Legislative Phase　This phase of policy development includes the "in-house" processes that take place in and around Cabinet as well as the formal process of voting by the entire legislature.

Post-Legislative Phase　The final phase happens after the enactment of the legislation. This is the implementation phase of policy. Legislation often involves a large amount of discretion on the part of senior bureaucrats regarding the policy implementation. Bureaucrats operationalize the policy implementation process that Cabinet approves as specific regulations that will guide the course of implementation (Thompson & Stanbury, 1979). Special interest groups may exercise some influence in this implementation domain and may also challenge the policy through the judicial system. Increasingly, the impact of legislation depends upon judicial interpretations of the legislation, especially in regard to provisions of the Canadian Charter of Rights and Freedoms (Dobell & Mansbridge, 1986; Thompson & Stanbury, 1979).

Debating the Place of Interest Groups on the Political Landscape

Lobbying by special interest groups is a pervasive reality within the Canadian political scene. Since Confederation, pressure has been brought to bear on government officials by persons representing their own self-interests and those of like-minded individuals. Connections to members of the business community and the power elite has always been an advantage to political officials and vice versa. However, today's interest groups, such as those representing consumers, women, students, and Native peoples, have their roots in the social movements of the 1960s (Pross, 1992). The scope of government policy formulation provides multiple opportunities for special interest groups and individuals to influence legislation and civil service hierarchy. Yet, debate over whether or how much interest groups should be involved in government processes such as social policy development continues (Dobell & Mansbridge, 1986; Pross, 1992; Sarapkaya, 1988; Thompson & Stanbury, 1979). The most often voiced concern involves the possibility that pressure group influence could favour narrow, specific interests over the views of citizens at large. The concern is that the democratic process can be subverted by groups possessing the time and money to pressure for self-interests rather than relying on the will of the people as expressed through voting for elected officials. This fear finds its basis in the historical operation of a power "elite" (i.e., political and economic power in the hands of a relatively few citizens) in Canadian politics. This concern is also fuelled by the more explicit presence and lobbying power of special interest groups in the United States.

Most analysis of pressure group influence supports this type of participation in the Canadian political process. Given the complexity of government and the scope of decision-making, special interest groups enhance rather than detract from the democratic process. Through their public awareness campaigns and their scrutiny of proposed policies, special interest groups bring policy decisions closer to the desires of the electorate. Pross (1992) indicates that "the ability of pressure groups to channel information to and from policy-makers can work to the advantage of society without jeopardizing traditional democratic institutions" (2). He contends that interest group participation in policy formulation and implementation enhances Canadian democracy.

The Policy-Making Process and Federal-Provincial Relations

A critical element in social policy decision-making in Canada is the status of federal-provincial relations. Since most social policy issues and programs involve federal and provincial jurisdictions, a further look at the federal-provincial relationship is warranted. The BNA Act specified that federal and provincial governments were to operate within certain spheres of influence, exercise certain roles, and act within prescribed parameters (Dobell & Mansbridge, 1986). The intention was that the two levels of government were to be complementary. The dual nature of Canadian federalism as prescribed by the BNA Act eventually gave way to the pragmatics of the current political model, with its give-and-take approach to financial responsibility. Given the scale of federal social expenditures to individuals and in transfer payments to the provinces, issues regarding social policy, funding, roles, and responsibilities grow in significance in times of fiscal restraint. Within such a fiscal context, concern increases for the "cost" to the federal government of maintaining federal-provincial conciliation and cooperation. The question becomes one of positioning for a strong federal role in social policy or a realignment of responsibilities to the provincial sphere of influence.

Current federal-provincial relations create a complex, competitive, and acrimonious environment for the participation of interest groups in social policy development and implementation. The divided jurisdictions over social policy areas necessitates pressure groups spreading their attention across a broad spectrum of players in social policy decision-making. The cost, in the form of time and money, to maintain lobbying efforts at both the federal and provincial levels may prohibit many interest groups from creating a significant and lasting impact. Interest groups must garner support from governments and the general public in order to obtain significant influence within the various spheres of policy deliberation (Dobell & Mansbridge, 1986). With federal-provincial relations in a state of flux regarding social policy, many interest groups may focus their energies on securing public acceptance of their positions and use this support as pressure for having their interests considered in future social policy decisions.

THE POLITICAL ECONOMY AND SOCIAL POLICY

Social policy decision-making has become part of an overriding socio-economic debate. Social policy concerns are being placed within a broader economic and environmental context; within the current economic climate "finance is the power in social policy" (Battle & Trojman, 1996, 52). For example, the chronology of the SSR indicates that statements and directions of the finance department and the minister of finance overshadowed the impact of this major social policy review initiative. It seems that the real impetus for change in social policy and programs is not coming from social advocates but economic advocates. Deficit reduction mixed with a tinge of anti-welfare ideology now dominates provincial and federal social policy ideas. In times of fiscal restraint, the prominence of economic issues over social concerns intensifies.

As social and economic factors as well as political preferences change, the social agenda and the ways and means of achieving this agenda also change (McGilly, 1990). Prominent among the constellation of economic, political, and socio-cultural obstacles to achieving the social agenda in the late 1990s are the status of federal-provincial relations regarding social policy responsibility and the relationship between debt/deficit spending and social programs. Pulkingham and Ternowetsky (1996) have reflected upon the relationship between the economic and social realities of the 1990s and the ability of governments to ensure the collective well-being of Canadians. They suggest that most political officials believe that the current social security system may no longer be affordable or fiscally responsible when the state is "groaning" under the weight of years of government debt and deficits. These authors highlight that the legacies of unemployment, underemployment, and poverty have proved difficult to dislodge even in the best of economic times—and these are the very social problems that provided the impetus for the creation of a national social security system in the first place. Their persistence over time and in spite of social policy initiatives has an impact on both the demand for government assistance and the government's ability to meet these demands.

Pulkingham and Ternowetsky (1996) have raised several important issues in their analysis of the current economically driven social policy context. What is the future of the Canadian social welfare system if all levels of government are committed to reducing costs? Given the interplay of global, federal, provincial, and local pressures, the present social security system is unlikely to remain intact. What social policy options best respond to current and future social planning needs of diverse groups in Canada? What collaborative and advocacy efforts are important in addressing social, economic, racial, and cultural inequalities?

The prediction has been made that a new "post-welfare state" model will emerge (Vaillcourt, 1996). This model will incorporate the values and principles of self-determination; increased consumer participation in decisions directly affecting their lives; and a decentralization with greater local-level control of service delivery with a greater mix of public, voluntary, and private sector involvement in the delivery of human services.

THE POLITICS OF INTEREST AND SOCIAL WORK

Social policies shape the lives of clients that social workers encounter every day in their practice. Social workers influence social policy formulation and implementation whether at the legislative, inter-agency, or agency level (Chapin, 1995). This makes all social work practitioners "policy practitioners." The decision to be made by social work practitioners is whether to take up this role in a conscious and conscientious manner. The social policy arenas within which social workers have a great deal to contribute include setting policy agendas, defining social problems, policy formulation and implementation, as well as assessing the impact of current policy upon the persons for whom it was enacted (Chapin, 1995).

Social policy "networking" can assist social workers in involving themselves as individuals and collectively with social policy change. Networking strategies may be considered as a social work mechanism in working for social justice—a prime directive of the social work profession. The social worker's role as educator may be used to give clients the knowledge and skills they need to manoeuvre within the complex social security system. Informed consumers of the social security system are able to exercise more control over service delivery (Dobell & Mansbridge, 1986). This may be more important with the movement to a more local or community-oriented basis for service delivery. The most needy in the public realm have often been the least involved when social policies are debated. The formation of consumer groups adds strength to the voices that are challenging the status quo for representation in consultation processes. This represents a "bottom-up" process and could have significant impact on social service policy and delivery. Associations such as Canadian Mental Health have modelled the efficacy of a consumer approach.

Given the socio-economic social policy context, social workers need to be aware of the economic issues facing their communities as well as provincial and federal governments. With changes in governments come new waves of consultation and consensus-building. Social workers may find themselves dealing with political and bureaucratic players with different attitudes. With this comes the opportunity for different groups and organizations to gain the ear of these political officials. Social workers need to be aware of the potential dilemmas they and interest groups will face. Important though lobbying is seen to be, including active relations with the media, there is concern that funding, usually from governments, can be jeopardized. Over-reliance on government funding can clearly be a limiting factor on the independence and objectivity of any interest group. The social policy consultation process is made more difficult by the overlap, and at times conflict, among the various levels of government involved with social policy. Social workers and clients may find themselves in the middle of such conflicts. Social workers require information from governments as to the location of decision-influencing and decision-making venues so that representation can be effectively directed. This means that social workers need to stay knowledgeable about social policy development and possible future directions. Gaining access to relevant social policy data is important.

FUTURE CONSIDERATIONS

In reviewing the current political processes involved in establishing social welfare policies and programs, some insights and trends have been identified which must be accounted for by social work practitioners who wish to be more involved in formulating and directing their activities. Primary among these is the fundamental shift in public attitude away from paying for universal social welfare programs. The so-called shift to the political "right" is a reality that will constrain and alter our practice into the twenty-first century. This, coupled with a clear movement away from a centralized federal government, is in some ways frightening but in others it provides new opportunities for creative and innovative programming.

A second trend, for which social work practice is well positioned to provide leadership, is the increased transfer of responsibilities to the local level. As communities demand and receive more involvement in program design and delivery, social workers are finding they have new roles beyond their traditional community organization functions. One such example is the major reorganization of family and children's services within the province of Alberta. This project is essentially a "grassroots"-driven restructuring of policies and services with extensive involvement of interested lay persons working side-by-side with professionals. In these activities, social work practitioners have become major partners in the restructuring processes rather than having the structures imposed from the top down.

Finally, one trend that appears to be emerging that is perhaps not unrelated to the coming together of volunteers and professionals in planning is the increasing recognition that many social issues transgress traditional partisan political boundaries. No political party has "the answer" and social work as a profession is not exclusively represented by any party. Many practitioners are recognizing greater power in the achievement of desired social change by aligning forces on specific social issues. Such a social issue focus brings together individuals and groups in a political process that heretofore may have been inhibited by perceived ideological differences. Some of the best examples of these newfound issues-focused activities may be found in the numerous alignments among business and social agencies in meeting community needs.

Local and regional political processes are becoming more accessible to social work practitioners as federal politics becomes less prominent. With this greater opportunity for involvement social workers should have more influence in helping to formulate the problem definition, to influence the debate, and finally to help shape the action plans for the next century.

REFERENCES

Battle, K. & Trojman, S. (1996). Desperately seeking substance: a commentary on the Social Security Review. In J. Pulkingham and G. Ternowetsky (Eds.). *Remaking Canadian social policy: social security in the late 1990s* (pp. 52–66). Halifax, NS: Fernwood.

Chapin, R.K. (1995). Social policy development: the strengths perspective. *Social Work, 40,* 506–514.

Dobell, A.R. & Mansbridge, S.H. (1986). *The social policy process in Canada.* Montreal, Quebec: The Institute for Research on Public Policy.

Guest, D. (1985). *The emergence of social security in Canada.* (2nd ed.). Vancouver, BC: University of British Columbia Press.

Jennissen, T. (1996). The federal Social Security Review, process and related events (December 1993–June 1995): a chronology. In J. Pulkingham and G. Ternowetsky (Eds.). *Remaking Canadian social policy: social security in the late 1990s* (pp. 30–32). Halifax, NS: Fernwood.

McGilly, F. (1990). *An introduction to Canada's public social services: understanding income and health programs.* Toronto: McClelland & Stewart.

Pross, A.P. (1992). *Group politics and public policy* (2nd ed.). Toronto: Oxford University Press.

Pulkingham, J. & Ternowetsky, G. (1996). The changing landscape of social policy and the Canadian welfare state. In J. Pulkingham and G. Ternowetsky (Eds.). *Remaking Canadian social policy: social security in the late 1990s* (pp. 2–29). Halifax, NS: Fernwood.

Sarpkaya, S. (1988). *Lobbying in Canada: ways and means.* Don Mills: CCH Canadian Limited.

Strain & Hum (1987). Perspectives on the welfare state. In J.S. Ismael (Ed.). *The Canadian welfare state: evolution and transition* (pp. 349–371). Edmonton: University of Alberta Press.

Thompson, F., & Stanbury, W.T. (1979). *The political economy of interest groups in the legislative process in Canada.* Montreal, QC: Institute for Research on Public Policy.

Thorburn, H.G. (1985). *Interest groups in the Canadian federal system.* Toronto: University of Toronto Press.

Vaillcourt, Y. (1996). Remaking Canadian social policy: a Quebec viewpoint. In J. Pulkingham and G. Ternowetsky (Eds.). *Remaking Canadian social policy: social security in the late 1990s* (pp. 81–99). Halifax, NS: Fernwood.

Wiseman, J. (1996). National social policy in an age of global power: lessons from Canada and Australia. In J. Pulkingham and G. Ternowetsky (Eds.). *Remaking Canadian social policy: social security in the late 1990s* (pp. 114–129). Halifax, NS: Fernwood.

GLOBALIZATION AND SOCIAL WORK PRACTICE

Glenn Drover and
Gail MacDougall

INTRODUCTION

The relationship between globalization and social work practice is complex. Part of the reason for the complexity is the meaning of the term *globalization*. As Zygmunt Bauman (1998) points out, globalization is "a fad word fast turning into a shibboleth, a magic incantation, a pass-key meant to unlock the gates to all present and future mysteries" (1). Notwithstanding the complexity of the term, however, we think that there are three essential elements of globalization about which most contemporary writers on the subject agree. The first is that globalization is anchored in the economic domain, specifically in recent developments of free trade agreements like the North American Free Trade Agreement and the World Trade Organization. Secondly, it is made possible by advances in information technology such that finance capital can be instantly shifted anywhere around the world and human capital is increasingly subordinated to the flexibility of the market. Thirdly, neo-liberalism is the underlying philosophy which gives force and everyday meaning to globalization: it justifies the allocation and distribution of societal resources through the market and the identification of social welfare with the sum total of individual welfare. In what follows, therefore, we link the three core elements of globalization—free trade, information technology, and neo-liberalism—to the basics of social work practice. We do so by highlighting how trade agreements are fundamentally shifting the justification of professional practice from a foundation based on knowledge and educational achievement to one based on competence and skill; how information technology is changing the medium of social work education as well as the forms of social work intervention; and how neo-liberalism is modifying the very language we use to justify and explain social work practice. Before turning to the specific impacts on practice, however, we begin with a brief discussion of the literature on globalization.

GLOBALIZATION

In general, the reactions to globalization can be divided into two types: those who welcome it and those who oppose it. For those who welcome it, globalization is an extension of the existing social order because trade and investment produce growing interconnectedness among national economies and improve living standards over time. For those who oppose it, globalization is a breakdown in the existing social order as states become increasingly subordinated to multinational corporations, markets are socially disembedded from their national moorings, and workers have less and less control over their lives. Paul Hirst and Grahame Thompson (1996) describe the first of these views as the new "inter-national" economy and the second as the "fully globalized" economy. Looking at globalization as an inter-national economy, the authors acknowledge the increasing integration of nations and world markets along with the growth of multinational corporations, but they also stress the ongoing importance of the nation state in policy-making. While less sympathetic to the fully globalized view of the world economy, they nevertheless recognize that it highlights the problematic of world governance as the roles of nation states and organized labour are increasingly transformed by the terms of international trade. The same two contrasting views of globalization are reflected in public debates in Canada, the first being closely associated with organizations like the C.D. Howe Institute (Lipsey, 1987; 1990) and the latter with the Canadian Centre for Policy Alternatives or the Council of Canadians (Barlow, 1990: Clarke, 1997).

In spite of differing (some would say polarized) views of globalization, writers agree that the global order is being fundamentally changed in three ways: free trade agreements, information technology, and neo-liberalism. The case for free trade is based on comparative advantage (Bryan, 1994, chapter 10). The idea behind comparative advantage is that each country gains from trade because each is likely to produce what it is best able to produce in a competitive international market. Hence, each country becomes more efficient at doing what it can do best and consumers in each country are better off because of that efficiency. On the other hand, comparative advantage does not presuppose that every person in each country will be better off or that income will be more equitably distributed because of the benefits of free trade. In fact, under certain circumstances, wages in one country (say for unskilled labour) can fall in the short term while those in another country can rise, although presumably in the long run, as wage differentials diminish, there will be a tendency toward equilibrium. Furthermore, the theory does not imply that no government interference or regulation will take place, particularly if labour standards or externalities, such as environmental pollution, are made worse by trade. Because of the uncertain effect of trade on wages, on the distribution of income, and on externalities like pollution, critics of free trade, such as environmentalists, challenge the notion of comparative advantage. On balance, however, the case in favour of free trade has usually been perceived as stronger than its limitations and as a consequence, both developed and developing countries have become increasingly open to free trade agreements in recent years.

Furthermore, while considerable debate rages about the intrusive nature of the trade agreements, particularly in terms of their impact on public policy, even the strongest opponents (Barlow, 1990; 2000) are not suggesting that countries return to economic protectionism and high tariffs. That was tried in the depression years of the '30s and failed miserably. Instead, they are calling for checks and balances to give full recognition to the rights of national governments to protect and maintain public services as well as labour and environmental standards. In addition, they wish to ensure that trade agreements, and multinational corporations in particular, will not override democratically elected institutions. Another challenge which free trade raises is how to extend democratic institutions to parts of the world where they do not currently exist and how to balance the prerogatives of individual states with their limited capacity to control capital. For those who favour comprehensive free trade agreements (Ohmae, 1990, 1995; Courchene, 1999), the nation states are less able to alter the course of economic and social development than they were before. Therefore, international agreements offer an advantage in that they impose common rules and regulations. As politics become more polycentric, different levels and functions of governance need to be tied together. In the process, some nation states may be more dominant than others (Hirst and Thompson, 1996, 183–4).

A second element of globalization is information technology. As with free trade, no consensus has been reached that the technology revolution is entirely beneficial, but few doubt that it has generated the instantaneity of market transactions and the movement of capital at the flick of a button. It is perhaps this aspect of globalization more than any other which is associated with the idea of the compression of time-distance relations. Known variously as the global information society, or the knowledge society, information technology has transformed the nature of transactions in the economy, perhaps most importantly in the form of production where there has been in a short period of time a shift from mass production in one location (Fordism) to multiple levels of production in many locations (Post-Fordism). Now, as a result of new technologies, a product or a service can be designed in one country, manufactured, in part or in whole, in several countries, and sold in still other countries. According to Harvey (1989, chapter 17), the impact of the technological revolution is not only a shift in production and accumulation but also a shift in the way we think of everything from fashions and products to values and practices. With time-space compression, there is less and less a sense of permanence or continuity in what we do or what we believe. Images are mass marketed instantaneously over space and time. The aura of political authority is ephemeral and fleeting. The cost of communication is invariant with respect to distance.

The speed and pace of change associated with the new technology have caused some to rail against it. Heather Menzies (1996) asks "Whose Brave New World?" is being created. She suggests that nothing matters less than people as corporations use the new technology to erode, deskill, and demean the workplace while using computers and computerization for the centralization of control. But Menzies also acknowledges that the new technology can be used to develop a critical discourse and further the advances of a civil society if it is viewed less as a medium of transmission for those in authority and more as a model of communication among communities of interest. In some ways, that is what happened when activists from around the world used the web to defeat the efforts of the Organisation for Economic Cooperation and Development (OECD) to create a new Multilateral Agreement on Investment (MAI) in order to extend the influence of multinational corporations over national governments. In a similar manner, the World Wide Web is being used to develop global public policy networks (Renicke, 2000) that watch-dog governments, develop new policy standards, broaden participation, and support local networks in ways which would not have been possible, or at least would have been more complicated, before the advent of the new technology. Hence, like the debate on free trade agreements, both proponents and opponents agree that the potential for transformation is significant and that new forms of communication are opening doors which were previously closed. The issue likely to prevail in the future, therefore, is not whether the new technology will be used (that is certain) but whether the technology will be used in a manner which is inclusive rather than exclusive (Howkins and Valantin, 1997).

A third element of globalization about which considerable agreement exists as to its influence, if not its benefit, is neo-liberalism. Neo-liberalism is a political ideology that derives its strength from neoclassical economic theory. It builds on the notion that the market is the optimal mechanism for the allocation of goods and services in society. The strength of the ideology is its set of plausible assumptions that are persuasive in their simplicity. First is the assumption that individuals, not governments or communities, are best able to decide their own welfare. Second is the idea that unimpeded markets, under conditions of competition, lead to an efficient and productive economy. A third assumption is that government is likely to interfere inappropriately in the market and distort efficiencies. A fourth is the primacy of private property rights to protect individual freedom. A fifth is that global markets without tariffs and non-tariff barriers enhance economic growth. Sixth, a morally just society is one in which people individually pursue their own goals and do not impose on others. Hence, the general good "consists principally in the facilitation of the pursuit of unknown individual purposes" and the "common good consists in the rule of law" (Plant, 1991, 80).

Writers like Kenichi Ohmae serve to make the tenets of neo-liberalism appealing to the general public. In his bestselling book, *The Borderless World*, Ohmae (1990) argues that national governments are obsolete, that multinationals are servants of the people, and that global markets overcome the protectionism inherent in national economies. In a similar vein, John Naisbitt (1994) talks about a global paradox in which the bigger the world economy is the more powerful the smallest players are.[1] At the other end of the spectrum, Gary Teeple (1995) highlights the negative impact of neo-liberalism on the deregulation of national economies, the downsizing of government, increasing income inequalities, and even the circumscription of civil liberties. Other writers (Clarke, 1997; Jackson and Sanger, 1998; Sinclair, 2000) associate it with a direct threat to democracy, since the individualistic free market values associated with neo-liberalism are antithetical to the community impulse of the political process. Globalization via free trade implies the allocation and distribution of resources based on private property while the collective political processes presuppose some capacity to allocate resources based on the common good or the public interest. Because of the democratic threat, many writers (Mander and Goldsmith, 1996) argue against globalization in favour of localization.

IMPACT ON SOCIAL WORK PRACTICE

At present, only a limited body of literature exists on the relationship between globalization and social work practice. Some interesting research is being done at the University of Southampton, in England, but it is in early stages of development. In Canada, most of the research to date has focused on the relationship between free trade and social services rather than social work. Drover (1988; 1989; 1995) outlined the implications of the Canada United States Free Trade Agreement and the North American Free Trade Agreement for the social services in the late eighties and early nineties. He noted how sections of the agreements

---

[1] The election of Margaret Thatcher in England, Ronald Reagan in the United States, and Helmut Kohl in Germany during the eighties helped to promote the acceptance of neo-liberalism on the world's political stage. By implementing monetarist policies and free trade agreements in their respective spheres of influence, neo-liberalism came to dominate the bilateral policies of their governments and the multilateral bodies under their control.

could lead to the contracting-out of social services and the commercial management of services that came within the orbit of trade. At the same time, others (Armstrong and Armstrong, 1992; Cohen, 1987; Gainor, 1992; Holm, 1988) were highlighting how the agreements would have an impact on services like health care, the environment, and education. Since the turn of the millennium, the same concerns are surfacing again as the governments of Canada, Mexico, and the United States spearhead a comprehensive Free Trade Agreement of the Americas (FTAA) and actively participate in the extension of the General Agreement on Trade in Services (GATS) within the World Trade Organization. Sanger (2000) states that the GATS will conflict with publicly provided health care. Barlow (2000) argues that the comprehensive nature of the proposed FTAA is a threat to social programs and social justice in Canada because it limits the right of governments to establish and maintain public services. Sinclair (2000) makes the same argument about the GATS and claims that it will require governments to justify the regulation of commercial services to protect the public interest. Outside Canada, individuals and organizations are raising some of the same concerns (Price, Pollock, Shaoul, 1999; People and Planet, 2000) about the threat of the GATS for the provision of health care and higher education.

On a more positive note, Midgley (1997) suggests that globalization is leading to greater international collaboration among non-governmental organizations and social security regimes as well as the treatment of refugees and the promotion of the well-being of women. He also notes that the internationalization of social work, through organizations like the International Federation of Social Workers, is increasing exchanges with colleagues in different countries and a search for professional identity. In a book on international social work, edited by Hokenstad and Midgley (1997), several writers identify the different ways in which the globalization of social work practice is occurring in areas like aging, ethnic conflict, and AIDS. In fact, they insist that many social problems confronting social work can only be addressed at a global level. Paul Wilding (1997) similarly identifies seven ways in which globalization affects social welfare, through the hollowing out of the nation state, the increased emphasis on competitiveness, and the priority given to the maintenance of social order. Mishra (1998) recognizes the constraints that globalization places on the autonomy of nation states. He concludes that it is important to re-create, at an international level, the mix of economic and social institutions that made the national welfare state possible. An example that he uses to illustrate his approach is the substitution of universal social rights (those rights that specifically relate to social service provision) by diverse social standards, the latter allowing for the application of rights at different levels of economic development. In a similar manner, Drover (2000) highlights the need to redefine social rights globally in order to encompass active citizenship, extra-statism, and diversity.

Khan and Dominelli (2000), in a paper presented at an international social work conference in Montreal, outline how globalization has created three sorts of challenges for the profession: external forces, ideological forces, and marginal forces. In reference to external forces, they point out that market criteria are being introduced into social service delivery in order to encourage efficency and promote innovation. Market criteria, in turn, lead to increasing fragmentation of public social services as programs proliferate through various contractual arrangements. They also lead to deprofessionalization as management practices reduce professional autonomy (Dominelli, 1996). In terms of ideological forces, the main influence is essentially counterfactual, in the sense that governments refer to globalization as the principle reason why they have to commercialize social services; hence, it is both cause and effect. With respect to marginal forces, Khan and Dominelli suggest that globalization has intensified the disadvantages experienced by more and more groups in society, and the diversity of social work clients, without the availability of additional resources. Jim Ife (2000), in an address to the same conference, highlights the relationship between globalization and social work by highlighting the potential for change. While he is mindful of the dilemmas and concerns raised by Khan and Dominelli, he dwells on the potential for rethinking social work practice in ways which link the global and the local, the personal and the political. Globalization, as he sees it, requires a re-examination of social work knowledge, values, and skills in order to embrace and influence it rather than reject it. In order to understand how social workers are actually responding to globalization, Rowe et al (2000) surveyed social workers in different regions of the world. They reported that globalization increased problems in terms of economic impacts but also opened opportunities for international cooperation through global communication, commitments to rights, and participation in international development.

It seems, therefore, that at both national and international levels, an awareness is growing that globalization has potentially both negative and positive consequences for social work, offering, on the one hand, challenges to the profession and, on the other hand, opportunities to move in new directions. A problem, however, with the existing literature is the relatively high level of generality in discussing the term *globalization*. In some ways, it has become a buzzword not only to explain economic restructuring but also to represent the woes of the welfare state and the social services. Alternatively, it has been used to legitimate political restructuring, ideological mystification, organizational change, and even professional disorientation. Faced with multiple meanings, the term *globalization* risks becoming an ambiguous and ambivalent term which loses conceptual clarity and fosters confusion. In reality, global interdependence results from diverse processes on various spatial scales and involves complex relations that need to be deconstructed in order to be understood. The three that we think are the most crucial and the most closely linked with globalization are international trade agreements, information technologies, and neo-liberalism. In the rest of the chapter, we attempt to show how social work practice in Canada is being affected, or is likely to be affected, by these three central elements of globalization. By taking this viewpoint, we attempt to show how the extension of international trade is shifting the justification of professional practice from a foundation based on credentials to one based on competence; how information technology is changing the medium of social work education and the forms of social work intervention; and how neo-liberalism is modifying the language social workers use to justify and explain their practice.

1. Impact of Trade Agreements

The two key international trade agreements of which Canada is a member are the World Trade Organization (WTO) and the North American Free Trade Agreement (NAFTA). The WTO was established in 1994 to replace the General Agreement on Tariffs and Trade (GATT). The WTO is the larger of the two agreements, in that it involves one hundred and forty nations (WTO Website, November, 2000) but is less comprehensive. NAFTA is essentially an agreement among three countries: Canada, Mexico, and the United States. Currently, proposals are being made to extend the WTO through the further liberalization of trade in services under the General Agreement on Trade in Services (GATS). Similarly, there are plans to extend and broaden the terms of NAFTA to all the countries of the American hemisphere under the Free Trade Agreement of the Americas (FTAA). The plans also include the further liberalization of the trade in services within the hemisphere. In general, the sections on services within the trade agreements are likely to affect social work, in part because of the potential inclusion of public services, in part because of the requirement to liberalize professional licensing requirements. The latter provision is likely to have an impact on social work practice in the short term and the former in the long term. To see why, we consider first the current service agreements under the GATS and NAFTA, then the debate around the expansion of the agreements.

The main reason why the service agreements are likely to have a long-term rather than a short-term impact on social work is that public services currently have some measure of protection under the GATS and NAFTA. At present, the GATS applies to a limited range of commercial services like finance, telecommunications, and transportation. The same is also the case in NAFTA. A key feature of both agreements is that the suppliers of commercially traded services must be treated in the same way in each member country regardless of the country of origin. Secondly, full transparency is required, which means that regulations and rules related to the provision of a services must be available to all potential suppliers so that foreign suppliers can be fully informed of their obligations. The two rules are relatively innocuous if they only apply to a restricted range of well-established commercial services, but they can be quite detrimental if they are applied to public services as they can no longer be protected from foreign competition. For that reason, the GATS currently exempts "services supplied in the exercise of government authority" (WTO, 1994, GATS, I), and NAFTA actually states that the agreement does not prevent the government of a country from providing or performing a range of public services, including social security and social welfare (NAFTA, 1994, 1201(3)). However, the agreements do not necessarily exclude components of public services which have been privatized or commercialized, such as medical laboratories, management services, or book publishers of educational material. And more importantly, both agreements specify that the service sector will be subject to further liberalization, meaning that the range of services to be covered will be extended beyond the initial list.

Because of the commitment to liberalization, pressure to include public services in the agreements seems to be mounting. The United States, a major provider of privatized health, education, and social services, is very open about its desire to have such services included in the GATS (WTO, 1998a). The WTO directorate is also promoting the expansion of services such as health, education, and social welfare in the current round of negotiations (WTO, 1998b). While the WTO claims that governments will still have the right to provide public services, critics of the new initiatives point out that even if public services remain an option, national governments will be increasingly restrained to develop and maintain them. In addition, they claim that the current agreements make it unlikely that national governments will develop new public services in areas like pharmacare or home care because they are required to compensate commercial providers of services which are already in the market. In a similar manner, critics of the FTAA claim that it will include "all public programs and gradually phase out all government barriers to international competition in services" (Barlow, 2000). They also claim that the United States will push to have the FTAA extended to allow corporations to sue governments directly for loss of profits resulting from national laws to protect health and safety. Hence, governments will be increasingly under pressure to justify public services by explicitly excluding them from the agreement and only then if they are offered exclusively by the public sector. A public service provided commercially or any public service offered in competition with commercial providers may not be excluded (Sanger, 2001).

Since the texts of the expanded GATS and the proposed FTAA are not available at this stage, it is not possible to confirm whether the worst fears of the critics will be realized. But even if they are, it is likely to take several years before the changes have a direct impact on social work practice. By contrast, one aspect of the free trade agreements which has had less debate, but which will have an impact on social work practice in the short term, are the provisions related to licensing and certification. Both the GATS and NAFTA state that licensing and certification requirements of member countries cannot be used as barriers to trade. Consequently, the agreements specify that each member country is obligated to ensure that any related measure "(a) [is based on] objective and transparent criteria, such as competence and the ability to provide the service; (b) is not more burdensome than necessary to ensure the quality of the service; and (c) does not constitute a restriction on the cross-border provision of a service" (NAFTA, 1994, 1210; WTO, 1994, GATS VII). In addition, NAFTA stipulates that each member country will be required to eliminate citizenship and residency requirements for the licensing and certification of professional service providers. Furthermore, it is stipulated that licensing and certification will be determined through competency and ability to provide a service rather than formal education. Largely because of the requirements of the international free trade agreements, the federal government of Canada, in cooperation with provincial and territorial governments, signed an Agreement on Internal Trade (AIT) in 1994. Under the AIT, Canadians who are qualified for an occupation in one provincial or territorial jurisdiction must be granted access to employment opportunities in another. Occupational standards, licensing, certification, registration, and residency requirements cannot be used to create barriers to labour mobility. The obligations of the agreement apply to all governments and non-governmental bodies that exercise authority to establish standards or requirements for licensing, certification, and registration. Fundamentally, the main point of the agreement is to ensure that each jurisdiction will adopt measures based primarily on competence. Social work, like other professions, is required to adapt.

To get some idea of the implications of the agreements, it is useful to look at the experience of nurses. Because the demand for nursing fluctuates considerably in different parts of North America, there is considerable mobility within the profession. To facilitate that mobility, a trilateral initiative, involving nurses from Canada, Mexico, and the United States, was established in 1994 (Oulton, 1998). The initiative initially involved representatives of 35 governmental and non-governmental organizations sitting down together and identifying similarities in nursing education, standards, and practice with a view to developing mutually acceptable criteria for licensing and certification. Subsequently, there has been a tendency to look at competencies rather than credentials for regulatory purposes, partly because governments are emphasizing competencies, and partly because nurses themselves wish to increase the potential for labour mobility while also assuring clarity of expectations for practice. Within Canada, nursing has also taken a lead in developing competencies in order to ensure that practice is of a high standard but is also applicable in a variety of practice settings. An example is the set of "entry-to-practice" standards developed by the Alberta Association of Registered Nurses (2000). Like social work across Canada, registration in Alberta is based on generalist practice, involves a theoretical base, necessitates an ability to undertake assessment, and emphasizes skill development. The association also is keen to use a competency-based standard of practice to assure a comparison of nursing data across populations, settings, geographic areas, and time, as well as to encourage its use in the development of curriculum in training programs. To achieve these broad goals, the association defines competence as "the ability ... to integrate and apply the knowledge, skills, judgement, and interpersonal attributes required to practice safely and ethically in a designated role and setting" (AARA, 2000, 4); frames practice within four categories (professional responsibility, knowledge-based practice, ethical practice, and provision of service); and associates the four categories with specific indicators and competencies. Most other nursing associations in Canada have followed a similar path in developing competency measures.

Like nursing, social work is gradually moving in the direction of competency, to establish basic standards of practice. The United Kingdom and Australia have already developed competency profiles. In Canada, there is, as noted above, a requirement under the AIT to develop competency as a basis of breaking down barriers to labour mobility between different jurisdictions in the country. As a consequence, the social work associations and/or registration boards of the provinces have signed an agreement for the mutual recognition of occupational qualifications (Agreement, 1999). In doing so, they committed themselves to break down barriers to employment opportunities for social workers across the country based on licensing, certification, or registration. In addition, they acknowledged, in accordance with article 707 of Chapter 7 of the AIT, that measures relating to licensing, certification, or registration would be based on competencies rather than credentials. In 2000, they went one step further and contracted a consultant to conduct a literature review of social work competencies. The consultant discovered that some professional associations like social workers in Australia and nurses in Canada had already developed competency profiles (NCA Associates, 2000). In addition, they suggested that since there was a high level of commonality among university and non-university social work programs in Canada, it would be feasible to assess them to determine the degree to which they incorporated core competencies characteristic of the practice of an entry-level social worker. One provincial association which has begun to explore core competencies is Nova Scotia (Beals, 2000).[2]

In spite of these and similar trends, however, it is important to note that competency-based practice is also causing debate and opposition. One of the more vocal critics is Lena Dominelli, a social work academic from Canada who teaches in Britain. Dominelli (1996) views the development of competency-based practice as the downside of globalization, part of the restructuring of the welfare state. Along with case management techniques, performance evaluations, and the contracting-out of public services, competency is viewed as an attack on professionalism, the affirmation of management control systems, and a major affront to progressive or anti-oppressive practice. The reasoning behind her critique is that professionalism based on competency decontextualizes practice and substitutes a highly technical set of tasks geared to product outputs and organizational (possibly political) interests, rather than a concern about people and relationships or community and transformation. Put another way, it replaces professional values and professional judgment by assessable outcomes circumscribed by employers and funding agencies. For these reasons, competencies represent both the tailorization of the profession (as tasks are subdivided into discrete elements which can be undertaken by less qualified personnel), and the proletarianization of social work (as the same tasks are streamlined into forms of commodity production). Rather than liber-

---

[2] The discussion of core competencies is at a deliberative stage in the association and therefore there is no official policy. The paper identifies ten core competencies and the requisite skills to realize them.

ating social workers and enhancing labour mobility as governments would have us believe, competency is viewed as a "mechanistic dissection of complex tasks and judgments" which "individualizes many of the collective values of social work" (Dominelli, 1996, 171).

2. Impact of Information Technology

Whereas free trade agreements represent the legal codification of globalization, information technology represents its operational foundation.[3] In fact, information technology is so central to the global project that one finds it difficult to imagine its potential without the availability of online communication. Economic development relies heavily on it in order to assure everything from finance and investment to product inventory and customer satisfaction. Social development also is becoming increasingly dependent in order to facilitate human communication and dialogue around the world. On the other hand, although the constituents of the information age—computers, communications, digital information, and software— are everywhere, it is important to remember that information technology has entered our lives in a very short period of time. The electronic computer is a little over fifty years old; the personal computer is about twenty years old; and the World Wide Web has been used by the public for about seven years. Because of the rapid development of information technology, many current users, including social workers, have necessarily become literate without becoming fluent. As the National Research Council of the United States points out, however, fluency is necessary in order to maximize the benefits of the technology, to ensure that people can express themselves creatively, reformulate knowledge, and synthesize new information (1999, 1–2). The challenge of the future, says the National Research Council, is to encourage more people to be fluent so that the applications of information technology enhance employment opportunities and equity in society. For this reason, they propose that information technology be sensitively and usefully integrated into all levels of education, from primary to university, basic to professional. Similarly, the Organisation for Economic Cooperation and Development (OECD, 1997) recommends that governments make information technology universally available so that it does not become the prerogative of an elite.

In spite of such optimism about the future of technology, there is also concern, especially among the social professions. David Livingstone (1997), of the Ontario Institute for Studies in Education (OISE), worries about information technology in the classroom, particularly if its use is controlled by corporations. He advocates publicly controlled, human-centred design of information systems in order to foster democratic education and society. Similarly, Jean Claude Couture writes of the pressure to assess competencies and educational outcomes in ways that can be measured by computers (the language of testing and performance assessment). As he sees it, the very notion of competence is equated with surveillance and is achieved through both external testing and self-administered performance appraisals. Education becomes a performative vision in which "what is worth doing is worth measuring" (Couture, 1997, 143). In like manner, Langdon Winner (1997) of Ryerson refers to a technoglobal assault through which the computer is used to redefine education as vocational training. The same reservations exist with respect to the impact of the new technology in the professional workplace. Some writers link the technologies with deskilling and deprofessionalization (Dominelli, 1996). Others "point to the use of computerized technology

---

[3] Information technology, as used here, refers to computer hardware, network systems, software, databases, and managing information systems (Rowley, 1996).

and networks to extend employer control over workers, even over long distances, and to create automatic systems that can replace the judgement and discretion of expert employees" (Meiksins, 1998, 152). On the other hand, the concerns about control and centralization may be overstated. The new technologies also make available to front-line social workers information that in the past would have been available only to managers. Because of the low cost of transmission, the potential for the dissemination of sophisticated information to individuals throughout an agency or organization is increased (Meiksins, 1998, 156). In addition, reliance on the technologies also presupposes that the social workers will be increasingly trained and upgraded in their use, thereby making the workers more capable of using the technologies for their own ends.

In reality, the management of social agencies has always been closely associated with information-based organizations (Drucker, 1989).[4] Because each unit within an agency tends to be a specialization with its own knowledge base, training, language, and values, it is in a strong position to use information technology to accommodate innovation and entrepreneurship. Social work organizations in health care have been taking advantage of information technology for some time, in order to provide administrative and clinical information as well as to advance management systems (Auslander, 1995; Breeding, 1996). Furthermore, the implementation of information systems depends not only on the technical design of management systems, but also the manner in which systems are introduced (Neugeboren, 1995). If they are introduced primarily for top management without consultation of professional staff, they will be primarily management driven. If, on the other hand, there is goal clarity, staff stability, resource availability, supportive leadership, and a perceived value to clients, professional staff are more likely to adopt information systems than reject them (Auslander, 1995). The perceived utility of the information system in dealing with accountability, reporting, improving quality of data, program monitoring, and clinical effectiveness is, therefore, the key to professional staff acceptance (Benbenishty and Oyserman, 1995). Social workers are also likely to be concerned about whether information technology is used primarily to assist clients or for purposes of surveillance and supervision. A Web site that seems to have been improving the potential for social work practice is Centrelink in Australia. Created by the Australian government, Centrelink is "one stop shopping" for income assistance, but it also enhances the opportunity for social workers to discuss client problems because matters related to income are handled by other staff on a routine basis (Humphries and Camilleri, 2000).

Another impact on practice is the training of social workers through distance education. Distance learning is gradually transforming the way in which social workers are educated and the way in which they relate to each other. Virtual universities and electronic libraries are multiplying rapidly. They provide choices that have hitherto been unavailable to social workers to link work and study, professional development and continuing education. They create the conditions for life-long learning, link the local and the global, the urban and rural. In response to demand from students as well as faculties, universities and college programs in Canada, including social work education programs, are turning to computers to test the benefits of interactive technology, assess the impact of cyberspace, communicate by email and listservs, engage in Web-based conferencing, and reframe pedagogic issues. Hence, the role of computers in social work education can be viewed from two powerful perspectives: as a

---

[4] The next two paragraphs are largely taken from Drover, Glenn (2001), Trends and issues in social welfare: the impact of globalization, in Francis Turner and Joanne Turner, eds., *Canadian Social Welfare*, Toronto, Pearson Education Canada.

tool to identify tasks and needs which have not yet been identified, and as a mechanism for knowledge development (MacFadden, 1995). Either way, there is an increasing reliance on the World Wide Web for professional information, electronic journals, and electronic databases, in addition to, or in place of, print material. Even the challenge of teaching communication skills online is being addressed by increasingly sophisticated software that allows for visual and simultaneous interaction. While face-to-face instruction is not likely to be totally replaced by online education, the trend to invoke and accept distance technologies is certainly growing. The trend is particularly strong among students who are employed full time or who do not have easy access to campus-based learning because of geographical location or time commitments which do not allow them to attend classrooms.

The least visible impact of information technology is in the area of direct practice, but even here, there are changes. Practitioners have moved from hesitancy and opposition to exploration and experimentation. After reviewing the literature on computer applications in practice, Berman and Phillips (1995) conclude that information technology can enhance professional practice without compromising its humanistic value base. To maintain control, they feel that it is necessary for social workers to be engaged in the design and evaluation of programs, not simply to be users. At present, several Web sites that are primarily informational in nature are available to social worker practitioners. Indeed, so many sites are now available to assist practitioners that search engines have been created to coordinate the information (e.g., www.socialworksearch.com). Aside from information sites, there are support groups, consultation services, case studies, diagnostic assessment programs, and even supervision sessions provided online. Probably the largest range of Web sites, however, are those that promote and advertise the services of social workers, since the Internet is increasingly becoming a primary port of entry for persons seeking services from the helping professions (giving birth to cyber-professionals and cyber-clients). Because of the developments, research is beginning to examine the impact of these changes. One recent study assessed an online support group to help social workers cope with work related stress (Meier, 2000). The study suggests that group development online is similar to face-to-face group development. However, the online group is less effective in providing coping strategies or engaging members in problem solving than a comparable face-to-face group. Another study (Galinsky, 2000) focuses on the implications of using telephone and computer technology for group practice. The benefits of the technology include increased accessibility, convenience, and anonymity; difficulties include fewer cues about group process. A similar study has tested a computer program known as Groups Support Systems for family therapy. It was found to improve brainstorming, reduce hierarchical status among participants, and increase self-reflection. Still another study (Cauble, 2000) reports that interactive multimedia training for child welfare workers is particularly useful in increasing knowledge and developing a sense of competency among practitioners.

The above is not to deny the existence of professional dilemmas in the use of information technology. Aside from problems related to the availability of computers and technology by income, gender, and age, a major challenge is confidentiality. Electronic record keeping and rapid changes in communication over the Internet may be outpacing the profession's capacity to maintain privacy (Gelman, 1999). The issue of privacy is so important that an international commission under the auspices of the United Nations was established to look into the matter as early as the 1980s (Michael, 1994). The commission concluded that the increasing use of information technology creates ongoing demands to redefine the meaning of privacy as well as the ethical and legal implications of technological innovation. In social work education, there is a related concern about developing cultural and racial sensitivity or anti-oppressive practice since the complicated and personal nature of the training pre-supposes a safe vehicle for student dialogue. A third dilemma relates to the misuses of the Internet through plagiarism or cyber-cheating (Gibelman, 1999). While the problem is par-ticularly acute in educational institutions because of the readily accessible "paper mills," the same potential arises with respect to report writing in professional agencies.

3. Impact of Neo-liberalism

Finally, we turn to the impact of neo-liberalism on social work practice.[5] The impact relates primarily to language and the justification of market provision of social services. As Khan and Dominelli (2000, 12) suggest, the language of welfare pluralism, of administrative flex-ibility, and provider competition come from a neo-liberal critique of the welfare state. To the extent that the welfare state is perceived to be inept, bureaucratic, costly, and inflexible, so are the social services of the state. The key reforms of the social services therefore necessarily involve the introduction of a market criteria, and quasi-market discourse, to accommodate demands for enterprise and competition, the introduction of new public sector management, the decentralization of decision-making, and the privatization of provision. The impact of these pressures and perceptions is the creation of tensions or contradictions since the values of the profession are based on justice and respect whereas the values of the market are based on effi-ciency and choice. A consequence is that "the need for public and private agencies to prove their efficiency in market terms may at times test the professional standards and ethics of those involved" (Barker, 1996, quoted in Kahn and Dominelli, 2000, 13). At an agency level, this testing of standards is evident in the fragmentation of services as the state engages in the contracting-out of services through tender. Agencies are forced to compete for limited resources, thereby leading to concerns about the securing of contracts rather than the coor-dination and comprehensiveness of services. At a client level, the impact of neo-liberalism is evident in the targeting of some groups for support and the downgrading of others, as well as the introduction of user fees for essential services.

In essence, neo-liberal social welfare policy has been advanced against Keynesian wel-fare policy since the late 1970s, but has been considerably invigorated by the advances of global trade in the last decade. Whereas Keynesian welfarism presupposes an active state to assure commitment to comprehensive social services, neo-liberal welfarism places greater reliance on the institutions of the market to ensure the maximization of welfare. Under the former, the client of the social services is perceived first and foremost as a citizen. Under the latter, he or she becomes a consumer. Under the former, there is an appeal to universality. Under the latter, an appeal to choice and preference. As a result of the reforms promoted by proponents of neo-liberalism, therefore, we are seeing the transformation of citizenship based on social rights to citizenship based on consumption. The medium of social interac-tion is not the state and civil society, but the market. Broad and Antony (1999, 11) argue that neo-liberal reform is obvious in cutbacks to the social services but also in increases in unem-ployment, underemployment, poverty, social polarization, privatization, deregulation, and

---

[5] It is important to distinguish between neo-liberalism, the focus of this section, and neo-conservatism. Neo-liberalism refers to the explanation and justification of laissez-faire capitalism. As a theory, it draws heavily on neoclassical economics. Neo-conservatism refers to the moral and political justification of individual and family responsibilities within society. While the two are complementary in some ways, they are not identical.

market instability. Hence, to the extent that social workers have fewer resources, because of cutbacks, to respond to the growing demands of the marginalized in society, they are being confronted in their practice by the impact of neo-liberal reform. At the same time, the welfare state is in a relatively weaker position to respond to the changing circumstances which social workers face because the financial resources upon which it can draw are diminished by its limited capacity to tax capital and income in a global market. Indeed, as Janine Brodie (1999) suggests, the diminished capacity of the welfare state is even used to establish neo-liberalism as the dominant paradigm in public management in order to promote individualization and familialization as well as privatization and decentralization. In some respects, she also equates individualization and familialization with the role of women as unpaid workers, since both presuppose volunteers to replace civil servants.

While all these changes clearly are having an impact on the social services, some negative, some positive, what do they mean in terms of practice? At the very least, neo-liberalism is changing the way in which practitioners speak about their workplace, their work, and themselves. In the workplace, the language of private sector management increasingly prevails. Whereas social workers twenty years ago spoke about cooperation and coordination, they are now more likely to talk about entrepreneurship and competition. Whereas, in the past, they used the language of public administration and voluntarism to frame their understanding of organizational behaviour, they now refer to management and accountability. An example of the shift is reflected in the recently formed Training Organisation for the Personal Social Services (TOPSS) in the United Kingdom. The aim of TOPSS is to work closely with, and on behalf of, employers to enhance the quality of staff and service in social care. As part of the mandate, TOPSS is writing national standards for different fields of service. One such set of standards for registered managers of adult care homes (TOPSS, 2000) is rife with the language of commercial analysis, including words and phrases like customer relations, quality management, agreements and contracts, strategic planning, monitoring, time management, business planning, benchmarking, marketing, and promotion. Even values are specified in managerial terms. The same market-driven language is used by TOPSS England (2000) in a document to describe a new national training strategy for social care workers. In it, the organization writes glowingly about quality assurance in training, performance management, information management, human resource development, and recruitment strategies instead of professional needs and resources.

In a similar fashion, practitioners use the language of the market to talk about their work and themselves. Clients are customers. Need is demand. Relationships are contracts. Social workers are providers. Services are products. Products are marketed. Inputs become outcomes. Fees and sales assure value-for-money. The major assumption behind these and like changes in language is that they reflect a new model of practice in which traditional client/professional relationships are replaced by consumerist expectations. Whereas the traditional model of care places the client in a patronized and powerless position with the professional in control, the consumerist model presumably puts the user in the driver's seat (Coppock, 1997). Faced with the power of the consumer, furthermore, social workers package their work in market terms so that the potential user can readily understand the product which is being purchased and the outcome which can be expected. In reality, of course, the consumerist model is frequently associated with fragmentation, limited access, and restricted care, but the image of market-driven demand is powerful and persuasive. It is an image which decision-makers and the business community understand. It is heard and read everyday in the media. It invokes a relationship which, albeit unequal, is justified in terms of equality. And above all, it places enormous weight on individual responsibility rather than professional judgment. As a consequence, social workers are increasingly called upon to justify themselves in terms of competence-based activities rather than academic credentials, not because the notion of competency enlarges or deepens the scope of their responsibility but because it makes explicit the products social workers deliver. In a market-driven world, social workers are being asked to identify their niche so that the consumer can be informed about the available products. In that way, according to neo-liberal thinking, supply will match demand, resources will be efficiently used, and preferences will be maximized.

CONCLUSION

We have highlighted, in this chapter, the impact on social work practice of three aspects of globalization: free trade agreements, information technology, and neo-liberalism. What we have tried to convey is that the changes are potentially profound, that they present a challenge to the profession, and that they are modifying the way we view ourselves, our values, and our work. But we also urge caution in coming to a premature conclusion that globalization is causing a radical shift in practice since the relative scarcity of literature on the topic of globalization and social work practice points to the need for research by both academics and practitioners. On the other hand, given what we already know, it does seem that emerging free trade agreements, with their potential to open the human service sector to increased provision by corporate services, will likely increase uncertainty for non-profit social service agencies as they compete with for-profit providers to deliver social services in the community. The Victorian Order of Nurses and Family Services Canada are already in the marketplace competing with for-profit providers of home care and employee assistance services. As more agency energy goes into developing business plans and marketing strategies, front-line workers may be forced to provide services with fewer resources than they believe to be necessary or desirable for their clients.

In a similar fashion, if community-based services are even partially replaced by corporate providers, the traditional responsibility of ensuring that clients are served within their own communities by community members will become attenuated. It is equally plausible that social services which are not marketable will not be funded, the nature and scope of practice being redefined on the basis of demand. An example of social work practice that may not be marketable in these terms is advocacy (case-based as well as social and political) since it will not have financial worth. What social workers professionally value may not be perceived to be valuable to employers in the private sector whose drive to achieve efficient and measurable outcomes precludes provision of "softer and less relevant services." Hence, the concern for fundamental social justice and human rights (an integral part of social work from its inception) may also be problematic for social workers in the future, as it may put them at odds with the corporate culture of which they may become a part. The fundamental values of neo-liberalism preferred by corporations are in some respects in contradistinction to the communitarian values that nurture social work.

A further challenge relates to the definition of social work. The lack of a simple, clean definition of social work may make it seem elusive to employers and for-profit services looking for service precision. Hence, it is possible that there will be encouragement to combine functions into new work-related professional definitions that are created to meet the specific needs of the market. An example is the rapidly emerging field of home care in which an employer wants one staff member in a visit to conduct an assessment of vital signs, give an injection, and provide specific counselling in relation to social and emotional difficulty. A new breed of worker who is trained in basic health assessment and social work is an "ideal employee" in that environment since he or she can provide a range of services in a cost efficient manner. Another example is a mental health practitioner who combines clinical social work and mental health nursing. Information technology similarly challenges social work. The technologies are advancing rapidly and social work is pulled along. We are already seeing how rapidly technology skills are being valued and demanded by employers in job postings. In a recent sector study of the human service occupations in Canada (www.socialworkincanada.org), employers state that they expect new social workers to have adequate computer skills to enable them to meet the needs of the job. In a transitional period, older social workers learn the basics on the job, but new workers will be expected to have some degree of literacy before they start. As new social workers who have skills in technology are employed, it is also likely that they will want (and indeed will be required) to explore alternative ways to utilize computers in the services they provide to cyber-clients.

We conclude, therefore, by suggesting that in the face of these and similar pressures brought on by globalization, social work practitioners will increasingly need to ask themselves the following questions:

1. Will social work have to be redefined and repackaged to accommodate the influence of neo-liberalism and market-based language? Where will that exercise take us?

2. Are social work values relevant to the new world of work that is emerging as a result of changing political and economic agendas?

3. To what extent are social work values challenged by information technologies?

4. To what extent are new forms of corporate responsibility, based on international networks, replacing community responsibility, based on informal and local networks?

5. In a world in which many professions are newly emerging, does the diversity of social work practice leave it vulnerable to being absorbed by other professions?

6. Do the existing ethical codes and instruments meet the needs of the cyber-practitioner and ensure an ethical basis of service to the cyber-client?

7. Will current provincial regulations of social work practice become obsolete as practice moves beyond provincial and national borders?

8. Can the profession adequately regulate cyber-practice and respond to concerns and complaints of clients who may be living in different countries and cultures?

REFERENCES

Agreement for the mutual recognition of the occupational qualifications of social workers, (1999). Ottawa: Signed by provincial associations and boards.

Agreement on internal trade, Chapter seven: labour mobility, (1994). Ottawa: Industry Canada.

Alberta Association of Registered Nurses (2000). *Entry-to-practice competencies*, Edmonton, Alberta: AARN.

Armstrong, P. and Armstrong, H. (1992). *Health care as a business: the legacy of free trade*, Ottawa: Canadian Centre for Policy Alternatives.

Auslander, G. and Cohen, M. (1995). Reliability issues in the development of computerized information systems, *Computers in Human Services, 12*(3–4).

Barlow, M. (1990). *Parcel of rogues: how free trade is failing Canada*, Toronto: Porter Books.

Barlow, M. (2000). *The free trade area of the Americas and the threat to social programs, environmental sustainability and social justice in Canada and the Americas*, Ottawa: Council of Canadians.

Bauman, Z. (1998). *Globalization: the human consequences*, New York: Columbia University Press.

Beals, H. (2000). *Competency profile for the entry-level social worker*, Halifax: Nova Scotia Association of Social Workers.

Benbbenishty, R. and Osyerman, D. (1995). Integrated information systems for human services: a conceptual framework, methodology and technology in J. Rafferty, J. Steyaert, and D. Colombi, eds., *Human services in the information age*, New York: The Haworth Press.

Berman, Y. and Phillips, D. (1995). Two faces of information technology: what does the social worker see in the mirror? *Computers in Human Services, 12*(3–4).

Breeding, W., Grishman, M., and Moreland, M. (1996). Implementation of computerized social work data base/assessments, *Social Work in Health Care, 23*(2).

Broad, D. and Antony, W. (1999). Citizenship and social policy: neo-liberalism and beyond, in Dave Broad and Wayne Antony, eds., *Citizens or consumer? Social policy in a market economy*, Halifax: Fernwood Publishing.

Brodie, J. (1999). The politics of social policy in the twenty-first century, in Dave Broad and Wayne Antony, eds., *Citizens or consumer? Social policy in a market economy*, Halifax: Fernwood Publishing.

Bryan, I. (1994). *Canada in the new global economy*, Toronto: John Wiley & Sons.

Calvert, J. and Kuehn, L. *Pandora's box: corporate power, free trade and Canadian education*, Toronto: Our Schools/Our Selves Production.

Cauble, A.E. and Thurston, L. (2000). Effects of interactive multimedia training on knowledge, attitudes, and self-efficacy of social work students, *Research on Social Work Practice, 10*(4).

Clarke, T. (1997). *Silent coup: confronting the big business takeover of Canada*, Ottawa/Toronto: Canadian Centre for Policy Alternatives and James Lorimer & Company.

Cohen, M. (1987). *Free trade and the future of women's work*, Toronto: Garamond.

Coppock, V. (1997). "Patient," "consumer," or "empowered user"?: the impact of marketisation on child and adolescent mental health services in the UK, *Youth and Policy, 58*, autumn.

Courchene, T. (1999). *Responding to the NAFTA challenge: Ontario as a North American region state and Toronto as a global city-region*, Los Angeles: UCLA Global City-Regions Conference.

Couture, J-C. (1997). Teachers' work: living in the culture of insufficiency, in Marita Moll, ed., *Tech high: globalization and the future of Canadian education*, Halifax: Fernwood Publishing and the Canadian Centre for Policy Alternatives.

Currie, W. (2000). *The global information society*, Chichester: John Wiley & Sons.

Dominelli, L. (1996). Deprofessionalising social work: anti-oppressive practice, competencies, postmodernism, *British Journal of Social Work, 26*.

Drover, G., (Ed.) (1988). *Free trade and social policy*, Ottawa: Canadian Council on Social Development.

—— (1989). Free Trade and Social Policy: The Canadian Debate, *Social Policy and Administration, 23*(2).

—— (1995). Politica social en Canada: ALC, TLC y mas alla, Teresa Gutierrez y Monica Verea, *Canada en Transicion*, Mexico: Universidad Nacional Autonoma de Mexico.

—— (2000). Redefining social citizenship in a global era, in *Social Work and Globalization*, Special Issue. Ottawa/Montreal: *Canadian Social Work, Canadian Social Work Review*, and *Intervention*.

—— (2001). Trends and issues in social welfare: the impact of globalization, in Francis Turner and Joanne Turner, eds., *Canadian social welfare*, Toronto: Pearson Education Canada.

Drucker, P. (1989). *The new realities*, New York: Harper and Row.

Gainor, C. (1992). Free trade and medicare in Jim Sinclair, ed., *Crossing the line*, Vancouver: New Star Books.

Gale, J., Dotson, D., Huber, M., Nagireddy, C., Manders, J., Young, K., and Carter, B. (1995). A new technology for teaching/learning marital and family therapy, *Journal of Marital and Family Therapy, 21*(2).

Galinsky, M., Schopler, J., and Abell, M. (1997). Connecting group members through telephone and computer groups, *Health and Social Work, 22*(3).

Gelman, S., Pollack, D., and Weiner, A. (1999). Confidentiality of social work records in the computer age, *Social Work, 44*(3).

Gibleman, M., Gelman, S., and Fast, J. The downsize of cyberspace: cheating made easy, *Journal of Social Work Education, 35*(3).

Grishman, M. (1995). Development of a computer management system, *Social Work in Health Care, 22*(2).

Harvey, D. (1989). *The condition of postmodernity*, Oxford: Basil Blackwell.

Hirst, P. and Thompson, G. (1996). *Globalization in question*, Oxford: Polity Press.

Humphries, P. and Camilleri, P. (2000). *Social work and technology: challenges for social workers in practice—a case study*, Paper presented at the Joint Conference of the International Federation of Social Workers and International Association of Schools of Social Work, Montreal.

Hokenstad, M.C. and Midgley, J. (Eds.) (1997). *Issues in international social work*, Washington, DC: NASW Press.

Holm, W. (Ed.) (1988). *Water and free trade*, Toronto: James Lorimer & Co.

Howkins, J. and Valantin, R. (Eds.) (1997). *Development and the information age: four global scenarios for the future of information and communication technology*, Ottawa: International Development Research Centre.

Ife, J. (2000). *Local and global practice: relocating social work as a human rights profession in the new global order*, Eileen Younghusband Memorial Lecture, IFSW/IASSW Biennial Conference, Montreal, July 31.

Jackson, A. and Sanger, M. (1998). *Dismantling democracy: the multilateral agreement on investment and its impact on Canada*, Ottawa: Canadian Centre for Policy Alternatives.

Khan, P. and Dominelli, L. (2000). The impact of globalisation on social work in the UK, *European Journal of Social Work, 2*, July.

Korten, D.C. (1995., *When corporations rule the world*, West Hartford, Connecticut: Kumarian Press and Berrett-Koehler Publishers.

Lipsey, R. (1987). The Canada-US free trade agreement and the great free trade debate, *Trade Monitor*, November, Toronto: C.D. Howe Institute.

—— (1990). *Canada at the US Mexico free trade dance: wallflower or partner?*, Toronto: C.D. Howe Institute.

Livingstone, D. (1997). Computer literacy, the "knowledge economy" and information control: micro myths and macro choices, in Marita Moll, ed., *Tech high: globalization and the future of Canadian education*, Halifax; Fernwood Publishing and the Canadian Centre for Policy Alternatives.

MacFadden, R. (1995). IT and knowledge development in human services: tool, paradigm and promise, *Computers in Human Services, 12*(3–4).

Mander, J. and Goldsmith, E. (Eds.) (1996). *The case against the global economy: and for a turn to the local*, San Francisco: Sierra Club Books.

Meier, A. (2000). A multi-method evaluation of a computer-mediated, stress management support group for social workers: feasibility, process and effectiveness, *Dissertation Abstracts International: The Humanities and Social Sciences, 60*(7).

Meiksins, P. (1998). Work, new technology, and capitalism, in Robert McChesney, Ellen Meiksins Wood, and John Bellamy Foster, eds., *Capitalism and the information age*, New York: Monthly Review Press.

Menzies, H. (1996). *Whose brave new world? The information highway and the new economy*, Toronto: Between the Lines.

Michael, J. (1994). *Privacy and human rights*, Dartmouth: UNESCO.

Mishra, R. (1998). Beyond the nation state: social policy in an age of globalization, *Social Policy and Administration, 32*(5).

Midgely, J. (1997). *Social welfare in global context*, Thousand Oaks, California: Sage Publications.

Naisbitt, J. (1994). *Global paradox*, New York: William Morrow and Company.

National Research Council (1999). *Being fluent with information technology*, Washington, D.C.: National Academy Press.

NCA Associates (2000). *The development of social work competencies: final report*, Ottawa.

North American Free Trade Agreement Text, (1994). NAFTA Secretariat Web site.

OECD (1997). *Towards a global information society*, Paris: Organisation for Economic Cooperation and Development.

Ohmae, K. (1990). *The borderless world*, London: Collins.

—— (1995). *The end of the nation state: the rise of regional economics*, New York: Free Press.

Oulton, J. (1998). International trade and the nursing profession, in S. Aarrilli and C. Kinnon, eds., *International trade in health services: a developmental perspective*, Geneva: UNCTAD/WHO.

The threat to higher education: a briefing on current world trade organization negotiations, (2000). London: People and Planet Web site.

Plant, R. (1991). *Modern political thought*, Oxford: Basil Blackwell.

Price, D., Pollock, A.M., and Shaoul, J. (1999). How the world trade organisation is Shaping Domestic Policies in Health Care, *The Lancet, 354*, Nov. 27.

Reinicke, W. (2000). Global public policy networks, in Katie Sjursen, ed., *Globalization*, Bronx: The Reference Shelf.

Rowe, W., Hanley, J., Moreno, E.R., and Mould, J. (2000). Voices of social work practice: international reflections on the effects of globalization, *Social Work and Globalization*, Special Issue. Ottawa/Montreal: *Canadian Social Work, Canadian Social Work Review*, and *Intervention*.

Sanger, M. (2000). *Reckless abandon: Canada, the GATS and the future of health care*, Ottawa: Canadian Centre for Policy Alternatives.

Sinclair, S. (2000). *GATS: How the WTO's new service negotiations threaten democracy*, Ottawa: Canadian Centre for Policy Alternatives.

Teeple, G. (1995). *Globalization and the decline of social reform*, Toronto: Garamond Press.

TOPSS (2000). *Introduction to the working draft of the national occupational standards of registered managers—adult care homes*, Leeds: Training Organisation for the Personal Social Services.

TOPSS England (2000). *Modernising the Social Care Workforce—the first national training strategy for England*, Leeds: Training Organisation for the Personal Social Sevices.

Wilding, P. (1997). Globalization, regionalism and social policy, *Social Policy and Administration, 31*(4).

Winner, L. (1997). The handwriting on the wall: resisting technoglobalism's assault on education, in Marita Moll, ed., *Tech high: globalization and the future of Canadian education*, Halifax: Fernwood Publishing and the Canadian Centre for Policy Alternatives.

WTO (1994). General Agreement on Trade in Services, *Final Act*, Annex 1B, World Trade Organization Web site.

WTO (1998a). *Health and Social Services, Communication from the United States*, World Trade Organization Web site.

WTO (1998b). *Health and Social Services, Background Note for the Secretariat*, World Trade Organization Web site.

C h a p t e r

THE HELPING
RELATIONSHIP

Nick Coady

This chapter's exploration of the helping relationship focuses on clinical social work practice, particularly on practice with individuals. This is because most of the theoretical and empirical writing in social work and other helping professions on relationship factors has centred on individual counselling. Due to this somewhat narrow focus, two issues should be clarified at the outset. First, I believe in a generalist framework for clinical social work practice (Coady & Lehmann, 2001) that includes sensitivity to environmental and sociocultural factors, and in the importance of intervention and advocacy on multiple levels (including the macro practice levels of community development and social policy). In fact, worker sensitivity to such issues is deemed necessary for the development of good helping relationships. Second, I believe that the same range and types of relationship skills (with some difference in emphasis) are important in micro and macro social work practice.

Within clinical social work practice, the helping relationship has long been considered the cornerstone of effective helping. Mary Richmond (1917) conceptualized the entire process of casework as the study and uses of social relationships. Other well-known social work writers have described the helping relationship as the "soul" (Biestek, 1957), "basic means" (Perlman, 1957), and "major determinant" (Hollis, 1970) of social work intervention. Although opinion within social work and other helping professions has changed over time with regard to what constitutes a good helping relationship, there is consensus currently that it is characterized by warmth, empathy, acceptance, genuineness, caring concern, mutual liking, and collaboration.

This chapter is divided into five sections. First, a historical review of the waxing and waning within social work and other helping professions with regard to the understanding of and emphasis placed on a good helping relationship will be presented. Second, current theory and research establishing that relationship factors are the most important determinants of client outcome will be reviewed. Third, the characteristics of good worker-client relationships will be described. Fourth, various issues concerning the development and maintenance of good helping relationships will be discussed. Finally, a case example with an excerpt of worker-client dialogue will be presented in an effort to illustrate how some of the relationship attributes and issues are manifested in practice.

HISTORICAL PERSPECTIVE ON VIEWS OF THE HELPING RELATIONSHIP

Early Social Work Practice

Although Mary Richmond (1917) emphasized the importance of social relationships in her early writing on casework, it would be misleading to suggest that clinical social work practice in the early part of this century embraced the same type of helping relationship that is valued today. This is because much of the early casework by Charity Organization Society (COS) "friendly visitors" was tainted by paternalism toward and moral judgments of the poor. In fact, it seems likely that the early community development practice by "live-in neighbours" of Jane Addams' Settlement House movement, which emphasized that people were poor through no fault of their own and that workers needed to work collaboratively to help people help themselves, was "kinder and gentler" than that of the COS workers. Although this may seem ironic, it helps to explain why social group work, which had its roots in the Settlement House movement, has always led clinical practice in valuing "authenticity, forthrightness, and abrogation of the mystique of professionalism" (Pappell & Rothman, 1980).

The moralistic elements of early casework gradually dissipated as the social work profession matured; however, elements of paternalism and social distance between worker and client were reinforced by the adoption of Freudian theory in the 1920s. Although classical Freudian theory made many positive contributions to social work practice, it advocated for a worker stance of neutrality, abstinence, and aloofness (Gelso & Carter, 1985), which is a far cry from the type of helping relationship that is promoted today.

The Functional School of Social Work

The first real wave of emphasis on a good helping relationship, as it is currently understood, did not begin until the 1930s when the functional (Rankian) school of social work arose to challenge the dominant diagnostic (Freudian) school. The functional school reacted against the Freudian preoccupation with the past and the emphasis on the worker as a socially distant authority. Instead, functional theory focused on the use of a warm, supportive, empathic worker-client relationship to release the growth potential of the client.

The debate between the diagnostic and functional schools lasted almost two decades, but the synthesis of perspectives that was eventually achieved included an emphasis on the power of the helping relationship. Perlman (1979) noted that relationship became "a mystique of treatment" (13) within social work in the 1940s and 1950s. Biestek (1957) suggested that it "became synonymous with the whole casework process" (10) in this period. Unfortunately, the emphasis on relationship factors within social work waned over time. Perlman (1979) noted that because the concept of relationship was not critically examined or researched in social work, by the 1960s it was "pushed off to the periphery of helping practice and theory" (17).

Client-Centered Theory and Research

The second major wave of interest in relationship within the helping professions was occasioned by Carl Rogers' (1957) famous and controversial assertion that the worker-offered relationship conditions (or "core conditions") of empathy, warmth, and genuineness were not only necessary, but also sufficient for constructive client change. Rogers went so far as to assert that theory and technique were unimportant except to the extent that they furthered the development of the therapeutic relationship. Although it is commonly overlooked, the parallel between Rogers' views on the importance of the helping relationship and those of the functional school of social work was more than coincidence. Early in his career, Rogers worked closely with social workers in the functional school and even held office in social work organizations (Rowe, 1986).

Rogers' (1957) assertions were accompanied by a challenge to the field to test his ideas empirically. Researchers responded enthusiastically in efforts to either prove or disprove Rogers' hypothesis. Although overall results of research on the core conditions offered support for their importance, later studies yielded less conclusive results than earlier studies. Unfortunately, continued resistance by the psychotherapy establishment to Rogers' controversial ideas, together with disenchantment with the methodological and measurement problems in the associated research, has limited the influence of client-centered theory on the field of professional helping since the mid 1970s (Gelso & Carter, 1985).

Therapeutic Alliance Theory and Research

The third major wave of interest in the helping relationship began in the mid 1970s with research on the concept of the therapeutic (or working) alliance. The concept of the therapeutic alliance is closely related to Rogers' concept of the helping relationship. The major difference is that the therapeutic alliance is conceptualized as a characteristic of the relationship between the worker and the client, not just as worker-offered conditions. Thus, there is the recognition that worker characteristics and behaviours interact with client characteristics and behaviours to influence the quality of the relationship.

The therapeutic alliance is defined generally as the ability of the worker and client to work together in a collaborative relationship characterized by mutual liking, trust, respect, and commitment to the work of counselling (Foreman & Marmar, 1985). Although the concept of the therapeutic alliance originated in psychodynamic therapy, partly as a reaction against the traditional analytic stance of aloofness (Greenson, 1967), interest in the concept spread quickly to other theoretical approaches.

It is likely that research on this concept was fuelled by two factors. One was the promising but controversial research results on the client-centered relationship conditions. Another was the cumulative finding, over two decades of research, that there were no significant differences in effectiveness among the variety of counselling approaches (Lambert & Bergin, 1994). This latter finding, commonly referred to as the "equal outcomes" phenomenon and still currently supported by research, supported Jerome Frank's (1961) long-held view that factors that are "common" across therapies (relationship factors in particular) may be more important than factors that are "specific" to the different types of therapy (i.e., theory-specific techniques). Frank argued that a good helping relationship was the major therapeutic factor and that its function was to instill hope and improve morale in the client.

Before moving to a review of therapeutic alliance research, it is important to note that interest in the concept has been confined largely to individual psychotherapy in the disciplines of psychology and psychiatry. It is clear, and unfortunate, that social work has been slow to embrace theory and research on the therapeutic alliance (Coady, 1993a). Social work's abandonment of its earlier emphasis on the helping relationship may be due to a number of factors. There is no doubt that for a number of decades social work has been preoccupied with the theoretical, technical, and scientific aspects of practice (Sheafor, Horejsi, & Horejsi, 1988). Goldstein (1990) has charged that the humanistic and artistic elements of social work practice have become devalued because of the profession's haste to achieve scientific respectability. Another factor may be social work's preoccupation with the field of family therapy, which has traditionally placed much more emphasis on technique than on relationship factors (Coady, 1992, 1993b). Also, there is no doubt that the managed care movement in the United States and similar economic and political forces in Canada have created tangible barriers to focusing on the helping relationship (e.g., increased caseloads and agencies' and employee assistance programs' limits on the number of counselling sessions).

Summary of Current Empirical Knowledge about the Importance of the Helping Relationship

Research on the therapeutic alliance has now spanned two decades. Cumulative research results provide strong support for the conclusion that a good relationship is necessary for good client outcome regardless of the model of counselling (Horvath & Symonds, 1991; Orlinsky, Grawe, & Parkes, 1994). These results have been consistent across a variety of outcome measures and client, worker, and clinical judge ratings of the alliance (Gaston, 1990). It has also been found that client and worker contributions to the alliance provide equally good predictions of outcome (Orlinsky, Grawe, & Parks, 1994). Client contributions to the alliance include being open, trustful, and non-defensive. Worker contributions to the alliance include warmth, interest, positive emotional involvement, and lack of negative attitudes.

One of the more controversial empirical findings is that relationship factors contribute more to outcome than technique factors (Lambert & Bergin, 1994). Based on reviews of research, Lambert (1992) has estimated that relationship factors account for about 30% of improvement in clients, whereas techniques account for about 15%. It is also striking that research suggests that the majority of client improvement is accounted for by factors that are extraneous to the actual work of counselling. Lambert estimates that 15% of client improvement is due to clients' expectations of being helped (placebo effect) and 40% is due to clients' personal strengths and environmental circumstances (e.g., social support). The latter estimates should function to keep all workers humbly aware of the fact that clients' personal characteristics and social circumstances have more impact on counselling outcome than the counselling itself. The former estimates reinforce the ideas of Rogers (1957) and Frank (1961) and should remind workers that the type of relationship they develop with their clients is likely more important than their use of theory and technique.

Although controversial, the fact that relationship factors seem to have more impact on counselling outcomes than technique factors should not be surprising. First, to the dismay of many professionals, research has shown that paraprofessional helpers who have requisite interpersonal skills but no academic credentials and little training, can often be as effective as highly trained and educated professionals (Christensen & Jacobson, 1994; Lambert &

Bergin, 1994). Second, it is clear that relationship factors have a "double-barrelled" effect. Not only can a good relationship directly strengthen the client's self-esteem, confidence, and morale, but it is also a precondition for lowering clients' defenses and facilitating their receptiveness to worker interventions (Orlinsky et al., 1994). Third, it is important to recognize that "to speak of the respective roles of technique (specific) versus relationship (nonspecific) variables is to participate in a misleading dichotomy" (Henry, Schacht, & Strupp, 1986, 31). It is not surprising that research has found meagre evidence of the association between therapeutic techniques and outcome, as techniques have been studied in isolation from the quality of the helping relationship. Research has attempted only recently to integrate the study of relationship and technique variables. Such research has yielded such common-sense findings as the positive impact of supportive self-disclosures (Hill, Mahalik, & Thompson, 1989) and the negative impact of hostile interpretations (Coady, 1991).

It should be acknowledged that because therapeutic alliance research has been confined largely to individual counselling, the extent to which implications can be generalized to family and group counselling is limited. Nevertheless, there is some evidence to suggest that relationship factors have similar associations with the outcomes of family and group counselling. With regard to family counselling, Pinsof and Catherall (1986) found a significant association between scores on their family therapy alliance scales and worker-rated client progress. Furthermore, in the conclusion to their review of research on family counselling, Gurman, Kniskern, and Pinsof (1986) stated that "refined relationship skills seem necessary to yield genuinely positive outcomes" (572). With regard to group counselling, it is generally accepted that cohesion (which is a concept closely aligned to that of the therapeutic alliance) is an exceptionally important therapeutic factor, although research on this issue has been plagued with conceptual and measurement problems (Bednar & Kaul, 1994).

CHARACTERISTICS OF GOOD HELPING RELATIONSHIPS

Currently there is little dissension about the fundamental elements of good helping relationships. Also, it is striking how the classic descriptions of good helping relationships that have been offered by prominent social work authors in the past (e.g., Biestek, 1957; Perlman, 1957, 1979) not only fit with current descriptions in the literature but also surpass many of them in terms of detail and thoroughness. For this reason, this section of the chapter will draw primarily on Helen Harris Perlman's writing on relationship attributes, with a focus on her 1979 book *Relationship: The Heart of Helping People*.

The worker-client relationship has always been afforded a significant role in Perlman's (1957) problem-solving model of casework. Perlman (1979) outlines five desirable relationship conditions that parallel the conditions that Rogers (1957) advocates in client-centered psychotherapy.

Warmth

Perlman (1979) describes warmth as a lively, positive, outgoing, and compassionate interpersonal manner. It suggests a spontaneous liking of and interest in others. Perlman surmises that warmth may be primarily a personal disposition that is the "product of early and repeated experiences of having been responded to in pleasurable and confidence-giving ways" (p. 55). She cautions that warmth may not be easily taught or cultivated, but that the other relationship attributes may function as substitutes.

Acceptance

Perlman (1979) advocates that workers accept and value clients as they are, although workers need not approve of clients' actions. She suggests that non-blaming is a more accurate term than non-judging. The worker may judge and challenge a client's actions or attitudes if this is accompanied by the worker's consistent acceptance of the client as a person. Perlman stresses that the frequently overlooked corollaries of acceptance and support are expectation and stimulation. The worker needs to "walk this fine line, both accepting the person's 'being' and expecting her 'becoming'" (55).

Empathy

According to Perlman (1979), empathy involves sensing and relating to the feelings that underlie clients' words and actions. This corresponds to the dictum of "putting oneself into another's shoes" or understanding things from the client's perspective. It is important to recognize that empathy involves not only accurate perception of clients' emotions but also communication of such understanding to the client. At the same time it involves not only identifying and commenting on immediately evident emotions but also underlying emotions. Although this sometimes occurs spontaneously it often requires the development of very sensitive listening skills, or "listening with the third ear" (57).

Perlman points out that the development of in-depth understanding of the client's feelings occurs in conjunction with the process of carefully exploring information provided by the client. Empathy deepens as the worker gets to know more details about the client's life situation and experience. Thus, one needs to guard against assuming too quickly that one knows how the client feels and to be tentative in identifying and displaying understanding of feelings.

Caring Concern

Perlman (1979) describes this as a nurturing display of concern for the personal and social well-being of clients. Concern for the personal well-being of clients involves caring about their emotional pain and general welfare. Concern for the social well-being of clients adds to warmth, acceptance, and empathy because it includes sensitivity to the welfare of other persons in clients' social systems.

Genuineness

Perlman (1979) contends that genuineness involves being free of pretension and suggests that, like warmth, it "is the product of...life experiences that made it possible to be self-observant, self-aware...and self-accepting" (60). Being genuine requires the admission that one does not have all of the answers and, when appropriate, the admission that one has made a mistake. Thus, the worker does not try to impress the client with technical jargon or knowledge. It is especially important to guard against the formality and stiffness that can result from hiding "behind professional masks" (Gitterman, 1988, 37). Genuineness also means that clients' problems or feelings are not glossed over with false reassurance. Rather, the worker acknowledges the seriousness of situations and offers realistic hope.

Summary

Perlman (1979) stresses that the various relationship attributes are interdependent; they "are expressed whole, received and responded to whole, felt as whole, with no measuring sticks for how much of which" (62). Perlman's view of relationship as "one expression of the heart's reasons" (203) reflects her belief that the worker's overt caring behaviour toward the client must flow from a genuine internal caring. It should also be noted that Perlman (1979) emphasizes the interdependence of the processes of relationship development and problem-solving: "Relationship is the continuous context within which problem-solving takes place. It is at the same time the emerging product of mutual problem-solving efforts; and simultaneously it is the catalytic agent" (151).

ISSUES CONCERNING THE DEVELOPMENT AND MAINTENANCE OF GOOD HELPING RELATIONSHIPS

Parallels and Differences Between Professional and Natural Relationships

Perlman (1979) stresses that the qualities of good professional helping relationships are the same as those that characterize good natural relationships. She does, however, differentiate between professional and natural relationships in a couple of important ways. Professional relationships, in contrast to natural relationships, are initiated "for the client." The exchange of rewards or gratification is expected to be reciprocal in natural relationships, but in the helping relationship the worker must be prepared to give attention and care to the client without expectation of reciprocation. Perlman points out that workers have the same tendency as others to withdraw from non-rewarding relationships. Research has documented that even highly experienced therapists tend to respond to difficult clients with counter-hostility in "the form of coldness, distancing, and other forms of rejection" (Strupp, 1980, 954). Clearly, workers need to be aware of such natural tendencies and to manage them in the best interests of the client.

The professional helping relationship is also more "controlled" than natural relationships in a couple of ways. First, although the worker needs to have caring concern and empathy for clients, emotional involvement needs to be controlled so that the worker is not overwhelmed by the client's issues and feelings. Second, the worker needs to take the responsibility of managing the process of social work intervention and must be comfortable in doing so.

There is, however, danger in talking about the "controlled" nature of professional helping relationships in both of these regards. With regard to controlled emotional involvement, although Perlman argues for an "objective" worker stance, she stresses that this does not imply detachment or neutrality. Rather, it is the recognition and management of one's own subjectivity in the best interests of the client. Also, she argues that the first step toward self-management is self-awareness: one needs to be aware of one's own emotional sensitivities and tendencies in order to manage them. With regard to the idea of managing the helping process, it should be stressed that it is more appropriate to construe the worker as "guiding" rather than "controlling" the process. Furthermore, it needs to be acknowledged that in guiding the helping process workers must often rely on creativity and intuition and are required "to develop the skills for finding courage in the face of the uncertain" (Papell & Skolnik, 1992, 22).

The Myth of the Unitary, Ideal Helping Relationship

Perlman (1979) argues against the myth that the professional helping relationship is an undifferentiated, unitary ideal relationship applicable to all combinations of clients and problems and all phases of the helping process. Rather, Perlman stresses that workers must continually adjust their approach to fit the changing needs of the same client over time, as well as the different needs of different clients.

Although this seems to constitute common sense, in a special section of a recent volume of the journal *Psychotherapy*, Norcross (1993) has noted that this has not been addressed adequately in the literature. In reviewing six articles that made up the special section of this journal issue, Norcross noted some points of consensus. First, there was consensus that universal relationship behaviours that hold across clients and across time include good listening, interest, and respect. Second, it was generally agreed that beyond the universal relationship behaviours it is often important to use different relational styles with different clients or with the same client at different points in time. This includes considerations such as degree of formality/informality, depth of warmth and empathy, level of activity and directiveness, and balance of support and challenge.

Beyond consensus on these basic issues, however, there are few guidelines to use in attempting to tailor relationship stances to client needs. One general suggestion by Lazarus (1993) that makes good sense is that unless there are indications that something different is required, the first and preferred mode should be that of empathy and kindness. Furthermore, as Shulman (1992) advises, even when challenge or confrontation may be necessary, it is important to first build "a fund of positive affect that is part of the working relationship" (140).

Another general strategy that can be helpful throughout the helping process in tailoring relationship stances to client needs is what Shulman (1992) refers to as "tuning in" or "preparatory empathy." This involves taking the time before meeting with the client to get in touch with the feelings and concerns that the client might be bringing to the session. Tuning-in is always tentative; however, it can help the worker to prepare to respond to client concerns in the most appropriate manner.

Diversity and the Helping Relationship

The existence of cultural differences between the worker and client (where culture is construed broadly as pertaining not only to ethnicity but also to gender, age, sexual preference, religion, class, disability, and so forth) not only may entail tailoring of relationship stance to client need, but may also necessitate dealing with issues of disadvantage and oppression. Unless the potential impact of difference and disadvantage/oppression is considered, the development of the helping relationship can be severely attenuated.

It is beyond the scope of this chapter to consider issues in and strategies for working across all the types of difference that may exist between workers and clients; however, some general strategies can be mentioned. There are a number of important issues that should be considered in tuning-in to prepare oneself to work with clients from any minority group. First, workers need to examine their own feelings and values to become aware of and deal with any discomfort or stereotypes of minority clients that may interfere with seeing clients as individuals. Second, workers should educate themselves as much as possible about the culture of the minority client, including issues of values, customs, experience of oppression, and so forth. Third, workers need to remind themselves that tuning-in to cultural differences is a tentative exercise because there is so much diversity within all minority groups. It is as bad to overestimate the effect of difference as it is to underestimate it. The key is to develop sensitivity to the possible impact of cultural differences and then to open oneself to understanding each client's unique experience.

Transference and Countertransference

Perlman (1979) explains that transference and countertransference are instances of "behaviour that indicate that one person is not seeing the other as he actually is; the behaviour seems inappropriate to what the realistic situation calls for... the indication is that the person's attitudes and reactions are being transferred from some past vital relationship (benign or malevolent) into the present one" (76). Transference refers to the client's projections whereas counter-transference represents the worker's projections.

Perlman stresses that the worker needs to be aware of the potential for counter-transference and that awareness of one's personal issues and sensitivities is paramount. It is particularly important to watch for and inhibit the expression of hostile and negative feelings toward the client. The worker must be able to put such feelings aside for later examination (in supervision, or in some instances, personal counselling). When dealing with hostile reactions from the client, the worker must consider "whether something in the here-and-now helping transaction is causing this problem and can be differently managed" (Perlman, 1979, 76). Thus, the worker must examine her own behaviour/motivations before attributing client hostility to transference reactions.

Perlman suggests transference can be indirectly curtailed by maintaining a focus on the present reality and the task at hand. If evidence of transference persists, Perlman recommends that the worker deal with it directly by gently exploring the meaning of the client's misperceptions while reaffirming acceptance of and respect for the client. Perlman emphasizes the need to understand rather than act defensively to client manifestations of transference. The aim is to redirect clients to the reality of the here-and-now and through your actions to show them that you will not treat them as others have in the past.

Recognizing and Dealing with Problems in the Helping Relationship

Beyond transference and countertransference phenomena, there are a myriad of possible problems that can get in the way of developing and maintaining productive helping relationships. Professional helping relationships can be as complicated as natural relationships. One of the main problems in both types of relationships is the difficulty in acknowledging and talking about the contentious issues.

As mentioned earlier, it has been documented that workers are prone to responding to client hostility and resistance with counterhostility (Strupp, 1980). On a more promising note, other studies (Foreman & Marmar, 1985; Safran, McMain, Crocker, & Murray, 1990) have found that workers can be effective in overcoming an initially poor helping relationship by directly addressing and working through concerns. Safran and colleagues (1990) have developed a common sense model for dealing with problems in the helping relationship, or "therapeutic alliance ruptures" as they call them. This model calls for workers to (a) watch for and be sensitive to clients' negative reactions, (b) encourage full expression of clients' negative feelings and respond empathetically, (c) validate clients' viewpoints and experiences, and (d) take responsibility and apologize for one's own contributions to the difficulties (see Safran & Muran, 2000 for a more in-depth consideration of alliance ruptures). In a similar vein, Barnard & Keuhl (1995) have proposed guidelines and specific questions for "ongoing evaluation" of the helping relationship in order to identify and work through potential problems. Although their article addresses family therapy in particular, the suggestions are also pertinent for work with individual clients.

The Development and Refinement of Relationship Skills

It is noteworthy that Perlman (1979) suggests that relationship skills may be to some extent "inborn or inbred" (58). As mentioned earlier, she suggests that receiving consistent nurturing and love in childhood may enable individuals to relate warmly to others. On a somewhat different note, another body of theory and research related to the "wounded healer" paradigm suggests that empathic and supportive abilities may develop from experiencing and working through personal/familial problems (Guy, 1987; Wolgien & Coady, 1997). Whatever the explanation, there are some people for whom relationship skills seem to come more "naturally."

The existence of natural relationship skills for some individuals does not preclude, however, the development and refinement of relationship skills through personal/professional development. On the personal front, and linked to the concept of the wounded healer, there is a prevailing belief in the professional helping field that personal psychotherapy for clinicians is important. In a recent qualitative study of social work students and practitioners who received personal counselling, all felt that it was valuable to the development of their helping abilities, but opinion was split on whether this should be required for clinicians (Mackey & Mackey, 1993). The cumulative outcome of research on this issue is unclear, however: "Because the reasons for entering therapy are so diverse and the effects so varied, the role of personal therapy on efficacy remains varied" (Beutler, Machado, & Neufeldt, 1994, 239). There is no doubt that self-awareness and psychological health are important to clinical ability. It is the author's contention, however, that many people can and do work through personal issues and develop self-awareness without professional counselling.

The refinement of relationship skills can also be fostered through training, supervision, and experience. There is evidence that relationship skills can be fostered through courses and workshops that use modelling, role-plays, supportive feedback, coaching, and reinforcement (Matarazzo & Patterson, 1986). Similarly, supervision that uses review of videotapes or process recordings to focus on worker-client relationship issues can also be helpful. In both instances, the quality of the relationship that is developed between the student/practitioner and the instructor/supervisor can facilitate or impede learning and skill development (Matarazzo & Patterson, 1986). Finally, there is no substitute for learning from experience, including one's mistakes. The key here is to solicit and be open to client feedback and to learn from mistakes. Much of such learning from experience involves the progressive development of a sensitivity or feel for interpersonal process and the ability to interact in more personal, open, supportive, and humble ways with clients (Coady, 1995; Wolgien & Coady, 1997).

Case

This case example is based on the author's recent work with an actual client; however, information has been modified to protect confidentiality. The client (Jim) is a 17-year-old male adolescent, an only child, who initially was pressured by his parents to seek counselling. One family interview was held but consensus emerged in this session that, due to emotional volatility in the family and Jim's developmental stage, it would be best to pursue individual counselling first. Initial sessions with Jim established that presenting problems included low self-esteem, poor peer relationships, and conflictual relationships with his mother and father that centred on issues of academic work habits and achievement, household chores, and educational/career aspirations.

The dialogue presented below has been constructed from memory of the overall work with Jim and is meant to pertain to a middle session of counselling (e.g., 6th of 12 sessions). Thus, it is to be assumed that the worker has established a good level of trust and rapport with the client by this point in time. Examples of relationship skills and issues are denoted in brackets.

At the start of this session the client has related that although things had been going better at home, there had been a major blow-up on the weekend. In this incident his parents had been "on his back" about his poor report card and disrespectful behaviour. This led to a heated argument that involved the threat of a physical confrontation between Jim and his father and which culminated in Jim holding a knife to his own neck to threaten self-harm. He was then able to use a "time-out" (he left the house to calm himself down) and returned to apologize for his behaviour. Initial discussion in this session determined that risk of harm to self or other was low and that this was a symbolic/dramatic event that the client felt quite embarrassed about.

> *Worker:* (After listening to Jim recount the incident) I can imagine that this incident scared the hell out of both you and your folks (empathy; caring concern for the client and his parents).

> *Jim:* Yeah, it did. I've never lost it like that before. I thought I'd been doing pretty well at controlling my temper with my folks for the last while but I guess I've gotten worse, not better.

> *Worker:* You were doing well but I can understand that a set-back like this makes it seem as if you're right back to square one (empathy, not glossing over difficult feelings).

> *Jim:* I'd say rock bottom—I'm not just a loser but a psycho too.

> *Worker:* There is no doubt that you could have handled yourself better during this blow-up but I know you well enough by now to know that you're not a loser or psycho (acceptance of the person but not the behaviour; genuineness).

> *Jim:* But why the hell couldn't I control myself?

> *Worker:* First of all you did control yourself...although you might have done it before things exploded, you did eventually take a time-out and you didn't get into a physical confrontation or hurt yourself (genuinely pointing out positives).... Secondly, I wonder if you'd been holding things inside to the point that pressure built up and exploded (empathy).

> *Jim:* Well I suppose so—but I just don't know what to do anymore—everything seems hopeless.

> *Worker:* I understand how you might feel hopeless (empathy) but I don't see it that way at all (genuineness)—I think it's very important that we don't let one incident undermine the progress that you've been making—set-backs are part of the normal process of making changes (normalization, instilling hope).

> *Jim:* Well I'm not so sure this is just a normal set-back. If it was just hassles with my parents that would be one thing, but I'm screwing up at school, I don't have a girlfriend, and I don't have any idea of where I'm going in life.

Worker: I understand that you're discouraged and that right now it seems that everything is going wrong (empathy). It may not seem so, but these are normal worries for guys your age and I struggled with many similar issues when I was younger (normalization, genuine self-disclosure). You show a lot of maturity in thinking seriously about these issues and in coming here to work on them (genuine crediting of client strengths).

Jim: Thanks, but I guess I'm just disappointed in myself right now.

Worker: I can understand that—it's just important that you don't lose sight of the progress you've already made. You've got a good heart and a strong mind. I'm confident that together we can continue to make progress in dealing with things that are bothering you (warmth, genuineness, caring concern, instilling hope, promoting collaborative work).

(The worker went on to explore Jim's feelings about their work together in the spirit of ongoing evaluation of the helping relationship, and then ended the session by brainstorming with Jim about how to handle future arguments with his parents more positively.)

There are obvious limitations to using a short piece of worker-client dialogue to illustrate relationship attributes and issues. First, it should be noted that the preponderance of worker speech in this excerpt is an artifact of the effort to illustrate relationship skills within space limitations. Although there is variation depending on worker and client characteristics and the stage of the counselling process, client speech should predominate in most worker-client dialogue. Second, it needs to be acknowledged that the worker responses reflect one person's style that was tailored to a particular adolescent client. Third, it is not possible to convey how some common relationship issues surfaced and were worked through over time. For instance, there was an initial period of exploring and working through normal client reservations around becoming engaged in counselling (e.g., clarifying that it was not about "headshrinking"). This also entailed some discussion of the potential impact of difference (e.g., in age, social status) on developing comfort in talking openly with one another. This was followed by some negotiation of personal versus professional relationship boundaries. Later, it was necessary at times to integrate some challenge and mild confrontation into the supportive nature of the work.

Finally, it is difficult to ascertain a sense of the cumulative impact of relationship factors from reading such a small piece of dialogue. It is the author's estimation, however, that the quality of the helping relationship was the major contributor to the improvement in social functioning and self-esteem this youth evidenced over time. Although some of the more theoretical/technical interventions (e.g., anger-management and conflict-resolution skills) did prove helpful, the genuine and mutual warmth, caring, and liking that developed in this helping relationship seemed to provide the boost in morale, hopefulness, and self-esteem that led to improved coping.

SUMMARY

This chapter has attempted to cover a wide range of issues with regard to the helping relationship. This has inhibited an in-depth exploration of issues and the reader is encouraged to do further reading (see reference list, below). It is hoped that this chapter has been successful in presenting two central arguments: (a) that the ability to develop and maintain helping relationships characterized by warmth, empathy, caring concern, genuineness, and acceptance is the cornerstone of effective helping; and (b) that this ability is more a matter of developing an empathic, collaborative, supportive heart/mind-set and expressing this in one's natural style than of developing sophisticated theoretical understanding and technical expertise.

REFERENCES

Barnard, C.P., & Kuehl, B.P. (1995). Ongoing evaluation: in-session procedures for enhancing the working alliance and therapy effectiveness. *American Journal of Family Therapy, 23,* 161–172.

Bednar, R.L., & Kaul, T. (1994). Experiential group research. In A.E. Bergin & S.L. Garfield (Eds.). *Handbook of psychotherapy and behavior change* (4th ed.). New York: Wiley, pp. 631–663.

Beutler, L.E., Machado, P.P., & Neufeldt, S.A. (1994). Therapist variables. In A.E. Bergin & S.L. Garfield (Eds.). *Handbook of psychotherapy and behavior change* (4th ed.). New York: Wiley, pp. 229–269.

Biestek, F. (1957). *The casework relationship.* Chicago: Loyola University Press.

Christensen, A., & Jacobson, N.S. (1994). Who (or what) can do psychotherapy: the status and challenge of nonprofessional therapies. *Psychological Science, 5,* 8–14.

Coady, N.F. (1991). The association between complex types of therapist interventions and outcomes in psychodynamic psychotherapy. *Research on Social Work Practice, 1,* 257–277.

Coady, N.F. (1992). Rationale and directions for an increased emphasis on the therapeutic relationship in family therapy. *Contemporary Family Therapy, 14,* 467–479.

Coady, N.F. (1993a). The worker-client relationship revisited. *Families in Society, 74,* 291–298.

Coady, N.F. (1993b). An argument for generalist social work practice with families versus family systems therapy. *Canadian Social Work Review, 10,* 27–42.

Coady, N. (1995). A reflective/inductive model of practice: emphasizing theory building for unique cases versus applying theory to practice. In G. Rogers (Ed.). *Social work field education: views and visions.* Dubuque, IA: Kendall/Hunt, pp. 139–151.

Coady, N., & Lehmann, P. (2001). An overview of and rationale for a generalist-eclectic approach to direct social work practice. In P. Lehmann & N. Coady (Eds.), *Theoretical perspectives for direct social work practice: A generalist-eclectic approach.* New York: Springer, pp. 3–26.

Foreman, S.A., & Marmar, C.R. (1985). Therapist actions that address initially poor therapeutic alliances in psychotherapy. *American Journal of Psychiatry, 142,* 922–926.

Frank, J. (1961). *Persuasion and healing: a comparative study of psychotherapy.* Baltimore: John Hopkins Press.

Gaston, L. (1990). The concept of the alliance and its role in psychotherapy: theoretical and empirical considerations. *Psychotherapy, 27,* 143–153.

Gelso, C., & Carter, J. (1985). The relationship in counseling and psychotherapy: components, consequences, and theoretical antecedents. *The Counseling Psychologist, 13,* 155–243.

Gitterman, A. (1988). Building mutual support in groups. *Social Work with Groups, 12,* 5–21.

Goldstein, H. (1990). The knowledge base of social work practice: theory, wisdom, analogue, or art? *Families in Society, 35,* 32–43.

Greenson, R.R. (1967). *The technique and practice of psychoanalysis* (Vol. 1). New York: International Universities Press.

Gurman, A.S., Kniskern, D.P., & Pinsof, W.M. (1986). Research on marital and family therapies. In S.L. Garfield & A.E. Bergin (Eds.). *Handbook of psychotherapy and behavior change* (3rd ed). New York: Wiley, pp. 565–624.

Guy, J.D. (1987). *The personal life of the psychotherapist.* New York: Wiley.

Henry, W.P., Schacht, T., & Strupp, H.H. (1986). Structural analysis of social behavior: application to a study of interpersonal process in differential psychotherapeutic outcome. *Journal of Consulting and Clinical Psychology, 54,* 27–31.

Hill, C.E., Mahalik, J.R., & Thompson, B.J. (1989). Therapist self-disclosure. *Psychotherapy, 26,* 290–295.

Hollis, F. (1970). Psychosocial approach to the practice of casework. In R. Roberts & R. Nee (Eds.). *Theories of social casework.* Chicago: University of Chicago Press.

Horvath, A.O., & Symonds, B.D. (1991). Relation between working alliance and outcome in psychotherapy: a meta-analysis. *Journal of Counseling Psychology, 38,* 139–149.

Lambert, M.J. (1992). Psychotherapy outcome research: implications for integrative and eclectic therapists. In J.C. Norcross & M.R. Goldfried (Eds.). *Handbook of psychotherapy integration.* Basic Books: New York, pp. 94–129.

Lambert, M.J., & Bergin, A.E. (1994). The effectiveness of psychotherapy. In S.L. Garfield & A.E. Bergin (Eds.). *Handbook of psychotherapy and behavior change* (4th ed.). New York: Wiley, pp. 143–189.

Lazarus, A.A. (1993). Tailoring the therapeutic relationship, or being an authentic chameleon. *Psychotherapy, 30,* 404–407.

Mackey, R.A., & Mackey, E.F. (1993). The value of personal psychotherapy to clinical practice. *Clinical Social Work Journal, 21,* 97–110.

Matarazzo, R.G., & Patterson, D.R. (1986). Methods of teaching therapeutic skill. In S.L. Garfield & A.E. Bergin (Eds.). *Handbook of psychotherapy and behavior change* (3rd ed.). New York: Wiley, pp. 821–843.

Norcross, J.C. (1993). Tailoring relationship stances to client needs: an introduction. *Psychotherapy, 30,* 402–403.

Orlinsky, D.E., Grawe, K., & Parks, B.K. (1994). Process and outcome in psychotherapy—Noch Einmal. In A.E. Bergin & S.L. Garfield (Eds.). *Handbook of psychotherapy and behavior change* (4th ed). New York: Wiley, pp. 270–378

Papell, C.P., & Rothman, B. (1980). Relating the mainstream model of social work with groups to group psychotherapy and the structured group approach. *Social Work with Groups, 3,* 5–22.

Papell, C.P., & Skolnik, L. (1992). The reflective practitioner: a contemporary paradigm's relevance for social work education. *Journal of Social Work Education, 28,* 18–26.

Perlman, H.H. (1957). *Social casework: A problem-solving process.* Chicago: University of Chicago Press.

Perlman, H.H. (1979). *Relationship: the heart of helping people.* Chicago: University of Chicago Press.

Pinsof, W.M., & Catherall, D.R. (1986). The integrative psychotherapy alliance: family, couple and individual therapy scales. *Journal of Marital and Family Therapy, 12,* 137–151.

Richmond, M. (1917). *Social Diagnosis.* New York: Russell Sage Foundation.

Rogers, C.R. (1957). The necessary and sufficient conditions of therapeutic personality change. *Journal of Consulting Psychology, 21,* 95–103.

Rowe, W. (1986). Client-centered theory. In F.J. Turner (Ed.). *Social work treatment: interlocking the-oretical approaches.* New York: Free Press, pp. 407–431.

Safran, J.D., McMain, S., Crocker, P., & Murray, P. (1990). Therapeutic alliance rupture as a therapy event for empirical investigation. *Psychotherapy, 27,* 154–165.

Safran, J.D., & Muran, J.C. (2000). *Negotiating the therapeutic alliance: A relational treatment guide.* New York: Guilford.

Sheafor, B.W., Horejsi, C.R., & Horejsi, G.A. (1988). Techniques and guidelines for social work prac-tice. Boston: Allyn & Bacon.

Shulman, L. (1992). *The skills of helping individuals and groups* (3rd ed.). Itasca, IL: Peacock.

Strupp, H.H. (1980). Success and failure in time-limited psychotherapy: further evidence. Comparison IV. *Archives of General Psychiatry, 37,* 947–954.

Wolgien, C.S., & Coady, N.F. (1997). Good therapists' beliefs about the development of their help-ing ability: the Wounded Healer paradigm revisited. *The Clinical Supervisor, 15*(2), 19–35.

11

THE NATURE
AND FUNCTION
OF PSYCHOSOCIAL
HISTORY[1]

Carol A. Stalker

HISTORY AND EVOLUTION OF THE
CONCEPT OF PSYCHOSOCIAL HISTORY

Not all social workers use the term "psychosocial history" to describe the gathering of information that is integral to social work practice. Mary Richmond (1917), in her pioneering efforts to describe social work practice, wrote that the initial process involved the collection of "social evidence." For her, the social worker formulated a social diagnosis based on inferences drawn from the social evidence, and the social diagnosis led to the development of a social treatment plan.

Several decades later, Florence Hollis (1972) wrote that the most suitable treatment plan always rested on a "psychosocial study." For Hollis, psychosocial study "is a process of observation and classification of the facts observed about a client and his situation with the purpose of securing as much information as is needed to understand the client and his problem and to guide treatment wisely" (251).

In the 1960s and 1970s, many social work writers and practitioners rejected the use of the word *diagnosis*, believing that it suggested an undesirable focus on individual pathology, and symbolized a "medical model" type of casework (Hollis, 1972). *Diagnosis* was frequently replaced with *assessment*, and conceptualizations of social work that borrowed from Dewey's principles of problem-solving gained favour (Compton & Galaway, 1994, 49).[2] Currently, many social work texts conceptualize direct practice as a problem-solving process, and the terms used to label the stages reflect this perspective. For example, Hepworth, Rooney, & Larsen (1997) describe the social work helping process as having three phases,

---

[1] As will become clear to the reader of this chapter, I argue that what some social workers term "psychosocial history" is essentially the same as what others call "data collection," or "exploring the problem." It is a basic component of social work assessment.

[2] Helen Harris Perlman acknowledged that she was "heavily indebted" to Dewey for the development of her ideas of problem-solving. (Perlman, 1957, p. 60).

the first one including exploration, engagement, assessment, and planning, the second involving implementation and goal attainment, and the third requiring termination and evaluation. Within this problem-solving framework, what was once called "the collection of social evidence" and later "psychosocial study" or "psychosocial history" becomes the gathering of "data" and "exploring the problem." This changing language reflects our profession's search for a more scientific approach to practice in a world that has put high value on the scientific method and on the ideals of objectivity and rationality.

The social work literature emphasizes that social work has a dual focus—the person in her/his environment. Attention to context and systems is essential, and consequently the worker must obtain information, including historical information, to adequately understand the interactions between the client system and its environment. Social workers, however, vary in the amount, detail and type of psychosocial history or "data" that they collect as part of the assessment process. The information that is considered relevant depends on such factors as the reason the client[3] comes for help, the nature of the practice setting, the client's wishes for service and the social worker's theoretical orientation. Furthermore, the gathering of information about the individual, couple, or family is not limited to the initial contacts. Social workers no longer see assessment as confined to the first phase of social work intervention, but rather as a process that continues throughout the interaction between the social worker and client. As the social worker conveys empathy and acceptance of the client, and the therapeutic alliance strengthens, the client often discloses additional information. Over time, as the worker seeks to understand the client and the situation more completely, she may ask for more detail about past events, or about how the client is currently perceiving and interpreting her or his experiences.

FACTORS AFFECTING THE NATURE AND FUNCTION OF THE DATA GATHERED

Mailick (1991), in an excellent analysis of assessment in clinical social work practice, notes that while "there is a basic unity in the principles of social work clinical practice," (12) different practice settings have different assessment processes. She also observes that in addition to the nature and scope of agency service, a social worker's theoretical and value orientation as well as the "unit of attention" are likely to have significant determining effects on assessment . Unit of attention refers to the level of complexity of the identified client. Is the social worker focusing on an individual, a couple, a family, or a small group?

The nature and scope of the agency service sets the parameters and focus of the social worker's relationship with the client. Consequently, it plays a primary role in the nature and function of the information and history that is gathered. For example, when the service being offered is one of primary prevention, the information required is usually limited to ascertaining that the potential client meets the criteria for inclusion in the program. A group program offered at a school for children in families experiencing marital separation or divorce may require only the parent's permission and confirmation that the child is one of the targeted group. During the course of the group, the worker might seek additional information from the parent, child and/or teachers (with appropriate consent) if a child seems especially troubled or upset.

---

[3] The singular is used here, but applies to situations where the "client" is a couple or family.

The collection of basic demographic data and recent history are usually required to determine whether an individual or family will even become a client. Information related to the nature or severity of the presenting problem is often necessary to determine whether the agency approached can provide the most appropriate service. Other factors, such as place of residence, ability to pay, current abuse of substances, or amount of previous intervention also can determine whether an individual will be accepted as a client or referred to another agency. Restrictions on the type of client problems served and residency requirements have recently become more common in Canada as agency funding has been decreased.

Space limitations restrict the degree to which all the possible combinations and interactions of practice setting, theoretical and value orientations, and the unit of attention can be discussed. Cases from two practice settings, focusing on different units of attention, and served by social workers with differing theoretical approaches will be used to illustrate how these factors interact to determine the nature and function of psychosocial history.[4] Common elements will be identified and discussed, and the chapter will conclude with a brief discussion of how postmodern and social constructivist perspectives have influenced social work theorizing about psychosocial history.

INDIVIDUAL PSYCHODYNAMIC APPROACH IN A MENTAL HEALTH CLINIC

Case 1

The client, Mrs. T., referred herself to a mental health clinic. The following is the information gathered in the initial interview.

> Mrs. T. is a 25-year-old married Caucasian woman who took a position as an executive assistant in a law firm about one month ago. Her husband is a computer analyst. They have no children. She is seeking help at this time because she has been depressed for approximately two months. She is sleeping more than usual, is having difficulty concentrating and is frequently tearful. When asked, she acknowledged that she has suicidal thoughts, but stated that she would not act on them. Her family physician prescribed antidepressant medication two weeks ago.
>
> Mrs. T. sought professional help for depressive episodes on two occasions while she was an undergraduate university student. She also saw a therapist at a local hospital for 3–4 sessions about 10 months ago when she described herself as being very depressed. She was placed on antidepressants at that time and seemed to recover quickly. On that occasion she had been depressed for approximately four months prior to seeking help. She says that previous therapists have used a cognitive-behavioural approach, which she felt was of some benefit, but she is now thinking that perhaps she needs a different approach. She feels that she lacks self-esteem and a clear sense of who she is and what she wants.
>
> Mrs. T. lives with her husband in an apartment in a small Canadian city. They have been married about two years. She describes her husband as loving and supportive. She indicated that they have a lot of debts, mostly related to their university educations. She

---

[4] The cases described are composites of several cases, and do not describe any one person or family. I wish to thank Kathleen Wheeler M.S.W. and Sheila Rodger-Faucher M.S.W. for their assistance in the composition of the case material.

feels that it is important that she work to help pay off these debts. They met when both were in university and lived together for about two years before marrying. Both families supported the marriage.

Mrs. T. is the second of three children. She has a brother five years older and a brother three years younger. Both brothers are married and apparently functioning well. She describes her mother as an introspective woman who was frustrated with her inability to pursue a career. Her mother suffered from a chronic painful illness. The client said, "We took turns looking after each other." The client reports that her mother sought psychotherapy for herself when she was a child, but was never hospitalized for emotional reasons. Her mother is still living, and she feels they currently get along well.

The client described her father as a hard-working executive who was very critical of co-workers and acquaintances. She recalls that her parents had few visitors. Mrs. T. feels that her father was more indulgent with her, but was very strict and demanding of her brothers. He died several years ago after a lengthy illness. Mrs. T. feels she was able to grieve her father's death.

She recalls that there was much conflict between her parents when she was an adolescent. Both parents would talk to her about their unhappiness with each other. Mrs. T. acknowledged that she felt caught in the middle and pulled both ways in terms of her loyalty. She also mentioned some struggles with her mother around food during adolescence, but she was never treated for an eating disorder. She currently finds it hard to eat when she is depressed or anxious.

The client said that she has always been a good student, although she had a difficult time with classmates in elementary school. She describes being the target of a lot of teasing and bullying. She has always been more comfortable with adults. She has an undergraduate degree in English, and training in human resource development.

Mrs. T. has had some difficulty coping with previous employment. Her first job, in a hospital, required that she spend long hours engaged in employee training. Because of the distance to the job, she lived separately from her husband during the week. She increasingly found the job very demanding. She describes becoming very depressed, and leaving the position after six months. A few months later, she was feeling better and took a short contract position, again involving staff development. She describes again working long hours, being treated poorly and feeling very unappreciated. Shortly after this contract ended she again became depressed, but did look for work and as mentioned is currently employed as an executive assistant. In the new job, she feels that she is performing adequately, but worries that her depression will interfere with future performance. She also sees this position as one that does not challenge her.

Mrs. T. sees herself as always having had low self-esteem and recognizes that she is very self-critical. She knows from her experiences with cognitive behavioural therapies that her negative thoughts about herself are not rational, but she finds she cannot change them. She does not wish to involve her husband in therapy. She sees the problem as largely her own.

Mrs T. impresses as above average in intelligence. She reports that her physical health is good, with no history of serious illness. She acknowledged that she values being independent, and having to seek help is difficult for her.

Why did the social worker gather this information, and not other kinds of information? As in any setting, the worker began by asking the client to share information about what brought her to the clinic, and how long she has been aware of the problem. Knowing how the client defines the problem, and how she has tried to solve it are important in assessing the client's strengths and in considering treatment options. In this case, the client has labelled herself as depressed. The worker asks for more information about what she means by this term, and learns that the client is experiencing some of the common symptoms of clinical depression. She also learns that the client has sought help from her family physician and is taking antidepressant medication. She appropriately asks about suicidal thoughts because it is important to assess suicidal risk, especially when individuals report feeling depressed. That the client has sought help from a mental health agency before, and experienced some benefit is helpful in understanding how the client has come to the conclusion that she may benefit from a "different" approach. Her statement that she lacks self-esteem and a sense of who she is suggests that she hopes to achieve change in these areas as well as in her level of depression.

That Mrs. T. came alone and not with her husband is an important factor. She is defining the problem as concerning herself, and not related to her relationship with her husband. The social worker, mindful that depression in women is often associated with marital problems, asked about her relationship with her husband, and saw questions about the history of that relationship and Mrs. T's feelings about her husband, as important. The worker did suggest that an interview with her husband might be helpful, but the client was quite clear that she preferred to work, at least initially, on her own.

The details that were gathered about the client's family of origin, education, and employment history can be seen as related to the worker's theoretical orientation.

Working from a psychodynamic orientation, this worker assumes that knowledge of early experiences with parents and siblings will be important in understanding this young woman's tendency to be self-critical and devaluing of herself. This information is also helpful in assessing her strengths and coping style, and the type of intervention that will be most helpful.

In this case, the history confirms that the client has many strengths. She is above average in intelligence and demonstrates initiative and determination. She has successfully negotiated post-secondary education, and has been able to secure employment in a difficult job market. She has sought help when her own efforts to cope with her depression have not been successful. The worker learns that the client felt that her father expected less of her than of her brothers, and that the only other female in the family, her mother, was a source of frustration to her father because he saw her as weak and dependent. This leads the worker to hypothesize that Mrs. T. may be dealing with conflicting messages about her ability to be successful in the world of work, or perhaps fears that becoming a successful career woman will be painful to her mother. Ambivalence about independence and powerful positions for women is a common theme in the traditionally patriarchal Canadian culture in which Mrs. T. has been raised. The family attitudes can be seen as reflecting that larger social structure.

The client's report of problems in relationships with other children indicates that internalized negative self and object representations may have contributed to problems in interpersonal relationships even in childhood. The nature of the problem in employment situations is unclear. The history suggests that the client pushes herself very hard but ends up feeling discouraged either with her own performance or with others' feedback. The worker wonders to what degree the client has been exposed to particularly unrewarding employment environments, and to what degree the client's expectations of employment may be unrealistic.

A clear environmental stress is the debt load that the client and her husband are carrying. The worker recognizes that it may be fruitful to explore further what this means to the client, and how much of her anxiety and sense of despair may be related to this pressure.

The history obtained about the client's experience with her family of origin also leads to some hypotheses about factors that may be contributing to her depression. It is possible that the client has learned to be very critical of herself, and possibly others, from her father's behaviour. Having become the confidante of both parents, she may have felt responsible to solve her parents' marital problems. Her inability to do this may have reinforced a sense of inadequacy. Her mother's illness apparently interfered with the mother's ability to be a consistent caretaker for the client. This may have contributed to doubts for Mrs. T. about her worthiness to be cared for, or possibly, discomfort around depending on others.

To summarize: in a mental health setting, a worker, using a psychodynamic theoretical orientation where the unit of attention is an individual, will gather information related to the client's understanding of the problem and her intra-psychic, interpersonal, and environmental experiences. Information about individual personality organization, past experiences, repetitive patterns, current functioning and family dynamics is the focus. (Mailick, 1991; Woods & Hollis, 1990). [5] This information guides the social worker as she talks with the client about the goals for treatment and the type of treatment likely to be of benefit. In the case described, the worker agreed with the client that the depression and tendency to be self-critical and self-devaluing seemed related. The history indicated that the client was able to reflect on her inner life, and already had some insight into the dynamics of her depression. The worker concluded that she would benefit from an insight-oriented approach where attention to the transference in the therapeutic relationship, and to patterns in her interpersonal relationships would clarify the key conflictual issues, and lead to their resolution.

A social worker employed in the same agency but working from a cognitive-behavioural theoretical orientation would gather similar information about the client's definition of the problem, her symptoms, the history of the depression, previous help-seeking, and physical health. However, conceptualizing that the depression is associated with "depressionogenic schemata" (Williams, 1984, 17, as cited in Schwartz & Schwartz, 1993), leading to negative cognitions, the social worker would focus more on the client's thoughts and assumptions about herself and her situation. The past is explored "only to the extent necessary to understand the present" (Schwartz & Schwartz, 1993, 248). Once it was established that the client was indeed suffering from depression, a standardized measure of depression might be administered to indicate the level of depression at the time of assessment and for use as a baseline measure from which to gauge change as treatment progresses.

FAMILY THERAPY IN THE CONTEXT OF A CHILD AND ADOLESCENT TREATMENT CENTRE

Family therapy is commonly used in settings in which the identified client is a child or adolescent. The history that is obtained and how it is used in such settings will vary according to the model of family therapy that the social worker finds most applicable. Below is a description of a family who was seen at a treatment centre for children and youth by a white, Canadian-born social worker with training in structural family therapy (Minuchin, 1974).

---

[5] In many mental health settings in Canada a psychiatrist will assign a formal diagnosis when the client's symptoms and functioning correspond to criteria for diagnosis according to DSMIV. Although social workers are familiar with this diagnostic manual, many provinces restrict the authority of social workers to formally diagnose.

Case 2

The intake worker at the treatment centre took the following information over the telephone:

> Mrs. B., an Afro-Canadian, called asking for help with her 15-year-old son, Jason. He is in Grade 10 at a local high school. The school has called Mrs. B. numerous times to report that Jason is absent. When he does attend school his homework is not done, and he has been disrespectful to teachers. At home, Jason spends most of his time in his room listening to music. Mrs. B. fears that he has been using drugs. On one occasion the police came to the house to interview Jason. Some boys with whom Jason spends time had been caught shoplifting, and the police wanted to question Jason as to whether he knew where they were hiding the stolen items. Jason insisted that he knew nothing about it.

> Mrs. B. explained that she had given birth to Jason as a single woman when she was 18 years of age and living in her native Grenada. Shortly after his birth she had come to Canada to work as a nanny, leaving her son in the care of her mother. Although she wrote and called frequently, she did not see him again until he was ten, by which time she had been able to put herself through nursing school and obtain a nursing position that allowed her to support them both. Two years ago, she married an Afro-Canadian man who has custody of his two children aged nine and twelve years. Mr. B. is an accountant. Because of his financial success, the family has moved into a more affluent neighbourhood and Mrs. B. is now working only part-time. At first it appeared that Jason liked his stepfather and new siblings, and was pleased about his mother's marriage. However, in the last year he has become more withdrawn and Mrs. B. finds he will not talk with her. The intake worker asked all family members, including Mrs. B., her husband, the two younger children and Jason, to attend the first session.

Prior to the first session, the worker assigned to the family met with her supervisor. Together they formulated the following hypotheses from the information obtained by the intake worker:

1. Mrs. B. is having difficulty allowing her husband to have a parental relationship with her son, and Mr. B. is having difficulty adjusting to the role of stepfather to an adolescent, especially since he has no experience with a child of this age. If Jason and his mother established some closeness during the three-year period that the two of them were on their own, they may both be having difficulty adjusting to the change from a single-parent family to a two-parent family. Jason may also be having difficulty accepting that his mother has a relationship with her husband that does not include him, and he may also resent having to share his mother with two other children.

2. The family move and the developmental issues of adolescence have reactivated for Jason unresolved feelings around the loss of his grandmother. He was able to tolerate this loss as long as his mother was continuously available to him and he felt she needed him, but as this seems to have changed and as he confronts the expectations that he be more independent, he is angry, afraid, and depressed.

3. Jason is experiencing academic and social difficulties in his new high school where issues of achievement and cultural expectations are different from those with which he is familiar, and where he is one of only a few black students. He may be experiencing discrimination, or fear of rejection because of race and cultural differences.

Structural family therapists stress the importance of joining and accommodating the family. In this case, the worker's efforts to join with the family were facilitated by the fact that the worker had informed herself of West Indian cultures by exploration of the literature and personal and professional experiences with members of these cultures. She knew, therefore, that in many of these cultures, the authority of the parents is highly valued and children are expected to demonstrate respect for their parents. In some families, children are taught not to establish direct eye contact when addressing parents and other adults. With this knowledge in mind, the worker greeted each family member warmly, and began by asking each of the parents to give their view of the problem. The worker then asked the parents if it would be acceptable to them if she were to ask the children to share their view of the problem. In this way, the worker acknowledged the parents' authority in the family, and her respect for their cultural norms.

The worker was keenly aware that the racial and cultural differences between herself and her clients were potential obstacles to an optimal "joining" with the family, and to an accurate assessment of the problem. Her appreciation of the racism and discrimination experienced by people of colour in Canada led her to recognize that the hypotheses she had formulated might need revision as she gained further understanding of how systemic injustices were impacting this family. She resolved to look for an opportunity to acknowledge this possibility, and to ask the family members about their experiences of discrimination.

As the family members discussed their perception of why they had come to the agency, the worker encouraged an "enactment" of interaction between and among family members. Based on observed interactions, she gathered evidence for or against the previously formulated hypotheses, at the same time considering the possibility that other hypotheses would be more accurate.

The worker observed that whenever Mr. B. attempted to offer a suggestion or idea to a discussion about Jason, Mrs. B. would interrupt him. Also, Jason was very quiet in the session, but did state that since his mother was so upset with him, he had been thinking of returning to Grenada. Mr. B. responded to this by saying that he felt that would be a mistake as the opportunities for a good education were much better here. Jason spoke of the "stupidity" of the teachers in his new school and how "boring" most of the kids were. At this point, 12-year-old Samantha said, "You're just scared they won't like you."

As the worker observed further interaction and responses to her questions, she concluded that there was support for the hypothesis that Mr. and Mrs. B. were having difficulty in establishing a functional parental subsystem in the "blended" family. There was also support for the third hypothesis. The new school, known for its emphasis on academics, was different from the school that Jason had previously attended. In the last school, Jason's academic achievements had been average, and he obtained a sense of accomplishment primarily from participation in sports activities. In the new school, Jason did not yet feel included in the athletic sphere, and appeared to be missing the sense of belonging he experienced in the previous school. The worker asked Jason directly about how it felt to be one of only a few black students in the new school. He acknowledged that he felt uncomfortable, scared, and sometimes afraid he would appear stupid.

The worker encouraged other family members to talk about their experiences with discrimination. She watched as Jason showed interest when Mr. B. shared his experiences of racist comments and more subtle forms of discrimination, and when he said he continues to feel very angry about the way young, black males are stereotyped. The worker thanked Mr. B. for his honesty, and asked Jason if he had found his stepfather's comments helpful. When Jason agreed that they were, the worker encouraged Jason to talk with his stepfather again when these experiences troubled him. She suggested that Mr. B. could be very helpful to Jason since he knew from personal experience what it was like to be young, male, and black. Mr. B. agreed.

The worker also encouraged each parent and the children to talk about their experience in the original families and the way they had done things before the creation of the new family. Mr. B. and his two children talked about some of the routines and rituals that they had engaged in when they were on their own. Similarly, Jason and Mrs. B. shared some of the patterns and habits they had developed together. All family members were encouraged to talk about the hopes and fantasies that each had for the new family. The intent was to help the family to more clearly recognize that everyone was feeling the loss of the old family, and to have more understanding of the specifics of each other's difficulties in making the adjustment to the new way of doing things.

In contrast to some other settings, the initial psychosocial history in this case was taken over the telephone by an intake worker. This practice allows the social worker to move quickly to the formulation and testing of hypotheses, and also to a greater focus on interaction patterns and dysfunctional family structures. In the first session with the family, the worker does not engage in a structured, fact-finding interview, but rather encourages an immediate "enactment" of family communication. In the course of the treatment of the family, the worker learns more about the family history of both parents, significant events in the histories of the children, and the norms, values, and "culture" of the family. But, in contrast to some other approaches, this is not the primary emphasis in the first interview, or even in later sessions.

Workers who follow what have been referred to as the "historically oriented approaches to family therapy" (Hoffman, 1981), such as that developed by Murray Bowen, would spend comparatively more time in the initial sessions gathering data about the history of the nuclear family and the history of the extended family system. The family diagram or genogram is often used to clarify patterns originating in the past which may be contributing to inadequate differentiation from the core families (Kerr & Bowen, 1988).

SUMMARY OF COMMON AND VARIABLE FACTORS IN DATA COLLECTION

A review of these two cases underscores the reality that the gathering of some data and background information is a crucial component of social work practice regardless of agency setting, theoretical orientation, or the unit of attention. One commonality is that the gathering of data begins with a search to understand the client's definition of the problem, and what the client has already done to help him or herself. Clearly, different settings and different theoretical orientations affect the language and emphasis of even this initial category of information. However, all approaches begin with attention to the problem that the client identifies.

A second common thread is that the social worker uses the data she collects to formulate hypotheses about what events, experiences, and attributed meanings are contributing to the client's distress. These hypotheses guide the focus of additional data gathering, and the decisions about what is relevant information.

A third common factor is that data collection continues throughout the entire helping process, and not just in the beginning phases. In both cases, the need for more and/or different kinds of information became apparent. As initial hypotheses are either supported or rejected, the worker reevaluates the need for more information, and modifies the direction of her response accordingly.

Although the idea that the psychosocial history leads to working hypotheses that lead to further data-gathering can be applied across agency settings, theoretical orientations, and units of attention, these cases also make clear that the worker's theoretical orientation and perspective on human development will significantly affect the nature of the hypotheses that she formulates, and the information that she will judge necessary to test her hypotheses. The most obvious continuum is that related to the attention given to past events, developmental milestones, and patterns across generations. But there are also differences related to the attention to specific thoughts, to specific behaviours, to discussion of feelings, and to the structure and process of the interview as opposed to its content.

The gathering of information from persons other than the client or family who presents for social work assistance is another aspect that varies. In mental health settings, a request for reports of previous treatment and hospitalizations, psychological testing, and medical reports is common. These are obtained only with the client's consent, and only when the client and worker agree that such reports will assist the current intervention. When children are involved, workers sometimes obtain information from a teacher or the family physician. In adult cases, information from an employer, member of the clergy, or a friend will assist the worker's understanding of how others perceive the client or family and her/their situation. Workers in child welfare settings and in a variety of other agencies regularly make visits to the homes of clients. This is another source of information about the socioeconomic and cultural realities of the individual or family. Observing the interaction of family members in their own territory frequently enhances the worker's understanding of the family system, the subsystems, and the individuals involved.

POSTMODERN/SOCIAL CONSTRUCTIVIST PERSPECTIVES

Ideas about the nature and function of psychosocial history, like other aspects of practice, have recently been influenced by postmodern perspectives and social constructivist philosophy. Social constructivists reject the concept of an objective reality, and stress the "intersubjectivity" of knowing. They argue that humans are "active shapers of their reality" (Weick, 1993, 18) so that knowledge "becomes a matter of the meanings assigned to experience" (Laird, 1995, 151), rather than incontestable fact or "truth." A social worker's perception and understanding is always filtered through previous personal and professional "stories" or "narratives" (theories). Likewise, it is the meaning that family members and individuals attribute to events or how they "story" their lives that determines their behaviour.

Applying the constructivist perspective, Michael White and David Epston have argued that problems should not be conceptualized as originating inside people or even in the relationship between people. Problems are seen as having been created or constructed by a dominant family, cultural, or societal ideology or narrative. A technique called "externalizing the problem" encourages the family to objectify and personify the problem that brings them to a helping agency, thereby turning its meaning into something less fixed and less limiting. (White & Epston, 1990, 38). The demonstration for family members that there are alternative ways of thinking and talking about the problem allows the family to adopt some perspective on the "dominant stories" that have been influencing their lives. Questions about when the problem has not occurred, that is, "historical unique outcomes," further demonstrate that there have been experiences that contradict or are incompatible with the dominant "problem-saturated" story, and that these unique outcomes can be used to construct an alternative story about the person's life. For example, when a family, including the "problem" child, is helped to recognize that the child does not always throw a temper tantrum when he is disappointed, they are one step closer to revising their personal and relationship histories, and withdrawing the negative labels and interpretations they have applied to the child.

Constructivist writers point out that traditional approaches to assessment, which assume that "facts" must be collected, have led to the development of structured formats for collecting information and psychosocial history (Dean, 1993). Following such structures may result in an account of the client and the problem that loses sight of the client's sense of what is important. "One of the major challenges in getting to know clients is to find ways to balance our questions, attempts at clarification and 'history taking' with their efforts to tell us what they consider important" (Dean, 1993, 135). Laird (1995) argues that terms such as *diagnosis* and *assessment* assume an "expert 'knower'" who is able to detect the meaning of the past and present experience of another (157). Such a mind-set, she argues, inhibits understanding because it leads to attempts to fit the client's narrative to the worker's "preunderstanding" and method of making sense of the world (157). Assessment, it is argued, should be defined as a collaborative approach to problem formulation, and the worker's role is "to raise questions that promote an exploration of the current situation (or concern) and expand the limits of understanding" (Dean, 1993, 131).

These changes in the language and the conceptualization of what we are doing with clients clearly do not change the need to talk with the client about her/his perception of the problem and the preceding events that seem relevant. Laird (1995) says, "The client's history is as important for its narrative as it is for its factual truth" (157). By referring to the client's history as a "narrative," this perspective makes clear that what clients tell us is an interpretation of experience rather than historical truth (Dean, 1993).

In the "modernist" era, the function of the psychosocial history was one of providing data for the generation of causal hypotheses, which if supported by further data, led to specific interventions. In the "postmodernist" era, the function of the psychosocial history is to initiate a conversation between the client(s) and the social worker which leads to discussions about whether there may be other ways of telling the story, or other meanings to be taken from it. Social work intervention becomes a working together with the client to revise the old story, and to find new ways of framing the dilemmas so that the client will be able to take new actions and recognize new possibilities.

Many social workers react to the discussion of the constructivist perspective by pointing out that the implications for practice derived from this perspective are not new, and that many of the ideas are familiar (Dean, 1993; Laird, 1995). This familiarity may be related to social work's historic emphasis on the "relationship" and on the principle of self-determination. Social workers have in common a basic socialization into the values of the profession which includes respect for the individual and her/his right to make decisions that affect her/his life. Perhaps the values of the profession have, at least to some degree, provided a balance to the modernist pressure to see ourselves as scientific, objective, and pursuers of "truth." The sensitivity to context which is a key idea in the constructivist position is certainly not new to social work. Furthermore, one can bring together constructivist practices with more traditional ways of working with clients. To do so, however, forces one to acknowledge that our knowledge is "constructed" and perhaps only applicable to certain contexts. Such a perspective leads to more humility and willingness to consider that other forms of knowledge and ways of interpreting the world may also be useful and effective (Dean, 1993).

In a country like Canada, which has historically attempted to be respectful of different languages, different values, different religions, and different ways of knowing, the constructivist perspective is not radical. And for the profession of social work, challenges to usual ways of thinking are not new. Mailick (1991) wrote: "a universally accepted principle in clinical social work practice is that it is important to gather some data about clients and their situations in order to provide service" (3). The cases and literature reviewed in this chapter support that statement. But there are only a few constants and considerable variation in terms of what kind of data is gathered. This chapter has attempted to identify the commonalities in the function of psychosocial history, and to demonstrate that the nature of the practice setting, the unit of attention, the theoretical orientation of the worker, and more recently, even the philosophical perspective of the worker determine both the nature of the data gathered, as well as how these data are used in social work practice.

REFERENCES

Compton, B.R., & Galaway, B. (1994). *Social work processes.* (5th ed.). Pacific Grove, CA: Brooks/Cole.

Dean, R.G. (1993). Constructivism: an approach to clinical practice. *Smith College Studies in Social Work, 63* (2), 127–146.

Hepworth, D.H., Rooney, R.H., & Larsen, J. (1997). *Direct social work practice.* (5th ed.). Pacific Grove CA: Brooks/Cole.

Hollis, F. (1972). *Casework: a psychosocial therapy.* (2nd ed.). New York: Random House.

Hoffman, L. (1981). *Foundations of family therapy.* New York: Basic Books.

Kerr, M. & Bowen, M. (1988). *Family evaluation: an approach based on Bowen theory.* New York: Norton.

Laird, J. (1995). Family-centered practice in the postmodern era. *Families in society*, 150–162.

Mailick, M.D. (1991). Re-assessing assessment in clinical social work practice. *Smith College Studies in Social Work, 62*, (1), 3–19.

Minuchin, S. (1974). *Families and family therapy.* Cambridge MA: Harvard University Press.

Perlman, H.H. (1957). *Social casework: a problem solving process.* Chicago: University of Chicago Press.

Richmond, M. (1917). *Social diagnosis.* New York: Russell Sage Foundation.

Schwartz, A. & Schwartz, R. (1993). *Depression: Theories and treatments.* New York: Columbia University Press.

Weick, A. (1993). Reconstructing social work education. In J. Laird (Ed.). *Revisioning social work education: A social constructionist approach.* New York: Haworth, pp. 11–30.

White, M. & Epston, D. (1990). *Narrative means to therapeutic ends.* New York: Norton & Co.

Woods, M.E. & Hollis, F. (1990). *Casework: a psychosocial therapy.* (4th ed.). New York: McGraw-Hill.

THE NATURE
AND FUNCTION
OF ASSESSMENT

Nora Gold

WHAT IS ASSESSMENT?

Out of the many different definitions of *assessment* that exist, one that stands out as particularly clear and concise is Ivry's (1992, 3): "gathering, synthesizing, and evaluating pertinent information to design an appropriate and effective intervention strategy." This definition reflects the traditional social work understanding of assessment as the first phase of the helping process, a necessary first step whose function is to prepare for "treatment," or intervention (Hollis, 1964; Perlman, 1957; Richmond, 1917). More recently, the term *assessment* has also been used to refer to an ongoing activity that continues throughout the entire process (Garvin & Seabury, 1997). While it is true that one is constantly collecting and analyzing new information (assessing), it is also true that once one moves out of the exploratory stage of work and into intervention and termination, the assessment that takes place is really only a gradual reshaping and modifying of the initial assessment—in other words, assessment on a very diminished scale (Hepworth & Larsen, 1997). This chapter, therefore, will concentrate on assessment in terms of the assessment of the client in the initial stage of work. *Assessment* as used here will also refer to the *process* of assessment, rather than the *product,* which is more accurately termed the *assessment statement*, the written output that usually concludes the assessment process.

The term *assessment* is also closely related to two other terms: *diagnosis* and *psychosocial history*, and it is important to distinguish at the outset between them, especially given the location of this chapter between these other two. *Psychosocial history* is one kind of social work assessment: the traditional social work assessment developed by Mary Richmond, and then built on by Perlman, Hollis, and others. However, it is only one kind, something that is sometimes forgotten, and like other forms of social work assessment, it has both its strengths and its weaknesses (Mattaini & Kirk, 1991).

The term *diagnosis* also came into social work through Mary Richmond (specifically with the concept of *social diagnosis*) (Richmond, 1917), and historically the terms *assessment* and *diagnosis* were considered virtually synonymous. In recent years, however, *diagnosis* has fallen into disfavour because of its "association with symptoms, disease, and deficits" (Hepworth, Rooney, & Larsen, 1997, 194). More specifically, there is concern about its association with the medical model, which focuses on individual problems rather than person-environment interactions, as well as the dangers of labelling people, which may result in stereotyping and/or stigmatization (Garvin & Seabury, 1997; Mattaini & Kirk, 1991).

Assessment is an essential part of social work practice, and precedes intervention at all levels, whether with individuals, families, groups, organizations, or communities. Regardless of the size of the client system, however, the process of assessment involves the same two activities: data collection and data analysis. Intimidating as these may at first sound, data is just another word for information, and both data collection and data analysis are activities that we engage in hundreds of times a day, often without even thinking about it.

For example, driving to work one day, you get within a few blocks of your office and notice that the streets are heavily lined with cars, which is unusual for that part of town (*data collection #1*). You interpret this as a problem, because if you have to spend ten minutes circling to find a spot, you will be late for your staff meeting, and you have already been late twice this week for work (*data analysis #1*). Frantically you look around, and up ahead you spot a parking lot you had forgotten all about (*data collection #2*). This seems to you to be a good solution to your problem, since paying for a day's parking is less costly to you than the cost to your professional credibility if you are late for the third time in one week (*data analysis #2*). As a result of this assessment process, you pull into the parking lot.

As this example illustrates, the two processes, data collection and data analysis, occur sequentially but often in very close succession (i.e., the data is analyzed seconds after it is collected, not days or weeks). We are constantly interpreting; and often (as in this example) there is a certain circularity in the interaction between the two processes, whereby the analysis (*data analysis #1*) may prompt the need to collect additional data (*data collection #2*). Despite the close and almost constant interaction between them, however, we will discuss these two activities independently in order to more deeply probe their properties. Accordingly, this chapter is divided into two sections: one on data collection and one on data analysis, and within each section, the issues of values and knowledge will be discussed. Before that, however, it is important to reflect on two factors pertaining to organizational context that also influence the assessment process, and these are the worker's setting and role.

THE WORKER'S CONTEXT: SETTING AND ROLE

The type of setting within which one works will significantly shape the data one collects as well as how these data are interpreted. Agencies often have their own assessment guidelines, and in some cases even their own forms, so clear are they on precisely what information they need in order to plan for intervention. Agencies may differ from each other on their assessments because of differences in mandate, philosophy, theoretical orientation, and intervention approach, and each agency collects data that will be relevant to the services it provides. For example, if the same client, Brian, goes to a social worker (1) at an alcohol relapse prevention program, (2) at his son's school, and (3) at a private clinic for marital counselling, he will be asked to provide significantly different data about himself, and these will be differently interpreted. Although there might be some overlap between them, the first assessment would focus primarily on his relationship with alcohol, the second on his relationship with his son and his son's behaviour problems at school, and the third on his marriage.

Furthermore, even the same agency will change the way it conducts its assessments if there is a change in any of the four variables mentioned above. For example, an agency known to this author "restructured" a few years ago, largely for financial reasons, and changed their intervention approach: instead of offering individual, marital, and family counselling, they began offering only groups to their clients. Within several months, their assessment forms were revised in order to include questions about clients' previous experiences with groups, and whether or not they would be receptive to groupwork intervention. Even more striking, however, was that whatever these clients wrote about themselves and their problems was interpreted in terms of their suitability for a group at the agency, and the vast majority of workers concluded in their assessment statements that the psychosocial needs of this particular client could be ideally met in one or another of the agency's groups! There is an old saying: "Give a kid a hammer, and the whole world will need hammering." Perhaps one could also say, "Give an agency a certain intervention approach...."[1]

Similarly, one's role in the agency will influence the assessment process. The same social worker in the same agency will collect different data and interpret them differently, depending on his or her role. Susan, an intake worker at a child protection agency, conducts her assessment in order to ascertain whether or not a certain applicant is appropriate for service. She will therefore ask questions about the nature of the problem (including, for example, if the child is at immediate risk), demographic criteria for service provision, such as the child's age or catchment area, and other questions consistent with this purpose. On the other hand, if Susan switches units and goes to work in long-term care within the same agency, she may well be conducting assessments in order to determine whether or not to remove children from their homes. Because of the difference in purpose related to her role, in this case she will need to collect significantly more information than she did as an intake worker, and she will need to analyze it far more comprehensively and in greater depth.

Role and setting, then, provide the organizational context within which assessment occurs, and influence both data collection and data analysis. These two processes will now be discussed in some detail.

DATA COLLECTION

What Data Do You Collect, *Why*, and *How*?

Although some beginning practitioners might think they should just try to gather as much information as possible about the client, there are two reasons to be selective in data collection, one practical, the other ethical. Practically speaking, time is limited, and especially in the current economic climate, leisurely in-depth assessments are increasingly a luxury most agencies cannot afford. Secondly, many of our clients come to us in crises or in stressful,

---

[1] One's setting will also affect one's assessment in terms of whether or not social work is the primary discipline there. A social worker in a hospital setting, for example, will have to interpret the data in terms that will be comprehensible and acceptable to his or her colleagues in that context.

Setting can also be more broadly interpreted in terms of the structure of service delivery. The introduction of managed care in the U.S., for example, completely altered the nature of private practice, including the assessment process (Brown, 1996). Political, social, and economic ideology all shape one's assessment (Brown, 1996); so in this sense the Canadian context, differing from the U.S. in its ideology and assumptions about the role of the State, can also be understood as part of this discussion on "setting."

oppressive life situations, and it is unethical to spend any longer than absolutely necessary collecting information about their problems before helping them to begin to solve them (Garvin & Seabury, 1997).

Data collection begins with seeking information about the presenting problem (the adage of "starting where the client is at"). This is important because clients' continuance in counselling is related to the perception that the content that is discussed, especially in the first session, is directly relevant to the presenting problem as they see it. This means that if a couple comes in because they are worried about their child's aggressive behaviour, and the worker chooses to explore their marital relationship with them, it is essential to explain in relatively straightforward, lay terms how this is connected to the presenting problem; otherwise the couple is likely to feel that the worker is simply prying into personal, but irrelevant, areas of their life.[2] The need to remain close to the presenting problem and to work within time constraints means that every question must be a "good" one, a question that will yield meaningful data and that can be defended in terms of its relevance.[3]

The data that is collected, therefore, is initially defined by the nature of the presenting problem. If the presenting problem is a child's behaviour, data is collected about this; if the problem is a drinking problem, data is collected about that.[4] One can collect the data in a variety of different ways. In a traditional psychosocial assessment, one may use face-to-face interviews, phone interviews, observation of the interaction of the client with significant others, collateral information from significant others and professionals, psychological tests, standardized social work instruments, questionnaires, ecomaps, and genograms (Berkman et al., 1999; Compton & Galaway, 1999; Garvin & Seabury, 1997; Hartman, 1978; Hepworth & Larsen, 1997; Johnson, 1995). Nowadays there are also numerous supplements or alternatives to these methods of social work assessment, including, for example, computerized assessment instruments (Compton & Galaway, 1999; Mattaini & Kirk, 1991). Whatever tools one makes use of, however, there is no escaping the complex issues associated with knowledge and values in data collection, and the theoretical and professional decisions the worker has to make in this regard. Some of these are now discussed below.

Theoretical Framework and Data Collection

The theoretical framework used by the worker has a major impact on the data he or she collects. To use the example referred to earlier, if a couple comes in with concerns about their son Johnny's behaviour, and the social worker, Caroline, views client problems from the perspective of social learning theory, she will ask them questions about Johnny's behaviour. When it turns out that the behaviour consists of hitting other children at school, she may explore how often this occurs (about once a month) and what happens after it does (the

---

[2] To the beginning worker, it may seem paradoxical trying to collect information about a problem while still trying to define what the problem is. Perhaps it's helpful to compare looking at a presenting problem with looking through binoculars and seeing a fuzzy picture. As you gradually adjust them, as time goes by and you learn more about the situation, things look less and less fuzzy, until finally what you see is very clear and sharp. The presenting problem wasn't "wrong," just incomplete. And to "complete" it, both exploration and maintaining focus were necessary.

[3] A good question is also a question that is asked well. A well-asked question results in a rich yield of information, and is more likely to be open- rather than closed-ended, asked in a way that is non-threatening, non-judgmental, and respectful, thus facilitating the building of the worker-client relationship and the process of "joining."

[4] For examples of how to collect data pertaining to different pieces of practice knowledge (e.g., social support, life cycle, coping, ego defense), see Sheafor, Horejsi, & Horejsi (1991), chapter 10. Also see Bisman (1999), Howe et al. (1999a), & Howe, Dooley, & Hinings (1999b).

school calls Johnny's parents in for a meeting, and he gets a lot of angry attention). The same situation will be assessed very differently by Michael, who works within the framework of family systems theory. Michael will likely collect data about the family's structure and dynamics, especially the relationship between the parental and the child sub-systems, and the ways in which the interactions between them relate to the presenting problem. Perhaps, for example, there is a great deal of conflict in the marital unit, but when Johnny gets into trouble, the parents stop fighting and pull together to help him through it. Hopefully, both Caroline and Michael are aware of the theoretical frameworks that underpin their work, they have considered the trade-offs of collecting precisely these data and not any other, and recognize the implications of this for the ways they define the problem and later intervene.

Unfortunately, however, this is not always the case. Consider, in contrast, Peter, whose preferred mode of intervention with pre-schoolers is psychoanalytically-oriented play therapy, but who initially assesses the children in terms of social learning theory because in his first field placement this was the way he was taught to assess. Much of the behavioural data Peter collects will end up not being used in his actual work with the children because of the profound inconsistency between these two approaches, both theoretically and practically. In a sense, then, there is little justification for collecting this behavioural data in the first place.

In the most efficient use of data collection, all of the information that is collected gets used, and this is most likely to occur when there is a high degree of consistency between the theory used for assessment and the one used for intervention. Using the same theory for both is ideal, or even a combination of theories, as long as whatever combination is selected is used throughout the entire process (i.e., for both assessment and intervention). Some theories integrate well together, and there is no problem with taking an eclectic approach and using more than one; however, the theories must be chosen in a thoughtful way such that possible inconsistencies between them are taken into account and they complement each other's strengths and weaknesses. This is quite different, however, from just using whatever one feels comfortable with because one has used it before, internalized it, and now it has the ring of "truth." No theory, however powerful, is *true*: the same problem can be looked at through the lenses of many different theories and, like different pairs of glasses, each one changes what one sees. Compare, for example, what Michael and Caroline "saw" when they looked at the same situation with Johnny.

It is therefore very important to choose one's theoretical framework, rather than being "chosen by it." Selecting one's knowledge base should be done carefully, since the theory one chooses will profoundly affect data collection as well as the interpretation of the data and the course of the whole case. In selecting a knowledge base, one should consider:

1. the appropriateness of the choice for the phenomenon being assessed (e.g., for a task group, one would not use the knowledge base developed for therapeutic groups),

2. whether or not the knowledge base is consistent with a social work approach (e.g., some theories are very deterministic and offer little hope for change), and

3. the nature of the power the knowledge base possesses (i.e., the extent and quality of its research base)

(Hollis, 1968, adapted by Johnson, 1995).

Being conceptually clear about what theoretical framework one is using, and why, is essential for collecting the most important data that one needs for one's assessment. It also lessens the worker's dependence on long lists of variables that have to somehow be included because, in the absence of conceptual clarity, one feels the need to try and "cover all the bases" in one's assessment. Thinking carefully and critically, therefore, about one's theoretical framework may not only increase the efficiency and effectiveness of the data collection, but also may be professionally empowering for the worker.

Value Issues in Data Collection

Values influence data collection in a number of ways: through the worker's values, the client's values, and the values of the profession. The worker's values affect how much of a situation and what parts of a situation are perceived: we tend to screen out information that is not congruent with our values or our thinking, and accordingly we may miss the unfamiliar or the different (Johnson, 1995). For example, we may simply not hear a client say that she is a lesbian if that is something we do not consider a possibility, or if the idea of a gay lifestyle conflicts with our values. Accordingly, it is very important to know what one's values are, and how they might limit or obstruct the accurate and complete collection of data.

Similarly, with reference to the client's values, it is important to learn as early as possible what clients' values are, in order not to waste time and energy exploring areas that are ultimately irrelevant or meaningless to them. For example, someone known to this author was interested in buying her first car, and asked her friends to help her collect information about safe cars with good resale value, since safety and resale value, she said, were her prime concerns in a car. After weeks of work, the choice came down to only two cars that met her criteria, and she spent another week trying to decide between them. Her friends were then completely stunned, and irritated, when suddenly she turned around and bought a car of a completely different make that had failed to pass muster on either of these counts. When asked to explain herself, she admitted with great embarrassment, "Well, I wanted a car that was red. I didn't realize that until I had to actually write the cheque, and neither of those two cars we came up with came in the colour red." Bizarre as this appeared at first, what it meant was that only at the final moment of the decision did she become aware enough of her own values to discard the "sensible, rational" factors in her decision-making, and recognize the essential value that outweighed all the others. If she had been aware of her true values when she began her search, she would have saved herself (and her friends!) a great deal of trouble and time. Similarly, with a client who says she wants to find a job, but who deeply believes that it is wrong to work outside the home when she has young children, there is no point gathering information for her about the different employment or job training options. Knowing a client's values, therefore, helps to clarify what data it makes sense to collect, and equally important, what data *not* to bother collecting.

In terms of the values of the profession, two of them in particular have implications for data collection. The first is the commitment to recognize and struggle against structurally-based oppression in all its forms, including racism and ethnic discrimination. In selecting one's assessment tools, it is important to be aware that standardized instruments are often problematic when used with ethnically diverse groups, due to problems with test bias (lack of "culture-fairness"), linguistic difficulties, and the fact that these tests have been normed only on subjects belonging to the dominant culture (Gold & Bogo, 1992). Because of these problems, standardized tests that are not sensitive specifically to cultural diversity can be seen as contributing to the perpetuation of the social and economic disadvantage of ethnic minorities (Ibid.). Accordingly, when selecting how to collect one's data, careful consideration should

be given to the implications of using one method over another with regard to clients from culturally diverse backgrounds, and if a certain standardized test is chosen, it should be assessed
for culture-fairness before it is used.

The other professional value relevant to data collection is the commitment to focus on
clients' strengths, and not only on their weaknesses (Compton & Galaway, 1999; Johnson,
1995; Hepworth & Larsen, 1997; Schriver, 1998). The implication of this is that strengths
have to be searched for, they are not always obvious, and that it is the responsibility of the
worker to find them.[5] If in a certain situation the worker has trouble seeing a client's strengths,
it is worth asking what it is about this client that is problematic for the worker, and which of
the worker's own value issues might be implicated (for example, issues about class, ethnicity,
or disability). Hepworth & Larsen (1997) are correct in noting that despite the change in terminology from *diagnosis* to *assessment*, many social work assessments still focus almost
exclusively on the pathology and dysfunction of clients. With the same concern, Miley,
O'Melia, and Dubois (2001, 230) suggest conducting assessments that focus on clarifying
competencies and resources, in order to discover "not causes or reasons" in clients, but "gold."

DATA ANALYSIS

The process of data analysis, or data interpretation, is in many ways the essential work of
assessment, to which data collection has been just the preparation. The process of analyzing data differs according to what kind of data one has collected. If the presenting problem
was depression, for example, and one has used a standardized scale to measure depression, then the data analysis of this scale may be little more than adding up the client's
score. However, a sound social work assessment will very rarely begin and end with standardized instruments. It almost always includes additional data whose purpose is to put
the problem in its social context ("person-in-situation"), and ordinarily draws on a variety
of other data sources that would help explain when, and why, this client gets depressed, and
how the depression expresses itself behaviourally. So even with the help of questionnaires,
computerized assessments, and various other tools, it is still up to the worker to synthesize
and make meaning of the data.

But how does one do it? How does one take the pile of data that one has collected, and
interpret it so that it *means* something—something that can serve as the focus of work with
the client? They key to interpretation is theory, but even with theory as a resource, data
analysis can be very challenging, because there are so many theories and therefore so many
interpretive possibilities to choose from. The same situation, the same collection of data, can
be analyzed in almost an infinite variety of ways. In the example alluded to earlier with
Johnny and his family, the problem may be defined as Johnny's behaviour, the parents'
marital difficulties, or the school's inability to handle aggression in the schoolyard. Similarly,
in a Native community with a high rate of teenage suicide, the problem may be defined in
terms of an educational system that limits the hopes and options available to Native youth,

---

[5] One group worker known to this author searched and searched in vain for some strength, competency, or skill in a
very quiet boy who was usually ignored in a group she was running. Finally, after much effort, she found out that he was
good at repairing things. For several group meetings she waited for something to break so that this boy could demonstrate his skilfulness and thereby earn some admiration from the group, but nothing ever broke. Finally, after a month
of waiting, this worker came early one day to work and broke the leg of the table in the room where the group met. Sure
enough, this boy set to work and fixed the table, and after that he was treated with considerably more respect by the group.

the absence of positive role models in the community, or in terms of the sociopolitical reality for Native people in Canada.[6]

It is initially hard, though essential, to grasp the neutrality of data, the idea that data, like tofu, has no real flavour of its own. It has no *intrinsic* meaning, or "truth." Without analysis, data doesn't *mean* anything; it is empty facts; it is only the interpretations we assign to it that give it meaning. For example, one child hitting another does not intrinsically mean anything; it is our social definition (or "social construction") of this behaviour as "aggressive" that makes hitting problematic. As Hamlet put it, "There is nothing either good or bad but thinking makes it so" (Act II, Scene II). The implication of this is not that one should become cynical about data interpretation since "after all, data can be made to say anything"; but rather to understand that the interpretive act is an act of power, and therefore one must approach data analysis with both ethical and intellectual rigour.

Essential to both is the ability to recognize that one *is* interpreting, and not simply seeing "reality as it is." Obvious as this may seem, most people automatically and unthinkingly translate from fact to interpretation without even realizing they are doing this. For example, a client named Fiona says to her social worker, Carla, that she is "no good at school." Carla therefore writes in her assessment statement that Fiona has "low self-esteem." However, this is interpretation, not fact. The only fact was that Fiona stated that she is "no good at school." And there are many other ways to interpret this than the way that Carla did. For example, Fiona's statement may be a simple descriptive statement, and one that is true, with absolutely no implications for how Fiona feels about herself. Self-concept and self-esteem are not the same thing: I may know I am not very good at car repairs, but I do not particularly value this activity, and do not evaluate myself in relation to this skill, therefore it has nothing to do with how I feel about, or value, myself. Fiona may know that she is not "good at school," but not care a fig about it, and have very high self-esteem because she thinks she is a good daughter and friend. Her statement may be nothing more than a factual and accurate response to Carla's question about how she does in school. In leaping from Fiona's statement (a fact) to an interpretation of it, without even realizing she has done this, much less checking it out with her client, Carla has inaccurately assessed Fiona, and in a way that may work to Fiona's detriment.

It is crucial, therefore, to recognize that interpretation is different from fact, and to know when one is interpreting. It is also essential, as this example illustrates, to use theory and knowledge in a critical and careful way when engaged in analyzing data.

Theoretical Framework and Data Analysis

The theoretical orientation that one brings to the analysis of the data is the intellectual mold which gives the data its shape. Just as gelatin poured into a triangular mold takes on the shape of a triangle, so data, in all their shapelessness, fit themselves to the mold of the theory one uses. An immigrant family's problems are defined in terms of stresses and coping behaviours if poured into the stress-and-coping theoretical mold; as a lack of social support is fitted into social support theory; and as role loss and role strain if analyzed using role theory. As

---

[6] Any one of these problem definitions is fine, but whatever one picks will significantly shape one's intervention. In terms of the second example, for instance, one may attempt to solve the suicide problem through the educational system, through community role models, or through political action and advocacy at the national level.

previously pointed out, theory influences the data one collects, so if one has conceptual-ized using these, or any other theories, then one has probably already collected the data in the shape of that specific mold (i.e., in this case by asking about stresses and coping strate-gies, or social support, or roles). In many instances, this is sufficient for beginning to work with one's client, and for finding "the meaning of the problem" (Meyer, 1993).

In other instances, however, the theory does not fit well enough with the data to proceed with the work. While on the one hand it is true that data can be poured into any theoretical mold, doing so does not always necessarily contribute to understanding the data. It does not open anything, it does not shed any light. A Marxist analysis will not fit meaningfully with the situation of a woman who two weeks ago lost her husband and is now in an acute state of grief. In some cases the mismatch may be due to error in selecting one's knowledge base. Alternately, it may be that what initially appeared to be the problem has shifted during the process of collecting the data, necessitating now a theoretical shift as well. It is also possible that this theoretical framework was not something that was selected specifically for this par-ticular situation, but rather was something that the worker always used, and this may have been the first time that, faced with a new kind of problem, this theory did not "work."

Whatever the case, the solution to the mismatch is to intellectually tinker with different theories, trying on numerous "pairs of glasses" until one finds one that fits. "Fitting" is also a relative term: when purchasing new glasses, one does not usually stop trying on different pairs the first time one finds one that looks okay; one keeps trying on others in the hope of finding something even better. In this spirit, playing around with different theories is useful not only where the data and the theory do not seem to fit; it is also helpful even if, at first go, one seems to have found an adequate match. *Yes, with stress-and-coping I understand quite a lot about this immigrant family; but what else might I learn if I try on four or five other the-ories as well?* This in no way insults or detracts from one's own favourite theory, but it does expand one's interpretive options and enriches one's understanding of clients-in-their-situations, both in breadth and in depth.

Having theoretical options also increases the likelihood of finding an understanding of the problem that is acceptable to clients, that matches *their* theoretical perspectives. Although an issue with all clients, this is an especially important point for involuntary clients (Rooney, 1992). Clients define problems in their own ways, and will often reject definitions of their situations that they find alienating or at odds with their values and beliefs. Some couples, for example, may resist feminist therapy, but will talk willingly about "gender roles in the fam-ily" from the perspective of role theory. Theoretical tinkering gives the worker considerable conceptual flexibility and an intellectual repertoire that facilitates a highly individualized and non-dogmatic approach to analyzing clients' problems.

Value Issues in Data Analysis

While theory is one's most important ally and tool in analyzing data, values enter data analysis more as a potential impediment, a problem to be neutralized. Probably the single greatest pitfall to avoid in analyzing data is interpreting the data, without realizing it, through the personal prism of one's own values. These values may be political, religious, cultural, or other, and significantly influence how we respond to people and the information we receive about them. Generally, one tends to feel closer to people who share one's values than to those whose values differ. If one is pro-choice, for example, a female client who shares this point of view will likely seem to you to be astute and sensible. If one is pro-life, on the other hand, this same client is likely to elicit a more mixed reaction. One may feel alienated from her, or a little cool. In some cases one may also experience a certain loss of respect, or even dislike, for the person.

Natural as these feelings are, it is important to recognize how these may affect our relationships with clients. Because of the power differential between worker and client, unless we are very careful, we may inadvertently disadvantage, or even "punish" clients whose values differ from our own. A social worker in child welfare, for example, goes to the home of a single mother to assess this woman's ability to care for her child. The house is extremely dirty, and the worker highly values cleanliness ("Cleanliness is next to godliness," etc.). The dirt is not so extreme that it represents a health hazard to the child, but it offends the worker's middle-class values. In her assessment report, when she makes her recommendation to the court, there is a certain coolness in its tone. She writes that this mother is capable of caring for her child, but she mentions the dirty house, and this is not the warm, wholeheartedly supportive report that she would have written about the same woman if the kitchen had been spic-and-span. The tone of a report may be a subtle thing, but it is sometimes quite significant, and in this case the worker's values have entered the situation and influenced her analysis of the data.

To complicate matters even further, some values that appear at first glance to be personal in nature may in fact relate also to larger societal values and norms (Gold, Benbenishty, & Osmo, 2001). The above example reflects a personal value on the part of the worker, but it also reflects the issue of class, and is typical of the classism that can creep, undetected, into the analysis of data. Similarly, one may think of it as "just a personal reaction" that, for example, one feels uncomfortable around disabled people, and does not know "what to say to them." But this feeling is closely related to societal values and norms which devalue disabled people, and define them as abnormal and less than fully human (Gold & Auslander, 1999). The same can be said regarding "personal" reactions to old people, gay people, people from racial and ethnic minorities, and girls and women. Canadian society can be sexist, racist, antisemitic, homophobic, classist, ageist, and ableist, and consequently all of us, even with the best of intentions, have internalized at least some of these oppressive attitudes. As a result, we may assess our clients in distorted ways, often without our even knowing it. For example, in a social skills group for adolescents, a girl who is sparring with a boy for the leadership of the group is seen by the worker as "domineering" and lacking in social skills because of the worker's sexist stereotypes about what behaviours are appropriate for girls. Two old people in a home for the aged fall in love, and are viewed by the social worker there with patronizing amusement, because of social misconceptions about old people as asexual. Or a gay man is labelled psychologically immature and unable to form intimate, meaningful relationships because he has never been involved with a woman.

In order to safeguard against this, the first step is to identify our own personal values, consider which of these in particular might affect our relationships with clients, and then, without being inauthentic, search for ways to respect and work with clients with different values in these areas. Secondly, we need to struggle with those of our values that relate to larger social oppression. In interpreting data, it is not enough not to be racist; one must strive to be *anti-racist* in one's assessments, and similarly "anti-oppressive" on the other dimensions discussed above.[7] One way to do this is to make a conscious effort to label in one's assessments

---

[7] See Milner & O'Byrne (1998), Ch. 5, for some specific ideas on this.

the specific structural oppressions acting on a particular client, and then ask oneself whether one is in any way supporting or reinforcing any of these oppressions.

Another strategy is to include in one's assessment reports the facts that underlie one's interpretation. For example, a worker known to this author was once assessing a 10-year-old boy from a culture where it was a sign of respect to lower one's eyes before figures of authority. In ignorance of this culture, the worker wrote in his assessment statement that the boy was "mistrustful, lacking in social skills, and introverted." If he had included the raw data in the report (the exact words and behaviour that he had observed), he would have written: "This boy refused to make any eye contact with me, and therefore appeared to me to be mistrustful, lacking in social skills, and introverted." In this case the reader, perhaps the client's subsequent worker, would have been able to dissent from the interpretation given to the data, while at the same time receiving important factual information about the client. Including the facts that underpin one's analysis also allows one to return at a later date to one's initial assessment statement, and reevaluate one's interpretation of the data in light of subsequent information about the client—something that is not possible if one has omitted the raw data from the assessment statement and presented only one's interpretation of it.

CONCLUSION

Beginning social workers often underestimate the importance of assessment, and think of the "real work" of social work as the intervention. The assessment, however, is the foundation of everything that follows, and it is in the assessment that the crucial conceptual groundwork is laid. If an assessment is done properly, intervention will be little more than the implementation of an agreed-upon plan. If it is not, the work will run into problem after problem because the foundation is cracked.

Given the importance of assessment, as well as the complex and challenging issues involved and the number of variables that one needs to take into account, it is easy for a beginning social worker to become quite intimidated by the topic. It is helpful, therefore, to remember that ultimately assessment is a relatively simple process, composed of two main activities: data collection and data analysis. This chapter has examined both of these activities in some detail, with particular emphasis on how they are shaped by the worker's values and theoretical framework. More specifically, it has stressed the importance of social workers becoming more versatile, comfortable and creative with theory, as well as developing strategies to prevent, insofar as possible, replicating in their assessments the oppressive values of the larger society.

REFERENCES

Berkman, B., Chauncey, S., Holmes, W., & Daniels, A. (1999). Standardized screening of elderly patients' needs for social work assessment in primary care: use of the SF-36. *Health and Social Work, 24*(1), 9–16.

Bisman, C.D. (1999). Social work assessment: case theory construction. *Families in Society, 80*(3), 240–246.

Brown, L. (1996). Theory and feminist therapy: where do we go from here? Keynote address presented at *Womanspan: Generating Bridges*. Annual Meeting of the Association of Women in Psychology. Portland, Oregon: March 15.

Compton, B.R. & Galaway, B. (1999). *Social work processes* (6th edition). Toronto: Brooks/Cole.

Garvin, C.D. & Seabury, B.A. (1997). *Interpersonal practice in social work: promoting competence and social justice* (2nd edition). Toronto: Allyn & Bacon.

Gold, N., Benbenishty, R., & Osmo, R. (2001). Risk assessments and recommended interventions in instances of suspected abuse or neglect in Canada and Israel: a comparative study. *Child Abuse & Neglect*, 25(5), 607–622.

Gold, N. & Auslander, G. (1999). Newspaper coverage of people with disabilities in Canada and Israel: an international comparison. *Disability & Society, 14*(6), 709–731.

Gold, N. & Bogo, M. (1992). Social work research in a multicultural society: challenges and approaches. *Journal of Multicultural Social Work, 2*(4), 7–22.

Hartman, A. (1978). Diagrammatic assessment of family relationships. *Social Casework*, 59, 465–476.

Hepworth, D.H., Rooney, R.H., & Larsen, J. (1997). *Direct social work practice: theory and skills* (5th edition). Pacific Grove, CA: Brooks/Cole.

Hollis, F. (1968). And what shall we teach? Social work education and knowledge. *Social Service Review, 42*, 184–196.

Hollis, F. (1964). *Casework: a psychosocial therapy*. New York: Random House.

Howe, D., Brandon, M., Hinings, D., & Schofield, G. (1999a*). Attachment theory, child maltreatment and family support: a practice and assessment model.* London: Macmillan.

Howe, D., Dooley, T., & Hinings, D. (1999b). Assessment and decision-making in a case of child neglect and abuse using an attachment perspective. *Child & Family Social Work, 5*(2), 143–155.

Ivry, J. (1992). Teaching geriatric assessment. In M. J. Mellors and R. Solomon (Eds.), *Geriatric social work education* (pp. 3–22). New York: Haworth.

Johnson, L. (1995). *Social work practice: a generalist approach*. Toronto: Allyn & Bacon.

Mattaini, MA. & Kirk, S.A. (1991). Assessing assessment in social work. *Social Work, 36*, 260–266.

Meyer, C.H. (1993). *Assessment in social work* (2nd edition). New York: Columbia University Press.

Miley, K.K., O'Melia, M., & Dubois, B.L. (2001*). Generalist social work practice: an empowering approach* (3rd edition). Toronto: Allyn & Bacon.

Milner, J. & O'Byrne, P. (1998). *Assessment in social work*. London: Macmillan.

Perlman, H.H. (1957). *Social Casework*.

Richmond, M. (1917). *Social diagnosis*. New York: Russell Sage Foundation.

Rooney, R.H. (1992). *Strategies for work with involuntary clients*. New York: Columbia University Press.

Schriver, J. M. (1998). *Human behaviour and the social environment*. Toronto: Allyn & Bacon.

Sheafor, B.W., Horejsi, C.R., & Horejsi, G.A. (1991*). Techniques and guidelines for social work practice* (2nd edition). Toronto: Allyn & Bacon.

THE NATURE AND FUNCTION OF DIAGNOSIS

Francis J. Turner

One of the more controversial terms in the professional vocabulary of Canadian social workers is that of *diagnosis*. This component of social work practice was at one time the heart of clinical practice, and the basis of methods teaching (Richmond, 1917). It has now lost much of its prior position of eminence. It is a concept ignored by many, and scorned by others. Initially it was viewed by social workers as a neutral pan-professional term to describe a very specific activity in our and other professions. However, for a variety of complex socio-political reasons, the term, like other items in our lexicon, became caught up in several of our inter- and intra-familial struggles. In so doing its precise meaning was greatly distorted, blamed for a host of deficiencies in practice, and like other scapegoats driven out into the desert of "unfashionableness" (Turner, 1994).

If struggles about the use of the term only constituted another example of an all too common parlour word-game among professionals, this terminological issue would be of little consequence. However, minimizing, or indeed excluding, this term and its conceptual meaning from our professional vocabulary can have the effect of making practice much less precise. This in turn can result in clients being underserved or indeed badly served (Fischer, 1970).

THE CONCEPT OF DIAGNOSIS

What then do we mean by *diagnosis*? It describes the process of a social worker or indeed any professional in organizing the range of information, observations, and judgments gained about a presenting situation in the assessment process so as to come to a conclusion, albeit tentative, as to the nature of the presenting situation upon which, or for which, action should and will be taken for which a practitioner is prepared to be held accountable. Implied in this of course is the possibility of a judgment that nothing need be done.

In many parts of the country the term *assessment* is viewed as synonymous with *diagnosis*. It is our opinion that it is important to separate these two critical yet different processes.

In assessment we are engaged in the very complex, broad-based scanning of a client's reality and its many facets to help sort out what, of the wealth of material available, is essential in the current reality. Obviously, assessment leads to diagnosis and, as processes, these two overlap and interface. The diagnostic component is the critical phase of making judgments, which leads us to taking action (Barker, 1988).

Diagnosis therefore is the outcome or the next step from the assessment process as discussed in Chapter 12. It is the conclusions to which our assessments lead us as they expand and deepen through the life of a case. In the assessment process through the life of the case we are continually looking at the broad spectrum of a client's reality, and sorting, clarifying, and ordering the data from the wide number of sources available to us. In the diagnostic process, we make judgments as to what are the essential and critical and required features of these assessments upon which professional action is to be taken.

As a process of coming to conclusions, diagnosis consists of saying to ourselves as professionals: "based on what I know now, this in my opinion is what I judge to be the critical reality here. And following from these judgments I am prepared to act in a particular way."

THE DIAGNOSTIC PROCESS

Diagnosis, like assessment, is not a one-time-only process; it is ongoing throughout the life of a case (Hollis, 1954). It frequently alters as we make new assessments leading to new judgments with new information, or new perceptions or new insights. Some diagnostic judgments will be made in the very first minutes with a client—for example, that some type of emergency exists for which instant action is required. At other times we will conclude that although I do not fully understand the situation as yet, I judge that it is safe for me, for the client, and for others in the client's life to continue even in this uncertainty. In such instances our diagnosis may remain highly tentative until we are clearer as to where we and the client are. But we need to be clear that we have made the critical tripartite judgments related to safety. We have diagnosed! Our diagnosis is not something that happens only after we have gathered and analyzed a quantity of material. It begins in our very first moments with a client. We are formulating diagnoses with each step or action we take or do not take during the life of a case.

But diagnosis is more than a process. It must also be a fact. By that is meant that we have a responsibility throughout the life of any case to periodically set out our diagnosis in a format that is accessible to other appropriate persons who may need to become involved in our case. In this way we diagnose for the profession and for society by providing a basis on which we can be held accountable for what we have done or not done.

DIAGNOSTIC DISCOMFORT

Without attempting to analyze all the factors that have led to the current discomfort with the term *diagnosis*, a few need to be noted to help understand why some colleagues so reject the term. It appears that most of the reasons for turning away from the concept stem from three principal sources, all of which are related to misuses or a misunderstanding of the term. First, this rejection of the term seems to relate to the perceived need of some of our colleagues to separate ourselves from an imagined over-identification with, and an over-dependency on, the medical profession. Since the term *diagnosis* is so important in the practice of medicine, our using it is viewed by some as a wish to emulate our colleagues in medicine. Hence it is to be rejected.

Second, social work did not in the past, nor indeed does it today, want to form its practice and concerns only on the problems and pathology of clients. Rather we have long wanted to build on the strengths and potential existing in people and situations. A narrow view of the term *diagnosis* views it as a process that describes a search for pathology or the classification of a problem or set of problems and thus as something to be avoided.

Third, our profession has always emphasized the need to be flexible and to view the client's situation as being flexible. Related to this is the misperception that a "diagnosis" takes away from this flexibility by locking the client in once and for all to an unchanging fixed categorization. In this way, diagnosis is mistakenly viewed as a search for a clinical label or labels such as are found in the various editions of D.S.M. Useful as this manual and the system it represents may be, it has little relevance for many activities in social work and when it does its lexicon only represents one aspect of our diagnostic judgments.

However, these and many of the other reasons that have been given as arguments against the use of the term stem from a misunderstanding of the term and a misuse of it. Because a term has been misused by a few it should not be rejected if a correct understanding and use of it is still important to practice. It is better to seek out and argue for clarity and precision. For example, consider how over the decades the term *social worker* has long been misused. However, because we have argued against its misuse and continue to give this term increasing precision and insist that it be used correctly, society is quickly coming to understand and indeed to view it in a delineated, exclusive, and highly respected manner (Woods & Hollis, 1990).

DIAGNOSIS: WHAT IT IS NOT!

To fully understand and appreciate just what is meant by a correct and precise use of the term, it is important to emphasize what diagnosis is not.

1. Diagnosis is not the exclusive property of any one profession. Many professions diagnose, and correctly use the term *diagnosis* as a component of their practice. This includes my car mechanic who, a couple of years ago when I took my car in to have him look at it, said I needed to have a full diagnosis done to see if there was anything needed. This was done with great seriousness and care. Recently, I noticed in the mail that the telephone company was going to start charging for "diagnostic services." Certainly physicians diagnose, but they do medical diagnoses. We rightly would object if our colleagues in medicine did social work diagnoses, just as we should not of course attempt to do medical diagnoses or telephone diagnoses or veterinary diagnoses or auto-mechanic diagnoses. However, we would also rightly object if these same professionals announced that they did not diagnose when we needed their opinions, judgments, and services.

2. Diagnosis in social work does not consist of the assigning of a label to a client, although of course labels, being descriptive nouns or adjectives, when accurately used have a place in our diagnosis and assessment activities. When we say a client is a man, we have used a label; when we say he is an elderly man, we have made the label more precise by using a modifying word. When we say he is an elderly man receiving a veteran's pension, we have further labelled him. We cannot communicate to each other about a client without using labels.

Obviously labels can be misused and become fixed stereotypical designations. Any of us who have practiced as social workers know the extent to which labels can be misused to the detriment of clients. But we also know that a position that says "I never label a client" is an impossibility, for even the act of referring to someone as a client is a labelling act. Such a position can lead to considerable under-service to a client and indeed can be a life and death matter.

3. The process of diagnosing in social work is not a search for pathology only. Any skilled diagnostician in social work knows that a critical component of a useful diagnosis is the identification of strengths in clients, not only of areas in a client's life where there are problems.

4. Diagnosis in social work is not a unidimensional process. Indeed one of the immense challenges for our profession is the reality of the intersystemic complexities of our clients' situations and the need to accurately assess how they interact and then come to a judgment about where and how to make ourselves and our resources available to them so as to minimize potential harm and maximize our ability to help. I suggest that there is no other profession for which the challenge of diagnosis is greater, because of the immensity and complexity of the spectra of which we need to be aware as we dare to involve ourselves in the bio-psycho-social lives of our clients. Our diagnostic skill comes in being able to view the spectrum of the clients' inter-influencing systems and decide with the client when and how to introduce ourselves into the system if indeed we need to become involved (Lehrman, 1954).

DIAGNOSIS: ITS ESSENCE AND QUALITIES

Let us now look again at what this term means. As was said above, it is the process of making judgments about the reality with which we are faced and of taking professional action for which we are prepared to be held responsible. It is a very difficult process, especially in social work. But it is that process which gives precision to our work. It gives clear direction to our intervention. It allows us and others to evaluate our work and our activities.

A possible reason that many social workers do not like this term is that it implies the making of *judgments*. In social work we have long held to the importance of not being judgmental. However, the making of judgments and being judgmental are two very different concepts. Any one who is committed to acting responsibly with clients is continuously making judgments about the person, the situation, and the process. If not, then a person is acting from feelings only or the frequently touted "gut reaction" approach to practice.

Many of the judgments we make about clients are almost intuitive yet they are critical. Many of these judgments are made in the very first few minutes in a professional situation. The skill of the responsible practitioner is to increase one's awareness of the range of these judgments and of the impact they have on our subsequent professional actions (Phillips, 1960).

An important reason that we do not often think about the necessity of recognizing many of the judgments we make in our professional activities is that they are similar to the judgments we make in any interaction with other people. As mentioned earlier, some of these are so basic and omnipresent that most of the time we are not aware that we are making them. However, if we reflect on this we will be begin to understand that as humans we are constantly in a process of diagnosing and taking actions based on our diagnosis. Our responsibility as practitioners is to develop processes in ourselves that bring to conscious awareness what judgments we have made and, just as critical, those that we have not yet made (Knight, 1996).

Following, is a chart that outlines the range of judgments that we need to make explicit to ourselves when we are in a situation of deciding what to do with and for a client. As indicated above, some of these, such as those concerning the overall mental status of clients, and their level of intelligence and perceived safety, we make very quickly in our first con-

---

A Diagnostic Checklist

The following are headings to be considered in formulating a first and ongoing assessment and diagnosis. The format presumes a single client and thus needs to be adjusted when the client is a dyad, family or group, or community situation.

1. Mental status

    i) Overall
    ii) Is client in crisis?

2. Intelligence

3. Basic personality characteristics

4. Safety

    i) In relation to self
    ii) In relation to others
    iii) In relation to therapist

5. Communication skills

6. Credibility

7. Basic value set

8. Significant role set

    i) Roles
    ii) Adequacy of role performance

9. Overall physical condition and status

10. Medication and its actual and potential effect on psychosocial functioning

11. Cultural, gender, racial, ethnic, religious factors

    i) Identity
    ii) Significance

12. Significant others

    i) Strength
    ii) Quality
    iii) Availability

13. Interpersonal network

    i) Strength
    ii) Quality
    iii) Availability

14. Significant social systems

15. Significant resources

16. Major strengths in

    i) Person
    ii) Significant environments

17. Major problem and stress areas in

    i) Person
    ii) Significant environments
    iii) Resources

18. Identified needs

19. Client's expectations and wishes

20. Required nature of help

21. Required availability of help

22. Present level of motivation

23. Prognosis

tact with them as we do in a meeting with any human being. Obviously, since diagnosis is a process, we will frequently change and modify our first diagnostic judgments through-out the life of a case as we get to know more. It is important that we be aware when we have made these alterations in judgment.

Obviously this is a highly generic outline. Practitioners working in various settings may also have to make judgments in other areas of a client's life or to be much more precise in some of the identified areas rather than including them under a very generic heading. Having a checklist such as this helps to insure that we have considered these aspects of a client's life. For example, the question of safety for ourselves and others is an important one in today's practice. There is strong evidence that many persons we meet in practice have active suici-dal thoughts or tendencies to violence, which are frequently well hidden. Even though this is so, over and over again one reads many case records without any indication as to whether the worker has even considered these as a possibility (Turner, 1969).

DIAGNOSIS: THE FACT

Many colleagues state quite assertively that they "never diagnose." However, when one talks to them about a case it is clear that they have thought about and have come to conclusions about many of the aspects of a client's life and situation included in the outline. Such per-sons have stressed the "process component" of diagnosis over the "fact."

In this regard it is important to remember that diagnosis is not only an ongoing process; it is also a fact. That is, more and more we have to build into our practices the discipline of setting out as accurately as possible the profile of judgments we have made about a client and on which we have based our decisions to proceed in a certain way. It is this critical fact of practice that has been so lacking in much of contemporary social work practice since the diminution of the importance of diagnosis. Without such statements there is no way of assessing whether practitioners are operating on the basis of some type of planned inter-vention or merely following their hunches and impressions.

What saves many of us over and over again from getting into serious difficulty in our prac-tice is the fact that many of the people we meet in practice are reasonably intelligent, well-functioning human beings who are going to be helped almost regardless of what we do. But that is not enough. For not everyone is functioning well and we will in our practices meet persons who turn to us in considerable pain and need. Often such people can present them-selves as comfortable and well functioning even though they are desperate and crying out for help. To fail such persons because we didn't even think of the possibility of suicide or abuse, for example, is a serious matter.

Of course, one of the principal risks of incorporating the fact of diagnosis in our prac-tice is that often we will be wrong. We will misjudge people for any number of reasons. But to help improve our practice and to help advance our knowledge it is just as important for us to give careful attention to cases of mis-diagnosis as to our successes. For only in this way can we learn where, as individual practitioners and as a profession, we need to become more alert, more knowledgeable, and more attentive.

Most people need only be in practice a short time to have developed highly effective skills at assessment. That is, we learn how to connect to people, how to hear them, and how to help them look at themselves and their lives in a manner that gives us the knowledge we need to be helpful in as short a time as possible. What makes us even more effective is to see that step beyond assessment where we move to a position of more precise and overt decision-making that pushes us to synthesize those assessments. This leads us to seek a position that says *based on my understanding of this situation at this time here is what I propose to do, here is why I propose to do it, and here is what I expect will happen* (Turner, 1978).

For some people this process is included in the term *assessment*. Indeed if practitioners include in their concept of assessment the further process of coming to discrete conclusions, a good case could be made for restricting the description of this component of practice to the single term *assessment*. However, I believe our practice becomes more precise, accurate, and effective if we view *diagnosis* as a separate yet essential concept. As well, I see it as politically and sociologically more empowering to ourselves and hence to our clients that we restore this term to its necessary place in our lexicon. There are six reasons for this:

1. *Diagnosis* is a term with a long and respectable history in our profession. It is one that marked our early commitment to building our interventions on knowledge and precision. To abandon it is to move away from our early roots in a manner that can be harmful to our clients.

2. It is very imprudent, indeed dangerous, to allow other professions to define our terminology. To say we do not diagnose because that is what physicians do is nonsensical. As mentioned earlier the term *diagnosis* is a neutral one in essence. It belongs to no one profession. There are just as many reasons for social work to use the term, as it correctly applies to social work, as there are for other professions.

3. In North American society at least, many people are covered by various forms of insurance, or are eligible for various designated services that are provided by social workers. Many of these situations require a diagnosis and prognosis to establish eligibility or to assure the payment of benefits. If we are not prepared to give such a diagnosis out of a misguided misunderstanding of the concept we may well deprive clients of needed help. Again we are talking about social work diagnoses, not the mimicking of those of other professions.

4. If we are prepared to reinstate this term to its rightful place in the profession it will give momentum to the much needed improvement of a commonality of terminology between and among colleagues. Diagnosis requires a commitment to precision and an abhorrence of vagueness. This in turn will lead to an increase in precision in our work, which in turn will better equip us to evaluate our interventions. In so doing, we can more clearly identify where we are effective and, of equal importance, where we are ineffective.

5. In spite of inter-professional turf struggles as to who owns such terms as *treatment, therapy, counselling, psychosocial, diagnosis, casework, social work*, etc., society and its legislative agents expect social workers to diagnose. Increasingly, society holds us accountable for the judgments we make or do not make. It we continue to declare that we do not make such judgments but only assess, then it could well occur that this responsibility will be assigned to other professions. This could result in a serious loss of our hard-won autonomy for making our own decisions about the appropriateness or lack thereof of particular actions and plans of intervention by ourselves and our colleagues.

6. *Diagnosis* is a powerful word both in its precise meaning and its sociological effects. We frequently talk about the need to empower our clients. We can only do so if we ourselves operate from an ever-strengthening base of power. To relinquish the power of this term for quite misguided sociological reasons, or because of a very distorted perception of the term, could indeed strongly influence our ability to empower our clients (Turner, 1995).

SUMMARY

The term *diagnosis*, once an essential concept in Canadian social work practice, has become embroiled in the many struggles of social work to ensure its place in the sun and to move away from a feared over-stress on a pathology base of practice. In so doing, the term has been incorrectly assigned a highly negative and restricted meaning that has then become the justification for its rejection. However, this aspect of the sociology of professions can and does have a potential negative impact on clients in depriving them of the precision of intervention that is their right, as well as at times limiting their access to needed resources.

As mentioned earlier, we are not suggesting that *diagnosis* replace the term *assessment*. The importance of this term is well discussed in Chapter 12. We are arguing that, in addition to the highly honed assessment skills that practitioners quickly develop, practice is enriched by the added process of sorting out, in as precise and concise a way as is possible, our judgments about what is essential to our assessment at any point in the life of a case. Thus, for example, one might say: *Based on my assessment to date, I have concluded the following, which is the basis for my proceeding in the following manner.*

Following are three examples of diagnoses that might be written in regard to three simulated cases. Each of these statements of diagnosis would be preceded by a general assessment of the critical issues in a clients life.

Case I

Based on the material presented in a first interview, in my opinion this 28-year-old single Caucasian heterosexual male of Irish/French descent appears to be in good mental and physical health. He is average or slightly above average intelligence. Although he has shown some low-level outbursts of anger with friends, he does not appear to be a person who will engage in assaultive behaviour, nor are there any indications of suicidal thoughts. He communicates well in a quiet, introspective, believable manner. Although not practising his religion he has a strong, or even over-severe conscience. He is strongly identified with his French-Canadian origins, which appear to be a source of considerable stress in his job. His personal and social network, although not extensive, is strong, varied, and supportive. He is experiencing a moderate level of stress with respect to the stability of his employment, which is further exacerbated by a rather large number of debts that he appears to be managing.

The major area of concern for which he is seeking help relates to a strong sense of uncertainly as to his life direction. He would benefit from a brief series of (3–4) one-to-one interviews aimed at helping him look at his strengths and alternatives from a Gestalt perspective. I think he will benefit considerably from this and will not require any further assistance.

Case 2

Mrs. G. is a 75-year-old woman of Chinese/East Indian origins, recently arrived from Ghana and living with her eldest daughter and family. The following stems from a series of four interviews, in two of which Mrs. G.'s daughter was present:

It appears that this woman is in good mental health but that her several physical problems related to arthritis and accompanied by a complex regime of medication have resulted in a slight restriction of spontaneity—the seriousness of which is greatly exaggerated by the daughter.

Her strong but small network of friends give her considerable support, as do her close associations with both the spiritual and social functions of her church. The very limited financial situation of the family appears to be in control and not affecting the mother-daughter relationship. Mrs. G. contributes much to the family as a skilled housekeeper and handiwoman.

The mild level of observed depression, confirmed by her physician, does not represent any threat to her. It is viewed by her physician as, and is also in my opinion, situationally caused.

Mrs. G. would like to feel more respected and appreciated and less infantalized by her daughter. The daughter appears to be a highly intact person, quite comfortable in looking at her interaction and considering modifications in it. Both are prepared to look at themselves and came to the agency with the strong urging of their pastor. The daughter is somewhat uncertain about the role of the agency and the nature of psychosocial treatment and will need some further learning in order to make full use of the relationship and our services.

This is a situation that could become more serious if the mother-daughter relationship deteriorates. However, with a present-centred, supportive, ongoing relationship, some role changes in both the mother and daughter appear possible. It may be that, in the future, an educationally focused self-help group of newly arrived women from other countries could further help the daughter better understand her own and her mother's psychosocial situation in a new country. I would view the prognosis of this situation to be moderately positive.

Case 3

Mr. G. is a 28-year-old Caucasian Canadian born of Polish/Scot parents. He has been medically treated for a diagnosed moderately severe schizophrenic condition since age 17 for which a carefully monitored program of medication permits him to function moderately well in the community. He appears to be of above-average intelligence and highly gifted and interested in music. He is no threat to himself or others although at times his severely bizarre behaviour, consisting mostly of verbal hallucinations, is of considerable stress to his family who have still not fully accepted or understood his condition. Nevertheless, his family is available to him and they are strongly supportive of him but not in a knowledgeable way.

He has few friends or acquaintances but is able to effectively use the network of services available in the community. He handles his money, provided by his family, reasonably well although he is frequently criticized by his mother for what she views as irresponsibility in travelling to concerts of interest to him or the purchasing of expensive audio equipment.

In my opinion, from a case-management perspective this young man will be able to function for many years living on his own. The approach should stress the provision of concrete services and problem-solving approaches as needed. He is not a person with whom a close therapeutic relationship should be attempted nor should he be invited to join a group. Rather, he will do well by knowing and being known by a service network composed of many helpful and available but not intrusive persons.

REFERENCES

Barker, R.L. (1988). *The social work dictionary*, Silver Spring Md.: NASW.

Fischer, J. (1970). Portents from the past: what ever happened to social diagnosis? *International Social Work, XIII.* (No. 2.) 18–28.

Knight, C. (1996). The impact of a client's diagnosis of AIDS on social worker's clinical judgements: an experimental study. *Social Work in Health Care, 23*, 35–40.

Lehrman, L.J. (1954). The logic of diagnosis. *Social Casework, Vol. XXXV* (5), 192–198.

Hollis, F. (1954). Casework diagnosis—what and why? *Smith College Studies in Social Work, XXIV*, (3) June.

Phillips, D.C. (1960). Of plums and thistles: the search for diagnosis. *Social Work, Vol. 5*, (Jan.), 84–90.

Richmond, M. (1917). *Social diagnosis.* New York: Russell Sage Foundation.

Turner, F.J. (1995) *Differential diagnosis and treatment in social work (4th ed.).* New York: Free Press.

Turner, F.J. (1969). The search for diagnostic categories in social work treatment. Paper presented to the Learned Societies of Canada. Toronto: York University (June).

Turner, F.J. (1978). *Psychosocial therapy: a social work perspective.* New York: The Free Press, 78–82.

Turner, F.J. (1994). Reconsidering diagnosis. *Families in Society, 75*(3), 168–171.

Woods, M. & Hollis, F. (1990). Assessment and diagnostic understanding in casework. In *Casework: a psychosocial therapy* (4th ed.). New York: McGraw Hill, Chapter 14, 288–304.

THE SETTING OF OBJECTIVES AND CONTRACTING

Leslie M. Tutty

INTRODUCTION AND HISTORICAL CONTEXT

While both assessment and diagnosis are activities for which the social worker takes the major lead, the setting of objectives and contracting, while guided by the worker, should focus on the needs and issues raised by the client. Assessment and diagnosis can look vastly different depending on the theoretical orientation and training of the social worker. For example, as was illustrated in Chapter 12, there are a number of assessment techniques that workers can utilize. However, with limited time, the choice between such assessment techniques as ecomaps, genograms, and family measures is made by the worker and is reflected by his or her orientation. Similarly, the question of whether or in what way a worker uses diagnosis, as described in Chapter 13, is based largely on training and theoretical background.

In contrast, the exploration and setting of objectives, while directed by the social worker, emerge from the needs of the client or family. This is where the uniqueness of the client and the circumstances surrounding the situation that brought him or her to treatment are given voice. The process basically entails asking the client system, "What do you want from treatment?" Such discussion should ultimately lead to an agreement between the client and social worker that either, "Yes, I can help you in working toward that," or "No, I cannot." This, in essence, is the therapeutic contract.

The setting of objectives and contracting are activities that have been commonly described across many theoretical approaches. In some theoretical models, the exploration of treatment objectives and developing the contract form the major focus of treatment. Behavioural therapy (Thomlison & Thomlison, 1996), reality therapy (Bassin, 1993), transactional analysis (Goulding, 1990), client-centred therapy (Rowe, 1996), and problem-solving therapy (Turner & Jaco, 1996) are approaches in which contracting with clients has been well described and is central. Similarly, social workers who use group work (Preston-Shoot, 1989; Wickham, 1993) and marital therapy (Shulman, 1992) often include contracting as an explicit step in the process of treatment.

But whether or not the description of treatment includes the setting of objectives and contracting as formalized activities, they will occur. Rothery (1980), paraphrasing Watzlawick, Beavin, and Jackson's famous phrase, "one cannot *not* communicate," proposed that "one cannot *not* contract." According to Rothery, the contract essentially negotiates the terms of the therapeutic relationship. As such, one can either be explicit about those terms or leave the rules undiscussed. From a consumer-oriented, client-focused perspective, it is preferable to open up these issues for discussion, as this allows the client more informed choices (Tutty, 1990).

Setting objectives and contracting are critical to the therapeutic process and are inter-related. In this chapter, the process of setting objectives will be considered as part of the contracting process, which will ultimately result in a therapeutic contract. The contract may be written or remain a verbal agreement. The process of setting objectives and contracting facilitates clients in being clear about what they want from counselling in such a way that they can easily assess whether they have achieved these.

Although the process may sound simple, it is during the setting of objectives and con-tracting activities that social workers guide the client away from identifying goals that are unobtainable or, indeed, may be a set-up for failure. It is important to note, also, that the worker's own training and values may intrude in the process in such a way as to render treatment a waste of time.

This chapter will suggest guidelines for setting objectives and contracting, attempting to provide social workers with both a sense of the complexity and importance of the process and how they might avoid common pitfalls. While this will first be discussed with a focus on how to facilitate individual clients and families through the process, the final section of the chapter will focus on the social worker's objectives and responsibilities and ways in which these may impede clients from both exploring their issues and developing achievable contracts.

SETTING OBJECTIVES

Presenting Problems: Tip of the Iceberg or Focus for Treatment?

The first question to consider is: With respect to which problem should a worker assist a client in setting objectives? A long-standing debate in the treatment literature is whether to accept the presenting problem, the one with which the client initially requests assistance, as the one around which to contract. Many decades of psychoanalytic literature have implied that the presenting problem is not necessarily the issue that is most pressing for the client, but repre-sents a trial balloon which the client uses to assess whether the worker can be trusted to deal with the "real" problem. Such discussion has led many social workers to regard the initial problem with distrust, leaving them looking for an underlying issue which may or may not exist.

In contrast, newer brief therapies do not typically include an in-depth assessment, and pro-ponents work with the presenting problem based on the systemic premise that change in the system with respect to one issue will also change how the system responds to other problems. From this perspective, one does not need to know a great deal about the client or their problems to initiate the change process.

However, many clients have issues that are not socially acceptable, nor are they likely to introduce them voluntarily in the initial session: wife assault, substance abuse, child abuse. The research on the extent to which incest victims who were clients of the mental health system were never asked about such victimization and continue to experience problems that they relate to their childhood experience must raise concerns about social workers taking a position that they need not know about past abuse history.

There is no question that clients or families often present with one problem while concealing more sensitive issues. Taking some time to assess for other issues such as the presence of wife assault, child abuse, substance dependence, or marital distress, and presenting feedback to the individual or family with respect to the assessment, may provide the clients with information that is both relevant to their objectives and gives them permission to address more serious concerns. For example, a 35-year-old woman did not realize that low self-esteem, her presenting problem, is common among victims of childhood incest, a circumstance that she revealed in response to questioning during the assessment phase. As in this example, the presenting problem is linked to the underlying issue in any case, but since most social workers would address low self-esteem slightly differently if a client identified having been sexually abused as a child versus feeling concerned about being overlooked for a job advancement, I would argue that the ideal is to set objectives that tie the presenting problem to other related and central issues.

Assisting Individual Clients in Setting Objectives

While social workers will likely be presented with a variety of client systems including individuals, couples, families, and even community groups, we shall begin the discussion of setting objectives with the "simplest" situation, an individual client or unrelated clients in groups. This is not intended in any way to imply that individual treatment is easier than working with systems of two or more people, but it greatly simplifies the discussion of setting objectives and contracting. A later section will describe these activities with more complex client groupings.

The first issue for consideration in setting objectives is whether the client's stated goals imply an objective of change. Much of the written discussion of setting objectives is from the psychotherapy literature that has clearly focused on the notion that clinical intervention entails some type of change. This might be a change in feelings, behaviour, thoughts, or beliefs on the part of the client. For example, an adolescent feeling unhappy about her life might focus on ways to change her feelings of loneliness. She could do this by behaving differently—by perhaps joining a club or sports team at school or at a community centre, instead of staying home all day, lying in bed with her curtains drawn. She could also examine her beliefs about why she considers herself unattractive and the way in which, when she feels lonely, her self-talk is critical and demeaning. Change could involve finding ways to interrupt this negative self-talk with more positive affirmations. In fact, change could easily involve setting objectives about feelings, behaviour, and beliefs.

However, social workers work in a variety of settings that are not expressly therapy-related, although the results could certainly have a therapeutic impact. The clients who seek or are directed to social work services are not necessarily seeking to change. They might wish to obtain information about a certain topic— parenting, for example. An objective to learn more about parenting stops short of stating that the person will change his or her behaviour. Another example of a non-change objective is with respect to interventions that focus on support, such as groups for women with breast cancer. In such cases, the women cannot change the medical fact that they have cancer; however, the empathy and encouragement from other group members facing the same crisis is often extremely helpful. A final example of a non-change objective is when clients are at such a level of crisis and chaos, often in reaction to previous change, that the most important objective for them is stabilization. Consider a woman who has left her assaultive partner to seek the safety of an emergency shelter. Before she can begin to decide whether to return to her relationship or to separate and begin an independent life, she needs a safe setting in which to calm down from the effects of the often-traumatic incident that resulted in her being in the shelter in the first place. If a social worker tries, too early, to encourage her to consider an objective that involves her changing or making a decision about her partner, this will be perceived not only as inappropriate, but also as disempowering.

The distinction between the different forms of objectives is important because the interventions for objectives of education, support, and stabilization typically entail different, less intrusive expectations of clients. In a parenting class, individuals would be expected to learn techniques to better manage their children's misbehaviour by using time-outs, for example. The parents might discuss how they could implement such strategies, but rarely would they be observed or coached in applying a time-out with their actual children, as might be the case in family therapy that has a clear objective to change parenting behaviour.

Nevertheless, one has to be somewhat careful about wording. Simply because a program is labelled "support," this does not mean that the objectives are to support rather than to change. For example, in-home family support programs are commonly utilized as ways to intervene with parents whose children are at risk of being apprehended by child welfare authorities because of abuse. The goals of such programs are clearly to change the parent's behaviour so that the children are protected. The term "support" in the title is there for the political reason that it sounds less intrusive and one hopes to engage the parents in actively working on changing their parenting behaviours.

The clarification of the type of objective is not separate from other aspects of setting objectives, but integrated into the process. The process of setting objectives is rarely a one-step, question/answer exercise, but in most cases will take the better part of a session to formulate, and in others will take even longer. Even your opening question over the telephone or in the first session can lead into a focus on client objectives rather than an open-ended and too-general discussion of your client's life story. This is not to suggest that allowing clients' stories to emerge is not a helpful part of therapy, but preferably the narratives should relate to the client's treatment objectives. Questions such as: "What did you come here to change?" "What prompted you to seek help?" and "How would you like to be different at the end of counselling?" lead directly into a discussion of the client's objectives in seeking help.

Some clients begin with clear statements of what they want to achieve in treatment. Examples of clear objectives include:

> "I want to stop being so 'nice' to other people that I end up always meeting their needs but not my own."

> "I want to decide whether to stay in my marriage or not."

> "I want to stop feeling so depressed."

Such clear initial objectives are rare, and, in fact, most clients need help in clarifying their objectives. As such, the process of setting objectives and contracting is, in itself, a major therapeutic intervention, involving an in-depth discussion of the factors involved in creating the problem and information about what interferes in achieving the objective to change.

Objectives must be rooted in the present and near future. It is important to differentiate between short and long-term objectives. In general, it is preferable to clarify the long-term goal, and to break the task into a number of smaller objectives that can be accomplished in the present, but which ultimately lead to achieving the larger objective. Similarly, one cannot change the distant past. Even though it will be essential to discuss issues of trauma such as child abuse, these must be linked to the present with questions such as "How does the fact that you were sexually abused as a child affect the problem you came with, improving your relationship with your husband?"

Objectives must be attainable. A 40-year-old woman with grade 10 education and no job experience who was in a shelter because she had been assaulted by her husband decided that what she wanted was to become independently wealthy in the next two years. This is a rather extreme example of an objective that is too grandiose to be attainable. As well, the long-term nature of the objective makes it difficult to achieve. More appropriate for this woman would be to see a career counsellor to explore what employment she might be best suited to and what education and training will be necessary to achieve this.

While the client's objectives may be focused on a general issue such as being more assertive, the discussion must focus on specific examples of when the client feels this to be a problem, how is he feeling (affect), what does he say to himself (cognitions and beliefs), and what does he do (behaviour).

Objectives must also focus on aspects of a problem over which clients have some control. The most obvious implication of this is that one cannot change another's behaviour, a common presentation to social workers. For example, a mother cannot stop her child from being aggressive with other children. She can, however, change her own parenting behaviour in the hope of the boy's reacting differently to her and ultimately changing his behaviour with others. For example, rather than spanking or slapping him if he hits another child, her previous parental intervention, the mother could use a time-out procedure. Alternatively, the social worker and the mother could consider an interactional form of treatment, family therapy for example, rather than continuing in individual treatment, often a preferable option for interpersonal problems, especially in working with couples.

The specific questions about client objectives will differ according to the theoretical approach utilized. For example, questions from a behavioural perspective will be with respect to the target behaviours that are the focus for change, identifying new antecedent events for each of the target behaviours and new positive consequences (Thomlison & Thomlison, 1996).

Here is an example of a series of questions that will initiate an in-depth exploration of therapeutic objectives (expanded from Goulding, 1990):

1. What do I want to stop doing?

2. What do I want to start doing instead?

3. What is in it for me to make the above changes? (What positive feelings or beliefs might result?)

4. How might I stop myself from following through with this plan? (How might I sabotage the plan?)

5. If I follow through with this plan, how might the important other people in my life react?

One can see the behavioural roots of these questions in the focus on changing behaviour rather than changing feelings or beliefs. While changing emotions and beliefs is considered essential to the change process, people typically feel more in control of changing their behaviour, which can result in changes to emotions and belief systems. If a client comes to therapy to stop being depressed, for example, clearly the major focus is changing their emotive state. However, an exploration of what they are doing that contributes to their depression, such as refusing to accompany friends to movies, sitting in a dark room for hours, and berating themselves for being a "failure," provides clues to behaviours over which they have control and the modification of which may result in initial relief from depression. It also may be helpful to ask the individual how she would know she is not depressed any more, for example, "What would you be doing differently if you weren't depressed?"

The behavioural focus does not preclude an exploration of feelings and beliefs. Questions such as "How do you feel after you turn down invitations to go out with friends?" and "What does it mean about you that your boyfriend broke off your engagement?" elicit information about emotional states and belief systems that are linked to behaviour and are important to discuss. Nevertheless, from this perspective, the change process is more easily accomplished by identifying and changing the behaviours associated with the feelings and rules.

The first two questions, "What do you want to stop doing" and "What do you want to start doing instead?" are obviously linked. Change involves not only stopping behaving in a certain way, but replacing that behaviour with another in order to avoid slipping back into familiar patterns. For the mother who has decided to change her parenting behaviours, it is not enough to simply identify the fact that she wants to stop spanking her son. A discussion of what she might do instead could involve questions such as, "How were you punished when you misbehaved as a child?" "What have you tried previously with Lucas?" and "What have important others (your husband, your mother, your doctor) told you to do?" Many clients may have already utilized an appropriate strategy, but stopped it too soon, or introduced it incorrectly. For example, the mother may have tried removing privileges before, but when her son was too young for this to be effective. This situation allows the worker to congratulate the mother for having identified a solution that may well work now.

The third question, "What is in it for you to make these changes?" speaks to motivation and is particularly important when clients come in with requests to stop behaviours that they believe they *should* change (called parent contracts in transactional analysis terms and easily identifiable by the inclusion of words such as "should," "have to" or "must" in the discussion). Such objectives typically imply that the individual is changing for someone other than him or herself or that he or she is ambivalent about changing. While stopping smoking, drinking, procrastinating, and overeating, are unarguably positive objectives, a discussion of the costs and benefits of changing these is critical. For example, a student may procrastinate at university in the same way that he avoided doing the chores that his overbearing mother set for him when he was younger. If the procrastination represents his secret rebellion at being told what to do, leaving him feeling powerful, deciding to give up this position may lead to depression. An exploration of other ways that he can feel powerful, and asking him to think about the benefits of stopping procrastinating ("Even your mother wants you to!") can prevent a seemingly simple contract from failing.

In other words, clients need to explore how changing their behaviour will be beneficial for them. From this perspective, the debate about whether it is possible to work with involuntary or mandated clients who are sent to treatment by someone else is misguided. Men who are mandated to group treatment because they have been abusing their wives are a good example. Although they often begin group work in an angry and even belligerent position and will openly resist the invitation to change their behaviour for their wives or the courts, skilful social workers can help them to realize ways in which their abusive behaviour is harmful not only in their marriage but with respect to their children, their relatives, and their friends. As such, the men need to identify their own objectives for change for treatment to be successful, but this is not necessarily as difficult as is sometimes implied.

The fourth question, "How might I sabotage this plan?" is one of the single most important questions in treatment. Often people smile when asked the question. The smile indicates that they clearly understand that part of them has been and will continue to resist changing. Often clients can come up with a quite elaborate list of the ways that they have sabotaged their own previous attempts to change. The question is key to the complexity of the change process, for if changing were as simple as merely deciding to stop one behaviour and replacing it with another, no-one would need to seek professional help.

For example, in exploring her objective to start being more assertive, a young women discovered that she continues to be unassertive because she fears that her co-workers will not like her if she comes across too strongly. Her fears have undermined her strength, but have also kept her safe from rejection by colleagues. As such, although she may plan to behave more assertively about saying no to colleagues when they ask her to take on extra work, she may also identify the fact that when faced with such requests she feels anxious and scares herself into not refusing. The part of her that has her heels dug in so as to protect herself must come to believe that real friends will still like her, and, in fact, may like her even more if she has the courage to say no. It is only when a client becomes aware that she typically sabotages her objectives in these ways that she has the option to stop and behave differently.

Despite one's own plans for change, each of us lives in a complex environment and we interact with many others. As such, a change, even a small one, may have a significant impact on the client's entire ecosystem. The fifth question, about how others will be affected by changing the behaviour, is therefore central and allows workers whose clients do not wish to or have been unsuccessful in involving their spouse or families to retain a larger systems perspective. As such, the worker asks individuals to predict how their spouse/child/parent may respond if they change this behaviour. It is not uncommon for clients to become aware at this point that their significant other may respond negatively to their changed behaviour and may, directly or indirectly, attempt to pull them back into the old familiar patterns. For example, several years ago, workers taught women who were abused by their husbands how to be more assertive without realizing that, rather than protecting the women, it put them at increased risk for being abused further. Had this question been asked as part of treatment, it would have become quite clear that behaving more assertively was potentially dangerous for some women. Role-playing is a useful technique to explore how significant others might react to changes, by having the client take on the role of the co-worker or boyfriend and react to the therapist who takes on the role of the changed client.

The responses to this question may lead to revising the previous plan. It may become quite apparent that family or couple therapy is more appropriate at this point. Or the objectives may shift to an assessment of the client's ecosystem. Perhaps the client should be changing jobs or considering whether to stay in the marital relationship, rather than trying to change his own behaviour.

In summary, while many questions can lead to the exploration necessary to set clear objectives for treatment, the preceding questions are a useful guide for new workers.

Problems in Setting Objectives with Individual Clients

The examples utilized in the previous discussion have already illustrated several common problems that arise when helping clients set their objectives for treatment: coming to treatment to change someone else, and coming to treatment because someone else wants you to change. Another common, more difficult situation for social workers involves clients who continually present in a state of crisis. Called "multiproblem" or "vulnerable" by Rothery (1993), these clients present in high states of anxiety, typically with a different crisis each session, shifting from issue to issue. They also tend to have multiple helpers and it is not uncommon for the helping system to become conflicted about the client's objectives in a way that mirrors the disorganization of the client system.

Three suggestions may be considered when faced with such clients. First, it is important to remember that as with Maslow's hierarchy of needs, basic needs such as food, shelter and safety must be available before clients are in any position to address other emotional and interpersonal issues. In such instances it is important for the social worker to adopt the role of case-manager, rather than therapist. Workers can inquire about these needs during the assessment phase of treatment and can provide information about and referrals to services that may address any gaps.

Second, when a client shifts issues from week to week, presenting each time in a new state of crisis, it is likely that the contract needs to focus on stabilization rather than on change. Reminding the client of the objectives that were set in the first session and asking how those are connected to the new incident may also lead to a shift from focusing on specific issues to focusing on a style of dealing with issues that is not working.

Third, look at the larger ecosystem. In cases with multiple helpers it is critical that workers from the diverse agencies meet to develop an agreement, a contract if you will, to clarify who is responsible for what aspect of treatment. Some agencies may wish to withdraw at this point so that workers are not either duplicating services or working at cross-purposes. Other workers will continue to assist with various aspects of the case, but, importantly, will act in liaison with the services that remain involved.

Setting Objectives with Families

Although setting objectives with families and couples is more complex than with individuals because of the potential diversity among family members, the process is analogous to that already described (McClendon & Kadis, 1990). However, several unique problems may emerge, including family members identifying different problems, identifying different objectives for treatment, and the presence of hidden agendas.

The first possible pitfall, family members identifying different problems, has the potential to halt treatment before it starts. Anderson and Stewart (1984) suggest several strategies to move a family beyond this impasse, including finding a new definition of the problem to which all members will agree or making the disagreement part of the problem. As such the problem becomes one of, "You see things differently, let's talk about how you disagree."

Similarly, when family members disagree about objectives, Anderson and Stewart suggest pushing for specificity by asking each member, "What exactly do you want?" Alternatively, the worker can label disagreement as normal in families and work with several objectives, the ideal being that they be related. For example, in a recently immigrated

Chinese family, an adolescent son wanted more freedom to socialize with his new Canadian friends from school, while his parents worried because he had disobeyed them several times by ignoring his curfew and his grades were beginning to slip. Although the son's objective to be more independent seemed to be directly opposed to the parents' objectives that he should live by the family's rules, the two can be linked in a way in which both can be accomplished. For example, the time of the curfew could be negotiated in session if the son improved his grades at school. Ultimately, one could suggest using a modality other than family treatment if the objectives remain widely divergent.

Hidden agendas are objectives that are at odds with the openly identified objectives of treatment and which, for therapy to be successful, must be unearthed. Probably the most common hidden agenda is when a couple presents for marital therapy but the secret intention of one partner is to separate. Another example is of a reconstituted family with sets of children from each parent. While ostensibly the objective was to get along better, the hidden agenda of the stepfather was that family therapy would fail and that the child who was creating the most problems in the family would move out.

Hidden agendas often become apparent when individuals seem to be resisting following through with plans or homework assignments that would achieve the contracted objectives. At this point, the worker can confront the family member(s) about his commitment to the previously agreed-upon objective, raising the possibility that perhaps not everyone is working toward the same objective. This opens a re-exploration of each individual's hopes, which may uncover central discrepancies between family members. The discrepancy then becomes the focus of the contract.

In summary, setting objectives is a critical process in therapy, one that may be revisited many times over the course of treatment. Social workers can be most helpful when they encourage an in-depth exploration of the issues, one that acknowledges the complexities of the problem in a way that is ultimately respectful to the client.

CONTRACTS

The term *contract* is not unfamiliar to social work practitioners, being widely used in both educational (Zapf, 1993) and treatment contexts (Russell, 1990; Thomlison & Rothery, 1984). For example, *group contracts* specify the rules, rights, and expectations for group members (Preston-Shoot, 1989), *homework contracts* set out what clients will do to achieve their objectives between sessions, and *no-suicide contracts* are an agreement between client and therapist that the client will not attempt self-harm (Stanford, Goetz, & Bloom, 1994). With the relatively recent acknowledgment of the serious nature of wife assault, therapists who work with couples where violence is of concern may utilize *no-violence contracts* as a condition of couple treatment (Stith & Rosen, 1990).

The literature on contracting is somewhat confusing because authors have described a number of different types of contracts. From my perspective, the most important distinction is between contracts that specify the objectives of treatment (*therapeutic* or *treatment contracts*) and contracts that set out the business arrangement between client and worker (*administrative*). The first, therapeutic or treatment contracts, spell out the objectives that the client/family have identified; where they would like to get to; what they want in coming to treatment (the material covered in the previous sections). Therapeutic contracts:

1. define the problem
2. set mutual, attainable objectives
3. describe how the individual/family might sabotage the plan.

Most social work authors emphasize the fluid nature of therapeutic contracts; that they must remain flexible as client needs change (Shulman, 1992). Throughout the course of treatment, as they achieve their stated objectives, clients may wish to set new ones and to recontract for further work. Rothery (1980), for example, has conceptualized contracting as a developmental process, as often the new contracts build upon learning that has taken place in meeting the previously agreed-upon objectives.

However, a second kind of contract used in social work treatment (Barker, 1987) is what Goulding and Goulding (1978) label an administrative contract. It is based on the assumption that it is important to be clear about the administrative issues regarding treatment, such as:

1. the time, length, and frequency of meetings
2. who will participate
3. the type of treatment modality to be utilized
4. the roles and responsibilities of both worker and client
5. payment and how it will be made
6. how and when the contract will be renegotiated
7. how the contract can be cancelled.

Both administrative and treatment contracts are important aspects of making the process of treatment more transparent and accessible to the client. Both types of contracts can be utilized with clients.

The Social Worker's Objectives

It would be misguided to discuss setting objectives and contracting from only the perspective of the client without acknowledging that there are circumstances with respect to the agency's mandate, the referral source, and the social worker's training and values that will affect, and may in fact interfere with, the contracting process. Such issues include worker/client differences in view of the problem, worker biases, utilizing worker knowledge in non-intrusive ways, clarifying who is the client when referral agencies are involved, and circumstances that take precedence over client contracts.

Client/Worker Differences in the View of the Problem   Seabury (1989) notes that clients and workers not uncommonly experience conflict when negotiating a contract, suggesting further that there are some situations when contracting may be impossible or contraindicated. An example of the first instance is where a client is in an acute psychotic state; an example of the second is when the urgent nature of the problem does not warrant the time to engage with the client in the contracting process.

Worker/client differences may occur because the client or family has a perspective on the problem that is vastly different from that of the worker. For example, a family with a very aggressive four-year-old may be convinced that these difficulties arise because of food allergies; however, the worker's focus is family interaction and parenting skills. The temptation for most of us is to attempt to convince clients that our perspective is the correct one and that theirs is incorrect, a strategy that will most likely fail; the clients will simply not return. Rather, it is important to acknowledge the discrepancies in viewpoint with a statement such as, "It seems that we are seeing the problem in very different ways. You suspect that food allergies may be causing Billy's aggressive behaviour, whereas in my experience such difficulties can often be helped by working with parents to set clearer limits." Once having clarified the different views, you can offer options, such as having the family work for a specified number of sessions on parenting skills to see if that has an impact.

However, when parents are firmly convinced that their view is correct, it is preferable to suggest that they explore their ideas first, with the invitation to return for treatment if that is unsuccessful. A dramatic example of how such worker/client discrepancies can be well handled was that of a recently immigrated family from Central America who sought help for their adolescent son who had begun behaving in a bizarre fashion. From a mental health perspective, he could be experiencing symptoms of schizophrenia or substance abuse, but the parents were firmly convinced that he was possessed by an evil spirit. The worker suggested that they continue with the steps that they had already taken to arrange a religious ceremony to exorcize the evil spirit, stating that if the exorcism failed, the worker would certainly be available to work with them to assess other possible explanations for their son's behaviour.

Worker Biases Social workers may insist on reframing the client's objectives to fit their particular expertise. The well-known phrase, "If all you have is a hammer, everything looks like a nail," is particularly apt in such instances. If the bulk of your training is in play therapy, for example, you are likely to see issues in terms of individual work with a child, whereas if you only have training in family therapy, you will see all child and adult issues from that perspective. An openness to acknowledging that your skills may not always be appropriate and a willingness to stay current in the treatment literature is key to overcoming the potential of your biases interfering in the client's achieving their objectives.

Similarly, there may be times when a worker's personal life prevents dealing effectively with certain problems or certain clients. For example, if a therapist is herself going through a divorce, this is likely not the best time to counsel couples who are questioning their own commitment to their relationship.

Who Is the Client, Anyway? Another common difficulty is when clients or families are referred by other systems or agencies with particular objectives in mind. Schools may refer families because their children are disruptive in class, or agencies may want an assessment of child abuse. The parents often come in with no idea of the agenda documented in the referral. In such instances, it is critical to contract with the referral source as well as with the family. In most cases, it will be important to clarify with the agency that although they made the referral, the needs of the family will take precedence over that of the school. In many cases, both can be addressed.

Circumstances that Take Precedence over the Client's Contract Finally, if issues of child abuse or potential harm to a client or another person surface in sessions, these must be addressed immediately. While shifting hats from a therapeutic role to that of an agent of social control may create resentment and confusion on the part of the client toward the therapist, we have no choice in making this shift because of the Social Work Professional Code of Ethics. For example, a woman being seen for depression mentioned giving her

13-year-old daughter "what she deserved" after the girl came in late one evening. The focus of the interview shifted immediately to assess what the mother meant exactly: Had there been an argument and what was said? Had the mother struck the daughter? If so, did she use her open hand? A fist? An object? Were there bruises on the daughter or did she require medical treatment?

In some cases, the shift can actually strengthen a therapist/client relationship. In one example, a woman came for help in improving her low self-esteem. During the assessment, she raised questions about her four-year-old daughter's recent behaviour. She had caught her daughter and the 15-year-old male babysitter French-kissing. At this point the worker asked more about the daughter's sexually explicit behaviour, learning that there had been another sexually-related incident at daycare with a preschool-aged girl. The worker was, however, reluctant to report the incidents to child welfare because she believed that the therapist/client relationship was, as yet, too delicate to withstand such action. In supervision, it became clear not only that the incidents must be reported, but that, in fact, it would make more sense for the mother to make the report with the support of the worker. This intervention actually validated the mother's perceptions, empowering her to feel better about herself (her original objective). The worker/client relationship was thus strengthened by the worker's willingness to acknowledge the mother's concerns and to assist her in taking steps to protect her daughter.

In conclusion, these examples of ways in which circumstances surrounding the worker, the problem, or other involved parties may have a significant effect on the contracting process are important to consider. Too often when contracts fail, we automatically blame the client, without consideration of the impact of other variables.

CONCLUSION

Setting objectives and contracting with clients is often the first opportunity for the client to get a sense of the process as one in which she is central and where her perspective and wishes will be acknowledged. These activities set the tone for the entire therapeutic process. To the extent that workers remain respectful of the client's wishes in a manner that does not preclude the worker utilizing her particular expertise to give permission to talk about uncomfortable subjects or to provide information about areas that would enhance and in many cases normalize the client's reaction to life events, setting objectives and contracting are the foundation for social work practice.

REFERENCES

Anderson, C.M. & Stewart, S. (1983). *Mastering resistance: a practical guide to family therapy.* New York: Guilford.

Barker, R. (1987). Spelling out the rules and goals: the written worker-client contract. *Journal of Independent Social Work*, *1*(2), 67–77.

Bassin, A. (1993). The reality therapy paradigm. *Journal of Reality Therapy*, *12*(2), 3–13.

Goulding, M.M. (1990) Getting the important work done fast: contract plus redecision. In J. Zeig & S. Gilligan (Eds.). *Brief therapy: myths, methods, and metaphors.* New York: Brunner/Mazel, pp. 303–317.

Goulding, R. & Goulding, M.M. (1978). *The power is in the patient: a TA/gestalt approach to psychotherapy.* San Francisco: T.A. Press.

McClendon, R. & Kadis, L. (1990). A model of integrating individual and family therapy: the contract is the key. In J. Zeig & S. Gilligan (Eds.). *Brief therapy: myths, methods, and metaphors.* New York: Brunner/Mazel, pp. 135–150.

Preston-Shoot, M. (1989). Using contracts in groupwork. *Groupwork, 2*(1), 36–47.

Rothery, M. (1980). Contracts and contracting. *Clinical Social Work Journal, 8*(3), 179–187.

Rothery, M. (1993). The ecological perspective and work with vulnerable families. In M. Rodway & B. Trute (Eds.). *Ecological family practice: one family, many resources.* Queenston, ON: Edwin Mellen, pp. 21–50.

Rowe, W. (1996). Client-centered theory: a person-centered approach. In F.J. Turner (Ed.). *Social work treatment: interlocking theoretical approaches* (4th ed.). New York: Free Press, pp. 69–93.

Russell, M.N. (1990). *Clinical social work: Research and practice.* Newbury Park: Sage.

Seabury, (1989). Negotiating sound contracts with clients. In B. Compton, & B. Galaway (Eds.). *Social work processes* (4th ed.). Belmont, CA: Wadsworth, pp. 495–502.

Shulman, L. (1992). *The skills of helping individuals, families and groups* (3rd ed.). Itasca, Ill: Peacock.

Stanford, E., Goetz, R., & Bloom, J. (1994). The no harm contract in the emergency assessment of suicide risk. *Journal of Clinical Psychiatry, 55*(8), 344–348.

Stith, S. & Rosen, K. (1990). Family therapy for spouse abuse. In S. Stith, M. Williams, & K. Rosen (Eds.). *Violence hits home: comprehensive treatment approaches to domestic violence.* New York: Springer, pp. 83–101.

Thomlison, R.J. & Rothery, M. (1985). Intervention with individuals. In S. Yelaja (Ed.). *An introduction to social work practice in Canada.* Scarborough, ON: Prentice-Hall, pp. 36–48.

Thomlison, B. & Thomlison, R.J. (1996). Behaviour theory and social work treatment. In F.J. Turner (Ed.). *Social work treatment: interlocking theoretical approaches* (4th ed.). New York: Free Press, pp. 39–68.

Turner, J. & Jaco, R. (1996). Problem-solving theory and social work treatment. In F.J. Turner (Ed.). *Social work treatment: interlocking theoretical approaches* (4th ed.). New York: Free Press, pp. 503–522.

Tutty, L. (1990). The response of community mental health professionals to clients' rights: a review and suggestions. *Canadian Journal of Community Mental Health, 9*(1), 1–24.

Wickham, E. (1993). *Group treatment in social work.* Toronto: Thompson.

Zapf, M.K. (1993). Contracts and covenants in social work education: considerations for Native outreach programs. *The Social Worker, 61*(4), 150–154.

APPENDIX A

Example of an Administrative Contract

Administrative Agreement between Marlene Smith, client, and Janet Dutton, M.S.W, therapist.

1. We will meet for counselling sessions once a week for one hour in the offices of Ms. Dutton. Times to be arranged.

2. Ms. Smith will attend on her own, unless both parties agree that other significant people should be invited for either individual sessions or for the remainder of the contract.

3. The intervention will utilize client-centred therapy with a feminist perspective.

4. The therapist will direct treatment and will be responsible for informing the client of any risks implicit in interventions and checking to ensure the client's willingness to comply with any directive. Ms. Smith will be responsible for informing the therapist of any discomfort or disagreement with any therapeutic interventions either within or between sessions.

5. Ms. Smith will be charged for sessions based on the agency's sliding fee schedule (attached). Payment will be made at the beginning of each session. Sessions may be cancelled with 24-hour notice, or, in the case of illness or emergencies, on the day of the meeting. Failing this, clients who miss sessions will be responsible for payment of same.

6. This initial contract is for eight sessions. During the eighth session the need/desire for a further administrative contract will be discussed.

7. This treatment contract can be cancelled at any time by the client, with 24-hours notice, or by the therapist if ethical dilemmas or unforeseen circumstances emerge. In both cases, information about the reasons for cancellation will be conveyed to the other party either by telephone or in writing.

APPENDIX B

Example of a Treatment Contract

Treatment Contract of Ms. Marlene Smith. Compiled after in-depth discussion in the first session on May 5th, 1996.

1. I want to stop being preoccupied with my weight, specifically: using diet medication containing barbiturates, berating myself for my size and appearance, avoiding outside activities because of my size.

2. Instead I will join Weight Watchers, start a walking program, start buying attractive clothes even though large-sized, and enrol in a singing class.

3. These changes may result in my feeling better about myself, even though I am heavier than I would like to be. As a result, I may speak my mind more at work, and have more fun by joining activities where I can meet new friends.

4. I would sabotage this plan by continuing to criticize myself for being overweight, scaring myself that if I go out people will avoid or mock me and by telling myself that no-one would want to be my friend.

5. If I follow through with this plan, my mother may continue to criticize my size and want to know what I am doing about my weight. If I don't tell her she may become angry. On the other hand, we may learn new ways to spend time together that do not focus on my size and that could result in an improved relationship. My co-workers and boss may be surprised to learn that I have some good ideas. I may meet new people who could become friends.

This Treatment Contract may be revised or refocused at any time with the mutual consent of client and therapist.

GETTING
READY TO
INTERVIEW

Catherine Mary Brothers

INTRODUCTION

After years of social work practice, it seems appropriate that I should be asked to prepare this chapter and the next one on the subject of interviewing by my first social work professor. I have never forgotten the frustration during the first few social work classes in Waterloo, Ontario during 1967, as Dr. Francis Turner talked enthusiastically about the process of interviewing. Impatiently, I wanted Dr. Turner to move beyond the details of preparing for an interview and talk about what I had come to study, namely "social work." It seemed like a teaser that he was discussing such matters as where one positions one's desk and whether one hangs one's professional degree upon the wall! I still remember the seat where I was sitting in class when "the penny dropped" and I recognized that interviewing is "it" in social work practice.

Interviewing is fundamental to all modalities within social work practice. Within the social work interview, we draw upon our vast reservoirs of knowledge, theory, and techniques, and really do "it." This chapter will discuss issues related to preparing for an interview. The following chapter will consider practical issues within the process of interviewing. It is a challenge to separate the skills of interviewing from the knowledge and content required for social work treatment. The interviewing skills discussed in these chapters must be applied within a context of social work theoretical frameworks. Interviewing skills are not honed in isolation; rather, they build on a solid social work knowledge base of assessment, diagnosis, treatment, and evaluation.

These two chapters on interviewing assume the social worker is using a broad-based and eclectic approach to treatment, drawing upon the best of techniques from many theories. Major theorists, such as Carl Rogers, Freud, and Maslow have greatly influenced the way social workers approach interviewing. As workers learn interviewing skills and techniques, they are challenged to integrate this learning with knowledge regarding the growing repertoire of credible theoretical frameworks, such as gestalt therapy, reality therapy, solution-focused therapy, cognitive therapy, ego psychology, and behavioural modification.

The social work interview is a professional conversation. It is deliberate, planned, and purposeful. It involves asking questions, listening, and talking. The interview is the medium for the exchange of information, and the expression of thoughts and feelings, through which the worker helps the client to gain mastery over his or her circumstances.

It is essential for the beginning social worker to conceptualize the difference between an ordinary conversation and the professional conversation that takes the form of an interview. Interviewing is not a chat over the back fence, nor a conversation with a friend. Such interchanges are usually more casual and unstructured. Participants in a conversation talk back and forth and frequently change the subject. Ordinary conversations involve two-sided sharing. Both parties can determine the topics of conversation, change subjects, and talk about themselves and their own ideas. There is usually a spontaneity to ordinary conversations that does not involve talking within a fixed time frame.

Social work interviews, on the other hand, focus on the person being helped. The helper shares little about him or herself. The worker has the responsibility to help the client. The social worker's words are all geared toward helping the other person gain mastery of his or her circumstances. The interview is a safe place where clients may work out problems, find solutions, and develop new skills. Within the interview the client relies upon the worker to maintain the professional distance required to understand what is going on and to redirect the interview as appropriate.

The social work interview comes in many forms, and takes place in many different types of agencies and settings. The client may initiate the request for help and come voluntarily to the interview. Or, the expectation that the client participate in the interview may come from somewhere external to the client. We speak of "involuntary" clients as those who have no choice and are required by others to participate, as can happen in psychiatric, criminal justice, and child welfare systems. The interview can take the form of a telephone interview, a formal office interview, an individual interview, a family interview, a group interview, a home visit, a hospital room visit, a prison range visit, a trip to the playground, an outing to the donut shop, a town hall meeting, an excursion in the city with a newly arrived immigrant, or a luncheon meeting between the social worker and a Member of Parliament. The fundamental skills needed to become an effective interviewer are common to all areas of social work practice, including community organization and development.

All social work interviews require a well thought-out plan. Thus, we turn to examining issues related to preparing for an interview and establishing the climate for successful social work interventions.

THE PHYSICAL SETTING

When clients first arrive to see the social worker, the general appearance and condition of the social agency, or setting, will begin shaping the helping climate. One cannot overestimate the importance of a warm and friendly receptionist. Clients frequently and discreetly ask the receptionist questions that prepare them for the interview. A positive, upbeat receptionist who values the social worker's activities will go a long way toward starting the interview on the right foot. The condition of the waiting room says a lot about the agency's attitude toward clients. Privacy, quiet, comfortable seating, clearly indicated washrooms, a water cooler, clean toys, a coat rack and boot tray, and up-to-date magazines with a range of choices appropriate to men, women, and children signal a client-centred agency.

In general, workers look for a private place, free from interruptions and distractions, in which to conduct their interviews. At the least, the physical setting should contain two chairs face-to-face, and a box of tissues within easy reach. In considering the physical setting and the establishment of a therapeutic climate, social workers strive to convey the seriousness of the interview, while at the same time establishing comfort and privacy.

In order to consider the many aspects of the physical setting that influence clients, social workers need to arrive for the interview before the client and set up for the interview in advance. In many settings there are multiple users of interviewing rooms, and social workers who expect to find the room in a certain order will be disappointed if they do not check in advance. Are there unrelated papers and materials in the room that can be disposed of? Is the room temperature comfortable? Are there distracting background noises? What can the worker do about colleagues in an adjoining room or hallway who are laughing or talking loudly? Are there ways to secure a table out of earshot from others in the busy donut shop? Is there some quiet place at the end of the hall, where the social worker can move the patient in a wheelchair away from a crowded hospital ward?

Everything in the social worker's office sends a message to the client. It is up to the social worker to make sure it is the message they want to send. The social worker needs to understand the goals of the setting in which he or she works and the nature of the clientele. For example, the same poster may not be appropriate in all settings. A female social worker in a family agency that was assigned a caseload of men, women, and children of all ages, placed her favourite poster on her office wall—"Women of the World Unite." While this poster may convey an encouraging and hopeful message to some clients, what messages might it convey to adolescent boys or men who are struggling with feelings of identity and assertiveness?

The choice of pictures for one's office can be tricky. I once had an abstract impressionist painting in my office which I considered to be pleasant, bright, and cheerful. The print was on the wall in view of seated clients. A young woman whom I had seen several times finally asked if she could remove the print during her visit. She had been severely abused as a child and she saw in the picture a large angry mother smashing a small helpless child on its head. Once she pointed out this image among the circles and lines that I had considered neutral, I could appreciate the woman's anguish, and regretted the lack of sensitivity in choosing this print for the office.

The choice of lighting in the interviewing room will influence the therapeutic climate. Often, social workers opt for lamps to replace the harsh glare of fluorescent lights. This arrangement might be quite suitable in daytime hours in offices with lots of natural light. It may, however, establish a seductive atmosphere when interviewing members of the opposite sex during evening hours. One male client did not return to a second interview with a female social worker because he was so distracted by the low lighting in her office. In a marital session with his wife, this client talked about his first attempt to seek help. According to the client, the very thought of sharing intimate feelings with a professional was threatening, and then to be in a setting that seemed so sexual was more than he could cope with.

Cluttered desks and bulletin boards convey a message to clients about the way a social worker looks after his or her business. A professional businesswoman who was going through a tough marital separation did not return to see her social worker a second time. Later, I received feedback from the woman that the worker's desk and bookcase were so messy that she decided he could not help her with her problems if that was the way he looked after his own business. While few social workers aspire to maintaining a desktop that is totally clear, all should give some thought to the message their desktop and bookcases are conveying to clients. To be sure, client trust and confidentiality are severely destroyed when identifying client information, files, or appointment times are displayed on one's desk. Computer terminals on social work desks pose new challenges related to ensuring confidentiality, as workers pull up appointment schedules on their computer screens with names identifying other clients.

Over the years, I have worked with many social workers who have bulletin boards in their offices and have always found the use of such boards confusing. It is rarely clear whether the bulletin board is for the worker's or the client's benefit. Often positioned over the worker's desk, the bulletin board has a hodgepodge of inspirational messages, "to do" lists, and practical resource information. Often, bulletin boards contain out-of-date memos and newsletters. One social worker, who ordinarily had excellent judgement, was even observed to have posted on his bulletin board the list of clients for whom he had outstanding case records. If bulletin boards are truly for clients, thought should be given to their position in the office, so that they are freely accessible to clients who must not be made to feel that they are snooping and reading the worker's business. If bulletin boards are for the use of the social worker, thought should be given to the impact they have on the client. The social worker who is relying upon a bulletin board might want to seek alternatives among other time-management and information-storage products.

Social workers need to be sensitive to the messages they send by displaying around the office mementoes from clients. A display of thank-you cards, client poetry, or client gifts, may inadvertently convey expectations the worker has of all clients, or such displays may suggest the neediness of the worker and his or her desire for validation and affirmation from clients. At the least, setting out client cards, writings, and other mementoes suggests that confidentiality is loose.

Displaying one's professional degrees, or even a graduating class picture, is usually viewed as helpful in establishing credibility and setting a professional tone to the social worker's office. On the other hand, displaying pictures of spouses, partners, friends, or children may influence the shape the interview takes, and will frequently divert the focus from the client to the worker. The social worker needs to think clearly about why they would want to display personal pictures and what impact such personal disclosures will have on the interview process. In some settings, where the social worker may be working with dangerous or threatening clients, the worker will want to avoid any disclosures that could put the safety of his or her family at risk.

Social workers give a fair bit of attention to where they position their desk in the office. Few social workers interview a client across the desk. The general thinking seems to be that unless you are trying to establish authority and control, move out from behind the desk. Social workers who need a desk between themselves and the client in order to establish authority and control probably will not succeed, as they fail to recognize the amount of authority that is inherent in their position, no matter where they sit.

Some social workers do prefer to sit at their desk, with the client sitting to the side of the desk, usually with the back of the desk against a wall. Other workers prefer to sit with the client at a round table of elbow height. Still other workers choose to arrange the chairs with a small coffee table in between. Sometimes, it is possible to offer the client a choice of seating arrangements. Always, it is possible for the social worker to plan and experiment with the seating arrangement in advance. It does seem that the people who purchase office furniture always buy one chair that has wheels on the bottom. More than one social worker has been thrown off by the client who enters the office and chooses the one chair with the wheels on the bottom. Which brings me to my point! Is it necessary for the social worker to sit in the chair with the wheels on the bottom? How much of a power and control gesture is such positioning? For sure, the client knows they have come for help, whether the worker sits in the chair with the wheels or not. Is it possible for the client to have a chair that also has wheels on the bottom? Could the worker leave the wheeled chair at the desk, and sit in the same kind of chair as the client? Perhaps minor details, these seating arrangements will, however, play a role in determining the climate for the interview.

Many social workers find it helpful to have a clock on the wall of their offices so that they can conduct their interviews within the allocated time frame and stay on schedule. The clock can be strategically placed on a wall where the social worker can see it throughout the interview without distracting the client. The end of the interview should not comes as a surprise. Looking at one's watch usually sends a signal to clients that either the worker is finished or the client is taking up too much time. With a clock placed on a wall, desk, or bookshelf, the social worker can be aware of the time throughout the interview and plan interventions with a definite sense of the time available, without distracting the client.

It is hard to imagine a social worker conducting an office interview without a box of tissue. Of course, not all clients cry, but for the many who do, it is considerate to have tissue easily accessible. In fact, one might want to give some thought to the size of the tissue that is kept in the social work office. Before I tuned in to the importance of this matter, I experienced several awkward moments as a hospital social worker with clients who were crying profusely and trying to use the tiny sizes of tissue provided as standard hospital supplies.

In considering the appropriate physical setting for interviews, social workers also need to plan for safety issues. Most agencies have policies that deter social workers from meeting with clients when there is no one else present in the building. It is the usual practice of most agencies to ensure that there is always someone else near to where the client and social worker are meeting. Social workers are careful not to interview abusive, assaultive, paranoid, or explosive clients in isolated areas. Social workers choose an interviewing room where they can attract the attention of others if they are in danger.

Another important aspect to preparing the physical setting and establishing a therapeutic climate involves planning in advance for the care of young children while parents are in an interview. While older children can sometimes wait comfortably and safely in the agency waiting room, this arrangement is impractical for young children. The receptionist or office support staff in most agencies have many responsibilities that make it impossible or inappropriate for them to care adequately for younger children. Beginning social workers are off to a bad start if they assume the agency receptionist is also the babysitter!

Another, not so obvious, aspect of the physical setting is the social worker's choice of clothing. The appearance of the social worker may have a tremendous impact on the client's perception of the worker's ability to help. In spite of the prevalence for many years of long, flowing, hippie-style skirts among female social workers, and beards on male social workers, there is no specific uniform or code of dressing for our profession. The specific setting and the age of clientele will help the worker determine appropriate clothing styles. Most importantly, the social worker strives to look clean and well-kept, without appearing overdressed and overbearing.

The need for a setting clear of distractions and interruptions was identified at the beginning of this section. Social workers need to conduct their interviews free from telephone interruptions. In these days of modern technology, all social workers should be able to turn off the ringers on their phones during interviews with clients. In some social work cultures, such as family service agencies, the practice is firmly established that social workers do not take phone calls during interviews. In other multi-disciplinary, fast-paced settings with a range of conflicting values and priorities, the challenge of having an uninterrupted interview is more daunting. This type of interruption does not convey a lack of respect for good social work practice so much as the complex and conflicting demands of busy institutions. The social worker is well advised to recognize these potential conflicts in advance and have clear guidelines for client-centred practices. I recall the secretary in a hospital social work department getting an urgent phone call from a harried head nurse who could not reach the social worker whose ringer was off during a session with a client. When the secretary patiently explained what was going on, the head nurse belligerently challenged, "I don't care if she's interviewing the Queen of England, I need to talk to her now!"

The social worker is also responsible for looking after distractions outside the interviewing room. (I once had an office along a busy hospital corridor, for example.) It would be irritating and inappropriate when a client was weeping sadly to have people standing outside the interview door talking and laughing. The social worker is expected to take charge of the interview and make a decision as to when it is in the client's best interests to step out into the hall or exterior waiting room and ask others to move along or quiet down.

Other interruptions that are even more disconcerting and challenging come with the ringing of unexpected fire alarms during the most emotional parts of interviews. To continue the interview with a distraught client during a fire alarm is clearly poor judgment; it is not only unsafe, but incurs the wrath of fire marshals and administrators. To march the client out of the office to join others in the designated "safe area" may be embarrassing and a real threat to confidentiality. On more than one occasion I have had the frustration of easing a tearful client out a hospital exit while fire bells were ringing, and an interview was terminated unexpectedly with the worst possible timing. This example is a reminder to social workers of the importance of recognizing and planning for external interruptions and distractions over which they may have little control.

The preceding discussion on the physical setting presumes that interviews will take place face-to-face between the social worker and the client. In rural and remote areas of Canada, face-to-face interviews are not always possible. For many clients, access to counselling is by telephone. Some exciting pioneer work has been done in this regard through Family Service Canada agencies. The Family Service agency in Thunder Bay operates a 1-800-number for credit counselling clients throughout Ontario who live in remote areas without ready access to a credit counselling agency. Using many of the same principles regarding attention to the therapeutic climate, counsellors are quite successfully helping clients to prepare budgets and take control of their money worries. Further, a new telephone counselling program has been initiated throughout Northern Ontario, through a coalition of Family Service agencies in North Bay, Sault Ste. Marie, Timmins, Elliott Lake, and Thunder Bay. Social workers are counselling clients by telephone 24 hours a day, seven days a week. A major difference between this service and the telephone counselling that has traditionally taken place in many social service settings is that the Northern Ontario telephone counselling is not intended as an adjunct to face-to-face counselling. It is the medium for helping when face-to-face counselling is not available. Through Employee Assistance Programs and 1-800-numbers that are available through Family Service agencies, such as in Toronto, Ontario, we see a positive response by clients to telephone counselling as an alternative to face-to-face counselling.

ADVANCE PREPARATION FOR THE INTERVIEW

Because the interview is a conversation with a purpose, it requires a plan and preparation on the part of the social worker. The social worker plans for the interview in advance and will have some questions in mind that relate to the purposes of the interview. Often these initial questions revolve around working with the client to establish the purposes of the interview. The social worker is challenged to approach each interview as if it is his or her only one for that day, and, for sure, the most important one. It does not help the client to hear how busy the worker is, or how far behind he or she is.

It is good social work practice to be on time for each interview, which also means finishing interviews within the scheduled time. Nothing establishes a negative climate of social worker control and disregard more quickly than leaving clients to wait in the waiting room beyond their scheduled appointment time. Embarrassing behaviours I have witnessed include social workers laughing and chatting to each other in clear view of clients who are waiting for appointments, and workers who go for "a coffee" during time they have scheduled for a client appointment. It is not too difficult to think of the negative responses these behaviours trigger in apprehensive clients who have busy schedules themselves. If it is apparent that the social worker is going to be more than a few minutes late for a scheduled appointment, consideration may be given to offering the client a choice of waiting or rescheduling.

Sometimes it becomes necessary for the social worker to change appointment times previously scheduled with clients. It sends a much more positive message when the client is given the choice of moving the interview time forward rather than backward. Delaying appointments suggests to the client that other priorities take precedence.

Prior to the interview, the social worker thinks about how he or she is going to convey a belief that the client can change. Usually, the social worker prepares for an interview by reviewing available client reports and "intake" or "face sheet" materials. Interviews, and a trusting relationship, are off to a better start when the social worker is straightforward with the client in stating what information he or she had access to in advance. Similarly, if the worker has not reviewed file material or consulted with others in advance of the interview, it is honest and congruent to let the client know this fact at the outset.

In preparing for the interview, social workers need to appreciate that clients do not wake up one morning and impulsively call a social worker for help. It is not easy to ask for help and it is not easy to open up to a social worker, no matter how wise and understanding that person may be. Not only the worker but clients too prepare for the interview by rehearsing what they want to say. Consequently, in reviewing advance material, the social worker needs to remind him or herself that this material may not reflect at all what the client is currently thinking and feeling. The social worker's responsibility is to be familiar with the background information, while at the same time retaining the focus of beginning "where the client is at." It can be helpful for the worker to plan beginnings that acknowledge the advance work that the client has done in getting ready for the interview. The social worker could give the client the opportunity to say what he or she has rehearsed in advance; for example, "I'm sure you've given some thought to what you'd like to talk about. Where would you like to start?"

Preparation for the interview also includes coming to grips, in advance of the interview, with one's own thoughts and feelings regarding the client's problems and circumstances. For example, if the social worker is to see an adult who is having an extramarital affair, a woman who has had an abortion, a child who has been abused, or an adult who has perpetrated a sexual offence against children, thoughts and feelings will be evoked which the worker needs to recognize. This self-awareness will help the worker to consider what impact their own feelings will have on the interview.

In preparing for interviews, a mistake that all social workers make at some point is to take literally the "presenting problem" or reason for referral. I have seen many interviews start off poorly because the social worker has looked at the "intake form" and picked up on two or three words such as "anxiety and depression," or "low self-esteem," and then started off on an interview with something like, "So, I understand that you have a problem with anxiety and depression," or "Can you tell me more about your low self-esteem?"

Given the circumstances for the interview, the social worker may wish to tell the client what information he or she has been given, but the social worker would be wise not to assume this "intake" information matches the client's perception of the problem or purpose of the interview. In hospital and school settings, "reasons for referral" are especially problematic since most often they are professional opinions, sometimes translated third and fourth hand, that have never been shared with the client. Unless the social worker has personally recorded the presenting problem, it will not be clear whether he or she is reading the client's words or someone else's opinion. Planning a starting point for the interview calls for thoughtfulness and sensitivity on the part of the social worker.

In planning for interviews, social workers are cautioned against asking clients to provide the same information several times. Such duplication conveys a lack of organization and a disrespect for what the client has already shared. For example, if a routine part of taking phone referrals involves asking clients their age, date of birth, marital status, and number of children, it does not make sense to have clients reproduce this same information on a form in the agency waiting room. It makes even less sense for the social worker to start out the interview by asking for this same information all over again.

Finally, in preparing for the interview, social workers are required to leave their own worries and office politics outside the interview. After a staff meeting, I was horrified to overhear a colleague's exchange with her client. As the social worker guided the client to her office, the client asked a polite "How are you?" The worker responded by saying, "There are big worries around here! We just learned that we might lose some of our jobs if a large part of our funding is cut." It is doubtful that this kind of stressed-out communication contributed in any positive way to establishing a helpful climate for the client interview.

TAKING NOTES DURING THE INTERVIEW

There is a wide variety of acceptable practice regarding note-taking during the social work interview. Usually, it is not necessary to write in detail during the interview, although it may be important to record specific facts or details. Many experienced social workers prefer to set aside a few minutes after the interview to make notes, while the content and process are still fresh in the worker's mind. To record notes at the end of a long day is difficult, and note-making, left for several days or even weeks, becomes stressful and yields records of questionable value.

When the social worker chooses to write notes during the interview, it is important to do so in a way that still conveys to clients that they have the worker's full attention. When taking notes, social workers can tell the client clearly what they are doing and why they are doing it. Workers can make the notes in an open manner whereby the client sees what they are doing. In fact, social workers may show the client what they have written and ask the client to confirm its accuracy. I have also seen examples where the social worker has suggested that the client may choose to keep his or her own notes as well. Some workers have a natural and open style of setting aside a few minutes at the end of the interview for taking notes. Again, this is acceptable practice as long as the social workers let the clients know what they are doing and why they are doing it.

The writer has noted an increasing practice among social workers of making the writing of the assessment and treatment goals a part of the interview process. The client actively participates in preparing the written document that becomes a treatment contract signed by both the worker and the client. Many clients take away a photocopy of this document, which remains on file.

It is essential for the social worker to plan how and when he or she will prepare notes on each interview. Recording should be done in the manner that is least distracting to both the social worker and the client. Always, the social worker should keep in mind the agency's expectations of good record-keeping, and the client's right to review file material.

INTRODUCTIONS

Interviews generally begin with friendly conversation and introductions aimed at making clients welcome and giving them a chance to sit down and become comfortable. Opening comments will establish the climate and chemistry for the interview. The social worker takes the lead with brief, clear introductions, an invitation to take a seat, and perhaps an offer to hang up the client's coat.

The role of food and eating in social work interviews is worth reexamining. Offering coffee, tea, or cookies has generally been seen as undesirable, as it establishes a social rather than professional tone. However, for clients of some cultural backgrounds, sharing food can be a sign of great trust and reciprocity. Social workers sometimes use food during interviews to highlight accomplishments and celebrate progress. I was moved recently when I observed the practice of a social worker in Ontario who had been working with an isolated and impoverished young woman, Darlene. As the end of treatment was approaching, the social worker asked Darlene how she would like to celebrate all the accomplishments made in her counselling sessions. Shyly, Darlene told the social worker that her favourite foods, which she rarely had, were fruit punch and Mars chocolate bars. The worker promised to bring these treats to the final session. The importance of this affirmation of Darlene's progress was highlighted when Darlene arrived at the interview with two glasses in her purse, neatly wrapped in handkerchiefs, and proudly produced these for the two bottles of fruit punch, which the worker had brought along. As an aside, Darlene's behaviour is a reminder of how important it is for the social worker to make only promises that they intend to keep!

It is appropriate for the social worker to offer a glass of water to a stressed client, especially when they have a dry mouth that is going to make talking difficult. The social worker is cautioned about using food and eating as a diversion in interviewing, or as a shift from a professional to a social encounter wherein one avoids painful issues. Nevertheless, there are times when food and eating can be a deliberate and purposeful part of the helping process.

The negative impact of opening comments is apparent in the example of a client who came into the interview apologizing profusely for being ten minutes late. This single parent had travelled to the agency, taking two buses with two young children in tow. The social worker responded to the client's apologies in a distant, matter-of-fact manner, saying, "Your lateness makes no difference to me. It's your hour and you've just lost ten minutes of it." Needless to say, walls went up and that client never came back to see that social worker again.

Introductions give an opportunity for social workers to indicate the name they prefer to be addressed by, and to ask clients how they prefer to be addressed. Before the interview bogs down in small talk, it is the social worker's role to focus the interview with a question such as, "Perhaps we can start out by asking you to describe what brought you here today?" or, "I understand you are here today because. . . . Can you tell me more about this?"

Sometimes, simple questions such as, "How are things going?" or, "Where would you like to start today?" are helpful beginnings to an interview. It cannot be stressed too much that the social worker is responsible for the direction of the interview. If the direction is not clear, or if the client seems to have a different agenda, it is the worker's responsibility to deal with what is going on. The more clarity there is at the beginning of the interview regarding client expectations and purpose, the more likely are the possibilities of successful problem solving and a satisfying termination.

It is essential that the social worker be frank with clients about the purposes of the interview and how anything they share might be used. The social worker must never lie, manipulate, or deceive clients about the purposes of the interview or how information might be used. The social worker establishes the trusting climate wherein the client is relaxed and comfortable. The social worker is calm and attentive. There is no room in a social work interview for being phoney or pretentious.

In some social work settings, it is necessary for the worker to establish fees for the social work service and to make arrangements for the collection of these fees. Sometimes clients complain that workers went to such elaborate lengths to establish and explain the fees that the client felt deprived of valuable interview time for solving their problems. The social worker needs to give some thought to the simplest, briefest, and most clear-cut manner of establishing and collecting fees.

Introductions to the interview might also include establishing the time frame for interviews. It is much easier to start and stop on time when the client is clear about the allotted time. Some social workers find it helpful to explain to clients that they may not solve their problems completely in the interview and it may be necessary to interrupt discussion in order to work within the available time for each interview. It can also be helpful to reassure clients that you know they will be thinking and doing "homework" away from the interview time. This direction helps remove the pressure to try to cover everything that is important within the limited interview time. It also reinforces the social worker's plan to start and stop on time.

Introductions in social work interviews take a different shape depending on who requests the interview. As a hospital social worker in both Toronto and Kitchener I was often in the position of introducing myself to patients upon the referral of another health professional, or calling family members of frail elderly persons and inviting them to interviews they had not requested. As a child welfare worker in London, Ontario, I was in a position of initiating interviews with parents when someone else had reported suspicions of child abuse. Or

again, as a social worker in a psychiatric clinic in Guelph and Orangeville, Ontario, I frequently interviewed either persons who were in attendance because someone else thought they
had a problem, or persons who thought they should be talking to a psychiatrist, not a social
worker. In the Waterloo Region family service agency where I am currently employed,
clients tend to request help on their own initiative and arrive for appointments prepared to
talk about issues of concern to them.

In each of the settings described above, the beginning of the social work interview is different. While there are common principles in interviewing, it is important for the social
worker to recognize the context in which the interview is taking place. When someone other
than the client has initiated the interview, it is helpful for the worker to start with as clear,
simple, and straightforward an explanation as possible regarding the purpose of the interview.
The social worker can expect that the client's perception will differ from those who requested
social work help on the client's behalf. The social worker does not easily start out with the
client's trust, and it helps to be as natural and non-defensive as possible. Fuzzy explanations from the social worker will ensure an awkward start. In fact, this introduction is so
important that I highly recommend that beginning social workers practise what they are
going to say, and, in particular, practise saying it out loud. If it does not make sense to the
social worker, it is not going to make sense to the client the social worker is interviewing.

CONCLUSION

At this point, the reader of this chapter will be wanting to get on with "it." We have established
the importance of preparation and attention to detail in establishing a therapeutic milieu.
Now it is time to move to the next chapter and explore what happens after introductions.

THE PROCESS OF INTERVIEWING Catherine Mary Brothers

The social work interview is a "time-out" for many clients—a safety island, whereupon the client talks things out, takes some risks in exploring thoughts and feelings, and plans new behaviours. This chapter will explore how the social worker helps the client through asking questions, listening, and talking. As a prerequisite for studying the process of interviewing, social workers will have considerable insight into their own personalities, strengths, and vulnerabilities. With this self-awareness social workers are able to adopt a comfortable interviewing style that suits their own personalities.

Social workers preparing for the interview process are reminded to consider how they themselves would like to be treated, or perhaps how they would want their parent, or best friend, to be treated in getting help from a social worker. When I was fifteen years old my first employment was as a cashier at A&P. A cashier was trained to treat every customer with great respect, as one never knew when the "mystery shopper" would arrive from head office. The unidentified mystery shopper would go through the cashier's line the same as any other customer, and when the transactions were all completed, the store manager would abruptly move in and close off the cashier's line. The surprised cashier would get an on-the-spot evaluation of her customer service, attitude, and accuracy. That experience had a lasting impact on my social work career. Each client is viewed as the "mystery shopper" challenging the social worker to put forward his or her best abilities.

Before beginning any interview, the social worker will consider who should be present in the interview. Will it be the individual, the couple, or perhaps the whole family? Are there significant others to include? Would it help the adolescent client to include a friend in the interview? It is always the social worker's responsibility to ensure that the client is safe in disclosing private matters when someone else is present in the interview.

There may be times when observers are present during the interview, especially in interviews of beginning social workers who are being closely evaluated and supervised. Social workers may produce audio or video tapes of interviews, another form of observation. In general, the presence of observers and taping equipment enhances the quality of the interview.

Interviews become more focused, purposeful, and disciplined. Clients forget about the observers when they have been introduced in a short, simple manner and their presence is explained in plain, honest language.

An interesting example of observation occurred when a social worker was interviewing a family of nine adult children and their spouses. All were concerned about their much-loved mother who was living alone and becoming increasingly frail and confused. Only one adult child, who lived in a distant city, was unable to be present. The family came to the interview with a tape recorder because they wanted the absent brother "to hear everything the social worker had to say." The social worker rose to the occasion and, under this pressure, conducted one of her most purposeful and focused interviews ever!

The language of the interview is important. The most successful social workers speak to clients in a comfortable, attentive manner, using a natural tone of voice; in fact, the same tone used in ordinary interactions. It is embarrassing to witness social workers speaking to clients with an affected and unnatural tone of voice. The receptionist in a social work setting can describe the tone of voice each social worker uses when he or she greets clients. It is easy to recognize when a worker is speaking in a patronizing, condescending, or authoritarian tone.

During the interview the social worker can increase the client's comfort and the bond between worker and client by using the client's own words, in a respectful manner, especially when summarizing what the client has said. The goal is to engage the client, not to raise credibility questions; thus the social worker does not want to appear unnatural in using the client's language. As examples, clients recognize the incongruence of a worker using the client's profanities, if this is not the social worker's usual way of speaking, and older social workers need to consider the impact of using language in vogue with adolescents. Sometimes youth have a particular pride in the language of their own culture, and the social worker needs to be respectful before crossing the boundary.

ASKING QUESTIONS

Most often the social worker asks questions as a technique for helping the client. The questions will be determined both by the purpose of the interview and by the worker's assessment of the client. The questions may be determined by the frame of reference the social worker is using for treatment. For example, a solution-focused social worker will ask questions related to discovering and reinforcing exceptional situations wherein the client has been successful. A social worker oriented toward encouraging insight into dysfunctional behaviour will explore past and present issues related to the problems. To give examples of questions based on theoretical orientation, the solution-focused social worker will deliberately frame his or her question as, "That's fantastic! You had one night last week when you did not drink! What was going on that night that made you so successful?" The problem-oriented social worker might ask, "Can you tell me more about how you were feeling before you started drinking?" In both approaches, the social worker can keep the flow of client involvement going with simple, encouraging questions, such as "And what else?"

Social workers stay away from closed questions that can be answered with one word, or a "yes" or "no," and which may leave the client with the impression that the worker is judging them. The goal is to stay with what is important to the client and ask open-ended questions which encourage the client to talk freely. Even when social workers think they know exactly what the client means, they will learn more, and the client will gain helpful insights, when the worker asks wide-open questions, such as "What was that like for you?" The social worker avoids pursuing an overabundance of factual information and conducting an interview that feels like a game of "Twenty Questions."

The social worker does not wish to become side-tracked by irrelevant details, or to bombard the client with questions that are not purposeful. Issues or feelings cannot be explored in adequate depth when topics are shifted abruptly. Workers often need to protect clients from revealing too much when they are vulnerable, especially in first interviews. Clients may withdraw if they feel they have revealed too much. Sometimes the role of the social worker is to slow the process down and respect boundaries and limits to the interview. The social worker does not have license to explore all aspects of the client's life and/or functioning, unless there is a clear purpose for doing so.

For a seasoned social worker, asking questions such as "Do you enjoy sex?" or "How much money do you have in the bank?" may seem entirely appropriate. For a client who has never discussed these private matters, and for whom their relevance is doubtful, these questions can be disturbing. Always, the social worker requires a purpose for his or her questioning and a keen sense of timing and context. The following case illustrates the importance of understanding the client before asking inappropriate and humiliating questions.

Jean, an intelligent, single, frail, isolated, eighty-five-year-old woman was admitted to hospital after a bad fall. She was helpless on the bathroom floor for twenty-four hours, unable to call for help. Jean had tremendous conflict and ambivalence. She feared for her safety living alone. She had been fiercely independent and private all her life. Her physician was urging institutional care. Jean was mentally competent and did not want to give up control of her own personal and financial affairs. She agreed to an interview with the social worker from the Home for the Aged.

The Home for the Aged social worker insisted at the outset of the first interview that several sheets of long forms had to be completed to determine Jean's eligibility. Until this was determined, the social worker stated there was no point in discussing Jean's concerns. Within three minutes, the social worker had asked Jean for the location, account numbers, and balances of all her bank accounts. Within five minutes the social worker had asked about the whereabouts of Jean's will and funeral arrangements. The social worker was firm that the Home for the Aged would not consider Jean's application until advance funeral arrangements were made, so that the Home would not "get stuck" with the bill for Jean's funeral. The impact of this interview on Jean was horrible. The social worker from the Home may not have had control over the content of the questions on the form; however, she certainly did have control over the timing and context in which they were presented.

During interviews, the general wisdom is to avoid questions that begin with "why." The "why" questions have a parental ring to them, and frequently lead to intellectual or defensive responses. Such questions may be seen as rhetorical or judgmental, and usually invite defensive responses, as in, "Why were you late?" or "Why didn't you pick up your dirty clothes?" Other questions, such as, "Can you help me to understand more about what is going on for you?" will be much more likely to engage the client.

The social worker can encourage the client to talk freely with such leads as, "Tell me about yourself." Questions that appear neutral, such as, "Do you go to school?" "Do you have a job?" "Do you have children?," may be distressing subjects for the client. Premature questions may inhibit the client from further disclosures and lead to pre-packaged defensive answers that are half-truths. The social worker who asks too quickly about a husband or wife may never learn that the client has a homosexual partner. When the social worker relaxes and works on conveying respect and acceptance, most relevant information will unfold naturally throughout the interview.

It is helpful for the social worker to verify that he or she is actually hearing what the client is saying. This can be done with uncomplicated and simple questions, such as "Are you saying . . .", or "I heard you say . . . . Did I get what you were saying?" Clients will try more than once to send the social worker a message when the worker misses the first signal. Clients will probe deeper with gentle questions and requests from the social worker to say more; for example, "Can you say more about that?" Premature statements, like "I understand" may limit the client's disclosure and self-exploration.

The social worker needs to recognize when the client is rambling in an interview. Asking a purposeful question will help the client to focus. It is helpful to remember that the importance of asking questions is not so much the information that the social worker gleans, as the change that takes place in the client as a consequence of the questions.

The more the social worker understands about assessment and diagnosis, the more purposeful and helpful the interview questions become. The social worker who has been unable to recognize the symptoms of clinical depression asks the depressed client to talk about his or her earliest childhood memories. Sadly, the client recalls feelings of fear, loneliness, and isolation, recounting the lack of friends and the mean teachers. The worker who is not thinking diagnostically gets caught up in a discussion about the faults of the educational system. The worker, who cannot recognize the gloominess associated with depression, fails to recognize that the client might have entirely different recollections if he or she were feeling better. The diagnostic and assessment abilities of the social worker are key ingredients in knowing how to structure the interview, and knowing when it is helpful to ask deliberate and focused questions. An eclectic approach to social work treatment is no excuse for a confusing jumble of questions.

Occasionally, clients will ask the social worker questions. Perhaps these are questions about the social worker's marital status, sexual orientation, age, religion, or parenthood status. The worker decides whether it is helpful to the client to answer such personal questions directly. In working with young children or adolescents a short, simple, direct answer is helpful. Usually with adults, however, the worker will want to refocus the question on the client, and avoid an ordinary two-way conversation that takes away from the professional nature of the interviewing process. There will also be times when clients ask the social worker for a personal favour, or for money. For example, a client leaving the social worker's office asked the worker for a loan so that she could play Bingo. Social workers need to anticipate and be prepared for such questions.

LISTENING

While social workers listen, they are paying attention to verbal and non-verbal communications; that is, both spoken and unspoken messages. When workers feel awkward or inadequate, their listening skills are impaired by tense physical mannerisms, a nervous posture, and lots of awkward gestures. Such fidgeting creates a tense climate, and the anxious behaviour of the worker may become contagious for a client who already feels ill-at-ease. Clients only tell the social worker what they think the worker can handle listening to. Good eye contact is encouraged in interviews. As with all techniques, it must be used sensitively, and the worker will ensure that eye contact does not become a leer or a stare.

The social worker builds trust with the client through giving feedback that paraphrases what the client has said. In listening, the worker understands that there is always "more to the story," and refrains from simple and naive interventions. As the client talks, the worker steps in only when there is a clear purpose. It is unhelpful for the worker to get drawn into some form of collusion wherein the client talks negatively about significant others not present in the interview. Clients require room to shift and change their attitudes as they gain more insight. The responsibility is on the worker to remain neutral, while at the same time listening with empathy, acceptance, and understanding.

While the worker is expected to be neutral in listening, it is entirely appropriate for the social worker to react with concern when clients talk about traumatic and awful things in their lives. It is not helpful if the worker is perceived as condoning abusive behaviour. For example, a sixteen-year-old girl told a professional that her father looked at her breasts a lot. There was much more to this story, but because the helper's reaction was "Do you think that you are the first teenager whose father has found her attractive?" the woman never told her tragic story to anyone else until she was in a psychiatric hospital twenty-five years later.

Silences play an important role in listening. The social worker develops a sense of timing that guides them in creating a comfortable atmosphere with silences. It is not helpful when the worker interrupts silences too soon. And silences that continue for too long can create an awkwardness, discomfort, or competitiveness that is not helpful.

It would be impossible for any social worker to pick up on all significant communication from the client during an interview. The more awareness the worker has of their own feelings, biases, and theoretical framework, the more purposeful will be the selections the worker does make to further explore observations or information.

Social workers using a reflecting technique selectively restate word for word what the client has said, showing that the worker is listening, and encouraging the client to continue talking. The client says, "I really feel that I can do it." The worker says, "You really feel that you can do it." The process of the interview will be influenced by what the social worker picks up on, for example, when the worker repeats statements that convey either hopefulness, or helplessness. The interview process is further influenced when the worker adds a "Good grief!" "Terrific!" or "Oh my!" to the beginning when repeating what the client has said. Even when the worker thinks he or she understands what the client is communicating, it can be helpful to get the client to go deeper by saying things like, "I'm not sure that I understand what you are saying, can you explain it more?"

When a worker senses that there is a negative chemistry between client and worker, it is usually helpful to acknowledge it in an accepting manner. It is not always necessary to process it or work through it. It is never helpful to get into a power struggle or a "win-lose" confrontation. The worker might say something like, "I am not sure what is going on, but I have a gut feeling that we are not connecting. I'd like to be able to help you." Sometimes just sharing this perception can be helpful, and may relieve the client's fears and ambivalence. There is a skill to challenging clients in a manner that is positive and does not cause the client to lose face. Growth and change are much more likely to occur when the social worker guides the client to the point where the client makes his or her own choices to change problematic attitudes and behaviours.

Clients report a validation and affirmation that comes from having the undivided attention of the social worker. In many ways the interview is a "mini lab" in which clients learn how to talk and be listened to. Talking and listening are fundamental skills, important to building all relationships. In this microwave age of instant everything, busy families and friends frequently have very brief verbal exchanges, often limited to conveying messages, scolding, and giving orders. The social worker who is listening will appreciate the uniqueness of each client and the dangers of assuming an understanding of the client's situation before the client has explained it from his or her singular perspective. Such listening does not involve superficially flattering clients, or avoiding areas where the exploration is more threatening. The worker wants to be positive and accepting, but not a dupe who does not understand the seriousness of the client's problems.

As social workers listen to the client, they will nod encouragingly from time to time, and use such supportive phrases as, "Uh-huh," "mm-hmm," "Great!" "Good work!" "Go on!" "Eh?" and "I see." It is annoying to hear a social worker adopt a few fixed phrases and use them repetitively. Such phrases, while reassuring at first, lose their sincerity and appropriateness when over-used. One social worker constantly conveys acceptance with the kind words "Okay, fair enough." With over-use, even an encouraging phrase becomes hollow-sounding. Likewise, it is distracting when the worker overdoses on Hollywood-style therapy platitudes such as "Do you feel like sharing. . .?"

The issue of listening to clients ventilate feelings is relevant to a review of listening skills. Annette Garrett's 1942 classic text on interviewing identifies the dangers in encouraging clients to express feelings in an undirected way. Garrett says, "In general, catharsis through talking is more effective the more the disturbing feeling is related to a fairly recent experience, and it becomes of dubious value the more the feeling is due to long repressed experiences" (Garrett, 43). Garrett's 1942 teaching resembles the emphasis in the 1990s on critical incident debriefing and solution-focused treatment. The social worker who is listening to the client ventilate feelings maintains the responsibility of directing the interview and ensuring that there is a clear purpose and focus for what the client is expressing.

Social workers who are not listening can send an interview off in a confusing direction. For example, the client says, "My mother has always put me down." The social worker responds, "Where does your mother live?" Another client says, "I am so angry that my husband works shifts." The social worker responds, "What kind of work does your husband do?" The hospitalized client says, "Nobody around here is telling me anything. It's my life. I have a right to know the test results." The social worker responds, mislabelling the client's feelings, "You seem hostile."

An interview may be heading in the wrong direction when social workers find themselves promising to do a lot of concrete tasks, or "helping things." It can be painful to explore feelings and problems. One of the worst mistakes I made as an inexperienced social worker involved interviewing a handsome young man who was sent by his employer for admission to a psychiatric hospital and an alcohol treatment program. The client was charming and convincing when he said that he had his substance abuse under control. He demonstrated no anxiety. He agreed to enter hospital to maintain his employment, but beyond that I could not engage him in any problem-solving. Groping for areas in which to connect with this articulate gentleman, I agreed that it would not be a wise idea for the client to leave hospital to get his car which was parked in the lot of a shopping mall. Suspending all good judgment and professional learning, I accepted the keys to the client's car, and together with another staff member, went to the shopping mall and brought the client's car to the hospital lot. My feelings of uneasiness were set aside with the rationalization that this was an important task to reinforce the client's motivation to stay in the alcohol treatment program. Within twenty-four hours, this client had left the hospital—in the stolen car that his social worker had so kindly brought to the hospital parking lot for him! This terrible mistake has served as an embarrassing reminder for the past twenty-five years as to what happens when one gives up on the process of an interview and settles for tasks. It also, of course, says a whole lot about a worker's failure to adequately assess and diagnose before jumping into treatment plans.

As workers listen to their clients, they need to come to terms with the issue of social workers crying during interviews. The suffering of clients can be so moving and so tragic that workers struggle with the impulse to express their own emotions with tears. Some workers report that they feel better after crying with a client, especially when parents have lost a child, or a young person is dying with a terminal illness. While the worker feels better after the tears, has this been a purposeful expression of feelings which helps the client? Parents of dying children express relief when they can share their deep-seated fears, losses, and emotions with the social worker, without the additional burden of protecting the worker from the tragedy. Young people with terminal illnesses report that they must console the worker who cries, and must avoid talking about their own feelings in depth. When clients are confronted with death or other tragic circumstances, the social worker's tears may enhance the friendship between worker and client, but they will also pose serious challenges to the professional helping relationship.

Social workers may work with clients who express a personal interest in the worker, one that goes beyond the professional relationship. The client may wish to socialize with or date the social worker. The worker recognizes that the client has misconstrued the worker's expressions of caring as the beginning of a more intimate or personal relationship. The worker is responsible for ensuring that he or she is not setting up false expectations or sending mixed messages. For example, a home visit to a client of the opposite sex may be misunderstood. Social workers need to thoroughly understand the Code of Ethics for their own profession as it relates to prohibiting personal and sexual relationships with clients. Workers also need to be tuned in to the possibility of a client's attempt to seduce them. For example, a young, enthusiastic, confident, male social work student was working with an older female client. The client phoned the worker in great emotional crisis, stating that she was going to kill herself. The eager and concerned social worker went immediately to the woman's home to rescue her. Imagine his surprise and discomfort when he was greeted by a naked woman who felt the only possible consolation would be to have sexual relations with her social worker!

TALKING AND TELLING

At times it is helpful for the worker to talk during the interview and tell the client some things. Such talking usually begins with "I" statements, such as "I want to give you my opinion," or "I want to suggest...." Such telling can have a powerful role in interviews; however, it is used sparingly and only when there is a clear purpose. Most frequently, the worker tells the client something when the client lacks essential information to come up with his or her own solutions.

Timing is essential in the process of interviewing, especially when the worker makes a decision to talk. When the social worker has a brilliant insight, it is not necessarily the time to share this insight with the client. It is generally more helpful for clients to reach their own insights. A client involved in extra-marital relationships referred to his wife by the wrong name. While this reference to another woman gave the worker an insight and something to consider later, there would have been no clear purpose in pointing out the slip to the client at that time when the focus was elsewhere.

Clients may find it helpful when the social worker talks about what they might experience between sessions. It is hardly ever helpful to reassure clients that everything will be all right. It is usually far more helpful to tell clients that things may become worse before they get better, and that, after talking, clients might feel more anxious, guilty, or angry. As part of the interview termination phase, it may be helpful to ask the client to focus on how they are going to deal with their reactions after the interview.

When the social worker talks too much it is rarely helpful. Short, simple sentences have the greatest impact! Talking should never be an excuse for by-passing self-determination through trying to persuade clients to do something against their will, or coaxing them to pursue a course of action that has been determined by the worker.

"Telling" can be used by the worker to convey hope. For example, almost fifteen years later, Sue looked up her social worker to tell her how she had lived through rough years. Sue came to the worker when she was a young mother with migraine headaches and three children under the age of four years. A series of medical specialists could offer no successful treatment for the headaches. Sue tearfully summed up her distress, saying, "Every morning other people get up and put on two socks. Every morning I get up with an enormous headache and I have to put on eight socks." After fifteen years, Sue recalled how the worker had accepted her distress, and then "told" her that these would be the hardest years of her life, and that in all likelihood the headaches would not end until the children were older. The worker also told Sue that she needed to look for as much support as she could, in order to get through these awfully tough times. Somehow, magically, those words had freed Sue up from the burdens of guilt and anxiety and given her hope for the future.

While talking and telling are used sparingly by social workers, it is important to recognize the influence that persons in positions of power and respect have when they "tell" something in an interview. Over and over again clients report that they never forgot the worker who told them, "I know that you are going to be successful."

Sometimes social workers fear being unmasked as a fraud and they are tempted to talk too much and pretend to understand things they do not know. It is sound practice for the worker to say "I don't know." This can be reassuring to clients, and can even give extra status to the client with a difficult problem. There will be areas for all workers where they feel deficient in interviews. Embracing our own shortcomings comfortably goes a long way to removing barriers between worker and client.

ENDING THE INTERVIEW

The end is a good and positive part of the helping relationship. The social worker has the task of preparing for termination in a manner that does not leave either the client or the worker with the stress of unfinished business and dangling ends.

Termination can be the most neglected aspect of practice. Why do so many clients terminate scheduled sessions before the worker expects it? What clues are workers missing that clients are not going to return? Do clients leave without notice because they have gone as far as they want? Do clients terminate unexpectedly because the worker is unhelpful? Failure to spend time managing the termination phase of the interview process may explain the high rate of cancellations and "no shows" for some workers.

The preparation for termination begins with the development of a plan that is mutually agreed upon by the client and the social worker. How can the worker or client know when they arrive at their destination if it is not clear where they intend to go? From the beginning, the worker can ask questions like, "How will you know when we are finished?" Such questions are helpful in preparing for termination and in establishing a focus and goals for interviewing. Workers find it helpful to conclude interviews with such questions as, "Have we talked about the things that are important to you?" "Was there anything else that you hoped we would talk about?" "Have things gone the way you hoped today?"

Starting and ending interviews on time is good social work practice. The worker has the responsibility to set time aside before the end of the interview to deal with termination and then to clearly signal the end of the interview. The worker may use such phrases as, "We can pick up from here when we meet next time" or, "You've done a lot of work in this session, and our time has come to an end." Many social workers find ten minutes an appropriate amount of time to review the work that has been done within the interview and to set some goals for the next session.

The social worker must be prepared for "door-knob" disclosures which frequently occur at the end of interviews. These disclosures of new and emotionally-laden material occur after the interview has come to an end and the client is taking leave. They also occur at a time when the next interview is scheduled, and the worker needs a few minutes for note-taking and preparation between interviews. The worker can deal kindly but firmly with clients who attempt to prolong the session when it is clearly at the end. These "door-knob" revelations do have meaning, and may suggest that the client is anxious, overly-dependent, or dissatisfied. To respond at a surface level to the client and engage in a whole new topic of discussion probably avoids the issue of what is going on with the client. In addition, the worker is going to become distracted and late for his or her next commitment. In anticipation of these comments, the worker might consider responses such as, "You are saying things that we can talk about next time, and you might want to write them down when you get home, so you won't forget what you want to talk about." Sometimes a clear, direct approach to ending is required, wherein the worker stands up and walks to the door, escorting the client on the way.

The matter of social workers accepting gifts from clients raises complex and sensitive issues which may be related to the topic of termination. In general, workers discourage gifts from clients. Many workers believe that gifts are symbolic of unfinished business between the worker and the client. Gifts may be perceived as manipulation and "pay off." Clients may believe that ongoing help is related to giving social workers generous presents. Clients may offer workers generous gifts that are beyond the means of the clients. There is cause for serious concern when the worker conveys to the client any expectation of a gift. Social workers have a responsibility to exercise utmost honesty and integrity in working with vulnerable and frail clients who wish to give gifts. In working with vulnerable clients, it is exploitative and unethical for the worker to accept gifts, or agree to inclusion in a will, or to profit from selling or purchasing personal effects of the client.

Even when clients insist that they want their personal property to go to the social worker, and there are no other apparent heirs, the worker ought to decline such clients' generosity and clarify the nature of the professional social work role. The worker knows the client through a professional relationship, and, when there is a temptation to accept gifts or profit from this relationship, the worker is advised to consult honestly and openly with his or her professional colleagues and superiors. It may make sense for the worker to accept a modest, well-intentioned gift, rather than insult the client, but in such cases the worker can make it clear that the gift is going to the agency or institution rather than to the worker personally. There will be times when the worker judges it prudent to accept small personal gifts by which clients demonstrate their appreciation. Even in such cases, workers need to consider how to graciously discourage gift-giving. Some workers seem to receive many gifts from clients. These gifts may not reflect a highly capable social worker, so much as a worker who has become dependent upon clients for reaffirmation and feedback. Clients are wonderful human beings who are sensitive to the needs of their social workers!

When the client does not appear to have feelings associated with termination, or does not perceive it as a significant experience, the social worker may facilitate a sense of ending with questions such as, "What thoughts do you have about ending?" or, perhaps, "How do you think the work you have done in our sessions will help you in the future?"

Mabel was a single, retired woman who lived alone, was inclined toward depression, and had a long history of physical illnesses. Mabel was always anxious during interviews, but she clearly valued the opportunity to talk about her thoughts and feelings. Mabel presented a different kind of "door-knob" challenge. After the interview was over, Mabel would return home and shortly thereafter telephone the social worker. Her question would be "So, how did you think I did today?" Mabel would ask the question as if she and the social worker were two colleagues discussing the well-being of a third person.

At all stages of the helping relationship, the social worker will review how the process of interviewing is unfolding. Specifically, the worker may review during each interview the plans for termination. In so doing, the worker encourages the client to express feelings regarding termination, such as rejection, sadness, loss, anger, accomplishment, happiness, mastery, and independence. Such expression of feeling should be purposeful in helping clients to reach a sense of completion and to grow in autonomy and self-confidence. This stock-taking and preparing for termination also emphasizes the client's responsibility for participation in the interviews and helps counteract the fantasy that something magical and mysterious will happen to the client as a result of social work treatment.

ETHNIC AND CULTURAL ISSUES IN INTERVIEWING

Canada is a country that places a high priority on multiculturalism wherein we promote and value diversity. This country's respect for cultural pluralism is deeply embedded in our history. In recent years, the arrival of new immigrant populations and an increasing breadth and depth of awareness and commitment to the values of diversity and multiculturalism have added new expectations and challenges to traditional social work practice.

Evident in many social work settings is an increasing recognition of the extent to which methods and styles of helping are culturally determined. There is growing recognition of the cultural differences and diversity among clients. Insight-oriented interviews that are core to Canadian social work practice do not make sense within the values of some of our multicultural client groups. Canadian social workers are recognizing that not all cultures place the same emphasis on the "individual." There is also growing respect and appreciation for the differences among clients who come from cultures wherein the family or the clan hold a greater priority than the feelings, wishes, or needs of the individual.

Social workers are engaging in "diversity training" in an enthusiastic manner. Family Services Toronto has provided leadership for all of Canada in remaking their agency to reflect the more than thirty languages and cultures of the clients they serve. Social workers are striving to recognize how their own cultural values, and deeply-held, but unconscious, prejudices and stereotypes get in the way of interviewing clients from minority and multicultural groups.

Social workers are recognizing the need to learn culturally appropriate helping skills, attitudes, and knowledge. Every culture has some concept of helping, but the concept of a helping interview is not universal. The concept of a specific time frame for helping is non-existent in some cultures, and the idea of a scheduled interview time with a beginning, middle, and end makes no sense within the cultural experiences of some of our clients.

In some cultures there is no distinction between a friend and a professional helper. This lack of distinction easily leads to confusion and a feeling of rejection when the social worker does not understand the client's frame of reference for a "helper." Social workers are learning that cultural barriers are just as important as language barriers, and that language interpreters only add to the confusion between worker and client if there is not an adequate understanding of the client's culture and how the concept of professional helping fits within it. The expectation that the worker will "start where the client is at" makes more sense than ever for social workers working with clients from a variety of ethnic and cultural backgrounds. The issue for many workers, however, is that they assume, based on their own cultural experiences, that they know where the client is at, and nothing could be further from reality. This is an area where inexperienced social workers are inclined to pretend. It is possible that the worker will work with a client from a country of which the worker is entirely ignorant. In such cases, it is important for the worker to spend extra time with the client in exploring and getting to know the client's cultural values and expectations. Clients respond positively when the worker displays an honest desire to build a trusting relationship and starts by asking the client for help in understanding his or her uniqueness. Consequently, workers need to consider the issue of the amount of time scheduled for interviewing clients of diverse ethnic and cultural backgrounds. Generally, multicultural counselling requires more time, and, consequently, resources. In addition to dealing with the client's specific present circumstances, the worker requires additional time to understand the cultural background of the client. In situations where an interpreter is used, the social worker must schedule additional time for preparing and debriefing the interpreter.

It is inadequate for a social work agency to announce that it is sensitive and accessible to multicultural groups. To have real credibility, the agency must also demonstrate its commitment to diversity. For example, an agency with a black social worker on staff will see a lot more black people coming to the agency. An agency with a Chinese social worker will see a lot more Chinese clients, and an agency with a Portuguese social worker will be sought out by many more Portuguese clients. After a while an agency earns a reputation of authenticity in serving multicultural clients, and it may not be so important to match workers and clients with like cultures. However, it is unlikely that an all-white, Anglo-Saxon or Francophone agency will bridge the gap in helping immigrant persons of diverse languages and cultures.

In working with community outreach support and educational groups for new immigrants within a family service setting, it has been my experience that the children of immigrants prefer to have such groups in English, while their parents prefer group leaders who speak the same first language. Children seem much more interested in activities that promote the similarities between cultures, rather than the differences. Again, these issues are important for the social worker.

One of the difficulties identified by both clients and social workers who belong to specific ethnic or multicultural groups, is that, based on similar appearances, homelands, or language, clients and workers often make premature assumptions of similarities and shared values. There is no doubt about the importance of understanding the attitudes, beliefs, and behaviours of particular cultures. Still, every individual is unique. It remains an uppermost priority for the worker to appreciate the individuality of each client, regardless of similarities or differences in cultural and ethnic backgrounds.

CONCLUSION

This chapter has concentrated on common skills that will help the social worker develop into an effective interviewer. I have not addressed skills specific to interviewing children or groups.

The extensive Outcomes Evaluation Project, initiated at Catholic Family Counselling Centre in Kitchener, Ontario in 1995, consistently finds that after social work intervention there are concrete, measurable, and observable changes and improvements in all areas of functioning which clients consider important. This client-driven outcomes project, which enhances the accountability of social work practice, has been adopted in family service agencies across Canada. While this project convincingly validates the outcomes of social work practice, it also provides positive reinforcement for continuous quality improvement in social work practice.

Over the next ten years there will be major shifts in the process of interviewing related to rapidly expanding technology. Video-conferencing will be a part of the way we do business. Voice-activated computers will lead to software programs that produce records, perhaps even assessments, of interview sessions. Telephone interviewing will expand further. Voice mail has opened up new communications with clients. E-mail and Internet capacities reveal new frontiers for counselling and challenges to rethink our concepts of interviewing and social work practice.

It is within the process of interviewing that we witness the powerful synergy between art and science. We see clients expressing deeply felt pain and suffering. We see clients demonstrating tremendous strengths and abilities to master their problems. We see the social worker demonstrating firmly rooted abilities that use knowledge and skills in a purposeful way. And we witness the dynamic exchange between social worker and client when the social worker's purposeful use of self is flexibly enhanced by artful and intuitive expressions of helping.

REFERENCES

Benjamin, A. (1981). *The helping interview* (3rd ed.). Boston: Houghton Mifflin Company.

Berg, I.K. & Miller, S.D. (1992). *Working with the problem drinkers: a solution focused approach.* New York: W.W. Norton.

Carrillo D.F. & Thyer, B.A. (1994). Advanced standing and two-year program MSW students: an empirical investigation of foundation interviewing skills. *Journal of Social Work Education.* Vol. 30. (Fall 1994), pp. 377–387.

Corey, G. (1996). *Theory and practice of counselling and psychotherapy.* (5th ed.). Toronto: Brooks/Cole Publishing Company.

Cournoyer, B. (1991). *The social work skills workbook.* Belmont, CA: Wadsworth.

De Jong, P. & Miller, S.D. (1995). How to interview for client strengths. *Social Work, 40*(6) (November 1995).

De Shazer, S. (1988). *Clues: investigating solutions in brief therapy.* New York: W.W. Norton.

Egan, G. (1994). *The skilled helper: a problem-management approach to helping.* California: Brooks/Cole Publishing Company.

Epstein, L. (1990). Some reflections on the therapeutic use of self. *Group, 14*(3), pp.151–156.

Epstein, L. (1990). *Talking and listening: a guide to the helping interview.* St. Louis, Missouri: Times Mirror/Mosby College Publishing.

Fetterman, D.M. (1995). *Ethnography: step by step.* Newbury Park, CA: Sage Publications.

Fox, E., et al. (1989). The termination process. *Social Work, 14,* (October, 1989), pp. 5–63.

Franklin, C. & Jordan, C. (1995). Qualitative assessment: A methological review. *Families in Society: The Journal of Contemporary Human Services,* May 1995.

Garrett, A. (1972). *Interviewing: its principles and methods* (2nd rev. ed.). Revised by Elinor P. Zaki and Margaret M. Mangold. New York: Family Service Association of America.

Gilliland, B.E., James, R.K., & Bowman, J.T. (1994). *Theories and strategies in counselling and psychotherapy.* Toronto: Allyn and Bacon.

Gordon, R.L. (1992). *Basic interviewing skills.* Itasca, Illinois: F.E. Peacock Publishers.

Hepworth, D.H. & Larsen, J.A. (1990). *Direct social work practice.* (3rd ed.). Belmont, Ca: Wadsworth.

Kadushin, A. (1972). *The social work interview.* New York: Columbia University Press.

Kell, B.J. & Mueller, W.J. (1966). *Impact and change: a study of counseling relationships.* New Jersey: Prentice-Hall, Inc.

Lee, J.L., Pulvino, C.J., & Perrone, P.A. (1993). *Dynamic counselling.* Madison, Wisconsin: Instructional Enterprises.

May, R. (1989). *The art of counselling.* (Rev. ed.). New York: Gardner Press.

Miller, S., et al. (1991). *Talking and listening together.* Colorado: Interpersonal Communications Program.

Okun, B.F. (1991). *Effective helping, interviewing and counselling techniques.* (4th ed.). California: Brooks/Cole Publishing Company.

Patterson, L.E. & Eisenberg, S. (1983). *The counselling process.* (3rd ed.). Boston: Houghton Mifflin.

Saleebey, D. (Ed). (1992). *The strengths perspective in social work practice.* New York: Longman.

Song, Miri & David Parker. (1995). Commonality, difference and the dynamics of disclosure in in-depth interviewing. *Sociology,* Vol. 29, (May 1995), No. 2. pp. 241–156.

Turner, F.J. (1978). *Psychosocial therapy.* New York: Free Press.

TERMINATION:
CONTENT
AND PROCESS

Jan B. Lackstrom and
Grant Macdonald

The two overriding goals of social work practice are to help our clients develop a new level of competence and to help them direct their own lives more confidently. As such, embedded within the first "hello" is the final "goodbye." The keystone of social work practice is termination. The foundation set during assessment and built upon during the working stage can be seriously challenged, if not lost, during termination. The social worker must attend to the ending stage if the client is to maintain the gains he or she has made and ideally continue to progress through the process of termination itself.

The moment termination is considered, two related issues come to the fore. Although most certainly found within the assessment and working stages, the meaning and quality of the helping relationship and issues of autonomy and separation become core issues influencing every aspect of the termination process. In this chapter, we will discuss the different types of termination, identify the stages of the termination process, and explore the role and tasks of the social worker during this critical phase. Attention will be given to problematic termination.

TYPES OF TERMINATION

Terminations fall into the two broad categories of planned and unplanned. Planned terminations can be further subdivided according to the length of the helping contract (i.e., time-limited or long-term). Unplanned terminations can be grouped according to three situations: (1) situations when a client unexpectedly and apparently prematurely withdraws from counselling or simply drops out; (2) terminations that are initiated by the social worker because of a lack of progress; and (3) terminations that sometimes occur when the social worker unexpectedly withdraws service because of a personal event unrelated to the helping process, for example a new job or an illness (Collins, Jordan, and Colerman, 1999; Levin, 1998). Planned terminations are recognized and mutually agreed upon by the social worker and the client, whereas unplanned terminations are unilaterally decided upon and unwelcomed by either the social worker or the client or both. The types of termination are presented in Table 17.1.

TABLE 17.1 Types of Termination

Planned and mutually agreed upon:

1. Time-limited, closed-ended counselling contract.

2. Long-term, open-ended counselling contract.

Unplanned and unilaterally decided upon:

1. Client terminates prematurely or drops out.

2. Social worker withdraws service because of lack of progress.

3. Social worker withdraws service for personal reasons.

THE TASKS OF TERMINATION

The tasks associated with termination are similar across all social work practice. The type of termination will shape the priority and emphasis of each task. There are generally four major tasks associated with termination. These include: (1) deciding when to terminate, (2) dealing with feelings associated with ending, (3) generalizing and maintaining gains made, and (4) evaluating accomplishments and the service provided. With the exception of deciding when to terminate, the tasks do not necessarily proceed sequentially to completion, but are ideally addressed in an integrated fashion, depending upon the client and the type of termination (Compton and Galaway, 1999; Kirst-Ashman and Hull, 1993; Henry, 1992; Hepworth and Larsen, 1990; Toseland and Rivas, 1995).

DECIDING WHEN TO TERMINATE

The social worker normally initiates the termination process, although it is not uncommon for a client to do so. In either case, the introduction to the termination should not be unexpected. At times the client's wish to terminate may in fact reflect a resistance to further work on a difficult issue. The social worker should be aware of this possibility and be prepared to explore the client's motivation to end the helping process. On the other hand, it is also important to trust the client's sense of timing and evaluation of his or her progress. One does not want to accuse the client of being resistant when in fact he or she is happy with the progress made and ready to move on. This does not mean that introducing termination does not cause anxiety. Both the practitioner and client may worry about the client's ability to manage without the helping process, even in the face of evidence that the client is managing well.

In time-limited work, the social worker introduces termination at the beginning of the contract, selecting a number of sessions appropriate to the task at hand or choosing goals that can be met in the time available. The date of the final meeting and the number of meetings left are regularly incorporated into the content of the counselling process and should be brought to the fore at least one or two sessions prior to the final session. The time-limit itself becomes one of the forces fueling the change process (Strupp and Binder, 1984; Horowitz, Marmar, Krupnick, Wilner, Kaltreider, and Wallerstein, 1984). The time-limit helps keep the client and the social worker focused on the tasks at hand. The end of the contracted time should mark the end of the helping process, regardless of whether the stated goals have been met. The client is welcome to return at some future date; however, at the moment, he or she should be encouraged to try to manage with what has been accomplished to date. With careful selection of clients and/or goals, the issue of extending the contract should be the exception rather than the rule. If the social worker and client know the contract can be extended, they may in fact negotiate a long-term contract under the guise of a series of brief contracts.

The drive to extend the contract can rest with the client or the social worker. Clients who appear overly anxious or regress at termination are often able to persuade the social worker that these "normal" reactions indicate that they are not ready to end the helping process. The social worker can be tempted to extend the contract of the client who seems to be making good progress and could be expected to continue. Practitioners sometimes extend a contract to continue to attempt to meet goals that were initially set too high. In this situation, the practitioner believes more time is needed to reach the goals, when in fact he or she should be reviewing the goals. Finally, social workers sometimes fail to terminate a brief contract because they are attached to the client and have difficulty withdrawing from the gratification they feel when working with him or her (Fortune, 1985). Studying the termination patterns of social workers using a brief model of practice, Fortune found that 41 percent reported that they extended the brief contract half the time or more and concluded that social workers tend to be "conservative and more willing to err on the side of too much treatment than to risk incomplete success" (Fortune, 1985, 656–657). The question remains whether this is the best practice. One wonders whether the client's or social worker's needs are being met.

When social workers employ longer-term open-ended contracts, they must guard against the tendency to lose focus. When the purpose of counselling is very broadly defined—for example, "I want to feel better about myself"—it can be difficult to determine when the work is complete. Before introducing the idea of termination, practitioners typically look for indications of improvement in the client's behaviour and intra-psychic functioning. They may assess the degree to which the client's goals have been achieved, look for a decrease in the client's need to consult with the social worker before identifying and solving problems, and assess the client's use of natural support networks (Fortune, 1985; Northen, 1988).

When in the social worker's judgment the client terminates the helping process prematurely, it is sometimes difficult to know what is happening, especially if the client drops out of counselling. It is important to remember that some clients are pleased with the progress they have made and, though they may end the helping process in an unorthodox fashion, they need not be considered treatment resistant or seen as denying their problems. However, it is also important to recognize that clients do unilaterally terminate counselling for a variety of reasons, some related to the social worker, some to themselves, and others to a combination of factors. Table 17.2 outlines common reasons clients terminate prematurely.

An outreach telephone call should be made to a client who drops out. The call signals the client that he or she is missed and important. The call provides an opportunity for the social worker to re-engage the client or encourage her or him to return for a final meeting. Educating the client about the importance of a final session is often helpful. The call also allows the opportunity to complete a limited evaluation of what has happened. Finally, speaking with the client does bring some semblance of closure and future planning in itself, as it allows the practitioner to recognize the client's decision and offer the consideration of a return to the service at some future time.

When, whether over the telephone or in a final office session, a client does agree to discuss his or her decision to leave counselling, the social worker must collapse the termination process into the limited time available. The social worker must balance exploring, chal-

TABLE 17.2 Reasons for Premature Termination from Individual, Family, and Group Counselling

1. Client is happy with improvements achieved, but doesn't tell the social worker.
2. Relationship problems between the social worker and client, which destroy the therapeutic alliance.
3. Client believes his or her needs are not being met or feels misunderstood.
4. Client is unable to tolerate the strong feelings evoked during counselling.
5. Client experiences negative reactions from significant others, which prohibits change.
6. Client leaves to avoid the ending process.
7. Conflicting expectations resulting from a poor introduction to the helping process.
8. Factors arising from concurrent therapies (e.g., individual and family therapy).
9. Factors the social worker and client cannot control (e.g., finances, work schedules, moving out of area).

Factors Specific to Group Counselling

1. Feeling out of place in the group.
2. Inability to form intimate relationships with others.
3. Fear of developing problems similar to those of other group members.
4. Inability to share social worker with group members.
5. Sub-grouping problems (e.g., scapegoating, exclusion).

Sources: Kirst-Ashman and Hull, 1993; Hepworth and Larsen, 1990; Fish, Weakland, and Segal, 1982; Yalom, 1975.

lenging, and supporting the client's decision to terminate. Challenging too agressively the client's reasons for terminating may result in the client becoming defensive or feeling victimized. Clients may be unable to reverse their decision even though they may want to. If they feel coerced to return, they will likely drop out again. Alternatively, clients might return feeling ashamed for thinking they had the ability to make an independent decision. Thus, the social worker's goal is to re-engage clients if appropriate. Clients should be aware of the social worker's concerns and reservations about the reasons for and the timing of termination, while also feeling supported and acknowledged for making their own decision. In this way, both clients and social worker are able to maintain their integrity and self respect.

Sometimes it is necessary for the social worker to terminate the helping process after determining it is failing, that the client is not achieving the identified goals or is perhaps even getting worse. This can be particularly difficult if clients believe that they are making progress. The social worker is best advised to be clear and direct about his or her observations and thoughts about the lack of progress. Clients may believe it is their fault that no progress is being made. The reasons for lack of progress are rarely perfectly clear and often rest in some combination of factors brought by both clients and the worker.

Of some concern is termination that arises out of the social worker's dislike of a client and belief that it is impossible to work with the particular individual, group, or family. On one hand, it is wise to terminate with a client one feels unable to work with, while on the other hand it is hoped that when the social worker begins to realize these interpersonal difficulties, he or she will seek supervision or consultation before ending the helping process. Each social worker has personal limitations and the ideal is to avoid those situations where possible. Realistically, this is not always possible.

It is important that the proper ending process occur when the social worker unilaterally initiates termination, because clients may be surprised, feel rejected and abandoned, and likely blame themselves for the termination. If the social worker fails to allow the time for clients to express these feelings, evaluate the work done to date, and consider a referral to a new practitioner, the feelings of rejection and abandonment can remain. With time to process the termination, clients can leave with a sense of completion and closure that will enhance their relationships. If clients drop out after hearing that the social worker is terminating their work, it is important that the social worker call to reassure the clients and attempt to re-engage them in the termination process.

In some instances, it will be impossible for the social worker to engage in the termination process. This might happen, for example, if the social worker is laid off suddenly or becomes acutely ill. At a minimum, the agency must facilitate the transfer of clients to a new worker who can process the unexpected loss of the original social worker and work with the clients to negotiate a new helping contract.

DEALING WITH FEELINGS ASSOCIATED WITH ENDINGS

The completion of the helping process focuses the social worker and client on the client's past and present losses. The loss of the therapeutic relationship, the loss of the client's "old self," and the reactivated memories of earlier losses in the client's life, serve to identify the themes of attachment and separation, dependence and independence (Hess and Hess, 1999; Strupp and Binder, 1984). This attention to loss and transition is placed within the context of the positive change that has prompted the initiation of termination. The practitioner must balance the recognition and celebration of accomplishment with the distress associated with the ending. Focusing exclusively on gains made can leave clients alone to cope with their distress about leaving the safety of counselling. Focusing exclusively on losses and anxieties can undermine clients' self-confidence. Most clients are able to identify their feelings of loss and anxiety and are usually pleased with their progress and confident in their ability to manage on their own. They are likely to feel somewhat sad about ending their relationship with their social worker and might be somewhat anxious about managing independently. Most clients are able to tolerate these feelings. They appreciate their experience and are ready to get on with their lives (Fortune, Pearlingi, and Rochelle, 1992).

Three primary factors influence a client's reaction to termination. These are the degree of the client's attachment to the social worker, the client's previous experiences with losses, and the circumstances of the termination. The greater the attachment, the poorer the resolution of earlier losses and the less complete the helping process, the greater the likelihood that the client will experience some difficulty. A summary of the factors that can contribute to difficult termination are presented in Table 17.3.

PROBLEMATIC REACTIONS TO TERMINATION

All clients can react to the separation brought on by termination. These reactions are often simply part of a normal reaction to a loss, and are easily identified and worked through.

TABLE 17.3 Factors Contributing to a Difficult Termination

Degree of Attachment to the Social Worker:

1. Long-term open-ended models of practice
2. High frequency of client–social worker contact
3. Counselling focused on personal problems
4. Client has limited personal support network
5. High level of emotional content
6. Client has poor sense of self

Client's Earlier Experience of Losses:

1. History of significant personal loss or losses
2. History of unresolved loss or losses

Circumstances of the Present Termination:

1. Unplanned ending
2. Treatment goals not achieved
3. Social worker-initiated terminations

Sources: Kirst-Ashman and Hull, 1993; Levinson, 1977; Fortune, Pearlingi, and Rochelle, 1992.

The response becomes problematic when clients' reactions are so severe or entrenched as to challenge their level of functioning and ability to relate. Unless the practitioner and clients are able to bring resolution to the problematic response, clients are in danger of regressing in their functioning and their ability to form close relationships.

Clients who have difficulty with termination are responding to the threat to their relationship with the social worker. Clients who regress or become more dependent on the social worker may be attempting to signal that they do not feel ready to manage on their own and as such they should remain within the helping relationship. Such clients may be attempting to reactivate their attachment to the social worker. In contrast, some clients reject the social worker and the helping relationship in an attempt to cope with the impending loss by appearing independent and self-sufficient. They are attempting to gain some sense of control and mastery by rejecting before they are rejected.

It is not uncommon for clients to deny that termination is even happening. A client may not speak of the impending loss and may repeatedly "forget" the date of the final meeting, all the while denying any feelings about the ending. The client may begin to act out feelings rather than speaking about them. For example, he or she may become non-participative in sessions, come late or miss appointments altogether. This may be an effort to avoid identifying and coping with the feelings associated with termination. Clients may become depressed and thereby be unable to participate in the process of termination. Alternatively, they might present with anger directed at the social worker or misdirected at family, friends, or the agency. Clients may use misdirected anger if they are afraid of how the social worker will respond to anger expressed directly. Some clients are afraid their anger will destroy the social worker, while others fear that the social worker will be angry with them and reject them for expressing their anger directly.

Some clients may marginalize the gains that have been made and others regress in their functioning. There may be a return of the behaviours or problems that brought them for help initially, or the social worker may be presented with new and urgent problems that, by implication, must be dealt with prior to termination. It is not uncommon for clients to express self-doubt and return to being dependent on the social worker to help them identify and solve issues mastered earlier.

Occasionally, clients may either idealize or devalue the practitioner and their experience together. Each stance puts the client in a "no win" situation. If the social worker and the helping experience are devalued, then the clients are unable to acknowledge either the pleasure of the relationship or the gains they have made. If clients idealize the social worker, then they deny their own contribution to the relationship and the work they have put into reaching their goals.

Another problematic reaction occurs when clients stop the helping process once termination is introduced. They may insist on ending the process quickly, deny that they are upset in any way, and focus exclusively on how well they are doing on their own now. These clients often have a history of difficult endings that have been poorly resolved. They may drop out of the termination process, either by not returning to the next session or leaving after expressing anger at the apparent rejection by the social worker. It is important to try to re-engage the client in the termination process. Some clients will leave the termination process by finding another social worker or natural helper in an effort to find someone who will continue to meet their dependency needs rather than challenge them to become more self-directing. Others will continue in their self-sufficient stance, avoiding future meaningful relationships.

THE SOCIAL WORKER'S ROLE IN RESOLVING FEELINGS RELATED TO TERMINATION

The social worker's role is to help clients resolve their feelings about termination and to help them recognize the accomplishments they have made. It is hoped that the client will complete the termination process with an increased sense of mastery of ending relationships and a willingness to emotionally invest in new relationships.

In preparation for termination the practitioner is wise to review the client's history of losses and endings, the nature of the present ending, and the quality of the present therapeutic alliance in an effort to hypothesize about the client's possible reaction to this ending. The social worker will also want to review the client's recent achievements and strengths. These strengths can be used during the termination process (Compton and Galaway, 1999).

The content of the termination stage focuses on the meaning of endings within the present helping relationship and the historical context. This provides the client with the opportunity to explore the impact of earlier losses on his or her present coping strategies and permits the possibility of bringing closure to old wounds. Depending upon the model of practice, reviewing the effects of historical losses can be made explicit or left unspoken. Regardless of model of practice, the successful completion of an ending in the present provides the client with a new experience to counter earlier problems and on which to build future relationships.

The practitioner should also focus the content of sessions on the progress the client has made and on a review of the way the client has met goals. This topic will be reviewed more thoroughly when discussing maintaining and generalizing gains made.

The counselling process should focus on helping clients to develop an awareness of the interaction between their thoughts, feelings, and behaviours. Clients should be genuinely encouraged to express their positive and critical feelings about ending the helping relationship. It is also important to normalize the entire range of feelings a client will have. The process of encouraging clients to identify and express their feelings prevents them from expressing their feelings in action. By putting feelings into words, both the social worker and clients have a greater chance to develop an awareness and understanding of the feelings. Feelings expressed in behaviours are open to misinterpretation and may be reactive, rather than purposeful. It is important for clients to know that the expression of feelings will not threaten the therapeutic alliance. Clients who either idealize or devalue the helping process and relationship will need help to develop a balanced view of their experience.

An often neglected task is that of helping clients learn to manage their upset feelings. Clients often become frightened by the strengths of their feelings. Learning how to tolerate strong feelings is important because it helps prevent them from reacting to their feelings. Strategies, such as pacing the expression of feelings, distracting oneself when distressed, thought stopping, reviewing thinking errors, and developing self-soothing techniques are particularly useful. They are easily integrated into the helping process and the techniques can be used to cope with any stressful situations in the future. The worker who has attended to this issue in the working stage of the helping process may have to remind the client of these techniques in the face of stress related to the termination.

The practitioner should work with clients' strengths during termination. Clients should be familiar with their strengths from the working stage of the helping process. The use of these strengths to cope with the stress of termination helps provide clients with a real life experience in which to use these skills and abilities. The social worker can help clients reflect back on their feelings, thoughts, and behaviours as they proceed through the termination process. Finally, the social worker needs to withstand the pull of regression or the push of rejection by clients. It is easy to minimize clients' strengths and ability to cope independently in the face of an increase in their fear, self-doubt, and an actual decrease in functioning. To give in to these fears can inadvertently reinforce clients' belief that they are not yet ready to become independent. It can be difficult to reach out to clients who are rejecting and angry. If the social worker does not reach out, the clients' worst fears—that they are worthless—can be confirmed.

Practitioners do make mistakes about the timeliness of termination. If the social worker is concerned by objective evidence that the client is not ready to manage independently, the counselling process can be renegotiated. Goals based on the evidence uncovered in the premature termination process should be included in the new goal setting. In the majority of cases, termination should proceed as planned. The client should be encouraged to try to use his or her newly developed skills and strengths, in returning for more counselling, if needed, but at some future time. It is helpful to review with the client the agency policies about returning for further counselling.

GENERALIZING AND MAINTAINING GAINS MADE

Ideally, the social worker and client have been working at anchoring the changes the client has been making throughout the entire helping process. Many clients relapse once they leave the helping process. Relapse appears to be related to clients not fully integrating the changes they have made and returning to an old, unchanged environment that fails to support the clients' new behaviours (Hepworth and Larsen, 1990). Termination is the final opportunity to reinforce earlier work and assess and challenge any threats to that work. Working through the emotional reactions to termination is designed to settle the threats derived from clients' anxiety about their own abilities. Clients must also prepare themselves cognitively for their independence and should know how they made the changes they did. The helping process must be demystified. Clients need to understand the techniques and skills they employ to solve their problems. It is essential that they do not believe their achievements are a result of the "magic powers ascribed to their worker" (Henry, 1992, 201). By carefully reviewing the work completed, the worker can help clients learn specifically how they have reached their goals. In this way, clients will develop a sense of competence and recognize the skills and tools they have developed.

The social worker and clients may identify one or two situations where clients remain unsure of themselves. It is helpful to have them confront these situations as much as possible during the termination process in order to increase self-confidence. The practitioner should be careful not to confuse solidifying progress with introducing new problems. The introduction of new problems is more likely related to anxiety about the ending and needs to be addressed in a different manner.

Clients need to know how to recognize and manage environmental stressors, both structural and interpersonal. The social worker can help them learn to anticipate future problems, to identify the approach to problem solution that they might take, and to anticipate and prepare for resistance to these solutions.

The social worker might also consider predicting slips and defining them as a natural occurrence. Labelling slips as "normal" helps prepare the client who does experience problems after termination. Clients who see slips as normal can focus on developing strategies, rather than ruminating about their failures. Hopefully, they are able to evaluate the slip and fine-tune strategies to deal with the situation. This labelling can help prevent small problems from turning into a full-blown relapse.

The practitioner can help maintain and generalize change by shifting the dynamic of the helping relationship. By encouraging and directing clients to increasingly rely on their natural support systems, the social worker is facilitating the separation from the helping process. Ideally, clients should be reporting what they have done, rather than processing what they should do. Meetings should be used to support clients and to "trouble-shoot." To a certain extent the worker should refrain from rescuing clients in favour of helping them to review their own decisions and actions after the fact.

Part of the process of creating distance within the helping relationship is encouraging clients to use their natural support. Clients may need help to develop the skills of asking for and accepting guidance and help from significant others. In some cases, they will need help accepting that some people are not going to change or be supportive. The client can learn specific strategies to manage differences and problems with individuals.

Clients can also be encouraged to use formal or informal support groups to get the confirmation that might be missing from their natural network. For example, a client who is shy might join a service club in an effort to meet new people, or an abandoned single adolescent mother might join a support group to get emotional support and help with parenting.

The social worker might also consider the use of booster sessions or follow-up contact to solidify and support gains made by the client. The contact, either by telephone or an office meeting, needs to be clearly negotiated. A brief assessment of how clients are coping will identify any problems they might be experiencing. Follow-up visits are helpful in preventing a slip from developing into a full relapse and will hopefully catch someone who has relapsed sooner, rather than later.

EVALUATING GOAL ACCOMPLISHMENT AND SERVICE PROVIDED

Social workers are continually evaluating the progress of their clients as they move through the helping process. Evaluation simply formalizes what every worker does as part of their everyday practice. Progress can be measured subjectively by simply reflecting on the process and goal-attainment and quantitatively by adding more objective measures such as standardized tests. The evaluation of the work accomplished by single clients can be combined and taken as an aggregate, giving the social worker an indication of the overall effectiveness of his or her practice.

Evaluation can focus on outcomes or on the helping process itself. Outcome evaluation is most rigorous when there are clear and objective measures of change. Typically the social worker and client have identified and collected baseline data during the assessment phase, which can be used to compare to data collected during termination or follow-up. A positive evaluation contributes to the client's identity and sense of competence.

A more subjective and less rigorous approach to evaluation involves the client and worker reviewing each goal and the progress made toward that goal. To help the client be more specific about changes it is helpful to ask for specific examples of changes made. The worker and client might consider eliciting information from fellow group members, family members, or significant others of the client to corroborate the evidence of change (Hepworth and Larsen, 1990).

Termination should also include an evaluation of the helping process. It is important for clients to recognize their achievements and to have an understanding of how they have accomplished these goals, if they are to transfer their learning to new situations. This new awareness also contributes to clients' sense of mastery and competence.

Clients should also provide the social worker with feedback about what the social worker did that was helpful or not helpful. This feedback can include the worker's personal qualities, such as attitudes and beliefs, as well as the skills and techniques employed. Due to the power imbalance, this feedback must be sincerely initiated by the social worker. This constructive feedback is especially valuable for practitioners as one way to evaluate their practice. It helps the worker confirm his or her strengths and identify weaknesses. This feedback can be done in person or as part of a written evaluation of the service provided. The evaluation should include an evaluation of the agency itself. The policies and procedures, the interaction with agency staff, and the environment might all be reviewed as supporting or hindering the helping process. Clients typically welcome the opportunity to provide feedback. The quality of the feedback will be good if the client believes the social worker values the critique and if the client is neither idealizing nor devaluing the helping process at the time of termination.

CONCLUSION

The process of termination is given little attention in the social work literature and in training programs. This is curious given the power the termination process has either to cement the changes made or to challenge and destroy those same changes. In this chapter we have identified the key types and stages of termination and discussed the role and tasks of the social worker. All clients must process the ending of the helping process and the helping relationship. Although the majority of clients seem to work through the process with little or no difficulty, there are a number of clients who are vulnerable to issues related to endings. These clients may present particular challenges to the social worker. In these situations, the social worker must pay particular attention to completing the ending process appropriately.

REFERENCES

Collins, D., Jordan, C., & Colerman, H., (1999). *An introduction to family social work.* Itasca: F.E. Peacock Publishers.

Compton, B.R. & Galaway, B. (Eds.). (1999). *Social work processes.* Toronto: Brooks/Cole Publishing Company.

Garvin, C. & Seabury, B. (1984). *Interpersonal practice in social work.* Englewood Cliffs: Prentice Hall.

Fish, R., Weakland, J., & Segal, L. (1982). *The tactics of change.* San Francisco, CA: Josey Boss Publishers.

Fortune, A. (1985). Planning duration and termination of treatment. *Social Service Review. 5*(8), 647–661.

Fortune, A., Pearlingi, B., & Rochelle, C. (1992). Reactions to termination of individual treatment. *Social Work. 37*(2), 171–178.

Henry, S. (1992). *Group skills in social work.* Pacific Grove, CA: Brooks Cole.

Hepworth, D. & Larsen, J. (1990). *Direct social work practice.* Belmont: Wadsworth Publishing.

Hess, H. & Hess, P.M. (1999). Termination in context. In B. Compton & B. Galaway (Eds.). *Social work processes* (pp. 489–497). Toronto: Brooks/Cole Publishing Company.

Horowitz, M., Marmar, C., Krupnick, J., Wilner, N., Kaltreider, N., & Wallerstein, R. (1984). *Personality styles and brief psychotherapy.* New York, NY: Basic Books.

Kirst-Ashman, K. & Hull, G. (1993). *Understanding generalist practice.* Chicago, IL: Nelson Hall Publishers.

Levin, D. (1998). Unplanned termination: pain and consequences. *Journal of Analytic Social Work, 5*(2), pp. 35–46.

Levinson, H. (1977). Termination of psychotherapy: some salient issues. *Social Casework. 5*(8), 480–489.

Northen, H. (1988). *Social work with groups.* New York, NY: Columbia University Press.

Strupp, H. & Binder, J. (1984). *Psychotherapy in a new key: a guide to time-limited dynamic psychotherapy.* New York, NY: Basic Books, Inc.

Toseland, R. & Rivas, R.F. (1995). *An introduction to group work practice.* Boston, MA: Allyn and Bacon.

Yalom, I. (1975). *The theory and practice in group psychotherapy.* New York, NY: Basic Books.

RECORD KEEPING
IN SOCIAL
WORK CLINICAL
PRACTICE

Cheryl Regehr

It is widely suggested that good record keeping is an essential component of clinical social work practice. Thorough documents allow social workers to maintain a record of their clinical assessment and clinical interventions in order to assist with ongoing work in the case and in order to clearly communicate their opinions, findings, and interventions to other members of the treatment team. In addition, careful records can be the key to ensuring that practice decisions are well considered and adequate measures are taken to ensure the safety and well-being of clients and others in the face of possible legal action in the future.

Record keeping consumes a substantial portion of social work time. Indeed, estimates from early research done in the 1950s indicated that social workers spent up to 25% of their time recording information in client files (Streat, 1987). More recent research estimates that between 10% to 60% of social workers' time is spent in the practice of documenting their work with clients (Ames, 1999; Edwards & Reid, 1989). Nevertheless, documentation is rarely a task that is approached with enthusiasm by social workers (Gelman, 1992; Tebb, 1991). As a result, when faced with time constraints, recording is often placed low on the priority list (Gelman, 1992; Kagle, 1984; Kagle, 1993; Streat, 1987).

Despite agreement regarding the importance of clinical records, and the time invested in this endeavour, surprisingly little has been written about what constitutes good recording practices and how to ensure that clinical records withstand court challenges. Several authors point to the lack of emphasis placed on recording in social work training programs (Gelman, 1992; Holbrook, 1983; Kagle, 1984). Others have criticized the quality of social work records, suggesting that they often contain information that is inaccurate, contradictory, and unsubstantiated, as well as opinions which are stigmatizing and insulting (Gelman, 1992). It has also been suggested that recording is a form of discretionary power and may be skewed in order to meet certain goals (Holbrook, 1983; Cochran, Gordon, & Krause, 1980). For instance, in order to have a client accepted into a particular group home, problematic issues are ignored and the assessment becomes overly positive. Few authors however, have offered guidelines for good recording practices. This chapter reviews the history of record keeping in social work, current expectations regarding recording, and legal issues related to the confidentiality of social work records in Canada.

HISTORY OF RECORD KEEPING IN SOCIAL WORK

Tebb (1991) does an outstanding job of outlining the history of social work recording. This history begins in the 1800s with the "friendly visitor" movement, initated by Mary Richmond (Coady, 1993) at a time when documentation consisted primarily of register-type records. These documents noted the name and address of the client, the name of the friendly visitor, a brief description of the problem identified, and resources that were distributed to the poor. At a later stage of this movement, which accompanied the work of Jane Adams in the Settlement Houses of the early 1900s, records were expanded somewhat to include both the verified facts of the case and the subjective opinion of the worker. This narrative record included not only the resources provided, but also the impact of these resources on the client, and it helped to justify the provision of services (Tebb, 1991).

Psychoanalytic theory, pioneered by Sigmund Freud in the 1920s, and the functional school initially developed by Otto Rank in the 1930s, led to the development of process recordings. In these documents, the therapist would describe the process of treatment and particularly the interaction between the worker and the client. In this way, workers could review their practice and plan intervention techniques. Later, recording moved from being a prospective tool for treatment planning, to a retrospective review of what occurred in treatment for the purposes of supervision. The extensive procedure of process recording gave way to summary recordings during the time when casework, as conceptualized by Helen Perlman, was the common mode of practice in the 1940s and 1950s. These summaries continued to be an opportunity to examine and evaluate practice (Tebb, 1991). Assessments continued to be highly subjective, and worker opinion played a central role in the document.

The contemporary social work record differs markedly from that of the past. The record now serves primarily to facilitate service delivery rather than to provide a basis for supervision. That is, a shift has occurred from analysis to action and from process to product (Kagle, 1983). As time constraints increasingly affect the ability of workers to invest time in recording, agencies are moving towards brief recording strategies such as outlines, checklists, or brief forms to replace long narratives (Kagle, 1993). Further, recording has become an important form of accountability for the practices of workers (Ames, 1999; Gelman, 1992). As workers are being held more responsible for the results of their decisions in both the criminal and civil courts (Alexander, 1995), recording practices have become increasingly focused on fact and less on opinion or conjecture. In addition, current legislation in Canada that permits client access to records, has resulted in the need to be concise and accurate, and to ensure that opinions are well substantiated by facts.

CURRENT EXPECTATIONS OF RECORDING

The Canadian Association of Social Workers' Code of Ethics (1994) makes the following statements regarding record keeping:

- 5.10: The social worker shall record all relevant information, and keep all relevant documents in the [client] file.
- 5.11: The social worker shall not record in a client's file any characterization that is not based on clinical assessment or fact.

The Ontario College of Social Workers and Social Service Workers (2000) provides more explicit guidelines, indicating that the records should be legible and systematic, that recordings should be made when the event occurs or as soon as possible thereafter, that record keeping guidelines apply to social workers employed in agencies and to those in independent practice, that records must be kept for a period of seven years, and that confidentiality of records must be ensured.

While the above statements suggest with little ambiguity that records must be kept, what is less clear is the question of what constitutes a good clinical record. Kagle (1983), in a study of 147 social agencies and social work departments conducted in 1979 in the United States, identified that the typical social work record contained (1) a social history; (2) the worker's assessment of the client's situation; (3) a goal statement; (4) a service plan; (5) progress notes; and (6) and closing summary. Guidelines offered by this and other sources (Kagle, 1984; OCSWSSW, 2000) are incorporated into the suggested framework found in Table 18.1.

TABLE 18.1 Aspects of a Clinical Record	
Assessment Phase	
Initial Information	• Name and contact information of the client
	• Reason for referral and referral source
	• Other agency involvement or outstanding legal issues
	• Client's perception of the problem
	• Any collateral information included in the assessment
Description of the client	• Brief personal history
	• Relevant relationships
	• Social/cultural factors
	• Current situation (stressors, supports, strengths, and limitations)
Formulation	• Summary of predisposing, precipitating, perpetuating, and protective factors
	• Worker's opinion
Plan	• Client's wishes
	• Goals for treatment
	• Tentative agreement
Intervention Phase	
Progress notes	• Relevant events in client's life
	• Summary of interventions
Additional data	• Record of any additional contacts with client or collaterals
	• Inclusion of any additional data obtained
	• Consents for release of information
Termination Phase	
Closing notes	• Evaluation of service
	• Referral, if any
	• Plans for follow up, if any

It is important to remember that recording practices must be adapted to meet the idio-syncratic purposes and constraints of various practice settings. For instance, shorter inter-ventions may require more concise and structured forms of reporting (Kagle, 1984; Streat, 1987). However, regardless of the setting, whether a worker is in a large institution, small agency, or independent practice, guidelines for recording should be established and fol-lowed in every case. At bare minimum, the record should contain identifying data of the client, a brief assessment, and dated notations of each contact (Kagle, 1984; OCSWSSW, 2000). The record should describe the treatment or intervention employed and the ratio-nale for selecting it (Ames, 1999). In addition, any significant clinical issues, such as a risk of harm to self or others and the relevant assessment and measures taken to ensure safety, must be documented. The reasons for any decision to breach confidentiality should be clearly noted (Ames, 1999; Glancy, Regehr & Bryant, 1998a). Recordings should be goal-directed and should relate directly to the problem identified. Interesting but irrelevant infor-mation should be excluded. Finally, it is critical to differentiate between factual information and worker opinion (Ames, 1999; Gelman, 1972).

CONFIDENTIALITY OF SOCIAL WORK RECORDS

The duty to protect the confidentiality of client information is a central tenet of social work practice. The Canadian Association of Social Workers' Code of Ethics devotes its largest chap-ter to this issue and states that:

> A social worker shall protect the confidentiality of all information acquired from the client or others regarding the client and the client's family during the professional relationship. (CASW, 1994, p.14)

The Code identifies several exceptions to the rule of confidentiality, including written autho-rization by the client, information required by a statute or order of a court of competent jurisdiction, threat of harm to self or others, and information obtained from a child of ten-der years, the disclosure of which the social worker determines to be in the best interests of the child (CASW, 1994). While these standards for practice appear clear, the actual appli-cation of the standards results in a number of dilemmas for social workers. Recent legisla-tive enactments and court decisions have further muddied the waters regarding which information is confidential and which information the social work practitioner ought to reveal (Regehr, Glancy, & Bryant, 1997; Glancy, Regehr, & Bryant, 1998b). This section will review current legal findings regarding confidentiality of social work records.

Client Access to Records

The Ontario Mental Health Act (1990) and a judgment of the Supreme Court of Canada (McInerney v. MacDonald, 1992) have established the right of clients to have access to all mental health and medical records regarding their care. This includes not only records com-piled in the treatment facility to which the request for access is directed, but also all records obtained from other facilities following the signed consent of the client.

If a treating professional has reason to believe that access to the information contained in a clinical record may be harmful to the client or a third party (such as a family member who has provided information), she or he may apply to the court to deny the request for access.

However, if the potentially dangerous information is contained in records that have been forwarded to another facility subsequent to a signed release of information form, the worker who authored the records may not be informed that the information is to be released and therefore may not have the opportunity to make application to have the information kept private.

While initially viewed with alarm by practitioners, client access to records is viewed by some as having benefits. For instance, clients are given the opportunity to correct or amend erroneous records. Further, when aware that clients will access records, social workers tend to ensure that records are better organized, shorter, more factual, and more goal-oriented (Gelman, 1992). It has also been suggested that involving clients in the production of case records can be an effective tool in the treatment process (Badding, 1989).

Parental Access to Children's Records

In Ontario, the Children's Law Reform Act (1990) and the Child and Family Services Act (1990) state that both custodial parents and non-custodial parents with access to their children have the right to review the clinical records of their child who is under the age of 16, without the child's consent. The exception to this is when the records relate to the counselling of a child aged 12–16. These requirements remind social workers that the clinical record must be written in a manner that respects the best interests of the client and his or her family.

Court access to records

Access to the treatment records of victims has been the centre of considerable controversy over the past few years (Regehr, Bryant, & Glancy, 1997). Arguments have focused on balancing the legal rights of the defendant, particularly in sexual assault trials, with the privacy rights of the victim. As a result of the vocal concerns of therapists and other victim advocacy groups, changes to the Criminal Code of Canada placed restrictions on access to victims' treatment records (Statutes of Canada, 1997). While subsequent court decisions challenged the legislation on the basis that it violated the Canadian Charter of Rights and Freedoms (1992), the provisions of the act have recently been upheld by the Supreme Court of Canada (R. v. Mills, 2000). Nevertheless, if victim records are determined to be relevant to the case, they can become a part of the criminal trial.

Civil court access to records

Individuals who initiate legal proceedings that put their treatment, medical condition, or health in issue are viewed as waiving the right to confidentiality and implicitly consenting to the disclosure of confidential information relevant to the action (P. (L.M.) v. F. (D.), 1994). Thus, the defendant in a civil action has access to records of the complainant's care. This has significant implications in cases where victims choose to sue their abusers.

Family court access to records

Family court proceedings may also result in court access to records. During a custody dispute, for example, a husband requested that the psychiatric records of his wife be disclosed to support his claim that she could not care for children (Gibbs v. Gibbs, 1985). The court ordered disclosure of records despite her doctor's conclusion that it would likely be harmful to her. The judge concluded that the potential harm to the children was the greater risk, thereby setting precedence for record disclosure in family court matters.

Protecting the Confidentiality of Records

As social workers in Canada are increasingly faced with limits to the privacy of client information, we must evaluate the effect of these changes on practice. New requirements have a significant impact on recording practices and remind social workers that clinical records must be written in a manner that respects the best interest of clients and their families. When recording, social workers should avoid speculation and record only details which are clearly pertinent to the assessment and treatment of clients. In particular, when workers provide treatment to victims or offenders, their clinical records must exclude any speculation as to the legitimacy of a victim's story or the culpability of the alleged offender. As always, it is important to clarify what is opinion and what is "fact" as presented by the client.

While information presented by the client is necessary for a comprehensive assessment, specific details of victimization or criminal activity should be avoided. As therapists attempt to reconstruct the client story from their notes and memory into an assessment, some facts can become distorted. These distortions may ultimately result in a miscarriage of justice, as it may appear that the client is providing inconsistent information. In addition, in sexual assault cases, information about the client's previous sexual history should not be recorded, in order to preserve her privacy should the notes go to court.

Barsky (1997) recommends the separation of client records for the various services that a client receives, such as vocational counselling and sexual assault treatment. Sexual assault care centres in hospitals have often elected to keep a set of records which is distinct from the main hospital record. Therefore, if the sexual assault chart is subpoenaed, the defendant does not necessarily receive all information about such things as psychiatric admissions or previous abortions. However, these records could be obtained by demonstrating relevance to the action before the court. Seeking legal advice is recommended prior to instituting a policy of separate records for any services rendered and certainly prior to making only a partial response to a subpoena. Further, the practice of keeping separate records clearly contravenes the CASW Code of Ethics which states that "The social worker shall maintain only one master file on each client." (CASW, 1994, Section 5.9). The master file, as defined by the Code, must include all information pertaining to the client The Code cautions that this document should be prepared with the anticipation that the file may be revealed to the client or disclosed in legal proceedings.

As a final point, notes, once made, should not be destroyed or altered in order to avoid the problem of court access. Such destruction has led to a dismissal of charges against an accused (Barsky, 1997). Destruction of records after the issuance of a subpoena could also lead to charges being laid against the record keeper for obstruction of justice, or to disciplinary proceedings.

When obtaining informed consent, social workers must be clear about the limits of confidentiality of social work records, particularly when the situation of the client may result in some type of legal action. Finally, social workers have an ethical duty to remain current about legal threats to confidentiality and to make all reasonable efforts to protect the privacy of our clients within the bounds of legal requirements.

CONCLUSION

Recording is a central component of social work practice which enhances case planning and the communication of assessment results and treatment methods to others, and allows for evaluation of the quality of services provided. It is the ethical and legal responsibility of all social workers to maintain records which accurately reflect a client's situation and all contacts between the social worker and the client. These records should be clear, concise, and focused on facts obtained from the client and other collateral sources. The social worker's opinion must be clearly differentiated and based on information gleaned about the individual client's situation, not based on pre-existing biases or assumptions. Records should be written with the view that they are not the personal property of the social worker or his or her agency but are fully accessible to the client. Finally, in the event that access of others to the record is made possible by a court order, the social worker must make every effort to ensure that confidentiality is maintained. In addition, he or she must ensure that the records will stand up to scrutiny should they be viewed in a legal context.

REFERENCES

Alexander, R. (1995). Social workers and immunity from civil lawsuits. *Social Work, 40*(5) 648–654.

Ames, N. (1999). Social work recording: a new look at an old issue. *Journal of Social Work Education, 35*(2) 227–237.

Badding, N. (1989). Client involvement in case recording. *Social Casework, 70*(9) 539–548.

Barsky A. (1997). *Counsellors as Witnesses*. Aurora, ON: Aurora Professional Press.

Canadian Association of Social Workers (1994) *Social Work Code of Ethics*. Ottawa: Canadian Association of Social Workers.

Canadian Charter of Rights and Freedoms (1982) Part 1 of the Constitution Act 1982, Being Schedule B to the Canada Act (U.K.), 1982, c.11.

Children's Law Reform Act, R.S.O. (1990), c.C.12, s.20(5)

Child and Family Services Act, R.S.O. (1990), c.C.11, s.184(1)(b

Coady, N. (1993). The Worker-Client Relationship Revisited. *Families in Society, 74*, 291–298.

Cochran, N., Gordon, A. & Krause, M. (1980). Proactive records. *Knowledge: Creation, Diffusion, Utilization*, 2(1) 5–18.

Edwards, R. & Reid, W. (1989). Structured case recording in child welfare: An assessment of social worker's reactions. *Social Work*, 34(1) 49–52.

Gelman, S. (1992). Risk management through client access to case records. *Social Work, 37*(1) 73–79.

Gibbs v. Gibbs (1985), 1 W.D.C.P. 6 (Ont. S.C.)

Glancy, G., Regehr, C. & Bryant, A. (1998a) Confidentiality in Crisis: Part I - The Duty to Inform. *Canadian Journal of Psychiatr,. 43*(12) 1001–1005.

Glancy, G., Regehr, C. & Bryant, A. (1998b) Confidentiality in Crisis: Part II - Confidentiality of Treatment Records. *Canadian Journal of Psychiatry, 43*(12) 1006–1011.

Holbrook, T. (1983). Notes on policy and practice: Case Records: Fact or Fiction? *Social Service Review, 57*(4) 645-658.

Kagle, J. (1983). The contemporary social work record. *Social Work, 28*(2) 149–153.

Kagle, J. (1984). Restoring the Clinical Record. *Social Work, 29*(1) 46–50.

Kagle, J. (1993) Record keeping: Directions for the 1990's. *Social Work, 38*(2) 197–203.

McInerney v. MacDonald, (1992), 2 S.C.R. 138.

Mental Health Act, R.S.O. (1990), c.M7, ss.29(2) and (3).

Ontario College of Social Workers and Social Service Workers (2000). *Code of Ethics and Standards of Practice.* Toronto, Canada: Author.

P. (L.M.) v. F. (D.) (1994), 22 C.C.L.T. (2d) 312 (Ont.Gen.Div.)

Regehr, C., Bryant, A. & Glancy, G. (1997) Confidentiality of Treatment for Victims of Sexual Violence. *The Social Worker, 65*(3) 137–145

R. v. Mills (1997) A.J. 891 (Alberta Crt of Queen's Bench

Statutes of Canada (1997) c.30 [Bill C-46, 1996] An Act to Amend the Criminal Code.

Streat, Y. (1987). Case recording in children's protective services. *Social Casework, 68*(9) 553–560.

Tebb, S. (1991). Client-focused recording: Linking theory and Practice. *Families in Society, 72*(7): 425–32.

TIME AS A FACTOR IN SOCIAL WORK TREATMENT

Jannah Mather

INTRODUCTION

Up until fifteen years ago, time in social work treatment was seen as a part of the "art" and "process" of the intervention approach. Length of time in social work treatment before this period was generally determined by the needs of the client and the approach to the treatment selected by the social worker to fit these needs. Longer-term therapy was seen as a requirement of psychoanalytic approaches and the use of short-term interventions was viewed as a short-cut substitute for treatment. Longer time periods in therapy, however, have now become a luxury restricted to clients who can afford to receive social work treatment interventions from funding sources other than those which set limits upon the numbers of sessions for which a client can be seen.

Despite the negative initial reactions to shorter approaches to treatment, research has begun to validate the usefulness of these shorter interventions. Studies by Monroe-Blum & Marziali (1995) on short-term group treatment, Thomlison (1984) on outcome effectiveness, and Giles, Prial, and Neims (1993) on the evaluation of psychotherapies all found that short-term approaches to treatment could be not only equally as effective as long-term approaches, but even more effective depending upon the issues with which the client is dealing. The results of these studies support the more short-term directive approach in social work treatment. Yet, the questions still remain as to the benefit of short-term treatment in all case situations as well as the role time can now play in the "art" and "process" of social work treatment. To answer these questions, it is important to examine all the meanings time has for the social work practitioner in treatment as well as to examine those areas of practice in which time plays a more significant part.

MEANINGS

Time in social work treatment does have more meaning than simply the number of sessions for which a client can be seen. Beyond the issues of the number and frequency of sessions, there are the factors of (1) the extent of time spent with the client or clients during each session, (2) the use of time in each session and its relevance for the client, (3) the time spacing between sessions, (4) the time of day, week, and month of the sessions, (5) the pacing of time in an interview, (6) the use of time as part of the techniques of the treatment approach, and (7) the implication of time as it affects cultural differences between clients. This chapter will examine these multiple aspects of time in social work treatment as well as address the initial concern of how administrative and funding structures produce short-term treatment as opposed to longer-term psychotherapies.

ADMINISTRATIVE AND FUNDING IMPLICATIONS OF TIME IN TREATMENT

Time is today a major source of concern for social work practitioners and the focus of time in many Canadian agencies has been more on the practitioner and the administrative issues of service than on the needs of the client and the relevance of time as part of the "art" and "process" in treatment. Time is what very few social workers have enough of when doing therapy today. The concepts of "limited sessions" and "short-term treatment" have brought new meaning to the word "time" in treatment. Most agencies and social work practitioners are having to contend with limited amounts of time in numbers of sessions authorized by extended insurance plans or by public funding sources. Additionally, accountability has added to the amount of time social workers now need to spend filling out forms to justify their approach to a client's treatment and their defined outcome goals.

Social work practice, from a traditional clinical perspective, is being restructured to meet the needs of the funding sources of clients rather then the actual needs of clients. The ethics of this situation have raised considerable concern among social work practitioners and social work agencies. Initial reaction to mandated shorter numbers of sessions was the belief that what social work practitioners could provide clients would be less then adequate. The real reaction to these changes was the feeling by social workers that they no longer controlled the type of interventions that could be given to clients. Despite the positive outcome studies of briefer treatments noted earlier, most social workers believe the "art" and "process" of the social work intervention is now being structured by external forces that do not understand the importance of the relationship between the worker and the client. There is a feeling that external funding is more focused on the efficiency of the outcome of the intervention than on the long-term change in the individual. Some of these fears may be well-founded depending upon the type of problem the client is experiencing. Test (1981) found in her study of the chronically mentally ill that structured continuity of care provided in an ongoing fashion was more effective to this client population than time-limited treatments. As will be seen in some of the following sections of this chapter, the use of short-term treatments may mean the more frequent return of clients to the social work agency.

LENGTH OF TIME OF TREATMENT (NUMBERS OF SESSIONS AND FREQUENCY)

The concerns over time-limited social work treatment now centre on how to provide clients with an intervention that is effective for them and limited enough to be authorized for care. As mentioned, the increase in the utilization of short-term, brief treatment interventions has focused the client on more changes in the here and now. Although the findings of studies on outcomes utilizing these briefer types of therapy approaches show positive results, not all cases will be as responsive to these methods. Having time controlled by external forces rather than by the psychological needs of the client has led many social workers to despair in their treatment approach and to be concerned over the kinds of care that can be provided. Although many clients can benefit from limited-term sessions, many need more of an ongoing approach to deal with deeper issues and/or pervasive problems which the client needs time to process. An interesting finding that is beginning to emerge in social work agencies is that those clients who need more service than the brief treatment model provides are returning with more frequency to the agencies to seek additional treatment.

A survey of social workers utilizing short-term treatment approaches indicates that clients are returning to their social work therapist at an increasing rate to pick up where the last intervention left off. The survey of fifteen private practice social workers indicated that their return rate of clients within a yearly period had more than doubled, compared to their earlier patterns of practice where clients worked in treatment longer but did not need treatment as often (Mather, 1996). What does this mean in terms of treatment? Well, apart from the fact that research in this area needs to be done on a more extensive basis, it indicates that the time spent in a short-term treatment process may only help clients with more than a situational problem. It would also appear that the client who receives short-term treatment may develop the sense that he or she has accomplished something, and hence want to pursue this further. Kalpin (1993) emphasized that the use of short-term treatment is not only good for funding reasons but also for giving clients a sense of accomplishment and a desire to continue their growth in treatment at a later time.

EXTENT OF TIME SPENT WITH CLIENT DURING EACH SESSION

The extent of time spent with an individual client during each session is dependent upon several factors. These factors are related to issues involved in the treatment as well as issues related to the client. Issues related to the treatment reflect what one is attempting to accomplish within an individual session as well as what point in the treatment process the social worker has reached. For example, trying to have an initial interview that lasts only fifty minutes may be effective in some cases, but most initial sessions require more time to build trust between the worker and the client. Gathering information related to the client's situation will begin in an initial session and continue on through the treatment process. Generally, the social worker will spend the first few minutes of the initial session creating a comfortable situation for the client before launching into discussing the issues that have brought the client in. This may include small talk, the offering of a beverage, or simply the sharing of the discomfort the client may be feeling in the initial visit. The social worker, in needing to gather information as well as build an empathetic, trusting relationship, will generally allow clients to spend their time in this initial session sharing what they are most comfortable with. This often means that the client does most of the talking during the first session and has an opportunity to disclose certain difficult issues. This does not mean that time parameters should not be set for the initial session, for the social worker will have other clients to work with. However, it is important in this initial meeting to allow clients enough time to become comfortable and to build their relationship with the social worker through this initial interaction.

On the other hand, the client may have a need for a more structured type of initial session and/or a shorter amount of time. For example, when working with children, we know their concentration span is less then that of an adult, and planning to see a child for greater than 20–30 minutes can be fruitless unless the session is structured around particular issues or play that will keep the child's attention. Children are not the only ones who may not be able to tolerate long periods in treatment. Individuals who are more easily frustrated, who become overwhelmed by their anger, or who cannot mentally concentrate on a particular area for long periods will need shorter sessions. It is important to remember that despite the external factors that may affect the numbers of sessions for which a client can be seen, the length of the sessions and the focus of these sessions should reflect the needs of the client.

USE OF TIME IN EACH SESSION AND ITS RELEVANCE FOR THE CLIENT

The use of time in each session is determined by the treatment plan and the desires of the client. When time in a session is not being used as planned, the social worker needs to examine both the issues being dealt with and the current situation of the client. Sometimes a recent occurrence in a client's life will require the social worker to deviate from the plan. It is important to remember that any issue in a session can be used to benefit the client. However, if the plan continues to be interrupted in each session by the client, this is an indication that the issues you are dealing with may be ones that the client is trying to avoid or that may not be relevant for the client.

Sensitivity to how this time is being used is critical in an ongoing assessment and evaluation of the treatment process. A good social work practitioner is prepared for each session and is not content to "just see what happens." The value of both the client's and social worker's time depends upon working toward the goals that have been set and accomplishing tasks that will reinforce and strengthen the client.

INTERVALS BETWEEN SESSIONS

The amount of time between sessions in social work treatment is often dependent not only upon the needs of the client but also on the availability of the social work therapist. In case situations where a client may need more intensive, frequent sessions because of his or her crisis state, it is important for the social worker to make a determination as to whether this kind of time can be provided to clients on an outpatient basis or whether it is best for the protection of the client that he or she receive inpatient treatment. If as a social worker you have any concerns that you may not be able to provide the client with the time they need to receive adequate care, additional arrangements should be made to aid them. As noted, this may mean they are seen on an inpatient basis or receive additional services from other resources which work closely with you on a collaborative treatment plan. For example, in a child welfare situation where one may be dealing with the possibility of mistreatment, the social worker has a responsibility to protect the child and provide the family with the resources they need not to abuse the child. If the social worker does not have the time to spend working with the family, then the protection of the child must take precedence. This is why programs like "family preservation," which supply intensive, 24-hour care from numerous workers, are so effective in child welfare situations. They allow the child to remain in the home because the family is worked with so intensively that the risk to the child becomes minimal.

TIME OF DAY, WEEK, AND MONTH OF SESSIONS

It may not occur to the social work practitioner that the day, week, or month of the treatment session can have an effect on the social work treatment itself. It is not unusual to find that client intakes and patient admissions to psychiatric hospitals increase with full moons, the aftermath of holidays, and/or the advent of the school year. Additionally, certain days of the week and hours of the day have been found to be more stressful on individuals and often result in an increased need for care at different times. It goes without saying in a treatment centre that often a Monday or a Friday will be the busiest time for social work practitioners. Generally this is a result of a long weekend in which family members have had difficulties or of a long work week where an individual may find that the stress of the work situation along with their other responsibilities comes to a point on this last work day of the week. Additionally, many social workers recognize that there are critical time periods during the day that affect individuals and families. Individuals seem less sure of themselves at night. Often they are alone or feel frightened of the night because of childhood histories.

Early morning and late afternoons before meal times tend to be the most stressful for families, and social workers will often find that they receive many of their phone calls from clients during these periods. It is also important for the social worker to be aware that there are certain periods of the day that can affect not only the client but also the social worker. Sessions immediately after lunch tend to be slower paced while sessions with children after they have sat in school all day tend to be more active. These are considerations that must be taken into account when the social worker plans his or her schedule for the day.

PACING WITHIN A SESSION

The pacing of a session is truly a part of the "art" of the treatment process. Depending upon the issues to be covered, the social work therapist must be constantly alert to the points in the session when it will be helpful to slow down. An understanding of this pacing becomes a natural part of the social worker's skill after having worked in the field for several years. One of the areas new social workers generally have much to learn about is the pacing of treatment and knowing the appropriate time to delve into specific issues.

Generally, a social work treatment approach will have stages or phases that the client will move through. Although there is flexibility in moving back and forth between these phases, the social worker must always be aware of the stage the treatment is in and how it is progressing. This is especially true in social work interventions employing brief or short-term treatments. If the social worker moves too slowly or too quickly for a client through these stages, they may lose all the accomplishments the client has made thus far. For example, take a situation where a client has just carried out a task assigned to him or her in a very appropriate manner. The client feels pleased with what he or she has accomplished and wants to spend some time sharing this with the social worker. The worker, however, is more concentrated on moving the client a step further and does not reinforce this accomplishment enough or spend enough time going over the actions the client took to reinforce his or her positive outcome. Very often in this type of situation the client can become discouraged and not put the effort into the next task he or she undertakes.

USE OF TIME AS A TECHNIQUE WITHIN A SESSION

The use of time within a treatment session is a critical technique used by the social work prac-titioner. Silence can be much more powerful than words. The social work practitioner must become comfortable with silence in a session and learn to help clients utilize it to understand the issues they are dealing with and make decisions to improve their situation. Many indi-viduals are uncomfortable with silence in stressful situations and will often talk out of their own discomfort. This is true for both the client and the social work practitioner. Yet, if the social worker is providing a model for the client on how to utilize and make the most of all their resources, he or she has a responsibility to demonstrate how silence is important to listening to their own thoughts and emotions before taking any action. Without being able to understand their thoughts and emotions, clients can make decisions and take actions which will not be productive for them. The length of time given for silence within a client session is a question often asked by new social work practitioners. The answer is, of course, dependent upon what is happening in the session and what is needed to help the client through the present situation.

Time also serves as a technique to move clients along in their treatment, according to Van-Bragt & Hesselink, (1993). Their study indicates that, in short-term, time-limited forms of treatment, time often serves as a force to help clients move forward and accomplish their plan. This finding was reflected in other studies which demonstrated that time itself could be a moti-vating factor in bringing about change in clients and in helping them accomplish their goals. An example of this can be seen in the case of Mary, a 22-year-old college student who has sought help in dealing with her anxiety regarding job interviewing. The social worker set up a short-term treatment plan which included working intensively with Mary immediately preceding a job interview. Both Mary and the social worker found the time before a job interview to be the most effective.

THE IMPACT OF CULTURE ON
TIME IN SOCIAL WORK TREATMENT

It is an important concept in social work treatment that the cultural background of the client is relevant to many aspects of the therapeutic process. Among these is time and how it is used within a session. A study by Semke, Stowell, and Durgin (1993) on the expenditure of time in a voluntary inpatient unit indicated that an Asian ethno-cultural background had a significant impact on how time was spent in treatment. The study highlights how the cultural back-ground of a patient can influence the use of time. In this study, the Asian cultural emphasis on "awareness of the social milieu" and "fatalism," or the acceptance of one's fate, influenced the length of stay in the inpatient unit. When a person views his or her life situation as his or her fate, their desire and urgency to change that situation is going to differ significantly from another individual who views his or her situation to be in his or her control (Ho, 1983).

Likewise, Aboriginals or Native Americans have particular issues related to time. These issues are connected with natural phenomena (especially in terms of moons and seasons or winters). Thus, a Native American may view the time or day of his or her session as significant to its success. This culture may also view many other things as more important than punc-tuality; thus arriving on time at a session may not have the same importance as some deep-seated issue related to treatment (Lewis & Ho, 1983).

Many minorities of colour who have experienced the oppression of living in a white-dominated ethnosystem can be significantly affected by the delays of time in being seen in a social service agency. From their perspective of powerlessness and discrimination, delays in receiving treatment are often interpreted as indifference on the part of the agency and the clients may drop out before their first session (Solomon, 1983).

CONCLUSION

Time as a factor in social work treatment runs richly throughout the "art" and "process" of the intervention whether the approach is long- or short-term. In so many ways, time can be the technique or factor which can make or break a therapeutic session or treatment plan. The social work practitioner's ability to be aware of all the differing aspects of time and to be sensitive to the client's needs regarding time will ensure a more positive outcome in social work treatment.

REFERENCES

Bryant, S.B. (1983). Social work with Afro-Americans. In A. Morales, & B.W. Sheafor (Eds.). *Social work: a profession of many faces*. (3rd ed.). Boston. Allyn and Bacon, Inc.

Giles, T.R., Prial, E.M., and Neims, D.M. (1993). Evaluating psychotherapies: a comparison of effectiveness. *International Journal of Mental Health, 22*(2).

Kalpin, A. (1993). The use of time in intensive short-term dynamic psychotherapy. *International Journal of Short Term Psychotherapy, 8*(2).

Lewis, R.G. and Man, K.H. (1983). Social work with Native Americans. In A. Morales & B.W. Sheafor (Eds.). *Social work: a profession of many faces*. (3rd ed.). Boston. Allyn and Bacon, Inc.

Man, K.H. (1983). Social work with Asian Americans. In A. Morales & B.W. Sheafor (Eds.). *Social work: a profession of many faces*. (3rd ed.). Boston. Allyn and Bacon, Inc.

Mather, J. (1996). Survey of private practitioners. Work-in-progress.

Monroe-Blum, H. and Marziali, E. (1995). A controlled trial of short-term group treatment for borderline personality disorder. *Journal of Personality Disorders, 9*(3).

Semke, J., Stowell, M., and Durgin, J. (1993). Influences on social work time expenditure in a voluntary inpatient psychiatric unit. *Health and Social Work, 18*(1).

Test, M. (1981). Effective community treatment of the chronically mentally ill: what is necessary? *Journal of Social Issues, 37*(3).

Thomlison, R.J. (1984). Something works: evidence from practice effectiveness studies. *Social work, 29*(1).

VanBragt, P.J. and Jesselink, A.J. (1993). Just before leaving: time and change in residential psychotherapy. *International Journal of Short Term Psychotherapy, 8*(2).

THE TECHNIQUES OF INTERVENTION

Luke J. Fusco

In social work practice, techniques of intervention do not exist apart from the professional helping relationship between the client and the social worker. In social work education, techniques cannot be explained or taught prior to the students having understood the nature of the relationship they will have with their clients.

The relationship is based on one fundamental principle, to help clients to manage themselves and their lives more effectively. The processes that define the techniques employed toward these ends are conditioned by the values of social work practice. Acceptance, purposeful expression of feelings, and a non-judgmental attitude help to create an atmosphere within which clients can feel safe and can trust the worker. Ensuring appropriate self-determination and confidentiality communicates respect for the clients' strengths and capabilities. Individualization emphasizes the uniqueness of each client. Controlled emotional involvement maintains the professional nature of the helping relationship.

These values and attitudes create a psychological and interactional environment within which specific techniques of intervention may be employed. The technology of intervention may be used in all modalities of social work practice. Practice with individuals, couples, families, small groups, and communities all utilize the techniques described below.

SUPPORT AND SUSTAINMENT

Clients approach the helping process with a great deal of uncertainty, anxiety, and ambivalence. The step of asking for help often follows many futile attempts at resolving the problem or adjusting to the situation causing difficulty. Having reached the decision to see a professional, and having made the appointment, people often experience increased apprehension and uncertainty. Who is this person called a social worker? What will she or he be like? Will the worker be able to help?

Ambivalence is usually present as people consider major changes in their lives. There are many possible sources for this ambivalence, including worrying that something is basically wrong with them (Hepworth & Larsen, 1993, 357). Clients, like anyone facing important life changes, do not know what the changes will actually bring. The ambivalence is the struggle between wanting things to improve and the fear that the changes will be worse than the current problems.

The task for the worker is to address all of the client's uncertainty about entering into a potentially intense relationship with this stranger. Rushing to solutions is a common mistake for beginning and even experienced practitioners. After all, they have gone into social work to help, and here is this person obviously needing and asking for help. It is understandable that a worker will want to try to alleviate the problem.

The appropriate responses emphasize techniques of sustainment and support. "Chief among these is interested, sympathetic listening, which conveys to the client the worker's concern for his well-being" (Hollis, 1972, 90). The social worker must give full attention to the client. He or she should sit at a conversational distance with no barriers, such as a desk or table, between them. The worker should maintain eye contact with the client. It is also important to convey, through positive facial expression and tone of voice, complete attention to the client's story.

In addition to asking for information about the client's problematic circumstances, support can be expressed through a question regarding the process the client went through in making the initial appointment. As the client describes these steps, the worker has an opportunity to reinforce the strength and even courage shown by the client in getting help. During the client's description of the process the worker can hear the ambivalence, uncertainty, and even fear about the results of obtaining assistance. The technique employed by the worker will be to address these feelings directly. In fact, they should be explored fully before moving to problem-solving.

Support and sustainment contribute to the establishment of the professional helping relationship. The client experiences a competent social worker who is focused on the client's feelings and is communicating an empathetic understanding of those feelings. Once that is accomplished, the work of exploring the problem areas can begin. Credibility must be established first. This fundamental principle applies whether the client is an individual who is depressed, a couple concerned about their relationship, a family with a chronically ill child, or a community group trying to get its local government to respond to its concerns.

The ultimate actions and changes must be accomplished by the clients themselves. If the worker has been able to create a positive, trusting relationship with the client, then the worker can more effectively push the client to consider alternatives to the problematic status quo. Sustainment and support establish a solid base that gives the client the security and confidence necessary to take the steps into the unknown future with all of its hope and lack of certainty.

EXPLORATION

Exploration occurs at several levels. In its most literal sense, *exploration* refers to the worker getting more detailed information from the client. Skilled interviewing involves helping the client to describe the physical, psychological, and emotional context within which the concrete events happened. The worker can then begin to construct the psychosocial history.

Exploration also includes helping clients to broaden their perspective on the problem. Patterns usually occur in our lives. A series of difficulties often represents a repeating theme in which the details may vary but the core event is the same. A common example is conflict with persons in authority, sometimes with one particular gender. Some brief exploration may reveal a pattern going back to parental conflict in adolescence, trouble with teachers and then with supervisors or employers. In that situation, exploration has broadened considerably the area for intervention. An alteration of a life-long pattern of interacting with authority figures will be more useful than simply helping the client to get along better with his or her current employer.

Feelings are always present in any situation. A social worker assisting a client to explore the problems that motivated the client to seek help will reach for those feelings. Sometimes clients will experience feelings that they are reluctant to express (Hollis, 1972, 103–104). Clients may require strong support from the worker in order to express a feeling. This is especially true if the client believes that the particular feeling is improper or forbidden. Feelings of anger toward a loved one may create a sense of guilt in the client. Some gentle exploration by the worker which validates the feeling may help the client to acknowledge the anger out loud. The worker's response to the client at that point can be crucial in the change process. The social worker's continuing acceptance and support of the client and what she or he is feeling can go a long way toward the client being able to recognize and express those feelings.

Hollis (1972) discusses another scenario where the client is talking openly and easily about him or herself without making any effort to effect changes (105). Here the worker can engage the client in a mutual exploration of the reluctance to consider personal changes or attempt to improve his or her overall situation. This pattern is related to the ambivalence to change discussed earlier.

REFLECTION, REFRAMING, AND EMPOWERMENT

Social workers and their clients may engage in reflection at any point in the change process. However, the social worker must take responsibility in managing how and when the reflection takes place. For example, clients who tend to blame themselves or are prone to feeling deep guilt over a problem relationship or situation ought not to be encouraged to dwell on such matters.

Conversely, when information and feelings are being expressed in a torrent of emotion, the worker may choose to interrupt the process and ask the client to pause and reflect on what she or he has been saying. The technique resembles a kind of self-analysis. The client is asked to listen to what he or she is stating, to bring some objectivity to his or her perspective.

As a rule, a social worker will do only what the client absolutely needs the worker to do. It is always preferable that clients work out their own understanding of their circumstances and ultimately their own solutions. All effective social work intervention includes helping individuals, families, and communities to develop skills and capacities that they may employ successfully in the future. Helping clients with a current problem, while of immediate benefit, is not as good an outcome as strengthening a community's ability to deal with all those setbacks that inevitably lie ahead.

If clients are unable or unwilling to engage in meaningful reflection on their problems, then the worker may initiate the process. Even then the worker's aim should be to have clients take over the process of reflection, or at least join in it, as soon as possible. The worker's reflections are useless unless clients are involved actively in the work. The social worker may begin the process, but ought not to become too enamoured with his or her own brilliance and neglect the client's participation.

Reframing (Watzlawick, Weakland, and Fisch, 1974) is a technique that may be used to stimulate clients first to react to another view of their situation and then to see things differently for themselves. Often associated with family treatment, reframing skills are useful in work with individuals, small groups, communities, and organizations. Reframing is one of the best ways to turn an apparently negative and even hopeless situation into one with at least some potential for change.

Clients come for help because on their own they see no way out of or around the problem. They have exhausted their usually reliable resources and hope that an "expert" will have some answers. Trying to provide solutions only reinforces the clients' sense of incompetence and is unlikely to be successful. The worker will never know as much about the clients' lives as they do. Reframing can be used to alter clients' negative perspectives on their circumstances. People need to see things in a more positive light and perceive the possibility for change before any improvement can take place. The worker may:

1. Reframe a problem so that clients can see that change is possible.
2. Convey a genuine belief in clients' ability to improve a situation they previously considered to be unchangeable (Hepworth & Larsen, 1993: 363).

Some examples can demonstrate how this technique can be highly effective. An individual may express the belief that either he or she or a partner is responsible for their failing relationship and that neither of them is capable or willing to acknowledge their part in the conflict. By focusing on what positive outcome the client ideally would want, the worker may gradually help the client to see his or her or the partner's behaviour patterns differently. The worker may point out how at a particular point in a typical fruitless argument the client could either take some direct responsibility for the problem or ask the partner what he or she would like to happen. Either way the pattern has been interrupted and a different response is required.

Sometimes the client's self-concept will not allow him or her to explore a problematic scenario. The worker may help by supporting a different view of the client's behaviour or sense of him or herself. The worker could, for example, point out how the client seems always to feel that he or she must be responsible for ending the dispute by giving in or compromising and then feeling frustrated and angry. That reframing of the situation can allow the client an alternative view of things and the possibility of new responses and a quite different outcome.

Much of the preceding discussion involves a steady empowerment of the client. Saleeby (1997) and others have written about the strengths perspective in social work practice. It is neither a theory nor a treatment model. The strengths perspective is more an affirmation of the innate capacity of humans to find ways to improve unacceptable situations.

Saleeby (1997) suggests categories of questions that will elicit recognition by clients of their own unacknowledged strengths (53). Survival questions cause the person to explore how they have managed up to now, despite all the challenges they have faced. Clients are asked to discuss the qualities they possess that have enabled them to endure. The worker would then attempt to build on those strengths.

Another kind of question delves into the person's support system. The clients are asked to identify who is helpful to them when they have troubles, and how they are helpful. There also may be groups or organizations which have been of assistance in the past. The aim then is to use those external supports and if necessary to develop a plan to build additional support systems.

Saleeby (1997) also discusses the importance of helping to build clients' self-esteem (54). The social worker asks the clients what good qualities others say they have. Clients are asked to describe those things about themselves, their life, and their accomplishments which they value and which give them a sense of pride. The worker guides the client into a more positive and optimistic view of the situation.

All three of these techniques—reflection, reframing, and empowerment using a strengths perspective—are designed to change how the client sees the problems that caused him or her to look for help. There also may be changes in how clients feel about themselves, about their perceived difficulties, and about the possibility that they can effect change in themselves and in others that will result in an amelioration of the stress they are experiencing.

ADVICE-GIVING

Perhaps the best advice to a social worker about giving advice to clients is, don't. Those who discuss this as a valid technique within the helping process list conditions and safeguards around its employment (Hollis, 1972; Brill, 1995). In general, advice-giving should not be the primary technique of providing help to another person. Even if the advice results in dramatic improvement, all the client may have gained is the sense that he or she will have to consult with someone else in the future when there are problems. Social work practice is about expanding people's own capacities and resources with a view to autonomous and independent living in the future.

In crisis situations, people are temporarily overwhelmed by a sudden, unexpected calamity. They simply cannot function because of the paralyzing emotions they feel. Intervention can take the form of taking over for the person, making decisions for him or her, and even being quite directive. Hence advice-giving can be appropriate and necessary.

However, clients usually approach a social worker when they are not in a crisis state. Often their expectation is that they will describe the problem and the worker will tell them what to do. We have all been conditioned by the medical model where a biological problem has a specific treatment or cure. As a result, clients often must experience social work intervention before they understand that they will play the major role in the change process and that the worker will not and cannot provide a cure.

There are times when workers may assist clients in formulating options and then making decisions about which course to pursue. In subtle ways, social workers can suggest various modifications in the problematic situation. However, the principle of client self-determination must condition all such suggestions. The clients should always make the final decisions about what they will or will not do in trying to make their lives happier or more acceptable.

In short we do not know what is best for other people. As professionals who know clients for a relatively short period of time, we cannot know the full meaning of a client's relationships. Therefore we cannot know whether two people should continue together or should separate. In cases of abuse, of course, the victim's safety comes first and protection becomes the priority. In non-abusive situations, suggestions, counselling, and even direct advice can be incorporated within the context of clients' managing their own lives. Social workers can think *with* their clients but not think for them.

AUTHORITY AND POWER

The use of authority in social work practice is one of the most modelled concepts within the profession. Before any meaningful discussion can occur, terms must be defined and used consistently.

Elsewhere the words *power*, *authority*, and *influence* are discussed in detail (Fusco, 1983). Briefly, power is communicated when a consequence is added to a statement. For example, saying to an adolescent child, "if you do not get home by midnight you will be grounded next weekend."

Power is present in social work practice when the agency and the worker can impose legal consequences on the client. That is often the case in the fields of corrections, child welfare, and public assistance, and at times in the mental health area. Clients seen within those fields of practice may be involuntary, adding another dimension of power to the relationship.

Power itself is not a technique, but its existence in a professional social work relationship may affect the ability of the worker to be seen by the client as a supportive helping person. Social workers whose agencies have legal power must become comfortable with that power, understand exactly what they will and will not do in various circumstances, and then communicate that information to the client. There must be no ambiguity in the explanation to the client. Everyone ought to be clear about the rules.

Professional social work authority can come from the position of the worker, within the function of the agency, or from the clients' view that workers are experts in their field, possessing both the knowledge and the skills required to help them with their problems (Compton & Galaway, 1989: 296).

The clients complete the authority relationship by believing in the worker's competence. The authority provides security to the clients; they are working with someone who will help them to make the kinds of changes required to effectively reduce or eliminate the problem.

Using that authority within the helping relationship is a vital part of social work practice. Social workers should be confident and optimistic about both the possibility of change and the client's abilities to effect the change. The authority is communicated not as prescription or direction but as belief in and support of the client's capabilities.

In circumstances where the client and the social worker have a legally mandated relationship, the helping process can occur only as the second part of a two-stage process. First, the social worker must explain the legal dimensions of his or her role and the requirements present. These are non-negotiable parts of what can be called the power relationship. That relationship will remain dormant as long as the client is in compliance with the law, court orders, and other related regulations.

Once that area is explained and clarified the mandated or involuntary client can be offered the opportunity to voluntarily make use of a professional helping relationship with the same social worker. (Some agencies have separated the two functions of supervision and counselling into two different units; either model can be used.)

The client can decline the second relationship and simply remain under supervision until the order is terminated by a court, parole board, or other legal body. The help remains available and the client only decides to initiate the helping process voluntarily.

The presentation of the legal contract by the worker must be done in a non-threatening, matter-of-fact manner. The technique employed here is one of belief in the client's capacity to behave appropriately and stay out of legal difficulty. The presentation should be clear and relatively brief. The emphasis should be on the client's potential strengths and the availability of help if the client decides that he or she wants that kind of assistance.

Social workers employed in the socio-legal areas of practice will have smaller caseloads of ongoing clients seen on a weekly basis within the larger workload composed of all the people assigned to them. The existence of power in these relationships cannot and should not be denied or misrepresented, but the power does not have to prevent the incorporation of more traditional social work authority utilized to assist these clients in the same way they would be helped in a voluntary family service agency or by a private social work practitioner.

PARTIALIZING

This technique in social work practice is an effective way for all of us to successfully manage anything that seems overwhelming. People often describe their problems as too much, too big, too complicated, or too many. "Such statements as, 'Everything is wrong' and 'There is nothing that can be done' reflect a totality that both overwhelms and immobilizes" (Middleman and Wood, 1990: 75).

Moving from the whole awful mess to individual tasks that can be accomplished involves more than just pointing out the obvious realities. In response to a client's description of a huge overwhelming situation, the social worker first should validate the client's feelings. Affirming that the burden is great and expressing understanding by stating that most people would feel the same way normalizes the client's feelings.

Partializing can be done by either worker or client but will be guided initially by the social worker. For example, if a client presents a scenario where he or she is concerned about a child's behaviour, the spousal relationship, job insecurity, and difficulty in sleeping, the worker may suggest that they explore each area separately. The client will have made attempts to work on each problem but will be hampered by all of the other areas impinging on those efforts.

Asking the client which of the areas is the most immediate problem, which is most important or most worrisome, will push her or him to giving order and priority to the totality of difficulties. Partializing begins to give the client control over the situation and provides some perspective on it. One thing at a time is often a good way to approach a "so much to deal with" situation.

As clients begin to make decisions and take action, their subjective perception of their difficulties starts to change. Improvement in one area will increase their sense of mastery, reduce the totality of the problem, and build a sense of competence. Things won't seem impossible anymore. The worker provides support and ought to congratulate the clients as they begin to sort out and manage their problems.

ADVOCACY

Advocacy can occur at any level of social work practice. Assisting an adolescent to be readmitted to school following expulsion is the kind of representation social workers make while working with individuals and families. Clients sometimes are not capable of presenting their needs effectively to another agency. Social workers can advocate for their clients—bearing in mind that the worker should only do what the client truly cannot do.

Communities of people can make use of the expertise of a social worker to both formulate and then carry out a plan, making their case to municipal or regional authorities. But again, good social work practice at the community level would include building these skills into the communities' own resources.

At the provincial and national levels, social workers and social work as a profession advocate for policies, regulations, and legislation protecting and guaranteeing the right of all people to have their basic human needs met and have the opportunity to pursue their growth and developmental needs.

The key to advocacy is not to maintain someone's dependency on a professional interceding for them. Advocacy can be incorporated into a more comprehensive approach to helping where the worker eventually becomes redundant and the client more and more independent and autonomous.

CHALLENGING AND CONFRONTING

Clients and their social workers must perceive reality in the same way if their mutual efforts are to result in positive changes. We too deny feelings and facts in order to make the reality more acceptable to us or to mitigate our own responsibility for any troubles.

A social worker may challenge clients' beliefs and confront the denials and distortions. If employed effectively the technique of confrontation can help to clarify what is really happening in clients' lives. Sometimes what the client says and what she/he communicates nonverbally are not consistent. The social worker may confront those inconsistent messages.

The words *confrontation* and *challenge* carry connotations of aggression and even hostility. Neither should be part of a social work use of these techniques. Confrontation can be firm but still gentle. It can be couched in supportive terms recognizing the clients' pain. "Sometimes it's very hard to admit to yourself that things are as bad as they really are" would be an example of a remark prefatory to the confrontation, "but you are going to have to recognize how serious this is before you can try and change things."

A community group might confront administrators in their municipal government about delays in promised action. A social worker hearing different accounts of the same event from clients and other parties might confront everyone involved in turn or together in order to clarify events.

On a one-to-one level, confrontation is best accomplished after the professional helping relationship has been established. People will accept confrontation less defensively if they know that the confronting person cares about them and is trying to help. Confrontation perceived as an attack is unlikely to achieve positive results.

ROLE-PLAYING

Role-playing, or behaviourial rehearsal as it is sometimes called, is an extremely effective technique used to help people learn and practise needed skills. Role-play can be used in work with individuals, couples, families, small groups, and communities. Role-play has obvious applications in the educational field and can be incorporated in the change phase of a social work intervention plan.

Simulated sessions can be used to demonstrate the existence of a problem. For example, an individual client can be asked to play the other person in a problematic relationship. The worker plays the client's role and attempts to manage as the client would. The dynamics are evident in the role-play. The client can then analyze the interactions (perhaps they might be taped) and consider alternative ways of responding. Again, role-play as a kind of rehearsal can be used to test out these new coping skills. Preparation and practice in response to several probable outcomes may have the effect of helping the client to develop new skills and to feel more confident about being able to effect change due to the practice he or she has had.

Similarly, couples can be asked to reenact their most recent argument or to try and work out a problem they actually have, in front of the social worker. Switching roles or trying new approaches with guidance from the worker can alter long-established patterns of communication. People will take risks in situations where they feel safe. Following the role-play, debriefing is important. Whether the clients have played themselves or other roles, they should discuss the thoughts and feelings present during the simulation. Discussion of the experience will lead to further modifications in the change plan.

Small groups are excellent modalities within which to incorporate the technique of role-playing. Various scenarios can be simulated, with group members either playing specific roles or providing reactions and suggestions. Since group members have similar problems or are in comparable situations, they can all benefit from the exercise regardless of the part they play. Social skills groups incorporate a combination of description, modelling, and role-playing into the specific skills which are to be improved or learned (Hepworth & Larsen, 1993, 455–458).

Community groups can use role-play to a variety of ends. The technique can be useful in managing problems within the organization itself. Rehearsal of a plan can be an effective way to prepare for a meeting with the city council, government officials, or other organizations. Members of the community group can play the roles of all of the various participants in the meeting. In carrying out this exercise, many of the obstacles or pitfalls that might be present can be exposed. The members will then be able to re-think their strategies and be ready to respond to the other participants more effectively.

The social worker can be an active player in behavioural rehearsals. Sometimes, especially in small groups and community organizations, the worker is more of a director or facilitator of the action. He or she can model or demonstrate a skill or a response and then later take the lead in debriefing the participants and extracting the understandings and insights which have resulted from the role-play.

MEDIATION

Conflict is present in many situations in which social workers practice. In cases involving couples, nuclear, blended, or extended families, neighourhoods, and larger communities, disputes or conflicts may be the major reason why social work intervention was requested. Among professionals, conflicts occur within therapy or research teams, in organizations, and among social planners. How effectively these various disputes are managed or resolved will affect how much energy can be re-directed into more constructive efforts.

Negotiation occurs when two individuals or groups (parties is the legal term) attempt to come to an agreement on an issue. The people directly affected meet face to face or they use representatives in the process of negotiation. A separating couple may discuss a co-parenting arrangement, neighbours may agree on a plan about a fence, a barking dog, or loud music, and community agencies may cooperate in developing a plan to share limited resources.

When people cannot negotiate a mutually satisfactory outcome on their own, they may choose to use the services of a third party, a mediator, to assist them. There are a range of third party processes described in the literature on conflict resolution (Barsky, 2000; Kruk, 1997). In this brief discussion (see Chapter 40 for a more detailed presentation) the focus is on situations in which a continuing relationship between or among the parties to the dispute is necessary.

The social worker's role in mediating disputes with a view to preserving the relationship is to assist the parties in identifying their fundamental interests and to help them to create a plan which accomplishes that end (Fisher, Ury, & Patton, 1997). Self-determination underlies successful negotiations. Mediators must respect the individuals' right to create their own outcome. Divorcing parents want to remain effective parents, neighbours want to live together harmoniously, colleagues want good working relationships, agencies prefer to focus on delivering services effectively, and communities hope to work toward improving their physical and social environment.

Social workers can use mediation skills as part of their broader helping roles whenever disputes arise. Some social workers may become specialists in dispute resolution. They may be employed by agencies, mediation being their primary role. Other professional social workers may be employed privately as mediators.

The key to mediation in most social work contexts is remaining focused on the importance of the future relationship between the parties. Once this is identified and agreed to there is added motivation to resolve the present conflict by mutually agreeing to an outcome. The individuals, groups, or organizations share common interests. Their future success as a family, community, or agency depends on successful conflict resolution.

Social workers have long played a mediating role in assisting individuals to live in their society (Schwartz, 1961). Today the mediating role can be sharply defined by more precise reference to the context and specifics of the dispute. Finally, the process of conflict resolution itself can assist those involved to better manage future disagreements. Successful mediation is potentially empowering for all those involved in the effort.

USE OF THE RELATIONSHIP

Elsewhere in this book there is a detailed discussion of the helping relationship (Chapter 10). However, in any discussion of techniques, it is important not to lose sight of the dynamics of the relationship between the social worker and the client or client system.

The classic works on social casework contain discussions of the phenomena of transference and countertransference (Hollis, 1972; Perlman, 1957). While these and other authors distinguish between social work practice and psychoanalysis in relation to transference, they do note the possibility of distorted or subjective reactions by clients and professionals.

Although once thought of as something to be guarded against, countertransference, the worker's distorted responses, are now seen as an inevitable aspect of the helping relationship (Hanna, 1993). Members of any client system can have transference responses to the social worker or to other clients in the group or community organization. Transference is part of family dynamics, as people bring issues from their own family of origin into their next family's relationships.

Social workers must develop a thorough understanding of their own reactions to other people and various human situations. Their own life experiences, relationships, problems, beliefs, and values will be the basis of their feelings and behaviours. Professional helpers should have a well-developed self-awareness and be able to identify their subjective reactions to events. Subjectivity ought not to obstruct the helping process. Good supervision, peer consultation, continuing education, and development are some of the safeguards that can support social workers in their professional roles.

The client's transference reactions can be used by the social work practitioner as part of the helping process. Aspects of the interaction between clients and workers may become part of the material that they explore and reflect upon. Interpretations by the worker and the expanding insights of the client broaden their perspective and understanding of the problem situation. While this approach is by no means available or appropriate in all social work practice, it can be productive with some clients. Transference is like rain: it's there. It is a potential source of information and should not be ignored.

CONCLUSIONS

A discussion of techniques is not a good place to begin a description of social work practice. The technology available to social workers has utility only after establishing a trusting relationship with the client or client system. The techniques then may be employed in order to help clients achieve their goals.

Clients' particular circumstances and needs and the workers' preferences and judgments are variables that determine which techniques will be used with which clients. Techniques are neither theories nor models. Workers pick and choose from a variety of approaches to a problem.

The concept of *equafinality*, from systems theory, can help to put the implementation of techniques in perspective. One can achieve the same result from different beginnings and through different means. If the system is open, then change can occur and the desired end be arrived at without initially prescribing the methodology needed to reach that end.

REFERENCES

Barsky, A.E. (2000). *Conflict resolution for the helping professions*. Belmont, CA: Wadsworth.

Brill, N. (1990). *Working with people: the helping process*. (4th ed.). White Plains, NY: Longman.

Compton, B.R. and Galaway, B. (1989). *Social work processes*. (4th ed.). Belmont, CA: Wadsworth.

Fisher, R., Ury, W., and Patton, B. (1997). *Getting to yes: negotiating agreement without giving in.* (3rd ed.). New York: Penguin.

Fusco, L.J. (1983). Control, conflict and contracting. *Public Welfare, 41*(1), 35–39.

Hanna, E.A. (1993). The implications of shifting perspectives in contertransference on the therapeutic action of clinical social work. Part II: the recent-totalist and intersubjective position. *The Journal of Analytic Social Work. 1*(3), 53–79

Hepworth, D.H. and Larson, J. (1993). *Direct social work practice theory and skills*. (4th ed.). Pacific Grove, CA: Brooks/Cole Publishing Company.

Hollis, F. (1972). *Casework: a psychosocial therapy.* (2nd ed.). New York: Random House.

Kruk, E. (Ed.). (1997). *Mediation and conflict resolution in social work and the human services*. Chicago, IL: Nelson-Hall Publishers.

Middleman, R.R. and Wood, G.G. (1990). *Skills for direct practice in social work.* New York: Columbia University Press.

Perlman, H.H. (1957). *Social casework: a problem solving process*. University of Chicago Press.

Saleebey, D. (Ed). (1997). *The strength perspective in social work practice*. (2nd ed.). White Plains, New York: Longman Publishers.

Schwartz, W. (1961). The social worker in the group. In *New perspectives on services to groups: theory, organization, practice*, 7–34. New York: National Association of Social Workers.

Shulman, L. (1992). *The skills of helping individuals, families and groups*. (3rd ed.). Itasca, Il: F.E. Peacock Publishers.

Turner, F.J. (1978). *Psychosocial therapy: a social work perspective*. New York. Free Press.

Watzlawick, P., Weakland, J., and Fisch, R. (1974). New York, W.W. Norton and Company.

C h a p t e r

THE

RESOURCES OF

INTERVENTION

Michael Rothery

GOALS AND APPROACH

A physician whose patient has an infected hangnail or a lawyer whose client needs to negotiate a separation agreement can take a relatively reductionistic approach to these tasks. The problems and goals are reasonably concrete and the interventions required are often straightforward.

A client who has been physically and emotionally abused by her partner and who is struggling with decisions about whether to leave him needs help of a different kind. Her social worker is required to work from a much more multifaceted assessment of her needs, and the resources that may be relevant in developing a helpful package of services for her are equally diverse.

The purpose of this chapter is to discuss the resources that Canadian social work practitioners use when they work with clients to make changes, a topic which poses certain difficulties. When complex needs are matched to diverse resources for intervention, the creative possibilities are endless. This represents a richness of opportunities for practitioners and their clients, but can also be daunting without a framework to organize our thinking and decision-making.

It is hoped that what follows is a practical aid to organized thinking in the complicated world of Canadian social work practice—useful generalizations about resources for intervention which retain respect for the complexities of the professional tasks that social work practitioners face. Throughout the development of the suggested framework for thinking about resources, two examples will be used.

Example 1

"Trudy"[1] was referred to a support group for women who had been subject to partner abuse by the social worker at a mental health clinic where she had received medical help and

---

[1] Both clients have agreed to the use of their stories in this chapter. Their names are, of course, fictitious and care has been taken to alter details to protect their identities.

counselling for depression. She had come to Western Canada from Ireland with her partner when he enrolled in a graduate program in a Prairie university. Violence toward her had begun with her first pregnancy, two years prior to their move to Canada. Her husband's mistreatment of her continued to escalate (as did his overuse of alcohol) culminating in an event in which he "went berserk" and threatened their son (now three years old) at the same time as he was attacking her. Insisting she could no longer stand "to live that way" she left their apartment and sought refuge in a shelter.

Trudy was so distressed emotionally during the initial few days of her stay in the shelter that she was referred to a mental health service for help with acute depression and suicidal impulses. As her mood improved, she became preoccupied with her relationship with her partner, acknowledging that it had become intolerable and dangerous for both her and her son but, on the other hand, insisting that he had considerable charms when he was sober and she wondered if she couldn't find a way to help him stop drinking so much so that she could stay married to him, enjoying his intelligence, wit, and rebellious spirit.

Example 2

Daniel is a 16-year-old Métis boy with a long history of substance abuse, including solvents such as glue and gasoline, alcohol, and various street drugs. When he was 15, he passed out in an alley on a bitterly cold night and was in a state of hypothermia when he was found and taken to hospital. His left hand was so severely frost-bitten that three fingers had to be amputated.

Daniel underwent residential treatment for substance abuse, and did well in this program. He then obtained support to enroll in a special program to provide job training for people with physical challenges. He did well in this program initially, but his performance began to slip and his teachers thought he was coming to classes mildly intoxicated on occasion. This was against program rules and his expulsion was being considered.

We will revisit these clients throughout this chapter, making the case that there is nothing simple about their situations or the resources for intervention that are potentially valuable to them.

For the social worker, the challenge is to offer help based on a complex understanding of these clients and their needs. If we act reductionistically, we might be content simply to refer Trudy to a group where she can learn about the cycle of violence, or arrange for Daniel to receive a second round of treatment for substance abuse. Such interventions may be appropriate, but if they are considered to be all that is required, they will almost certainly prove insufficient, leading to future failures and frustration for the clients and their workers.

FRAMEWORKS

While the dangers of reductionism are clear, risks are also associated with the relatively holistic approach that social work practitioners are trained to employ, as the familiar verse about the centipede suggests:

> The centipede was happy, quite,
> Until an ant, in fun,
> Said: "Pray, which leg comes after which?"
> This worked his mind to such a pitch,
> He lay distracted in the ditch,
> Considering how to run.

We can become immobilized by complexity. If we are to retain a broad and complex view of our clients' situations and the possibilities for intervention which those situations suggest without becoming ineffective, a sound framework is required. The criteria appropriate for such a framework are that:

- It should encourage a sufficiently broad or comprehensive perspective,
- It should provide a sense of direction and focus, and
- It should be open rather than closed.

The last criterion recognizes that practice is highly creative. As necessary as frameworks are, they can work for or against creativity. Frameworks that are open to new knowledge acquired as we grow professionally, and which can be adapted to the unique aspects of each new situation our clients present, will help us organize ourselves creatively—adapting to new information and fresh problems. Relatively closed frameworks have the opposite effect, tending to give our work a rigid, prescribed quality.

RESOURCES FOR INTERVENTION IN AN ECOLOGICAL FRAMEWORK

Social work practice has always been informed by frameworks that focus on people and their environments. Recently, this multi-leveled perspective has been effectively expressed and elaborated by the adoption of ecological and systems theory, which emphasizes "goodness of fit" or the adequacy of the many relationships that link individuals and families to their social (and physical) environments (Brower & Nurius, 1993; Germain & Gitterman, 1996; Gitterman, 1996; Meyer, 1988).

In our relationships with our environment, we deal with constant demands for adaptive responses: these demand factors may be called stresses, or needs, or problems.

Our linkages to our environment also provide us with access to supports, which we use when we adapt to demands. When the supports we have at our disposal are rich enough that we can cope effectively with the demands in our lives, our goodness of fit with our environment is likely to be satisfactory, and we should be leading reasonably successful lives. Conversely, to the extent that our supports are deficient we feel less able to cope and are more likely to experience distress—emotionally, physically, or socially.

However, the equation is not so straightforward as I have just implied, since the balance of demands with supports is mediated by differences among individuals and their families. Given the same set of demands and supports, differences in how we perceive our situations, our beliefs about ourselves and our world, and our competencies will all affect how well we meet our needs.

Figure 21.1 illustrates the ecological relationship of people and their families with their environments. Their "goodness of fit" in relation to stresses and supports is emphasized, but the figure also stresses that these issues and relationships must be thought about in context. Context is defined by many possible factors (any aspects of the physical, social, and cultural environment) whose importance will vary across time and place. I have included gender, culture, and the life cycle in the diagram to recognize their importance to contemporary Canadian social work practitioners.

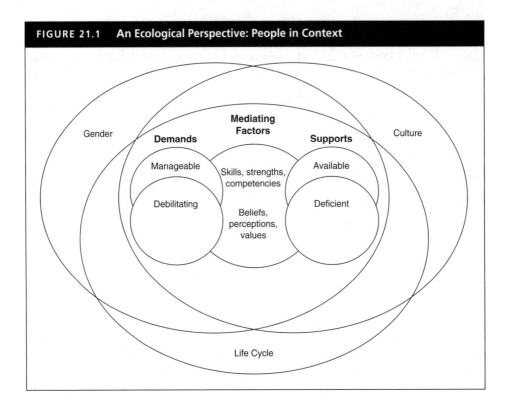

FIGURE 21.1   An Ecological Perspective: People in Context

All the circles in the figure overlap, which recognizes the extent to which the factors identified are interdependent. While it is useful to separate out variables like demands, beliefs, supports, gender, culture, and life cycle stages for purposes of discussion, at the level of experience we can all recognize how much each of these affects the other. The impact of a particular stress may not be the same for women and men, may be different for children and elderly people, and may be more or less relevant for someone from an Irish as opposed to a Métis (or English, Chinese, or Italian) cultural background.

The balance of demands and supports, mediated by beliefs and competencies (and the myriad effects of the cultural, political, and physical context) is the ecological model writ large. The next task is to explore selected elements in detail, and consider their implications regarding resources for intervention.

Supports and Demands

The ecological framework as presented to this point suggests certain generalities about resources for intervention. First, some resources are helpful in the straightforward sense that they shield us from stress (or reduce its impacts). Trudy will benefit from entering the shelter for the simple reason that it provides her respite from escalating physical and emotional abuse.

Stress reduction is often a matter of strengthening the client's supports, and some resources for intervention are important because they accomplish this. If Daniel is finding his job-training program increasingly difficult to manage, it may have to do with the loneliness of being the only Métis person in his class, isolated from his friends and culture. If so, emotional supports to reduce his feelings of isolation may benefit him. (To emphasize a point made earlier, context is vital: Daniel is from the Métis culture, he is male, and he is sixteen years old—all of which lends uniqueness to his needs.)

The supports people use to cope with demands come in four general types and from two general sources (Cameron and Rothery, 1983; Rothery, 1993). These distinctions are somewhat arbitrary (not all writers organize matters the same way), but they should be sufficient for our practical purposes. The four types of support are:

- *Concrete, instrumental supports*—the goods and services we use to cope with life's demands. For example, Trudy required financial assistance and help finding accommodation when her stay at the shelter was ending. The availability of such resources had a major impact on her ability to consider living independently rather than returning to an abusive spouse out of economic necessity. She also needed help with child care, especially when her emotional state was at its worst and she required times when she could focus on her own needs.

- *Information, knowledge, and skills*—supports which come to us in the form of knowledge about the demands we face and our options in responding to them. Daniel stood to benefit from training which could help him overcome an unsettled childhood and physical disability, and achieve greater self-esteem and economic security through employment. At a more subtle level, he also might be helped by information about racism, social isolation, and their impacts on minority-group members working in mainstream settings. Similarly, Trudy would benefit from information about the cycle of violence, and the skills associated with setting boundaries in relation to abusive former partners.

- *Emotional supports*—opportunities to express and discuss emotionally charged aspects of our experiences in a relationship where we will be understood and feel safe. Both Trudy and Daniel are isolated from friends and family with whom they have established understanding and trust—relationships within which emotional support is normally found.

- *Affiliational supports*—which supply us with validation, or messages to the effect that we belong, and are considered important and competent. A major part of this is access to meaningful social roles; another is recognition of our right to occupy those roles and our competence to meet the expectations attached to them. Having left her homeland for Canada, Trudy had no work, no close friends, no connections to a church or club. In her own view she had two roles: wife and mother. The first of these was in shambles and she had nobody in her life to validate her with respect to the second. For his part, Daniel had a network of friends (though he was geographically somewhat distant) and extended family providing him with roles in which he felt recognized. He was not at all sure he belonged or was seen as capable of fulfilling the expectations associated with his student role—he had been the object of occasional racist "jokes" from his classmates, and told his social worker that he thought his instructors tacitly colluded in this teasing. He also thought, when he made mistakes performing tasks or answering questions, that he was seen as incompetent and that this was linked to pejorative stereotypes of his culture.

The resources for intervention on which social workers draw when they work with clients to strengthen the supports in their lives come from two general sources: formal and informal (Cameron, 1990; Erickson, 1984; Whittaker and Garbarino, 1983). Trudy received a good deal of emotional support from the professionals she encountered as a result of her crisis. These are *formal* sources, since they consist of people who are paid explicitly to provide that kind of service. What is noticeably lacking in Trudy's life is emotional support from *informal* sources. She has counsellors to confide in but no friends, and (for reasons having to do with her beliefs) she has been unwilling to communicate with her family and friends in Ireland about her difficulties.

We cope best in life when the demands placed upon us are manageable, and this is likely to be true (in part) when we have adequate supports of each of the four types described above. Further, we will be more secure in our ability to cope effectively when we draw supports from a variety of sources. Linkages to friends, family, neighbours, colleagues in the workplace, and others, as well as access to the formal services we need, suggests a level of security that not everyone enjoys. Not only is the level of support we receive likely to be greater, but our sources are more secure. The loss of a role or a friend will not have the same potentially devastating effect as it would for someone like Trudy, who is dependent on very few resources to meet her support needs.

The resources for intervention that social workers use must take these considerations into account. When Trudy is in the most acute stage of her emotional crisis, support from formal services will be vital to her. The emotional support that clinical social workers and others provide her can contribute greatly to her survival and eventual relief of her depression. However, her ability to maintain those gains will be compromised if, after the formal helping relationships end, she has no ongoing resources in place which will continue to assure that her support needs are met. She will still need people to talk to after her social workers join her in celebrating her recovery and turn their attention to someone who needs it more.

As a mother in her late twenties who has just left an abusive partner, Trudy faces a host of demands. We cannot discuss them all, but two are immediately apparent and will be enough for our purposes. First, she has been brutalized (and her child threatened) by someone she had emotionally committed herself to. Her own emotional needs resulting from the impact of this experience are necessarily considerable. Secondly, she feels a strong need to make a decision about the future of her marriage.

TABLE 21.1 Supports and Resources for Intervention		
Supports	**Examples of Formal Resources**	**Examples of Informal Resources**
Concrete, Instrumental	Agencies supplying goods and services: financial assistance, churches, food banks	Extended family, friends
Information, Skills	Psychoeducational programs, books, media, counselling and therapy	Peers, neighbours, colleagues, family, etc.
Emotional Supports	Psychotherapeutic relationship	Intimates
Affiliational Supports	Programs preparing for social roles, the workplace, clubs, community groups, churches	Extended family, networks that provide validation

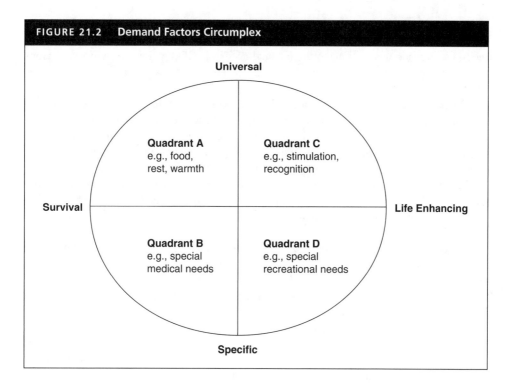

FIGURE 21.2   Demand Factors Circumplex

As a generalization, demands vary with respect to their meaning for us: at one extreme, demands have implications for our survival, stability, safety, and basic comforts; at the other, demands are important for our growth, self-actualization, and enjoyment of life. If one also considers that some demands are common to most if not all people (universal) while some others are more or less specific to subgroups or individuals, a simple circumplex suggests itself (Figure 21.2).

Clients facing demands that are in Quadrant A will rightly regard those demands as priorities, and the social worker will likewise give first importance to resources for intervention that meet those needs. The same is true for the kinds of demands that are indicated by Quadrant B, the only difference being that Quadrant A refers to needs that are relevant for all of us, and Quadrant B to needs that are specific to particular groups or individuals. Special needs of select groups are common issues for social workers searching for interventive resources. The safety needs of assaulted women like Trudy, or the educational needs of people with physical impairments like Daniel are just examples—hundreds more could be offered.

The more specific the need, the harder it may be to find appropriate resources for intervention or to convince potential sources of support of their importance. The need for food, warmth, and sleep is easy for all of us to identify with, since it is part of our shared experience. The need of a client who suffers from extreme environmental sensitivities for expensive resources offering protection against a range of potentially deadly allergens may be a different problem. The required resources may be difficult to locate, and other people will not always readily identify with the client's plight, which decreases their motivation to respond supportively.

Further, the more oppressed or marginalized the person or group experiencing a specialized need, the more difficult it may be to locate or develop necessary resources (some of the more ungenerous reactions to the medical needs of AIDS patients provide an obvious example). It is for this reason that public education and advocacy are an important part of the social work practitioner's role.

Quadrant C refers to universal needs that are more relevant to one's quality of life—to growth, self-actualization, learning, and pleasures. These are very important to our fulfilment as people, but if they are not satisfied we will not consider our safety, survival, or basic comforts to be compromised. We may not be eating gourmet fare in the company of stimulating companions, but we are not going hungry either.

Many resources that we draw on in our work with clients are targeted as needs of this sort. Recreational programs, programs to improve family communications, and programs to enhance human growth and potential are examples of such resources which social workers regularly utilize.

Quadrant D recognizes needs that are life-enhancing and specialized. Someone with a taste for wines, for example, reads that the Taylor's 1992 vintage port has received glowing reviews and a perfect numerical rating (100 points) by a recognized expert (Parker, 1995, 767), and feels that such a bottle is a necessary addition to his cellar. Such a need may well seem irrelevant to people with more sensible priorities, and it is unlikely to be a professional concern for a social worker (unless the taste for port leads to personal, familial, or occupational problems). Resources that meet the specialized growth needs of other people or groups are not irrelevant to our profession, however; consider, for example, the work that is often done respecting the life-enhancement needs of immigrant groups, or impoverished single parents, or troubled teenagers, or institutionalized elderly people.

Responses to Demands

When we confront demands, we find ourselves reacting in different ways (see Figure 21.3), and the resources for intervention that a social worker uses with clients must respect that fact.

When our belief is that the demands we must respond to are manageable (given the resources we have at our disposal), we adapt: we problem-solve and work through whatever changes are required in ourselves, others, or our situation to assure that our needs are met. If we are less confident that we can cope—demands are too severe or resources too thin— we may find ourselves becoming more rigid in our responses. Rather than looking at adaptive changes, we look for ways to simply maintain stability. If you ask a colleague how she is managing and she reports that she is "hanging in there," she is suggesting that her life is harried and her goal is to maintain stability rather than anything more creative.

If you ask a colleague how his work is going and he bursts into tears before retreating to his office, locking his door, and refusing to come out to talk further, you can safely conclude two things. First, things are going rather badly; second, his response is a disorganized one— he is not adapting to the demands in his life, nor is he maintaining stability. He is, colloquially, "throwing in the towel."

Some resources for intervention are suited for use in situations where a client's priority is to regain or maintain a sense of safety or stability. When life becomes chaotic or dangerous, we all place a high premium on help to help us achieve these basic goals. This often suggests concrete supports like a safe place to stay, or the security of dependable relation-

FIGURE 21.3   Types of Response to Demands

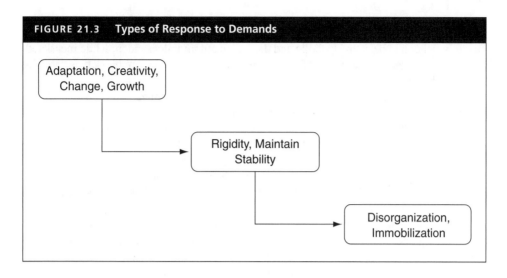

ships—when someone's distress is extreme it can even mean constraint in a secure, structured setting for a period of time.

A mismatch of interventive resources to needs in this respect can have serious consequences. At the point where she entered the shelter, Trudy was clearly overwhelmed. Her
depression and the threat of suicide constitute an extreme example of immobilization and disorganization. It is important to recognize that at that point, Trudy does not require help becoming more empowered, improving her self-esteem, or learning about the cycle of violence.
These are worthy goals, but should wait until her needs for safety and stability are sufficiently
well met. Resources such as the safety of a protected setting, medical care, and even time to rest
will be more attuned to her needs than will resources that are more relevant to making changes.

However well-intended, resources having to do with problem-solving (a change-oriented agenda) could be experienced by Trudy as threatening when she is in crisis, and they
could make her feel worse rather than more empowered. The reason for this is that her
instinctive need, at this time, is for stability. Change is always to some extent destabilizing, and change-oriented interventions can therefore run counter to Trudy's needs as she
experiences them while she is in an emotional crisis. Resources which she will welcome
later, when she is ready to consider creative change, may make matters worse for her if the
worker's timing in presenting them is bad.

Whether demands have a destabilizing or immobilizing effect on us is partly a function
of the amount of stress we are managing (balanced by our resources). It is also partly due to
individual differences. For example, Daniel has, in the past, immobilized himself with drink
and other substances. He is tempted to respond the same way to some of the demands associated with attending his job training program. On exploration, he offers that what has most
often triggered a temptation to drink has been feeling upset when he makes mistakes in performing tasks, or when he cannot answer questions posed by the instructor. While it may not
be immediately obvious why demands that are quite ordinary in educational settings should
have a disorganizing impact on him, there are sound reasons why this is the case. These
have to do with his beliefs, factors which mediate the balance of demands and resources
and their impact on our lives—and it is to these factors that we now turn our attention.

Mediating Factors: Beliefs

Daniel's father had been an alcoholic and died in an automobile accident while inebriated. He was a capable man, but would often, when he was drinking, refer to himself as "nothing but a dumb Indian."

The father's internalization of painful racist beliefs was replicated in the son: Daniel recounts that when he is in school and encounters a problem he can't solve or is asked a question he can't answer, he becomes anxious. He worries about whether he incurred brain damage through substance abuse, and questions whether he belongs in school. Worse, he hears his father's words: "Nothing but a dumb Indian."

Trudy described her mother as "a rock." She (the mother) had drawn strength from her deep Irish Roman Catholic faith and had endured poverty and her husband's alcoholism to raise six children—all of them well-educated and leading diverse, interesting lives as adults. In Trudy's view, her mother's life had been one of self-sacrifice in the service of the family, inspiring admiration and gratitude. When she looks at what she regards as her own "failure" to keep her family intact, she feels weak and incapable by comparison.

The image Trudy has of her mother exacerbates the feelings of unworthiness that are already part of her depression. It was mentioned earlier that she did not contact her family in Ireland about her marital situation and this is why: she thought they would agree with her own harsh assessment of herself, and this would make her misery even more acute.

Resources for intervention that can impact on clients' lives at the level of such pernicious beliefs can have a very important and lasting effect on their well-being. Conversely, it is not uncommon that interventive resources have a limited impact because, although they are relevant enough, they fail to touch the painful beliefs which underlie the client's problems. Daniel could become highly qualified, develop a career, and still question his right to belong if internalized racist slurs continue to haunt him. Trudy might divorce her abusive partner and establish a successful life for herself but still remain prone to depression if she retains the belief that in doing so she has failed to measure up to her mother's standard of strength, self-sacrifice, and family loyalty.

The potential for interventive resources to impact on problematic beliefs is a subtle issue. Properly timed and targeted, all of the types of resources we have discussed to this point can affect beliefs in helpful ways, even when this was not the primary reason for accessing them. Concrete supports, relevant information, a sympathetic ear—these are beneficial in their own right. When conditions are auspicious they may also help someone like Trudy to see herself as worthy of other people's caring, or someone like Daniel to see himself as competent. Such an impact on beliefs makes the effect of resources stronger and longer-lasting. Similarly, if, as a result of trying new behaviours, a client not only solves a problem but acquires a new sense of personal power, benefits are realized at more than one level.

The resources for intervention that are specifically designed to impact on beliefs include therapeutic help from clinical social workers or other professionals trained to work in this domain. Training in counselling and therapeutic skills provides workers with professional resources for intervention which enable them to facilitate change at the level of beliefs: repairing damaged self-esteem, or helping clients discover a sense of personal efficacy, for example.

Daniel's belief that he was incapable and did not belong in his educational program was approached at a number of levels. One was clinical work in which he was helped to articulate and explore those painful ideas. Medical information ruling out brain damage from his prior drug usage was obtained. His instructors were apprised of some aspects of how he saw himself in their program, and were able to agree to look for ways to be more supportive toward him (and to discourage the racist "jokes" which some students in the class indulged in). Finally, an uncle who Daniel liked agreed to spend time with him talking about his father's "demons"—the self-hatred and self-destructiveness that racial oppression had engendered.

With the most acute phase of her depression behind her, Trudy was also helped to identify and modify her tendency toward self-denunciation. Subsequently, she joined a self-help group for abused women. As is common with such resources, the discussions afforded her an opportunity to explore new ways of seeing herself and her former marriage—acknowledging the seriousness of the abuse she had suffered, clarifying and strengthening her commitment to values affirming her right (and her son's) to have a non-violent family, and respecting her power to make decisions that were in her own interests. Other similar educational resources that impact on beliefs include psychoeducational groups and programs. A client like Trudy might benefit from such a resource focusing on her knowledge of violence, alcohol abuse, and the role that sexism plays in making it difficult for women to assert their right to have their demands for safety and respect met.

Group services like this, together with the clinical services provided in response to her depression were supplemented with help Trudy received from her family. As noted earlier, she delayed contacting them because of her belief that she had failed to measure up to their standards of success (self-sacrifice in the service of the family). Exploring this issue with her social worker, she was able to acknowledge that she was cutting herself off from a vital source of support by assuming they would be angry and would reject her. In fact (and fortunately), they applauded the action she had taken and validated her decision to make her safety a clear priority.

Mediating Factors: Competencies and Skills

Competencies and skills are another category of mediating factors, closely related to beliefs. Levels of demand will have varying degrees of impact on us, depending in part on how competently we can use available supports in mobilizing an effective, adaptive response.

When we speak of *competencies*, we are referring to abilities that are both cognitive and behavioural. Cognitively, people respond effectively to demands when they have the knowledge they need, an understanding of their own efficacy (or personal power), and an ability to plan and problem-solve. Trudy and Daniel will cope better with their difficulties to the extent that they have knowledge of the reality of their situations (the cycle of violence, or the forms that racial oppression take, for example), about their needs, and about their abilities to get those needs met.

Skills are the active aspect of competencies: the behaviours we use to reach our goals. Whatever cognitive understanding of the cycle of violence Trudy acquires, she will translate this into complete competencies only when she works out its behavioural implications—learning to exercise her power to take care of herself by setting and enforcing clear limits to her involvement with her former partner, for example. Daniel's cognitive understanding of how racist labelling could undermine his sense of his capabilities and entitlements (and his father's before him) is central to competencies which must, nevertheless, be operationalized through skills associated with self-assertion, confrontation, and maintaining supportive relationships.

This understanding of competency suggests that the relevant resources for intervention will include knowledge resources and help with skill development. Most if not all of us profit from clarification of our needs and values, and knowledge of our environment and the resources it contains. We all cope better to the extent that we have skills that enable us to access relevant resources and use them effectively. Further, we all benefit if our behavioural repertoire includes the ability to *generate* supports of the types discussed earlier, to meet our own needs and the needs of others. Possession of the competencies that make us providers as well as consumers of supports is essential to the development of reciprocity in our relationships, which, in turn, is necessary if relationships are to endure.

Skill training programs have been developed in profusion in recent decades, and are used as interventive resources to help clients with various areas of their lives, such as parenting (Thomlison, 1990), partner relationships (L'Abate, 1990), assertiveness, and many others (Thomlison & Thomlison, 1996). In any urban Canadian centre, resources exist to teach basic life skills (dealing with universally important competencies) through specialized skills addressing special needs that only some clients will find relevant (for example, anger management). Skills can address needs for basic security (self-defence and safety skills for women, for example), or they can be more relevant to needs for growth and life-enhancement (such as communication skills designed to enrich partner relationships by enhancing openness and trust).

Of course, in drawing on skill-development programs it is necessary to consider each individual in her or his unique context, roles, and demands. The competencies that Daniel will employ to avoid sliding back into substance abuse are different from those Trudy will use to free herself from an abusive relationship—there will be similarities, to be sure, but the details and patterning of such issues are always unique from one person's situation to another's.

RECAPITULATION AND CONCLUSIONS

We began this chapter by recognizing the complexity of the professional demands that social work practitioners face. As other writers have emphasized (see Meyer and Mattaini, 1995), client needs and problems can include addictions, violence, racism, isolation, poverty, and neglect. The resources workers draw on in serving their clients are found in our profession, agencies, other community organizations, and among the natural helpers in families and social networks. Our profession has developed knowledge of how to intervene at different levels: implementing social policies relevant to the needs of clients like Trudy and Daniel, promoting community responses through education and resource development, and working clinically as change agents in networks, small groups, families, and with individuals. We employ knowledge generated by a range of schools of psychotherapy, community development, and political action to serve the core purposes and values of our profession and the infinitely diverse needs of our clients.

The context within which Canadian social workers exercise their professional mandate has also always been diverse. Urban lifestyles contrast with the different priorities and values that prevail in rural settings. Different languages, world views, and traditions for responding to life's challenges have coexisted among the range of First Nations, and cultures of immigrants from every continent on the globe. As our cultural mosaic continues to become more varied, the demands our clients present and the resources for intervention on which we draw will necessarily change as well.

In a world of such diversity and change, it is not really possible to catalogue the resources for intervention that social workers utilize—any list would necessarily be incomplete and quickly outdated. Instead, it is useful to explore a framework for thinking about constantly changing resources for intervention in a systematic way. Hopefully, a framework suggesting a focus on demands and resources, mediated by beliefs and competencies, and sensitive to the context provided by culture, gender, and the life cycle will serve two purposes: supporting direction and focus while preserving openness and respect for the complexities of clients' needs and possibilities.

The ecological framework recommended for thinking about resources for intervention suggests that supports of different types can be considered: concrete, instrumental supports; information; emotional support; and affiliation (or access to rewarding roles). Such supports can come through formal sources (such as professional helpers) or informal sources found in the family, neighbourhood, or workplace, with a combination of these being desirable.

Some of the demands that face us are common to all people, and the relevant resources are universally familiar: we all get hungry, and we can all appreciate the importance of food. Other demands are specific to particular people, and relevant resources will be specialized. In any event, resources for intervention are relevant to the extent that: (1) they provide clients with the tools they need to deal with the demands in their lives, (2) they prevent and ameliorate the deleterious effects that demands can have when they are frightening, painful, or threaten to be overwhelming, and (3) they have an impact at the level of mediating factors, enabling clients to modify painful beliefs or to reinforce their competence and skills.

Further, the framework suggests that we think in terms of resource packages, rather than provision of single services or supports. To the extent that Daniel and Trudy are provided with resources for intervention that address their needs at several levels they are likely to make sustainable changes.

Our analysis of demand factors also suggests that timing matters. Sensitivity to the impacts of demands and other issues affecting readiness to change can be vital to the development of a true alliance between worker and client. Very generally, when demands are experienced as debilitating, interventive resources that will contribute to safety, security, and stability are the priority. Once these issues are sufficiently well attended to, resources designed to promote change (evaluating beliefs and developing competencies) will become more appropriate.

Finally, a point that deserves reiteration in closing is that developing and mobilizing resources for intervention is highly creative: the diversity of the needs we are called on to address is such that there can be no formula for matching resources with problems. An adequate framework can help us respond more systematically and comprehensively. However, each client comes to us with demands, possibilities, beliefs, and competencies shaped by culture, gender, development, and other contextual issues into something unique. Resources for intervention are therefore rethought, reconfigured, and even reinvented with every client we encounter.

REFERENCES

Brower, A. & Nurius, P. (1993). *Social cognition and individual change: current theory and counseling guidelines*. Newbury Park, CA: Sage.

Cameron, G. (1990). The potential of informal support strategies in child welfare. In M. Rothery & G. Cameron (Eds.). *Child maltreatment: expanding our concept of helping*, Hillsdale, NJ: Lawrence Erlbaum, pp. 145–168.

Cameron, G. & Rothery, M. (1985). *An exploratory study of the nature and effectiveness of family support measures in child welfare*. Toronto: Ontario Ministry of Community and Social Services.

Erickson, G.D. (1984). A framework and themes for social networks intervention. *Family Process*, *23*, 187–204.

Germain, C. & Gitterman, A. (1996). *The life model of social work practice: advances in theory and practice.* New York: Columbia University Press.

Gitterman, A. (1996). Life model theory and social work treatment. In F.J. Turner (Ed.). *Social work treatment: interlocking theoretical approaches* (4th ed.). New York: The Free Press, pp. 389–408.

L'Abate, L. (1990). *Building family competence: primary and secondary prevention strategies.* Newbury Park, CA: Sage.

Meyer, C. & Mattaini, M. (Eds.). (1995). *The foundations of social work practice.* Washington, DC: National Association of Social Workers.

Meyer, C. (1988). The eco-systems perspective. In Dorfman, R. (Ed.). *Paradigms of clinical social work.* New York: Brunner/Mazel.

Parker, R. (1995). *Parker's wine buyer's guide* (4th ed.). New York: Simon and Schuster.

Rothery, M. (1993). The ecological perspective and work with vulnerable families. In Rodway, M. & Trute, B. *Ecological family practice: one family, many resources.* Queenston, Ontario: Edwin Mellen , pp. 21–50.

Thomlison, R. (1990). Uses of skill development and behavior modification techniques in working with abusing/neglecting parents. In M. Rothery & G. Cameron (Eds.). *Child maltreatment: expanding our concept of helping.* Hillsdale, NJ: Lawrence Erlbaum, pp. 127–143.

Thomlison, B. & Thomlison, R. (1996). Behavior theory and social work treatment. In F.J. Turner (Ed.). *Social work treatment: interlocking theoretical approaches* (4th ed.). New York: The Free Press, pp. 39–68.

Whittaker, J. & Garbarino, J. (1983). Social support networks: informal helping in the human services. New York: Aldine.

INDIVIDUAL

TREATMENT

Rose Marie Jaco

INTRODUCTION

Although we are surrounded by other people, life is essentially encountered on an individual basis. Even when societal forces are widely experienced, either adversely or positively, the consequences are felt one by one, person by person. People may be embedded in a web of connections with others and with the institutions of society, but every life is experienced uniquely, and its quality is determined solely by the person living it.

Quite early in its development, the social work profession adopted the position that each human life has its own special value. Through their efforts to alleviate the suffering of people caught in situations of poverty, misery, isolation, and despair, the pioneers of social work became aware that enduring relief could come only by effecting change at both the societal and personal level, altering those aspects of society that were detrimental, and strengthening individuals so that they could live their lives more effectively (Bellamy and Irving, 1995; Turner, J.C., 1995). From these early beginnings, the individual method of social work intervention has evolved substantially. This chapter contains a discussion of the place direct social work with individuals has in the profession, from the perspective of rationale, theoretical foundation, goals, and interventive approaches.

As social work endeavoured to improve the human condition, various forms of social activism were developed to effect changes in society, while social casework evolved as the method for helping individuals deal with their problems in living. Although casework has changed greatly over the years, the early practitioners succeeded in constructing a method of helping individuals that has remained stable to this day in its purpose, values, and commitment, but capable of incorporating new theories and ways of intervening that promote personal growth and change. These more recent approaches are based on deeper understandings of individual psychology and of the interactions human beings have with their physical and social environments than were available earlier, resulting in the incorporation into social work thought of the current bio-psychosocial perspective. This view of human existence proposes that the problems people experience in their lives may be rooted in their inner psychological world, the social environment, the biological self, or any combination of events in these spheres (Turner, 1984, 8). Additionally, recent social work theory places much more importance on having a social worker approach clients with sensitivity to their unique cultural and situational factors including ethnicity, race, language, religion, gender, age, social class, and sexual orientation. In casework, the result of combining the original, stable base of goals and values with openness to current developments in knowledge and helping skills has enabled succeeding generations of social workers to gradually re-shape this traditional model of helping individuals without losing its unique strengths.

THE RATIONALE FOR SOCIAL WORK WITH INDIVIDUALS

That old argument, known as the "cause-function" debate (Johnson, 1995, 5), about where social work should place its emphasis and resources, is still lively. Specht (1990) speaks for a group of social work thinkers who fear that social work practice is about to be absorbed into the world of individual psychotherapy and so lose its identity. He states that "there is good reason to expect that the profession will be entirely engulfed by psychotherapy within the next twenty years, and social work's function in the public services will become negligible" (146). His argument is based on the fact that increasing numbers of social workers are in private practice or are using various psychotherapeutic approaches in their social agency practice, to the neglect of group work and community development, and with the additional result that less well-trained people are working with the frail and needy. Specht (1990) further laments the loss of social work's role as the "conscience of the community" for he believes that it is the healthy community that forms the healthy person (153). There is some power in this argument, and it calls for a response.

In establishing the essential question as one where a choice has to be made between either changing society or changing individuals, a false dichotomy is established. We do not have to choose one and reject the other; we can and must choose both. To create caring and humane communities is an essential goal of social work. To assist people in forming groups where social support is available to them is an indispensable tool for helping. To aid couples and families in negotiating troubled relationships is a necessary contribution to human well-being. And helping each individual who needs guidance, counselling, sustainment, and knowledge from a social worker is a fundamental function of the profession and a testament to its respect for human life. This does not mean that the longer-range goals of preventing social ills and creating a caring society are less important than helping people in the here-and-now. But it does mean that when social work has the knowledge and tools to assist clients in coping with distress, problems, and crises in their daily lives, it would be unconscionable to refuse them aid.

As well, the systemic nature of social work with individuals may well have a substantial impact on preventing social dysfunction and creating supportive communities. Granted that it would likely be an impossible task to change society simply by working with people on a one-to-one basis, we still need to recognize that the ripple effect resulting from individual change certainly alters the small social system within which a client moves, and so must ultimately have a cumulative effect on changing the nature of society. Individuals may be seen alone by the social worker, but a horde of other people are crowded into the interview with them, invisible though they may be; clients bring not only themselves in present and past time, but also their partners, children, parents, siblings, friends, neighbours and workmates, and even grandparents, because it is with these people that they experience stress, conflict, frustration. Any increase in clients' abilities to relate positively, to play their social roles effectively, to become forces for just and fair social exchange in the community, to work, play or study productively must eventually elevate both their own and others' quality of life.

DEFINITION OF TERMS

Casework with individuals refers to a method of social work intervention in which the worker intentionally creates a helping relationship with a client that enables dialogue, interaction, and influence to occur, with the purpose of effecting positive changes in client thought, feeling or action, or in the social environment he or she inhabits. Casework is designed to help clients attain goals they have identified as desirable, such as strengthening their ability to cope with environmental demands, to use societal resources, to improve problem-solving and interpersonal skills, to enhance their sense of self worth, and to resolve relationship conflicts (Gambrill, 1983, 1–5).

Clinical social work is a newer term for this same activity, but one that more clearly includes linking clients to resources, coordinating services, and advocacy (Swenson, 1995). *Direct practice* is a term that is used in a similar way to refer to helping interventions at the micro-level provided to individuals, couples, or families, in contrast to indirect or macro-level practice which takes place at the level of community or policy change. Direct practice consists of "helping or social treatment through services such as therapy, counselling, education, advocacy, provision of information, referral, and certain aspects of community organization such as social action and mediation" (Pinderhughes, 1995, 740). *Therapy* is defined by Woods and Hollis (1990) as "work in which social and psychological means are used to enable individuals (singly or in family or formed groups) to cope with environmental, interpersonal and/or intrapsychic dilemmas—and the interactions among these—that are causing personal distress" (6). Each of these approaches shares a common concern with both the internal and external worlds of the client and the manner in which these spheres interact, as well as a common goal, which is to strengthen the client to cope with pressures and demands from within and without, for the purpose of achieving a sound level of social functioning.

SOCIAL WORK WITH INDIVIDUALS: GOALS AND PROBLEMS

In working with individuals, the question of their personal level of social functioning is a central issue, and this focus ensures that the work always proceeds with one eye on the context surrounding the client. This allows a worker to intervene in the social surroundings if changes there could improve the capacity of clients to manage their lives well. Siporin (1975) provides interesting insights into the nature of social functioning. In his view, it refers to the way in which individuals "behave in order to carry out their life tasks and meet their needs" (17). This involves the performance of age and context-related tasks and roles, which have "situational, relational and behavioral dimensions" (17). *Task* refers to "a unit of work, a set of actions to get a job done" (17), and *role*, a more complex concept, involves the carrying out of tasks as well as the development of relationships that are associated with the specific role status. Being unable to function well in their social roles prevents people from meeting their needs and is a primary reason people seek social work services. In Siporin's (1975) analysis, poor social functioning is often caused by

> . . . a lack of complementarity, a mismatching, an unequal exchange or ecological imbalance between people and their environments. For both the individual and the social system, expectations and tasks may be too stressful, demanding, ill-timed, conflicting, or discrepant; obstacles may be too severe; resources may be lacking; capabilities or competence may be impaired or undeveloped (18).

Any of these conditions may become the focus of helping interventions in social work with individuals.

The inability of a client to function well, or of society to afford the conditions that make that possible, results in problems for both the client and those with whom he or she interacts. What kinds of problems bring a person to a social worker for help? A typical recent office log of a private practitioner contained the following requests for service from individuals.

> *Bill* is a young adult of twenty-two who asks for help to disentangle himself from a very needy family where the parents have a conflicted relationship and a sister suffers from serious mental illness. He has accepted so much responsibility over the years for keeping the family in balance by mediating their conflicts and being the message exchange centre for others that he has been unable to achieve his own goals of establishing a lasting relationship with a partner, or developing his career, as that would take him away from daily contact with his family. He is anxious, depressed, and has feelings of being trapped in a situation without solutions.

> *Gloria* is a childless widow in late middle life who seeks to resolve her feelings of acute grief for a husband who died accidentally five years ago. Her unrelenting sorrow interferes with her ability to relate to a man who wishes to form a friendship with her and to whom she feels attracted. It also drains her of the energy she needs to give to her work. She has just been told that her performance has to improve or she will lose her job.

> *Angela* is a young woman in her twenties who has finally decided to deal with the consequences of sexual abuse inflicted by an authority figure when she was a child. Her extreme shame has kept her completely silent on this issue until recently when she told a clergyman, who made a referral for counselling. She recognizes that the abuse has impaired her life, robbing her of spontaneity and joy in her activities, creating distance between herself and family members, and preventing her from trusting men enough to begin to date.

> *Gerard* is a man in late middle age involved in an extremely stressful home situation. His wife refuses to see a counsellor or a physician, but from his description she shows signs of paranoid thinking, although on some days she appears normal. He is the target of groundless accusations from her of infidelity and financial dishonesty. He is feeling uncertain about how to obtain for her the help she obviously needs, but totally rejects, and is unsure about whether he can remain in the marriage if she does not get treatment. The quality of his life is poor and he has feelings of despair and hopelessness. His daughters will not visit the home because their presence seems to trigger mother's angry statements against their father and he is becoming increasingly isolated from the family and the community.

Although these situations differ in detail, they all strongly challenge clients to make sound decisions about changing a difficult life situation in ways that will enable them to function with freedom, dignity, and a reasonable prospect of satisfaction with their lives. It is clear that the range of situations for which individuals seek help varies greatly, but that any problem which interferes with people's ability to function fully in their social roles; which impairs their capacity to form rewarding relationships with partners, parents, children, or friends; which impedes the performance of developmental tasks as the stages of life unfold; or which erodes satisfaction with their quality of life, may be brought to a social worker. Specifically, clients may ask for help to solve a practical problem, such as budgeting or the use of resources to support a child with special needs in the home. More likely, the issue is one of a conflicted, confused, or empty relationship that the person wants to redesign, or if that is not possible, to relinquish. The question of self-esteem and self-worth is usually involved in an individual's quest for help. The very fact of being caught in a problematic situation can erode a person's sense of competence, power, and esteem, and interventions that provide the client with ways of exerting some control over changing certain aspects of his or her life can create or restore a sense of efficacy and worth. In general, individual work is designed to enable clients to use their own powers of judgment, discernment, understanding, emotional attachment, and will to evaluate their problematic situation or relationship, review their options, and choose a path that promises the most satisfaction, while operating on principles that are fair and just to the other people who inhabit their world.

Planned change, which is the general focus of all treatment, is often achieved more readily by including significant others in the client's life in order to help them all work through an issue that is causing distress. There is no inflexible rule stating that individual clients must always be seen alone. If people need to solve a problem that involves their whole family, a spouse, partner, sibling, or friend it is often advisable to include in the interview the people with whom negotiation or the clarification of perspectives and positions needs to occur. With a social worker present to set the ground rules for productive communication, and to act in the role of an objective inquirer into the situation, people are often able to gain insights, share viewpoints, ask for changes, and respond in ways that would have been very difficult, and perhaps impossible, without a joint meeting.

HISTORICAL DEVELOPMENT OF THEORY FOR HELPING INDIVIDUALS

In order to fully appreciate the richness and power of the elements that have combined to create social work practice with individuals, it is helpful to briefly consider the origins and growth of this method over the decades. Much of this historical overview is based on material from a work by Woods and Hollis, *Casework: A Psychosocial Therapy* (1990), and from Goldstein's review of social work thought in her book, *Ego Psychology and Social Work Practice* (1984). The first texts on the casework approach to helping, *Social Diagnosis* (1917), *What is Social Casework?* (1922), were written by Mary Richmond, who established the theoretical foundation for change-oriented work with individuals. Woods and Hollis (1990) state that

> she stressed the development of a strong, trusting relationship through which a worker could influence a client toward activities and decisions that would be in his or her best interest. Suggestion and persuasion were predominant techniques, but there was also discussion of the need for frankness and honesty in the relationship and on the client's participation in decision-making, which seems to suggest rational discussion, though this term was not used (11).

Over subsequent decades, the developing field of individual psychology strongly influenced social work practice. By the end of the 1930s, two theoretical positions known as the diagnostic and functional approaches had emerged, based on different understandings of human nature. The diagnostic perspective, rooted in Freudian psychology, emphasized the influence of childhood and past experiences on people's present functioning, and the need to take a thorough social history in order to understand the psychological and social aspects of clients' lives, diagnose their problem, and propose a treatment plan. The functional school, based on Rankian psychology, operated in a present time frame, emphasized the power of an individual's will and ability to act, change, and self-determine, and used the tools of time and agency structure to motivate clients to deal with their problems (Woods and Hollis, 1990, 12–13; Goldstein, 1984, 27).

In later years, the diagnostic school was criticized for being too deterministic, relying on a medical or disease model of human behaviour, and focusing so strongly on the past that the current problems that concerned the client were not addressed (Goldstein, 1984, 26). Functionalism was criticized in its turn for creating the possibility of a power struggle between client and worker as the nature of agency service became the yardstick by which the individual's need was measured. If the client did not wish to use services in the way in which they were offered, this was likely to be seen as a form of resisting help, and terminating the case might well result (Goldstein, 1984, 27).

From these early strivings to find the keys to helping others, some central features emerged, and these became essential components of later social work theory. One was the influencing power of a trusting relationship between client and worker. A second was the right of clients to determine their own goals and select ways of attaining them within the confines of ethical and realistic behaviour. A third was the need for a careful assessment of the "person-in-situation," including the psychological make-up of the client, the nature of his or her relationships, social interactions, physical and societal environment, and potential resources available for problem-solving. One of the most enduring contributions to these early efforts was Biesteck's (1957) codification of casework values, which gradually became a guideline for professional behaviour in working with clients, and which still strongly influences practice. These values include individuality, purposeful expression of feeling, controlled emotional involvement, acceptance, non-judgmental attitude, self-determination, and confidentiality. Building on these basic concepts, and on both the diagnostic and functional approaches, a surge of intellectual activity occurred among social work thinkers in the 1950s and 1960s, resulting in some landmark works. Although these do not focus solely on work with individuals, they have had a profound effect on modifying the original casework method toward more flexibility and eclecticism.

In *Social Casework: A Problem-Solving Process* (1957), by incorporating the structured steps of problem-solving in the dialogue with the client, Perlman attempted "to bridge the lingering dispute between diagnostic and functional caseworkers" (32), as well as to offer correctives for practices that she viewed as dysfunctional for the client "such as long waiting lists, high drop out rates and help which was not focused on the client's stated needs" (Goldstein, 1984, 32). Hollis, in *Casework: A Psychosocial Therapy* (1964), synthesized a variety of helping interventions drawn from casework theory and practice, thus enabling practitioners to learn a comprehensive, integrated system of helping, based on positions drawn from psychodynamic and ego psychology perspectives. Systems theory entered the field in the 1960s as a framework which provided "a larger perspective on the interaction between the individual and the environment" (Rodway, 1986, 516), thereby permitting workers to conceptualize the connections people had with each other and with society, and to develop interventions that reached out simultaneously to modify both person and surroundings. This resulted in several unifying works such as that by Pincus and Minahan, *Social Work Practice: Model and Method* (1973), and *The Life Model of Social Work Practice* (1980), by Germain and Gitterman, in which the ecosystems approach to helping was outlined in depth.

An approach to helping individuals, families, and couples that combined behavioural, cognitive, and problem-solving concepts was formulated by Reid and Epstein. In *Task-Centred Practice* (1977), they provided a structured approach to change, based on a set of tasks to be performed by clients, which were designed specifically to resolve their problems, and around which they had entered into a contract with the worker. Throughout the decades, gradual advances in the field of ego psychology had offered social work theorists new perspectives that emphasized the potential people have to grow through adversity by using their powers of reason and will. Reason allowed people to understand their situation and will enable them to take the actions necessary to cope with it. These views were set forth in an integrated practice approach by Goldstein in *Ego Psychology and Social Work Practice* (1984). Maluccio, in *Promoting Competence in Clients: A New/Old Approach to Social Work Practice* (1981), proposed that social workers should encourage growth and capability in clients by helping them act on their own behalf, and then consciously experience the learning and power associated with their own actions. As a result of these changing perspectives the current focus of intervention with individuals is on empowering clients to assess their situation realistically and to solve their inevitable problems-in-living with wisdom.

At one stage, the casework method was sharply criticized as being an ineffective method of helping (Fisher, 1973; Mullen and Dumpson, 1972), although it was subsequently argued that the evaluation methods used by the critics were flawed. Nevertheless, partially in response to the challenge, the 1980s witnessed an explosive growth of theory resulting in movement toward a more eclectic mode of practice in which the worker could select an approach from a wide range of possibilities, depending on client circumstances. Of this period, Hepworth and Larsen (1982) note that "ever-increasing research efforts and expanding definitions of skills have combined to infuse practice with scientific vitality. Practitioners have a widening array of available interventions and increasingly rigorous criteria to aid them in selecting the most promising intervention" (4).

SELECTING THEORY: THE ECLECTIC APPROACH

As a consequence of this increased activity in the area of theory development and research, social workers currently practising with individuals draw from an ever-changing pool of choices. Some theory and practice is well-tested and rooted in social work tradition, but other approaches have developed from new research in various fields of the profession. Additional options spring from increased opportunities for the cross-pollination of ideas from psychology and psychiatry, made possible by the expanded availability of communication channels and publications. There are few secrets in the world of professional helping, nor should there be. This diversity and cross-flow of ideas means that social workers face a major challenge in choosing and blending interventive, explanatory, and predictive theories in ways that best serve their clients. As an example of this diversity, Payne (1991) lists ten commonly used social work practice models, based on a variety of theories. These models are: psychodynamic or psychosocial, crisis intervention, task-centred, behavioural change, systems and ecological, social psychological and communication, humanist and existential, cognitive, radical and Marxist, and empowerment. In Turner's latest edition of his text

Social Work Treatment (1996), there are twenty-seven theories and methods examined, along with their implications for social work practice, and these include constructivism, feminist theory, and client-centred theory. In addition to these positions, the following developments are significant emerging perspectives for practice: ethnically and culturally sensitive social work (Bloom, 1990; Compton and Galaway, 1994), the multi-generational approach (Freeman, 1991; Satir, 1988), and brief or solution-focused therapy (Cade and O'Hanlon, 1993; de Shazer, 1994).

Every social worker who practises with individuals must first have in place a foundation for understanding and intervening drawn from the tested methods of practice. They must also be able to incorporate recent advances from developing approaches and techniques, especially those that have been empirically tested for effectiveness. What are the most important perspectives to develop and how does the practitioner know which route to take among the many divergent paths that beckon?

Some years ago, Fisher (1978) considered this problem in a way that is still useful. He divided theories broadly into two categories—those that explain the "why" of human behaviour and those that answer the question of "what" to do in order to produce change (52). In his view, the social worker who must select approaches from what is now an immense body of knowledge is best "guided in practice by what is most effective for our clients" (68). This position is supported by other writers, including Hepworth and Larsen (1982), and Payne (1991). Hepworth and Larsen (1982) describe a social worker who chooses this approach as follows:

> A systematic eclectic practitioner carefully selects from models and techniques those that best match the problem/situation of a given client, according the highest priority to techniques that have been empirically demonstrated to be effective. Far from being a jack of all trades and master of none, the systematic eclectic practitioner must be knowledgeable about many theories and techniques as well as deliberate and thoughtful in making choices according to the needs of each client. Systematic eclecticism is thus most demanding, requiring the practitioner to keep abreast of emerging theories and research findings. In our judgment this approach to practice holds the highest promise of being efficacious with a broad range of clients and problems. (9–10)

Social workers who base their work with individuals on a broad range of theories of human development and professional intervention need a framework to guide their choices. Fisher (1978) sets out some principles for the eclectic practice of social casework, which are equally applicable to those who consider themselves clinical social workers or direct practitioners. It should be noted that his emphasis on having research-based evidence of effectiveness as a criterion for choice leads him to favour behavioural approaches, but his guidelines are also useful for those who prefer interventions based on other theories. He discards any notion of achieving *theoretical* integration, but proposes "an atheoretical integration grounded in certain values and propositions which cut across theoretical domains and are integrated at the level of *professional* (rather than theoretical) practice" (71). The dimensions he proposes are designed to help social workers evaluate and select theory, and to integrate the chosen approaches in a practice model that is individualized for both client and worker.

The first principle of eclecticism is that the theories used will reflect the *major values* of social work, namely respect for the dignity and worth of the individual and our mutual responsibility toward each other as human beings. This emphasis on individualized helping in the context of community counteracts impersonalization and alienation. The second principle is that the theories used should focus on the *domain of social work*, which is enhancement of the social functioning of people and the ability of the environment to respond supportively to their needs. A third position is that theories of intervention should be *useful*. Therapeutic procedures should be specified so that workers know what they must do in order to extinguish unwanted behaviour and help the client develop desired behaviours. In addition to this focus on individual change, social workers need to know methods for eliciting supportive responses from the communities and societal institutions with which clients interact. A fourth principle is that when *research validates* an approach, it should be seriously considered as one to add to the social worker's repertoire. For this workers need to be able to evaluate the adequacy of research design and findings, and the extent to which they can be generalized to a client's life (Fisher, 1978, 71).

PROMOTING CHANGE:
INTERVENTIVE SKILLS AND METHODS

It is probably safe to say that few people voluntarily seek help from a social worker unless they are suffering some distress or discomfort in their lives. While non-voluntary clients make up a fairly high percentage of all of those seen by social workers in both public and private agencies, their presence is motivated by someone else's distress, usually persons who have sufficient influence to bring the reluctant individual into the professional helping process. Problems, challenges, crises, and coercion open individuals to the possibility of change, whether or not they came totally of their own free will. While people seek change as a solution to their difficulties, personal change is often resisted because it appears unfamiliar and even dangerous. However, changing others seems to be a much easier task, and clients often ask their worker to help them change a significant person in their social network, rather then presenting themselves as a person in need of change. One of the first lessons workers teach clients in their role of guide and counsellor is that people only have the power to change themselves, but if they will make that effort, the change effect is likely to ripple through their interactive system and trigger changes in those with whom they interact.

There are many equally difficult lessons to be taught and learned in social work with individuals. The only factor that makes the teaching-learning, intervention-change process tolerable is the relationship that workers consciously foster with their clients. Relationship is created through the intentional use of communication skills and behaviours that create trust and attachment (Hepworth, Book, and Larsen, 1997, chap. 5). More is written about relationship in this text, so it is sufficient to say here that without the supportive and energizing effect of a warm, caring, and challenging relationship offered to clients by a worker, clients are not likely to take the risk of changing significant aspects of their lives. Goldstein, Hilbert, and Hilbert (1984) state that planned "change is the consequence of a complex and often enigmatic process" (296) with the general intent of freeing people "to search for, define and risk fresh, creative and ethical solutions to their problems in living" (296). In general, people seek change when some aspect of their way of functioning or of the circumstances of their lives is no longer rewarding or acceptable to them or to others.

Social workers can encourage individuals to make changes in their lives in a great variety of ways, many of which will be covered in the chapter on intervention in this text. Intervention, in the words of Johnson (1995), means a "specific action by a worker in relation to human systems or processes in order to induce change" (83). When practitioners are attempting to sort their way through the confusion caused by having access to many theories and approaches, it helps to remember that the selection of interventive techniques depends upon the client's stated goals for change, the worker's assessment of the client's problem, and the evaluation of what needs to be changed in order to bring about the desired results. In addition, the work of intervening to create change is conducted within a context of ethical behaviour on the part of the worker, and is strongly shaped by sensitivity to the cultural, religious, and ethnic values of the client.

Clearly, there are some aspects of people's lives that are not amenable to change. Such events as the death of a loved person, one's health status, aging, the loss of a job, or having endured a childhood history of abuse, violence, or neglect cannot be altered. Despite the immutable nature of some present and past events, clients always have some choice about how they react to their situation, within the limits set by reality. The worker seeks to open up the range of possible responses from which clients may choose, and to help them select the response most likely to lead them to their stated goals. The path to individual change may require alterations in any of the following spheres: the person's attitudes, beliefs, perspectives, actions, reactions, or patterns of relating. Although many specific areas may be selected as targets for change, they can be categorized as follows: the client's view of the situation, the client's view of the self, and the client's actions taken in response to his or her situation. Interventions initiated by the worker to effect the desired changes may be directed toward any or all of the three categories of situation, self, or response. It should be noted that these three divisions, while logical, have been chosen to help manage the complexity of human life, and so are artificially simple. Real lives tend to have unexpected elements and developments that are hard to categorize.

CHANGING THE VIEW OF THE SITUATION

Changes in a client's view of his or her situation can mobilize the person to feel and act more positively and hopefully. Reconceptualization or reframing as a technique is based on communication and constructivist theory, in which "It is the *nature* of the client's verbalizations and thinking about the problem, interacting with relevant sociocultural values, norms and definitions, that constitute the reality of the problem, and hence the focus for treatment" (Carpenter, 1996, 157). Interventions designed to help people revise their point of view about their life or situation often enable them to make profound changes in thought, feeling, and action. Goldstein (1984) states that if clients "can think about their problem differently, then they will treat it differently" (87) and Kelley (1996) notes that narrative treatment "may involve helping the client to challenge the problem-saturated dominant story as the only truth, and to find other aspects of his or her life which may also be true" (465). Cognitive approaches are used to help effect this change in how a client views his or her world. The basic position is that behaviour and emotion are rooted in thinking, and that the human mind "can modify and control how stimuli affect behaviour" (Payne, 1991, 184). Workers using this approach intervene to create cognitive change through "conceptual reorientation" where they "act as a model for new ways of thinking and understanding, give information and advice, help the client connect their thinking with the things that they have experienced, and pull out from the client any conceptions which are inhibited by others' expectations" (195). Specific techniques of reframing a client's present and past reality may include:

- *self-examination*, in which clients are encouraged to look closely at their daily lives to gain insights about their patterns of thought, feeling, and action;
- *explanation*, which involves the social worker in giving new information, interpreting actions and feelings, confronting resistance, reflecting, giving feedback, questioning to encourage a wider exploration of the situation and the self, and offering suggestions;
- *self-demonstration*, which consists of role-playing or reflection on real-life situations in which clients can perceive themselves as acting differently;
- *modelling*, where the client is invited to copy the behaviour or reactions of others, including the worker, or of people they respect or have read about (195–196).

Through selecting appropriately from among this array of interventions, the social worker hopes that the client will gain a revised view of his or her situation, which opens up new opportunities for action and problem-solving.

Counsellors and psychotherapists who work with traumatized individuals have a range of relatively new techniques available to them which use principles of energy psychology to free people from the symptoms associated with trauma and post-traumatic stress disorder. This approach treats psychological problems by using the body's own energy systems to create shifts in feelings, cognition, and behaviour. Included are techniques such as Eye Movement Desensitization and Reprocessing; meridian tapping therapies, which use accupressure applied by the client; and Thought Field Therapy. In the most general terms, these psychobiological techniques are focused on healing traumatic memories by having the client intently focus on the recall of the event and the emotions associated with it, while the body's energy is being activated by bilateral stimulation of the brain or by releasing energy through tapping on specific meridian points. Some research is now available on these approaches, which indicates that for certain clients the sense of relief is rapid, real, and profound. Clearly, special training is needed for each technique, and there are indicators which aid the therapist in selecting appropriate clients, for these interventions are not suitable for all personalities (Shapiro, 1995; van der Kolk, 1996).

CHANGING THE VIEW OF THE SELF

Current social work approaches encourage the development of client strengths and competencies as well as treatment for any specific difficulties. Traditional assessment during the interview as well as consultation with the referral source and other key people in the client's life enable the worker to capture a sense of client abilities and disabilities.

Assessment interview outlines are widely available in the literature relating to specific problems in living. For example, social workers may consult books and articles on assessment and treatment of people who have experienced childhood sexual, physical, or emotional abuse; those who are grieving the death of a significant person; individuals with a history of conflicted interpersonal relationships; or people who appear to be depressed. These conditions, and a host of others, have clearly developed assessment protocols that guide the focus of the interview, as well as treatment plans flowing from the assessment.

An additional method for determining the nature of individual difficulties is to administer questionnaires that measure client dysfunction in a variety of areas. Simply administered and marked within minutes, they give the practitioner reliable indicators of such conditions as depression, anxiety, fear, eating disorders, or characteristics such as levels of self-esteem and sexual satisfaction (Corcoran and Fischer, 1987). When a comprehensive assessment has been made, and with client collaboration, the worker designs an interventive approach, which has three purposes: it reinforces those aspects of social and personal functioning that work well, it helps clients learn ways of overcoming specific dysfunctions, and it helps them to operate generally with more power and effectiveness as people in charge of their own lives.

A recent exploration of empowerment theory consolidates much previous thought about this aspect of social work practice. DuBois and Miley (1996) state that "Empowerment implies exercising psychological control over personal affairs, as well as exerting influence over the course of events in the socio-political arena" (26). They provide some guidelines for ways in which social workers can help their clients achieve more power in their personal and social lives. In the following list, the elements whereby empowerment theory is operationalized are set forth. Social workers should:

- foster relationships that reflect empathy
- affirm clients' choices and self-determination
- value individual differences
- emphasize collaboration
- promote communication that respects dignity and worth
- consider individual differences
- remain client-focused
- uphold confidentiality
- seek solutions that encourage client participation
- inform clients of their legal rights
- reframe challenges as opportunities for learning
- involve clients in decision-making and evaluation
- reflect standards of the social work profession
- adhere to the profession's code of ethics
- involve clients in professional development research and policy formulation
- redress discrimination, inequality, and social justice issues.

An additional way of encouraging people to see themselves as creative and powerful is by helping them grow in their levels of self-esteem. "Self-esteem is the need to hold oneself in positive regard, to value oneself, and to feel valued by others" (Pearlman and Saakvitne, 1995, 72). When the ability to affirm the worth of the self is absent, people are filled with anxiety and self-doubt. They question every act or decision they make and give themselves little recognition for successful efforts so that the quality of the person's life is greatly diminished. Personality theorists have used cognitive theory and developed methods of enabling people to restore and maintain good levels of self-esteem. Creating a pattern of self-talk that is positive and affirming is encouraged, while the person learns simultaneously to silence the critical inner voices that are destroying their peace of mind (McKay and Fanning, 1992).

CHANGING ACTIONS AND RELATIONSHIPS

People need certain skills to help them operate effectively, even if they do succeed in feeling more powerful and hopeful. Three essential competencies that social workers can teach their clients focus on problem-solving, communication, and relationship-building. The ability to follow a logical process in solving the problems of daily living is a vital skill which many people have not been able to learn, and indeed, their difficulties in this area may account for their seeking help from a social worker. Compton and Galaway (1994) set out a series of steps for social workers to follow as they problem-solve with the client, but also emphasize that the approach can be taught to clients as it unfolds in practice in a way that allows them to incorporate problem-solving into their daily lives (Chapter 2).

Communication is a valuable skill because it creates the interpersonal world of the individual by defining the nature of specific relationships. Satir was a pioneer in analyzing the nature of sound communication, and in developing methods of teaching good communication skills and principles to clients (Englander-Golden and Satir, 1991). Many resources exist for the teaching of communication skills, based on some of the extensive research that has been done in this field. Approaches may be general in nature (McKay, Davis, and Fanning, 1990), or directed toward couples (Miller, Nunnally, and Wackman, 1986). There is an extensive literature on how to create and maintain relationships that are equal-sharing and supportive in nature, and much of this exists in the form of self-help books for clients (Gray, 1993), and in more academic texts that guide workers in their teaching role with clients (Hoffman, 1981; Beavers, 1985; Carter and McGoldrick, 1980).

CONCLUSION

In the work of helping individuals, our goal as social workers is an ambitious one. It is no less than helping them in their life's work of building a life that is rewarding to themselves and to others. The planned change that comes about as a result of a client-social worker encounter is designed to support and strengthen people as they strive to accomplish their goals in life, from the most modest to the most significant, from getting through a stressful day, to parenting well. Helping people adapt to demands, change, and responsibilities is central to the mandate of working with individuals, as is the challenge of assisting people to develop what Goleman (1995) refers to as "emotional intelligence," or the capacity to become self-aware, to control negative impulses, to persist at tasks, and to relate to others with warmth and empathy. From the early days of social work these have always been the challenges of helping individuals. The practitioners of today are most fortunate in having a wealth of theories and interventions available to assist them in their work.

REFERENCES

Bellamy, C. and Irving A. (1995). Pioneers. In F.J. Turner and J.C. Turner (Eds.). *Canadian social welfare.* Toronto: Allyn and Bacon.

Beavers, W. (1985). *Successful marriage: a family systems approach to couples therapy.* New York: W.W. Norton.

Biesteck, F. (1957). *The casework relationship.* Chicago: Loyola University Press.

Bloom, M. (1990). *Introduction to the drama of social work.* Itasca, IL: Peacock Publishers.

Cade, B. and O'Hanlon, W.H. (1993). *A brief guide to brief therapy.* New York: W.W. Norton.

Carpenter D. (1996). Constructivism and social work treatment. In F.J. Turner (Ed.). *Social work treatment.* (4th ed.). Chapter 7. New York: Free Press.

Carter E. and McGoldrick, M. (1980). *The family life cycle: a framework for family therapy.* New York: Gardner Press.

Compton B. and Galaway, B. (1994). *Social work processes.* Pacific Grove, CA: Brooks/Cole.

Corcoran, K. and Fischer, J. (1987). *Measures for clinical practice: a sourcebook.* New York: Free Press.

deShazer, S. (1994). *Words were originally magic.* New York: W.W. Norton.

Englander-Golder, P. and Satir, V. (1991). *Say it straight.* Palo Alto, CA: Science and Behaviour Books.

Fisher, J. (1973). Is casework effective? A review. *Social Work, 18*, pp. 5–20.

Fisher, J. (1978). *Effective casework practice: an ecclectic approach.* New York: McGraw-Hill.

Freeman, D. (1991). *Multigenerational family therapy.* New York: Jason Aronson.

Gambrill, E. (1993). *Casework: A competency-based approach.* Englewood Cliffs, NJ: Prentice Hall.

Germain, C.B. and Gitterman, A. (1980). *The life model of social work practice.* New York: Columbia University Press.

Goleman, D. (1995). *Emotional intelligence.* New York: Bantam Books.

Goldstein, E. (1984). *Ego psychology and social work practice.* New York: Free Press.

Goldstein, H., Hilbert, H., and Hilbert, J. (1984). *Creative change: a cognitive-humanistic approach to social work practice.* London: Tavistock Publications.

Gray, J. (1993). *Men, women and relationships.* Toronto: Harper Collins.

Hepworth, D.H. and Larsen, J.A. (1982). *Direct social work practice: theory and skills.* Homewood, IL: The Dorsey Press.

Hepworth, D.H., Book, R.H., and Larsen, J.A. (1997). *Direct social work practice: theory and skills.* (5th ed.). Homewood, IL: The Dorsey Press.

Hoffman, L. (1981). *Foundations of family therapy: a conceptual framework for systems change.* New York: Basic Books.

Hollis, F. (1964). *Casework: A psychosocial therapy.* New York: Random House.

Johnson, L.C. (1995). *Social work practice: a generalist approach* (5th ed.). Boston: Allyn and Bacon.

Kelley, P. (1996). Narrative theory and social work treatment. In F.J. Turner (Ed.). *Social work treatment.* (4th ed.). Chapter 19. New York: Free Press.

McKay, M., Davis, M., and Fanning P. (1990). *Messages: the communication skills book.* Oakland, CA: New Harbinger Publications.

McKay, M. and Fanning, P. (1992). *Self-esteem* (2nd ed.). Oakland, CA: New Harbinger Publications.

Maluccio, A. (1981). *Promoting competence in clients: a new/old approach to social work practice.* New York: Free Press.

Miller, S., Nunnally, E., and Wackman, D. (1986). *Talking together.* Littleton, CO: Interpersonal Communication Programs.

Mullen, E.J. and Dumpson, J.R. (Eds.) (1972). *Evaluation of social intervention.* San Francisco: Jossey-Bass.

Payne, M. (1991). *Modern social work theory: a critical introduction.* Chicago: Lyceum Books, Inc.

Pearlman, L. and Saakvitne, K. (1995). *Trauma and the therapist: countertransferance and vicarious traumatization in psychotherapy with incest survivors.* New York: W.W. Norton.

Perlman, H.H. (1957). *Social casework: a problem-solving process.* Chicago: University of Chicago Press.

Pincus, A. and Minahan, A. (1973). *Social work practice: model and method.* Itasca, IL: Peacock.

Pinderhughes, E. (1995). Direct practice overview. In *Encyclopedia of social work* (19th ed.). Washington, DC: National Association of Social Workers.

Richmond, M. (1922). *What is social casework?* New York: Russell Sage Foundation.

Richmond, M. (1917). *Social diagnosis.* New York: Russell Sage Foundation.

Reid, W.J. and Epstein, L. (1977). *Task-centred practice.* New York Columbia University Press.

Rodway, M.R. (1986). Systems theory. In F.J. Turner (Ed.). *Social work treatment* (4th ed.). New York: Free Press.

Satir, V. (1988). *The new peoplemaking.* Palo Alto, CA: Science and Behaviour Books.

Shapiro, F. (1995). *Eye movement desensitization and reprocessing.* New York: Guilford Press.

Siporan, M. (1975). *Introduction to social work practice.* New York: Macmillan.

Swenson, C.R. (1995). Clinical social work. In *Encyclopedia of social work* (19th ed.). Washington, DC: National Association of Social Workers.

Turner, F.J. (1996). *Social work treatment* (4th ed.). New York: Free Press.

Turner, F.J. (1984). Mental disorders in social work practice. In F.J. Turner (Ed.) *Adult psychopathology: a social work perpsective.* New York: Free Press.

Van der Kolk, B., McFarlane, A., and Weisaeth, L. (Eds.) (1996). *Traumatic stress.* New York: Guilford Press.

Woods, M.E. and Hollis. (1990). *Casework: a psychosocial theory* (4th ed.). New York: McGraw-Hill Publishing.

Turner, J.C. (1995). The historical base. In F.J. Turner and J.C. Turner (Eds.). *Canadian social welfare* (3rd ed.). Toronto: Allyn and Bacon.

FAMILY

TREATMENT

Elizabeth Ridgely

Understanding the context of problems is a primary tenet of social work practice. Historically, the profession has considered culture, socioeconomics, community, and family in understanding problems and in working with clients. Social work practice deals with the family as well as the child, and the community as well as the family, within the parameters of social justice and the distribution of power, money, and services. Advocacy, community organization, research, education, and clinical work are all different aspects of the profession. Out of this tradition grew theories, research, methodologies, and literature specifically related to families and their treatment. Social work with families takes place in many areas including neighbourhood centres, women's shelters, child welfare, schools, hospitals, correctional institutions, and children's mental health centres, to name a few. Major contributions have been made by Canadian social work practitioners in the field of family treatment. Their influence permeates this chapter.

THE CONTEXT

This chapter discusses family treatment with children specifically referred to children's mental health centres in Ontario. These mental health centres offer treatment services to children from early childhood to late adolescence and to their families. The centres have a multidisciplinary staff and full funding from the provincial Ministry of Social Services and provide a variety of services ranging from assessment and community-based treatment to day treatment and residential programs.

Children's problems may include psychosis, conduct disorders, depression, suicidal ideation, learning difficulties, school avoidance, phobias, and antisocial behaviours. The problems range from severe to moderate. The child may have been identified by the family or by the community (school, child welfare, court, family physician, etc.) as having difficulty managing and the child's behaviour is disturbing both in the family and in the community.

The treatment of choice lies with the child's family and significant others, for two main reasons. The first reason is that the child's well-being is tied to the family. It is very difficult for a child to reach full potential in a family burdened by problems. The child's identity, sense of belonging, safety, and security all develop from the relationships within the family unit and the child's place in that unit, and children who must leave their family remain at risk even into adulthood. Children have the most invested in the future of the family and may attempt in many ways to maintain its functioning, even under the most difficult circumstances—for example, children who are abused and do not report it or children who unconsciously take on the "job" of keeping the parent focused on him, lest problems such as divorce, poverty, or loneliness overwhelm the adult.

The second reason relates to distribution of power. In a family, a child has far less power than an adult and has less capacity to change her circumstances. To work with a child outside of his context leaves any gains in a precarious state if the context of the problem stays the same.

Family therapy with children follows the same guidelines as adult family therapy. When dealing with violence and abuse, family members are not seen together. The intimidation of being in treatment with the abuser may cause the victim to be unable to talk freely with the practitioner. As treatment enters its final phase, family members can be seen together to discuss what went on and the effect it had on all members.

Having called for an appointment for their child, often at the suggestion of the school or some other concerned party, the whole family is invited to attend the first appointment to discuss their concerns. Appointments need to be made, as much as possible, around the family's work schedule. As the incidence of separation and divorce continues to climb, the number of single parents continues to rise. It is important to ask the single parent who is calling, usually the mother, if the father could come to the first session with the family so that both parents may plan for the child. The parent may agree or may prefer to wait until the second session. From the beginning, the problem is flagged as possible underinvolvement of the non-residential parent or as continuing conflict between the separated parents. Treatment of separated families, therefore, always includes ways of managing parenting. In fact, the problem itself may be one way the child has developed to facilitate a reconciliation or to see the non-custodial parent more frequently.

Although most families come of their own volition, many are referred when a child is being readmitted to school, for example, or when being returned home from a child welfare placement. Thus, there is often a combination of voluntary and involuntary aspects to the referral. It is important to acknowledge this with the family and to find a way to work with it. "I guess if the school had not said you had to come here as part of your child being readmitted to school, you might not have come. Right? So what can we do together to reassure the school that your child is ready to return and to learn?"

OVERVIEW OF THE THINKING

Family treatment brings many theories of behaviour together to help in understanding the individual within the family system and the family system itself. Working with families is treating the context of the problem along with the actual problem.

The major idea that family treatment introduced to the field of child treatment was the use of systems theory for understanding the context of the problematic behaviour of the child (Minuchin, 1974; Ackerman, 1967; Satir, 1983; Aponte, 1994). The idea that the whole was larger than the sum of the parts and that another's behaviour had a circular influence on one's own behaviour developed a new direction for treatment. Lyn Hoffman (1981) describes the presenting problem as a warning flag indicating a need for change in the system while, at the same time, preventing change. An adolescent's refusal to go to school may be a signal that the family needs to make some changes to allow the child more independence but, at the same time, may prevent this by attracting more parental vigilance. Minuchin (1974, 1981) taught that the presenting problem was always the "wrong" problem. If the family had the "right" problem they would be able to solve it themselves. He believed that the problem lay in the structure of the family, which is to say, within the organization of the parts of the system, which prevents the system from finding new solutions required at new developmental stages. He had much respect for subsystems, accompanied by clear generational boundaries, always looking at spatial relationships among family members. Who is too close to see clearly and who is too far away to act? How would the problem be addressed by different persons? From the very beginning, Minuchin was interested in the peripheral person and in enlisting that person's help with the problem. He sought to involve fathers differently in the working of their families (Minuchin, 1967). Aponte (1994) developed ways to expand the family system to include the school and to develop a clearly articulated definition of the problem in underorganized, poor families.

At the same time, Ackerman (1967) and Satir (1983) were developing, respectively, a psychodynamic and communications approach to family treatment with children. Don Jackson and Gregory Bateson were exploring cybernetics, feedback loops, and sequential steps of interactional patterns to better understand the strength of systems, the forces of inertia, and what level of intervention would be useful to make any change in a social system.

Understanding the interactional patterns in a family system reaches beyond the nuclear family and into the family of origin and larger kinship system (Andolfi, 1989, 1994; Braverman, 1981; Freeman, 1976, 1977, 1978; Bowen, 1966; Boszormenyi-Nagi, 1984; Framo, 1976; Williamson, 1991). Just as one considers spatial relationships in the nuclear family, it is necessary to consider the nuclear family in relation to the extended family, and to look at forces that keep the family isolated and vulnerable, such as cutoffs, losses, feuds, distance. Again, the solution to the problem may be to involve different people, to rearrange the spatial relationships among nuclear families. The father who is struggling with his adolescent son may, in fact, be struggling with his own unsuccessful relationship with his father. Including the grandfather as part of a session may connect the father differently to his father which in turn affects the relationship with his own son. Increasingly, grandparents are enjoying a longer life with more opportunities to support and rearrange their relationships with their grown children and grandchildren. This connection among different generations, as well as same age generations, adds enrichment and resources to problem solving. Having the father's brothers come to a session with their sons also provides a forum of consultation among family members that enhances a shared belonging, a common history, and different ideas to avoid impasses with the next generation.

In addition to the whole, comes attention to the part. Developmental theory (Erikson, 1968; Fraiberg, 1959; Kagan, 1984; Gilligan, 1982; Blos, 1979) of the individual is an element of all family treatment thinking. Families must change to accommodate the developmental stages of its members. Mothering a six-year-old requires a different arrangement between the parts than mothering a sixteen-year-old. The equilibrium of the whole is in constant flux as it grapples with the growth and development of the parts. The family must be flexible and respond to the changing needs of its members while it maintains a core of stability to facilitate a sense of identification and belonging.

Social work with families includes the larger systems within which the family functions (Hartman, 1979, 1983). Understanding the individual fabric of the family requires a small immersion course by each family of each family practitioner. In Canada, with its diverse population and new immigrant populations regularly arriving, the traditions, culture, finance, and domestic organization of the families encountered will often be very different from the practitioner's own experience. It is essential to have an anthropological stance and be educated by the family in order to guard against bringing one's own traditions into the treatment site (Falicov, 1988; McGoldrick, 1991). By combining the family's tradition with the practitioner's tradition, together with theory and practice, a third system may be created. The therapeutic system is the joining of the professional and family systems for the specific task of developing its own unique way to work with each other on behalf of the child.

Feminist-informed thinking has more recently permeated the family treatment field (Myers Avis, 1986, 1991, 1992; Walters, Carter, Papp, and Silverstein, 1988; Goodrich, 1988, 1991; Goldner, 1985, 1988, 1991; Bograd, 1984, 1986). The distribution of power, finance, and housework, which reflect the dominant patriarchal culture, are sources of difficulty for men, women, and children in families. These issues, often leading to depression, divorce, abuse, and acute anxiety in the children, are explored through a subsystem participation within generations and across generations. A major contribution to understanding family systems theory, from this group of women, was the recognition that the parts are not equally weighted in family systems. Also the assumption is that until the parts are more equal, there will always be problems. Symptoms will be needed to prevent families from splitting apart (Goldner, 1988).

OVERVIEW OF THE WORK
Joining the Family

At the first interview, parents inevitably feel they have failed as parents and as a family. Having a child in a struggle with life is painful for parents and often a source of shame. The family may feel that they have had no say in the referral because of pressure from the school or child welfare agency. It is important to realize that most families have been sent to treatment by a third party. They come to the first interview filled with anxiety, at times hostility, and fear of being judged inadequate. Families, by and large, have no idea what to expect. They may know very little about the agency. It is important to introduce the family to the setting: the room, the toys, the video cameras, the services available, and the name of the interviewer. The more information the family has about the agency and about the practitioner, the more at ease the family will feel.

The purpose of the first interview is twofold: to increase the comfort level of both the family and the practitioner and to begin the work around a shared definition of the problem. This shared definition will include ideas from the family and from the practitioner. This is the beginning of the development of the therapeutic system, in which the family and the practitioner alternately lead and follow.

To accomplish this, the practitioner must meet each family member at the individual's developmental stage. The work of "joining" is relevant to the task at hand. It is not social. It is purposeful—the age, the work, the grade, the fit of the adult with her work and the fit of the child with his school, the country of origin. The practitioner's careful attention to detail allows the family to appreciate the interest in their personhood first: how difficult working hours are, the experience of being unemployed, managing these issues; how difficult it is to have a mean teacher, to have no friends, to have friends whom your parents do not like. This inquiry allows the professional to meet the family's competence, strength, accomplishments, and the particular story of the family prior to the discovery of where they think they have failed.

Family treatment is possible when the practitioner has found a point of identification with each individual accompanied by a sense of the patterns of the whole. From a position of competency, the child and the family have then begun treatment with a different view of themselves in relation to the problem. From this strength, the discussion of weakness takes on a new meaning.

To define the problem, the practitioner should enlist the child as a guide to the troubled areas of the family—for the child, for the siblings and for the parents (Andolfi).

Interviewing the child first shows the practitioner's respect and interest in hearing about the problem from the child's point of view. Usually, in our culture, we ask the parent to talk about the child. This is not useful for enhancing the competence of the child or for engaging the child, who assumes her story will then be of secondary importance.

When asked, parents will give the practitioner permission to start with the children. It gives them an opportunity to hear their child and, as the child explains the situation to the practitioner, to feel some pride in their child's observations and opinions. There are many ways to include parents without giving them the floor; eye contact, smiling, shared enjoyment of the child's view, and the occasional requested comment for a point of clarification or an acknowledgment of the child's competence in describing the people in the family and the worries they might be experiencing. Parents can supplement the story, but the narrator is the child.

This invitation to the child and to the sibling subsystem begins individually with clarifying the names of the therapist and the children. Most children do not "hear" the name of the therapist the first time. "I would like to start with the children. My name is Libby and your name is...? Susan. I like that name. I have an Aunt called Susan. So, Susan, just remind me how old you are and what grade you are in. And your brother beside you? I'd like to talk to all the kids first and find out about yourselves and your family. O.K. by you?"

Clinical conversations with children are no different than with adults. They start from the outside and move to the inside. With children, depending on their age, areas of interest include their extra-familial life at school, with friends, with teachers, sports, music, dress, hobbies, activities, and their familial life. "What kind of work does your mother do outside of the house? Does she like it? Is it difficult? How tired does she get? How can you tell when she is tired? Do you worry about her then? Do you try to help her? Who else helps her? What about your grandmother? Does she help? And your father? What is the story about him? What worries you most in the family? How do you try to help out? What are your parents' worries about you? Who should come to the next session? What other people can help with this problem? When should they come?"

A child will become involved with the therapist when the questions are relevant to the child and when the therapist stays with the child in the interview. It is very difficult for children to speak after their parents because of the conviction that the adults will stick together and the child's voice will be unheard. Further, children have the largest investment in the family as it determines their entire childhood and adolescence. With attentiveness from the therapist, the child will guide the therapy in the direction necessary for change.

Course of Treatment

Family treatment is a series of conversations between different combinations of people, listened to by other combinations of people. The more varied the groups, the more interesting the conversations—interesting in the sense that the persons involved in the problem have changed. This provides the opportunity for new solutions, less predictability, and a jump start to a system that has become repetitive and predictable.

As well, with different people come different conversations that are expansive and not restricted to "the" problem but can include other problems. The main systems idea here is that process becomes more important than content. Participation from different persons frees the family from the impasse that brought them to treatment. At the time of the referral, the family has been talking about the same thing (the child) in a predictable fashion, which has been maintaining of the system and the problem. To add more people to one session, reduce the number for the next, add gender (mother/daughter; father/son) for the following session, subsystem (husband/wife, siblings) the next session, and invite friends to another session adds to the treatment a variety of resources that belong to the family but which, over time, have become underused by the family. The treatment needs to be unpredictable, confusing, and interesting. If the family can predict the conversation in the next session, they might as well have the conversation at home in their own kitchen.

The course of treatment is determined by the family as they decide who they want to include in the next few sessions, who else can help them with this problem. The therapist is interested in expanding the system to add flexibility and to reduce the isolation that comes with defeat. The process is the strengthening of the family resource system rather than the adoption of the family by the professional system. Many families go through difficult times with a child without outside help. When families use outside help, it is usually a sign of depletion of their own resources.

Family of Origin

The North American idea that nuclear families must be self-sufficient has put enormous pressure on small families to be everything to each other: grandparents, aunts, uncles, brothers, sisters. It is not unusual for families not to "burden" other family members with their problems. Also, it is not unusual for other family members to respect their "privacy" and not ask about the problem. As the problem becomes more difficult, the tendency to withdraw from larger family functions takes over.

This tendency may occur in the complex world of raising children and working, with time at a premium and fatigue at a maximum. It also may come from unresolved relationships within the family of origin that continue to generate feelings of discomfort and are to be avoided. For others it comes from geography, through relocation for work or immigration. The result is "orphaned" nuclear families, too distant to offer each other support, confirmation, humour, babysitting, an extra hand, a casserole, or a conversation. As a parent explains the reason she has not told her mother and siblings about her dismay, her loneliness becomes apparent to both the speaker and the listener. Having identified the source of loneliness, the conversation moves to what it would take for this mother to invite her family to a session to act as a consultant to the practitioner on her behalf. "These are the people who know you the best and for the longest and it may be that they can help me help you." The immediate success of the session is that the woman asks her sisters and her mother to come in to help. This is the beginning of giving up the isolation stance that so often accompanies family problems. The actual session provides a look at intergenerational relationships. The question of "How do you want to use the session?" leaves room for the family to direct the session.

The practitioner asking the visiting member to tell her about her grown daughter/sister and how she has changed over time allows the person to begin and end the story as she chooses. All family members are invited to these sessions to hear about their mother/wife from the grandmother/aunts/in-laws.

The larger a context the family has, the more opportunity for varying solutions to problems. The stronger one's support, the more normalized one's problems become. Thus, the course of treatment is to attend to the missing resources of the family, to understand how the family became out of balance and how to support a new equilibrium.

Balance is a useful way of thinking about families: a lack of balance can lead to a different intensity between the child and family which impedes solving the problem. Imbalance comes from loss—loss through death, divorce, unemployment, immigration.

When a child attends a session with the family, it is important to listen for whom the child and/or family is not including. An example of this is a separated or divorced family where the child has no contact with one parent and that parent's entire family. This might affect the child in many ways: conflicted loyalties, abandonment, rejection, anxiety regarding the absent parent. All of these ingredients are part of the therapeutic conversations.

Lack of balance comes from eliminating a part of the whole, leaving the whole lopsided. Lopsidedness from cut-offs, losses, or distance in the family's life leads to an internal familial intensity that impedes the family's finding new solutions to the problem. Including significant others redresses the balance. When family is not readily available, friends can be good substitutes.

A twelve-year-old boy admitted to a short-term residential unit for increasingly bizarre and dangerous behaviour, had been on "home instruction" for nine months with no sign of improvement. In the family, the father suffered from manic-depression and the sister was severely brain damaged from an accident when she was three. I suggested to the mother that she bring an "army" of women to the next session. This burden was too much for one woman to carry.

She brought her mother and sister to the next session and her sister returned with her for another session. This "army" had always been there for her but their inclusion in a family session led to a different discussion of the problem, including her reluctance to ask for help from her family.

Friends

As well as other members who are part of the larger fabric of the nuclear family, friends are important reference points for sharing difficulties, normalizing problems, and offering support. When a family becomes bogged down with a recurring problem, exhaustion often takes over their entire life. They stop doing fun activities. They stop going to restaurants because of the child's behaviour. They stop visiting. Attending to work and looking after the child are all they can manage. With the attendant isolation comes an amplification of the problem, with no relief in sight.

It is important to reintroduce their friends (Andolfi and Haber, 1994) into the family for support, confirmation, an alternative view, and different activities. Initially, families consider it strange to invite non-family members to a session. They have concerns about privacy and may be embarrassed; this mirrors how, over time, they have moved away from others.

The practitioner, asking about friends of the family, introduces the idea of inviting someone who knows them well and cares for them to come as a consultant to the practitioner on how they see the family managing in this crisis. It becomes very interesting for the family to consider who they might ask to come to a session. The children can be very useful in suggesting people who they know are important to their parent.

A session with friends involves a history of the friendship—the events they have shared together, the concern they have for their friend now, the advice they wanted to give but felt unable, or uninvited, to offer. The process is an expansion of the system and a strengthening of it. The content is less important. Having a friend at the session immediately reduces the isolation, renews the friendship, and allows the family to be securely located among its own resources.

It may be that the family cannot think of anyone to bring to the session. A single mother who was struggling with her ten-year-old only son and who could manage only her job and her son, was at a loss to think of someone to invite. Such isolation had become part of the problem for these two. With encouragement from the practitioner, she agreed to find someone. She asked a woman with whom she sat at their son's hockey games. The woman was pleased to be invited and expressed surprise that the mother was having trouble with her son. She thought that he was a great kid! At the session, the woman contributed much information about her view of the son and also of the mother from their contact at the arena. The two women began to expand their friendship beyond hockey, to the benefit of the son who was less worried about his mother's loneliness.

Friends of the child can also be a resource. A single mother from Grenada was very worried about her only daughter and the dangers she perceived in the school and in the malls. She became frantic if her daughter did not call her at work immediately after school, and battles occurred regularly. The daughter was invited to bring her two best friends to the next session to talk about safety. These thirteen-year-old girls were very clear about how to avoid fights, bad kids, and other perils of attending a large school with many social problems. They were clear about their family rules and where they were allowed to go and where they were not. This was reassuring for the client, who thought she was the only one with rules and that her daughter was lying about her activities. For the next session, we invited the girls' mothers to discuss this again. One other mother, who also was an immigrant to Canada, attended and the two mothers shared concerns in the presence of the daughters, with the daughters periodically reassuring them.

The input of friends can ease the immediate impasse. The remaining work continues on understanding other aspects of the story and how they impact on the present dilemma. This particular family had a lot of abuse from the past, which clouded the present, as well as multiple losses from migration.

Family Treatment and Schools

The second most important area for the child is school and school life. The child's growing sense of self comes from membership both in the family and in the school. Tentative membership in either area puts the child at risk. When a child is referred for treatment, the school has exhausted its own capacity to be helpful. The school is also looking for help. It is not unusual for the school and the family to be on opposite sides—the family blaming the school for the problem and the school blaming the family.

Part of the work with children is to bring the school and the family together in a new way that offers alternative solutions for both. This can be a very delicate operation. Learning problems and disruptive behaviour disorders are extremely taxing for the child, the family, and the school. Often, the school would like the child transferred to a treatment facility.

Here, the role of the practitioner is advocacy for the child and the family within the school system. Not only does the family require a new view of themselves and their child, but so does the school. These children are known to the whole school in that they are so easily identified by their behaviour: the principal, the vice-principal, the homeroom teacher, the teacher on recess duty, the special education teacher, the consultant to special education— all know the child and some things about the family. The Internal Placement Review Committee (I.P.R.C.) planning conferences take on a military air with an army of people in attendance. The family is out-numbered and has the least input at these meetings.

The family treatment practitioner must discover the competence of the family and of the child in the planning of educational goals and must present this information to the school until such time as the family can do so themselves. As the work proceeds with the family, sharing the view of the problem and ideas for the school becomes an ongoing process shared by the practitioner, the family, and the school.

Just as the family needs to find some hope for change, so does the school. Part of the practitioner's job is to make the child "likable" again to the school: likable, teachable, reachable. This process is subtle, in that it includes new views of the child with an emphasis on strengths, the unusual and interesting aspects of the child, and areas where the teacher might connect with the child. Availability to the school is crucial as part of family work. It is useful for the practitioner to see the school in which the child is trying to find a place and for the child and family to be aware that the practitioner knows the school first-hand.

ENDING WITH SEMICOLONS

Family treatment ends when the family feels qualified to manage and prepare for the next developmental stage. Ending with families is always with a semicolon; the family is free to call for a chat, a booster shot, a consultation, or a series of meetings when they feel it would be useful.

Growth and change are regular parts of family life and ongoing for life; though this chapter ends with a period, the reader is invited to contemplate the idea of a "semicolon-ending" that would point to all those other adventures still to come.

REFERENCES

Ackerman, N. (1967). *Treating the troubled family*. New York: Basic Books.

Andolfi, M. (1983). *Behind the family mask: therapeutic change in rigid family systems*. New York: Brunner Mazel.

Andolfi, M. (1989). *The myth of atlas: families and the therapeutic story*. New York: Brunner Mazel.

Andolfi, M. & Haber, R. (Eds.). (1994). *Please help me with this family: using consultants as resources in family therapy*. New York: Brunner Mazel.

Aponte, H. (1994). *Bread & spirit: therapy with the new poor.* New York: W.W. Norton & Company.

Avis, J.M. (1992). Where are all the family therapists? Abuse and violence within families and family therapy's response. *Journal of Marital and Family Therapy,* July 1992.

Avis, J.M. (1992). Current trends in feminist thought and therapy: perspectives on sexual abuse and violence within families in North America. *Journal of Feminist Family Therapy,* 1992.

Avis, J.M. (1986). Feminist issues in family therapy. In F. Piercy & D. Sprenkle (Eds.). *Family therapy sourcebook.* New York: The Guilford Press.

Benjamin, M. & Irving, H. (1992). Toward a feminist-informed model of therapeutic family mediation. *Mediation Quarterly, 10,* 1992.

Benjamin, M. & Irving, H. (1989). Shared parenting: critical review of the research literature. *Family & Conciliation Courts Review, 27,* 1989.

Blos, P. (1979). *The adolescent passage: developmental issues.* International University Press, 1979.

Bograd, M. Family systems approaches to wife battering: a feminist critique. *American Journal of Orthopsychiatry, 54,* 1984.

Bograd, M. (1986). A feminist examination of family systems models of violence against women in the family. In M. Ault-Riche (Ed.). *Women and family therapy.* Rockville, MD: Aspen Systems Corporation.

Bograd, M. (1990). Female therapist/male client: considerations about belief systems. *Journal of Feminist Family Therapy,* 1990.

Boszormenyi-Nagy, I. & Spark, G.M. (1984). *Invisible loyalties.* New York: Brunner Mazel.

Bowen, M. (1966).The use of family theory in clinical practice. *Comprehensive Psychiatry, 7,* 1966.

Braverman, S. (1981). Family of origin: the view from the parents' side. *Family Process, 20,* 1981.

Braverman, S. (1995). Intergenerational work as an adjunct to psychoanalysis and psychotherapy. *Journal of the American Academy of Psychoanalysis, 23,* 1995.

Braverman, S. (1995).The integration of the individual and family therapy. In *Contemporary Family Therapy: An International Journal, 17,* 1995.

Braverman, S. (1990). Long-term family therapy: a developmental approach. *Contemporary Family Therapy: An International Journal. 12,* 1990.

Braverman, S. (1982). Family of origin as a training resource for family therapists. *Canadian Journal of Psychiatry. 27,* 1982.

Braverman, S. (1980). Family therapist: technician or practitioner? *Canadian Journal of Psychiatry, 25,* 1980.

Byles, J., Bishop, D., & Horn, D. (1983). Evaluation of a family therapy training program. *Journal of Marital & Family Therapy. 9,* 1983.

Carter, E.A. & McGoldrick, M. (Eds.). (1980). *The family life cycle: a framework for family therapy.* New York: Gardner Press.

Erikson, E.H. (1968). *Identity and the life cycle.* New York: W.W. Norton & Company.

Falicov, C.J. (1988). Learning to think culturally. In *Handbook of family therapy training and supervision.* H. Libble, D. Breunlin, and R. Schwartz (Eds.). New York: The Guilford Press.

Fraiberg, S.H. (1959). *The magic years: understanding and handling the problems of early childhood.* New York: Charles Scribner's Sons.

Framo, J.L. (1976). Family of origin as a therapeutic resource for adults in marital and family therapy: you can and should go home again. *Family Process, 15,* 1976.

Freeman, D.S. (1976). Phases of family treatment. *Family Coordinator, 25,* 1976.

Freeman, D.S. (1976). A systems approach to family therapy. *Family Therapy. 3,* 1976.

Freeman, D.S. (1976). The family as a system: fact or fantasy? *Comprehensive Psychiatry, 17,* 1976.

Freeman, D.S. (1977). The family systems practice model: underlying assumptions. *Family Therapy, 4,* 1977.

Freeman, D.S. (1978). Person to person communication in the family. *Family Therapy, 5,* 1978.

Gilligan, C. (1982). In a different voice: psychological theory and women's development. Cambridge: Harvard University Press.

Goldner, V. (1985). Feminism and Family Therapy. Family Process, *24,* 1985.

Goldner, V. (1988). Generation and gender: narrative and covert hierarchies. Family Process, *27,* 1988.

Goldner, V. (1991). Feminism and systemic practice: two critical traditions in transition. *Journal of Strategic & Systemic Therapies, 10,* 1991.

Goodrich, T., Rampage, C., Ellman, B., & Halstead, K. (1988). *Feminist family therapy: a casebook.* New York: W.W. Norton & Company.

Goodrich, T.J. (Ed.).(1991). *Women and power: perspectives for family therapy.* New York: W.W. Norton & Company.

Hartman, A. (1979). *Finding families: an ecological approach to family assessment in adoption.* Sage Publications.

Hartman, A. (1983). *Family centered social work practice.* New York: The Free Press.

Hoffman, L. (Ed.). (1981). *Foundations of Family Therapy.* New York: Basic Books.

Irving, H. & Benjamin, M. (1989). Therapeutic family mediation: fitting the service to the interactional diversity of client couples. *Mediation Quarterly, 7,* 1989.

Kagan, J. (1984). *The nature of the child.* New York: Basic Books.

Kenyon, E. (1988). Treatment of families with sexually abused children: systemic dilemmas. *Children's Mental Health, 1,* 1988.

McGoldrick, M., Anderson, C. & Walsh, F. (Eds.). (1991). *Women in families: a framework for family therapy.* New York: W.W. Norton & Company, 1991.

Minuchin, S., Montalvo, B., Guerney, Jr., B., Rosman, B., & Schumer, F. (1967). *Families of the slums.* New York: Basic Books Inc.

Minuchin, S. (1974). *Families and family therapy.* Cambridge: Harvard University Press.

Minuchin, S. & Fishman, H.C. (1981). *Family therapy techniques.* Cambridge: Harvard University Press.

Philipp, R., Cohen, J., Gelcer, E., & Steinhauer, P. (1990). Family therapy training: quo vadis? *Canadian Psychology*, *31*, 1990.

Satir, V. 1983). *Conjoint family therapy*. (3rd ed.). Palo Alto, California: Science and Behavior Books, Inc.

Turner, F.J. (1978). *Psychosocial therapy: a social work perspective*. New York: The Free Press.

Walters, M., Carter, B., Papp, P., & Silverstein, O. (1988). *The invisible web: gender patterns in family relationships*. New York: The Guilford Press.

Williamson, D. (1991). *The intimacy paradox*. New York: The Guilford Press, 1991.

C h a p t e r

SOCIAL GROUP WORK PRACTICE: THE CANADIAN EXPERIENCE[1]

Ellen Sue Mesbur

Social group work, as a modality of social work practice, is central to the repertoire of the social work profession. With roots in the settlement movement of the late 1880s, social group work as a method of practice dates to the 1930s, when social work struggled to gain professional and public recognition. Falck (1993) reflected that social work with groups was born in troubled times, with a mission to better social life and build competence in each and every individual who comes to our attention. This mission continues to influence social group work practice: "group practice in social work today is perhaps best character-ized by its breadth, which spans purposes, populations, practice settings, practitioners' roles, and practice approaches" (Schopler and Galinsky, 1995, 1130). Changing societal conditions, expanding knowledge, and a proliferation of practice contexts require adaptations of social group work to an increasing variety of populations and life situations.

Social group work practice in Canada has evolved toward an integration of different models and a consensus that within each model certain characteristics are common to all group work practice. Each model includes strengths that assist practitioners in developing their skills for current practice. Today, social group work is grounded in the humanistic approach to practice, encompassing democratic processes, mutual aid, and common goals.

THE EVOLUTION OF SOCIAL GROUP WORK: 1900–1950

During the first half of this century, social group work evolved from British and American practices, incorporating their collective knowledge and practice wisdom into the Canadian experience. The Industrial Revolution, and the social upheaval that emerged from it, led to social conditions unprecedented in Canadian society. The dramatic shift in population from rural to predominantly urban settings, and the resulting plague of inhumane working con-ditions, widespread poverty, and social upheaval, became catalysts for social action. Breton

---

[1]This chapter was written with the research assistance of Frank Marra, Cheryl Webb, and Sarah Torontali, B.S.W. students, Ryerson University, School of Social Work, Toronto, Ontario.

(1990) describes the early social group work tradition as situated within three social movements: the settlement movement, the recreation movement, and the progressive education movement. These movements all fostered a belief in the primary importance of social action and the individual as a political entity.

THE SETTLEMENT MOVEMENT

The settlement movement engaged individuals as members of social groups and, as such, perceived them to be affected by the social, economic, and political conditions of the period (Breton, 1990). Early settlement houses, such as London's Toynbee Hall (1884) and Chicago's Hull House (1889) were established to "fight for improved housing, better working conditions, and increased recreational opportunities" (Schopler and Galinsky, 1995, 1131). It was a reform movement following rapid industrialization and the growth of cities and responding to "the myriad of social evils that sprang out of rapid social transformation" (Irving, Parsons, and Bellamy, 1995, 206).

Canada was a latecomer to the settlement movement, as the full effects of the Industrial Revolution were not felt until the early 1900s (Irving, Parsons, and Bellamy, 1995). Evangelia House, the first settlement in Canada, was established by Sara Libby Carson and Mary Lawson Bell in Toronto in 1902 as a cooperative venture between the two women and the Dominion Council of the YWCA. In 1907, with donations from philanthropists, a new home for Evangelia House was opened by Canada's Governor-General, Earl Grey, "enhancing the prestige and public acceptance of Canada's first social settlement" (Irving, Parsons and Bellamy, 1995, 28).

The Presbyterian Church established a chain of settlement houses in Canada's larger cities: St. Christopher House in Toronto (1912), Chalmers House in Montreal (1912), Robertson Memorial House in Winnipeg (1913), St. Columba House, Point St. Charles in Montreal (1917), Vancouver Community House (1918), and Neighbourhood House in Hamilton (1922). These settlements were founded by the church's social gospel movement and provided practical social services in urban slum areas. The broader aspects of reform were not viewed as appropriate matters for the church.

> Consequently, St. Christopher House and the five other settlements in the chain concentrated their energies in those early days on neighbourhood services, with little or no involvement in civic action or reform movements such as had distinguished the early social settlements in Great Britain and the United States (Irving, Parsons, and Bellamy, 1995, 73).

Other settlements included Toronto's University Settlement House (1911) and Central Neighbourhood House (1911). The aims of University Settlement House were to "bring the university students into direct contact with those living amidst the unfortunate conditions of our modern cities and thus broaden the one and elevate the other" and also to carry out "all sorts of social work and investigations" (Irving, Parsons, and Bellamy, 1995, 85). Central Neighbourhood House was conceived as a secular settlement that would include activities such as clubs, educational classes, and health clinics, but would also "play an activist role unlike anything undertaken by the other early Toronto settlements" (Irving, Parsons, and Bellamy, 1995, 104). This was an action-oriented era that ultimately led to the movement becoming integrated into the mainstream of the emerging social work profession in the 1930s (Shulman, 1992).

The Recreation Movement

The recreation movement held a multi-dimensional view of group members that also focused on action in the form of planned activity. Groups gave specific attention to the accessing of a group member's strength in a conscious effort to engage individuals to be more than victims (Breton, 1990). Neva Leona Boyd, a pioneer of the recreation movement, urged group workers not to overemphasize verbal expression while ignoring play and action as therapeutic tools for group work. Boyd believed in the creative use of activity, geared to members' needs, to support group work in therapeutic settings. Her work contributed substantially to early group therapy developments (Brown, 1991).

The Progressive Education Movement

The progressive education movement formalized many of the era's sociological and philosophical notions of reciprocity between the individual and society and between the small group and society. Group services, mainly found in leisure-time agencies, were linked to progressive education (Brown, 1991). This movement was strongly influenced by John Dewey and Charles Horton Cooley.

Dewey contributed philosophical positions on the ideal forms of government, on citizen participation, and on the potential for education in groups (Breton, 1990). He saw the potential of voluntary groups for creative learning. Through his association with Jane Addams at Hull House, he was "instrumental in moving group work toward a more scientific method" (Brown, 1991, 30).

Cooley was responsible for "developing the concept of the primary group" (Brown, 1991, 30). His research into the nature of the primary group provided a profound rationale for the social uses of human togetherness (Gitterman and Shulman, 1985). Cooley formulated ideas about the nature of small groups and viewed group life as a "basic social fact to be understood and taken into account in formulating a theory of democracy and the state" (Shapiro, 1991, 9).

Summary

In the early days of social group work "there was an assumption that all humans could engage in group life for developmental, self-help, mutual aid, social action, social sustenance, and personal enhancement purposes" (Lang, 1978, 247). Lang characterizes the infancy of social group work as a period situated within democratic values and group member inclusion. Group work practitioners viewed democratic group forms and democratic processes as essential to individual fulfilment and vital to a participatory citizenry.

MODEL BUILDING: 1950–1970

By the 1950s, when social group work could longer be encompassed within one descriptive framework, theorists developed models to deal with the complexities of practice (Lang, 1978). Schopler and Galinsky (1995) summarize this era by pointing out that group work theorists identified the common tasks that social workers must perform in their work with groups. They state that the "three major conceptions of social group work that emerged in this era—the social goals model, the reciprocal model, and the remedial model—were a driving force in the development of social group work" (132).

The Social Goals Model

The social goals model emphasized the enhancement of individual growth through democratic participation and social responsibility and reflected the traditionalists who wished to preserve social group work's social action dimension (Brown, 1991; Mesbur and Jacobs, 1989; Schopler and Galinsky, 1995). This model "aimed to influence groups toward democratic values, social conscience, and social action for the 'common good'; to encourage socialization; and to enhance individual growth, development, and learning" (Middleman and Goldberg, 1987). The social goals model "because of its view of social work as a 'cause' and because of its relevance to contemporary struggles for human rights, continues to influence all of social work practice as well as its group work component" (Garvin, 1997, 7).

The Reciprocal Model

The reciprocal model, influenced by Phillips and conceptualized by Schwartz, was grounded in social systems theory and field theory and "directed the worker to mediate the engagement of individual and society as each reached toward the other for mutual self-fulfilment. This model introduced the terms 'contract' and 'mutual aid' into the vocabulary of social group workers" (Middleman and Goldberg, 1987, 715). Through continued refinement of his original concepts of reciprocal interactions in group work, Schwartz's model evolved into the mediating model and finally the interactional model.

The Remedial Model

The remedial model emerged at a time when group work was moving into rehabilitation settings (Garvin, 1997). This model emphasized the use of the group for remedial or corrective purposes, whereby through a process of diagnosis and treatment, groups are formed that have the greatest potential to help the individual (Mesbur and Jacobs, 1989). Formulated by Vinter and his associates, the remedial model "was grounded in psychoanalytic concepts, ego psychology, and social role theory and used the group to alter and reinforce individual behaviour change" (Middleman and Goldberg, 1987, 715).

Summary

The characterization of the 1950s to the 1970s as a model-building era reflects upon and expands the influence of humanistic and democratic values and the further understanding of group dynamics through an infrastructure in the form of models. The dialogue between theoreticians and practitioners is continuously centred on a negotiation between social group work's traditional value base and history, and the evolution of group work practice.

THE DIVERSIFICATION OF SOCIAL GROUP WORK: 1970–PRESENT

Papell and Rothman (1980), through a distillation of the three models of group work practice, attempted to integrate their commonalities into what they called "the mainstream model of social work practice with groups, a term they borrowed from Lang" (Middleman and Goldberg, 1987, 717). They suggested a "pluralistic use of knowledge and skills" (Papell and

Rothman, 1980, 7). It is this conception of social group work practice that most accurately informs our current practice, characterized by "common goals, mutual aid, and non-synthetic experiences" (Papell and Rothman, 1980, 7).

The Mainstream Model is primarily a framework for practice rather than a clearly defined model. It emphasizes the interaction of the member, the group, the worker, and group activities. Each of these components, although important in itself, cannot be isolated from, and is interactive with, the others. Central to the mainstream group are four core elements: the group as a mutual aid system, externality, group development, and diversity of group types and target populations.

Building on the foundation of social group work theories, many writers have contributed significantly to social group work literature. Shulman (1979, 1991, 1992), focuses on the group as a whole as the unit for intervention and on the worker as a mediator between the members and their environment. Balgopal and Vassil (1983) apply systems theory and an ecological perspective to work with groups. Brown (1991) emphasizes group work with disadvantaged populations within a wellness perspective. Garvin (1987, 1997) focuses on groups to enhance individual functioning and task-centred group work practice. Glassman and Kates (1990), within the context of a humanistic approach to social group work, define and illustrate practitioner behaviours necessary to operationalize humanistic values and norms. Northen (1988), incorporating systems theory, provides a theoretical foundation for a psychosocial model of social group work. Toseland and Rivas (1984, 1995) offer a systemic approach to group work practice, integrating individual, group, and organizational/community collectivities with societal concerns. Berman-Rossi (1993) and Berman-Rossi and Kelly (1999) expand on the worker role in relation to stages of group development. Schopler and Galinsky (1984) articulate the way in which open-ended groups mature and function. Lee (1987, 1994), Pernell (1986), Middleman and Wood (1990) Gutierrez (1990), and Gutierrez and Lewis (1999) formulate concepts of competency and empowerment as key processes for group work and social action. Gitterman (1989), Gitterman and Shulman (1994), and Steinberg (1997) further concepts of the distinctive dynamics of mutual-aid practice.

Major contributions from the Canadian literature include Lang (1972, 1978, 1979a, 1979b, 1981, 1986), Breton (1985, 1988, 1990, 1992, 1994, 1995, 1997), and Shapiro (1977, 1986, 1990, 1991). Lang distinguishes the social work group from other types of groups often seen in social work, and characterizes the social work group as one in which group process is the major means of offering professional help (Home, 1985). Much of Lang's work has focused on delineating "a continuum of social organizational forms in use or available for use in the profession of social work, and to explore their capability for helping purposes" (Lang, 1986, 8). She suggests that the notion of "collectivity" as a social form that possesses some, but not all, of the features of a fully-formed group, should be acknowledged as viable and potentially helpful.

Breton "views the 'political factor' as central for group workers" (Shapiro, 1991, 18). Her writing is characterized by a strong emphasis on the need for social workers to maintain the combined focus on the individual and society (Breton, 1990). According to Breton, social change and political commitment must be included as an integral aspect of all social work practice models (Breton, 1990). Breton expands on the concept of empowerment in groups, illustrating the theory with her own practice with homeless women. She challenges social group workers to "reclaim our own historical 'Option for the Poor'" (Breton, 1992, 259). Social group workers must engage in liberation activity which involves a real sharing of power and responsibility. Most recently, Breton uses an empowerment framework to identify some elements of group work practice in what she terms "a post-empowerment era" (Breton, 1997). This "model assumes that groups are the instrument of choice for both the process and the goal of empowerment.... Empowerment requires transformations at personal and structural/political levels" (Breton, 1997).

Shapiro's work focuses on mutual helping as distinct from professional helping. He maintains that groups have the potential for mutual helping between peers, and that group members both give and seek help in a climate of support and mutual responsibility (Shapiro, 1977).

Shapiro (1990) also develops the notion of the social work group as a social microcosm:

> ... social work groups, like other types of groups, can be expected to be 'social microcosms' in that prevailing structures and dilemmas in the area of social relations will be reflected. Relationships in the group can be seen to be embedded in the 'current social, intergroup and interpersonal crises'. Social, political, ideological, and cultural processes in contemporary society enter into concrete forms of human relationships in all of their manifestations, and in substantial ways are mediated through the frames of reference carried with them by members into groups or evoked in members by the group experience (5).

This underlying notion of groups as social microcosms is also the central tenet for engagement and change within social group work. Social work groups exist as social microcosms and, therefore, have the capacity to change individuals as well as society.

SPECIALIZATION AND DIVERSIFICATION: SOME PRACTICE EXAMPLES FROM THE CANADIAN LITERATURE

The 1990s were a time of tremendous change in the needs and situations of the Canadian population. The economic crisis and subsequent severe cuts in social programs disproportionately affected disadvantaged groups, rendering them even more vulnerable. Unemployment amongst the middle class defined a newer vulnerable population, one which traditionally has not been viewed as "disadvantaged." New populations, such as refugees, women and children fleeing domestic violence, and de-institutionalized psychiatric patients, joined the ranks of the excluded (Home, 1996).

The Canadian literature illustrates the way in which Canadian theorists and practitioners have responded to social change as reflected in shifting population demographics and emerging social needs. Adaptations of traditional models of social group work practice have addressed current concerns of a broad range of populations.

A review of the literature indicates the following diverse and multi-dimensional approaches to Canadian social group work practice: groups for institutionalized and non-institutionalized elderly (Kirsh and Edelson, 1987; McNicoll and Christensen, 1995; Singer, et al. 1988; Sulman, et al. 1986); groups in health care (Bothwell and Eisenberg, 1987; Clarke, 1987; Hamlet and Read, 1990; Israel-Ikeman and Rotholz, 1987; Levitt and Lewis, 1995; Moffat and Kay, 1992; groups for women, including groups for abused women (Breton, 1979, 1988; Breton and Nosko, 1997; de Jong and Gorey, 1996; Home, 1988; Lawlor, 1992); groups for abusive mothers (Lovell, et al., 1992); groups for lesbian women (Travers, 1992, 1995); womens' groups for social change (Home, 1981; 1991); groups for male batterers (Caplan and Thomas, 1995; Currie, 1983; Farley and Magill, 1988; Nosko and Wallace, 1988; Palmer, et al, 1992); multi-family and family support groups (Brown and Shields, 1992; Cassano, 1989a, 1989b; Home and Darveau-Fournier, 1990, 1995; Power, 1988;

Stokes and Gillis, 1995); neighbourhood support groups for child abuse prevention (Fuchs and Costes, 1992); groups for offenders (Wright, 1993, 1997); groups for adolescent sexual offenders (Helde, 1995); group work with Caribbean youth (Glasgow and Gouse-Sheese, 1995); support groups for life stresses (Cohn, 1987; Reynolds and Jones, 1992; Rodway, 1992; Warren, 1987); groups for adult children of alcoholics (Efron and Moir, 1996); workforce transformation groups (Gladstone and Reynolds, 1997); and groups for HIV education and support (Rivers, 1992).

The literature is generally descriptive in nature, problem-focused, population-specific, and favours the view that social group work results in positive outcomes for a variety of populations in a wide range of life situations and, in fact, is the intervention modality of choice. It demonstrates the adaptiveness and creativity of practitioners working within agency contexts that may or may not be supportive of the delivery of group services. Often the populations served are amongst the most vulnerable (e.g., abused children and women, the frail elderly, and seriously ill individuals). Themes of social support, mutual-aid, competence-building, the value of educational components, and the mastering of specific skills permeate the literature. A variety of group structures were cited, including time-limited, open-ended, closed, and semi-structured.

A range of practice from limited uni-dimensional to multi-dimensional groups is described. Those writings that demonstrated a multi-dimensional approach to social group work practice reflected work with the individual, the interactional, and the societal levels. Multi-dimensional social group work practice reflects multi-purpose, multi-bonding amongst members, the capacity of the group experience to influence various phases of the members' lives, and a member-focused group with assistance from the worker to achieve mutually-developed goals.

Three studies of social work practice with groups in Quebec (Home and Darveau-Fournier, 1982; Paquet-Deehy, et al., 1985; Turcotte and Lindsay, 1995) concluded that within the commonalities of social group work practice, is a diversity of group goals, populations served, service settings, worker roles, and structure. A typology of social work practice with groups was identified: personal change groups, development groups, and social change groups. These group types were analyzed along four dimensions: the intervention process, group structure and influence, group goals, and worker and member roles.

The diversity of Canadian social group work was also illustrated in Mesbur's (1996) informal study of thirty-two social agencies in Metropolitan Toronto. Ninety groups illustrated trends in the pattern of group service types and delivery that are also reflected in the Canadian literature. Similar to Turcotte and Lindsay's (1995) findings, most of the groups were of a short duration (sixteen weeks or less) with the majority meeting for ten to sixteen weeks. In Mesbur's study, open-ended and time-limited groups were equally valid options, while Turcotte and Lindsay found that more than one-half of the groups were closed. Both studies revealed an overwhelming trend toward support and personal development, with social action groups almost non-existent.

Most recently, the program of the 22nd Annual International Symposium of the Association for the Advancement of Social Work with Groups, held in Toronto, Ontario in October 2000, reaffirmed this profile of group work practice in Canada. The symposium theme, *Social Work with Groups: Social Justice Through Personal, Community and Societal Change*, resonated for participants, with over fifty papers and workshops presented by Canadian practitioners and academics. Presentation themes still highlighted a problem-focused and population-specific approach to social group work; however, an increase in the number of groups focused on various aspects of diversity and capacity-building provides hope that social group work in Canada is beginning to move back to its traditional mandate (Altimira, 2000; Blum & Bellamy, 2000; Cato & Charles-Fridal, 2000; Fay, 2000; Goodman, 2000; Green, Tilly, & Lemen, 2000; MacDiarmid, 2000; Maurice, 2000; McNicoll, 2000; Moffat, 2000; Paoletti & King, 2000). Reflected, also, are innovative approaches to practice, including online computer groups (Neilson, 2000; Nicholas, 2000); meal-planning and cooking groups (Mishna & Muskat, 2000; Moldolfsky & Devor, 2000); and adopted children and their families (Reid & Wattie, 2000; Streeter & Fenton, 2000).

Summary

The specialized social work groups as described in the Canadian literature could be viewed as a divergence from group work's traditional mandate of unique societal engagement toward specialized clinical issues. Workers are faced with an increasing number of populations to serve who have major deficits of ego functioning, who are experiencing extreme social fragmentation in their lives, and who are victimized by the lack of social supports and decreasing financial assistance from government sources.

Multiple and intersecting elements of social group work practice and a social justice agenda were reflected in the 22nd Annual International Symposium of AASWG. Canadian presentations consistently identified the common context for struggle faced by disadvantaged and oppressed populations, promoting a greater focus on empowerment and social action through innovative and creative approaches to social group work practice.

COMMON ELEMENTS OF SOCIAL GROUP WORK PRACTICE

Current conceptual frameworks for social group work practice:

> offer a core set of interlocking values and concepts that give group work its unique identity and integrity as a social work method. The myriad frameworks in social work with groups are joined by adherence to (1) a systemic perspective, (2) an understanding of group dynamics, (3) common concepts of intervention, and (4) processes important to a sequence of intervention (Schopler and Galinsky, 1995, 1133).

These values and concepts are essential to today's practitioners, for ignoring one may be to the detriment of the needs of the group and the group members. Eclecticism in its most positive sense may assist practitioners in making the most effective intervention choice for a particular group. What is critical is that the practitioner be well-versed in social group work theory, be grounded in the humanistic and democratic values of social group work, and be guided by the purpose of the group and the needs of the members. This then allows the practitioner to differentially apply specialized knowledge and skill to each group situation and avoid rigid adherence to one approach. Shapiro (1990) takes the position

> that within any 'broad-range model', frames of reference with regard to relationship-types, group-types, and group development types vary widely in both content and context, and that group structures and developmental processes may vary accordingly. Social group workers have a particular responsibility—and opportunity—to help members engage sensitively with both the content and context of their frames of reference and, through this engagement, to shape the structure and development of their own group as a 'person/group/structure-sensitive' task (18).

TYPES OF GROUPS

It is the purpose that determines whether groups are formed as treatment or task groups. Purpose will guide the planning process, from group composition, structure, and activities to worker role. As defined by Toseland and Rivas (1995),

> the term treatment group is used to signify a group whose major purpose is to meet members' socio-emotional needs.... In contrast, the term task group is used to signify any group in which the major purpose is neither intrinsically nor immediately linked to the needs of the members of the group. In task groups, the overriding purpose is to accomplish a mandate and complete the work for which the group was convened (14).

It is important to acknowledge and value the contribution of both treatment and task groups as part of our repertoire of social work with groups. Demand for group services within agency contexts, the increasing pressures for interdisciplinary collaboration in treatment and task teams, consultation and training roles with self-help groups, and our ability to adapt to new professional roles require practitioners to apply their knowledge of social group work practice in ways that will not only result in effective service, but will also further our conceptualization of practice with groups.

INTERVENTION PROCESSES

Underlying all social group work practice is a basic core of knowledge, values, and techniques. Emanating from need and purpose, all interventions with groups require that the worker attend to the following intervention processes: composition, structure, timing, assessment, goal setting and contracting, programming, evaluation, and ending (Schopler and Galinsky, 1995; Shulman, 1992). A solid foundation of small group theory, including stages of group development, role theory, communication/interaction, norms, cohesion, and the development of group culture, contributes to the practitioners' ability to make strategic choices as they work with their groups (Brown, 1991).

In groups where mutual aid is fostered and is considered an important goal, the worker must consider the theoretical basis for conceptualizing groups as mutual-aid systems and using these concepts in all aspects of the group (Glassman & Kates, 1990; Steinberg, 1997). This includes group-specific interventions to promote and foster mutual aid through goal-setting, democratic participation, problem-solving, use of authority, developing common ground, and acknowledging and working with differences.

COMPOSITION

Composition "...refers to the selection and modification of the membership of the group system" (Schopler and Galinsky, 1995, 1135). Group size, heterogeneity and homogeneity of descriptive and behavioural attributes of group members all must be considered. The determination of which characteristics to consider as important will vary with each group and will be guided by its purpose (Shulman, 1992). There are no prescriptions for group composition. The extent of members' pain, the common denominator that brings people together for a particular purpose, may override wide differences in age, ethnicity, and ability.

The purposeful selection of group members in pre-group planning plays an important role in mutual-aid groups. Thus, composition includes factors of goodness of fit between the needs of the potential members and the group's purpose; capacity to communicate and inter-act, and ways in which commonalities and differences will enhance group members; and ability to make connections with one another (Steinberg, 1997).

STRUCTURE

A group must be structured so as to enable group members to meet their needs and to assist the group to achieve its purpose (Toseland and Rivas, 1995). "Structure refers to the planned, systematic, time-limited interventions used to help clients change in desired directions" (Toseland and Rivas, 1995, 240). During the formation period of a group, structures must be established to promote group development (Garvin, 1997). Communication structure needs to "become one in which the maximum numbers of members participate and in which members respond to each other" (Garvin, 1997, 86). Sociometric structure, power structure, leadership structure, and role structure require the worker to encourage participation amongst all group members and to address the manifestations of these structures as they impact upon the group's beginnings and later upon the group's ongoing development (Garvin, 1997).

TIMING

Timing refers not only to the number of times a group will meet and the length of meetings, but also to the strategic use of time as an intervention technique (Alissi and Casper, 1985). As Shulman (1992) notes, the worker must "draw on common sense, the experience of the agency, and the literature, and all must be related to the group purpose" (306).

Time is a specialized aspect of structure. The importance of time to effective group work practice needs to be underscored. Often, decisions regarding the length of time for a particular group are not made based upon research and practice wisdom, but are framed in relation to trends and "fads." While time-limited methods have been shown to be effective for many types of populations and problems, there are some needs which require longer term groups (Toseland and Rivas, 1995).

ASSESSMENT

Assessment is ongoing throughout the life of the group and requires that the practitioner focus simultaneously on the individual members in the group and the group as a whole. Assessment is both a process and a product and varies according to the type of group being conducted. It requires attention to the strengths and deficits of the group, the individual members, and the environment (Toseland and Rivas, 1995).

> Assessment of the members in the group makes use of the practitioner's perceptions and empathy—as well as knowledge and values—to guide the use of techniques.... The practitioner considers the stage of development of the group, along with salient group needs and member commonalities that enable cohesion (Glassman and Kates, 1990, 215).

Glassman and Kates (1990) emphasize the importance of stage theory in understanding member behaviour. They suggest that "change in member behaviour is in some ways shaped by the stage of development the group is in, and that member behaviour is not to be viewed apart from the stage context" (216). As Garvin (1997) notes, there is no consensus amongst group work theorists regarding theoretical frameworks for assessment. Group workers will therefore "use behavioral, ego psychological, role, or other theoretical systems in the same manner as other social workers" (78). Toseland and Rivas (1995) caution that group workers may tend to focus on content of members' participation rather than on the group process and, like Glassman and Kates, urge practitioners to assess group process as well as the group's environment.

UNDERSTANDING PURPOSE AND GOAL SETTING

Understanding purpose and goal setting are interrelated and guide intervention. Goals are defined as "the ends that members pursue individually and as a group. Goals are formulated through a process of finding common ground among the various expectations of the members, the agency and the social worker" (Schopler and Galinsky, 1995, 1135). Goals provide the standard by which progress in the group is assessed.

A humanistic, interactional view of social group work requires that the practitioner consider the goal-setting process as the necessary interaction between the member, the worker, the group, the agency, and the environment.

Steinberg (1997) notes that developing a group purpose speaks to one of the major obstacles of mutual aid. A clear conceptualization of purpose is crucial for group development, to help members identify a common cause and begin their work together to act as a "reference point for carrying out and evaluating process and progress (p. 55).

CONTENT

Programming refers to the "planned use of action-oriented experiences to facilitate the group's work together" (Schopler and Galinsky, 1995, 1136). The use of programming is one of the distinguishing features of social group work practice and is an important part of the group's enhancement and transformation of social functioning (Glassman and Kates, 1990). Middleman's (1982) work on the use of activity in social group work highlights the richness of creative expression through activity and play. Program activities provide a medium through which to assess members' functioning and as a means of specific therapeutic intervention (Toseland and Rivas, 1995). Shulman (1992) suggests that "to dichotomize 'talking' and 'doing' is a mistake" (561). A "mixed transactional model," whereby all mediums of activity are included as "exchanges in which people give to and take from each other" (Shulman, 1992, 562) should guide the interventions of the social group work practitioner.

Thus, content is the means toward achieving the group's purpose (Kurland & Salmon, 1998). Frequently, group purpose is confused with content, resulting in confusion on the part of group members and lack of focus on the part of the worker. Content refers to the "what" of an activity, while purpose refers to the "why" of an activity.

EVALUATION AND ENDING

Evaluation is an ongoing process throughout the life of the group, a mutual process between worker and members that focuses on both process and outcome. Toseland and Rivas (1995) describe four broad types of evaluation in social group work practice: (1) planning a group, (2) monitoring a group, (3) developing a group, and (4) testing the effectiveness and efficiency of a group method (368). Evaluations may be formal or informal, but with the increasing push for accountability and empirically validated practice, there is considerable pressure for group workers to become practitioner-researchers (Toseland and Rivas, 1995). Sullivan (1995) recognizes the richness of our practice wisdom, promoting the value of qualitative research through "ethnographic inquiry" or "ethnographic content analysis."

Steinberg (1997) suggests that evaluation is complex and requires a two-pronged approach, which attends to how the group process reflects mutual aid in action and how group members feel they were helped as a result of that process. "It is the personal characteristics of the group itself—the personalities of the members, their unique needs and strengths, the nature of the group's purpose, the challenges it has overcome in its group-building process, the specific nature of the help that has taken place, and the skill of the practitioner—that will provide the most meaningful food for thought" (Steinberg, 1997, p. 181).

CONCLUSIONS

Emerging from a rich tradition of over 75 years, social group work practice in Canada is on the threshold of a new era. From the early group work methods of the 1920s, focusing on recreation and education as primary goals to enrich community life, to the 1940s and 1950s when social group work was employed as a method of practice for populations with particular, problematic needs in hospitals, mental health centres, public welfare agencies, and residential institutions (Sullivan, 1996), to the model building of the 1960s and 1970s, and to the diversification and specialization of the 1980s and 1990s, our history and our practice have remained inextricably intertwined. As Garvin (1997) states:

> Group work, as a social work method, has evolved and changed in the three-quarter century since its origin. These changes result from altered circumstances, increased knowledge, and an expansion in the number and variety of practice settings. A consensus has developed during this period as to what constitutes social work with groups, although different practice models have been created and coexist within this broad consensus (1).

With models at hand, we are challenged to continue to expand our conceptual frameworks and develop rigorous research approaches to examine group work processes and outcomes in order to build theoretical foundations based on empirical data (Schopler and Galinsky, 1995). Adaptiveness, flexibility, and inclusiveness should characterize our practice as we respond to current and emerging practice conditions.

> In highlighting aspects of social group work, group therapy, and social work with groups, it is not clear whether one is putting a period on an era of history in social work practice—precious, unique, and influential—or whether one is placing an asterisk on social work with groups to signify a new aura of attention that will lead to a broad, dynamic, and informed practice with groups by social workers (Middleman and Goldberg, 1987, 714).

The power of the group in the helping process is fundamental to social group work practice. The collective force of interaction, the focus on strengths and capabilities, and the promotion of social well-being through mutual aid provide practitioners with unique and creative opportunities for social group work intervention.

REFERENCES

Alissi, A. and Casper, M. (Eds.).(1985). *Time as a factor in group-work: time-limited group experiences*. New York: Haworth.

Altimira, I. (2000). From parenting to capacity building: immigrant women take charge. Paper presented at the 22nd Annual International Symposium of the Association for the Advancement of Social Work with Groups. Toronto, ON.

Balgopal, P.R. and Vassil, T.V. (1983). *Groups in social work: an ecological perspective*. New York: Macmillan Publishing.

Berman-Rossi, T. (1993). The tasks and skills of the social worker across stages of group development. In S. Wenocur, P. Ephross, T. Vassil, and R. Verghese (Eds.). *Social work with groups: expanding horizons* (pp. 69–81). New York: Haworth.

Berman-Rossi, T. & Kelly, T. (1999). Advancing stages of group development theory: the case of institutionalized older persons. *Social Work with Groups, 22*(2/3), 119–128.

Blum, E. & Bellany, K.J. (2000). Laughter & language: Group work with immigrant women. Paper presented at the 22nd Annual International Symposium of the Association for the Advancement of Social Work with Groups. Toronto, ON.

Bothwell, M. and Eisenberg, C. (1987). Planned collectivity: an entity that works for cardiac patients. In N. Lang and J. Sulman (Eds.). *Collectivity in social group work: concept and practice* (pp. 69–79). New York: Haworth.

Breton, M. (1979). Nurturing abused and abusive mothers: the hairdressing group. *Social Work with Groups, 2*(2), 161–174.

Breton, M. (1985). Reaching and engaging people: issues and practice principles. *Social Work with Groups, 8*(3), 7–21.

Breton, M. (1988). The need for mutual-aid groups in a drop-in for homeless women: the sistering case. *Social Work with Groups, 11*(4), 47–61.

Breton, M. (1990). Learning from social group work traditions. *Social Work with Groups, 13*(3), pp. 21–33.

Breton, M. (1992). Liberation theology, group work, and the right of the poor and oppressed to participate in the life of the community. In J.A. Garland (Ed.). *Group work reaching out: people, places and power* (pp. 257–269). New York: Haworth.

Breton, M. (1994). On the meaning of empowerment and empowerment-oriented social work practice. *Social Work with Groups, 17*(3), 23–37.

Breton, M. (1995). The potential for social action in groups. *Social Work with Groups, 18*(2/3), 5–13.

Breton, M. (1997). Empowerment practice in a post-empowerment era. Manuscript submitted for publication, University of Toronto.

Breton, M. and Nosko, A. (1997). Group work with women who have experienced abuse. In G.L. Greif and P. Ephross (Eds.). *Group Work with Populations at Risk* (pp. 134–146). New York: Oxford University Press.

Brown, L. (1991). *Groups for growth and change*. White Plains, N.Y.: Longman Publishing.

Brown, R. and Shields, R. (1992). Making foster group homes work: using the group to support foster parents. In D.F. Fike and B. Rittner (Eds.). *Working from strengths: the essence of group work* (pp. 227–242). Miami: Center for Group Work Studies.

Caplan, T. and Thomas, H. (1995). Safety and comfort, content and process: facilitating open group work with men who batter. *Social Work with Groups*, *18*(2/3), 33–51.

Cassano, D.R. (1989a). Multi-family group therapy in social work practice—Part I. *Social Work with Groups*, *12*(1), 3–14.

Cassano, D.R. (1989b). Multi-family therapy group: research on patterns of interaction—Part II. *Social Work with Groups*, *12*(1), 15–39.

Cato, C. & Charles-Fridal, F. (2000). Working with "at-risk" black youth. Paper presented at the 22nd Annual International Symposium of the Association for the Advancement of Social Work with Groups. Toronto, ON.

Clarke, E. (1987). The use of single session collectivities with families of spina bifida children. In N. Lang and J. Sulman (Eds.). *Collectivity in social group work: concept and practice* (pp.103–111). New York: Haworth.

Cohn, S. (1987). Themes in group work with separated individuals. *Social Work with Groups*, *10*(1), 49–60.

Currie, D.W. (1983). A Toronto model. In B.G. Reed and C.D. Garvin (Eds.). *Groupwork with women/groupwork with men* (pp. 179–188). New York: Haworth.

de Jong, T. and Gorey, K. (1996). Short-term versus long-term group work with female survivors of childhood sexual abuse: a brief meta-analytic review. *Social Work with Groups*, *19*(1), 19–27.

Efron, D.E. and Moir, R. (1996). Short-term co-led intensive group work with children of alcoholics. *Social Work with Groups*, *19*(3/4), 117–129.

Evans, D. and Shaw, W. (1993). A social work model for latency-aged children from violent homes. *Social Work with Groups*, *16*(1/2), 97–116.

Falck, H. (1993, October). *Central characteristics of social work with groups—a socio-cultural analysis*. Paper presented at the 15th Annual Meeting, Association for the Advancement of Social Work with Groups, New York, N.Y.

Farley, D. and Magill, J. (1988). An evaluation of a group program for men who batter. In G.S. Getzel (Ed.). *Violence: prevention and treatment in groups* (pp. 53–65). New York: Haworth.

Fay, J. (2000). You can't check your privilege (or power) at the door: lessons in cross-sectoral social justice group work. Paper presented at the 22nd Annual International Symposium of the Association for the Advancement of Social Work with Groups. Toronto, ON.

Fuchs, D. and Costes, T. (1992). Building on strengths of family and neighbourhood social network ties for the prevention of child maltreatment: a groupwork approach. In D.F. Fike and B. Rittner (Eds.). *Working from strengths: the essence of group work* (pp. 191–210). Miami: Center for Group Work Studies.

Garvin, C.D. (1987). *Contemporary group work* (2nd ed.). Englewood Cliffs, N.J: Prentice Hall.

Garvin, C.D. (1997). *Contemporary group work* (3rd ed.). Boston: Allyn and Bacon.

Gitterman, A. (1989). Building mutual support in groups. *Social Work with Groups, 12*(2), 5–21.

Gitterman, A. & Shulman, L. (Eds.). (1994). *Mutual aid groups and the life cycle.* Itasca, IL: Peacock.

Gitterman, A. and Shulman, L. (Eds.) (1985). *The legacy of William Schwartz: group practice as shared interaction*. New York: Haworth.

Gladstone, J. and Reynolds, T. (1997). Single session group work intervention in response to employee stress during workforce transformation. *Social Work with Groups, 20*(1), 33–49.

Glasgow, G.F. and Gouse-Sheese, J. (1995). Themes of rejection and abandonment in group work with Caribbean adolescents. *Social Work with Groups, 17*(4), 3–27.

Glassman, U. and Kates, L. (1990). *Group work: a humanistic approach.* Newbury Park: Sage.

Goodman, D. (2000). From treatment to social action: an adolescents-in-care empowerment group—a road less travelled. Paper presented at the 22nd Annual International Symposium of the Association for the Advancement of Social Work with Groups. Toronto, ON.

Green, J., Tilley, A., Urback, M., & Lemen, C. (2000). Group work practice with women who are disadvantaged and at risk: changing populations and group work. Paper presented at the 22nd Annual International Symposium of the Association for the Advancement of Social Work with Groups. Toronto, ON.

Hamlet, E. and Read, S. (1990). Caregiver education and support group: a hospital based group experience. *Journal of Gerontological Social Work, 15*(1/2).

Helde, K. (1995). Sexual offenders group treatment: The ESAT experience in Toronto, Canada. In R. Kurland and R. Salmon (Eds.). *Group work practice in a troubled society* (pp. 177–188). New York: Haworth.

Home, A. (1985). Intervention with groups. In S. Yelaja (Ed.). *Social work practice in Canada* (pp. 69–87). Toronto: Prentice-Hall.

Home, A. (1988). Les groupes de femmes: Outils de changement et de développement. *Service Social, 37*(1–2), 61–85.

Home, A. (1991). Mobilizing womens's strengths of social change: the group connection. *Social Work with Groups, 14*, 153–173.

Home, A. (1996). Réussir l'intervention de groupe dans un contexte difficile: mission impossible? *Intervention, 102*, 20–33.

Home, A. and Darveau-Fournier, L. (1982). A study of social work practice with groups. *Social Work with Groups, 5*(3), 19–34.

Home. A. and Darveau-Fournier, L. (1990). Facing the challenge of developing group services for high-risk families. *Groupwork, 3*(3), 236–248.

Home, A. and Darveau-Fournier, L. (1995). Respite child care: a support and empowerment strategy for families in a high-risk community. In R. Hess and W. Stark (Eds.). *International approaches to prevention in mental health and human services* (pp. 69–88). New York: Haworth.

Hurley, D.J. 1984). Resistance and work in adolescent groups. *Social Work with Groups, 7*(4), 71–81.

Irving, A., Parsons, H., and Bellamy, D. (Eds.). (1995). *Neighbours: three social settlements in downtown Toronto.* Toronto: Canadian Scholars' Press.

Israel-Ikeman, B. and Rotholz, T. (1987). The single-session waiting room group. In J. Lassner, K. Powell and E. Finnegan (Eds.). *Social group work: competence and values in practice* (pp. 113–125). New York: Haworth.

Kirsh, E. and Edelson, J. (1987). Collectivities in a minimal care residential setting: The residents' floor meeting. In N. Lang and J. Sulman (Eds.). *Collectivity in social group work: concept and practice* (pp. 81–89). New York: Haworth.

Kurland, R. & Salmon, R. (1998). *Teaching a methods course in social work with groups.* Alexandria, VA: Council on Social Work Education.

Lang, N. (1972). A broad-range model of practice in the social work group. *Social Service Review, 46*(1), 76–89.

Lang, N. (1978). The selection of the small group for service delivery: an exploration of the literature on group use in social work. *Social Work with Groups, 1*(3), 247–263.

Lang, N. (1979a). A comparative examination of therapeutic uses of groups in social work and in adjacent human service professions: Part I. The literature from 1955–1968. *Social Work with Groups, 2*(2), 101–115.

Lang, N. (1979b). A comparative examination of therapeutic uses of groups in social work and in adjacent human service professions: Part II. The literature from 1969–1978. *Social Work with Groups, 2*(3), 197–220.

Lang, N. (1981). Some defining characteristics of the social work group: unique social form. In S.L. Abels and P. Abels (Eds.). *Social work with groups: proceedings 1979 symposium* (pp. 18–50). Louisville, Kentucky: Committee for the Advancement of Social Work with Groups.

Lang, N. (1986). Social work practice in small social forms: identifying collectivity. In N. Lang and J. Sulman (Eds.). *Collectivity in social group work: concept and practice* (pp. 7–31). New York: Haworth.

Lawlor, D.E. (1992). Strength within a women's support group for survivors of childhood sexual abuse. In D.F. Fike and B. Rittner (Eds.). *Working from strengths: the essence of group work* (pp. 243–256). Miami: Center for Group Work Studies.

Lee, J. (1987). Social Work with oppressed populations: Jane Addams won't you please come home? In J. Lassner, K. Powell E. and Finnegan (Eds.). *Social work with groups: competence and values* (pp. 1–16). New York: Haworth.

Lee, J.A.B. (1994). *The empowerment approach to social work practice.* New York: Columbia University Press.

Levitt, Z. and Lewis, E.I. (1995). Treating the chronically ill in an outpatient hospital setting: does group work work? In M.D. Feit, J.H. Ramey, J.S. Wodarski, and A.R. Mann (Eds.). (1995). *Capturing the power of diversity* (pp. 173–183). New York: Haworth.

Lovell, M.L., Reid, K., Richey, C.A. (1992). Social support training for abusive mothers. In J.A. Garland (Ed.). *Group work reaching out: people, places and power* (pp. 95–107). New York: Haworth.

MacDiarmid, A. (2000). Group work in a multi-cultural environment. Paper presented at the 22nd Annual International Symposium of the Association for the Advancement of Social Work with Groups. Toronto, ON.

Maurice, J. (2000). Rebalancing injustices experienced by Aboriginal persons through social work with groups. Paper presented at the 22nd Annual International Symposium of the Association for the Advancement of Social Work with Groups. Toronto, ON.

McNicoll, P. (2000). Current innovations in social work with groups to address issues of social justice. Paper presented at the 22nd Annual International Symposium of the Association for the Advancement of Social Work with Groups. Toronto, ON.

McNicoll, P. and Christensen, C. (1995). Making changes and making sense: social group work with Vietnamese older people. In R. Kurland and R. Salmon (Eds.). *Group work practice in a troubled society* (pp. 101–116). New York: Haworth.

Mesbur, E.S. (1996), with Marra, F. and Webb, C. Survey of social group work in Metropolitan Toronto. Unpublished raw data.

Mesbur, E.S. and Jacobs, J. (1989). *Understanding and working with groups.* Toronto: Ryerson Polytechnic University.

Middleman, R. (1982). *The non-verbal method in working with groups: the use of activity in teaching, counseling, and therapy.* An enlarged edition. Hebron, CT: Practitioners Press.

Middleman, R. and Goldberg, G. (1987). Social work practice with groups. In *Encyclopedia of Social Work* (8th ed.). A. Minihan (Ed.): 714–729. Silver Spring, M.D. Practice with Groups National Association of Social Workers.

Middleman, R. and Wood, G.G. (1990). *Skills for direct practice in social work.* New York: Columbia University Press.

Mishna, F. & Muskat, B. (2000). Food for thought: the use of food in group. Paper presented at the 22nd Annual International Symposium of the Association for the Advancement of Social Work with Groups. Toronto, ON.

Moffat, P. (2000). The last chapter: group work with family carers in a chronic care hospital. Paper presented at the 22nd Annual International Symposium of the Association for the Advancement of Social Work with Groups. Toronto, ON.

Moffat, P. and Kay, N. (1992). The new patient mix: group work and chronic disorders in an acute care hospital. In B.L. Stempler, and M.S. Glass (Eds.), with Savinelli, C.M. *Social group work today and tomorrow: moving from theory to advanced training and practice* (pp. 57–69). New York: Haworth.

Moldofsky, Z. & Devor, S. (2000). Meals made easy: a group program at a food bank for parents of young children. Paper presented at the 22nd Annual International Symposium of the Association for the Advancement of Social Work with Groups. Toronto, ON.

Neilson, B. (2000). Group work without walls: an international computer group in the health care field enables social justice for patients with bladder exstrophy. Paper presented at the 22nd Annual International Symposium of the Association for the Advancement of Social Work with Groups. Toronto, ON.

Northen, H. (1988). *Social work with groups* (2nd. ed.). New York: Columbia University Press.

Nosko, A. and Wallace, B. (1988). Group work with abusive men: a multidimensional model. In G.S. Getzel (Ed.). *Violence: prevention and treatment in groups* (pp. 33–51). New York: Haworth.

Palmer, S.E., Brown, R.A., and Barrera, M. (1992). Group treatment program for abusive husbands: long-term evaluation. *American Journal of Orthopsychiatry, 62*(2), 276–283.

Paoletti, D. & King, K. (2000). The GAP group (gay and positive): transformative group work with HIV+ gay and bisexual youth. Paper presented at the 22nd Annual International Symposium of the Association for the Advancement of Social Work with Groups. Toronto, ON.

Papell, C. and Rothman, B. (1966). Social group work models: possession and heritage. *Journal of Education for Social Work, 2*(2), 66–77.

Papell, C. and Rothman, B. (1980). Relating the mainstream model of social work with groups to group psychotherapy and the structured group approach. *Social Work with Groups, 3*(2), 5–23.

Paquet-Deehy, A., Hopmeyer, E., Home, A., and Kislowicz, L. (1985). A typology of social work practice with groups. *Social Work with Groups*, *8*(1), 65–78.

Pernell, R. (1986). Empowerment and social group work. In M. Parnes (Ed.). *Innovations in social group work: feedback from practice to theory*. New York: Haworth, 107–117.

Power, R., (1988). Differential models of social work groups with family violence. In G.S. Getzel (Ed.). *Violence: prevention and treatment in groups* (pp. 9–31). New York: Haworth.

Reid, D. & Wattie, L. (2000). Negotiating the minefield: a group to help adopted teens and their families survive adolescence. Paper presented at the 22nd Annual International Symposium of the Association for the Advancement of Social Work with Groups. Toronto, ON.

Reynolds, T. and Jones, G. (1992). Trauma debriefings: a one-session group model. In B.L. Stempler and M.S. Glass (Eds.), with Savinelli, C.M. In *Social group work today and tomorrow: moving from theory to advanced training and practice* (pp. 129–139). New York: Haworth.

Rivers, P.E. (1992). Being non-deliberative on "A hot winter's night": confessions of a creative practitioner. In B.L. Stempler and M.S. Glass (Eds.), with Savinelli, C.M. *Social group work today and tomorrow: moving from theory to advanced training and practice* (119–127). New York: Haworth Press.

Rodway, M.R. (1992). Self-examination of loneliness: a group approach. *Social Work with Groups*, *15*(1), 69–79.

Schopler, J. and Galinsky, M. (1984). Meeting practice needs: conceptualizing the open-ended group. *Social Work with Groups*, *7*(2), 3–19.

Schopler, J.H. and Galinsky, M.J. (1995). Group practice overview. In *Encyclopedia of Social Work II*, pp.1129–1142. Washington, D.C.: National Association of Social Workers.

Schwartz, W. (1985). The group work tradition and social work practice. In A. Gitterman and L. Shulman (Eds.). *The legacy of William Schwartz: group practice as shared interaction* (pp. 7–27). New York: Haworth.

Shapiro, B.Z. (1986). The weak-tie collectivity: a network perspective. In N. Lang and J. Sulman (Eds.). *Collectivity in social group work: concept and practice* (pp. 113–125). New York: Haworth.

Shapiro, B.Z. (1977). Mutual helping—a neglected theme in social work practice theory. *Canadian Journal of Social Work Education*, *3*(1), 33–44.

Shapiro, B.Z. (1990). The social work group as a social microcosm: "frames of reference" revisited. *Social Work with Groups*, *13*(2), 5–21.

Shapiro, B.Z. (1991). Social action, the group and society. In A. Vinik and M. Levin (Eds.). *Social action in group work* (pp. 7–21). New York: Haworth.

Shulman, L. (1979). *The skills of helping individuals and groups*. Itasca, Ill.: F.E. Peacock Publishers.

Shulman, L. (1991). *Interactional social work practice: toward an empirical theory*. Itasca, Ill.: F.E. Peacock Publishers.

Shulman, L. (1992). *The skills of helping individuals, families, and groups* (3rd ed.). Itasca, Illinois: F.E. Peacock Publishers, Inc.

Singer, C., Wells, L., Basu, R., Szewczyk, L., and Polgar, A. (1988). Social action oriented groups in institutions for the elderly: a theoretical framework. In M. Leiderman, M.L. Birnbaum, and B. Dazzo (Eds.). *Roots and new frontiers in social group work* (pp. 177–189). New York: Haworth.

Steinberg, D.M. (1997). *The mutual-aid approach to working with groups.* Northvale, NJ: Jason Aronson Inc.

Stokes, N. and Gillis, J. (1995). Effective treatment strategies with adult incest survivors: utilizing therapeutic group work methods within the context of the immediate family. In R. Kurland and R. Salmon (Eds.). *Group work practice in a troubled society* (pp. 189–201). New York: Haworth.

Streeter, B.A. & Fenton, P. (2000). Group work, social justice, and the adoption community. Paper presented at the 22nd Annual International Symposium of the Association for the Advancement of Social Work with Groups. Toronto, ON.

Sullivan, N. (1996). A qualitative research study of the development, nature, and significance of 'family-like' features in a social work group. Unpublished doctoral dissertation: University of Toronto, Toronto, Ontario.

Sullivan, N. (1995). Who owns the group? The role of worker control in the development of a group: a qualitative research study of practice. *Social Work with Groups, 18*(2/3), 15–32.

Sulman, J., Fletcher, J., Gayler, C., and Sokolsky, A. (1986). A collectivity of impaired elderly in an acute care hospital: Practice and research. In N. Lang and J. Sulman (Eds.). *Collectivity in social group work: concept and practice* (pp. 59–67). New York: Haworth.

Sundel, M., Glasser, P., Sarri, R., and Vinter, R. (Eds.). (1985). *Individual change through small groups* (2nd. ed.). New York: Free Press.

Travers, A., (1992). Redefining adult identity: a coming out group for lesbians. In B.L. Stempler and M.S. Glass (Eds.), with C.M. Savinelli. *Social group work today and tomorrow: moving from theory to advanced training and practice* (pp. 103–118). New York: Haworth.

Travers, A. (1995). Adversity, diversity, and empowerment: feminist group work with women in poverty. In R. Kurland and R. Salmon (Eds.). *Group work practice in a troubled society* (pp. 139–156). New York: Haworth.

Toseland, R. and Rivas, R. (1984). *An introduction to group work practice.* New York: Macmillan.

Toseland, R. and Rivas, R. (1995). *An introduction to group work practice* (2nd ed.). Boston: Allyn and Bacon.

Turcotte, D. and Lindsay, J. (1995). The recent evolution of social work practices with groups in Quebec: a comparative study. Paper presented at the Seventeenth Annual Symposium on the Advancement of Social Work with Groups, San Diego, California, October, 1995.

Warren, P. (1987). The social therapeutic club: a collectivity for ex-psychiatric patients. In N. Lang and J. Sulman (Eds.). *Collectivity in social group work. Concept and Practice* (pp. 91–101). New York: Haworth.

Wright, M.M. (1993). Family-like group in a correctional setting. *Social Work with Groups, 16*(4), 125–135.

Wright, M.M. (1997). Group work with offenders. In G.L. Greif and P.H. Ephross (Eds.). *Group work with populations at risk* (pp. 206–224). New York: Oxford University Press.

COMMUNITY SOCIAL WORK PRACTICE ACROSS CANADA

Ken Banks

INTRODUCTION

For over one hundred years, community work has been a set of practices that has resonated with those social workers who want to facilitate social action for community change. In Canada, the earliest community work traditions were established by church workers and settlement workers in the city cores. Practices were articulated in rural areas as well, over time, and community workers have developed a range of approaches that may be applied to support the strengthening of living conditions wherever there is a need and where there are assets to work with.

In this chapter, we will examine five exemplary contemporary practices. These practices share the three central precepts of community social work: (1) the local identification of need, (2) the local identification of solution, and (3) the mobilization of collective response. The case examples examined here are drawn from sets of community work practice known as (in order of their appearance): (1) community economic development, (2) social animation, (3) participatory research, (4) rural social work, and (5) social support. These are drawn from five regions of Canada, starting with the Maritimes and proceeding to the West.

This book has already dealt with the range of theories and practices that constitute a great deal of social work with individuals and groups in Canada. Community social work practitioners can make use of most of those theories and practices in addition to drawing heavily on consciousness-raising approaches developed in the field of adult education (Freire, 1993). The core practices that constitute community social work are present in all of the following, but each area has its own fingerprint, just as the practitioners have their own ways of organizing these essential practices. So will you, should you decide to become a community social worker.

With the exception of Father Moses Coady of the Antigonish movement, the practitioners whose stories are presented below identify themselves as professional social workers. Dr. Coady was a priest and adult educator, but most of the approaches that he used have been applied throughout the world in the name of community and economic development, so I have no hesitation in including the practices of the Antigonish movement in this chapter. His approach to community economic development and the practices of other notable community workers specializing in social animation, participatory action research, rural social work, or social supports (such as advocacy, self-help, and mutual aid) constitute the foundations of community social work in Canada today. Through these closely related approaches, community social work applies core social work practices in unique ways.

The thing to remember here is that all social workers try to start with an understanding of what the client thinks the problem is. We then draw on both our own and the client's knowledge and experience, exploring possible solutions with a goal of contracting with the client to act on changes that may bring about solutions. The techniques or tools that we use have been described to you throughout this book. They range from assessment to change and evaluation of the outcome, and we all use them, but in community work we apply the tools in order to strengthen collectivity in groups. Here social work tools are used to construct social conditions, such as local cooperation, that are outside the control of one individual.

There are three precepts of community social work practice:

1. The worker identifies locally perceived community needs. Here the community worker uses interview skills and identifies local concerns. It is necessary to gather people together based on common interests and to assess their needs. The community worker will also establish a group and create an enriched environment of new ideas and strategies in the community.

2. The worker identifies locally perceived solutions. Again, using the requisite group-building skills, the worker will encourage groups to discuss needs and identify goals for change. Community workers then support groups in acting on these commonly held goals. Many workers will develop a wagon-wheel (Murray Ross, 1963) model of organization, where a multiplicity of service exists. Where local solutions exist, utilize them; where they do not exist, explore new solutions. Here you can build a broad-based "hub" of people committed to community development and who can attach themselves to tasks that challenge them if such a community association does not already exist. You can also support "spoke" organizations, where related tasks are being addressed. These organizations may be committed to strengthening an existing service to begin a new initiative.

3. A collective response is built. This can take many forms. At the beginning of a project it is almost impossible to predict what communities will produce.

The narratives that follow will give you an idea of the range of action that community groups take.

FIVE REGIONS, FIVE MODELS OF COMMUNITY SOCIAL WORK PRACTICE

All the following models are derived from a broad range of education and psychosocial theory; so I will identify the range of theories and ideas used in these examples of community social work as I go.

The Antigonish movement draws heavily on the literature of adult education. Raising local people's consciousness of the international, corporate cause of their poverty and deprivation in the depression years was a central task of the extension workers of St. Francis Xavier University in Antigonish, Nova Scotia. Building self-esteem with clients is a perennial problem for social workers. The esteem-building study groups organized through the rural regions of Nova Scotia in the 1930s are still nurtured in the 1990s by churches, unions, and other local citizens. They are mobilized by local pride, a strong sense of belonging, and a locally controlled means of improving conditions. (CBC, Dec. 1996)

Model 1: Social Movements for Community Economic Development

Father Coady believed that rural people were often at a disadvantage in the increasingly modern world, because they did not have a liberal education. He saw that massive cultural changes were just surfacing in the 1930s in Nova Scotia and that an exceptional effort was going to have to be made to prepare these farm-based local people to be mutually support-ive in the industrial age. The most effective tool that he saw for that purpose was a cooper-ative study club, organized by St Francis Xavier University extension workers in scores of farming villages in Nova Scotia.

The following is Father Moses Coady's description of the organization of the study clubs:

BOX 25.1	Father Moses Coady and Community Economic Development

The first logical step in this process was for someone to round up the people, so to speak. This involved the mass meeting. After some preliminary advertising, through press and pulpit, the people of a given community were brought together and addressed by a member of the Extension Department. At these first meetings, fundamental, homely philoso-phies were placed before the people. They were shown that man (sic) made progress through the operation of his mind, and that the mind counted much more than muscle. The people were also shown the great possibilities for life around them everywhere, if they would only condition themselves to the point where they could realize them. The story of what common people had done in other parts of the world was told.

The mass meeting features the human personality, and nothing can replace the person as an instrument of the dissemi-nation of knowledge. True, people can be educated by books and the informa-tion they themselves gather, but philos-ophy and ideas come and go by human beings.

Study Clubs:

Out of this general mass meeting, dis-cussion groups or study clubs were formed. Sometimes a whole community would respond enthusiastically. In other places—and this was the general thing—only a few groups would be formed. A leader was selected for each group. He (sic) was not to be a teacher but rather a secretary of the group whose business it was to round up the people, to see that they got the literature and that they attended the meetings. The next step was to get the people who formed the little discussion groups to meet once a month in a larger group called an associated or federated study club. This was done in a belief that the success attending the operations of some little groups would stimulate further interest in the members of all the groups. Furthermore, it was a common meeting ground where people could talk about their difficulties and their problems. It afforded an opportunity for recreation and cultural activities, and it gave the people a chance to hear inspirational speakers who attended these rallies. This direct and purposeful organization of the people is a short-cut to results.

Leadership and Cooperation:

The success of this procedure depended upon a somewhat unknown quantity; the local leader. If he could be found, all would be well. Often he was the clergyman of the community. Sometimes a schoolteacher or other socially-minded individual would come to the fore. There were instances, however, where no such individual was found, but the people themselves successfully applied the technique.

Large Scale Volunteer Movement:

It must be said, however, that, in the experience of the Antigonish movement, clergymen played a big role. Workers from the Department of Agriculture and Fisheries were important to the scheme also. It thus happened that from the very beginning the St. Francis Xavier Extension, which had only two men officially connected with it for field work, had a large staff of hundreds of people scattered all over the country. This fact brought a new enthusiasm to the work. A great social and educational technique was thus accidentally discovered. The idea dawned upon everybody that all over Canada were tens of thousands of free men and women with good education who could be involved in this work. It became clear to the Extension leaders that democracy could survive if its human assets could be organized to work for it. In all past time these human beings had not released their total energy for the good of society (Laidlaw, 1971, 91–92).

The three precepts of community work are implicit in Father Coady's Community Economic Development movement:

1. Identify locally perceived community needs.

   Organize study groups, "a common meeting-ground where people could talk about their difficulties and their problems."

2. Identify locally perceived solutions.

   By meeting with thousands of Nova Scotia people in their home communities, they "accidentally" discovered a social and educational technique that identified local solutions to the problems identified.

3. Build a collective response.

   The Antigonish movement built farming, fishing, and financial cooperatives in the 1930s that are successful areas of the economy of Nova Scotia today.

Community Economic Development (CED) practices were the result of Father Coady's vision that people of no great material wealth could learn to better themselves if they had access to knowledge and worked cooperatively. This worked so well that for a time the Antigonish movement members believed they were on the way to solving world poverty. However, other economies driven by the profit motive have limited the growth of the cooperative CED movements. CED is still encouraged and, in skilled hands, brings propriety to local communities around the world where, for example, government decides to target unemployment with local initiatives.

Next, I will introduce you to social animation, an approach to community work found in Quebec, initiated by Michel Blondin, a social worker.

Model 2: Social Animation

In social animation, where Blondin draws on French applied sociology, a somewhat charismatic worker is needed to rally the local people. Once local issues are determined, field research is organized, and the group participation is focused upon solutions, local autonomy in making change becomes possible. The Catholic Church, United Way, and Quebec government have encouraged social animation to varying degrees over the past thirty years. Paradoxically, other practitioners have noted (Alary, 1987) that this approach receives less support from these dominant interests in Quebec society when participants are most successful in achieving a strong independent voice in local communities. This success leads to motivated, critical, and involved communities of people, an outcome that institutions and democratic governments desire in theory but find hard to tolerate in practice. This paradox is a characteristic that has tempered the popularity of community social work in all jurisdictions over the years (Banks and Mangan, 1999).

The following excerpts are taken from a monograph that Michel Blondin wrote on social animation:

BOX 25.2	Michel Blondin and Social Animation

Maximum Involvement of Local People:

During 1962–63, the Conseil des Oeuvres (Montreal Council of Agencies) drew up a preliminary inventory of the situation of the disadvantaged districts of Montreal, comparing the efforts and the results of the various agencies working in those districts, including the family service and specialized agencies. They were forced to admit that the results were meagre indeed, so the Conseil des Oeuvres decided to explore other forms of action. The approach they chose had two characteristics: first, it had to be a community approach and second, it had to rely on maximum involvement of the local people.

Participation and Autonomy:

The necessity for group action became apparent when the limitations of the individual approach were seen. In addition, the new approach sought to reintroduce the need for action to change the environment, without which all efforts might come to nothing. Thus two complementary approaches would be developed. Such a choice leads automatically to maximum involvement of the local population, *because it is impossible to accomplish any change in the people of the district unless some of them start the ball rolling and are willing to become active in their district.** We knew only too well how useless it is to hand over to people other than those closely concerned the responsibility for solving problems, as was done in the past. Thus participation emerged as our objective. (*emphasis mine)

One of the fondest ambitions of social animation is to achieve self-determination in a group of the population so that it becomes autonomous, that is, freed from its besetting automatisms and determinisms. Autonomy means the ability to make decisions and choices freely and to take the consequences.

Role of the Animator:

1. The animator as an agent of rationalization (organizational structure)
   - The course of action followed by the group under the leadership of the animator is as follows:
   - analysis of the situation,
   - search for solutions,
   - carrying out the action by identifying the tasks, and
   - supervision—assessment of the results.

   The first role of the animator also includes training of the group in the basic techniques to be used by the [citizen's] committee: agenda, minutes, sub-committees, duties of president and secretary, and so forth.

2. The animator as an agent of socialization (group process)

   The group owes its existence to the cohesion which is formed between all the individuals which belong to it.
   - First it is necessary to foster the expression of a thinking that is common to the group and shared by the members of the group…

   - As a cohesion is not only a rational phenomenon, the animator must make it easier for persons with differing sensitivities and emotional make-ups to get along together…
   - Our recent experiments have led to the discovery that a genuine action of social transformation can only become a reality when there is an intense group spirit…

3. The animator as a channel of information

   The group cannot draw from within itself all the knowledge it needs. It must acquire a working knowledge of the techniques which it will have to use regularly to secure further information…

4. The animator as an instigator of participation

   Finally, the animator must firmly believe in the objective he (sic) is seeking to achieve in this work, namely participation, and must identify all of the possible implications of it as he goes about his daily work…

Facilitation, not control:

If through small and apparently insignificant acts, the animator betrays attitudes which mean that he takes responsibilities for this group, it can be expected that genuine participation will not be engendered (Blondin, 1968, 1,2,8,9).

Once again, the three precepts of community social work are implicit in Michel Blondin's approach to social animation:

1. Identify locally perceived community needs.
   Michel Blondin calls this "analysis of the situation."
2. Identify locally perceived solutions.
   In social animation this is known as the "search for solutions."
3. Build a collective response.
   Blondin's communities "carry out the action by identifying the tasks."

Social animation practices in Quebec are built on the principle of maximum involvement of the local population. Autonomy and self-determination for local communities are of critical importance as well. Blondin prepared his workers, the "animators," more formally as professionals than Coady did. He saw the skill of the animator as essential, creating conditions for developing an "intense group spirit." The skill was in group support or facilitation, not in her or his control of the group. The community groups that Blondin's animators worked with in the 1960s and early 1970s were effective in negotiating for much better housing and recreational and educational facilities for their communities, as well as in providing many direct supports for people who were struggling in conditions of poverty.

Model 3: Participatory Research

As you can see, community social workers start by finding out what local people need once a project area is selected. They then draw out what solutions local people have in mind for those needs. I have worked with groups in Toronto and Southwestern Ontario, several of which lacked a multiplicity of services, and so lacked organized community health centres. Another large project was facilitating a community concerned with displaced youth. The people in the community organized a residential placement centre. My list of projects over the years includes establishing resident associations in low-income areas, and clothing depots and English as-a-second language programs in districts where many immigrants were arriving and local people wanted to help them. In all cases, we had to define clearly what was needed and what options there were for collective action to solve the problems. The project participants needed a method through which to systematically and thoroughly identify local perceptions of need and solution. In addition, individual, corporate, or charitable decision-makers required data regarding needs and outcomes in order to approve funds.

I will describe a research-driven approach to community social work that is close to my heart, in the hope of bringing into focus the natural mutuality and strength that I have experienced in many localities. It is a stretch but, yes, collective practices do work in Ontario.

BOX 25.3	Ken Banks and Gail Wideman on How to Begin Participatory Research

Our intent is to learn, through dialogue with communities, about the strengths and weaknesses of mutual aid relations engaged in (or not) by local people...

...First of all, three possible sites in the city [of Cambridge] were proposed for the project and 32 open-ended interviews were conducted with key informants. These included social workers in the area, school principals, business leaders in the chamber of commerce, and housing officials, all of whom we saw as important community gatekeepers. The site we chose has a downtown that

has just experienced some renovations, although many of the store-fronts remain vacant as they have for some years.

Underlying Problem:

Since the fabric and washing machine industries moved south where labour was cheaper, in the late 1960s, this once-thriving community has suffered visibly. The construction of a highway isolated the site from its traditional neighbouring communities, although regionalization of municipal government has imposed a much-resented bond with these communities. The introduction of home-delivered mail in 1969 obviated the need for people to come downtown every day, so they stopped shopping there almost overnight. New housing proliferates and the commuter-residents that this housing attracts have no time to invest in or explore local traditions and long-standing relations.

Snowball Sample:

The beginning strategy was the fore-mentioned traditional community development leadership influence survey. Through this we attempted to sound out professionals and business leaders as to their perception of needs in the community. We also asked these key informants to recommend local people whom they thought would make good interviewers, based on the strengths of their social network in the community, their capacity to keep a confidence, their perceived stability, flexibility, and general street knowledge of the important segments of the community. Through the informant interviews we paid special attention to the older people, youth, women, and cultural and linguistic minorities in the community.

We decided to use a snowball sample, for much the same reasons that we did the influence survey of the key informants. The five interviewers whom we recruited had experience in one or more of the interest groups mentioned above. We started an interviewers' training group where we collaborated to construct the interview question guidelines. We also solicited the interviewees from among the interviewers' personal networks. After some preliminary "trial" interviews, the local interviewer-participants noted that the most productive interviews took place with those contacts of their network who were informal but were not too familiar. Very close relatives and friends were not included in the sample because even the most innocuous issues were often too

enmeshed for siblings and parents, etc. This strategy enabled the interviewers to remain focused on the more general structural aspects of the respondents' social networks...

No Imported Agenda:

In order to avoid bringing an agenda for action with us into the community, we asked each of the 160 people that we interviewed what they perceived as the needs of the local community. It was very hard for the trained community developers not to go out to the local churches and community associations to encourage the start-up of programmes that we identified as being needed in the community. It was also very hard not to advocate on behalf of what appeared to us to be blatant injustices that we observed as we worked out of our site office on the main street. We did not follow our community-development 'instincts', theorizing that if you impose your expert-driven programme on the community, you had better be prepared to own and pay for it, and we felt that there was no money to do that. The second part of our theory is the assumption that if ideas for action do come from community members and if they do act on implementing some notions that strengthen their network, they will own and maintain the continuing action. The research team (community social workers) strives to provide for the most part process that is constructed from, and later facilitates, the actions of local participants. This requires a set of (two) techniques that are sensitive to the ways that local people gather:

1. Listen carefully when local people are talking. We keep field notes on significant conversations, record and transcribe group meetings. We listen until they end the conversation whenever possible.

2. Be very non-directive in the early stages of any group meeting. Later in meetings, issues that members agree are worth working on will be treated with propriety. Conversation, story telling, banter and over-talking are informal ways for diverse people to build relationships. (Banks and Wideman, 1996,21–23).

The three precepts of community social work that were implicit in my participatory research model are:

1. Identify locally perceived community needs:

   Recruit and train five local people to conduct interviews, as part of the research team.

2. Identify locally perceived solutions:

   Provide a planning process that is constructed from ideas for action voiced by community members.

3. Build a collective response:

   Facilitate the action of local participants, in this case, building inter-class and inter-generational linkages through schools, community celebrations, an environmental action group, a strengthening of service organizations, and through publishing books, newsletters, and CDs about ways to build community.

Participatory research starts from the premise that the community worker probably doesn't know what is most needed in the community that has been selected for community development. A research process that will draw out the local perceptions of need gives one confidence that community members will become engaged in a local improvement process. When you listen to their solutions and support implementing some of them, enthusiasm reigns!

If local people own the focus and the outcome of a community development process, their participation is assured and the project will reflect local priorities.

Model 4: Rural Social Work

The next example of community social work focuses on practice in rural conditions that disadvantage women and First Nations people in particular. An approach that is sensitive to local culture is absolutely necessary for a rural community social worker to be effective. A keen eye is essential to spot local resources, and a capacity to listen carefully is valuable, so that ingredients for a locally acceptable solution to problems can be assembled.

The following story gives an idea of the range of practices drawn upon by Ken Collier, the only social worker in his area for hundreds of miles.

BOX 25.4	Ken Collier and "The Delta Fort Outlaws"

In the Northern Saskatchewan Métis town I will call Delta Fort, juvenile delinquency was an ongoing and growing problem. Courts frequently sentenced the young to juvenile holding units in southern cities. They came back to hero's welcomes, carrying with them more sophisticated knowledge of crime than when they were sent away.

On the occasion I will tell you about,

seven girls aged 14 to 18 years old spent a late spring evening smashing most of the windows in buildings on the main street. The Royal Canadian Mounted Police (RCMP) quickly apprehended the culprits. A progressive and culturally aware judge asked me for a pre-sentence report. Instead of the usual individual approach to work up the reports, I decided to meet with them all together. I said I knew what happened when young people got sent south to city institutions. They knew it also. They did not want to be sent out. They said they had merely been bored and angry.

I said the judge must sentence them to something, and if they had anything better to suggest than southern (holding tanks), they should say so now. The girls said they should do something for the community—something for their elders.

"Like what?" I asked. "How about gardening, for food?" they replied. It was their way to bring food, wood, water or fish to their elders. We decided on a community garden which the girls would dig up, seed, water, and weed during the summer. The food they would give first to their grandmothers. If there was extra, they would give it to their grandfathers if they had no wife living. If there was still some left, they would give to some aunts and uncles and others that might be in need of food.

This group called themselves the Delta Fort "Outlaws." We put all this in a collective pre-sentence report to the judge. The RCMP Corporal was enraged at this approach, especially the group name, saying it merely encouraged more youth crime and was just a slap on the wrist. Nonetheless, the judge made the order to carry out the garden project.

Through the summer a Métis elder, who was also a town counsellor and an uncle of most of the girls, supervised the garden, because I did not live in that town. I only drove or flew in each week for two days. The girls first thought the

project was just a lark, a bit of fun, but as the garden began to grow, they took ownership, got very protective, and commented on how much work it was in the hot sun, and how nasty it was on cool and windy days. The girls took early lettuce and radishes to their grandmothers and other relatives. Some of their brothers got jobs fixing the broken windows, and the girls learned how much trouble and expense they had caused.

By September they had harvested the garden, taking bags of very nice carrots, potatoes, onions, cabbages, peas and beans to their kin. While the garden was ripening, they also picked berries which flourished in the bush on the riverbank, bringing the fruit to the senior citizens' home and to those too old to go picking berries. Sometimes they pushed their elders in wheelchairs to the edge of the bush or garden so they could watch and talk. Many of the old and young had never talked much to each other before, and these occasions became times of telling of the old ways; of how plants grew, of the medicines and who could harvest them. The girls learned of the sweet grass, used ceremonially to make purifying smoke. The girls told their grandparents of their hopes and wishes.

After the summer was finished, and the sentence was over, the judge asked for a report. Though the RCMP grudgingly admitted there might be something to this method of dealing with some young people who broke the law, I did not recommend it as a standard practice, for some of the young had no intention of co-operating with a scheme like this, and would have sabotaged the garden. But this group clearly benefited, and, to my knowledge, did not re-offend.

It was a nice combination of community work in a rural setting and a recognition of cultural connections which could be exploited productively" (Collier, 1996).

The three precepts of community social work are evident in Ken Collier's work with the "Delta Fort Outlaws':

1. Identify locally perceived community needs:

   A progressive and culturally aware judge asks the social worker for a pre-sentence report grounded in local values.

2. Identify locally perceived solutions:

   The social worker involves the offenders in designing an appropriate resolution.

3. Build a collective response:

   An uncle of one of the girls, who is a town counsellor, supervises while the girls share food with their relatives in a way that is traditional and healing to them and to the community.

Community social workers have to keep their eyes and ears open for local solutions to problems. Engaging the energy for good in a community promotes healing in relationships. People who will benefit from talking to each other are brought together to solve a local problem. Here the institutions of our society initiate the process, but the identification of the particulars of the problem and solution are left up to the local community. The community then acts and owns the solution, often without the expenditure of money in a rural economy that is not wealthy.

The next approach builds on the technologies of counselling that are germane to clinical social work. Collectivity and local sensitivity can promote personal growth when people are strong enough to trust and reach out. When the individual work is coming to an end, it is beneficial to refer a client to a program that cautiously phases people back into community relationships.

Model 5: Social Support

Madeline Lovell, Jennifer Newman, and others drew on the work of several women's projects in Washington State, much of it grounded in the work of psychologists and psychotherapists who understand and support the particular needs of women through "The Friendship Group." This program features a combination of advocacy and modelling of successful approaches to relationships in a protected environment, conditions that drive most self-help and mutual aid efforts. They often enhance learning of social skills that are a mystery for many people who feel alone and angry in the middle of our impersonal, mass society. Yes this too is community social work. Workers identify people who have similar problems and who find social skills baffling and elusive and heretofore achievable for others but not for themselves. The workers encourage them to gather together and work on mutually achieved solutions.

The following report outlines the approach of the friendship group.

BOX 25.5	Social Support: "The Friendship Group"

An effort to address isolation:

In our work with parents of abused children, we have been struck repeatedly by how lonely many are and how few posi-tive social interactions they appear to have.... The nature and form of [our] curriculum have been developed over time. In an initial effort to address the isolation seen in the parents with whom they worked, colleagues at Childhaven, a therapeutic day nursery in Seattle, Washington, decided some years ago to begin a group for parents that would focus on common problems in parenting and daily life. However, we found that bringing parents together in a weekly group meeting seemed to have little effect on relationship development. While parents had the opportunity to get to know other parents, they rarely made friendships that they considered significant. Rather most parents continued to prefer to interact primarily with staff members (Lovell & Hawkins, 1988). In determining why parents shied away from other parents and sought out staff, we realized that staff made much more rewarding network members. They offered the praise, attention, and concrete help that was rarely forthcoming from other parents. It was as if the majority of parents did not know how to be a rewarding friend.

Experiential social skill training:

We decided that experiential skill training was an essential step in helping parents learn to be more rewarding as friends. Just talking about common concerns with people in a similar plight was clearly insufficient. Parents also needed guidance in learning how to be less vulnerable to those who took advantage of their loneliness. Unfortunately, most traditional social group-work approaches with the population fail to teach the necessary interpersonal skills. Not only are parents thus hampered to their interactions within the group but they are also unable to take away from the group competencies that would enable them to build better relationships in the community. Being in groups that fail to provide basic skill training may only make them more

dependent on professional help for their support needs.

Manual helps with safety and trust:

("The Friendship Group" provides a manual with curriculum materials as a kit for participants in the program). The manual included modules on the nature and stages of relationships, communications skills, assertiveness, and access to community resources for network development. Because many parents have had highly negative experiences with friends and family, their ability to trust is very fragile. This approach devotes considerable time to initially helping participants determine whether a relationship or situation feels safe. Knowing how to protect themselves when they feel unsafe is a necessary precursor to reaching out to make changes in their networks.

Firm-up existing friendships first:

Our follow-up data suggests the participants do not necessarily use these skills to go out and immediately make new friends, although that certainly is possible. Instead parents appear to value the friendships they already possess differently as they begin to work out issues with present network members. They value their social contacts more and place less reliance on family members. They are empowered in their relationships with friends. For some people, the group offers beginning information on how to act, think, and feel in new ways with friends....We attempt to normalize seeking ongoing help to deal with relationship problems that appear resistant to change and have offered follow-up on an individual basis to support the achievement of network goals. (Lovell, 1991; Lovell and Hawkins, 1988: 175-183)

The three precepts of community social work are at work in this model, but here the role of the social worker is both supportive and directive:

1. Identify locally perceived community needs.

   Social workers perceive that lonely people don't make local friends.

2. Identify locally perceived solutions.

   Social workers help project participants determine what feels safe in relationships.

3. Build a collective response.

   Participants learn how to act, think, and feel with friends, ways that empower their relationships with friends. With more successful relationships in the community, local people who have been vulnerable can be more confident and more in charge of their lives.

Social workers can work in counselling settings, yet use collective approaches that draw on the three precepts of community work. "The Friendship Group" workers did an assessment and developed a treatment plan for each individual participant; yet what the participants learned about relationships built healthy, trust-based collectivity outside of the project's sphere of influence. The capacity to have strong friendships made the individuals less vulnerable, and the need for individual dependence on the social work program was greatly reduced.

THE PRACTICES OF COMMUNITY SOCIAL WORK

What is unique for community workers is our orientation to mutuality and collectivity. This is grounded in the view of humankind that many social workers share with Paulo Freire and Moses Coady, one that was best articulated over 100 years ago by celebrated zoologist and biologist Prince Peter Kropotkin:

> The mutual-aid tendency in man (sic) has so remote an origin, and is so deeply interwoven with all the past evolution of the human race, that it has been maintained by mankind up to the present time, notwithstanding the vicissitudes of history.... New economical and social institutions, in so far as they were a creation of the masses, new ethical systems, and new religions, all have originated from the same source, and the ethical progress of our race, viewed in its broad lines, appears as a gradual extension of the mutual-aid principals from the tribe to always larger and larger agglomerations, so as to finally embrace one day the whole of mankind, without respect to its divers creeds languages, and races (Kropotkin, 1989, 223-224).

Skeptics abound, but the principles of mutual aid work well with the principles of self-determination, and together those ideas inform the practice of community social work. As long as our free society allows practices to be grounded in diverse and apparently conflicting ideologies, the practice of social work with individuals will do the work that must be focused on individual need, and the practice of community social work will carry on where the collective ideas and energy of mutuality can solve community problems.

REFERENCES

Alary, J., et al. (Eds.) (1990). Trans. Susan Usher. *Community Care and Participatory Research.* Montreal: Nu-Age Editions.

Banks, C.K. and Mangan, J.M. (1999*). The company of neighbours: revitalizing community through action research*. Toronto: University of Toronto Press.

Banks, C.K. (1997). Community development research in Canada. In Hubert Campfens, *Community development: an international perspective*. Toronto: University of Toronto Press.

Banks, C.K. and Wideman, G. (1996). The company of neighbours' building social support through the use of ethnography. *International Social Work, 39*(3), pp. 317 – 328.

Blondin, M. (1968). *Social animation: as developed and practised by Le Conseil des Oeuvres de Montreal* Ottawa: Community Funds and Councils of Canada, monograph.

CBC (Dec. 26, 1996). Morningside Toronto, Peter Gzowski sharing recipes with a study group in Antigonish, honouring father Moses Coady and the continuing movement.

Collier, K. (1997). *The Delta Fort Outlaws*. Edmonton: Athabasca University.

Freire, P. (1993). *Pedagogy of the oppressed*. New York: Continuum

Kropotkin, P. (1989). *Mutual aid: a factor in evolution*. Montreal: Black Rose Books.

Lovell, M. (1991). *The friendship group: learning the skills to create social support. A manual for group leaders*. Vancouver: The Social Support Training Project, School of Social Work, the University of British Columbia, monograph.

Lovell, M. and Hawkins, J.D. (1988). *An evaluation of a group intervention to increase the personal networks of abusive parents*. Seattle, Washington: Children and Youth Services Review.

Laidlaw, A. (Ed.) (1971*). Writings and speeches of M.M. Coady: The man from Margaree*. Toronto: McClelland and Stewart, Ltd.

Ross, M. (1963). *Community organization*. Toronto: University of Toronto Press.

Turner, J. and Turner, F. (Eds.) (1986). *Canadian social welfare*. Don Mills: Collier Macmillan.

SOCIAL POLICY

PRACTICE
Anne Westhues

Of all aspects of social work practice, social policy analysis is the most firmly grounded in the Canadian context. While policy analysis is the primary practice modality selected by only a small number of social workers, it is an integral part of the work that the rest of us do. In recognition of the critical role that policy plays in shaping how effectively we can meet the needs of our clients, the most recent version of the Canadian Association of Social Workers' Code of Ethics includes a section on ethical responsibilities of professional social workers with respect to social change. The introduction to this section reads: "A social worker shall advocate change (a) in the best interest of the client, and (b) for the overall benefit of society, the environment and the global community" (CASW Code of Ethics, 1994, 24). The Code then goes on to mention specific areas that are to be addressed, such as elimination of discrimination; equal distribution of resources; advocacy for equal access of all persons to resources, services, and opportunities; advocacy for a clean and healthy environment; and the promotion of social justice.

In this chapter, I will provide a fuller understanding of this area of practice, and in particular why it is necessarily so culturally specific. To do this, I will first explore what is meant by social policy, and social policy analysis. This will be followed by a discussion of the dimensions of social policy, how one would go about influencing policy development, and the skills required to be an effective policy analyst. In closing, I will discuss the limitations of policy analysis as a means of effecting change in the best interest of our clients.

DEFINING SOCIAL POLICY AND POLICY ANALYSIS

There has been a longstanding debate within the literature as to what is meant by the term *social policy*. The central issue that frames this discussion is how inclusive is the domain of social policy. Does it encompass only those areas that have been described as the "personal social services" like income security, child welfare, and counselling (Kahn, 1979)? Does it include related human services like education and health care, or an even broader range of what some consider economic policies such as labour legislation, decisions with respect to the reduction of the budget deficit, or free trade agreements with the United States and Mexico? Does it include only decisions made with respect to the allocation of rights and resources by governmental bodies, or does it also include decisions made by transfer payment organizations or by nongovernmental collectivities such as unions? Is the role of the policy analyst that of the detached, dispassionate observer, or does he or she have a responsibility to advocate for a value-based position? While the debate may seem somewhat esoteric, the position that one takes defines how broad is the range of policy issues about which you believe social workers have a responsibility to be informed, and on which we have an ethical obligation to try to effect change.

Canadian authors have tended to emphasize a broader definition of social policy, though a few have taken a midpoint on the spectrum. Yelaja (1987), for instance, offers this definition: "Social policy is concerned with the public administration of welfare services, that is, the formulation, development and management of specific services of government at all levels, such as health, education, income maintenance and welfare services" (2). In the same vein, Brooks (1993) says: "Many of the most expensive activities carried out by the state in advanced capitalist societies are associated with the area of social policy. These functions include public education, health care, publicly subsidized housing, and the provision of various forms of income support to such segments of the population as the unemployed, the aged, and the disabled" (184). At the opposite end of the spectrum, in keeping with Rimlinger and Wilensky and Lebeaux, McGilly (1990) suggests: "The least misleading simplification of social policy is to define it as society's struggle to keep up with the consequences of advancing industrialization" (12). This broader definition, which recognizes the unequivocal linkage between social policy and economic policy, is reflected in the writing of Canadian social workers such as Alan Moscovitch (1981, 1991), Glenn Drover (1981), Ken Collier (1995), Andrew Armitage (1988), Graham Riches and Gord Ternowetsky (1990), Frank Tester (1991, 1992), Ernie Lightman (1991), Brian Wharf and Brad McKenzie (1998), and John Graham, Karen Swift, and Roger Delaney (2000). As we have unmistakenly shifted into a global economy over the past twenty years, it has become clear that social policy can no longer be discussed in a meaningful way without understanding the economic context of policy decisions.

At the same time that there has been a shift to defining policy issues in a more global context, there has been a parallel shift to thinking about policy as it relates to practitioners locally. Pierce (1984), writing from a social work perspective, suggests that there are eight levels at which social policy is made that shape our work as practitioners. These include the three levels of federal, provincial, and local government, which political scientists such as Pal (1992) and Brooks (1993) include in the domain of public policy. Pierce also suggests that they include "small scale policy systems" (Flynn, 1992) like social service organizations and professional associations. This reflects his understanding that an integral part of practice is the development of operational policies that define how a client will experience a policy which is generally set at a larger system level, for instance "minimum intervention" into the lives of families with children, "normalization" for people who have disabilities, or a commitment to the equality of women.

Pierce (1984) includes the family and the individual practitioner as relevant system levels to understanding social policy as well. He argues that decisions made by the individual practitioner in relation to the implementation of public policy define how clients experience social services and the social policies which shape those services. Every worker has some discretion in how they interpret policy. For instance, a social assistance worker may or may not choose to accept, as part of a recipient's work requirement, volunteer time at his or her child's school. Or a childcare worker determining the eligibility of clients for social assistance may choose to advise them on how they could become eligible for subsidy by buying a refrigerator on credit rather than saving for it. How the worker chooses to act in these two instances gives a very different message to clients about the social policies affecting them. Similarly, decisions taken by a family with respect to the care they are willing to provide to an elderly family member or a child with a disability will have an influence on social policy.

Flynn (1992) reinforces the importance of this broader perspective for the social work practitioner. Citing Kahn, he says that policy shapes and delineates what the practitioner does, how he or she relates to the client group, and the manner in which discretion is allowed or exercised. Further, he argues that understanding how policies at the agency, or even individual, level affect what the practitioner may or must do, and how they can be changed, is a way to empower practitioners.

Another important issue discussed in the current literature is the role of the policy analyst. Mirroring the debate in the social sciences about whether positivist, constructivist, or critical theory approaches are most appropriate for social science research today (Newman, 1994; Maguire, 1987; Kirby & McKenna, 1989; Strauss & Corbin, 1990; Cresswell, 1994; Lincoln & Guba, 1985), the question explored is whether the role of the policy analyst is to provide information to decision-makers that will help them make more informed decisions (Friedemann, 1987), or whether the analyst has a responsibility to engage in some form of social action with his or her analyses (Moscovitch, 1991). As we saw above, this latter position is consistent with the Canadian Association of Social Workers' Code of Ethics.

So what is social policy? Following Pal (1992), I would define social policy as "a course of action or inaction chosen by public authorities to address a given problem or interrelated set of problems" (2). My definition of "public authorities" would be very broad, however, including decisions taken not only at the various levels of government, but also by the social service organization, and collective agreements, in order to implement policies intended to address social problems. Further, I would add the phrase "which deal with human health, safety or well-being" (Flynn, 1992) to the end of the definition to differentiate social policy from the broad range of public policy issues that governments address.

If social policy is action taken to address a given problem, policy analysis is "the disciplined application of intellect to public problems" (Pal, 1992, 38). Pal differentiates between academic policy analysis and applied policy analysis, the domain of social work practitioners. The academic is primarily concerned with theory, explanation, understanding policies and how they came into being, and attempts to retain some objectivity in making the analysis. The practitioner, by contrast, is more interested in specific policies or problems than theory, in evaluation rather than explanation, in changing policies, and in advocating for the interests of our clients (Pal, 24). Moroney (1981) explains this difference in orientating between the traditional academic approach to policy analysis and the practice-based approach as being about making value-based choices. In support of this position, Kelley (1975, cited in Flynn, 1992) suggests that there are three criteria that must be considered in all policy analyses. These include adequacy, the extent to which a specified need or goal is met if program objectives are carried out; effectiveness, the extent to which the outcomes obtained are a result of policy intent and program activity; and efficiency, the measure of goal attainment in terms of the expenditure of the least amount of resources. Other values that may be basic to social policy issues include impact on client identity and impact on self-determination. Values that may guide the process of policy development might include informed decision-making, public accountability, procedural fairness, and openness and accessibility to the process (Ogilvie, Ogilvie & Company, 1990).

MODELS OF POLICY DEVELOPMENT

Another way in which academics and practitioners have tried to understand social policy and policy analysis is through the conceptualization of a model that captures the complexity of the policy-making process (Kahn, 1969; Mayer, 1985; Meyerson & Banfied, 1955; Pancer & Westhues, 1989; Perlman & Gurin, 1972; Pierce, 1984; Westhues, 1980; Wharf & McKenzie, 1998; York, 1982). The earlier models, as one might expect, were less detailed than are more recent ones. Meyerson and Banfied (1955), for instance, defined only three stages in policy development: (1) the decision-maker considers all options open to him or her, (2) the consequences of adopting each alternative are identified and evaluated, and (3) the alternative that seems to have the best fit with the valued ends is selected.

As the social sciences moved into a period in which positivism and rationality were highly valued, models became more detailed and emphasized the technical skills of the policy analyst as researcher (Kahn, 1969; Mayer, 1985; York, 1982). When our competencies in these areas developed more fully, concern arose that insufficient attention was now being given to the political aspects of policy development, and models were proposed which attempted to rectify this imbalance (Gil, 1981; Perlman & Gurin, 1972; Wharf & McKenzie, 1998). A model that is sufficiently useful for helping us to think about the policy-making process in each of the systems and domains we will explore in this chapter is: (1) defining the problem, (2) agreeing on goals, (3) identifying alternatives, (4) choosing an alternative, (5) implementing the policy, and (6) evaluation.

POLICY DIMENSIONS

One of the reasons that it has been difficult to develop a model that captures the complexity of the policy-making process is precisely that it is such a complex process. Social policy can be made at the international level, at the federal, provincial, and local levels of government in Canada, as well as within the agency setting. The policy initiative may fall into one of four subsystems within each of these systems: the strategic framework, the legislative framework, the program framework, or the internal management framework (Ogilvey, Ogilvey & Company, 1990). These dimensions of social policy are explored in more depth below.

Traditionally, we have thought of social policy issues in a national context. The generosity of the safety net that a country puts into place has been related to its level of industrialization, its level of affluence, and the extent to which its cultural values have supported the assumption of a collective responsibility for the well-being of all citizens (Moscovitch & Drover, 1981). As we have moved into a period of global capitalism (Collier, 1995; Teeple, 1995), however, international policies have begun to have important influences on our social and economic well-being. Following the introduction of the Free Trade Agreement between Canada and the United States in 1989, and the North American Free Trade Agreement between Canada, the United States, and Mexico in 1992, for instance, it has become evident that there are economic and political pressures to "harmonize" social policy in all three countries. While ideally that may have meant that American and Mexican social policy would come to look like Canadian social policy, in fact the safety net that was so carefully woven over a period of at least fifty years in Canada is gradually being weakened, taking on the appearance of its less sturdy American cousin.

United Nations agreements like the U.N. Convention on the Rights of the Child of 1989 also shape social policy initiatives in Canada. Article 8 of the Convention, for instance, says that "State Parties undertake to respect the right of the child to preserve his or her identity, including nationality, name and family relations as recognized by law without unlawful interference." This entitlement, which Canada had agreed to by becoming a signatory to the Convention, has implications for international adoption, for instance. If children have a right to maintain their identity, Canada must now ensure that information is gathered on the children's background, and that there is a mechanism for passing this information on to them at some specified age, in both nonidentifying and identifying forms.

Policy at the international level may be made in each of the four subsystems identified above. The strategic framework includes development of a vision and mission statement, goals and objectives, and is associated with what we have come to call strategic planning. The legislative framework includes legislation and the regulations, directives, and guidelines that are intended to facilitate its implementation. The program framework involves program design, the service delivery structure, and the implementation plan. This area of policy is sometimes called program planning. Lastly, the internal management framework includes human resources policies, budgeting, and defining an operating structure, the policy domain that we have traditionally associated with administration. (Ogilvie, Ogilvie & Company, 1990). This policy may be set through bilateral or multilateral agreements such as free trade legislation, or through administrative agreements between Canada and individual countries with respect to a policy issue such as international adoption. International policy may also be made by international organizations like the United Nations or the newly formed World Trade Organization.

Social policy in Canada is shaped by what is called the "divided sovereignty" (Van Loon & Whittington, 1976) of the British North America Act of 1867, and now the Constitution Act, 1982. This means that jurisdiction has been given to the federal government for some areas of policy development and to the provinces for others. Provinces are responsible for "the establishment, maintenance and management of public and reformatory prisons in and for the provinces," and "the establishment, maintenance and management of hospitals, asylums, charities, and eleemosynary institutions" (Splane, 1965). While it is generally agreed that the intention of the legislation was to limit the role of the provinces, and to create a strong federal government, judicial interpretations of the legislation have, over time, limited the role of the federal government in the direct provision of human services.

Depending upon the policy area of concern, then, the federal government may play a greater or lesser role. Legislation pertaining to young people in trouble with the law, the Young Offender's Act, for example, falls within the federal jurisdiction. Each province has enabling legislation to serve as an implementation guide, however. In all cases this is a section of the province's child welfare legislation. By contrast, the federal government has no jurisdiction within the area of child welfare. This means that it cannot pass legislation that will shape the provision of child welfare services. The one way in which the federal government has influenced child welfare is through the provision of federal funding for approved child welfare services. The Canada Assistance Plan was the mechanism for this provision until recently. It allowed for the federal government to match provincial spending on approved child welfare services, a so-called cost-sharing agreement. This federal-provincial agreement was replaced in 1996 with the Canada Health and Social Transfer. This legislation will still allow for the transfer of federal funds to the provinces, but the transfer is now in the form of a block grant, meaning that the provinces will have more control over how the funds are allocated within the areas of health, education, and social services than under the Canada Assistance Plan or the Established Programs Financing Act, which facilitated the flow of money to the provinces in the areas of health and education. In addition to policy being possible within the legislative framework at both the federal and provincial levels, policy may also fall into the areas of the strategic framework, program framework, and internal management framework.

Local governments have a limited policy jurisdiction with respect to social services in all provinces in Canada (Tindal & Tindal, 1984). Their primary areas of responsibility include land use, water, roads, and recreation. In most provinces, they do not deliver any social services, and so not only have no legislative jurisdiction, but therefore have no reason to set policy within the strategic, program, or internal management areas. Ontario and Nova Scotia municipalities have some jurisdiction in the area of social services, a jurisdiction which has increased in the past few years in Ontario to include responsibility for the delivery of social assistance, child care, long-term care, social housing, and community health. In addition, in Ontario, local government must contribute 50% of the spending on social assistance, long-term care, and child care subsidies, and the full cost of social housing and community health (Melchers, 1999). This means that local governments play a key role in determining the annual budget for services in these areas. Policy initiatives at the local level are primarily in the strategic, program, and internal management areas, with the province setting legislation.

Service delivery in all provinces is through some mix of government offices and transfer payment agencies; that is, organizations that enter into purchase of service agreements, generally with the provincial and local governments. A few small agencies provide service without government funding. The programs of these agencies are shaped by the legislative framework defined by the province, or sometimes the federal government. The domain of their policy work tends to fall within the strategic, program, and internal management frameworks, though they may assume a responsibility to advocate for policy changes within the legislative framework set by the provincial or federal governments. These dimensions of social policy are summarized in Table 26.1.

INFLUENCING POLICY DEVELOPMENT

Social work practitioners, as noted above, have a responsibility to advocate for social change that will improve the well-being of our clients. A key way in which this can be done is by attempting to influence the policies that shape their experience of the services we deliver. To be able to do this effectively, one must first identify which is the appropriate system to be addressed for the policy issue of concern. If you are interested in changing some aspect of child welfare legislation, making it easier for an adopted person to obtain identifying information about his or her birth parents, for instance, the appropriate system would be the provincial government, not the local Children's Aid Society. While it may be useful to have child welfare organizations supporting your efforts, they are not the decision-makers on this issue.

TABLE 26.1	Dimensions of Social Policy
Policy System	**Policy Domain**
International	• Strategic • Legislative • Program • Internal Management
Federal Government	• Strategic • Legislative • Program • Internal Management
Provincial Government	• Strategic • Legislative • Program • Internal Management
Local Government	• Strategic • Program • Internal Management
Agency	• Strategic • Program • Internal Management

Once the appropriate system has been identified, it is necessary to understand the policy-making process within that system. Figure 26.1 outlines this process in detail for the provincial level. Figure 26.2 provides even more detail on this process, specifying the approvals required for each type of policy change: whether a change to legislation, regulations, or operational policy, procedures, or guidelines. What is striking about these two figures is how many approvals are required before any change can be effected.

At the federal level, the process of effecting change is even more complex, with the additional approval of each of the provinces required. The failed agreement on the Meech Lake and Charlottetown Accords are testimony to this complexity, though the recent agreement on the Social Union demonstrates that it is possible (Mendelson, 1999). At the local level, it is much simpler, generally requiring only the approval of the social services department, the commissioner of social services, the social services committee, and regional or municipal council. At the agency level, the process is similar, with approvals required by the program unit, executive director, and the board of directors. Depending on the model of board governance, approval may be required by a standing committee of the board and the executive committee before the matter is presented to the board of directors itself (Carver, 1990).

What these models fail to convey is the politically charged environment in which many policy decisions are made. While Bell and Pascoe (1988) identify the first step in the policy-making process as the ministry initiating a policy submission, in fact there is often considerable political activity, sometimes over a prolonged period of time, before a ministry sees an issue as a sufficient priority to address it. These political efforts are sometimes conceptualized as social advocacy, or community organizing (Ross, 1967; Taylor & Roberts, 1985; Tropman, Erlich, & Rothman, 1995), and planning and policy analysis are described as more rational processes. Further, it is important to understand that both internal and external politics are influential in this process, that is, not only various stakeholders, but the bureaucrats making decisions themselves will promote different interests (Tindall & Tindal, 1984).

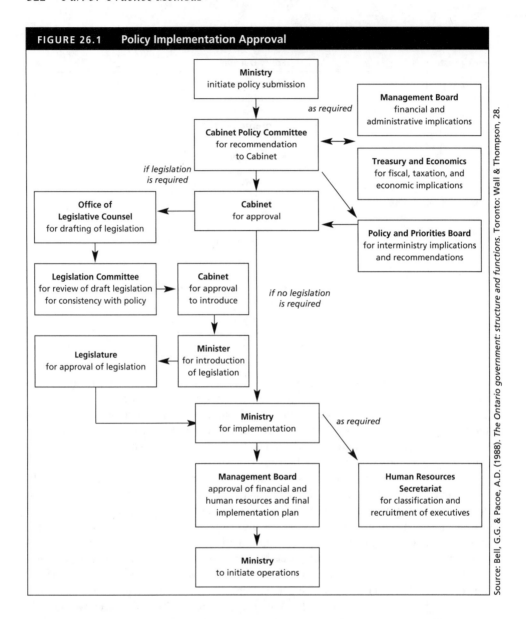

FIGURE 26.1   Policy Implementation Approval

Ministry
initiate policy submission

as required

Management Board
financial and
administrative implications

Cabinet Policy Committee
for recommendation
to Cabinet

*if legislation
is required*

Treasury and Economics
for fiscal, taxation, and
economic implications

**Office of
Legislative Counsel**
for drafting of legislation

Cabinet
for approval

Policy and Priorities Board
for interministry implications
and recommendations

Legislation Committee
for review of draft legislation
for consistency with policy

Cabinet
for approval
to introduce

*if no legislation
is required*

Legislature
for approval of legislation

Minister
for introduction
of legislation

Ministry
for implementation

as required

Management Board
approval of financial and
human resources and final
implementation plan

**Human Resources
Secretariat**
for classification and
recruitment of executives

Ministry
to initiate operations

Source: Bell, G.G. & Pacoe, A.D. (1988). *The Ontario government: structure and functions.* Toronto: Wall & Thompson, 28.

Efforts to educate the general public about wife assault are a good case example of this political process, one which is lucidly described by Gillian Walker (Walker, 1990). Through the women's centres set up to raise consciousness about women's rights in the early '70s, it soon became evident that a major concern of women experiencing relationship difficulties was being assaulted by their partners. In response to this concern, women's shelters began to spring up across the country as places for women to take refuge when they were under attack. To obtain funding for these shelters, it was necessary to convince the United Way, and local and provincial governments that wife assault was a sufficiently widespread problem to warrant funding for shelters. Walker makes an insightful analysis of the process of defining the problem of wife assault, and the conflicting politics of feminists and professionals in defining the issue. For feminists, it was an instance of women's oppression, grounded in the patriarchy, which influences family relationships and social institutions like the law. The only possible remedy, for them, was fundamental social change, with the objective being a system that supports social, political, and economic equality for women. For professionals, by contrast, the problem was defined as that of outdated sex roles, traditional attitudes, and inadequate institutional procedures. Their remedy was to develop programs that educate men and women about gender equality, and therapeutic interventions to deal with the trauma of assault.

SKILLS REQUIRED

Whether policy analysis is a social worker's primary job responsibility or a secondary one, two sets of skills are required: what have been called process (Rothman & Zald,1985), interpersonal (Tropman, 1995), or interactional (Perlman & Gurin, 1972) skills; and task (Rothman & Zald,1985), intellectual (Tropman, 1995), or analytic (Perlman & Gurin, 1972) skills. Figure 26.3 outlines both the analytic and interactional skills required at each stage in the policy development process. The analytic skills identified draw heavily from an earlier article by Pancer and Westhues (1989).

In addition to the general skill of thinking analytically, at the initial stage of the policy development process, when *the problem is defined*, analytic skills are needed in two areas: values analysis and needs assessment. To complete a values analysis, the analyst must know how to conduct opinion polls or to cull useful information from opinion polls conducted by others; carry out key informant interviews; use group techniques like the nominal group

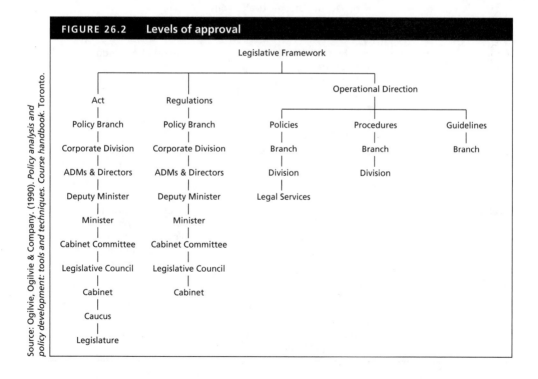

Source: Ogilvie, Ogilvie & Company. (1990). *Policy analysis and policy development: tools and techniques. Course handbook.* Toronto.

FIGURE 26.2   Levels of approval

FIGURE 26.3	Skills Required at Each Stage of Policy Development	

Stage in Policy Development	Analytic Skills	Interactional Skills

Defining the problem	Values analysis
	• opinion polls
	• key informant interviews
	• group approaches
	  (nominal group technique,
	  Delphi, community forum)
	• preference scaling
	
	Needs assessment
	• social indicators approaches
	• surveys
	• group approaches
		Leadership
		Creating a safe environment
		Ensuring participation
		Active listening
		Public speaking
		Clear, concise writing

Agreeing on goals	Goals Analysis
	• Goal formulation: surveys,
	  community forums, rating
	  of goal characteristics
	
	• Priority Setting: estimate-discuss-
	  estimate procedure, Q-sort,
	  paired comparisons, multi-attribute
	  utility measurement, decision-
	  theoretic analysis
		Engaging people in process
		Clarifying intent
		Brokering
		Mediating
		Persuading

Identifying alternatives	Policy Logic Analysis • review of theories of causation • review of outcome evaluations in policy area • concept development	Sharing Knowledge Facilitating
Choosing an alternative	Feasibility Study • investigation of funding sources • cost-benefit analysis • cost-effectiveness analysis • PRINCE analysis • administrative feasibility assessment	Sharing Knowledge Facilitating Guiding
Implementing the policy	Implementation Assessment • Gantt charts • milestone charts • PRT-CPM networks	Information gathering Manufacturing commitment

Evaluating the Policy	Process
	• collection of data from
	  Information systems
	• peer review ratings
	• client satisfaction surveys
	
	Outcomes
	• experimental approaches
	• quasi-experimental approaches
	• single case design
	• social impact assessments
	• client satisfaction surveys
		Sharing of expertise
		Safe environment
		Ensuring participation
		  in developing design
		Communication of results

technique, the Delphi, and community forums; and do preference scaling. To complete a needs assessment, the analyst has to know how to identify and interpret social indicators, carry out surveys, and use the group approaches identified above. Interactional skills required at this critical first stage of the process include leadership in setting up a process that will allow for the exchange of ideas on the issue; the ability to create a safe environment so people feel they can express their feelings about the issue; skills for ensuring that all stakeholders have an opportunity to participate in the process of constructing the problem; active listening skills, to ensure that the nuances of different stakeholder perspectives are not missed; public speaking skills if one is going to advocate for a particular policy position; and clear, concise writing skills, whether one is playing the role of neutral internal policy analyst at some level of government or that of community-based advocate.

At the next stage, *agreeing on goals*, analytic skills are again needed in two areas: goal formulation and priority setting. To formulate goals, skills are needed to carry out surveys, conduct community forums, and rate goal characteristics. Procedures like the estimate-discuss-estimate procedure, the Q-sort, paired comparisons, multi-attribute utility measurement, and decision theoretic analysis can be used to set priorities. To support the analytic tasks, interactional skills are needed which permit the analyst to engage stakeholders in the process of reaching agreement on goals, as well as skills in clarifying, brokering, and mediating. If the analyst is acting as an advocate, she or he will also need to be skilled in persuasion.

Policy logic analysis, a variant of program logic analysis, can be used to facilitate the *identification of policy alternatives* which, in light of a specified theory of causation of the identified problem, could be expected to achieve the policy goals agreed upon. A review of any outcome evaluations of these policy alternatives would identify empirical evidence that could either support the implementation of a particular alternative, or suggest that it would not, in fact, achieve the anticipated outcomes. Theory often precedes practice, so another skill required by the analyst is the ability to discern the practice implications of a particular theoretical perspective for policy development. The interactional skills required at this stage include being able to summarize and share knowledge in a way that is both interesting and concise, and the ability to facilitate discussion to generate alternative ideas.

Feasibility studies provide information which assists in *choosing among policy alternatives*. Assessing feasibility includes determining whether funds would be available for the various alternatives, completing cost-benefit or cost-effectiveness analyses on each alternative, completing a political feasibility assessment using a technique like PRINCE, and assessing the administrative feasibility of the alternatives. Good skills in presenting information in an interesting and concise way are required at this stage as well. In addition, the analyst must be able to guide the process in such a way that it is possible to reach a decision with respect to which alternative to select.

An implementation assessment permits the analyst to identify how much time would be required to implement the alternative selected, which jurisdictions would need to be involved, and which approvals would be required. Pressman and Wildavsky (1973) alerted us to the importance of this stage thirty years ago when they discovered that many policies never have their intended effects because they fail to make it through the long string of decisions necessary for the policy to be implemented. Analyzing these approval processes beforehand, and identifying potential blocks will provide greater assurance that the policy will, in fact, be implemented. The primary interactional skills required at this stage are the ability to gather information on complex systems, and to manufacture commitment on the part of service providers to the new policy alternative so that it will, in fact, be implemented as intended.

Finally, any policy must be systematically evaluated to assess what has happened in light of its intended effects. Process evaluation includes a review of who has been served, for what reasons, and what service they have received. Peer reviews are made of cases to determine whether defined standards of care have been met. Client satisfaction surveys assess whether the client received the service expected, in a timely fashion, and whether they found it helpful. Outcome evaluations may focus on individual goals or program goals, and are intended to assess the extent to which the changes that are intended to occur for the client have, in fact, occurred. The interactional skills required of the policy analyst as evaluator include the ability to share his or her knowledge about how evaluations may be designed, to create a feeling of safety with respect to the evaluation, to ensure that all those affected by the evaluation participate in its design, often to engage service deliverers in the data collection process, and to communicate the results of the research to all those involved.

LIMITATIONS OF POLICY ANALYSIS

With all of its promise for improving the well-being of our clients, what are the limitations of policy analysis as an area of practice? First, the process may be exceedingly slow. Even within an agency setting, to make a change in policy may take a year or longer from the point at which a concern is identified until a new policy has been implemented. If the local, provincial, or federal government is the focus of change, it is likely to be much longer yet. This means that a commitment to effect change must be a long-term one.

Second, efforts to make changes in policy can be very resource-intensive. It takes time, energy, and money to raise awareness about an issue. The more complex and controversial the issue, the more resources will be required. It is essential to learn to build coalitions, to create organizations where none exist to advocate for an issue, and to identify and link with existing ones which might share your concern. It may also be necessary to raise funding to support your policy change initiatives. This means that a commitment to effect change is an opportunity to develop a set of social work skills that are quite different from those within the clinical domain.

Third, even with the investment of considerable resources, it may not be possible to effect changes that are consistent with social work values at a particular time in history. In Ontario and Alberta, for instance, the governments have recently introduced mandatory workfare. While most social workers support the development of job training opportunities for people on assistance, requiring people to work in return for benefits is in conflict with the value we place on self-determination. Data are abundant that show that most people work when given the opportunity. Job readiness programs offered by the various levels of government in Canada have typically been oversubscribed. In spite of this empirical evidence, the ideology continues to exist that people on assistance are lazy, and that we need to be coercive to get them to accept work. As long as a government is in power which holds this belief and refuses to alter it in light of evidence to the contrary, efforts to change this particular social policy are unlikely to be fruitful. This means that a commitment to effect change may not always be successful in the short run, and can be the source of considerable discouragement if a longer-term perspective is not maintained.

Finally, for the policy analyst working within an organization or at some level of government, it is essential that there is a clear understanding between the policy analyst and his or her employer about which kinds of political activity are acceptable. Traditionally, the role of government employee was defined as that of a rational, apolitical analyst. Political activity was not only discouraged but could be the grounds for dismissal. While that has now changed, there may still be limits on what is allowed. An employee at the local government level may be free to engage in efforts to change provincial legislation with respect to regulation of social workers, for instance, but not to lobby his or her member of parliament to withdraw the mandatory aspect of the workfare program. This means that a commitment to effect change requires a careful assessment of one's work environment, and clear communication about the boundaries on political activity.

CONCLUSIONS

Social workers have come to accept social policy development as an essential component of our work as professionals. While the prospect of trying to change legislation, the vision of an organization, or agency policy with respect to service delivery may seem daunting, our successes in these efforts not only provide us with an opportunity to develop a set of skills that are complementary to those we use as clinicians; they also teach us that it can be done. Whether we choose to focus on issues at the international, federal, provincial, local, or agency level, our efforts improve the well-being of individual clients, build a sense of community, and empower us as individuals and as a profession. Ultimately, the values we stand for, infused in social policy, will shape and give definition to the vital, ever-changing culture that we know as Canadian.

REFERENCES

Anastas, J.W. & MacDonald, M.L. (1990). *Research design for social work and the human services*. Toronto: Maxwell Macmillan.

Armitage, A. (1988). *Social welfare in Canada: ideals, realities and future paths*. Toronto: McClelland & Stewart.

Bell, G.G. & Pacoe, A.D. (1988). *The Ontario government: structure and functions*. Toronto: Wall & Thompson.

Brooks, S. (1993). *Public policy in Canada: an introduction*. (2nd ed.). Toronto: McClelland & Stewart.

Canadian Association of Social Workers. (1994). Code of Ethics. Ottawa.

Carver, J. (1990). *Boards that make a difference: a new design for leadership in nonprofit and public organizations*. San Francisco: Jossey-Bass.

Collier, K. (1995). Social policy versus regional trading blocs in the global system: NAFTA, the EEC and "Asia." *Canadian Review of Social Policy , 35*(1), 50–59.

Cresswell, J.W. (1994). *Research design: qualitative and quantitative approaches*. Thousand Oakes: Sage.

Flynn, J.P. (1992). *Social agency policy: analysis and presentation for community practice*. Chicago: Nelson-Hall Publishers.

Friedmann, J. (1987). *Planning in the public domain: from action to knowledge*. Princeton, New Jersey: Princeton University Press.

Gil, D.G. (1981). *Unravelling social policy*. (3rd ed.). Cambridge, Massachusetts: Schenkman Publishing Company.

Graham, J., Swift, K., & Delaney, R. (2000). *Canadian social policy: An introduction*. Scarborough: Prentice Hall Allyn and Bacon.

Guest, D. (1985). *The emergence of social security in Canada*. (2nd ed.). Vancouver: University of British Columbia Press.

Kahn, A.J. (1969). *Theory and practice of social planning*. New York: Russell Sage.

Kahn, A.J. (1979). *Social policy and social services*. (2nd ed.). New York: Random House.

Kirby, S. & McKenna, K. (1989). *Experience, research, social change: methods from the margins*. Toronto: Garamond.

Lightman, E. (1991). Support for social welfare in Canada and the United States. *Canadian Review of Social Policy , 28*(2), 9–27.

Lincoln, Y.S. & Guba, E.G. (1985). *Naturalistic Inquiry*. London: Sage.

Maguire, P. (1987). *Doing participatory research: a feminist approach*. Amherst Mass.: University of Massachusetts, Centre for International Education.

Mayer, R.R. & Greenwood, E. (1980). *The design of social policy research*. Englewood Cliffs, New Jersey: Prentice-Hall.

Mayer, R.R. (1985). *Policy and program planning: a developmental perspective*. Englewood Cliffs, New Jersey: Prentice-Hall.

McGilly, F. (1990). *Canada's public social services: understanding income and health programs*. Toronto: McClelland & Stewart.

Melchers, R. (1999). Local governance of social welfare: Local reform in Ontario in the nineties. *Canadian Review of Social Policy. 43*(2), 29–57.

Mendelson, M. (1999). The new Social Union. *Canadian Review of Social Policy. 43*(2), 1–11.

Meyerson, M. & Banfield, E.C. (1955). *Politics, planning and the public interest*. New York: Free Press.

Moroney, R.M. (1981). Policy analysis within a value theoretical framework. In R. Haskins & J.J. Gallager, (Eds.). *Models for analysis of social policy: an introduction*. Norwood, NJ: Ablex Press, 78–102.

Moscovitch, A. & Drover, G. (1981). *Inequality: essays on the political economy of social welfare*. Toronto: University of Toronto Press.

Moscovitch, A. (1991). Citizenship, social rights and Canadian social welfare. *Canadian Review of Social Policy , 28*(winter), 28–34.

Multiculturalism and Citizenship Canada. (1991). *Convention on the rights of the child*. Ottawa: Minister of Supplies and Services Canada.

Neuman, W.L. (1994). *Social research methods: qualitative and quantitative approaches*. (2nd ed.). Toronto: Allyn & Bacon.

Ogilvie, Ogilvie & Company. (1990). *Policy analysis and policy development: tools and techniques. Course handbook*. Toronto.

Pal, L. (1992). *Public policy analysis: An introduction*. Toronto: Nelson Canada.

Pancer, S.M. & Westhues, A. (1989). A developmental stage approach to planning. *Evaluation Review, 13*(1), 56–77.

Perlman, R. & Gurin, A. (1972). *Community organizing and social planning*. New York: John Wiley and Sons.

Pierce, D. (1984). *Policy for the social work practitioner*. New York: Longman.

Pressman, J.L. & Wildavsky, A.B. (1973). *Implementation*. Berkeley, Los Angeles: University of California Press.

Riches, G. & Ternowetsky, G. (1990). *Unemployment and welfare: social policy and the work of social work*. Toronto: Garamond Press.

Ross, M.C. (1967). *Community organization: theory, principles and practice*. New York: Harper and Row.

Rothman, J. & Zald, M.N. (1985). Planning theory in social work community practice. In S.H. Taylor & R.W. Roberts (Eds.), *Theory and practice of community social work*. (pp.125–153). New York: Columbia University Press.

Snyder, L. (2000). Success of single mothers on social assistance through a voluntary employment program. *Canadian Social Work Review, 17*(1), 49–68.

Splane, R.B. (1965). *Social welfare in Ontario 1791–1893: a study of public welfare administration*. Toronto: University of Toronto Press.

Strauss, A. & Corbin, J. (1990). *Basics of qualitative research: grounded theory procedures and techniques*. Newbury Park: Sage.

Taylor, S.H. & Roberts, R.W. (1985). *Theory and practice of community social work*. New York: Columbia University Press.

Teeple, G. (1995). *Globalization and the decline of social reform*. Toronto: Garamond Press.

Tester, F.J. (1991). The globalized economy: What does it mean for Canadian social and environmental policy? *Canadian Review of Social Policy, 27*(1), 3–12.

Tester, F.J. (1992). The disenchanted democracy: Canada in the global economy of the 1990's. *Canadian Review of Social Policy, 29/30*(1/2), 132–157.

Tindal, C.R. & Tindal, S.N. (1984). *Local government in Canada*. (2nd ed.). Toronto: McGraw-Hill Ryerson.

Tropman, J.E., Erlich, J.L., & Rothman, J. (Eds.), *Tactics and techniques of community intervention*. (3rd ed.). Itasca, Illinois: F.E. Peacock.

Tropman, J.E. (1995). Policy management in the social agency. In J.E.Tropman, J.L. Erlich, & J. Rothman (Eds.). *Tactics and techniques of community intervention.*(3rd ed.). Itasca, Illinois: F.E. Peacock.

Van Loon, R.J. & Whitington, M.S. (1976). *The Canadian political system: environment, structure and process*. (2nd ed.). Toronto: McGraw-Hill Ryerson.

Walker, G.A. (1990). *Family violence and the women's movement*. Toronto: University of Toronto Press.

Westhues, A. (1980). Stages in social planning. *Social Service Review*. (September), 331–343.

Wharf, B. & McKenzie, B. (1998). *Connecting policy to practice in the human services*. Toronto: Oxford University Press.

Yelaja, S.A. (1987). *Canadian social policy*. (Rev. ed.). Waterloo, Ontario: Wilfrid Laurier University Press.

York, R.O. (1982). *Human service planning: Concepts, tools and methods*. Chapel Hill: The University of North Carolina Press.

ADMINISTRATION

AND

SOCIAL WORK
Colin Maloney

In the halls of agencies, there is often heard, "I became a social worker to assist people and instead of working with clients I have become an administrator, lost in a blizzard of forms, recording, documents, accounts, messages, and reports." Most social workers do not see themselves as administrators. Social workers will see themselves as counsellors, therapists, group or community workers, advocates, consultants, and trainers, but very seldom as administrators. Social workers must develop the skills to be good administrators not only in order to be effective but to survive.

In this chapter on administration and social work, we shall reflect on the following questions:

1. What is administration?
2. How does administration differ from the notion of management?
3. In what way is a social worker a manager?
4. In what way is a social worker an administrator?
5. What skills does a social worker need in order to be a successful administrator?
6. How does personality and organization culture shape the individual's personal administrative style?
7. How is technology creating new possibilities and demands for administration?

WHAT IS ADMINISTRATION?

The word *administration* comes from Latin and means "to render a service to someone, to carry out an activity according to a set pattern or rules, for example, to administer medicine, justice, etc." Administration is a process of organizing resources to get work done. Administration differs from doing the actual work in its emphasis on the process of organizing resources. At this abstract level, resources can be people or things. This process of organizing resources can be for a unique event or an ongoing process related to specific tasks. We might say "I'll organize the party." This is a limited kind of administration. Usually, we consider administration not just in relation to a single event or process, but rather as the sum of many different processes by which the total activities are directed toward achieving a common goal. For example, an organization's staff are directed toward achieving the stated goals.

There is also a view of administration that describes the management of an organization. Similarly, titles for the head of an organization may be chief executive, chief administrator, or executive director. In these cases, administrator or director can be seen as synonymous titles. Does this mean that *administration* and *management* are synonyms? The dictionary defines them as synonyms; however, in today's world, the word administration tends to be more narrowly considered as paperwork and/or processes that support or facilitate an organization's direct delivery of service rather than as management. Thus, administrative services in an organization are often viewed as support services rather than as direct work with clients. When we hear *administration*, we often think of the various departments such as finance, human resources, public relations, and information services. There is no doubt that all of these departments support and make possible an organization's delivery of its services to clients. Administration often has the connotation of paperwork or tasks that are necessary but are not the fundamental purpose of an organization that delivers human services centred in social work.

Administration is frequently associated with bureaucracy in a negative way. This results in the perception that administration is bound by its own rules and regulations and not focused primarily on the facilitation of service delivery. Thus, standards such as employment and accounting are normative for administration processes no matter what the service needs. This view of administration is reinforced when an organization specifies the administrative costs as distinct from the cost of the delivery of the social service.

HOW DOES ADMINISTRATION DIFFER FROM THE NOTION OF MANAGEMENT?

The concept of administration is much more limited than that of management. Management includes the management of processes and staff, whether in administrative services or direct delivery of services. The essential quality of management is that results are achieved through the work of others. Thus, the activities and the responsibility of the manager of a group of carpenters are quite different from the activities of the carpenters who actually do the work of sawing the wood and hammering the nails.

A note of authority or power, and being in charge and responsible for the results of others is implied in the coordination of resources. Another characteristic of management is the variety and fragmentation of its activities within the context of the goals of the organization. It is important to remember that the central characteristic associated with management is that it involves achieving results through others. Thus, since one must work through other people, management is highly interpersonal in that it must lead, set directions, create a vision, plan, allocate resources, hold people accountable, resolve conflicts, motivate, and encourage.

At the centre of these various tasks and processes is the need for information that lets people know what is happening and why. Information is fundamental to assessment, planning, and accountability, which will be discussed later in this chapter.

IN WHAT WAY IS A SOCIAL WORKER A MANAGER?

Let's explore who management is within an organization. Managers are usually considered to be those people who are responsible for the direction and supervision of the work produced through other staff. Often included in an organization's management category are those professional staff, such as human resources, who work closely with the direct service manager and can influence management policy development but who do not themselves supervise other direct service staff. The first level of management is often called the supervisory level, that is, the level which directly manages front-line staff. Thus, front-line staff who directly deliver the service and administrative staff would be called *non-management*. In many organizations, front-line and administrative staff are in a bargaining unit represented by a union.

In social work, this understanding of management is ambiguous since the social worker is usually considered a non-manager, yet his or her work is basically to manage others. Front-line social workers are essentially managers because of their responsibility to achieve results through others. Similar to managers described above, front-line social workers have responsibilities to direct, support, motivate, access, and coordinate resources, and train and hold accountable their clients. Most of the time, since social workers need to work through others, the desired outcomes, such as protection of a child or changes in the adult's behaviour, are not in their hands directly. These goals are not something they can directly achieve. The achievement of the goals is primarily in the hands of the clients whom the worker is expected to manage or supervise. In fact, the worker may have twenty to forty cases to manage, e.g., families, parents, or children.

The National Association of Social Workers (NASW), in their standards for social work case management, define case management as follows:

> Social work case management is a method of providing services whereby a professional social worker assesses the needs of the client and the client's family, when appropriate, and arranges, coordinates, monitors, evaluates, and advocates for a package of multiple services to meet the specific client's complex needs.

> A professional social worker is the primary provider of social work case management. Distinct from other forms of case management, social work case management addresses both the individual client's biopsychosocial status as well as the state of the social system in which case management operates. Social work case management is both micro and macro in nature: intervention occurs at both the client and system levels. It requires the social worker to develop and maintain a therapeutic relationship with the client, which may include linking the client with systems that provide him or her with needed services, resources, and opportunities. Services provided under the rubric of social work case management practice may be located in a single organization or may be spread across numerous agencies or organizations.

In the definition of case management, all the processes and expectations of a manager come into play. The basis of achieving the goals or outcomes depends primarily on establishing a relationship of trust, partnership, and teamwork. There will be the need to set objectives, agree upon a plan of action, review the plan from time to time, allocate resources, evaluate outcomes, motivate and encourage problem-solving, and support clients in order that they may achieve their goals. To be sure, a social worker has to be a skilled manager, but since clients are not paid staff under contract, we do not usually consider front-line social workers as a part of management. Instead they are called case managers.

Although it is clear that a desired outcome is not directly in the hands of the social worker, as it would be in the case, for instance, of a carpenter building a house, this does not imply that the work and the tasks of the social worker are not crucial for the outcomes. In some ways, the results depend directly on the case manager in terms of expertise in assessing and making crucial decisions. These decisions may raise questions for the social worker such as whether a child should be apprehended or returned home, whether an adoption is advisable, and questions regarding court involvement and allocation of resources.

All of this is really what management is about. Ultimately if the task is to be achieved it is only because the client does the work. The various stages of the process (assessment, setting of objectives, crucial decision-making) have to belong to and be understood by the client. I believe this is why social work has become consumer-driven. This is illustrated in the Family Decision Making Model, which originated in New Zealand, the "Wraparound," so strongly advocated by Dr. John VanDenBerg, and the Brief Solution Focus Therapy of Insoo Kim Berg, which are all built around the reality that the client is the doer and the social worker the front-line case manager.

Understanding social work from the managerial perspective does not reduce the therapeutic role of the worker, the need for social work expertise, or lessen our responsibility. This concept can clarify roles and responsibility and frame the appropriateness of how decisions are made. This clarity of the case management role does not, of itself, dictate how this role will be fulfilled and practiced. The practice ranges from the authoritarian to the self-managing, from high control with permission and rules to significant autonomy with appropriate accountability and flexibility.

So far, we have looked at administration and management and how these concepts differ in present social work practice. We have also considered how a social worker, in a true sense, is a manager. This primary focus is often called case management.

This perspective on social work, focusing on its management role, does not imply that all management roles are the same or equal. The executive director's role brings with it a responsibility, power, and authority that no one else has in the organization. Thus, the role of senior management differs from the that of supervisors, which in turn differs from the managerial role of the front-line worker. This difference should not obscure the management function common to all of these levels. Perhaps one may object to calling a social worker a manager because, as a front-line social worker she does not have authority to hire and fire as a manager does. Of course, authority differs at each level. I would like to quote again from the NASW: "At all stages of client intervention, it is crucial that the social work case manager be granted sufficient authority to access, allocate, monitor, and evaluate service and fiscal resources. Such authority is a prerequisite of effective case management practice."

A front-line worker who has authority to close a case has an authority analogous to that of other managers. A good manager excels more through inspiration, vision, relationships of trust and respect, achieving something which is meaningful through recognition and reward rather than through authority. Thus, the exercise of authority through such actions as firing an employee is more of an exception than a rule in management practice. The large majority of cases are managed in partnership and collaboration. Similarly, in child welfare a social worker, by way of exception, may use authority to apprehend a child or take someone to court.

HOW IS A SOCIAL WORKER AN ADMINISTRATOR?

It is clear that social workers are managers. It is not so clear that they are also administrators. While in general the words *manager* and *administrator* are used interchangeably, I would like to use the more narrow definition of administration that focuses more on organizing processes than people. From this administrative perspective, I would like to focus on the front-line social worker rather than the organization administration. First, we will consider the organization's administration only from the perspective of how a worker must learn to engage and use that administration. Second, we will consider how the organization's administrative culture shapes the worker's style of administration.

The most essential resource in social work administration is the worker's time. Consultants, or those being paid by the hour or involved in managed health care, are inundated by time-management accountability.

The framework for a worker's management of time obviously is the organization in which she works. The organization's business hours in themselves create a block of time that we have at our disposal, especially if the organization is government-run with set hours, more or less, from 9 to 5. This gives order and helps to balance one's private life. However, from a management perspective (i.e., the social worker's management perspective which is to engage, to create client ownership, and to motivate) we must always ask if the organization's hours support the worker or the client. For example, does the organization function like a bank, which creates its hours to suit itself, so that consumers are the ones who must adapt?

There is pressure for an organization to have more and more flexibility and to respond to the client's non-work hours, i.e., weekends, evenings, and nights, which raises the question, "How can a worker find balance between her family's private life and work?" While the organization's business hours set the framework for the worker within the time frame of the hours allocated, a worker with so many cases and so many tasks must manage her time as best she can. The various demands that all workers face include attending meetings with clients, attending team meetings, as well as responsibilities with regard to supervision, training, court, documentation, and travel.

Clearly in social work there is always much more that needs to be done than there is time allocated. The basic problem with time allocation is that the heart of social work is built on relationships, and it takes time to build the understanding, trust, and motivation essential to good relationships. Instead, administration focuses on paper work, forms, and meetings. Indeed, there seems to be a continual tension between administration and work with clients.

WHAT SKILLS DOES A SOCIAL WORKER NEED IN ORDER TO BE A SUCCESSFUL ADMINISTRATOR?

From an administration point of view, the worker's most difficult decision is the allocation of the most expensive resource, which is his time. Time management is planning and allocation of worker time. How does one plan one's work, and adapt to the changes, surprises, and crises that dominate social work? The skills involved in worker time management are similar to those we use in our personal lives, for such tasks as shopping, raising children, studies, etc. People tend to be consistent. Some are very careful, write lists, are very punctual, and are aware. Others are very charismatic, spontaneous, and respond to the moment. Time management style tends to be reflected both in how we live and how we work, and is determined by our personalities rather than just the demands of the task.

In a strange way, life is a continuous training ground in time management. We have already created our own time management style by the time we commence social work practice. And we use resources that support our style, such as the appointment books or planners, which help us plan, prioritize, and remember. These resources often include additional space for notes, follow-up activities, financial costs, and notes to be expanded when we do our recording. Loss of our case notes is a disaster.

Obviously, choosing priorities is important. Many priorities, such as mandatory training, meetings, and supervision, are set by the organization. Sometimes, our allocation of time is set by others or by the court. Time management is not the management of that unstoppable flow or movement of the minute hand, but the management of one's life. There are basic patterns and values that frame and govern how we manage time. We are, if nothing else, consistent in how we manage time and how we manage our own lives. To change one is to change the other.

The problem is that the number of demands coming from so many different directions can overwhelm our sense of being able to respond, or at least being able to respond appropriately. This is more and more true as governments cut back, increasing worker case loads, and as the expectations of managed care increases the demands on the social worker. Obviously, we presume that a worker has the appropriate expertise and knowledge to be able to assess and set priorities. What is most often missing is the appropriate support and resources. What is most important is workers' ability to remain centred, to trust in their ability, to be free to weigh priorities, to make decisions, and to be clear without being afraid to face conflicts.

A supervisor must be able to assist a worker in being centred, and be able, when we lose our centredness, to show how to regain it. Often, the supervisor who listens and reflects on what has happened can quickly refocus the worker. For many people, there needs to be a time of stillness, just to let all concerns and worries go and to have some emotional distance from them in order to come back to being centred. For some people, breathing is a major factor in keeping or finding their centredness. The more uncentred we are, usually the shorter and less deep our breathing. Whatever happens, to be centred is the most fundamental priority for social work—otherwise demands can overwhelm and scatter our emotional freedom and our ability to prioritize with a sense of hopefulness.

The second and most important aspect of time management is clarity. At the intake/assessment, there is a lack of clarity as to what needs to be done and by whom. We always begin in a state of ignorance and with a lack of clarity. With assessment, listening, and supervision, we begin to achieve clarity. Part of the process is dealing with the lack of clarity. The difficulty is in not being aware that we lack clarity. This is the essential beginning of clarity. So many forms are filled out by workers in a hurry because they are not clear what is being asked. This can be a major waste of time.

A vital issue in time management is to be conscious of what we don't like or what we are afraid of or feeling insecure about. There is always a tendency to avoid this issue, which in the end wastes much time and energy. This must have a priority. Plus, we need to be careful and attentive to why the fear and insecurities are there. The issue is not the fear and insecurity. The issue is being centred in confronting our fears and insecurities, so that we are able to prioritize our time in an effective manner.

With centredness and clarity comes a sense of freedom. There is a need to contextualize our responsibilities and the overwhelming needs of the client. The sense of being responsible for the situation, but not feeling in control of it, not being able to do directly what needs to be done, requires that we trust the client. For some people, there is a very religious sense of trusting in life, providence, or fate, so that there is truly a freedom in the face of the high risks and difficult decisions that a worker must make. Without this freedom in the face of injustice and crises, the risk is great that our work will invade our personal lives and result in burnout.

At present, in the social work field there is a major shift in the question of time management, since the most costly resource an organization has is usually worker time. In fact, 85% of an organization's expenses goes to cover the cost of staff time. In many organizations, unless there is the need to bill for appointments, counselling, etc., there is very little known of how workers spend their time. Mostly, the organization demands that workers account for their activities but not for their time. Studies have been done that give a brief snapshot, such as a week or a day, of a worker's time. In child welfare, many studies show that workers are fortunate if 30–40% of their time goes to direct work with clients.

The health management movement in the United States manages these major time costs by assigning a limit to the amount of time an intervention may have. For instance, if there is to be counselling, only five sessions are allotted and in those five sessions certain outcomes are expected. Organizations, especially government agencies, are in large part accountable for activities, but not for productivity in the use of the most precious of resources, the worker's time. Thus, this new demand for accountability flows over into cost effectiveness, productivity, and the demonstration of outcomes. In conclusion, the fundamental administrative task that a worker has is to be a good administrator of time.

With government cut-backs, a growing demand on workers' time, greater accountability, the needs for collaborative case conferencing, greater contracting with collaterals, and more meetings, time becomes more and more difficult to manage. It is incumbent upon us to become much more skilled at being centred, to achieve clarity, understanding, and freedom.

HOW DO THE ORGANIZATION'S VALUES AND CULTURE SHAPE THE WORKER'S PERSONAL ADMINISTRATIVE STYLE?

Our lifestyle and character shape not only our process of administration but also the values we have in terms of priorities. Our values are also shaped by the values of the organization. For example,

- Is the priority of the organization being on time, attending to paperwork, meetings, procedures, administration?
- How much priority is given to the client?
- How much flexibility am I given in terms of responding, adapting our program, our work, to the needs of clients?
- How much is my work shaped by an authority that is there not only to hold accountable but to be truly of service to the front-line worker?
- Is the organization's authority mostly to control and to make all the decisions?

The values of the organization are reflected in the style of how the worker administers her own time, resources, and priorities. While there can be some dissent, some uniqueness and individuality within certain boundaries, it is difficult to remain in the organization and be a maverick. It is therefore necessary to come to some compromise with organization values, and its use of authority, because as workers are treated, so will the workers treat others. If one works in an authoritarian organization, casework will be authoritarian. If it is a paternalistic or maternalistic organization, casework and management style will be paternalistic or maternalistic. If priority is given to administration, programs, and paperwork, the client will not come first. The client loses on all levels because his uniqueness is ignored, nor does he receive the trust and support he needs, and programs are inflexible.

The tension between personal values and organization values is compounded in those organizations where the government exercises a profound control through funding, policy, rules, and supervision. The organization can also have a tension of values between the expectations and political demands of the funding body and the desire and values of the organization in terms of service to be delivered. Thus, in the relationship between the authority governing the organization and the authority of the organization governing the worker, there is truly an echo effect. One cannot live for long with the dissonance of being a collaborative partnership in an organization that is driven by paternalistic authority. Many organizations live with this tension of paternalistic authority of government. This same echo makes impossible the expectation of client empowerment. Clients are unable to take ownership of the decision and it becomes impossible to form a true partnership in the context of values that are paternalistic.

HOW IS TECHNOLOGY CREATING NEW POSSIBILITIES AND DEMANDS FOR ADMINISTRATION?

While we have always had such instruments as our case notes and our appointment books to help us manage our time, the technological revolution brings greater demands and many more possibilities in terms of the many uses of the telephone, messaging, conferencing, mobile phones, and laptop computers. All of these technologies are shaping how a worker manages time, prepares documentation, and accesses and receives information.

Just as the telephone shaped social work communications seventy-five years ago, so today technology is truly revolutionizing how we work, how we manage, and how we administrate. Initially many feared that the telephone would depersonalize social work. Now the telephone is being extended by the fax, the laptop, video camera, tele-conferencing, and the Internet.

These technologies are reshaping how social workers, as administrators, manage their work. Our relationships, knowledge, skills, and resources are the basis of our work. Much of what we are able to do depends upon the management of information. Organizing and sharing of information are the most significant administrative tasks that we have to do as social workers besides managing our time.

From intake through assessment, diagnosis, planning, recording, evaluating, conferencing, court, supervising—all are based on the management of information. How timely, accessible, and communicable our information is will dictate the quality of much of our work.

In the past, most of this administration of information was through a file in which there were many forms, assessments, letters, and documents. The belief was that the worker owned the file. But now the paper file has been replaced by cyberspace. We now expect information to be available whenever it is needed, and more people have access to it. "My case" quickly becomes "our case." Information systems have deprivatized casework, which used to be much more in the worker's hands, being at the most shared with the supervisor. Initially, these new resources and demands were seen as burdens instead of as instruments that help in the administration of information.

So often, technology is used to control and make available an ever-increasing amount of data that management wants. It should be the instrument that truly supports and facilitates workers' case management and administration so that their work is enriched and much more accountable. Unfortunately, technology is very seldom front-line driven, but usually management driven.

Technology has transformed the nature of accountability. Previously, the file belonged to the worker and was physically in her file cabinet or carried with her. All of a sudden, technology is creating a system in which information is open and available to anyone who has authority at the press of a button. It is now shared information and open to public scrutiny by fellow workers. The technology allows the worker to record what is essential in a way that is precise, clear, and helpful. Yet, most training hardly ever gives the skills necessary to use this technology and to use it wisely, thus causing tremendous loss of time and efficiency. The appropriate technology allows a team to be able to share the information, communicate with each other, be accountable to each other, and work more and more as a team. If a worker gets sick, or if one is out of the office, we are able to access and manage information so that time and space are less and less relevant to the management of information.

Technology also creates a possibility that the organization will become a learning organization. Databases are created that allow a worker to review how similar cases were successfully handled, what the resources were that would be available for this type of case and what the outcomes were that could be legitimately hoped for. The possibility is there to have a database open to all workers to seek resources and expertise. Technology can create an ongoing learning situation in organizations where this has never been possible to this degree before. Technology not only changes how we manage our time and information, it increases the possibility of learning. It has also transformed the nature of accountability and outcomes.

One of the primary questions that a social work organization faces is: What difference does an organization's intervention make? This question has always been with us, but the answer is now more widely and urgently demanded. The fields of education and health are no less under the gun of accountability for outcomes.

The problem with defining outcomes is that most of life's development or healing, whether in education, health, or social work, is a self-development and a self-healing. While we as case managers only support, clarify, allocate resources, give leadership, and advocate, the results are ultimately not in our hands but primarily in the client's hands. A teacher can teach, but only the student learns. No longer can we just say a student fails, but must say the school failed also. We can no longer just say that the client was unmotivated, uncooperative, etc. We have to review our strategies and our customization of programs and interventions. While social workers are being pushed through technology, weakened by cut-backs, and faced with the competition of managed health care, we are expected to demonstrate that we manage and administer successfully, cost-effectively, and with outcomes that are acceptable.

CONCLUSION

As we have mentioned, our primary resource is our time. However, there are many resources a worker is called upon to organize and prioritize. How should we assign a volunteer? When should we encourage the use of groups? When should we advocate for access to a program? The decision of a child welfare worker to bring a child into care, the decision to go to court to seek crown wardship—all of these issues involve the allocation of millions of dollars. Very seldom do we see these decisions as resource allocation as we strive to do what is in the client's best interest. This is all a part of our administration. It is not enough to do counselling, to make a visit, nor is it enough to say that I have done these activities. The question remains, were they the right activities? What were the outcomes? How effective were they? These are more and more the kind of questions that are crucial to good social work administration and case management.

We have clarified that an essential way to understand social work is from a management/administration perspective. From this perspective, a social worker's management skills of supervising others, such as listening, motivating, planning, and holding accountable, are primary. We have affirmed that the key to managing is the relationship of trust and partnership between a worker and a client. This partnership is shaped by the worker's values but, above all, by the organization's values and management style.

We have covered the essential double role of administration: organizing and allocation of resources, especially time, and the management of information. A good social worker is a manager and an administrator, as an effective manager and administrator can then be accountable and effective in his or her therapeutic and advocacy roles.

CLINICAL PRACTICE EVALUATION

Barbara Thomlison and
Cathryn Bradshaw

Recent literature suggests that the use of evidence-supported practice guidelines and technology to augment direct practice interventions with clients is becoming more common (Meenaghan, Gabriel, & Holden, 2000). Both of these influences have increased awareness and sensitivity to addressing practice effectiveness and accountability. *Practice competence* may be defined as a set of attitudes, skills, knowledge, and beliefs necessary to work effectively with clients (Corcoran, 2000). As a consequence, technology has provided social workers access to extensive online research and practice interventions and the opportunity to critically examine established practice applications and knowledge.

The proliferation of evidence-supported literature reviews is the science of research synthesis and has enhanced knowledge or provided more reliable evidence of the effects of interventions, thereby allowing social workers to take advantage of knowledge that was previously not readily available (Chalmers, 1999). Social workers can access libraries, full-text articles, and other sources of practice information on the Internet for practice methods for common problems. Now, most student social workers take at least one or more courses fully online or partially assisted through online research (Meenaghan, Gabriel, & Holden, 2000). Such knowledge is important for social work practice accountability and extends beyond individual workers to the systems and agencies that deliver services. These influences are increasingly important issues for various stakeholders, particularly for social workers who, at treatment termination, will need to provide evidence of practice effectiveness as well as of maintenance and generalization of gains. Accessing best practices through the Internet helps practitioners to keep abreast.

The purpose of this chapter is to assist clinical social workers in developing an explicit practice evaluation approach, based on using evidence-supported interventions. The concept of *evaluation* is used broadly to include any method that collects data in a reliable and valid way to describe the client's characteristics and functioning (Jordan & Franklin, 1995). The context of accountability, including the cultural context of social work practice, is considered first. Then, matters such as the importance of practice evaluation, practice evaluation assumptions, evaluation as a client service, guidelines for establishing case-level evaluation, choosing appropriate measures, and integrating evaluation into practice intervention are considered.

CONTEXT FOR ACCOUNTABILITY

As a professional social worker, you are accountable to yourself, to your profession, to your clients, to the agency you work in, and to other stakeholder systems, such as funders or other collateral agencies. In fact, accountability for the provision of quality service delivery has long been part of social work values and ethics. Elements of the Canadian Social Work Code of Ethics (Canadian Association of Social Workers, 1994) pertain to the professional obligation of all social workers to engage in client self-determination, to individualize service, and to provide effective social work practice to clients as well as contribute to social work knowledge-building. Effective clinical practice is important because clients underutilize services, delay utilization, and often prematurely terminate utilization of health and mental services, and this is often attributed to a lack of competence on the part of service providers (Potocky-Tripodi, 2001). However, there is a need to demonstrate even more competent practice for ethnically diverse populations. Practice evaluation is therefore considered to be an essential and ethical element of social work practice. A "good" intervention is one that works. And a quality service is one that achieves its intended or desired outcome and is delivered in an efficient manner. Clients have a right to effective and efficient service (Corcoran & Vandiver, 1996). Practice evaluation is important since the results can be used to revise client treatment plans, profile clients for referrals, formulate practice guidelines, as well as shape or improve clinical intervention services. Achieving change, maintenance, and generalization of treatment gains are part of this process.

Establishing evaluation as an essential treatment plan activity for each client system allows good practice to become better and reduces the likelihood of social workers reaching unsupported claims about client change. When evaluation is viewed as a measure of quality assurance for the provision of services, resources can then be better targeted in order to meet both the quantity and quality of services needed to address the situations and problems facing Canadian families. Practice evaluation can ensure quality services as well as program service fidelity. Clients and social workers need to know to what extent contracted goals and objectives have been achieved. Funders need to know the skills, approaches, methods, information, resources, and strategies used to accomplish the goal and objectives that are most effective.

As Canadian social workers encounter increasing diversity in practice, it is also important to consider ethno-cultural aspects of evaluation. The evaluation approach that is most free of bias is single-system assessment or evaluation. There is nothing inherent in the single-system approach that limits it to a specific clinical problem or situation. Single-system evaluation can be applied to many different populations and issues. In this regard, it is particularly well-suited to diverse populations such as Canada's, and may be preferred to other evaluation methods.

CULTURAL COMPETENCE IN EVALUATION

Delivering culturally appropriate services to diverse clients is a challenge. Demographic trends in Canadian society, such as immigration patterns and a large aging population base, mean that an increasing proportion of the clients in social service, health, and mental health agencies will present social workers with challenging practice issues. Social workers need to be sensitive to unique cultural patterns, whether the service rendered involves individual, couple, or family intervention, or developing community programs consistent with ethnic reality. Cross-cultural practice situations are usually conceptualized and viewed in terms of comparing dominant group members with the culturally different group members. When faced with cross-cultural practice situations, we are challenged to consider uniqueness and commonality at the same time social workers are called to value and appreciate the diversity as well as the interrelatedness and interconnectedness of human expression and experience. (Dana, Behn, & Gonwa, 1992; Sue, Arrendondo, & McDavis, 1992).

Practice guidelines assist service providers but need to be more specific. Development of practice guidelines for culturally competent practice is derived from two sources: empirical evidence and expert consensus (Potocky-Tripodi, 2001). Guidelines are intended to offer help to practitioners to make the best choices among intervention strategies. Guidelines for cultural competence are based on expert consensus and the Canadian Association of Social Workers has not yet worked out guidelines, such as those developed by the American Psychological Association (APA), for providers of services to ethnic, linguistic, and culturally diverse populations (APA, 1990). Social workers adhere to the following practice principles derived from experts:

Principles pertaining to attitudes and beliefs

- Respect client beliefs and values as they impact their worldview, psychosocial functioning, as well as ways of expressing distress.
- Respect helping practices and help-giving networks important to the culture.
- Value diversity.
- Develop self-awareness of own assumptions, values, and biases and understand the source of these cultural values and biases.

Principles pertaining to knowledge

- Understand how social work practice may be in conflict with various cultural values and practices of clients.
- Have awareness of system barriers that impede access to and provision of appropriate social work services for ethnically diverse populations.
- Identify potential cultural and language biases in various measurement techniques and instruments, and use and interpret measurement data in a culturally appropriate manner.
- Access information about cultural stories such as family structures, hierarchies, immigration histories, values, beliefs, experiences of discrimination, and community characteristics, as well as natural helping resources.
- Develop awareness of community, policy, and institutional discriminatory practices.
- Understand that both individual and collective experiences impact problem generation, problem solutions, and evaluation methods.

Principles pertaining to skills

- Engage in various verbal and nonverbal helping responses.
- Assess the impact of discrimination on the presenting issue.

- Consult with other professionals or persons significant in the particular culture.
- Provide service in the preferred language of the client, such as through the use of interpreters, or refer the client to more culturally appropriate services when available.
- Adapt practice interventions in designing helping strategies.
- Provide information to the client regarding intervention and evaluation practices.
- Work to eliminate clinical and social practices that are biased, prejudiced, or discriminatory.

The competent social worker considers the elements of diversity of clients that are a source of cohesion, identity, and strength as well as a source of strain, discordance, and strife. Therefore, both the context of diversity and elements of culture are considered in case-level practice evaluation. The reader is referred to the case of Nora (see Appendix) to illustrate issues of diversity and practice evaluation at the case level. Nora is an Aboriginal teenager receiving family reunification services. This case example will be referred to throughout this chapter.

PRACTICE EVALUATION

Practice evaluation is primarily concerned with effectiveness and efficiency. *Effectiveness* is concerned with identifying which practice activities or interventions are associated with better outcomes. *Efficiency* pertains to how cost-effective practices are. Effectiveness is emphasized here and the reader is referred to Corcoran and Vandiver (1996) for a complete discussion of efficiency. The purpose of practice evaluation is to obtain information about a client (case-level) or a service (program-level) to assist in decision-making. There are a number of ways to define *practice evaluation*, but in general it refers to a planned, systematic way of collecting, analyzing, and reporting information about change. When there is a broader evaluation focus, information relates to program-level activities and is used for program decision-making in the quality improvement process. As used here, practice evaluation will refer to information focused on change at the case level—that is, the client's problem(s) or situation and the progress toward the treatment goal (Corcoran & Vandiver, 1996).

ISSUES IN PRACTICE EVALUATION

Evaluation is an integral part of social casework planning and is necessary for both practical and ethical reasons. Nevertheless, social workers consistently express difficulties in evaluating practice and frequently do not do it. Often social workers claim they do not know how to go about identifying and tracking case progress and therefore must be encouraged in management, supervision, and practice policies. More importantly, clients have a right to effective treatment, and social workers an ethical responsibility to inform clients about effective interventions and their outcomes. When agency management encourages evaluation at all levels, social workers are more likely to receive support for evaluation of cases as part of routine practice.

Some social workers may even feel distress or believe that practice evaluation methods interfere with their ability to work effectively with their clients. Some do not realize that systematic and planned evaluation is a form of practice monitoring related to social work knowledge building. Evaluation provides benefits not only to clients but also to you as a social worker. Evaluation shows clients that you care about their progress and wish to keep them fully informed. The potential benefits to clients and social workers are opportunities to improve skills of helping.

Still others may think practice evaluation methods are intrusive, time consuming, and unnecessary. In reality, evaluation serves to facilitate implementation and replication. During the intervention phase, evaluation serves as feedback to both the client and worker. For the client, evaluation information will promote motivation and involvement in change. For social workers, evaluation data informs clinical decisions regarding the continuation of specific intervention strategies. Social workers are able to design and implement follow-up strategies that can encourage the maintenance and generalization of achievements across time and across life settings. Evaluation as a client service thus promotes improved performance standards, provides feedback to numerous constituents, and also acts as a form of staff training about evidence-supported interventions.

Kazi and Wilson (1996) offer five reasons for using evaluative strategies in clinical social work practice:

1. Evaluation assists the social worker and the client system in identifying and assessing the impact of problem situations.

2. Evaluation provides evidence of improvement to the client system and the social worker, as well as to other stakeholder systems, such as family, school, work, or others. Regular feedback in the form of review and evaluation can be instrumental in helping everyone maintain an effective motivation level and commitment to the change process.

3. Evaluation recognizes that ongoing appraisal will provide the social worker with objective information to report at case conferences and other collaborative efforts.

4. The agency's credibility with both clients and funders can be enhanced through its social workers' commitment to evaluating the outcome of their services.

5. The consistent use of evaluation strategies promotes a more objective and systematic approach to the delivery of social work services to individuals, families, groups, and communities.

The important principle for practice evaluation is that clinical social work service must be empirically based in order for quality services to occur. The context of effective social work practice relies on logically linking the planned treatment intervention to the presenting client problem. Clinical social workers make many decisions throughout the treatment process, and planning for practice evaluation at the beginning of client contact assists in this task. Evaluation is a necessary part of quality client service. That is, it is important to determine whether the client improved, treatment goals were achieved, and the maintenance of gains resulted.

EVALUATION IS A CLIENT SERVICE

Evaluation is a client service. It is an essential clinical activity within the practice continuum of assessment, contracting, intervention, evaluation, and termination. From the initial encounter with a client system and throughout the course of service, evaluation activities require social workers to structure treatment and change processes into well-defined steps. While most practice evaluation is not particularly concerned with attempting to demonstrate cause and effect relationships of common client problems and change, it does allow social workers to evaluate approaches to service interventions and thus to maximize client outcomes.

Depending on the purpose, there are different types of evaluation. Two common and useful types, for most practitioners, are *monitoring* and *summative* evaluation. *Monitoring* involves ongoing data collection to obtain new information and/or the need for a change of interventions. This is usually done to provide continuous output information about the client's problems. Social workers may collect data on client characteristics, problems, and services provided, as well as changes during treatment, at termination, and even after discharge. Such data are useful in focusing intervention activities with clients. Thus, continuous or formative evaluation functions as a feedback system for both the client and the worker in order to modify and improve intervention activities. Tracking client goal achievement can facilitate a continuous identification of service effectiveness, service gaps, and service activities or strategies. Ongoing evaluation ensures that treatment procedures are implemented according to the client's goals and professional social work standards, and that the appropriate match is achieved between the level of service and the severity of the problem.

Evaluation can also occur periodically. *Summative* evaluation occurs infrequently and usually on a one-time basis. It is usually done to assess outcomes and may occur a long time after the delivery of direct services. The results of summative evaluation provide feedback to programs at a particular point in time, such as at the completion of a service cycle. Thus, *periodic* evaluation may not be of particular, direct benefit to the client and worker, but it can facilitate program improvement. Program review and evaluation strategies assist the agency in program planning, service development, and resource allocation. The most helpful evaluative design to the clinical social worker is the single-case system design, which asks the question "Did the client improve during the course of treatment?" This design provides basic information for key decisions in case-level practice.

CASE-LEVEL EVALUATION

There are numerous books (Gambrill, 1997; Tripodi, 1994) on how to evaluate case practice. Case evaluation is well defined. It closely parallels the social work practice problem-solving framework: assessment, planning, intervention, and evaluation. Evaluation informs social work case practice by providing information about human behaviour as well as social problems and the solutions to these problems. The informed social worker uses this knowledge base to assist in making the myriad of clinical judgments as part of daily practice.

Evaluative research is concerned with two questions: (1) Were the expected outcomes achieved?, and (2) Are the outcomes attributed to the interventions provided? It is the effectiveness of the intervention or treatment procedure that is being tested. That is, how strong is the relationship between the intervention and the outcome reported? Evaluation demonstrates whether this association can be made. The social worker is involved in a set of activities that go well beyond determining whether expected outcomes were achieved. These evaluation research activities will need to take into account the complexities of most social work clinical contexts, as well as the tasks and practice methods of social work and whether the desired outcome was achieved. The emphasis of the two approaches is slightly different.

Using the single-case approach demands planning with the client system and perhaps other helping systems to develop strategies matched to client strengths, diversity, and abilities. Case service and intervention activities need to be stated in clear, precise, goal-focused behavioural terms for ease of measurement. Hudson (1982) noted that the best way to retrieve this information is to ask clients or to observe clients directly. This moves social work practice from *implicit* to *explicit* evaluation. Information collected as part of standard casework practice is then useful for case decision-making with the client when assessed against the planned treatment goals.

CASE EVALUATION PROCESS

The process of evaluation parallels the clinical problem-solving process as follows: (1) problem identification and specification; (2) evaluation planning in the form of determining the mode of evaluation; (3) collection and analysis of the data; and (4) sharing of the knowledge gained. The simplest and often the most feasible evaluative design for clinical social work practice is a single-case design, the AB design being perhaps the most widely used. The AB design has two phases. The A phase is comprised of establishing a baseline (a rate of the outcome measure) at the time of assessment or just prior to the beginning of intervention. The B phase represents the implementation of the intervention strategies designed to promote the desired changes.

The chosen measurements are repeated at specified points throughout the assessment, intervention, and follow-up periods. The results are recorded in such a way as to facilitate change comparisons. Zastrow (1995) summarizes six steps in the utilization of single-system evaluation. An example from the case of Nora (see Appendix) is provided with each step:

1. *Specify the goal.* Goals need to be formulated in specific, concrete, and measurable terms. A specific goal should reflect the presence of, rather than the absence of, something. Well-formulated goals will concretely state what will be different when treatment has been completed. A concrete goal is measurable and usually involves a change in *behaviour* (thoughts, actions, feelings, or attitudes), a change in the *quantity and/or quality of relationships*, or a change in some aspect of the *environment*, such as a change in living arrangements or school situation.

   Specifying Nora's goals. The general goals for this case were: (1) to expand the availability of Nora's family network; (2) to increase Nora's coping abilities surrounding family relationship issues; (3) to increase the continuity of family contact; (4) to improve the quality of family relationships; and (5) to strengthen Nora's sense of identity. An example of a specific goal was to expand the availability of Nora's family network to include contact with her biological father.

2. *Select suitable measures.* One of the most challenging tasks in intervention planning is determining how you will measure the degree of outcome change. Selecting a suitable outcome measurement tool for the goals involves considering how you can quantify the desired outcomes. For example, has change occurred: yes or no? This would represent the most basic means of evaluating change. However, most outcome evaluations include various levels or degrees of change. A number of evaluation or measurement tools are available to social workers. The strengths, needs, and diversity of the client system, as well as the agency requirements must be taken into account in selecting appropriate ways of measuring outcomes. Measurement methods have been grouped under the categories of: (1) rating scales, to determine an internal state, (2) rapid standardized assessment instruments, to provide a basis of comparison against known groups, and (3) behavioural obser-

vations for a direct measure. Whenever possible, social workers should choose those measurement instruments that have reported reliability and validity. Examples for each of these types of measures for social workers are readily available in social work texts (see Fischer & Corcoran, 1994; Hudson, 1982; Tripodi, 1994; Zastrow, 1995).

Selecting suitable measures for Nora's goals. (See Appendix: Figure 28.1) For each of the goals listed, the following measures were selected:

Goal: Expand the availability of Nora's family network: measure selected was the use of a genogram;

Goal: Increase Nora's coping abilities surrounding family relationship issues: measure selected was a questionnaire developed for foster parents, family reunification worker, and the child, Nora;

Goal: Increase the continuity of family contact: measure selected was monthly contact calendars recording number of contacts between family members by visits telephone, or written communication.

Goal: Increase the quality of family relationships: measure selected was the Hudson Index of Family Relations Scale and the Index of Sibling Relations Scale.

Goal: Strengthen Nora's sense of identity: measure used was My Preferences Scale, family genogram, and Consumer Satisfaction questionnaire.

3. *Record baseline data.* The baseline establishes the level, stability, and trend of the client's functioning prior to any specific intervention. During the assessment period, this usually requires a minimum of three data points, or until a stable data pattern is obtained. This becomes the standard against which any changes accompanying intervention can be evaluated. If the client system is in crisis or danger, immediate intervention is essential. In such circumstances, the social worker would proceed with intervention and repeatedly measure the client's progress during the B or treatment phase.

   Recording baseline data in Nora's case. Multiple baseline data for each goal was recorded prior to family reunification services being initiated. Baseline for number of family members identified in the genogram ranged from 27 to 35 family members for Nora prior to closing of services. The nature of family reunification services did not permit repeat of the baseline measures prior to service. Only one baseline measure was possible.

4. *Implement intervention and continue monitoring.* At specified intervals, such as every month or every week, the same measurement tool would be given as for the baseline. This provides information on whether progress is being made and can be valuable information for deciding if revision of change strategies or objectives needs to be made.

   Intervention and monitoring in Nora's case. The interventions included family locator approaches, behavior modification techniques including role and response rehearsal for child and birth parents, recasting family history for child and birth parents, negotiating contacts, and supporting contacts through teaching parent-child and family activities and relationship techniques for communication. Interventions were monitored throughout the treatment phase.

5. *Assess change.* Creating a chart or graph from the data collected facilitates a visual analysis of the social worker's measurements. This visual representation of change can provide important information to both you and the client regarding whether change is taking place in the desired direction.

Assessing change in Norea's case. Each goal was monitored throughout the baseline, 6-month, 12-month, and 18-month period, including follow-up. Measures on the Hudson scales showed continual change in a positive direction. The 12- and 18-month follow-up continued to show positive change in all family reunification goals for Nora.

6. *Infer effectiveness.* Making an inference about whether your intervention was responsible for client outcomes involves determining whether other explanations for the changes might be found. Possible sources for change besides your intervention include: history (events which occurred during the time of treatment but were not related to the treatment), maturation (the effects of time), multiple-treatment interference (more than one treatment received), and statistical regression (high and low scores on measures tend to move towards the mean or average score when retested) (Zastrow, 1995). All of these factors, known as threats to validity, need to be eliminated if you are to infer that your intervention caused the observed change. More complex single-system research designs than the AB design will help you to have confidence in the link between your interventions and the outcomes. For a discussion of more complex designs for social workers see Tripodi (1994).

Inferring effectiveness in Nora's case. Based on the results of Nora's measures, the birth parent responses, and foster parent and family reunification worker responses to measures and questionnaires, the introduction of family reunification services changed Nora's involvement positively with her biological family. These results are confirmed (see Figure 28.1). It is quite certain that with the introduction of services at this time, the change can be attributed to the intervention.

7. *Follow-up.* It is important that the social worker analyze the results of the intervention program to assess the maintenance and generalization of change by contacting the client after three months and six months. "The purposes of follow-up are to determine whether the positive changes during intervention persist on removal of the intervention, the problem recurs or relapses, new problems appear, and/or the social worker should reinstitute intervention" (Tripodi, 1994: 86). Follow-up determines whether the gains made during the intervention process are maintained over time or across life settings. Issues of follow-up such as generalization and maintenance of outcomes need to be of concern to all social workers. Common follow-up activities include stabilizing success, firming up social supports, and transitioning to the future (Ivanoff & Stern, 1992; Zastrow, 1995). Outcome achievements need to be integrated into the daily functioning of clients for maximum stabilization of success. This is best accomplished throughout a clinical process where emphasis is placed upon practising learned skills and behaviours in a variety of situations and across common life settings or domains. This type of clinical process will promote client self-confidence rather than implying that the skill resides only with the social worker. Reviewing successes and strengths assists clients in feeling more confident in approaching related issues in the future. Support networks outside that of formal social services are important for maintaining changes accomplished during the intervention phases.

Questions that may help you frame follow-up strategies for your clients include:

• Will there be further contacts planned before termination is completed?

• Who will be responsible for initiating these contacts?

- If no contacts are planned, can the client contact the social worker if need arises?
- Does the agency have a formalized follow-up procedure as part of its program evaluation process?

Social workers can expect that evaluation is an ongoing process that needs careful planning. There are different kinds of single-case designs and the reader seeking more extensive information is referred to Gambrill (1997) and Tripodi (1994) for a complete discussion. The next section addresses considerations for finding a measure.

MEASUREMENT METHODS

Incorporating evaluation into the intervention process requires deciding what will be measured, when, by whom, and how the information will be shared. Deciding what to measure is primarily grounded in what the client considers important. Types of change measured include:

- change in circumstances, such as return of Nora from foster care to home of biological family;
- change in attitude, such as increased self-respect and family identity;
- change in skills, such as increased parenting skills;
- change in behaviour, such as increased contact with birth parents, increased life satisfaction.

Two general methods or approaches to outcome measurement are identified in the social work literature: the use of empirical measures and the use of pragmatic indicators of practice effectiveness. Empirical measures include tests, questionnaires, rating scales, checklists, inventories, and any instrument that is systematically used between the client and social worker. This includes the use of charting or log recording techniques. These measures will have uniform administration and scoring procedures, resulting in increased assurance that you are measuring what you think you are measuring. Pragmatic indicators include reliance on client statements or clinical impressions. This method is considered less systematic and prone to bias. Many social workers use a combination of pragmatic and empirical strategies for evaluating client change. In preparing to measure change, the social worker needs to go through the following process:

- Start with the question, "What information is needed?"
- Choose goals (outcomes) that are simple, practical, and meaningful to the client
- Measure one or two things well
- Involve the client in defining the outcomes to measure
- Review and revise the measure with the client who will be using it
- Build on what the client is prepared to document
- Measure often.

It is important to remember that measurement is not an end in itself but an important way in which you and the client can gain clarity about the focus of change and how both of you will know when change has occurred. The success or failure of measurement depends on how you present the measurement task to the client. Fischer and Corcoran (1994) have compiled a list of measures for adults, children, and couples related to a number of psycholog-ical, behavioural, and interpersonal difficulties. The measures have been reproduced in their text and you can examine them to find one suitable for clinical practice.

USING A MEASUREMENT TOOL

You should follow several guidelines when using any type of measurement method in your practice:

1. Be familiar with how the measurement works. Try the task yourself first and practice on friends or colleagues. Know how it works and how long it will take to complete.

2. Assure the client of the importance, the purpose, and the use of the information obtained from the task. One of the most important messages that you as a social worker can con-vey to your client is that you have confidence in the value or importance of obtaining the client's responses.

3. Reassure clients that there are no right or wrong answers. Always stress accuracy and honesty.

4. Review the entire measurement task with your clients before they need to complete it on their own. Be sensitive to the educational, social, and cultural background of clients, such as reading and language difficulties. Remember that the objective of measurement is to obtain information that will assist you and your client in evaluating progress towards goal achievement.

5. Review the results with the client. Explain their significance and/or how you will use them. This shows respect for the client and decreases the "expert mystique" of the social worker.

    Use the individual items or details provided by the measurement task to discuss strengths as well as areas for further development. Do not just use the total score or gross out-come. Remember, all measurement needs to be simple, practical, unobtrusive, culturally appropriate, and of importance to client and social worker.

LESSONS LEARNED

1. Practice evaluation is part of routine social work practice.

2. Practice evaluation is in the best interests of clients and should be an essential right of clients.

3. Practice evaluation promotes client involvement, a focus on client strengths, and empow-erment.

4. Practice evaluation using single-system approaches is particularly suited to culturally diverse populations.

5. Research indicates that positive client outcomes are related to intervention techniques that facilitate the client's active role in the evaluation process.

6. Practice evaluation allows you to make explicit judgments about whether your inter-vention is working, and assists in ways of improving information about client outcomes.

7. Practice evaluation educates clients about the processes of interventions.

8. Be knowledgeable of evidence based practice interventions regarding the population being served.

9. Recognize ethnicity and culture as significant parameters in understanding problems and intervention processes while respecting clients' religious and or spiritual beliefs.

10. Interact in the language requested by the client or make an appropriate referral.

REFERENCES

American Psychological Association (1990). *APA Guidelines for providers of psychological services to ethnic, linguistic, and culturally diverse populations.* Washington, DC: Author. www.apa.org/pi/guide.html.

Canadian Association of Social Workers (1994). *Social work code of ethics.* Ottawa, ON: CASW.

Chalmers, I., Macdonald, G., Grimshaw, J., Clarke, M., & Oxman, A. (1999). *How might the Cochrane Collaboration facilitate international collaboration to prepare and maintain systematic reviews of the effects of social and educational interventions?* Paper for the meeting at the School of Public Policy, University College London, July 15–16, 1999.

Corcoran, J. (2000). *Evidence-based social work practice,* Springer.

Corcoran, K., & Vandiver, V. (1996*). Managing the maze of managed care: Skills for mental health practitioners,* New York: Free Press.

Dana, R., Behn, J., & Gonwa, T. (1992). A checklist for the examination of cultural competence in social service agencies. *Research on Social Work Practice, 2,* 220–233.

Fischer, J., & Corcoran, K. (1994). *Measures for clinical practice* (2nd ed.). New York: McGraw-Hill.

Gambrill, E. (1997). *Social work practice. A critical thinker's guide.* New York: Oxford University Press.

Hudson, W. (1982). *The Clinical measurement package.* Homewood, IL: Dorsey Press.

Ivanoff, A. & Stern, S. B. (1992). Self-management interventions in health and mental health settings: Evidence of maintenance and generalization. *Social Work Research & Abstracts, 28*(4), 32–38.

Jordan, C. & Franklin, C. (1995). *Clinical assessment for social workers. Quantitative and qualitative methods.* Chicago, IL: Lyceum Books.

Kazi, M.A.F. & Wilson, J.T. (1996). Applying single-case evaluation methodology in a British social work agency. *Research on Social Work Practice, 6,* 5–26.

Meenaghan, T., Gabriel, M., & Holden, G. (2000). *Technologies on the horizon of clinical social work.* Commission on Educational Policy Millennium Project. Council on Social Work Education.

Potocky-Tripodi, M. (2001*). The development of practice guidelines for culturally competent practice.* Paper presented at the Annual Program Meeting of the Council on Social Work Education, Dallas, TX. March, 2001.

Sue, D., Arrendondo, P., & McDavis, R. (1992). Multicultural counselling competencies and standards: A call to the profession. *Journal of Counselling and Development, 70,* 477–486.

Tripodi, T. (1994). *A primer on single-subject design for clinical social workers.* Washington, DC: NASW.

Zastrow, C. (1992). *The practice of social work* (4th ed.). Pacific Grove, CA: Brooks/Cole.

APPENDIX

Case Example—Nora

The Family Networks Program study used in this case example provided family reunification services to children and youth who had Permanent Guardianship Order (PGO) status. Nora, a 15-year-old Aboriginal youth, had been living in the care of child welfare for 12 years. She had two treatment family-based foster care placements in the four years since PGO status had been granted. Cultural or diversity issues for Nora included reconnecting with her biological family, traditions, and community, as well as issues concerning identification with her foster and biological family systems.

Nora identified her biological father as her priority contact. She did not want to pursue contact with her mother. Nora had minimal contact with two of her siblings. As her contact with her father increased, so did that of her siblings with her father and Nora with her siblings. Nora was supported in taking the initiative in relationships as well as assessing when further contact was not in her best interest. Nora's relationship with the foster family deteriorated by the end of the program. This was more the result of the foster mother's inability to deal with the changed dynamics of including the biological family. Nora struggled with a sense of divided loyalty throughout the first two phases of the program but made a clear choice for biological family involvement when a choice became evident. Today, Nora lives in a supported independent apartment with consistent contact with father and siblings, and some regular contact with extended family members.

FIGURE 28.1 Data Summary for Nora

Goal	Baseline	6-Month	12-Month	18-Month	Comments
Expand family network—genogram.	27 "family" members	96 "family" members	37 "family" members	35 "family" members	At 18-month follow-up, Nora was living in a supported independent apartment. Her genogram reflected a decreased identification of foster family members and an increase in biological and extended family members
Increase coping abilities—observations	Foster parent and child ratings were very similar	As parental contacts increased, foster mother felt more and more left out	Expressions of anger and sadness were interpreted by the foster mother as indicating that the reconnecting was not positive for Nora	Nora was in new living situation and was coping well with a roommate situation. She had very little contact with foster family	Nora demonstrated an increased ability to handle stressful situations and express emotions than prior to program
Continuity of family contact—calendar entries (identified biological father as priority for contact)	0 contacts with father	37 contacts with father (phone, visits in the community and at father's home)	34 contacts with father (phone, visits in the community and at father's home)	61 contacts with father (phone, visits in the community and at father's home)	Nora's relationship with her father had been labelled as "hostile" by child welfare prior to program. Nora established weekly visits with her father as well as regular phone calls
Quality of family relations: Hudson scales (the lower the score the more positive the family relationship)	*FF: 40 - 25 = 15 BF: None	FF: 34 - 25 = 9 BF: 68 - 25 = 43	FF: 28 - 3 = 25 BF: 53 - 25 = 28	FF: 137 - 112 = 25 BF: 48 - 23 = 25	Nora was very reluctant to complete the measure for the foster family at the 18-month follow-up. She had moved to a supported independent situation. As Nora's biological family relationships improved, the quality of her foster family relationships decreased
Sense of identity—My Preferences Scale	16 / 20	19 / 20	19 / 20	19 / 20	Perceived expectations of self and others as similar and enjoyed doing things with group rather than on her own after reconnecting with biological family.

* FF = foster family; BF = biological family

THE STRUCTURE AND NATURE OF SERVICE DELIVERY

Donald M. Fuchs

INTRODUCTION

This chapter will help the reader understand the practice challenges emerging from the rich and complex diversity that marks the structure of the social service delivery system in Canada. It presumes the reader is familiar with general information about the facets of the system. The reader unfamiliar with the general aspects of the Canadian social service system may wish to consult Armitage (1996), McGilly, (1990), and Mullaly (1993), who provide some background information about the general elements of this system. This chapter aims to expand on this knowledge as it relates to practice. It discusses how this highly diverse system can assist clients and how it can hinder meeting clients' needs. It presents the requisite skills of the practitioner in knowing the system and knowing how to function within it in the diverse roles required. The author examines the concept of networking and meshing formal and informal helping strategies, and discusses the role of practitioner as broker, mediator, referral agent, and advocate, and the popularity of case management as a strategy.

In particular, the Canadian service mosaic is viewed as an ever-evolving entity requiring practitioners to be continually updating their knowledge and skills in manipulating service structures for the benefit of the client. The range of skills required in this component of practice, including consultation and network-building skills, will be discussed. To begin the discussion of how this highly diverse system assists and hinders clients in meeting their needs, it is helpful to examine some of the practice challenges emerging from the structure of the Canadian social service system.

COMPLEX PRACTICE CHALLENGES EMERGING OUT OF THE STRUCTURE OF THE CANADIAN SOCIAL SERVICE DELIVERY SYSTEM

The structure of the Canadian social service delivery system and the devolution of governmental responsibilities for social policy and the provision of social services represent two of the major factors that generate the complex practice challenges facing social work practitioners.

Both Armitage (1988) and McGilly (1990) have clearly demonstrated that the present array of Canadian personal and community social services was not designed as a total system. As a consequence, they are dominated by a series of independent and competing service enterprises. Armitage (1988) and Wharf (1992) indicate that the current complex of social service delivery systems have some intrinsic merits, the foremost of which is the developed ability of some of the separate parts to provide good services to their clients. In addition, Wharf (1990) maintains that the separate identities have provided clients with some choice of service; the client who did not like the services received from the child welfare agency might do better with the services received from a family service or mental health agency. The separate services have provided independent foci for growth and political support; hence the resources they have in total may be greater than could have been obtained by a unified approach. Finally, the independent services have provided the context for the development of specialized professional expertise.

Notwithstanding the merits of the system, Armitage (1996) argues that the existing array of major delivery systems has two major defects. The first is that none of the individual delivery systems provides the basis for comprehensive services. This is particularly true for minority and poor clients. Each is built around particular sectional interests and most share a social-problem/residual-services approach to service design. The second defect is that the existence of a series of independent systems, serving overlapping populations, produces enormous inter-system boundary problems. These include such major problems as service interconnection, gaps, and coordination; they also include intersystem competition for resources, professional rivalry, and excessive administrative costs. In response, there has been a widely used strategy of reorganization of the personal social services with the intent to find simpler and more economic means of service delivery.

Dubois and Miley (1996) maintain that the current approach establishes the social service system as a collection of discrete program options that are available to eligible clients. This system, fraught with fragmented and limited service options, is a smorgasbord of programs constrained by categorized funding and rigid eligibility requirements. Ultimately clients must accept available, often limited services to relieve at best their immediate problems. Available services are frequently restrictive or so overburdened that clients must place themselves on waiting lists to participate in appropriate best-service options. Clients often fall in the cracks of the system because barriers to access, including physical, cultural, and financial barriers, exclude them from getting appropriate services to meet their needs.

Because of the existing competition fragmentation amongst social service systems, social work practitioners need to develop specific skills in linking and advocating for their clients within the diverse range of public, private, formal, and informal helping resources that exist within the social service structure.

For the past two decades neoconservative ideological approaches to social policy and social services have brought about an increasing shift to a residual model of social services aimed at providing the minimal service for those defined as most needy (Pulkingham & Ternowetsky, 1996). This has resulted from federal/provincial and municipal governments attempting to control and reduce deficits. Many neoconservative policy makers believe that a great deal of health and social services are not necessary and that they create dependency. Therefore it is felt that they should be cut back and provided only to the most needy. All levels of government have been devolving their service responsibilities to the individual, to families and locally-based voluntary service organizations, or to other forms of informal helping structures at the community level.

Members of visible minorities, single parents, the poor, young people, and the elderly continue to be affected the most by deficit reduction and service devolution (Scott, 1996; Graham, Swift, & Delaney, 2000). The neoconservative arguments are that the poor and disadvantaged minorities must bear their share of the pain of deficit reduction. They continue to be seen as having caused their poverty and as needing to take responsibility for themselves and their children in the alleviation of their poverty. This has resulted in the cutbacks to essential social services for all, including the most needy, and has led to the greater marginalization of single parents, Aboriginal peoples, and visible minorities.

These residual approaches have led to the rapid movement in the privatization of social services. Privatization results when governments support private nonprofit and for-profit social services rather than expanding their government-based public services. Through the purchase of service contracts, income maintenance vendor payments, and low cost loans, various levels of government have ushered private business and industry into the social service delivery network as mainstream providers of social services.

Increased devolution of social services has resulted in increased competition for funding rather than collaboration among social service agencies. This often works directly against the provision of effective and efficient service to consumers (Mullaly, 1993, Pulkingham & Ternowetsky, 1996). Funding competition also leads to agency protectionism. Protection of agency self-interest, or agency turf, often centres around disputes about which agency should gain funds to provide certain types of services or work with particular types of clients. While some agencies offer comprehensive services under their broadly stated missions, others use single-focus approaches that limit the types of services they provide or the clientele that they serve (Wharf, 1992). In reality, agencies may develop new programs only because funds are available, not because these programs match their mission or the needs of the consumers of their services.

The nature of the Canadian social service system is such that it provides a number of unique practice challenges. The increased devolution of services and movement to the privatization of Canadian Social Services has led to further fragmentation of services. It has greatly limited the access to services and reduced the quality and benefit levels of the available social services (Graham, Swift, & Delaney, 2000). For some clients the major block to meeting needs is a lack of resources. Sometimes these resources are available but the client is not aware of them or does not know how to use them. Sometimes the resource is not responsive to all or some of the client's needs or client groups and more groups are falling into the cracks between service systems. In a complex and diverse society all resources are not responsible to all clients. One part of the social worker's understanding of a community is knowing which resource can meet the needs of which clients in the rapidly changing arrays of social services. Consequently, an increasingly important part of the social worker's interventive repertoire is the ability to match clients and resources and to enable the client to use the available resources.

REQUISITE KNOWLEDGE AND SKILLS

According to Johnson (2000, 310), to help clients use the resources that may be available to them, workers should have knowledge and skill in four areas: (1) they should have a thorough knowledge of the service delivery systems of the community in which they practise and the community in which the client lives and functions; (2) they should have knowledge of and skill in the use of the referral process; (3) they should understand the appropriate use of the broker and advocate roles and have skills in filling these roles; and (4) they should know how to empower clients to take charge of their life situation.

To effectively serve clients in the rapidly changing social services context social workers must understand the general features of the social service delivery systems and the unique characteristics of their community's network of services (DuBois & Miley, 1996). Practitioners work in many different types of practice settings, including organizations such as agencies and associations. These settings can be public or private, primary or host, sectarian or nonsectarian, nonprofit or for-profit settings, or independent practice settings. Each particular community has its own array of social services that reflect the values of the local community. These services have their own eligibility requirements and other structural arrangements, which may make access to service and utilization difficult if not impossible for many at-risk populations. Practitioners must be familiar with these structures to help clients get access to, and effectively use, the formal helping services of the community to meet their needs.

Increasingly, practitioners need to develop skills in linking clients to appropriate formal and informal helping services that are client-focused and that respond to clients' needs in a holistic manner. This means developing flexible, responsive, and unique configurations of formal and informal service provision for effectively responding to clients' needs.

KNOWLEDGE AND SKILLS FOR LINKING CLIENTS TO FORMAL HELPING SERVICE SYSTEMS

According to Kirst-Ashman and Hull (2001), there are a number of basic skills for understanding and working within the complex web of ever-changing social services. More specifically, advocacy, brokerage, and consultation skills are essential skills necessary for social workers to negotiate the difficult social service structures to help clients obtain needed resources. They argue that one of the most important objectives of social work is to help people obtain needed resources from the formal helping system. Often this occurs through social workers serving as consultants and brokers of services. These roles require that the social worker help clients by connecting them to appropriate agencies or services. Further, they indicate that the social worker often must act as a mediator between the consumer and the resource.

Also, in many situations social workers are called upon to serve as advocates. Barker (1991, 7) defines advocacy as the "act of directly representing or defending others; in social work championing the rights of individuals or communities through direct intervention or through empowerment. Social workers use their position and professional skills to exercise leverage for needed services or resources on behalf of individual groups." Advocacy is often seen to take one of two forms as either case or cause advocacy. Case advocacy refers to activity on behalf of a single case. It is usually employed in situations where the individual is in conflict with an organization, perhaps over benefits that have been denied. Case advocacy can be seen as involving individual, family, or small group; cause advocacy involves social workers' efforts to address an issue of overriding importance to some client group (Kirst-Ashman & Hull, 1993, 466). Cause advocacy usually involves advocacy relating to social issues that affect multiple groups of clients or potential clients.

The role of broker has become an increasingly necessary role for practitioners in the fragmented social service context. Connaway and Gentry (1988) maintain that linking of client systems to needed resources is a major component of the brokerage role. The assumption has been that after assessing a client's needs, the worker then connects the client to available resources. They maintain that becoming effective in the role of broker requires, first, knowledge of agencies and their eligibility criteria; second, it requires familiarity with many different types of resource systems, e.g., social assistance family support; third, it requires that the worker develop a network of contact people to whom clients may be referred.

Kirst-Ashman and Hull (2001) identify the following six steps in brokering or linking: identifying and assessing client needs, identifying and assessing potential resource systems, helping the client select the best resource system, making the referral, helping clients use resource systems and follow-up, and evaluation of resource systems.

Rothman (1994) maintains that professional linking does not consist of simply suggesting a referral. It also means making an effective connection, including doing whatever is necessary to ensure that the client actually receives the needed aid. It calls for a wealth of knowledge about the human service system: accurate, up-to-date information on policies, programs and procedures; contingencies and "loopholes;" and the costs and benefits of different options. The practitioner also needs to arrive at constructive working relationships with varied agencies and institutions to actualize service outcomes.

Many authors point out that linking to formal services is not a one-time event (Compton & Galaway, 1994; Johnson, 2000; Fuchs & Lugtig, 2000). Once clients have been connected with services, their personal needs may change, requiring that they be tied in with other appropriate resources. For example, a discharged patient may be referred initially for emergency housing to a shelter and to stabilize a medical condition. Once the individual makes progress with this condition the practitioner could move toward linkage for job retraining and then for job placement. Even in making a given agency connection, linkage is a process rather than a single action.

Rothman (1994) points out that for effective linkage to occur for vulnerable client populations there are a number of other factors that need to occur. That is, there first must be a connection with resource identification. For linkage to occur, community resources must be noted and appraised. This requires the identification of all programs available from local community and government resources. The practitioner needs to be aware of what services exist in order to begin the process of linking. If the resource identification area is weak, the linkage function is undermined. Rothman also speaks of the importance of monitoring and advocacy connection with inter-agency coordination to enhance linkages with formal organizations.

KNOWLEDGE AND SKILLS FOR LINKING CLIENTS TO INFORMAL SUPPORT NETWORKS

When the social worker is taking action to enable clients to use the resources available, the function of the social worker is to link people to the resources they can use in meeting their needs and thus enhance their social functioning and coping capacity. When identifying components of the service delivery system, workers usually begin by identifying social service agencies and services provided by other professionals (Johnson, 1995). A far broader view needs to be considered. Within many neighbourhoods, communities, and ethnic groups, a helping network outside the formal system exists. This "natural helping system" is becoming known to social workers as they attempt to stretch the scarce resources of the formal systems in a time of economic stress (Green, 1999). There is, however, much that needs to be learned about how to work cooperatively with this system.

The natural helping system is made up of a client's family, friends, neighbours, and co-workers. Often these are the people to whom a person in need goes for help first (Lugtig & Fuchs, 1992; Warren, 1992). Often social workers can strengthen or support the natural helpers rather than take over the helping completely (Lugtig & Fuchs, 1992). The extended family has always been an important part of the helping system for many ethnic groups and in small towns and rural areas. For example, in many situations in working with Aboriginal people, if the extended family or informal helping system is not involved, the clients may not be able to use any of the help offered. Many practitioners have developed approaches that mesh formal and informal helping approaches (Lugtig & Fuchs, 2000; Marsh & Crow, 1996; Pennell & Burford, 1996).

The work of Lugtig and Fuchs (2000), Pennell and Burford, (1996), and Warren (1992), supports the use of family, neighbours, and kin as a helping resource. They describe neighbourhood ties as useful because of the speed of response to need. The person seeking help has face-to-face contact that is immediately available. The person in need is continually observed and help is provided quickly when situations change. Family or kin are particularly helpful because of the long-term relationship that exists. For example, they are a resource for the care of children when a parent dies or when persons face long-term medical care or institutionalization. Friendship groups are useful because there is free choice. The relationships among kin or friendship groups often have strong emotional ties and thus are most useful in the provision of a wide range of social support.

Also, natural helping networks are composed of natural helpers in the community, community benefit organizations, and self-help groups (Green, 1999). Natural helpers are those persons who possess helping skills and exercise them in the context of mutual relationships (Lugtig & Fuchs, 1996). These are usually persons who make helping a part of their everyday life. Rothman (1994) maintains that natural helpers have a number of attributes that make them most helpful to individuals in their social contexts. These people are: hardworking and optimistic about people being able to change; mature and friendly, and have often had the same problem as those they are helping; trustworthy and keep confidences; available and share a sense of mutuality with others. They usually have had similar life experiences and have similar values as the person they are helping. Furthermore, people in the neighbourhood, small communities, or ethnic groups usually know who these persons are. However, it is often difficult for professional people to identify them without help from those who are part of the community system.

Rothman (1994) identifies four types of informal support networks including networks of families, friends and neighbours, community-based groups, and self-help groups. Gottlieb (1988) identifies size, helpfulness, intensity, durability, accessibility, proximity, and reciprocity as important attributes of socially supportive network ties. He integrates these concepts by identifying types of networks for different purposes and circumstances. For example, if a client is reserved and private, low or medium density situations might be preferred initially. If the client has a variety of different needs that have arisen at different times and places, a large network with individuals who divide tasks may be the best choice. If the client is highly active and capable, a reciprocal arrangement might be called for.

In working with clients, practitioners must understand the unique nature of the natural helping context of available resources for helping clients, and they must increase their skills for working with these informal helping systems.

MESHING FORMAL AND INFORMAL HELPING SYSTEMS

Increasingly, practitioners are being called upon to bring informal and formal helping resources together to work in new partnerships to meet clients' needs more effectively. The challenge for practitioners is to recognize and work with informal and natural helping systems, meshing the resources of both the formal system and informal systems.

In looking at linking practice to mesh informal and formal helping resources to effectively serve clients, Rothman (1994) maintains that there are five guidelines that should direct practice in working with formal and informal helping resources. These include, first, defining the clients' networks through an assessment of all the natural helping sources, their attributes, and their potential. Second, clients needs and helping resources must be specified. Some of the support functions can be categorized in four areas which include friendship and socialization, emotional support, practical assistance, guidance, and advice. Gottlieb (1988) also includes feedback or critical appraisal.

Third, in assessing the potential of help-giving sources it is important to assess factors that influence the capacity or potential for each support unit to deliver assistance. Some of the important factors include the willingness to help, frequency (intensity) of contact, proximity, accessibility, durability (or continuity) of helping, and expectation of reciprocity for assistance (which might be considered a cost) (Gottlieb, 1988; Lugtig & Fuchs, 2000).

Fourth, making and maintaining linkages involves sensitive relationships with people who do not have professional experience and skills in providing human services. Understanding and motivation need to be engendered. Confidentiality has to be weighed and explained. Fifth, Rothman maintains that an important focus for informal linkage efforts is aimed at strengthening the helping capacity of networks and network members. After initial assessment of the helping capacity of the helping network the practitioner might move on to improve the helping capacity of the network.

There is a wide range of informal helping resources. Fuchs and Lugtig (2000) assert that in the meshing of formal and informal helping systems practitioners are called upon to serve in new consultative roles and relationships with informal helping systems. For example, social workers are being called on to take on new practice roles in the area of working with self-help groups (SHGs) (Fuchs & Costes, 1990). SHGs are useful in developing connectedness to others at a time when isolation may be a felt problem. These groups are useful in encouraging growth and redefinition of self (Powell, 1987). Some also work for social change regarding social impacts that affect the resolution of the common problem of the group members. These groups involve persons who have lived through problems and are helping those who currently have the problem to find their own solutions. Help is given modelling positive reinforcement, and emphasis is on the here and now. Examples of these groups are the anonymous groups like Alcoholic Anonymous, cancer-support groups, and life-transition groups such as widow-to-widow groups.

The relationship between self-help groups and formal human service organizations is often problematic because of the different ways of functioning (Powell, 1987). Such variables as the client group on which the service is focused, the need for resources from outside the system, and the relationships of helper and those receiving help are usually quite different. Also, relationships between self-help groups and human service organizations vary a great deal. Yeheskel Hasenfeld and Benjamin Gidron (1993) identified five relational patterns: competition, referral, coordination, coalition, and cooptation. The ideal relationship would be one of coordination and/or coalition. Powell (1987) contends that regardless of relational patterns, in order to maximize the use of self-help groups, social work must be aware of the relational pattern that exists and, when appropriate, work to facilitate a different pattern.

Dubois and Miley (1996) maintain that in working with natural helping systems, social workers must be aware that these systems are primary groups that use an informal personal means of interaction. To attempt to work with natural helping systems using the strategies and techniques of formal bureaucratic systems often blocks any meaningful interaction or coordination. Two results that take place are: (1) the natural helping system may give up its help and allow the formal system to do the helping—in this situation the natural helping system is destroyed; (2) the natural helping system may withdraw from the formal system and go underground—in this situation the social worker is unable to coordinate and cooperate and the two systems may offer help that does not allow clients to use either system effectively.

Lugtig and Fuchs (2000) maintain that the peer-consultative or partnership approach and enabling stance seems to be the most appropriate way of functioning with natural helping systems. Social workers must be creative and seek a means of linking formal and informal networks if the use of resources of the natural helping systems is to be maximized. The most important consideration in this linkage is the maintenance of communication without undue interference with the functioning of either formal or informal systems.

LINKAGE MODEL FOR PROMOTING ACCESS TO ETHNICALLY SENSITIVE SOCIAL SERVICES

Of growing importance for social work practice in the increasingly diverse Canadian society is knowledge and skill for linking clients to ethnically sensitive formal and informal helping systems. Schwager, Mawhinney, and Lewko (1991) and Green (1999) note that cultural assumptions are so implicit in our behaviour that we are usually not aware of them. The uniformity of our cultural environments prevents us from seeing that culture is greatly variable and open to question. In that regard cultural assumptions are like speech accents; we note them in others, not ourselves. Rather than seeing social work for other groups as minor variants of our own mainstream and culture-free approach, we should become aware of and learn to analyze the pervasive cultural underpinnings of our own programs and practices. Cultural limitations and idiosyncrasies apply not only to groups other than our own, but also to our own community and subgroups within it.

In working with the relevant social service delivery for diverse ethnic groups Bernard and Thomas (1991) maintain that it is important to be attentive to a bridging approach. In this model, mainstream agencies hire workers from different ethnic-cultural backgrounds in order to provide multilingual, multicultural services for a wide variety of client groups. Matsuoka and Sorenson (1991) maintain that the essential aspect of this approach is that it links mainstream agency resources to the ethno-cultural communities, cross-culturally sensitizing both the agencies and the communities, and generating resources from the communities through community development strategies. As these resources develop, they are in turn more likely to become coordinated with existing mainstream services. In other words, the bridging model considers members of the ethno-cultural communities not only as potential recipients of services, but also as a source of strength and a resource for service provision.

Further Matsuoka and Sorenson (1991) argue that the bridging model has several advantages over other approaches. It prevents ethno-cultural communities from becoming peripheral by maintaining links with mainstream agencies and by developing links with other communities associated with the other mainstream agencies. Such associations can serve as the basis for collective action against such problems as racism. Another advantage is that this model may provide a way to introduce immigrants to mainstream agencies by allowing them to discover existing services through the agency of ethno-cultural community workers who can offer explanations and advice.

Simply hiring workers from ethno-cultural groups does not always ensure sensitive services. Matsuoka and Sorenson (1991) found in their research with workers at settlement agencies that some clients prefer not to see a worker from their own ethnic group because they fear that personal information will be divulged to the community. This again points to the difficulty in obtaining confidence from all members of the service outlet for the group. In some cases, referring the client to the mainstream agency can be the answer. Through utilization of the bridging model, if the cross-cultural sensitization of the mainstream agency worker is effective, such referrals can easily be accomplished and the service is more likely to be appropriate.

Devore and Schlesinger (1996) contend that one of the most effective ways to implement the bridging model is to ensure that there is appropriate cross-cultural sensitization and training among staff. This is most important to avoid the creation of unnecessary divisions between mainstream and ethno-cultural workers. In addition, to effectively implement the bridging model, it is necessary to bring staff on board from the ethno-cultural communities. This is important to assist social service organizations to adapt and to reduce barriers to access to social services for consumers from different ethno-cultural communities.

CASE MANAGEMENT AS AN EMERGING STRATEGY

In various Canadian social service sectors case management approaches to practice have emerged to cope with the increasing privatization, devolution, fragmentation of, and reduced accessibility to, social services. Rose (1992) maintains that the need for case management constitutes an indictment of existing organizational and interorganizational patterns of service design and delivery. Many authors argue that case management would not exist if there were integrated systems of care; comprehensive, integrated coverage across organization sectors as diverse as income, housing, mental health, psychosocial rehabilitation, employment; or client-centred providers supporting people to identify their own needs and goals and negotiating systems to acquire or produce the resources required to live stable, positive lives in communities (Armitage, 1996, Rothman, 1994, Johnson, 1995). As a consequence of the absence of these social prerequisites, case management must become a system reform strategy with responsibility for direct practice with individuals and/or families.

Kisthardt and Rapp (1993) maintain that case management is an approach to service delivery that attempts to ensure that clients with complex, multiple problems and disabilities receive all the services they need in a timely and appropriate fashion. They suggest that it is a boundary-spanning approach in that, instead of providing a specific direct service, it utilizes case managers who link the client to the maze of direct service providers. These case managers are expected to assume ultimate responsibility for seeing that the service delivery system is responsive to all the needs of each client. Case management has been used in various fields of practice, especially in mental health with the chronically mentally disabled, in the care of the aging and of those with physical or developmental disabilities, and in child welfare (Rothman, 1994).

Both Loomis (1992) and Rubin (1992) argue that although the emphasis in case management is on linkage, case managers in theory do whatever it takes—whether brokerage, advocacy, or resource development—to ensure that all clients' needs are met; they may even provide missing services themselves. Holding one worker responsible for the overall fate of the client and for the responsivity of the entire service delivery system is a strategy for overcoming the neglect and fragmentation that are thought to typify the way in which myriad service providers have historically dealt with multi-problem or profoundly impaired clients. In other words, designating one person as the case manager is an attempt to ensure that there is somebody who is accountable and who is helping the client hold the service delivery system accountable, someone who cannot pass the buck to another agency or individual when and if services are not delivered quickly and appropriately (Rapp, 1998).

Rose (1992) maintains that social work and case management share two essential features. Both occur historically when the social structure of society creates "surplus" populations that cannot be integrated within existing resources and patterns of resource allocation. And each has a dual practice responsibility to individual clients or families, on the one hand, and to social reform in producing more supportive environments on the other. Often, particularly in health and mental health settings, restrictive funding guidelines or conventional practice models limit or restrain these responsibilities (Rose & Black, 1985). Both case management and social work are confronted with problems of direction and assertiveness, with conflict over funding and legitimation in relation to advocacy and system change.

Rubin (1992) argues that within the diversity of case management roles, five typical case management functions regularly appear: needs assessment; service or treatment planning; linking or referring; monitoring; and advocacy. Few constructions of case management leave out any of the five task areas, although the advocacy function rarely receives the same amount of time and attention as the other four when compared in most models.

Rothman (1994) maintains that denial of either aspect of case management's dual focus on clients and on system reorganization inadvertently becomes a form of betrayal to the clients. The most common form of betrayal, failure to advocate for needed system intervention, obstructs the possibilities for clients' social development or capacity to gain independence from the service providing system. The economic and social context that forms the basis for most case-management clients' lives demands advocacy either to arrange resources that clients need in a more responsive, coordinated manner, or to produce vitally needed resources such as safe, affordable housing when none exists. These are the very areas in which clinical social work has resisted intervening, despite the fact that concrete needs structure and organize everyday life.

Further, Rothman (1994) points out that social work has participated in both client-driven and provider-driven paradigms. It has varied its focus on the dual practice commitments. Internal obstacles and external barriers to the development of needs-focused, client-driven approaches have inhibited the meeting of clients' needs. The primary internal deterrent is the emphasis on individual-defect explanatory paradigms and psychotherapeutic intervention coupled with the trend toward private practice. At the external level is the ongoing fiscal crisis and its impact on policies of the welfare state. These problems interact to produce a scenario that emphasizes cost containment through the reduced use of institutional settings in all service fields, the absolute need for alternative community-based support systems, and the urgent need for advocacy in both direct practice and policy, planning, and program evaluation—all shaped by ecological approaches to human behaviour and social work practice.

Rose (1992) argues that an advocacy/empowerment case management approach is the model most consistent with the value base of social work practice. It requires a dual commitment to deliver direct services to vulnerable clients and to challenge dysfunctional service delivery systems. The advocacy/empowerment perspective assumes that the very existence of case management approaches constitutes a very serious indictment of system functioning. Put somewhat differently, if there were comprehensive service planning coupled with adequate and appropriate resources; if there were integration of diverse service system components; if there were highly responsive provider systems with both facility of access and appropriate modes of intervention; and if there were client-driven supportive services tied to adequate material resources such as safe, affordable housing, there would be no need for case management. Rose (1992) and Rothman (1994) assert that the appearance of case management in numerous service sectors attests to the universality of system deficits, fragmentation, and irrationality.

Rose (1992) maintains that advocacy/empowerment case management sees case management differently than the more fragmented agency-driven approaches. It requires clients' active involvement in producing or defining their own goals and in designing their implementation strategies. A corollary assumption values the setting for living as the most interdependent environment possible for each person. In this perspective, needs assessments come from clients' goals. Needs establish what must be acquired, confronted, accomplished, or developed at the level of the client, the family, or the social network or system to produce client-defined or desired outcomes. Parallel to the advocacy dimension, the rules, roles, and routines of service providers are not the central concern.

He suggests that the advocacy/empowerment model regards effective case management as client-driven rather than provider-driven. He suggests that the following four assumptions should govern an advocacy/empowerment case management model. First, case management clients are seen as whole human beings living in a social context. Second, people can grow and develop when provided with the necessary material, social, and emotional supports, and validation to live stable, positive lives. These people who actively participate in transforming their environments, at whatever level their capacity allows, change themselves in the process. Conversely, people coerced into adapting to debilitating environments are forced into managed identities or roles that sustain dependency. Advocacy/empowerment case management has a commitment to supporting clients' change from objects, known and acted upon, to subjects who know and act (Rose & Black, 1985). Empowerment, the active, continuous process of determining and setting goals and working to produce them, or living as a subject, characterize the relationships advocacy/empowerment case managers seek to build.

The third assumption is that growth and movement occur in the context of relationships characterized by honesty, clarity of goals, and continuity between goals, purposes, and shared plans of action. Fourth and finally, diagnosis does not determine the person's entire future development or capacity to live more fully than the provider's roles permit. Human development, the capacity for growth and change as a human being, cannot be restricted by diagnostic categories and providers' definitions of clients' roles. Advocacy/empowerment case management presumes that clients have a potential for development. This potential is tied to the participation of the client in producing direction and meaning-centred goals, articulated in deriving needs, and expressed through sharing responsibility for change or movement.

Case management approaches are proliferating within the Canadian social service system at a very rapid rate. Practitioners need to be constantly vigilant of the impact of the different orientation of case management approaches for meeting clients' needs and their capacity to serve as barriers for clients in their efforts to access social service. The advocacy/empowerment model discussed in this chapter provides practitioners with some frame of reference for the continued monitoring and development of case management approaches that effectively meet the needs of clients.

CONCLUSION

This chapter has examined the complex practice challenges for social workers that have emerged out of the evolving Canadian social services. It has discussed the knowledge and skills necessary for social workers in their efforts in working with clients to meet their needs. It has examined the need for practitioners to expand knowledge and skills in linking clients to both formal and informal helping systems. It has presented some innovative notions of how the formal and informal helping systems might work together to meet clients' needs. Further, it has put forward a linkage model for increasing access to ethnically-sensitive social services. Finally, it has discussed the rapid growth in case management approaches as the Canadian social service system becomes increasingly more fragmented and inaccessible, and has presented an advocacy/empowerment approach to case management as an effective means of maintaining a focus on meeting clients' needs and reducing barriers to service.

REFERENCES

Armitage, A., (1988). *Social welfare in Canada: ideals, realities and future paths (2nd ed.).* Toronto: McCelland & Stewart.

Barker, R.L. (1991). *The social work dictionary (2nd ed.).* Silver Spring, MD: The National Association of Social Workers.

Berard, W.T. & Thomas, G. Social service sensitivity training program. *Canadian Social Work Review.* *8*(2), pp. 237–245.

Compton, B. & Galaway, B., (Ed.). (1994). *Social work processes.* Pacific Grove, Ca.: Brooks/Cole Publishing.

Connaway, R. S. & Gentry, M.E. (1988). *Social work practice.* Engelwood Cliffs, N.J: Prentice-Hall.

Devore, E. & Schlesinger, E.G. (1996). *Ethnic-sensitive social work practice (4th ed.).* Boston/London: Allyn and Bacon.

Dubois, B. & Miley, K., (1996). *Social work: an empowering profession (2nd ed.).* London: Allyn and Bacon.

Fuchs, D. & Costes, T. (1990). Building on strengths of family and neighborhood social network ties for the prevention of child maltreatment. In D. Fike & B. Rittner. (Eds.). *Working from strengths: the essence of groupwork.* Miami, Florida: Centre for Group Work Studies.

Graham, J.R., Swift, K.S., & Delaney, R. (2000). *Canadian Social Policy: An Introduction.* Toronto: Prentice-Hall Canada.

Green, J.W. (1999). *Cultural Awareness in Human Service: A Multi-ethnic Approach.* Boston: Allyn and Bacon.

Gottlieb, B. (1988). *Marshalling social support.* Beverly Hills. CA: Sage.

Hasenfeld, Y. & Gidron, B. (1993). Self-help groups and human service organizations: an interorganizational perspective. *Social Service Review, 67*, 217–236.

Herberg, D.C. (1993). *Frameworks for cultural and racial diversity.* Toronto: Canadian Scholars' Press.

Kirst-Ashman, K. & Hull, G. (2001). *Generalist Practice with Organizations and Communities.* Belmont, CA: Wadsworth Thompson Learning.

Kirst-Ashman, K. & Hull, G. (1993). *Understanding generalist practice.* Chicago: Nelson-Hall Publishers.

Kisthardt, W.E. & Rapp, C. (1992) Bridging the gap between principles and practice: implementing a strengths perspective in case management in Rose, S. (Ed.) *Case management and social work practice.* New York, New York: Longmans.

Loomis, J.F., (1992). Case management in health care. In Rose, S. (Ed.). *Case management and social work practice.* New York, New York: Longmans.

Johnson, L. (2000). *Social work practice: a generalist approach* (Canadian Edition). Toronto: Prentice-Hall.

Johnson, L. (1995). *Social work practice: a generalist approach* (5th ed.). London: Allyn & Bacon.

Lugtig, D. & Fuchs, D., (2000). *Building on the strengths of local neighborhood social network ties for the prevention of child maltreatment.* The Final Report of the Neighborhood Parent Support Project. Ottawa: Justice Canada.

Marsh, P. & Crow, G., (1996). Family group conferences in child welfare services in England and Wales. In J. Hudson & B. Galaway (Ed.). *Family group conferences: perspectives on policy and practice.* (pp. 152–166). Leichhardt, NSW Australia: The Federation Press

Matsuoka, A. & Sorenson, J. (1991). Ethnic identity and social service delivery. *Canadian Social Work Review. 8*(2), pp. 255–268.

McGilly, F. (1990). *Canada's public social services.* Toronto: McClelland & Stewart.

McIntyre, E.L. (1986). Social network potential for practice. *Social Work,* November– December, pp. 421–426.

Mullaly, R. (1993). *Structural social work: ideology, theory and practice.* Toronto: McClelland and Stewart.

Pennell, J. & Burford, G. (1996). Attending to context: family group decision making in Canada. In J. Hudson & B. Galaway (Eds.). *Family group conferences: perspectives on policy and practice.* (pp. 206–219). Leichhardt, NSW Australia: The Federation Press.

Powell, T.J. (1987). *Self-help organizations and professional practice.* Silver Spring, Maryland; National Association of Social Workers.

Pulkingham, J. & Ternowsky, G. (1996). *Remaking Canadian social policy: social security in the late 1990s.* Halifax: Fernwood Publishing.

Rapp, C.A., (1998). *The Strengths Model: Case Management with People Suffering from Severe and Persistent Mental Illness.* Oxford: Oxford University Press.

Rothman, J. (1994). *Practice with highly vulnerable clients: case management and community-based service.* Englewood Cliffs, New Jersey: Prentice-Hall.

Rubin, A., (1992). Case Management. In Rose, S. (Ed.). *Case management and social work practice.* New York, New York: Longmans.

Rose, S. (1992). Case management: an advocacy/empowerment design. In Rose, S. (Ed.). *Case management and social work practice.* New York, New York: Longmans.

Rose, S.M. & Black, B.L. (1985) *Advocacy and empowerment: mental health care In the community.* London/ Boston: Routledge & Kegan Paul.

Schwager, W.K., Mawhiney, A., & Lewko, J. (1991) Cultural aspects of prevention programs. *Canadian Social Work Review, 8*(2), pp. 246–254.

Scott, K., (1996). *The progress of Canada's children 1996.* Ottawa: Canadian Council on Social Development.

Wharf, B., (1993). *Rethinking child welfare In Canada.* Toronto: McClelland & Stewart.

Wharf, B. (1992). *Communities and social policy in Canada.* Toronto: McClelland & Stewart.

Wharf, B. (1990). *Social work & social change in Canada.* Toronto: McClelland & Stewart.

Warren, D.I. (1992). *Helping networks of the aging and retired.* Queenston, Ontario: Edwin Mellen Press Ltd.

Wilson, S.F. (1992). Community support and community integration: new direction for client outcome research. In Rose, S. (Ed.). *Case management and social work practice.* New York, New York: Longmans.

Chapter 30

SERVICE DELIVERY IN PRIVATE PRACTICE

William Rowe

THE CONTEXT OF PRIVATE PRACTICE

Private or independent practice in the delivery of social services in Canada has, until the past decade, been regarded as a minor if not aberrant form of social work practice. It was confined to a few areas of service (i.e., psychotherapy, counselling, consultation) and often seen as a part-time or occasional activity for an otherwise "employed" social worker. Although relatively little literature has been generated on the topic of private practice in social work, it has been referenced and studied in both the U.S. (Wallace, 1982) and Canada (Lewin & Leginsky, 1989) for over 60 years.

Acceptance in the U.S. came much earlier, partly due to a tradition of consumer or third party payment for health and counselling services. By the mid-1970s, many students were entering graduate schools of social work with the express purpose of pursing a career in private practice. This has been a more recent phenomenon in Canada but is becoming more common with the increasing privatization of health and social services (Bell-Lowther, 1988; Hurl, 1986).

The early discussions appeared to centre on the concern that social workers as private practitioners would be abandoning their traditional commitment to the poor, the oppressed, and the marginalized in favour of higher-status clients, greater prestige, higher wages, and more autonomy. Later, some argued that some forms of private practice, i.e., employee assistance programs, were antithetical to the social change mission of the profession and, in fact, helped support oppressive organizations (Carniol, 1987). Finally, with wholesale moves toward privatization of health, social services, and even prisons, many have raised alarms about the protection of high quality services to the most vulnerable groups (i.e., disabled, elderly, poor immigrants, and refugees) in society (Bell-Lowther, 1988; Gandy & Hurl, 1988).

While the above arguments have raised some important cautions that must be thoughtfully considered, many have recognized that the private practice of social work has gained increasing acceptance because social workers are providing needed, desirable, and unique services that clients and organizations are ready to contract for. Words such as consumer, proprietorship, vendorship, and entrepreneur have entered the social work lexicon and are likely here to stay (Saxton, 1988; Reichert, 1977). Increasingly, social workers are exploring models of private practice that respond to needs well beyond traditional counselling and psychotherapy. Some of these include practice with the frail elderly (Fauri & Bradford, 1986), family practice (Greene, Kruse, & Arthurs, 1985), discharge planning (Wenston, 1982), rehabilitation services (Matkin, 1983), corrections, adoption, bereavement, and critical incident debriefing.

The private practice of social work is expanding at an extraordinary pace and as such it is necessary to consider how this model of practice complements and, in fact, enhances overall social services. This chapter reviews the general nature of private practice in social work, the parameters that are being promoted by professional associations, the locus of private practice, and finally some thoughts about trends and implications.

THE NATURE OF PRIVATE PRACTICE IN SOCIAL WORK
Type of Worker

Not every social worker is prepared by temperament or training to be successful as a private or independent practitioner. The worker must posses an entrepreneurial nature and a proclivity for working with uncertainty. Private practitioners must be flexible, open to change, and able to discern opportunities for involvement when they are not otherwise readily apparent. Unlike the agency worker who often limits his or her activity to specific agency mandates, the individual worker may have to redefine his or her role as expressed needs change and evolve.

Defining Your Practice

Defining your practice is the first and possibly most important task facing the social worker in the initial stages. Very few people can relate to or understand what services a generalist social work practitioner would offer. Rather, people relate to the specific services one might offer, i.e., psychotherapy, mediation, family, or couple counselling. While you might define your practice quite broadly, you will quickly become known for what you do well (the most common referral source is a satisfied client) or by a needed or unique service (gay couples counselling, abuse survivor therapy, grief and bereavement counselling, and so on). This will often determine the kind of referrals you get.

It is important to define your practice within the limits of your knowledge, experience, and competence while at the same time being aware of the marketplace needs (i.e., what needs are not being met by current services). Some agencies require that you not provide the same services on a private basis that you perform for the agency—at least in the agency's catchment area. This may not be a problem because part-time private practitioners often want to provide a service that they do not have an opportunity to provide in their agency. If you are a supervisor, administrator, or educator, you may want to keep your skills sharp by engaging in counselling and psychotherapy a couple of evenings a week, or if you practice casework all day you may want to offer groupwork services occasionally.

Type of Practice

An equally important decision involves whether to practice by yourself, in a partnership, a group or a consortium. Each has its advantages and disadvantages. Partnerships and consortiums can broaden your referral base, decrease your overhead, and provide much needed professional exchange. They can, however, have professional, economic, and legal liabilities that must be carefully considered. It is best to consult a lawyer when establishing a partnership because you could become responsible for your partner's debts. If a member of your group or consortium has a poor reputation it could tarnish yours by association.

A solo practice, on the other hand, affords the most autonomy, which is one of the things that attracts social workers to private practice. In a solo practice you can shift your emphasis, decrease or expand your client volume, and make independent decisions about your location or office set-up without negatively affecting partners or associates.

Location of Practice

Where you practice can have important implications as well. Obviously your available resources will be a central determinant. Some part-time practitioners make arrangements with their own agencies or institutions to rent space. A conflict can arise if the practitioner is seeing clients who might also or otherwise be served by the agency or if the agency is seen to be sanctioning the practice. In such a case, the client must have a clear and distinct contract with the private practitioner and not the host agency by inference.

Some practitioners are able to negotiate space as part of their contract with a host agency. An example of this is corrections, where clients have to be seen in a correctional facility, or adoption, where the child welfare agency is involved. Some use space in their own home which, while providing some cost and tax advantage, can be problematic for privacy reasons or if your client is extremely troubled or dangerous.

Where resources permit, the preferred option is an office suite in a professional building or multi-service centre that has good access, public transportation, and/or parking. Depending on the client volume, an answering service or a part-time receptionist may be useful. If you are in a group practice or consortium, pooled resources can decrease your overhead costs. It is wise not to incur significant overhead commitments until your volume allows for it. Otherwise you may find yourself pressured to take contracts and cases that aren't necessarily appropriate for you.

Relationship to the Client

In situations where there is no third-party payment the client is much more a customer or consumer than in regular agency practice. While this shouldn't affect the quality of the service it can have significant ramifications for the nature of the engagement and contracting phases of treatment (Wallace, 1982). It may also have an impact on the number and frequency of the sessions. Issues such as length of sessions and missed appointments take on a new dimension, and if clients are allowed to run up large bills it can negatively affect the nature of the therapeutic relationship.

Without agency mandates or precedents the social worker must clearly define the parameters of service with each client and ensure that there is no perceived conflict of interest or role confusion. Private practice often lacks the same rigorous intake process that exists in agency practice. It is best not to be in multiple roles with the clients, but if you are, you must be extra careful to define roles when friends, co-workers, or acquaintances become clients, or vice versa.

Referral Sources

Referrals are the life blood of a private practice. At one time the vast majority of referrals came via recommendations from current or former clients who were satisfied with the service they received. Curiously, a significant number come through an advertisement in the yellow pages. Many individual practitioners, partnerships, and consortia now maintain Web sites, and people in need of service are increasingly using the internet as their first point of inquiry. Increasingly, traditional agencies are contracting out more and more of their services and private practitioners are being engaged on an hourly fee or in some cases a retainer to provide assessment and counselling services to individuals, families and groups, court reports, or home care. Consultation notes, assessments, progress notes, and termination notes must be timely, regular, and well written since they in part form the basis on which agencies or referral agents will continue to use your service.

Referral agents appreciate receiving a concise brochure that describes your service and qualifications, and which they can pass on to potential clients. Distributing an annual letter describing any changes (i.e., fees, type of service, new partners, location) will help keep you networked and your referral sources up-to-date.

Fees

It is important to carefully consider your fee scale before you begin to see clients. The best way to sort this out is to put together a proper business plan that takes the factors of overhead, market, and competition into account. Some practitioners use a sliding fee scale that is based on the client's ability to pay. A consultation with a qualified accountant can be very useful at this point. Whatever level you set your fees at, it is wise to have a coherent rationale because clients or referral agents will appropriately raise questions if there are different fees levied for the same service.

In Canada, a social worker in private practice must have a business number and collect appropriate GST, PST, or HST. Social work associations including the CASW are arguing for exemption as a health profession, but this has not yet been achieved.

Some agencies or organizations negotiate a lump sum or the equivalent of a retainer that allows them to budget a maximum amount for the year and save the time and cost of negotiating a new contract every time they need a few hours of service. This can also be helpful to practitioners in planning their budget year.

Some practitioners trade service for a commodity or another service. This is normally unwise because of the tax implications and the potential for boundary or role confusion. As a social work practitioner you are often privy to sensitive information or are cast in a powerful helping role that can be misunderstood or clouded with transference issues. This would be especially problematic if the practitioner were dissatisfied with the commodity or service traded.

Some social workers find negotiating fees or payment schedules uncomfortable or unseemly. It is important to deal with the issue of fees and billing arrangements at the outset so that there is no confusion or misrepresentation. Some practitioners print a schedule of services and fees, which can be handed out to clients and referral sources. If there are any changes, everyone must be notified well in advance so they can make an objective decision whether to continue with the service or not.

Third-party payment through insurance or employee assistance plans bypasses the fee discussions with the client but often places limits on the number of sessions or the funds available. If your judgment about the recommended length of treatment differs markedly from what the third party will reimburse it is important to inform your client before beginning so that he or she can make an informed decision.

PARAMETERS OF PRIVATE PRACTICE
Qualification

Minimum qualifications and credentials for engaging in private social work practice are as yet not well defined or agreed upon. As such they remain highly variable. The National Association of Social Workers in the United States has had a voluntary register of clinical social workers since the mid-1970s. In Canada, some provinces regulate practice by law while others have only voluntary registration or association. Some provincial associations have set up voluntary private practice rosters that can provide some assurances to the public. The Canadian Association of Social Workers publishes a National Registry of Clinical and Non-Clinical Social Workers in private practice every year (CASW, 01). The national registry will take on central importance in internal trade, which requires that common qualifications be recognized across provinces and territories.

A voluntary register usually has a set of qualifications and standards that the registrants agree to. Many assert that an MSW from an accredited school of social work and a number of years of supervised practice should be the minimum qualification. While this is laudable, the reality is that a number of social workers with a BSW and many years of supervised practice and/or specialized training currently provide high quality service. Those who are establishing rosters are therefore providing for exceptional circumstances to include such individuals. Where private practitioners claim to offer specialized services such as addictions counselling, sex therapy, or hypnotherapy—specializations not normally offered in schools of social work—it is expected that they would seek out such training and supervision and achieve the qualifications deemed appropriate.

It is especially appropriate in private practice to display your diplomas and certificates where clients can see them. Clients should be encouraged to inquire about your qualifications and professional affiliations and certifications, and you should be ready and willing to discuss or explain them in a clear, jargon-free manner.

Supervision and Continuing Education

Private practitioners are strongly encouraged to make arrangements for supervision or consultation on a regular basis. If you hold off until you have a particular difficulty with a client, the situation could become less retrievable. Some provincial associations require evidence of such arrangements to maintain your place on the roster. Article 3.3(e) of the Saskatchewan Association of Social Workers on standards for the private practice of social work asserts the following:

> Members of the Roster shall commit to the use of ongoing professional consultation (by a professional deemed acceptable by the association) when necessary and be prepared to submit documentation if required (SASW, 1996).

Some private practitioners form or join supervision groups where they can benefit from mutual consultation, support, and networking. Whatever arrangements are made, this is clearly an important aspect of independent practice that is too often overlooked.

Increasingly, continuing education is becoming an accepted norm for registered or certified social workers. The requirement to acquire a minimum number of continuing education credits per year is common in many professions. The number of credit hours varies but 40–50 per year is not uncommon. This can be achieved by attending scheduled courses, conferences, training sessions, specific supervision by a recognized expert, or even an organized journal club. Given the changing social work landscape—new laws, new policies, new client issues—continuing education is not only desirable but necessary to remain informed.

Liability and Record-Keeping

Liability insurance is required for those who choose to join the roster of qualified private practitioners, and where it is not required it is strongly recommended. It is wise to have both general liability (accident insurance) and malpractice insurance. There have been very few successful actions against social workers in Canada to date and, as a result, malpractice insurance premiums are extremely low compared to some other professions. There is a changing mood, however, by clients and courts—especially in highly contentious areas like mediation, adoption, abuse survivors, false memory allegations, and offender release counselling. There is potential for liability suits in almost any aspect of social work practice and malpractice insurance has therefore become a normal part of the private practitioner's portfolio.

Record-keeping is closely related to liability by virtue of the fact that in a suit, records are one of the first things subpoenaed. Uniform record-keeping has become the norm in most social work agencies at this point. Most agencies recognize that assessments, recommendations, and transfer notes can be viewed as legal documents and require their social workers to keep them up-to-date and professionally written. There is more variability in progress notes, but these should at least be internally consistent.

No less should be expected of the private practitioner even though the same formal structures are not in place. The practitioner should establish a uniform method of record keeping and store the records in a secure, accessible place.

Some clients engage the services of a private practitioner specifically because they do not want a public agency to have a record of their involvement. Public officials, police officers, and other professionals are some examples. While there can be great variability about the amount of detail you choose to include in a note, under no circumstances should you meet with a client and not record the time and date of the meeting. Such an omission can have serious consequences in a legal action.

Record keeping can easily fall behind when there are no supervisors or administrators to account to, but you do so at your peril and that of your client.

TRENDS AND IMPLICATIONS

At one time it was clear that the vast majority of all private practice preferred by social workers was strictly clinical in nature. Consultation, supervision, training, and organizational development covered most of the others (Wallace, 1982; Lewin & Leginsky, 1989). Industrial Social Work or Employee Assistance Programs, as they came to be known, expanded in the 1970s and 1980s to become a clear career choice for social workers. Schools of social work, such as those at McGill University and the University of Maryland, for example, developed courses and initiated programs with large companies and institutions to provide field placements and research opportunities. Social workers through the same period set up private practices and clinics for family and couple counselling, divorce mediation, child custody and access, and private adoption services. It is difficult to know at this point what percentage of social work services are delivered by private practitioners, but it is clear that it is increasing at an astonishing rate.

The Saskatchewan Association of Social Workers defined private practitioners in the following manner:

> Private practitioners are social workers who, wholly or in part, are engaged in the independent practice of social work without the benefit of supervision provided by an employer or board of directors. They are solely responsible for their actions in whatever field they practice, i.e. clinical practice, social administration, social work research, social work education and contract work.
>
> The private practitioner's professional identity is social work and they set their own conditions of payment with clients (SASW, 1996).

Given this definition we are likely to see more and more social work described as private practice. For a number of years there has been a clear trend for governments, public agencies, and child welfare services to contract out for specific service rather than maintain whole departments and staff. This trend has accelerated greatly in the past few years as governments are attempting to grapple with deficits through cutbacks and downsizing (Bell-Lowther, 1988). This has significant implications for social workers and private practice for a number of reasons.

1. The downsizing has affected middle managers and supervisors more than front-line workers. Often these social workers have considered or flirted with private practice and the prospect of unemployment has motivated them to make a commitment to private practice. This is made more possible in light of the fact that these individuals often receive generous severance or early retirement packages that give them time to build a practice.

2. For those coming into the job market for the first time there are fewer full-time positions available. Graduating social workers have to accept limited-term positions (filling in for a temporary absence) or contract out their services for a number of part-time activities. The long experience and high qualifications that are recommended for private practitioners may have to be reconsidered when the only possible employment is to facilitate a group, do some independent assessments, or contract for a few cases.

3. As hospitals close and rehab units shift more of their residents to the community, more private practitioners will be providing more diversified and more decentralized care. This has already occurred with the wholesale deinstitutionalization of developmentally-delayed persons and is likely to happen in many other arenas.

In spite of all the reorganization, people are still in need and there is still a lot of social work to do. With no reversal in sight of the current political and economic trends of divesting the community and family of health and social services, the private delivery of services is sure to become mainstream social work activity in the near future. Clearly, we must do more in our educational programs to prepare graduates for what is coming rather than what is past, and we are likely to see courses and seminars in topics related to private practice in the near future.

SUMMARY

In this chapter we have taken a brief look at the background, nature, and parameters of the private practice of social work in Canada. We have reviewed some of the practical aspects of building and maintaining a private practice and some of the key issues that private practitioners have to address.

Those who have paved the way for the expansion of private practice options have demonstrated risk-taking, independence, and entrepreneurship. As private social work practice becomes more normative there will likely be a wider range of social workers involved and more aspects of social work service included. Given the current and unfolding trends toward privatization of health and social service, the debate is no longer whether there should or should not be private delivery of services but how can they be properly utilized to complement the ever-shrinking public provision of health and social services. Issues of standards, qualifications, and accountability must be addressed in a more systematic fashion, and graduating social workers should be prepared to embrace the new economy and find ways to market their services while maintaining a commitment to serving the poor, the oppressed, and the marginalized.

REFERENCES

Bell-Lowther, E. (1988). Privatization: increasing government efficiency or dismantling the welfare state? *The Social Worker, 56*(3), pp. 101–104.

The Canadian Association of Social Workers *National Registry of Clinical and Non-Clinical Social Workers in Private Practice*, http://www.casw-acts.ca/NRSWPP.htm

Carniol, B. (1987). *Case critical: challenging social work in Canada*. Between the Lines: Toronto.

Fauri, D.P. & Bradford, J. (1986). Practice with the frail elderly in the private sector. *Social Casework, 67*(5), pp. 259–265.

Gandy, J. & Hurl, L. (1987). Private sector involvement in prison industries: options and issues. *Canadian Journal of Criminology, 29*(2), pp. 185–204.

Greene, G., Kruse, K., & Arthurs, R. (1985). Family practice social work: a new area of specialization. *Social Work in Health Care, 10*(3), pp. 53–73.

Hurl, L. (1986). Keeping on top of government contracting: the challenge to social work educators. *Journal of Social Work Education, 2*, pp. 6–17.

Lewin, R. & Leginsky, P. (1989). Independent social work practice in Canada. *The Social Worker.* Canadian Association of Social Work, *57*(3), pp. 155–159.

Matkin, R. (1983). Legal and ethical challenges in the private rehabilitation sector. *Rehabilitation Literature, 44*(7–8), pp. 206–213.

NASW. (1976). *Register of Clinical Social Workers* (1st ed.). Washington, D.C.: National Association of Social Workers.

Reichert, K. (1977). The drift toward entrepreneurialism in health and social welfare. *Administration in Social Work, 1*(2), pp. 123–132.

SASW. (1996). *Standards for the private practice of social work*. Regina: Saskatchewan Association of Social Workers.

Saxton, P.M. (1988). Vendorship for social work: observations on the maturation of the profession. *Social Work, 33*(3), pp. 197–201.

Wallace, M.E. (1982). Private practice: a nationwide study. *Social Work, 27*(3), pp. 262–267.

Wenston, S.R. (1982). Social work consultation for small hospitals. *Social Work in Health Care, 8*(1), pp. 15–26.

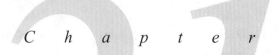

THE ROLE OF
VOLUNTEERS

Glenda E. McDonald

INTRODUCTION

There are many areas of compatibility between the profession of social work and the field of volunteerism. Both have a dual concern with the delivery of service and advocacy for equity, accessibility, and quality of service. Both are practised in a broad range of settings and fields of service. Both operate from a similar value base founded on humanitarian and egalitarian ideals.

Both are frequently associated with "good works" directed to the disadvantaged or disenfranchised of society. Each has a history of working with the other. Volunteers have played an important role in delivering a wide range of social and health services. Many who have chosen social work as a career entered the field through volunteer experience (Perlmutter, F.D.,1990; Wigdor B.T. & Foot D.K.,1988).

However, the association between volunteers and social workers, although obvious, is also problematic. At times, the roots of volunteerism have caused the social work profession to be defensive of its professional territory. This is due to a wish to create distance from the benevolent past (Parsonnet & Weinstein, 1987). In an attempt to assert professional training and skill, there has been a tendency on the part of social work practitioners to view volunteers as useful but peripheral in terms of their contribution to service. Similarly, some volunteer movements are irritated by professionalism in the field. Professionals are seen by some to have a vested interest in maintaining the status quo and consequently diverting attention from the social or structural analysis of problems.

This chapter will discuss several aspects of the role of volunteers in social work practice. It will begin with a brief historical perspective on the development of the social work profession from its roots in the voluntary sector; provide an overview of the Canadian volunteer; review some specific roles that volunteers tend to have within the human services; and conclude with a discussion of some ethical issues associated with the role of volunteers as they relate to social work practice.

HISTORY OF VOLUNTEERS AND SOCIAL WORK

The strong historical link between social work and volunteerism dates back to the beginning of the nineteenth century and the connection between industrialization and the development of charities established to meet the needs of the poor and disabled. The forerunners of many social work functions can be found to a large extent in the volunteer movement: the Friendly Visitors of the Charity Organization Societies who stimulated the writings of Mary Richmond; the early community activists who participated in the development of the settlement house movement; and the progressive thinkers who were the architects of many of our current social welfare programs. The contributions of these individuals may have preceded the emergence of social work as a profession, yet their work was motivated by some of the principles that later became incorporated into the definition of the social work profession (Perlmutter, 1990). Some contend that social work, as an occupation, could be said to represent the "professionalization" of volunteerism.

Volunteers have played a historic role in Canadian social welfare history. Few of these pioneers had any professional training in social work. Those people who made significant pioneering achievements in the past were not usually graduates of schools of social work and represented many facets of society. Robert Mills, Charlotte Whitton, and John Howard Toynbee Falk are prominent volunteers who pioneered the development of several social welfare programs and services that still exist today. However, given the complex tasks relegated to the voluntary sector at the turn of the century, the lack of training and accountability intrinsic to the volunteer role was seen to be problematic. Recognition of the increasing need for formal training for many of the functions that volunteers had been performing led to the evolution of the volunteer role from the "well intentioned" to the "well educated." J.J. Kelso, an Irish immigrant, journalist, and child welfare pioneer, articulated the need for formal university education for people interested in social work as a career. In 1914, the first such course in Canada was established at the University of Toronto (Bellamy & Irving).

Thus, the important distinction between the role of the volunteer and the social worker was initiated. The professional social worker now had to operate from a defined body of knowledge that included formal training, experience, and expertise. Although the volunteer role could augment social work practice, it would now be seen as distinct from it.

A PROFILE OF THE CANADIAN VOLUNTEER

Volunteers are an important human resource in the Canadian social service system. According to Statistics Canada, in 1992 people who participated in organizational or other voluntary work averaged around 2.75 hours a day on these activities. As Figure 31.1 illustrates, people of all ages participate in some form of volunteer work.

Of particular note is the substantial proportion of middle aged and senior people who participate in formal unpaid volunteer work. In 1992, 19% of all people aged 65 and over as well as those aged 45–54 were involved in volunteer activity. For those aged 55–64, almost 25% were engaged in volunteer work. In fact, these groups were more likely than people in age groups under age 45 to be involved in formal volunteer work (Statistics Canada, 1997). Clearly, volunteering is one of those activities that people do more as they get older. Perhaps older people have more free time to offer to worthy causes than their younger counterparts. With the aging of the Canadian population, this is a trend that will likely increase in years to come (Foot, D.K.,1996).

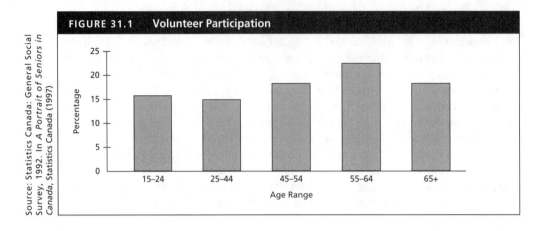

Source: Statistics Canada: General Social Survey, 1992. In *A Portrait of Seniors in Canada*, Statistics Canada (1997)

FIGURE 31.1   Volunteer Participation

This retired or pre-retirement individual will represent quite a sophisticated volunteer. They possess a wealth of experience for the volunteer sector to rely upon. These will be for the most part people who have had productive careers, and their skills and abilities will augment the activity of many volunteer agencies. "[M]any seniors are enjoying the freedom to do volunteer work that they enjoy. [These people] are the mainstay of dozens of charitable and cultural organizations ... from meals on wheels to political party offices, many are using talents they never had time to use before" (Lonetto & Duncan-Robinson, 1989, 15; Wigdor B.T. & Foot D.K., 1988).

The cohort of employed professional volunteers includes people who are employed but are willing to "donate" their time and services to agencies. While for some this may be an expectation of their position (e.g., corporate executives), overall the motivation of this group may derive from the need for increased personal satisfaction. As the new millennium progresses, more and more of the baby boom generation will discover that they have plateaued in their careers. This realization may motivate some to consider the satisfaction of working for a worthy social cause. For this group, consideration will have to be made for the fact that they are still working and consequently under severe time constraints. The availability of the older, experienced volunteer augurs well for the future of nonprofit organizations. These are complicated organizations to run and are likely to become more complicated as governments back out of the delivery of services, leaving us more dependent than ever on nonprofit organizations for many social services (Foot, D.K., 1996).

Current social and economic trends point to another group of potential volunteers. For the well-educated 20 to 30-year-old who is under or non-employed, volunteer work may represent more than experience and social contributions. These individuals may look to the volunteer sector to make productive use of their time and for their activities to translate into "experience" for the paid labour market (Wigdor B.T. & Foot D.K.,1988).

The student volunteer will continue to be an important type of volunteer. These volunteers will be looking for volunteer experiences to augment their formal education. Their motivation may be related to the issue of employment preparation but may also relate to the issue of developing unique interests and social responsibility. Gaining an understanding of the potential pool of volunteers is critical to successful volunteer recruitment and utilization. The organizations that are most adept at preparing for and accommodating themselves to this valuable resource will reap its rewards.

TYPES OF VOLUNTEER WORK

This chapter will review three types of volunteer work as they relate to social work practice:

1. *The volunteer as service provider.* Volunteer work to augment clinical social work practice.
2. *The volunteer as association member.* Volunteer work to augment organizational practice in order to further the mission, goals, aims, and values of an association.
3. *The volunteer as initiator of service.* Volunteer work to develop organizations, specifically self-help networks.

Before describing these types of volunteer work, some elements common to all volunteer structures will be reviewed. These components include: organizational controls, volunteer motivation, volunteer recruitment, retention, and termination, and the relationship between volunteers and paid professional staff.

Organizational Controls

Organizational controls refer to those formal practices, policies, and procedures that reside in the structure of the agency or program (Richan, 1961). These controls ensure congruence between the values, missions, and aims of the agency and the activities of the volunteers. The structure needs to make the volunteer role a productive and satisfying one (Perlmutter, 1990). This includes an explicit accountability structure for the volunteers, and identification of the appropriate roles and functions for volunteers, including clarification of the standards and skills required. It includes a need for the organization to examine the population being served or tasks to be done and to match these to the skills, abilities, and interests of the potential volunteers. It includes the development of policies and procedures around such issues as confidentiality, conflict of interest, and limits to volunteer participation. It includes the development of clear volunteer position descriptions, which incorporate review mechanisms, wherein mutual expectations can be explicitly defined and regularly reevaluated.

Volunteer Motivation

Understanding volunteer motivation is crucial to the successful integration of volunteer activity to an agency or service. It is critical to anticipate and understand both the general and individual motivation of prospective volunteers. Motivation is a complex concept and includes factors such as self-actualization, professional development, community status, networking opportunities, and job experience. Perlmutter (1990) discussed volunteer motivation from the theoretical perspective of the social exchange theory—the relationship between the altruistic (cost) and egoistic (rewards). She noted that, although initially the volunteer's interest may be motivated by altruism (to help someone else), the motivation to continue may be reassessed in terms of return (what do I get out of this). Understanding motivation from this perspective helps to underscore the importance of developing strategies to maintain volunteer motivation. Volunteers constantly need to be helped to understand, anticipate, and accept the reality of their activity and the relevance of its contribution to the organization.

Volunteer Recruitment, Retention, and Termination

There is agreement in the literature that this is an overlooked and underrated skill in the area of volunteer management (Perlmutter, 1990; American Society of Association Executives,

1982). The skill required for the successful recruitment and retention of volunteers must not be underestimated. Finding the right volunteer for the right task requires a clear understanding of the agency's needs with respect to volunteers. The clearer the needs, the more likely the possibility that one will find a match between the qualifications and schedules of the volunteers and the demands and requirements of the services to be provided.

The retention of volunteers can also be related to social exchange theory. Volunteers tend to get discouraged when there is limited feedback about the effectiveness or quality of their contribution to the agency or program. Without this recognition or support the costs to the volunteer may exceed the rewards, which in turn leads to "dropping out." The initial response when a volunteer quits is to be frustrated with the volunteer. However, the resignation may speak to a lack of "return on investment." Retention needs include such activities as orientation, supervision, continuing education, and recognition.

A delicate issue in the area of volunteer management is the termination of a volunteer. Because one should never underestimate the impact on the individual of being turned down or terminated from a volunteer position (as well as the impact on the program), it is a situation which has to be handled with the utmost skill, awareness, and sensitivity (Sues & Wilson, 1987). The issue of termination speaks to the critical importance of establishing a probationary and regular review system for a volunteer position. Frequently, misunderstandings between the volunteer and the program can be traced back to the initial recruitment process. The need to have a clear understanding of the expectations of the volunteer as well as make clear the expectations of the agency cannot be overstated.

Volunteer Relationships with Paid Professional Staff

The relationship between professional social work staff and volunteers will differ depending on which type of volunteer one is working with. The relationship may be supervisory, collegial, hierarchical, or employee-employer, as in the case of the relationship between an executive director and members of the board of directors.

Regardless, the key is to educate staff in how to work with volunteers effectively. A prerequisite to the successful integration of volunteers is that the staff mustn't perceive the volunteers as a threat to their jobs. The clear delineation of roles and responsibilities of the volunteers and staff is required so as not to increase staff resistance. Seeing the relationship between volunteers and paid staff as a partnership helps the professional focus on areas that require social work skill and training while the volunteer focuses on those areas that regular staff cannot deal with (Barnsteiner, J.H., Cady, C.C., & Hagelgans, N., 1992).

THE VOLUNTEER AS SERVICE PROVIDER

Several examples of innovative and creative use of volunteers in direct services appear in the social work literature. Reports describe volunteers being used in supportive interventions with families, in patient transportation services, as friendly visitors, in recreation activities, and in orientation activities. Many examples are from the hospital sector and a few will be reviewed here for illustrative purposes. It is expected that these examples could easily be replicated in the community agency context.

Recent changes in the delivery of health services are placing extraordinary and often conflicting demands on hospital social work departments. Development of volunteer services as an adjunct to practice may be a way to meet some of these conflicting demands (Sues & Wilson, 1987).

The benefits that such a program can provide include significantly increasing the volume and variety of work efforts in a cost-beneficial way, thus leading to an increased appreciation of the contribution of social work in health care settings. Additionally, for patients and families, the volunteer can represent a valuable link with the community, someone who can provide a normalization of the experience of hospitalization by not focusing on the sick role and, most important, who can contribute the precious commodity of time (Parsonnet & Weinstein, 1987).

There is a strong body of literature describing the value of volunteers providing patient and family support in the areas of cancer, surgical, and critical care. The main form of intervention provided by these volunteers is emotional support to the patient and/or family, assistance in social activities, and provision of limited non-medical information (Parsonnet, L. & O'Hare, J., 1990; Wurlitzer, F.P. & McIvor, A.C., 1996; Fusco-Karmann, C. & Tamburini M., 1994; Morey-Pederson, J., 1994; Barnsteiner J.H. et al., 1992; Schlosberg, A., 1991). Frequently, these volunteers are former patients or family members of former patients. They can be trained to identify high-risk families so that social workers can better organize their time with families requiring professional efforts. These programs represent a partnership between social workers and volunteers, which brings together different skills and abilities. The social worker brings clinical skills and judgment, the volunteer the experience of "having been there." An additional benefit of the volunteers who are themselves former patients or families of patients is that they provide an identification with wellness, showing that recovery, survival, and constructive coping are possible.

At Mount Sinai Hospital in Toronto, the workplace of the author, a social worker has developed a "Parent Buddy Program" in the Neonatal Intensive Unit (NICU). This Unit cares for the approximately 500 premature infants born at the hospital each year. Mount Sinai is an acute care teaching hospital in downtown Toronto, designated as a Regional Perinatal Unit specializing in high-risk pregnancies. The premature infants may weigh as little as 500 grams with a gestational age as young as 23 weeks. The mortality rate for these infants is high and even if they survive, many are in hospital for several months and may have subsequent physical, developmental, and cognitive limitations. Many of the parents, though from the metropolitan area, must travel long distances to visit their infant. The "Parent Buddy Program," initiated in 1990, represents a collaborative effort by social work, nursing, and parent volunteers from the Mount Sinai Hospital Parent Association, which is also a voluntary organization. The program utilizes parent volunteers, who have had an infant in the NICU, to be available to "new" parents to offer support, encouragement, and non-medical information. As coordinator of the program, the NICU social worker screens, trains, and matches the buddies and parents, and acts as an ongoing consultant to the parent buddies. Parents and buddies are matched on several parameters, including weight and age of infant, family constellation, and culture. As Toronto's cultural diversity has increased in recent years, the cultural match has become critically important to the program. It helps to ensure that cultural issues as they relate to the NICU, the care of the infant, and coping styles of the parents are not missed or misunderstood. The Parent Buddy Program has freed the social worker from providing day-to-day emotional support to parents and allowed him or her to focus on the more severe and complex psychosocial issues these families face. The parent buddies have demonstrated an ability to use themselves and share their personal life experiences in a way that professionals cannot. It has also offered the parent buddies a sense of mastery, hope, and support (Ardal, F., 1996).

Although hospital volunteerism is seen as a way to compensate for cost containment and health reform challenges, the effort required to develop and maintain these programs should not be minimized. Ideally, such a program should demonstrate a creative extension and enrichment of social work service rather than a replacement for tasks which are no longer possible within the new fiscal realities. All hospital volunteer programs described within the literature stress that volunteers must be carefully selected, trained, supervised, and evaluated. These volunteers require unique skills and competencies to manage complex situations and systems with which they will be confronted in the hospital environment.

Parsonnet & Weinstein (1987) outline some of the considerations that should be attended to when developing such a program. They stress the need for a good match between needs of programs and quality of volunteers. Ideally, the screening and training of the volunteers is incorporated into the social work function. One should screen for such attributes as self-awareness, warmth, empathy, commitment to patient confidentiality, an ability to relate to professionals as well as to the patients and families, a willingness to learn, a non-judgmental manner, and a sense of humour. Most critical is that volunteers have an awareness of their own reaction to stress and how to seek help when appropriate and that they know from whom to get such help.

A constant challenge is to design and implement systems where volunteers give assistance to professionals by performing tasks that can safely be done by volunteers. Determining those activities that can responsibly be delegated to a volunteer requires critical evaluation and assessment. W.C. Richan (1961) developed a theoretical schema for determining differential roles for professional and non-professional personnel. His theory was developed as a result of the paucity of trained social work personnel in social service agencies in the early 1960s. At that time, the majority of positions in the social welfare field were filled by non-professional workers. The need to differentiate the role of the professional from that of the non-professional permeated the social work literature of the time.

Although Richan's work was not intended for use in the voluntary sector, it would seem to have some applicability to the current discussion. Richan identified the importance of determining the extent of professional controls required for certain situations of client vulnerability. He defined professional controls as those controls that reside in or are internalized by the practitioner and include competence based upon a body of theoretical knowledge and skills assimilated over an extended training period. He defined client vulnerability as the susceptibility of clients to damage or exploitation stemming from incompetent or unethical behaviour. According to Richan, the more vulnerable the client, the greater the need for professional controls.

In the current application of Richan's model to the determination of appropriate roles for a volunteer, professional control was expanded to include professional accountability and is defined as the differential use of professional skills and abilities, based upon a body of theoretical knowledge, in problem identification and resolution and/or a legal mandate conferred upon the profession (e.g., child protection, domestic violence, capacity assessments). Demonstration of professional accountability is evidenced through adherence to a professional code of ethics, which regulates relationships between professionals and their clients and explicitly identifies duties, obligations, and responsibilities.

Client need is added to the definition of vulnerability to reflect the possibility that the need for professional service is dependent upon the complexity of client need as well as their vulnerability. Figure 31.2 outlines the relationship between these two concepts.

By putting these two concepts together, we are able to begin to distinguish a number of different roles. In situations requiring a high degree of professional accountability, coupled with situations of high client need or vulnerability, the greatest level of professional social work skill

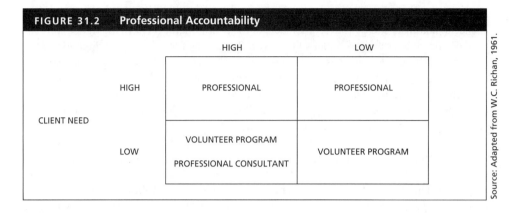

FIGURE 31.2   Professional Accountability

Source: Adapted from W.C. Richan, 1961.

and autonomy is required. In such situations, it would not be appropriate to utilize the services of a volunteer. For example, volunteers should never give medical information, advice, counselling, do crisis intervention, or conduct complex psychosocial assessments. In short, no act within the scope of practice of a social worker should be delegated to a volunteer.

There may be situations of high client need for which a set number of predetermined policies and procedures must be in place and which essentially require technical skills. In this situation, a social work intern or student under the supervision of a professional social worker might be appropriate.

In situations of client need that is low in terms of complexity and severity, the services of a volunteer may be quite useful and appropriate. The determination of whether or not the volunteer requires the consultation or supervision of a professional is determined by the aforementioned need for professional accountability. Volunteer programs with unpredictable outcomes or the possibility of escalating client need would require the availability of the social work professional as a consultant, as in the previously described Parent Buddy Program.

Situations of low client need and low professional accountability would require the most limited responses from the social work professional. In fact, in Richan's typology, he acknowledged that this area would be consistent with volunteer utilization.

THE VOLUNTEER AS ASSOCIATION MEMBER[1]

Since its inception, volunteers have led the association movement. For the purpose of the current discussion, *association* is intended to refer to nonprofit membership organizations whose organizational structure is best exemplified by the concept of administration by democracy. Such organizations may not necessarily have the word *association* in their title. These associations are first and foremost membership organizations which represent, protect, encompass, and promote the interests of diverse members (American Society of Association Executives, 1982).

Associations are composed of a board of directors, committees, association staff, and members. The key constituency of the association is its membership. Members frequently pay a fee to belong to the association or are involved in fundraising to maintain the fiscal viability of the organization. The greatest element of "membership'" is the opportunity and right

[1] This section was written with the assistance of Mary Ann Chang, M.S.W., Executive Director, Alzheimer Society for Metropolitan Toronto.

of members to influence an organization through the ability to cast votes. Members have the chance to nominate and/or vote for members of the board. Members have the right to present by-law amendments and resolutions that may influence the functioning and direction of the association. The association's raison d'être lies within the interests of its membership. The function of the association is to carry out the programs and policies that are common to all or most members. Some examples of common interests around which associations may be developed include health issues (e.g., Cancer Society, Alzheimer Society, Association for Community Living), professional interests (e.g., Association of Social Workers), public policy issues (e.g., Greenpeace), and social concerns (e.g., One Voice, Pensioners Concerned).

Associations seek out and strive to develop voluntary leaders to serve effectively on boards and committees of the association. These leaders help shape the issue or profession they represent. They establish short- and long-term goals, set policy, establish budgets, monitor programs and priorities and furnish expertise (American Society of Association Executives, 1982).

Committees are created to further the goals or operations of the association and are made up of members of the association, appointed or recruited from the membership. Committees are frequently delegated certain responsibility and authority. This sharing of responsibilities is essential as staff resources alone are usually insufficient to accomplish the goals of the association.

Voluntary organizations tend to be communally directed, with a board of directors that is drawn from the community at large. The directors have a trusteeship role with respect to the mission of the association, and the quality and extent of services provided is a dominant responsibility rather than financial gain (Perlmutter, F.D. & Adams, C.T., 1990). The board of directors carries the legal responsibility and sanction for the association that it governs. As such, the board of directors is the major decision-making body within the association. A balanced board of directors will mirror its total membership in composition in order to compose a group that will reflect the interests of the members at large. Much has been written about how boards of organizations can be more effective and in recent years it has been common for members of boards of directors to participate in workshops and seminars to learn more about improving their performance in this area.

Among the proponents of effective board leadership is John Carver (1996), who distinguishes the differing roles of board and staff. He assigns to the board what he calls the Policy Governance Model with an emphasis on values, vision, and the empowerment of both board and staff. He advocates that the board have a vision of its own job as "trustee-owner," as opposed to that of a "volunteer-helper" or "staff-watchdog." Within the Policy Governance Model, the board crafts its values into four types of policies: (1) ends, which are the definitions of which human needs are to be met by the association, for whom and at what cost? (2) executive limitations: Carver refers to the staff of an association as its Executive. Executive limitations are the boundaries of acceptability within which staff methods and activities can be left to staff decisions; (3) board-executive linkage, which clarifies the manner in which authority is delegated to staff and how staff performance will be evaluated; (4) board process, which determines the philosophy, accountability, and specifics of the board's job (Carver, 1996). In short, by defining the "ends" of the organization and focusing on long-range planning, the board is able to set "executive limitations," which define the way authority is delegated to the staff, and by which staff performance is monitored. Here, of course, the word "staff" primarily refers to the CEO, as it is assumed that the other staff are directed by the CEO to perform in a way that helps to accomplish board directives. The board is responsible for determining policies and priorities (governance) and the staff is responsible for implementing these policies (operations). Despite widespread acceptance of Carver's model, these distinctions are far from cut and dried (Perlmutter, 1990). Nevertheless, for effective association functioning it is critical that the board members be oriented to the difference between these two concepts and translate this awareness into their work as a board. Policy governance represents a substantial evolution in how board leadership is expressed (Carver, 1996). However, these concepts are still relatively new, and most organizations have boards which, at best, are only in the process of becoming a governance-oriented board.

Just as with volunteers who are service providers, the effectiveness of the volunteer contribution in associations is dependent upon rigorous and thoughtful recruitment, retention, training, monitoring, and evaluation strategies. The goal is to encourage productive participation by all members. In view of the changing nature of the board's role, as articulated by Carver's Governance Model, the characteristics of volunteers recruited for the board need to be carefully reviewed. The qualities that help to accomplish goals in this model are substantially different from the hands-on programming boards that many organizations still have. A powerful tool that administrators have at their disposal is the ability to influence the composition of the board. This opportunity often represents high-level volunteer recruitment and systems management. The administrator should encourage board participation from those members who will be able to reflect the direction and processes the administrator deems appropriate for association growth and development (Perlmutter, 1990).

THE VOLUNTEER AS DEVELOPER OF SERVICE

The development of self-help networks or groups is a growing phenomenon. Hundreds of self-help networks are started annually by ordinary people who have a little bit of courage, a fair amount of commitment, and a lot of care to give (CCSD, 1989). A self-help/mutual aid group or network is usually more loosely organized than an association. They rarely have any paid staff. However, many a self-help group has been a predecessor to association development. Self-help networks are usually started by a group of people linked together by a rare illness or situation (e.g., Friends of Schizophrenics, Mothers Against Drunk Driving, etc.). Through a model of mutual aid, these networks can ease the sense of isolation, powerlessness, hopelessness, and stress of a situation. They can provide emotional support, valuable information, and opportunities for advocacy. Their purpose is usually to raise awareness and to raise funds for research into treatment. They often start out as self-help groups but evolve into advocacy groups as they discover that social conditions often perpetuate the problems people have.

Self-help groups are usually based on the values of inclusivity and empowerment. The groups have a non-competitive, cooperative orientation with an anti-elite, anti-bureaucratic focus. A shared, circulating leadership is frequently developed. There is an emphasis on the fundamental belief that people who have a problem know much about it from the inside, from experiencing it, and members are being helped through helping. Helping is at the centre—knowing how to receive help, give help, and help yourself. The group is the key and de-isolation is critical (CCSD, 1989). Because of this accent on empowerment, an optimism about the ability to change evolves.

The relationship between professionals and the self-help movement is often one of measured antagonism. Self-helpers often view the professional as pretentious, purist, distant, and mystifying. Self-helpers prefer simplicity and informality. Professionals have often viewed the self-help movement with a skeptical and patriarchal eye. It is recognized that work is needed to improve the cooperative relationship between the professional and the self-help systems. A discussion is needed about the knowledge, attitudes, and skills professionals need in order to work effectively with self-help and mutual-aid groups. The first requirement is that professionals have to believe that they have much to learn from the experience of self-helpers. Riessman (1989) contends that both systems can benefit most from their interactions if they recognize both their oppositional and complementary dimensions. In other words, both need to gain an awareness that they can learn from each other. Professionals have specific training, which contributes to their knowledge and understanding of certain conditions. Self-helpers, on the other hand, have an "inside" understanding that comes from experience and empathy. Professionals need to listen and learn and modify at least some of their traditional practices and style. They need to be willing to move away from their professional tendencies to medicalize and pacify. Self-helpers need to be willing to see a role for professionals in the treatment and prevention of the illness or condition. Each needs to see the other as a potential partner, particularly in advocating for social change.

VOLUNTEERS AND ETHICAL ISSUES

There are some important sociological, political, and ethical issues to consider in the relationship between volunteerism and social work. The first concerns the potential for a volunteer program to promote elitism and to perpetuate systemic inequity based on culture. Volunteerism is frequently associated with education, income, and occupation. The higher the status of these three, the higher the rate of volunteerism. It has been documented that the non-white, lower educated, and lower socioeconomic status individual may be underrepresented in the volunteer pool (Perlmutter, 1990). It may well be that the cultural dimension has been seriously neglected within volunteerism. In a step toward ethnically sensitive practice, an adequate appreciation of cultural patterns, values, and norms of the population served should be ensured. This concern has implications for the increasing cultural diversity of the Canadian population. At its most basic, volunteerism is people helping people. Therefore, volunteers should reflect the population they serve from the cultural as well as the other human dimensions. Whether the volunteers are service providers, association members, or self-helpers, understanding the cultural issues associated with their particular cause is of critical importance. Issues of language and the constructs of a helping relationship have unique cultural manifestations. In volunteer programs, the potential for systemic racism in the recruitment process must be evaluated. Even though it may not be intentional, carrying out routine institutional procedures within volunteer activities and recruitment practices may reflect dominant cultural values and be reinforcing stereotypes and perpetuating acts of unwitting racism (Thompson, 1993).

There is also the potential for volunteerism to be viewed as a feminist issue. Gender is a fundamental dimension of the human experience and as such gender inequity occupies a central place in sociological discussions (Thompson, 1993). There has been a traditional role of women as volunteers. Some authors contend that this perpetuates a view of women that continues to position them outside the economic structure (Perlmutter, F.D., 1990). Another gender-related issue is the type of volunteer work done by women as opposed to that done by men. Some reports, albeit anecdotal, support the notion that women are over-represented among volunteers associated with service provision, whereas men are over-represented in the association movement, particularly on boards of directors. This may represent a perpetuation of the power imbalance between genders in the social service sector.

The aim of identifying these issues is simply to raise the consciousness of the reader and to promote further study and discussion in order to gain a better understanding of the issues, in particular as they relate to the complex interrelationship between racism and sexism within voluntarism

The final ethical issue to be discussed is the potential for exploitation within volunteerism. This issue relates to the unemployed professional—specifically, the unemployed social work graduate, who wishes to volunteer his or her services to an agency or program. These individuals may be willing to volunteer their services in order to gain some measure of experience which in turn may aid their employment prospects. One must at least address the possibility that it may be exploitative to use the services of a trained social work graduate to perform social work services for which there is no longer a budget. Additionally, one cannot ignore the possibility that this practice could lead to the extinction of some publicly-funded social services. This issue is of current concern as governments lessen their support for the universality of certain health and social programs. This practice may escalate tensions between volunteers and the professional community, who do not want to return the responsibility of social work services to private philanthropy. Creative solutions will have to accommodate all areas of concern. There are obviously no clear answers to this dilemma. As social work administrators are in a unique position to contribute to effective development and utilization of volunteers, including bridging the gap between volunteers and professionals, this will be an area for further deliberation and research.

CONCLUSION

In contemporary society, the tradition of voluntarism is strong in the social services and a broad spectrum of activities exists in which volunteers can be engaged. Volunteers continue to play multiple roles of provider, director, interpreter, funder, need identifier, and advocate of social services. Their altruism, commitment, and enthusiasm can enhance the quality and quantity of a variety of social services. It is recognized that some issues are still associated with the volunteer movement that prevent social workers from seeing them as colleagues. However, as social work has a fundamental responsibility for constantly exploring means of maximum utilization of all helping personnel, the challenge continues to be to embrace this aspect of our past, not to be encumbered by it, and to recognize the creative and collaborative role that volunteers do, can, and will play in contemporary social work practice.

REFERENCES

American Society of Association Executives (1982). *Fundamentals of association management: the volunteer*. Washington: American Society of Association Executives.

Ardal, F. (1996). A continuum of care through a parent support program for parents of prematures. Unpublished.

Barnsteiner, J.H., Cady, C.C., and Hagelgans, N. (1992). Auxiliary personnel can increase productivity. *Nursing Management. 23*(7), 103–104.

Canadian Council on Social Development. (1989). *Initiative: the self-help newsletter, 5*(2).

Carver, J. (1996). *Board Leadership*, Volume 23.

Carver, J. (1996). *Board Leadership*, Volume 25.

Foot, D.K. (1996). *Boom, bust & echo*. Toronto: MacFarlane Walter & Ross.

Fusco-Karmann, C., and Tamburini, M. (1994). Volunteers in hospital and home care, *Tumori*. *80*(4): 269–272.

Lonetto, R., and Duncan-Robinson, J. (1989). *Age is just a number*. Scarborough: McGraw Hill Ryerson Press.

Madara, E. (1989). Starting a support network for persons with a rare illness. *Initiative: the self-help newsletter*. Canadian Council on Social Development, *5*(2), 1–2.

Morey-Pedersen, J. (1994). When the waiting is difficult: surgical waiting room volunteers aid families. *Journal of Post Anesthesia Nursing*, *9*(4), 224–227.

Parsonnet, L., and O'Hare, J., (1990). A group orientation program for families of newly admitted cancer patients. *Social Work*, *35*(1), 37–40.

Parsonnet, L., and Weinstein, L. (1987). A volunteer program for helping families in a critical care unit. *Health and Social Work*, *12*(1), 21–27.

Perlmutter, F.D., and Adams, C.T. (1990) The voluntary sector & for-profit ventures: the transformation of American social welfare? *Administration in Social Work*, *14*(1), 1–13.

Perlmutter, F.D. (1990). *Changing hats: from social work practice to administration.* Washington: NASW Press.

Riessman, F. (1989). Professionals and self-help: a dialectical relationship. *Initiative: The Self-help Newsletter*. Canadian Council on Social Development, *5*(2), 9.

Richan, W.C., (1961) A theoretical scheme for determining roles of professional and non-professional personnel. *Social Work*, *6*(4), 22–28.

Schlosberg, A., (1991). Seven-year follow-up of an adolescent volunteer program in a psychiatric hospital. *Hospital and Community Psychiatry*, *42*(6), 632–633.

Statistics Canada (1997). *A portrait of seniors in Canada*. Ottawa: Statistics Canada.

Sues, A.M., and Wilson, P.A., (1987). Developing a hospital's volunteer program. *Health and Social Work,* *12*(1), 13–20.

Thompson, N. (1993). *Anti-discriminatory practice*. London, England: The MacMillan Press.

Wigdor, B.T. & Foot, D.K. (1988). *The over forty society: issues for Canada's aging population*. Toronto: James Lorimer & Co., p. 121–122.

Wurlitzer, F.P., and McIvor, A.C., (1996). Short-term volunteer staffing of a hospital, *Southern Medical Journal*, *89*(1), 46–50.

WORKING
WITH INFORMAL
HELPERS

John Cossom

INTRODUCTION

This chapter focuses on the significance of natural helpers and informal helping networks in people's lives. It speaks of how everyday forms of social support can nourish and sustain us, and act as a buffer against stress, illness, and personal difficulties. Because of the great importance of supportive relationships for people's well-being, it is imperative that social workers understand the integral parts they play in human ecology. It is also essential that social work practitioners shape their work so as to complement and nurture informal support in helping people deal with life problems.

Informal and formal help are contrasted to show their potential relationship and complementarity. Barriers that block social work's effective use of informal help are addressed, as are obstacles and antagonisms that militate against the positive integration of professional and informal worlds of support. The significance of informal helping for social work practice is discussed in the context of contemporary social work theory. The major practice and policy implications of working with informal helpers and support networks are presented. Finally, a practical example of a social support map and grid are provided, as tools that can be used to advantage by social workers.

By design, this chapter does not address the related subject of volunteer helpers. *Volunteer* is taken to mean a designated role in the context of a formal agency or organization providing sanctioned services to clients or consumers. Neither is attention given to the multitude of organized self-help and mutual aid organizations and groups that provide enormous quantities of lay care and assistance in our society. Rather, this chapter deals with spontaneous and natural informal relationships and networks that occur amongst family, friends, neighbours, and other helpers—where support, advice, compassion, advocacy, and all manner of practical aid are given freely, outside of any formal organizational boundaries.

THE ROLES OF INFORMAL HELPING AND SUPPORT SYSTEMS

From practice wisdom and intuition social workers have long known of the significance of social support. Indeed, professional social work foundations are solidly ensconced in marshalling social support for those facing personal difficulties and social disadvantage. This was particularly evident in settlement house, community, and group work practice. These approaches emphasized practical community-based help, group and neighbourhood mutual assistance, and attention to socio-economic and political forces that affected residents' lives.

For the past three decades research findings have supported practice wisdom by telling us that informal helping relationships and social support are indeed critical factors for our lives and health. Cobb (1976) defined *social support* as "information leading the subject to believe that he is cared for and loved, esteemed, and a member of a network of mutual obligation" (300). For Gottlieb (1983) social support consists of "verbal and/or nonverbal information or advice, tangible aid, or action that is proffered by social intimates or inferred by their presence and has beneficial emotional or behavioral effects on the recipient". Tracy and Whittaker (1990) refer to social support as "the many different ways in which people render assistance to one another: emotional encouragement, advice, information, guidance, tangible aid, or concrete assistance" (462).

Social work practice also has had growing awareness of the preventive and curative power of *social support networks*. "Networks are interconnected relationships, durable patterns of interaction, and interpersonal threads that comprise a social fabric" (Garbarino, 1986, 31). Social support networks are defined as "a set of interconnected relationships among a group of people that provides enduring patterns of nurturance (in any or all forms) and that provides contingent reinforcement for efforts to cope with life on a day-to-day basis (Whittaker & Garbarino, 1983, 5). People who are well connected to such networks (e.g., through a church, synagogue, or temple; as part of an extended family group; a friendship group; in a work setting; or in a self-help group) are more likely to cope well when confronted with everyday problems of life or unexpected events that turn into crisis. Being part of a social network of relationships and having social resources available has positive, stress-buffering effects on people's well-being (Cohen & Wills, 1985; Garbarino, 1986). Conversely, the absence of social support has been demonstrated as a negative factor in people's everyday social functioning (Van Meter, Haynes, & Kropp, 1987, 70).

We take it for granted that social relationships and support networks are essential to our well-being and provide us with a sense of self-identity. Research supports this, demonstrating that supportive social relationships play important roles, preventing social dysfunction, maintaining our physical and mental health, aiding recovery from illness and regaining stability after crisis.

> The conclusion that supportive interactions among people are important is hardly new. What is new is the assembling of hard evidence that adequate social support can protect people in crisis from a wide variety of pathological states: from low birth weight to death, from arthritis through tuberculosis to depression, alcoholism, and other psychiatric illness. Furthermore, social support can reduce the amount of medication required and accelerate recovery and facilitate compliance with prescribed regimens. (Cobb, 1976, 310)

Since Cobb wrote this we have discovered many new ways in which supportive relationships have positive effects on our health. For example,

Women with medically at-risk pregnancies suffer only one-third the complications at birth if they are well-connected socially, with more friends and relatives in frequent contact. Men experiencing life changes (such as unemployment) report greater psychological well-being if they have the support of wives and friends.

A study of people who had been abused as children showed that those who had strong and active social networks were much less likely to repeat the abusive pattern in their own childrearing than those without such a support system. (Garbarino, 1986, 34)

We may not know exactly what the essential preventive or remedial ingredients of social support are, how they immunize us against stressors and threats to our health, and reduce the impact of others. However, there is mounting agreement that support from natural relationships acts as a buffer or mediator against the effects of stress, and as a positive factor in disease prevention, health promotion, and recovery from illness (Caplan, 1974; Cobb, 1976; Cohen & Wills, 1985; Gore, 1978; Gottlieb, 1981).

Caplan (1974) identifies three major forms of help that can come into play through social support.

...[They] help the individual mobilize his psychological resources and master emotional burdens; they share his tasks; and they provide him with extra supplies of money, materials, tools, skills, and cognitive guidance to improve handling his situation (6).

Maguire (1991, xv–xix) reviews resources that can come through social support. He identifies five that are important for social workers to understand.

1. *A sense of self.* Providing an opportunity through non-judgmental, genuine acceptance for people to come to a better understanding of themselves, to talk about the difficulties they face, and to figure out solutions that are best for them.

2. *Encouragement and positive feedback.* Offering someone a sense of being valued and having worth, especially at a time of stress when self-worth may be under significant threat.

3. *Protection against stress.* Simply being available to a person under stress, and offering support seems to be an ingredient that makes a difference in how someone deals with stressful situations (e.g., job loss, death of a loved one, divorce, or the onset of illness).

4. *Knowledge, skills, and resources.* These can range from giving information about formal services, to practical support like driving a friend to an appointment, providing meals or house cleaning at a time of crisis, and providing direct financial help.

5. *Socialization opportunities.* Often at a time of great stress we can be vulnerable to isolation. Friends, relatives, and workmates can provide opportunities for simple social interaction and an opportunity to sustain or reconnect social relationships.

The focus of social support and social support networks studies is predominantly on their positive roles. Social workers know all too well that the picture is not always an encouraging one. A person can be solidly embedded in a social network that has more negative than positive social influences. Out of the same social source can flow both help and hindrance. Social workers often find a focus in their practice is helping individuals who want to free themselves from the negative influences of a powerful social network. One has only to think of the effect of peer group interplay on the actions of delinquent boys, or any number of other self-defeating behaviours that can flow from group interactions. Not all social exchanges are socially supportive, nor do they necessarily support socially positive behaviours (Van Meter, Haynes, & Kropp, 1987). Also, simply having more social network resources does not automatically lead to a greater resource of social support (Tracy & Whittaker, 1990, 462).

Social support and helpful networks are certainly no panacea for a trouble-free existence. The question of informal help and social support is much more complex than simply that of whether people have access to this resource or not. Most people have access to some sort of social support through family, friendship, work, leisure, or religious networks. The clients we see are usually not completely isolated. However, the availability and nature of social support can vary dramatically in many dimensions, such as cultural and ethnic norms, one's personal and social skills at maintaining relationships and using support, the degree of stigma and social distance that one's situation conveys, and so on.

WHY AN INCREASED INTEREST IN INFORMAL HELPING SYSTEMS?

As noted, in the past three decades informal helping and social support has increasingly held the interest of researchers and professional practitioners. Why is this so? One reason is the growing fiscal restraint, political disenchantment, and withdrawal of support from social programs of the welfare state. With these factors have come shortages in professional personnel to deliver social services. These economic and social policy realities have forced attention to and interest in finding cost-saving interventions.

Paralleling these trends there has also been widespread emphasis on de-institutionalization, moving people previously housed in hospitals, prisons, and facilities for the physically and mentally disabled into community-living situations. Usually these community-based alternatives have been under-resourced and at least in part dependent on unpaid, informal, and non-professional helpers. Bottom-line issues have naturally drawn politicians and policy makers to pay much more attention to approaches that draw on voluntary, informal, free human resources, and increased their perceived attractiveness as ready solutions to pressing and persistent social problems.

As we have already seen, as an accompaniment to these economic drivers there has been a growing research awareness that informal helpers are vital in people's lives, and offer different and equally significant kinds and qualities of help compared to professional helpers. After all, spontaneous help from family, friends, neighbours, and workmates has been present throughout all human history. Even in a post-industrial world, with intensifying reactionary responses to the ubiquitousness and cost of the welfare state, most social care takes place outside of human services. Warren (1981, 49) suggested that of the entire helping that takes place in the U.S., only 12% occurs under the aegis of formal service agencies or professionals. This means that for each contact with a formal helper there are eight with informal helpers. In his survey of over 1500 urban residents he found that in seeking help for concerns they turned to spouses, friends, and other relatives, in that order of preference. Other research has shown consistently that people go first to friends, relatives, neighbours, and other lay helpers such as hairdressers and bartenders for information and help (Garbarino, 1986, 35). Social workers ignore such a powerful and extensive natural resource of social care at their own and their clients' peril.

Another factor shining a spotlight on informal helping has been its challenge to the effectiveness of traditional forms of professional help. For example,

Evaluation research shows that on the average, self-help or mutual aid groups can be as effective or even more effective than casework or individual therapy approaches in dealing with child maltreatment. In terms of cost-effectiveness, they are the clear winners. (Garbarino, 1986, 35)

Also, as discussed in more detail later in this chapter, new paradigms of social work practice have emerged that place far more attention on environmental situations and the interaction between person and social environment, as opposed to a focus on individual, person-centred approaches (Tracy & Whittaker, 1990). This naturally centres some attention on help-givers and supporters of all kinds.

Not surprisingly then, a confluence of these and other factors has increased attempts to understand how informal helping and natural helping systems work, and how they can be harnessed. From this impetus has come proposals, projects, and injunctions to further study and experiment with better linkage between informal care and professional social work practice.

PROFESSIONAL AND INFORMAL HELP: DIFFERENCES IN STRUCTURE, STYLE, AND MEANING

Although both informal and professional helpers are often concerned with the same human dilemmas, there is agreement in the literature that there are significant differences in form, substance, and style between their approaches to help-giving (Ayers, 1989; Caplan, 1974; Hoch & Hemmens, 1987; Lepman, 1982; Patterson, 1977; Patterson, Germain, Brennan & Memmott, 1992; Tracy & Whittaker, 1990).

In general, informal helping is characterized by spontaneous relationships and offers of assistance; flexibility as to when and what help is given; freely giving of one's time and labour; an absence of organizational auspices, implying a freedom from constraints in this regard; help given primarily on the basis of life experience; mutuality, interdependence, and reciprocal approaches in giving and receiving help, reflecting an exchange of help and an approximately equal relationship status; and freedom from the stigma often associated with being "the client" of a formal helping organization. Informal social support tends to be more natural, accessible, culturally valid, and acceptable to many people than are often poorly-known services from professionals and social agencies.

Paid helpers, on the other hand, offer assistance within the bounds of their publicly recognized and sanctioned specialities. They are—with the exception of most private practitioners—tied to an organizational structure that sanctions and prescribes what they do and whom they serve. This usually means that professional helpers relate to a particular target population (e.g., mentally ill adults, sexual abuse survivors, the frail elderly). They have social and professional legitimacy, power, and funding associated with their status; they use specialized knowledge and training; they rely on professional objectivity as a hallmark of helping; and they offer a relationship that has inherent elements of unequal status between helper and client, despite the efforts of many social workers to reduce this social distance and hierarchy as much as is possible.

It is obvious and inevitable, then, that these two kinds of helping differ in form and meaning for helped and helper along many dimensions. Not the least of these is power, by reason of the different authority relations that exist (e.g., between friend and friend, as opposed to social worker and client). The question is, can these differences be partnered while retaining the essential strengths, advantages, and integrity of each?

INFORMAL AND FORMAL HELPING: CO-EXISTENCE, PARTNERSHIP, OR DISCONTINUITY?

An important series of questions—some old, some new—have emerged about possible relationships between formal and informal systems of care (Froland, 1980; Miller, 1985; Hoch & Hemmens, 1987). At first glance it seems that helping bureaucracies and natural helping networks should be able to operate with positive complementarity. It is obvious that they have existed side-by-side for a very long time. Yet our knowledge of partnering processes is far from complete.

Non-organizational, small-scale, informal care has not diminished as organized social welfare has grown exponentially in the past century. It remains the first line of defence for most people in need. Yet not everyone has access to a caring network. Nor is there enough natural care for everyone. If there were, would such a complex array of social and health services have emerged? Help from friends and neighbours is often strained because of limits in continuity, reliability, access to knowledge, skill, and resources.

Can professional and informal care be integrated? Or are they so different that they are destined to simply co-exist in parallel form, concerned with many of the same human dilemmas, yet approaching them with different values, assumptions, and approaches toward help? Are these two phenomena like oil and water?

Most writers agree that the essential differences between these two forms of caring produce tensions between them. Hoch and Hemmens (1987) see two essential problems: rational incompatibilities and power differences. They challenge authors (Collins, 1980; Froland, Pancoast, Chapman & Kimboko, 1981; Patterson, 1977) who take the position that partnership is readily achievable, and argue that aid offered by informal helpers and professionals "differs significantly in kind and meaning ... and differences easily become conflicts when the partners do not possess equivalent authority" (437). These writers emphasize the fact that natural helpers offer aid not on the basis of need, but of friendship—a totally different footing than that of professional paradigms of helping. Hoch and Hemmons (1987) draw on research to demonstrate that when professionals and lay helpers combine, the result is almost always unintended co-optation of the indigenous helper, and superimposition of the "instrumental focus of the organized care system" (433). Examples of "partnerships" between the two worlds can often reflect an unrecognized co-optation by professionals, raise more questions than they answer, and have usually been implicitly conducted from the vantage point of professionals. This is because efforts to link natural and professional helping reflect the rational, instrumental focus of the organized care system. Hoch and Hemmens wonder whether efforts to integrate these two realms of help do not increase antagonisms between them, and "endanger the social integrity of existing types of informal care" (433). It should hardly be surprising that there can be a decided power imbalance between the formal, organized strength, knowledge, and expertise of professionals, and the loosely-connected, informal attributes of natural helping processes.

CONCEPTUAL FRAMEWORKS FOR WORK WITH INFORMAL HELPERS

1. Ecological-Systems Theory

A framework that plays an important part in supporting the inclusion of informal helping and social support into the social work knowledge base is ecological-systems theory. Human ecology theorists (Bronfenbrenner, 1979; Garbarino, 1986; Germain & Gitterman, 1980) have built on biological studies of interrelationships between organisms and their environment in attempts to formulate a better understanding of the complexities of people in relation to their social environments. Ecological-systems theory puts emphasis on social workers viewing their practice through a wide (person-environment) lens, rather than simply through a narrower (individual) focus. This theoretical perspective has led social workers to more careful scrutiny of connections and transactions between people and their family, friends, neighbourhood, workplace, religious and educational institutions, and even broader features of their habitat including social structure, geography, climate, laws, institutions, and values (Garbarino, 1986).

In this ecological theoretical framework, life stresses are seen as an expression of a particular person-environment interaction—the stressor in the environment and the person's social, emotional, and physiological responses to it (Germain & Patterson, 1988). How one copes with life stress depends in large measure on the availability of resources—material, informational, and socio-emotional support in one's environment. This paradigm has logically pointed social workers in the direction of natural helping systems, and shifts intervention toward the person's environment, including involvement with informal helpers and social networks.

2. Social Treatment

Building on an ecological perspective, Whittaker (1974) provides a social treatment practice framework that emphasizes the interface of formal and informal helping. This is not a new framework for social work practice. It has a long tradition, stretching back to social work's formal origins. However, Whittaker further delineates this paradigm for social work. He defines social treatment as

> [An] approach to interpersonal helping that uses direct and indirect strategies of intervention to aid individuals, families, and small groups in improving functioning and coping with social problems. (49)

The major conceptual emphases of this framework are on:

1. *Social functioning and social problems.* Starting with the social problem as experienced by the client, but seeing problems as the result of individual and environmental interplay.
2. *Direct and indirect intervention.* Social treatment assumes that helping includes direct work with clients as well as environmental change done on clients' behalf.
3. *Interpersonal helping.* A focus on work with individuals, families, and small groups.
4. *An eclectic view of practice methods.* Using a range of helping strategies drawn from different theoretical bodies of knowledge (Whittaker, 1974, 49–61).

In Whittaker's elaboration of social treatment he identifies social work roles that fit it well: treatment agent, teacher-counsellor, broker of services and resources, advocate, network/system consultant. All these roles have potential for combining formal and informal strategies of helping. But it is in the network/system consultant role cluster that Whittaker sees special opportunities for us to work with existing or contrived informal support systems to assist clients (1986, 46). Examples he gives of social workers playing these roles with informal helpers are:

1. Teaching basic crisis intervention and marital counselling skills to "community gatekeepers": e.g., beauticians, barbers, physicians, police officers, school crossing guards, and bartenders.

2. Enlisting elderly citizens in "foster grandparent" programs for mentally disabled children.

3. Consulting with an informal network of day-care "neighbours" to improve preventive and protective services for children.

3. Exchange theory

Studies of informal help stress that it usually takes place through a reciprocal relationship. "Helping is a social process with three equally important elements: giving, receiving, and repaying" (Miller, 410). This is important for understanding informal helping. People participate in reciprocal exchanges that they feel will have benefit for them and which offer them a measure of equality in a relationship, with potential to return the help at some point (Lewis & Suarez, 1768). A professional helping relationship is not built upon this expectation of reciprocity. One of the potential dilemmas for a client is that there is no ready way to "repay" the helper for a public or free service. Theoretical perspectives on the nature of social exchange are important for professional practitioners to understand. They shed light on the inherent differences between their help and what friends, family, and neighbours offer. There are social ingredients of informal helping relationships that have important implications for professional practice.

Related to the concept of reciprocity of exchange is Reissman's (1965) helper-therapy principle. In his study of self-help groups and processes Reissman saw that people were greatly helped through helping others. This is an important part of a natural helping exchange—it benefits both receiver and giver. While most professional practitioners would agree that there is great benefit in being a helper, this is not a raison d'être of professional helping, and substantially distinguishes it from informal helping.

MAJOR IMPLICATIONS FOR SOCIAL WORK

What are the implications for social work that flow from the growing knowledge and theory about informal helping and social support? How can social workers respond? In this section we look at implications of social work relationships with informal helpers for social work practice, education, and social policy.

1. Practice

There are no panaceas or foolproof guidelines. Much remains to be done to strengthen the knowledge base that allows for better integration of these resources, while preserving the integrity and strengths of each. One principle seems clear. It is essential that effective awareness of and liaison with informal helping occupy a central, integral place in social work practice. This means putting as much emphasis on social and environmental intervention as we do on person-focused elements of practice, such as talk therapies and personal healing. With evidence piling up on the significance of natural help and social support, another way of saying it is that the "social" in "social work" should be given a higher priority. If informal social support is to be used in social work practice frameworks, it should be seen as an integral part of practice, not simply an add-on approach or another "method" of practice.

Informal social support is not a miracle solution for the social problems of the 21st century (despite the wishes of some politicians). Nor is professional intervention. Neither formal nor informal care alone can respond to demands for help in isolation from one another.

These two responses to human need will continue to co-exist in the face of pressing social problems. Can they do better than co-exist? Is there potential for professional and informal help to cooperate to the advantage of clients in need? Can they accomplish more in partnership than in isolation?

Let me propose some general themes that have to be addressed if more than parallel co-existence is to occur; if informal help is to be seen as an essential resource by social service workers. First, the formal social services cannot and should not forsake their legitimate responsibilities for responding to human need. Nor should

> the swing to voluntarism...[result] in government and professional abdication of their responsibilities to provide resources, services and coherent welfare policies. Community networks must not be expected to provide life-belts for the victims of the government's economic policies. (Olsen, 1986, 21)

However, social workers can be better prepared to take risks and reach out to informal helpers as partners in practice. We not only ignore working with these resources at our peril, but also to the disadvantage of our clients. The challenge is to work with people in less powerful, largely unsanctioned roles without dominating, overpowering, supplanting, or co-opting them in professional paradigms. Informal helpers do not have the same knowledge, assumptions, and approaches as professionals. Their expertise is different, based on experience. Like professional helpers, there are many problems that they cannot help with, many things they cannot do, resources they cannot access. Together, however, professionals and informal helpers can often combine to strengthen the client's resources. Informal helpers may be able to act as a bridge between citizens and social services. Professionals can link clients to social supports in their natural environments.

This assumes that workers and agencies are open to and active in pursuing information about informal helping networks in their communities and in their clients' lives. Antagonism toward or disinterest in grass-roots helpers occurs all too often. Of all professional helpers, social workers should be most willing to familiarize themselves with clients' community context, and ready to link to and support informal help.

We should not expect liaisons between formal and informal care always to be free of conflict, given the two different worlds they represent. There is no shortage of troublesome areas that emerge in this regard. For example, what information is shared by the professional agency in working collaboratively with informal helpers? How are members of a social support network effectively involved in case planning? Challenges to collaboration are more likely to be heard when statutory agencies are involved that offer service to clients on probation or parole, or where children's safety and well-being is under scrutiny. In many cases information can be readily shared with the client's permission. In others, there may be considerable tension around this decision. These examples illustrate that the wish to collaborate is sometimes easier than its practice, given the different responsibilities of partners in helping.

2. Policy

While the focus of this book is not on social policy, it is hazardous to discuss this subject without brief reference to a few sample policy issues that impinge upon the relationship between informal and formal helping resources. After all, social work practice is greatly influenced by the nature and shape of social policy, both in its commission and omission.

If we are to value the everyday contributions made to human well-being by natural caregivers and helpers, how can social policy be framed to express support for this social and health resource? For example, how well do we support helpers and caregivers by providing respite services for them? Is enough emphasis placed on such things as day-care opportunities and other services for disabled individuals that lift pressure from their caregivers, at the same time as providing normalizing, out-of-home opportunities?

Are there adequate tax benefits for those who give social support and act informally as caregivers to relatives, friends, and neighbours? There are certainly tax benefits for those whom government considers "productive" business people. Are we much more reluctant to reward the productivity of those who day-by-day carry out important community social support roles? Is this a productivity double standard? Are social assistance regulations made in such a way that those dependent on the state are recompensed for important work done supporting friends, neighbours, or family members in need of care? Is the helper-therapy principle recognized and supported in welfare policy?

One cannot leave even a brief discussion of policy issues without drawing attention to feminist analysis of informal community and family care. While men do occupy caring and informal helping roles, a majority of these responsibilities are carried by and assumed to belong to women: wives, mothers, sisters, and daughters (Cossom, 2001). For example, with a distinct demographic shift toward an older population in Canada, it is noteworthy that "community care" tends to mean the unpaid care of female family members (Aronson, 139). Similarly, most care of the sick and severely disabled is likely to fall to women. Simultaneously, the shrinking size and multiple forms of the contemporary family, the still-increasing participation of women in the labour force, geographic mobility, and high divorce rates raise pointed questions about what is happening to the major source of informal care. Given these pressures faced by most women, what resources do they have left for demanding caregiving roles? Public policy statements asserting that the family is the best source of support usually ignore key questions like "How do we provide for the needs of all, and not at the expense of women?" (Segal, 1987, 242).

There are two worlds of care, the organized and the communal, "the public world of the bureaucrat and the private world of mothers" (Abrams, 1978). It seems that these two worlds are now operating in more complex, proximal relationship, without fully understanding one another, or meshing to each other's advantage. Yet neither of these two systems of care can meet human need by itself; neither can perform successfully without the other. Our expanding expectations of informal helping services mean there is no shortage of policy questions and no simple answers.

3. Social Work Education

One important way social work practice is influenced is by the paradigms and practice models that are taught in professional schools. Miller—based on a literature review of how professional social workers use informal resources—makes recommendations on how social work education can prepare students to see lay helpers as equal partners (Miller, 1985). She calls for explicit curriculum content on informal helping as reciprocal exchange; types of lay resources; exposure to natural helpers in classroom and field practice; and orientation to the different, valid roles and knowledge that lay and professional people have, and the strengths and limitations of each.

Theoretical orientations and ideologies that are taught in a social work curriculum go a long way to frame students' perspectives on their roles and their potential attitudes toward lay helpers. So careful attention is needed here.

TOOLS FOR UNDERSTANDING AND ASSESSING SOCIAL SUPPORT

If social workers are to work more closely and collaboratively with informal helpers and social support networks, we need to have techniques to better understand and assess these resources as they affect people's lives.

Social workers have had more and better tools available to help them understand and assess the personal psychological problems of individuals than they have had for adequately comprehending people's complex environments. This is so despite social work's long-claimed practice concern and focus on people in their social environment. With a shift in some quarters from an individual/clinical mode of practice to stronger socio-ecological and structural perspectives, and approaches that are more amenable to collaboration with informal helping sources, attention is being given to ways of assessing and working that are more inclusive and ecological. Accompanying this shift has been the development of assessment tools to help social workers better understand and work with the client's social world. One of the problems with many tools is that typically they have been cumbersome, time-consuming to use, and often yielding little of immediate, practical use to practitioners.

The eco-map is one device that has been available for two decades, designed to illustrate an individual's or family's connections and relationships with the social environment (Hartman, 1978). Another frequently used device for mapping family support is the genogram (McGoldrick & Gerson, 1975). Maguire (1983, 1991) has described a Personal Networking Assessment Instrument that can be used to engage clients in mapping both the structure and qualities of social support relationships in their lives.

A more recent instrument that shows promise, consisting of both a social network map and grid, was developed as part of The Family Support Project in Seattle, Washington (Tracy & Whittaker, 1990). It is specifically designed to generate information with clients about their support networks, both in structural measures (the existence and quality of relationships), and functional terms (the various types of supportive exchanges in these relationships). The project reports that the social network map and grid was well received by practitioners and clients, and yielded useful information on

> (1) Existing informal resources, (2) potential informal resources not currently used by the client, (3) barriers to involving social network resources, and (4) factors to be considered and weighed in the decision to incorporate informal resources in the formal service plan (Tracy & Whittaker, 1990, 462).

Because this tool has potential direct application in practice, can support practitioners' understanding of and relationship to informal helpers, and relates in a practical way to the themes of this chapter, the social network map and grid are included in the appendix to this chapter with instructions for their use.

CONCLUSION

This chapter has explored the importance of natural helping relationships for social work. It is clear that whatever directions social policy takes, and whatever approaches professional social workers use, informal helping will continue as a major feature of support for people facing crises and coping with the day-to-day demands of life. The challenge is for social workers to recognize, understand, and support these forces for health and well-being wherever they exist, and to help people build and nourish them where they are absent or strained.

It seems to me that social work, of all professions concerned with personal and social change, is most strongly placed to work with natural helpers in its practice. Seeing ourselves as partners with informal helpers has great potential for practice that empowers clients (individuals, groups, and communities) to have control over their destinies, and that strengthens rather than distances the relationships between social workers and consumers.

This approach to practice has relevance for all fields and populations, ethnic and cultural groups. The form and substance of help may vary quite substantially in different contexts, (e.g., in a particular First Nations community; amongst AIDS patients; in families supporting children with disabilities; by elderly spouses and friends dealing with those suffering from Alzheimer disease; or in an urban, ethnic community). However, informal patterns of support will exist, and there is a choice for social workers and their agencies to reach out and collaborate, or to operate in isolation from these resources.

Although there is much yet to learn about informal help and how we can work alongside it without overpowering or co-opting it, the challenge is for us to adopt a practice mind-set that sees formal and informal support as allies, rather than as competitive, separate social entities.

REFERENCES

Abrams, P. (1978). Community care: some research problems and priorities. In J. Barnes & N. Connelly (Eds.). *Social Care Research* (pp. 18–99). London: Bedford Square Press.

Aronson, J. (1991). Dutiful daughters and undemanding mothers: contrasting images of giving and receiving care in middle and later life. In C.T. Baines, P.T. Evans, & S.M. Neysmith (Eds.). *Women's caring: feminist perspectives on social welfare* (pp.138–168). Toronto: McClelland & Stewart.

Ayers, T.D. (1989). Dimensions and characteristics of lay helping. *American Journal of Orthopsychiatry, 59*, 215–225.

Bronfenbrenner, U. (1979). *The ecology of human development*. Cambridge, MA: Harvard University Press.

Caplan, G. (1974). *Support systems and community mental health*. New York: Behavioral Publications.

Cobb, S. (1976). Social support as a moderator of life stress. *Psychosomatic Medicine, 38*(5), 300–314.

Cohen, S. & Wills, T.A. (1985). Stress, social support, and the buffering hypothesis. *Psychological Bulletin. 98*(2), 310–357.

Collins, A.H. (1980). Helping neighbours intervene in cases of maltreatment. In J. Garbarino & H. Stocking (Eds.). *Protecting children from abuse and neglect* (pp. 133–172). San Francisco: Jossey-Bass.

Cossom, J. (2001). Informal helping and mutual aid. In J.C. Turner & F.J. Turner (Eds.). *Canadian Social Welfare* (4th ed.). (pp. 346–361). Scarborough, Ontario: Allyn & Bacon.

Froland, C. (1980). Formal and informal care: discontinuities on a continuum. *Social Service Review, 54*(4), 572–587.

Froland, C., Pancoast, D.L., Chapman, N., & Kimboko, P. (1981). *Helping networks and human services*. Beverly Hills, California: Sage Publications.

Garbarino, J. (1986). Where does social support fit into optimizing human development and preventing dysfunction? *British Journal of Social Work, 16*, Supplement, 23–37.

Germain, C.B. & Gitterman, A. (1980). *The life model of social work practice.* New York: Columbia University Press.

Germain, C.B., & Patterson, S. (1988). Teaching about rural natural helpers as environmental resources. *Journal of Teaching in Social Work, 2*(1), 73–90.

Gore, S. (1978). The effects of social support in moderating the health consequences of unemployment. *Journal of Health and Social Behavior, 19*, 157–165.

Gottlieb, B.H. (Ed.). (1981). *Social networks and social support.* Beverly Hills, California: Sage Publications Inc.

Gottlieb, B.H. (Ed.). (1983). *Social support strategies: guidelines for mental health practice.* Beverly Hills, California: Sage Publications Inc.

Hartman, A. (1978). Diagrammatic assessment of family relations. *Social Casework, 59*, 465–476.

Hoch, C. & Hemmens, G.C. (1987). Linking informal and formal help: conflict along the continuum of care. *Social Service Review, 61*(3), 432–446.

Lepman, A. (1982). Formal and informal support: a conceptual clarification. *Journal of Applied Gerontology, 1*, 141–146.

Lewis, E.A. & Suarez, Z.E. (1995). Natural helping networks. In R.L. Edwards (Ed. in Chief). *Encyclopedia of social work* (pp.1765–1772). Washington, D.C.: NASW Press.

Maguire, L. (1983). *Understanding social networks.* Beverly Hills, California: Sage Publications Inc.

Maguire, L. (1991). *Social support systems in practice.* Silver Spring, Maryland: NASW Press.

McGoldrick, M., & Gerson, R. (1985). *Genograms in family assessment.* New York: W.W. Norton.

Miller, P.A. (1985). Professional use of lay resources. *Social Work, 30*(5), 409–416.

Olsen, M.R. (1986). Integrating formal and informal social care—the utilization of social support networks. *British Journal of Social Work, 16*, Supplement, 15–22.

Patterson, S.L. (1977). Toward a conceptualization of natural helping. *Arête, 4*(3), 161–171.

Patterson, S.L., Germain, C.B., Brennan, E.M., & Memmott, J.L. (1988). Effectiveness of rural helpers. *Social Casework, 69*(5), 272–279.

Reissman, F. (1977). The helper-therapy principle. *Social Work, 10*(2), 27–32.

Segal, L. (1987). *Is the future female? Troubled thoughts on contemporary feminism.* London: Virago Press.

Tracy, E.M. & Whittaker, J.K. (1990). The social network map: assessing social support in clinical practice. *Families in Society: The Journal of Contemporary Human Services, 71*(8), 461–470.

Van Meter, M.J.S., Haynes, O.M., & Kopp, J.P. (1987). The negative social network: when friends are foes. *Child Welfare, 66*(1), 69–75.

Warren, D. (1981). *Helping networks.* Notre Dame, Indiana: University of Notre Dame Press.

Whittaker, J.K. (1974). *Social treatment.* New York: Aldine.

Whittaker, J.K. (1986). Integrating formal and informal social care: a conceptual framework. *British Journal of Social Work, 16*, Supplement, 39–62.

Whittaker, J.K., & Garbarino, J. (1983). *Social support networks: informal helping in the social services.* New York: Aldine.

APPENDIX

INSTRUCTIONS/SCRIPT FOR SOCIAL NETWORK MAP[1]

Step One: Developing a Social Network Map

Let's take a look at who is in your social network by putting together a network map. We can use first names or initials because I'm not that interested in knowing the particular people and I wouldn't necessarily be contacting any of the people we talk about.

Think back to this past month, say since [date]. What people have been important to you? They may have been people you saw, talked with, or wrote letters to. This includes people who made you feel good, people who made you feel bad, and others who just played a part in your life. They may be people who had an influence on the way you made decisions during this time.

There is no right or wrong number of people to identify on your map. Right now, just list as many people as you come up with. ...

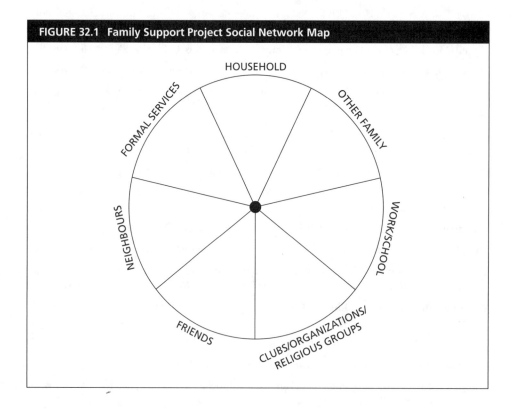

FIGURE 32.1 Family Support Project Social Network Map

---

[1]Adapted from Tracy, E.M. and Whittaker, J.K. (1990). The Social Network Map: Assessing Social Support in Clinical Practice. *Families in Society: The Journal of Contemporary Human Services, 71*(8), 461–470.

First, think of people in your *household*—who does that include?

Now, going around the map, what *other family members* would you include in your network?

How about people from *work* or *school*?

People from *clubs, organizations,* or *religious groups*—who should we include here?

What *other friends* haven't been listed in the other categories?

Neighbours—local shopkeepers may be included here.

Finally, list professional people or people from formal agencies whom you have contact with.

Look over your network. Are these the people you would consider part of your social network this past month? (Add or delete names as needed.)

Step Two: Completing the Social Network Grid

(If more than 15 people are in the network, ask the client to select the "top fifteen" and then ask the questions about only those network members. For each of the questions use the appropriate sorting guide card. Once the client has divided up the cards, put the appropriate code number for each person listed on the network grid.)

Now, I'd like to learn more about the people in your network. I'm going to write their names on this network grid, put a code number for the area of life and then ask a few questions about the ways in which they help you. Let's also write their names on these slips of paper too; this will make answering the questions a lot easier. These are the questions I'll be asking (show list of social network questions), and we'll check off the names on this grid as we go through each question.

The first three questions have to do with the *types of support* people give you.

Who would be available to help you out in concrete ways—for example, would give you a ride if you needed one, or would pitch in to help you with a big chore, or would look after your belongings for a while if you were away? Divide your cards into three piles—those people you can hardly ever rely on for concrete help, those you can rely on sometimes, and those you'd almost always rely on for this type of help.

Now, who would be available to give you *emotional support*—for example, comfort you if you were upset; to be right there with you in a stressful situation; listen to you talk about your feelings? Again, divide your cards into three piles—those people you can hardly ever rely on for emotional support; those you can rely on sometimes; and those you almost always can rely on for this type of help.

Finally, whom do you rely on for *advice*—for example, who would give you information on how to do something, help you make a big decision, or teach you how to do something? Divide your cards into the three piles—hardly ever, sometimes, and almost always—for this type of support.

Look through your cards and this time select those people, if any, in your network who you feel are *critical* of you (either critical of you or your lifestyle or of you as a parent). When I say "critical," I mean critical of you in a way that makes you feel bad or inadequate. Divide the cards into three piles—those people who are hardly ever critical of you, sometimes critical of you, and almost always critical of you. Again we'll put the code numbers next to their names.

Now look over your cards and think about the *direction of help*. Divide your cards into three piles—those people with whom help goes both ways (you help them just as much as

FIGURE 32.2 Family Support Project Social Network Grid

Name #	Area of life 1. Household 2. Other family 3. Work/school 4. Organizations 5. Other friends 6. Neighbours 7. Professionals 8. Other	Concrete support 1. Hardly ever 2. Sometimes 3. Almost always	Emotional support 1. Hardly ever 2. Sometimes 3. Almost always	Information/ advice 1. Hardly ever 2. Sometimes 3. Almost always	Critical 1. Hardly ever 2. Sometimes 3. Almost always	Direction of help 1. Goes both ways 2. You to them 3. They to you	Closeness 1. Not very close 2. Sort of close 3. Very close	How often seen 0. Does not see 1. Few times/yr 2. Monthly 3. Weekly 4. Daily	How long known 1. Less than 1 yr 2. 1–5 yrs 3. More than 5 yrs
01									
02									
03									
04									
05									
06									
07									
08									
09									
10									
11									
12									
13									
14									
15									
1-6	7	8	9	10	11	12	13	14	15

they help you), those who you help more, and those who help you more. OK, let's get their code numbers on the grid.

Now think about how *close* you are to the people in your network. Divide the cards into three piles—those people you are not very close to, those you are sort of close to, and those you are very close to—and then we'll put a code number for them.

Finally, just a few questions about *how often* you see people and *how long* you've known the people in your network. Divide the cards into four piles—people you see just a few times a year, monthly, weekly, and daily (if you see someone twice or more than twice a week, count that as "daily"). OK, we'll put their numbers on the grid.

This is the last question. Divide the cards into three piles—those people you have known less than a year, from 1 to 5 years, and more than 5 years.

Now we have a pretty complete picture of who is in your social network.

ORGANIZATIONAL FACTORS IN SOCIAL WORK PRACTICE

Glenn Thompson

ORGANIZATIONAL FACTORS—WHAT ARE THEY?

The practice of social work, like any human activity, is certain to be affected and influenced by the organizational framework within which it occurs. Social workers should be conscious of their capacity, by virtue of their professional training, to understand their organization's environment and to influence change in that environment in ways that can facilitate service to their clients.

I began my social work practice in a maximum security correctional institution. The medium was intended to be the message, and usually was, for those confined there. Frequently, they were persons who had acted out in other less secure centres and were transferred in for that reason. The maximum security environment did not impede our capacity to practice psychiatry, psychology, nursing, social work, teaching, or trade training, but the requirements of all staff, especially correctional staff, to ensure secure management, meant that the environment was an important and often very useful springboard for the therapeutic process. After all, it would have made little sense to work with these individuals and not recognize their propensity to act out their anger and frustration and the ever-present physical consequence of that behaviour.

Most social work practice will not be conducted in such spartan surroundings and within an organizational environment that has such evident physical manifestations. Nevertheless, it is important to analyze the organizational environment at the start of any new practice initiative to ensure that its client and practice impacts are recognized and whenever possible made use of in, or altered for the benefit of, the client-worker relationship.

I had the good fortune over a sixteen-year period, as a Deputy Minister in the Ontario Public Service, to be the senior staff member responsible for six different ministries. And different they were! These organizations, while a part of the same government with the same administrative and political philosophy, had very different organizational factors exerting an impact upon their workers and their consumers. Some of these organizational factors can be listed as follows:

- the task to be accomplished
- the clarity of the organizational mandate
- the political policy agenda of the time, both in general and specific to that Ministry
- the interest of the political arm of government and the public in the Ministry's task
- the stage of the then current economic cycle
- the publicly perceived need for the products that are the organization's raison d'être
- the funding available to address the task
- the policy and planning processes—strategic and tactical—being utilized
- the number, experience, and training of staff to address the task
- my management style and that of my predecessor deputy minister
- the standards and ethics in practice
- the labour-management relationship
- the Ontario cultural scene at the time
- the expectation of evaluation of output
- the physical environment in which the task was carried out
- the area of Ontario in which the workplace was located.

One can define organizational factors more or less broadly. For purposes of this discussion, organizational factors will be considered in a broad context. For example, I see the dynamics of Canadian and Ontario social and cultural evolution as having a significant impact upon organizations, especially governmental ones. Undoubtedly, those factors were having an impact upon both the staff and the customers of the six ministries in which I worked. They helped to create the social and organizational milieu—the dynamic tensions in which our policies were developed. At times, Ontario's social and cultural changes were the rationale behind legislative and policy change that became a part of the job to be accomplished and, in some cases, changed the service to be delivered.

ORGANIZATIONAL FACTORS IN ACTION —IN A GOVERNMENT CONTEXT

In 1995–1997, Ontario witnessed some of the boldest and most rapid legislative and organizational change in the province's history. The public voted for a government that had set out its deficit reduction and smaller-government agenda very clearly before the June 1995 election. The ensuing change process affected every organization funded by government. It is one of the predominant organizational factors of this time period.

During the 20 years that I worked in the Correctional Services Ministry, our efforts were carried out in a social environment where the public had become ready for community corrections. There was an opportunity and a mandate to create a spectrum of services for offenders, from probation to rehabilitative incarceration, followed by temporary absence and parole. We seized the moment, and our organization and its services to offenders changed very rapidly and dramatically.

One of the most vivid examples of organizational factors impacting upon Correctional Services programs and behaviours occurred while I was Superintendent at a women's correctional centre. At the old Mercer Reformatory for Women, built in 1881, many women acted out in a self-destructive manner, carving their bodies or slashing themselves. This behaviour had long been commonplace in training schools for girls and carried over with some of those individuals who later came through the adult court to the Mercer Reformatory. They influenced others with this contagious behaviour.

In 1969, the Mercer Reformatory, a unitary-style building with residential corridors, a school, workshops, staff offices, etc., all in the same building, was closed and replaced with the newly constructed, cottage-style Vanier Centre for Women. The new setting was introduced with a modified therapeutic community environment, based upon 24-bed cottage units. The physical surroundings were attractive, well furnished, and anything but oppressive.

From the day we relocated the residents from the old institution to the new, the self-mutilating behaviour ended. It didn't taper off and end, it ended in one day—a dramatic display of the message sent by good accommodation as an organizational factor to women offenders whose self-esteem is typically very low. This also speaks of the benefits of the altered therapeutic program, which allowed a much closer, daily and personalized contact between all sectors of staff and residents who met daily in small cottage-based groups. Smaller groups, living in distinctly separate buildings, along with enhanced supportive staff-resident interaction, created very different organizational factors, which influenced changed behaviours. Over time, the self-mutilating behaviour did not return.

In the early 1980s, while I was in the Energy Ministry, oil and gas shortages were forecast and that expectation drove very rapid development of conservation and alternate energy programs. The public had begun to accept that an energy shortage was imminent, and for the Energy Ministry, that created an organizational factor that dramatically altered its focus and expenditures.

In the Government Services Ministry—responsible for the government's more than 6,000 buildings, its major computer installations, and the purchase of supplies—we developed our mission as the work environment ministry for government. It was our belief that we could be a major influence in creating a workplace that could make a major difference in the working environment of our 90,000 workers and their clients. We could have a major impact upon vital organizational factors.

In the Municipal Affairs Ministry, we saw an opportunity for municipal government to be much closer to the public and to be the hub of most direct service delivery. The changes underway as this book goes to press, which place responsibility for much more service delivery at the municipal level, will be one of the predominant organizational factors in the social services, and in some health services, for years to come.

In the Labour Ministry in the 1987–89 period, the Liberal-NDP Accord spawned a myriad of worker-focused initiatives. These changes in legislation were initiated to improve health and safety in the workplace and to strengthen the employment standards that govern the employer-worker relationship. It was a very interventionist period on the part of government legislators and of their staff as implementors. And now, in the 1995–2001 period, we have witnessed a dramatic shift toward deregulation by government and to self-regulation by employers. The intent is to lower government costs in carrying out these tasks and to make Ontario more attractive to industry and commerce through a lighter regulatory cost burden. Whatever one feels about either approach, these recent actions have created an organizational environment quite different for social workers functioning in Ontario workplaces and for the workers and their families who are their clients.

The new political, legislative, and fiscal environment has become a paramount organizational factor in many industries and in their associated communities.

In the Housing Ministry, from 1989 to 1991, we were involved in the largest social housing construction program in Canadian history. The task was clear, large, and well funded. There was a political belief on the part of the party in power that better housing for the public, who could not afford to improve their own housing situation, would enhance not only the social condition of those particular families but that of Ontario society in general. On the political level, housing was viewed to be a right.

Our staff were skilled and ready for the occasion, having developed many smaller-scale projects in the years preceding. The Ministry head office physical environment was quite positive, as was that of the many regional offices in Ontario. We had a high level of knowledge and lengthy experience in our management team. Evaluative mechanisms were in place. The organizational factors were right for the adventure.

Social workers employed at the delivery end of the affordable housing chain would have experienced these demanding, but thematically consistent, organizational factors. In fact, many were involved in the advocacy and consultative processes leading to the new developments and in client placement in the new settings when they were built.

Organizational factors cover a wide spectrum of processes, including political, cultural, administrative practice, managerial style, workplace environment, and management of change.

ORGANIZATIONAL FACTORS AND THE MANAGEMENT CYCLE

If we accept organizational factors in their broadest context, it is also useful to consider their interaction with the management cycle in the organization. Understanding the elements of the typical management cycle will help social workers to visualize environmental factors as they interact with that cycle. Indeed, it will be possible to influence the organizational factors within your organization more effectively if you focus on particular components of the management cycle.

The following 1981 Ontario government graphic (Figure 33.1) sets out the basic elements of a typical management cycle. Examination of it in relation to one's own place of employment will assist in determining best points to impact upon the organizational factors in your workplace.

ORGANIZATIONAL FACTORS—PRACTICE CONSIDERATIONS

Social workers should be attempting to have an impact upon the political and cultural influences facing their client group and, if they are successful, they may alter some of those organizational factors in ways that can improve the lot of their clients. Organizations are very prone to seizing upon new management philosophies. From time to time, any organization needs a breath of fresh air, a new way to look at itself. However, the rush from one guru to the next can be very disruptive given the turmoil that is created for workers and clients alike. It is better to have an ongoing and considered process in which all staff and consumers can participate to determine the best organization for the job at hand.

Social workers should see organizational factors as changeable and their training should enable them to be workplace leaders in the change process. Organizational factors are never static. Their impact, and their ability to be impacted upon by both worker and client, will depend to some degree on the level at which the social worker is functioning and the intensity of service in which the client is involved. Nevertheless, client groups and teams of workers at any level can have a powerful impact if appropriately led.

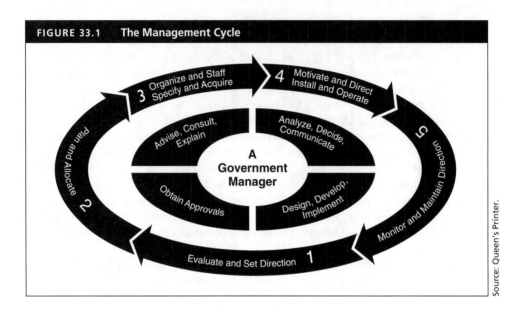

FIGURE 33.1   The Management Cycle

Source: Queen's Printer.

Social work practice should involve using organizational factors as a part of the therapeutic/training/learning process for and with clients. A graphic example of such an opportunity occurred at a therapeutic community psychiatric hospital in England where I was employed in 1964 as the senior social worker. There was no psychiatric medication and no individual therapy used in the hospital. All of the therapeutic process occurred in groups and the Patient Council were co-leaders with staff in that process. The patients were described as delinquent psychopaths. The therapy was the practice involved in helping to run this therapeutic community, in helping one's fellow patients to examine their successes and failures in functioning in this "society." A daily meeting of all staff and patients was used to focus upon group and individual behaviour.

This program used almost every available organizational factor as a component of the therapeutic process. The community was constantly trying both to assist its individual members and to transform itself. Social, work, and interpersonal behaviours formed the therapeutic stage. Contrast this milieu and its organizational factors with those in a typical hospital.

ORGANIZATIONAL FACTORS AND MENTAL HEALTH REFORM

The mental health field in Canada, like the criminal justice system, is full of examples of organizational factors that influence the delivery of services to consumers in very negative ways.

Since the writing of the Graham Report in 1988 in Ontario, the field has been attempting to overcome its lack of integration. The New Democratic Party, while in power in Ontario from 1991 to 1995, adopted Putting People First as its policy for mental health reform. That policy continues in effect with the current Progressive Conservative government. Over the intervening ten years there have been several very significant breakthroughs, in specific communities, where barriers have fallen and a comparatively seamless service has been developed and maintained. Unfortunately, these examples are notable for their scarcity. Organizational factors continue to impede development of the seamless system which consumers deserve and taxpayers expect. Dollars are not the main impediment for the current client group. The $1.3 billion spent annually on mental health services in Ontario could provide good care for the majority of those currently identified as having a serious mental illness, but not for the many others who avoid care because of the stigmatization of this illness or the inefficiencies of the system they confront.

Mental health is full of organizational boundaries. General practitioners providing primary care, psychiatrists, general hospital psychiatric units, specialty psychiatric hospitals, the ten provincial psychiatric hospitals with their multifaceted services, and the community-based nonprofit agencies do not link well together for the benefit of their clients.

The Health Services Restructuring Commission has responded to these deficiencies in two of its earliest completed reports. In Northeast Ontario, a Mental Health Agency will be created to lead the integrative process. At least in that area, there will be a governance body with a clear mandate to integrate the disparate parts and which will have the leverage to control most, if not all, of the funding envelope. Psychiatrists and primary care physicians providing mental health services appear likely to elude this round of reform inasmuch as they will remain outside the funding envelope.

Mental health service networks will be created across Ontario in appropriate geographic, population, and service agency clusters. In some measure these service networks may be modelled upon the Community Care Access Network approach already selected for the reform of long-term care.

Organizational factors such as centralized funding, policy leadership, administrative control, and responsibility for evaluation will do much to pull the mental health fragments together. Equally important will be the labour strategies adopted under the leadership of the new agencies. Personnel constitute the main asset and cost centre in mental health. Retraining all current staff for their new roles and responsibilities will be essential. Teamwork doesn't happen by chance. Leadership, below the regional agency level, in sub-networks, will be an essential organizational factor for success.

Involvement of consumers and their main support persons—in many cases their family members—in the mental health reform and operational process at every level has been recognized as an essential factor in recent years. It has been said that, unless consumers recognize a difference in their care, the reform process will have been in vain. Their involvement at the planning, design, delivery, and evaluative stages will be one of the most important organizational factors in ensuring success.

The establishment of case management services and the separation of the assessment/placement staff into a separate responsibility centre should lead to greater role clarity and provide different evaluative criteria for this staff group. Evaluation of their success should attempt to weigh their success in channelling consumers to the most appropriate, economic and, where appropriate, community-based care. Primary care physicians should be seen—and should see themselves—as a central component of this screening and first-stage care process.

Adequate preparation for work in an integrated mental health system will be essential for all caregivers so that their vision of their role and their practice values will have the consistency and high standards that can assure quality service.

THE LITERATURE—WHAT THE AUTHORS SAY

Now let us look at some of the literature that relates to organizational factors. In a study entitled "Client Careers and Structure of a Probation and After-Care Agency," the authors demonstrate that the "careers" of some offenders may be shaped by the organization of a probation intake system (Hardiker & Barker, 1985). Career, as a sociological concept, refers to the regular sequences associated with particular social statuses, i.e., marriage, courtship, engagement, child-rearing, etc. Role requirements are central to a career concept, though entering "career positions" may have consequences for the self-identity of the occupant (Goffman, 1961; Smith, 1979).

Client careers can refer to the sequence of statuses and relationships that people have with service agencies; many offenders have no contact with the probation service, but those who do have such contact enter a "career" which may terminate at the pre-applicant or applicant phase, or much later when their files are closed (Hardiker et al., 1985, 602).

In this project, the intake process was separated from the ongoing probation supervision functions. Probation staff were assigned to perform that role alone and not to function in other aspects of probation work. The evidence presented in this paper suggests that the establishment of a court Intake and Assessment Team influenced some dimensions of probation practice quite significantly, though not necessary always in ways intended (Goffman, 1961).

"But the process by which certain characteristics of probation agencies shape the 'client careers' of offenders will need to be delineated and the concept of organizational boundary is one means of examining these" (Hardiker et al., 1985, 602). "Systems theory is particularly useful in calling attention to the crucial interplay between an organization and its environment" (Miller and Rice, 1967; Pugh, 1971). "Agencies must draw resources from their environment in order to survive; these include finance, personnel and the clients who will be processed through the service provided by the agency" (Hardiker et al., 1985, 604).

Organizational factors appeared to underline these changes in probation practice. The officers became clearer about the purposes of social inquiries as they tried to maintain their credibility with colleagues; they had to negotiate a client status for offenders across organizational boundaries, and they experienced terrific pressures. Second, some aspects of service delivery changed with the introduction of the intake system. The officer gained increased control over the duty office and referrals from court, and social agencies were processed smoothly; the new system narrowed the boundaries of the helping relationship offered to offenders at the social inquiry stage and changed the processes by which they were inducted into the client role (Hardiker et al., 1985).

An article by Daly and Jennings et al., entitled "Effective Coping Strategies of African Americans," looks at organizational factors in the historical, cultural context. They state that, "the Africentric paradigm proposes that in African culture, humanity is viewed as a collective rather than as individual and that this collective view is expressed as shared concern and responsibility for the well-being of others" (Daly, Jennings, Beckett, & Leashore, 1995, 241).

These authors submit that the Africentric orientation to coping and resolving problems is different. These coping mechanisms are reviewed across system levels. At the organizational level, Schiele (1990) identified an Africentric model that diverged in three ways from mainstream organizational theory. He stated that mainstream theories (1) focus on productivity and efficiency, (2) use materialistic achievements as the major criterion for measuring success, and (3) view human beings individualistically with communal and family relations most likely perceived as potential interference in corporate matters. In contrast, Schiele (1990) stated that an organization shaped by the Africentric paradigm is characterized by how the group preserves itself, rather than its productivity. Goal attainment is defined in the context of survival. Therefore, resource procurement and use replace efficiency and productivity as standards. The communal view of human identity may lead to the sharing of similar tasks in the workplace rather than an extensive division of labour. Group consensus in decision-making is preferred over strict hierarchical structure. Finally, the organization is open to its environment because it is concerned with preservation. Boundaries between the organization and the community are less marked; the survival of the community and the organization are related.

Another study has suggested that African-American managers not only increase their support to staff in response to environmental turbulence but that they tend to increase their problem-solving communications to a greater extent. White managers, while supportive, did not change their communication patterns (Schiele, 1990).

In an article entitled "The Organizational Context of Empowerment Practice," ways are suggested in which social work administrative practices can create an organizational culture that can support empowerment practice. The analysis suggests several barriers (including funding, social environment, and interpersonal factors) and three supports (staff development, collaboration, and leadership) to empowerment practice. "Organizations that empower workers by creating an employment setting that provides participatory management will be better equipped to empower clients and communities" (Gutierrez, Glenmaye, & Delois, 1995, 251). These authors go on to state that political conditions that limit control over resources and policies severely limit the use of participatory management in public welfare settings.

In a study entitled "Interpretations of Stress in Institutions: The Cultural Production of Ambiguity and Burnout," Meyerson (1994) considers how organizational cultures reflect and reinforce institutional conditions that have been negotiated in the interaction of individuals.

In "Treatment Teams that Work—An Application of Hackman's Group Effectiveness Model to Interdisciplinary Teams in Psychiatric Hospitals," Diane Vinokur-Kaplan (1995) sets out the organizational and group factors that contribute to team effectiveness. The value of teamwork has long been an emphasis in medical institutional settings. "More recently, the value of such teams has been noted in such high-burnout fields as community mental health, because the teams provide greater continuity of treatment for long term patients and mitigate the impact of frequent staff turnover" (Vinokur-Kaplan, 1995, 305). The more recent models of team effectiveness have gone beyond earlier laboratory and T-group based models which focused more on the internal dynamics and development of groups (e.g., Tuchman and Jensen, 1977) to focus more on the organizational environment in which teams are established and must perform (e.g., Ancona and Caldwell, 1988; Wheelan, 1994; Vinokur-Kaplan, 1995, 306).

This ecological perspective looks more closely at a team's interface with such various organizational structures as the reward and boundary system (e.g. Sundstrom and Altman, 1989; Sundstrom et al., 1990; and Vinokur Kaplan, 1995; Vinokur-Kaplan, in press) and considers the role of the organization in supporting or undermining a team's effectiveness. The author cites Hackman (1990) as noting the importance of having teams set up right in the first place or having initial conditions of group structure that promote competent work on the task. These structural features include a task structure that is (a) clear and consistent with the group's purpose, (b) a group composition that provides an appropriate size and mix of talents and interpersonal skills needed for communication and coordination with one another; and (c) core norms that regulate member behaviour and promote ongoing performance evaluation (Vinokur-Kaplan, 1995, 306).

Vinokur-Kaplan quotes Hackman (1990) as follows: "those who create and lead work groups might most appropriately focus their efforts on the creation of conditions that support effective team performance as opposed to attempting to manage group behaviour in real time." "The positive contributions of both initial conditions and enabling conditions to team outcomes should encourage organizational consultants and educators to address a comprehensive range of organizational, professional, ecological, and inter-group factors to enhance team effectiveness" (Vinokur-Kaplan, 1995, 323).

This study uses standards met, cohesion of team, and individual well-being (contribution of the team to the members themselves) as the three specific outcomes to be examined. It sets out the factors that clinical treatment team members view as contributing to their overall team effectiveness in developing and implementing treatment plans. "The findings of this study underscore the importance of attending to ecological concerns and conditions (cf. Ancona, and Caldwell, 1988; Sundstrom and Altman, 1989) in addition to the traditional focus on the team's dynamics" (Vinokur-Kaplan, 1995, 324).

For the purposes of this chapter, it is important to note that it was the mutual influence of the treatment unit type and the hospital setting that reflected the greatest difference in success; they were the critical organizational factors.

The health care system in Ontario is in the early stages of the most profound set of changes in its history. A Health Care Restructuring Commission has been authorized to order measures to effect integration of hospital services and to reduce expenditures. In some cases, hospitals have already been moving to less bureaucratic and hierarchical structures. These organizational factors present tremendous opportunities and challenges for social workers. In an article entitled "Social Work and the New Integrated Hospital," Globerman and Bogo (1995) suggest that social work can be a champion in the new, integrative, less bureaucratic hospital. I would suggest that the same impact can be achieved by social work in community-located health care. The authors note that, "systems theory and the ecological perspective are the key theoretical approaches to social work in health care" (Germain, 1984; Bogo and Taylor, 1990; Bogo, 1991; Globerman and Bogo, 1995, 3). "In fully integrative organizations, discipline-specific departments are eliminated to allow a focus on collaboration, coordination, interconnection, shared resources and integration" (Charms and Tewksbury, 1993; Globerman and Bogo, 1995, 4).

The authors rely heavily and to advantage on Drucker (1991, 1992) who suggests "that the modern organization must recognize knowledge as its primary resource. [Drucker] emphasizes the need for decentralized, integrative organizations to function as teams to enhance opportunities for knowledge generation. They must be made up, Drucker says, of an organization of equals" (Globerman and Bogo, 1995, 6).

Thus, according to organizational theorists (Drucker, 1991, 1992; Peters, 1992), to maintain its power, its relevance and its currency, the new integrative hospital must recognize the value of knowledge generation. Drucker (1992) suggests that the modern organization, if it is to survive, "must be organized for continuous self-improvement, must exploit its knowledge-generating ideas, promote research and education, and must learn to value innovation and change" (Globerman and Bogo, 1995, 7). "Knowledge workers and service workers learn most when they teach" (Drucker, 1991, 78; Globerman and Bogo, 1995, 15). "The integrative hospital values patient-focused, accountable and responsible professionals. Collaboration, a flattened hierarchy, and a focus on innovation and the creation of new knowledge are the means to that end" (Globerman and Bogo, 1995, 18).

In an article entitled "Organizational Resource Mobilization: A Hidden Face of Social Work," a case is made that organizational factors influence the very content of social work practice. The author argues that what social workers do, in actual practice, "bears little resemblance to the main precepts of the social work literature or the content of much social work training" (Davies, 1993; Wilding, 1982; Specht, 1985; Parsloe, 1986; Bar-On, 1990, 133).

This study reports that organizational factors cause social workers to deal only for one-third of their time with clients in face-to-face contact. "Most social work activity is devoted to interacting with persons who are not one's clients, such as collaterals, managers and administrators in one's own or other agencies, or members of clients' informal networks" (Bar-On, 1990, 146).

While the findings are only exploratory, and should therefore be interpreted with caution, they suggest that the bulk of social workers' targets of intervention are not their clients but other service providers whose resources they mobilize to help their clients. In other words, it would appear that social work practice is less about "people changing" than it is about "people processing" or case management.

"Adopting an influence perspective does not deny social workers a clinical framework. Rather it should help them to develop and manage their non-clinical interactions, which currently pose considerable constraints on their need-meeting efforts" (Pearson, 1975; Mawby, 1979; Epstein, 1981). To do so, however, social work must first take up an appropriate language of discourse, such as that of power-dependence or transactional theories, which direct attention to the environmental means and resources social workers can exploit to better meet their clients' needs, identify and establish the necessary competencies to do so, and facilitate the acquisition of appropriate behaviours and skills (Bar-On, 1990, 148). This article questions what our organizations actually demand of social workers in terms of what services should be delivered. If this author's evaluation is correct, social work training should include elements from other disciplines such as business management and public administration.

SUMMARY

Both my experience and the growing literature relating to the impact of organizational factors on social work practice reinforce the need for every social worker to examine these factors in their practice. We should move boldly to influence them and to ensure a better service delivery system and environment for our clients. Whenever feasible, we should ensure that our clients themselves are presented with opportunities to influence the organization that serves them.

REFERENCES

Bar-On, A.A. (1990). Organizational resource mobilization: a hidden face of social work practice. *British Journal of Social Work, 20*(2), 133–149.

Daly, A., Jennings, J., Beckett, J.O., & Leashore, B.R. (1995). Effective Coping Strategies of African Americans. Rutgers U, School of Social Work, *40*(2), 240–248.

Globerman, J. & Bogo, M. (1995). Social work and the new integration hospital. *Social Work Health Care U.S. 21*(3), 1–21.

Goffman, E. (1961). *Asylums.* New York, Anchor Books: Doubleday.

Gutierrez, L., Glenmaye, L., & Delois, K. (1995). The organizational context of empowerment practice—implications for social work administration. *Social Work, 40*(2/3), 249–258.

Hardiker, P. & Barker, M. (1985). Client careers and the structure of a probation and after-care agency. *British Journal of Social Work, 15*(6), 599–618.

Meyerson, D.E. (1994). Interpretations of stress in institutions: the cultural production of ambiguity and burnout. *Administration Science Quarterly, 39*(4), 628–653.

Miller, E.J. & Rice, A.K. (1967). *Systems of organization: the control of task and content boundaries.* London: Tavistock.

Pugh, D.S. (Ed.) (1991). *Organizational theory.* Harmondsworth: Penguin Books.

Schiele, J.H . (1990). Organizational theory from an afrocentric perspective. *Journal of Black Studies,* (21), 145–161.

Smith, G. (1979). *Social work and the sociology of organizations* (rev. ed.). London: Routledge and Kegan Paul.

Vinokur-Kaplan, D. (1995). Treatment teams that work: an application of Hackman's group effectiveness model to interdisciplinary teams in psychiatric hospitals. *Journal of Behavioural Science. 31*(3), 303–327.

ETHICAL

ISSUES

Kathy Jones

INTRODUCTION

There is perhaps nothing that a social worker struggles with more than weighing ethical dilemmas. No matter what the practice setting, social workers face situations regularly that demand that they have a clear sense of their ethical obligations and responsibilities. But how does the competent social worker ensure that he or she not only is meeting the requirements set out in the Code of Ethics but also has knowledge of the multitude of factors that need to be considered in making decisions? How does the social worker navigate through all of the ethical obligations—to a social work code, to codes affecting specific areas of practice, to provincial regulations in provinces that have social work legislation, or to regulatory bodies some of which have their own ethical guidelines? In addition, how does the social worker answer to workplace obligations or to legislated responsibilities? An initial view of these complex issues creates uncertainty for the beginning social worker and often discomfort for the experienced practitioner. The purpose of this chapter is to provide a broad sense of the ethical umbrella under which social workers practice in Canada. The role of a code of ethics, with particular emphasis on the Canadian Association of Social Workers (CASW) Social Work Code of Ethics (1994), will be discussed. Mention will be made of the diversity of codes in the Canadian context. Direct advice is then offered in areas such as how the Code and regulations interact with such issues as legislated responsibilities, followed by a proposed framework for ethical decision-making. Illustrations are used to help the reader's understanding and appreciation of the processes that they need to employ in weighing ethical dilemmas. These examples include some increasingly complex ethical issues that are realities of Canadian practice. The importance of consultation is addressed, along with the resources that are available to Canadian social workers. Ethical discomfort, which is experienced by all practitioners, receives attention. Finally, the concept of the tripartite ethical responsibility of the practitioner to the client, to the profession, and to society will be explored.

THE ROLE OF A PROFESSIONAL CODE

It is suggested that professional ethics serve normative, aspirational, and prescriptive functions (Levy, 1992). Ethics are normative insofar as they identify what the expected standard should be. Ethics are aspirational insofar as they identify the principles which social workers should attempt to reach, and prescriptive in that they identify absolute behaviours to which professionals are to be held accountable. It is recognized by many disciplines that ethical codes serve the following key purposes:

1. To provide a statement of moral principle that helps the individual professional to resolve ethical dilemmas;

2. To help establish a group as a profession;

3. To act as a support and guide to individual professionals; and

4. To help meet the responsibilities of being a profession (Sinclair, Poizner, Gilmour-Barrett, & Randall,1991).

The first purpose, a provision of a statement of moral principle, assists the professional in attempting to balance conflicting principles. For example, the 1994 CASW Code gives a bottom-line statement in its definition of the "best interest of client" (CASW, 1994). The essence of this statement is that all actions will be taken with the belief that the client will benefit and that the client is respected.

This definition was included in the 1994 Code to provide a benchmark of moral principle. All other sections of the Code flow from this statement. This allows social workers who find themselves in an ethical dilemma to refer to this principle in determining their action.

In helping to establish the group as a profession, codes provide a philosophical framework and identify what makes the profession unique. For example, social work codes describe the profession as having a holistic view of clients and describe the broader commitment of the profession as an egalitarian ideal. The CASW Social Work Code of Ethics has in its preamble a definition of the profession:

> The profession of social work is founded on humanitarian and egalitarian ideals. Social workers believe in the intrinsic worth and dignity of every human being and are committed to the values of acceptance, self-determination, and respect of individuality. They believe in the obligation of all people, individually and collectively, to provide resources, services, and opportunities for the overall benefit of humanity... (CASW, 1994).

As a support and guide for the individual professional, codes set out obligations and responsibilities to which the professional will be held accountable. In doing this, codes advise the professional as to what specific conduct is expected. The professional can then use the document as a guide when faced with ethical dilemmas. It is important to point out, however, that there are limitations on how a code can answer specific questions. Often codes contain principles or ethical standards that in isolation would not raise questions. At times when standards are considered together—which in essence is what a dilemma amounts to—obligations to both cannot be upheld (Reamer, 1982). The importance of using professional judgment and consultation cannot be overemphasized at such times.

Clients, workplaces, and society need to know what can reasonably be expected of a professional or a professional body. Many professions now have the ability to self-regulate either through mandatory registration dictated by legislation or through voluntary membership. Professional associations and colleges of practice that govern social work practice establish codes to serve not only as guides for the practitioner, but also to serve as benchmarks for the evaluation of ethical practice, particularly in conduct complaints (Levy, 1992). Codes not only assist a profession as it monitors itself but also as it addresses client rights. Specifically, social work codes set forth what clients reasonably can or should expect from a social worker. For example, what is the limit of confidentiality? What are the expectations of a "competent" social worker?

It is critical that codes are subject to review and change. With rapid changes in issues such as information technology, it is imperative that codes keep pace. Processes that continuously document and reflect such changes are a necessary function of ethics committees of both professional associations and colleges of practice. Continuous knowledge of these issues can then be used for revisions to ethical codes. Codes thus must become "living documents" that are revised formally at regular intervals.

THE CANADIAN CONTEXT

Across Canada, various regulatory bodies serve to hold professional social workers in their respective jurisdictions to ethical standards and principles. The leadership document for social work practice in Canada is the Canadian Association of Social Workers (CASW) Social Work Code of Ethics (1994). This code was completed following an extensive debate across the country. While the majority of Canadian provinces adopted the 1994 CASW Code, a few did not. Quebec, for example, continued to use its own well-established Code of Ethics. Some provinces, such as Alberta, began the process of developing ethical standards. Therefore, in determining the exact ethical standards and principles that the social worker must follow, the first reference point should be jurisdiction. Second, social workers will need to examine other existing documents, such as standards that may accompany legislation. One province that incorporates the CASW Code directly into its regulations is Prince Edward Island.

Besides codes that specifically govern social work practice, areas under which social workers practice may also have their own codes. Such areas include mediation (Code of Conduct Family Mediation Canada), and the code governing marital and family therapists. Workplaces often have codes of conduct for employees.

Despite the diversity of codes that exist across Canada, it is largely the precise details that are diverse, not the general content. Consequently, I will use the CASW Code (1994), the most comprehensively used document in Canada, as reference.

THE CASW CODE

The CASW Social Work Code of Ethics (1994) provides the three functions identified previously—norms, aspirations, and prescriptions. There are two distinct areas—ethical duties and ethical responsibilities. The first of these, ethical duties, are more prescriptive in nature, while the latter are more aspirational and normative. Ethical duties are owed to a client while ethical responsibilities are owed to persons other than a client. A breach of an ethical duty would be subject to disciplinary action whereas a breach of a responsibility alone would not. A breach of an ethical duty would occur either through an omission or by commission. A breach of a responsibility occurs through a lack of appropriate action.

The 1994 Code's ethical duties include: primary professional obligation to the client, integrity and objectivity, competence, limit on professional relationship, confidential information, and outside interests (CASW, 1994). It is important to recognize the significance of the use of the word "shall" in these sections as well as in other parts of the Code. "Shall" implies an absolute duty whereas words such as "will" or "may" are more futuristic and less absolute. Ethical responsibilities are to those in the workplace, to the profession, and to social change.

As stated earlier, there are many codes in Canada, including those specific to areas of practice and individual workplaces and organizations. It can be confusing if the social worker is not clear as to their first point of reference when faced with differing responsibilities. The CASW Code states that whenever a conflict arises in the obligations that a social worker (bound by the Code) is faced with, the Code takes precedence (CASW, 1994).

This does not mean that other codes, for example workplace codes and employer requirements, cannot set standards that are higher than what is articulated in social work codes. The social worker would still be expected to follow those expectations. It is also important to point out that the standards in any code state the minimum expectations. Social workers can by personal choice raise their standards higher.

It is important to recognize that a code is a collection of ethical standards and principles that assist in guiding the practitioner in ethical dilemmas. The exact use of the standards—the selecting and ordering of which standards apply in a specific ethical dilemma—involves a process that the social worker must undertake. This will be discussed later in this chapter.

THE INTERRELATIONSHIP OF THE CODE WITH LAW

Having said that a code of ethics is the first reference point for the social worker, what about situations where it appears that the principles in the code conflict with the law, particularly with legislated practice responsibilities? How does the social worker maintain ethical principles in such situations? What about situations where someone—either the client or a third party—is clearly at risk? Does the social worker uphold the principle and obligation of confidentiality or does the social worker breach confidentiality to protect a third party? If the social worker breaches an ethical obligation, how does he or she justify such action?

Codes of ethics do attempt to integrate legal considerations in situations involving risk to others. It is important that the social worker be clear as to how law and ethical codes interrelate. It is also important that the social worker understand how to balance conflicting ethical standards and legal considerations and how at times the law may override.

The CASW Code attempts to provide a level of balance between legal considerations and ethical standards and principles. For example, a number of sections speak to risk situations where confidentiality may not be absolute. Chapter 5, sections 5.25 and 5.26, describe situations of potential harm to self or others as circumstances where confidentiality would need to be breached.

These sections state:

A social worker shall disclose information acquired from one client to a member of the client's family where the information involves a threat of harm to self or others...(CASW, 1994).

In addition, section 5.26 states:

> A social worker shall disclose information acquired from a client to a person or a police officer where the information involves a threat of harm to that person (CASW, 1994).

The Code also attempts to clearly distinguish practice situations where primary obligations can be confusing. Because primary obligations flow from the client, the 1994 Code attempted to differentiate the multitude of different scenarios. For example, the definition of *client* includes those who are clients as the result of legislated responsibilities. Such clients would include non-contractual clients, defined as:

> A person, family, group of persons...on whose behalf a social worker provides or agrees to provide a service...as a result of a legislated responsibility (CASW, 1994).

This clearly indicates that not all clients may agree with the provision of social work services, but still binds the social worker to uphold ethical obligations to this client group. Another definition of *client* attempts to clarify those situations where the social worker is completing a court ordered assessment, such as in custody disputes. This definition refers to the judge as the client in those situations. That means that the primary obligations are directed to that entity. It is important to be clear that in any situation, while the primary duties may be directed to a specific entity, the social worker still has ethical obligations to whomever is being served. For example, integrity and competence obligations do not disappear.

Other areas that consider legal issues include the best interests statement, the client definition, and other sections of the confidentiality chapter. With this in mind, we will now turn to how the interrelationship of ethical codes and law is illustrated in practice.

There are situations where the social worker has to be clear that the first obligation is to a relevant piece of legislation. While the competent social worker will attempt to balance all of the obligations, the bottom line in some situations may not allow the clear upholding of all ethical principles. By far the clearest situation where the law would override any code would be where legislated responsibilities exist. Perhaps the most prevalent of these situations is in child protection. Recent inquiries occurring after tragic events have clearly shown that the social worker's primary consideration in these cases is the well-being of children (Gove, 1995). For several years, the philosophical thrust in child protection was one of family support. Legal considerations are now pushing more social workers in the direction of balancing family preservation with the need to protect. What does this all mean for social workers in terms of their ethical responsibilities?

First, the act of balancing the principles in social work codes with areas of practice such as child protection must ensure that the legislation is followed. The legislation under which a social worker functions takes precedence over any code or other regulatory document. This does not mean, however, that social workers can or should "throw their codes out the window" when practising in such situations. Social work ethical principles are critical in the practice of child protection. Areas such as worker-client relationships must follow ethical guidelines. An area that some social workers struggle with is confidentiality and how this at times creates confusion when considered in light of legislated responsibilities. For example, how much information can be revealed to a collateral contact when completing a child protection investigation? It is suggested that while there may not be a precise script for each scenario, the first reference point is the child protection legislation. This is complementary to the 1994 Code that supports confidentiality unless information is released under the authority of a statute:

A social worker shall protect the confidentiality of all information acquired from the client or others regarding the client and the client's family during the professional relationship unless...the information is released under the authority of a statute or an order of a court of relevant jurisdiction (CASW, 1994).

This would also include those social workers required by provincial statute to report cases of suspected child abuse.

Another area of law which social workers must pay attention to is the Criminal Code of Canada. While most practice would not necessitate that the social worker refer to the Criminal Code, one area that has in recent years raised questions is that of assisted suicide. Some social workers have expressed confusion about what the possession of knowledge of a possible assisted suicide of a terminally ill patient may mean for them criminally. As of writing this chapter, it is not an offence under the Criminal Code to possess such knowledge. It is a criminal offence to partake in the assistance of a suicide. The CASW statement on euthanasia and assisted suicide would be of interest to those facing such situations. An area of practice where this issue has received considerable focus is HIV and AIDS.

A further area of consideration is case law pertinent to professional groups. While it is not realistic for all social workers to have direct knowledge in this area, it is important to keep abreast of areas that could potentially have impact. This should be within the knowledge base of any legal counsel that the social worker may need to consult. One such area that has received considerable attention both in U.S. and Canadian case law is the concept of "duty to warn." This concept applies to professionals who have knowledge that another individual may be at imminent risk. This idea arose from a California case, Tarasoff v. Board of Regents of the University of California, in which a psychologist had a client state to him that it was his intent to harm another individual. The concept was considered and is quoted in the 1994 Code. The implications of this concept have relevance to those social workers who may have a client make such a statement to them. For example, a social worker working in a mental health clinic could have such statements made to him or her in a therapy session. The social worker would be obligated to find out if there is a threat, whether the danger to the intended victim is severe, real, and imminent, and whether the victim is identifiable (Kagle & Kopels, 1994). The key in this is "assessment of imminent harm." This necessitates that the social worker check out even veiled threats (Kagle & Kopels, 1994). If it is assessed that the potential victim could come to harm, then the overriding principle is not confidentiality but the duty of the social worker to warn. This can be done by either contacting the victim directly or by contacting the police. The social worker should seek consultation before carrying out such an action and should document all actions with a clear rationale. A section of the 1994 Code (5.25) speaks to the necessity of the social worker overriding considerations of confidentiality in such situations. Critical in this is the importance of advising the client at the outset that confidentiality in the social worker–client relationship is not absolute. The Code sets out in Chapter 5, section 5.5 that:

The social worker has the obligation to ensure that the client understands what is being asked, why and to what purpose the information will be used, and to understand the confidentiality policies and practices of the workplace" (CASW, 1994).

Recent writings have discussed the relevance of "duty to warn" in the area of HIV/AIDS (Taylor, Brownlee, & Mauro-Hopkins, 1996). Also, the area of impaired driving by clients leaving a professional's office has received attention (Slovenko, 1992).

More and more case law is dictating that professionals cannot "hide behind" their codes, particularly in situations of imminent risk. The ethical social worker in these situations will balance the risk to the other individual against the feasibility of advising the client that confidentiality will be breached. In all cases, where feasible, the social worker should seek consultation. It is important to remember that the "duty to warn" concept does not absolve social workers of their ethical obligation to their client but instead permits breaches of confidentiality where assessed to be necessary (Kagle & Kopels, 1994).

In all situations, written law takes precedence over a professional code of ethics. However, the social worker is obligated to balance the need to uphold the law with the principles dictated in the code of ethics. In addition, drafting of new codes, standards of practice, or regulatory documents must take current legal issues into account.

THE PROCESS OF ETHICAL DECISION-MAKING

Thus far, this chapter has focused on codes of ethics and the intersection of the code with the law. Attention will now be paid to the process involved in weighing ethical dilemmas.

How often do professionals aspire to find the one right answer to a complex situation? While experience teaches that only "best" answers exist in practice, even the seasoned social worker has been known to agonize over that one answer. It is important to remember that inherent in any social work practice, there are frequently conflicts. Reasonable differences of opinion do exist (Reamer, 1982). Such different opinions usually focus on how differing variables are weighed rather than on the exact decision made. The process that a social worker employs to weigh ethical dilemmas is what is critical, not the rank ordering of the principles or even the outcome. In any given situation, the social worker must keep in mind two things: what a reasonable social worker would do in this situation, and the importance of weighing actions before they are made. Canadian inquiries into social work practice focus not on the eventual outcome of the actions of social workers but on the process that was employed for making the decision (Koster and Hillier, 1996).

So how then do difficult ethical decisions get made, particularly when the nature of practice often demands expedient action? A variety of literature exists concerning models of ethical decision-making, both specific to social work and to other professions. Most contain similar elements, including:

1. Identification of the ethical dilemma;
2. Identification of conflicting ethical principles and standards;
3. Development of different courses of action, including possible risks or consequences;
4. What other issues may impact upon the decision (for example, legal considerations);
5. Choice of action;
6. Evaluation of action.

In all models, careful documentation not only of the eventual decision but also of the process utilized in reaching the decision is critical. As well, consultation and documentation is important. It is crucial to remember that what the social worker will be evaluated against is not so much the outcome of a decision but the process that the social worker used in reaching the decision and whether that process falls within acceptable practice. Being able to explain the way that the decision was reached, including the principles that were considered, is key. It is the professional judgment of the social worker in weighing these principles that will ultimately result in effective decision-making.

Illustration 1

You are a social worker in a family service agency. You are currently seeing Mr. Davis for individual counselling to deal with his depression associated with his recent marital separation. You have fulfilled your ethical obligation at the start of the counselling by advising Mr. Davis of the boundaries of confidentiality. During the second session, Mr. Davis advises you that he believes that his wife has been having an affair, that he knows who this individual is, and that he is planning to kill this person. What do you do ?

What is the dilemma?   The client is advising the social worker of a plan to harm another individual. The social worker has confidentiality obligations to the client. The worker also has a duty to warn the intended victim. Does the worker breach confidentiality or respect the confidentiality rights of the client? If the worker breaches confidentiality, how does he maintain the therapeutic relationship with the client?

What are the ethical principles?   The conflicting principles in this case are the client's rights of confidentiality within the social work relationship and the duty-to-warn responsibilities of the social worker. In addition, while not an ethical obligation, the social worker will be concerned about the continuation of the therapeutic relationship with the client.

Possible courses of action   The social worker could maintain confidentiality and attempt to work with the client to reduce the hostility toward the third party. If the social worker is unsuccessful and the third party is harmed, there would be ramifications for the social worker. The social worker could decide that the party needs to be warned and proceed with that action immediately. Alternatively, the social worker could further assess the client's "plan" or intent. Should the social worker determine that there is imminent risk to the third party, the social worker could proceed to warn the identified victim and, depending upon the presentation of the client, advise the client in advance of this action.

Other issues which impact the decision   Clearly, if the social worker has assessed that the third party is at imminent risk, then the "duty-to-warn" obligation discussed earlier in this chapter is paramount. The social worker should assess the duty-to-warn obligation by weighing the factors identified earlier in this chapter—is the victim identifiable? Is the threat real, severe, and imminent?

Choice of action   Clearly, the social worker, having assessed the potential risk as high, has a duty to warn. Breaching of confidentiality in such situations is covered in section 5.25 of the CASW Social Work Code of Ethics. The social worker should attempt to consult with a supervisor or agency administrator prior to taking such action. This should be documented. The client should be advised of the necessity, unless it is believed that such advance warning may increase the risk to the third party.

Evaluation   In this situation, the third party was not harmed. The social worker did seek consultation, which confirmed that the duty-to-warn obligation was the paramount consideration. Documentation of this action was made. The client decided to terminate the relationship with the social worker.

Illustration 2

You are a social worker in a small multi-practice agency in a rural area. A co-worker has become ill and will be off work for the foreseeable future. Your employer directs you to take over the caseload. The majority of this caseload is marital therapy. Your practice has not been in this area and, in fact, your last marital case was during a field placement twelve years ago. Your employer insists that you take this caseload.

What is the dilemma?   You have been directed by your employer to work in an area of practice in which you do not have competence. The practice setting is a rural community, and therefore other options for these clients may be limited. The social worker has certain obligations to the employer, however, and should not become involved in cases if the ability to offer a competent service is questionable.

What are the principles?   The Code of Ethics speaks to competence in Chapter 3: "The social worker shall have and maintain competence in the provision of a social work service to a client." The other principles involved here are the ethical responsibilities a social worker has to the workplace, as set forth in Chapter 8 of the code: "A social worker shall advocate for workplace conditions that are consistent with the code." The struggle for the social worker in this situation will be how to maintain a positive relationship with the employer (not to mention employment) but first and foremost to maintain ethical principles.

Possible courses of action   The social worker can refuse to provide service. If this decision is made, the client should be referred elsewhere. Often in rural communities "elsewhere" does not exist. The social worker could attempt to gain competence in this area by obtaining training. If the client would suffer harm in the interim, the social worker should not make such an attempt. The social worker could enter into the area if training is available and if consultation with a colleague competent in this practice area is available.

Other issues impacting the decision   Clearly here there are no overriding issues such as legal ones.

Choice of action   Sections 3.1., 3.2, and 3.3 of the Code may provide further assistance to the social worker in this situation. Section 3.1 states: "The social worker shall not undertake a social work service unless the social worker has the competence to provide the service or the social worker can reasonably acquire the necessary competence without undue delay, risk or expense to the client." Section 3.2 allows for referral if the social worker cannot reasonably acquire the competence while 3.3 allows the social worker to obtain advice with the agreement of the client. This provides the social worker with a few options. First and foremost, the social worker should continue the discussion of this issue with the employer. The social worker should indicate that it is necessary to advise the clients of the social worker's lack of competence in this area. If available, assistance can be obtained through consultation with another social worker who has competence in this area. All of this must be done with the full knowledge and agreement of the clients.

Evaluation   In this situation, the social worker with the full agreement of clients was able to continue service. Consultation was obtained from a colleague with competence in this area. The clients were able to remain with the agency and the worker was able to fulfill the employer's expectations.

Illustration 3

You are a social worker in a community health centre. The centre has a code of conduct for its employees. One section of this code speaks to limits on employee relationships with clients. Specifically, you are prohibited from having any personal relationships with clients. This includes former clients. A client whom you had seen for marital counselling five years ago invites you to lunch. The client advises you that its been a long time since you have seen each other and that you have been missed. What do you do?

What is the dilemma?   The question here is can the worker have a personal relationship with the client after five years? Does the invitation to lunch constitute a "personal relationship"? Does the comment about the client "missing" the social worker demonstrate a boundary issue?

What are the principles?   The social worker can refer to the CASW Code which states: "a client ceases to be a client 2 years after the termination of a social work service" (CASW: 1994). The social worker here is also bound by the workplace code.

Possible courses of action   The choice here is whether or not the social worker accepts or rejects the client's invitation. The social worker also needs to be clear that accepting the invitation without clarifying the comment about the client missing the worker is not appropriate.

Other issues   Clearly the workplace code impacts the decision.

Choice of action   The social worker in this situation may be confused as to which obligation takes precedence, the workplace code or the social work code. As cited earlier, codes set minimum expectations. This does not mean that there will not be other higher expectations on the social worker either by way of other codes or personal choice. The social worker here is also bound by a workplace code that sets its standard higher. This does not conflict with the CASW Code, but sets a higher standard. The worker needs to be clear in setting boundaries with present and former clients. In this situation, the worker politely explained the workplace requirements. The worker also explored with the client what the client's comment meant. It was ascertained that the client had few personal supports and that the worker was able to facilitate a referral to a local mutual aid group.

Evaluation   The social worker here has fulfilled the standard stated in the social work code as well as a higher workplace standard without compromising either. In addition, as a practice issue the worker explored the comments made by the client and was able to help the client to find more appropriate supports.

ETHICAL DISCOMFORT

Problem-solving ethical dilemmas brings with it discomfort. Part of resolving this discomfort is learning to tolerate the ambiguity that exists in these situations (Kitchener, 1986). The new social work practitioner (and often the veteran) experiences anxiety when faced with this ambiguity. Searching for the right answer increases this anxiety. Part of learning to resolve ethical dilemmas is dealing with one's own emotions. Experience helps in this regard. However, reassurance also comes from the process of weighing ethical principles. Using decision-making processes, such as the model described earlier, is vital. While the outcome of actions taken by social workers is important, evaluation will focus more on the process of decision-making used before the action was taken. Social workers are often faced with "fallible decision making about futuristic human behaviour" (Thompson, 1996). Such predictions are complex and often expediency is necessary in such decision-making. The social worker who takes the time to consider the significant principles, weigh the possible courses of action, and think through possible outcomes will be comforted in part by being able to explain what he or she did. Detailing actions in documentation can also relieve the stress in complex choices. A professional support system will also assist the social worker in the decision-making process. Find someone with whom you feel comfortable to discuss such dilemmas, whether it be your supervisor, a colleague, or a mentor. Such discussion not only assists in releasing some of this discomfort but also fulfills the important role of consultation.

THE ROLE OF CONSULTATION

While consultation has been mentioned in this chapter, it is important to point out the resources that the competent social worker will use when faced with ethical questions. As helping professionals, whether they are new graduates or seasoned veterans, social workers need consultation and should never fail to seek it out when faced with difficult decisions. Colleagues are often a first source of consultation, particularly for the new practitioner. Supervisors or social work administrators can play a vital role, especially when decisions are of a nature that client rights may need to be overridden—for example, in duty-to-warn situations. Many agencies have legal consultation available for questions involving legal considerations. A source of quality consultation can be the provincial or local social work association or regulatory body. While all of these bodies can serve an important resource function for the social worker, many have actual practice resources in the form of standards committees. Regulatory bodies also possess knowledge of how similar issues may have been evaluated by disciplinary committees. Often these organizations are aware of how similar issues have been handled by other professional groups. The use of any consultation should be carefully documented. This serves to justify the action taken if the action is evaluated after the fact.

MULTIPLE RESPONSIBILITIES

Thus far, discussion has been centred on the ethical obligations of the social worker. It hasn't included discussion of the broader responsibilities of which the social worker must be mindful. There has perhaps never been a time in Canadian social work practice when the ethical responsibilities of social workers have been put to as great a test. As our Canadian welfare state slowly erodes in the face of government deficit-cutting, social workers are faced with demands as never before. As cited earlier, the Code of Ethics clearly lays out the ethical philosophy of the social work profession as: *"... being committed to the obligation of all people to ... provide resources ... for the overall benefit of humanity"* (CASW, 1994).

This clearly calls upon social workers to act in a manner that is consistent with this philosophy. Advocacy is a critical component of the social worker's obligations. Chapter 10 of the Code speaks to the social worker's responsibility to advocate for equal access to resources, services, and opportunities, and for the equal distribution of resources. In stating this, social workers must demonstrate that they uphold such values. This can include activities such as seeking opportunities to educate those with influence about these principles and actively demonstrating them. Social workers must also advocate for social justice.

In addition to ethical responsibilities to society, social workers have ethical responsibilities to their profession. Chapter 9 of the Code of Ethics speaks clearly to this responsibility. Issues such as the reporting of any breach of the Code by another social worker, the promotion of excellence in the social work profession, and the actions of a social worker in relation to others are covered. This concept rests on the belief that social workers must strive to uphold the reputation of their profession. While not directly mentioned in the Code, this conceivably includes participating in activities that strengthen the profession, such as working with professional associations or regulatory bodies.

There are times when the obligations one has to a client, to one's profession, and to society may come into conflict. While the Code clearly outlines the difference between obligations and responsibilities, and while most duties are owed to a client, it is still critical, as with any dilemma, that the social worker carefully weigh these competing issues. Social workers must remember the fundamental goal of their profession—to work toward a society that is more tolerant, more compassionate, and more socially just. To overlook this responsibility is to negate that which makes the profession unique.

A BRIEF NOTE ON INFORMATION TECHNOLOGY

As illustrated in the earlier-mentioned illustration, the area of information technology and the ethical ramifications for the social work profession are extremely complicated. By the time of the drafting of the 1994 CASW Code, this issue had become so complex that very broad obligations were written into the Code. The reasoning behind this was that more limiting obligations would put social workers into precarious situations. Unfortunately, professional codes have not kept pace with the rapid growth in information technology. Social workers need to exercise caution in this area. In all situations, the broad guidelines in the Code must be followed. In addition, the social worker should keep in mind the philosophy of the profession, which respects the client's right to confidentiality. These rights begin and end with the client, and agencies should not put in place any practices that negate this principle. If the social worker is placed in such a position, the local chapter of the professional association should be able to help.

SUMMARY

This chapter has focused on the broad umbrella of ethical principles under which Canadian social workers must practice. The complexity of weighing ethical dilemmas has also been discussed. In the end, Canadian social workers must continuously seek to expand their competency in making ethical choices and decisions. The significance of being able to explain what you have done is becoming increasingly important as the complexities of practice increase. While the social worker will always experience a degree of discomfort in weighing ethical dilemmas, as experience is gained and confidence grows, ethical dilemmas should be welcomed as challenges for learning.

REFERENCES

Abramson, M. (1996). Reflections on knowing oneself ethically: toward a working framework for social work practice. *Families in Society: The Journal of Contemporary Human Services, 61*, 195–202.

Canadian Association of Social Workers. (1994 Revised). *Social work code of ethics*. Canadian Association of Social Workers.

Canadian Association of Social Workers. (1994). *CASW code of ethics 1994 Implementation Document*. Unpublished.

Gove, T.J. (1995). *Report of the Gove inquiry into child protection*. Victoria: British Columbia Ministry of Social Services.

Gross, D.R. & Robinson S.E. (1987). Ethics, violence, and counselling: hear no evil, see no evil, speak no evil? *Journal of Counseling and Development, 65*, 340–344.

Kagle, J. & Kopels, S. (1994). Confidentiality after Tarasoff. *Health and Social Work, 19*, 217–222.

Kitchener, K.S. (1986). Teaching applied ethics in counsellor education: an integration of psychological processes and philosophical analysis. *Journal of Counseling and Development, 64*, 306–310.

Koster, A. & Hillier B. (1996). A report prepared for the Honourable Russell H.T. King, M.D., Minister, Department of Health and Community Services, New Brunswick (The Turner Report), unpublished.

Levy, C. (1992). *Social work ethics on the line*. New York: Haworth Press.

Mappes, D.C., Robb, G.P., and Engels, D.W. (1985). Conflicts between ethics and law in counseling and psychotherapy. *Journal of Counseling and Development, 64, 246–252*.

Meara, N., Schmidt, L., & Day, J. (1996). Principles and virtues: a foundation for ethical decisions, policies, and character. *The Counselling Psychologist, 24*, 4–77.

Nicolai, K.M. & Scott N.A. (1994). Provision of confidentiality information and its relation to child abuse reporting. *Professional Psychology: Research and Practice, 25*, 154–160.

Reamer, F.G. (1982). Conflicts of professional duty in social work. *Social Casework, 56*, 579–585.

Reamer, F.G. (1990). *Ethical dilemmas in social service*. New York: Columbia University Press.

Rhodes, M. (1992). Social work challenges: the boundaries of ethics. *Families in Society, 73*, 40–47.

Sinclair, C., Poizner, S., Gilmour-Barrett K., and Randall, D. (1992). The development of a code of ethics for Canadian psychologists. *Companion manual to the Canadian code of ethics for psychologists, 1991*. Canadian Psychological Association, 1–11.

Slovenko, R. (1992). Confidentiality versus the duty to protect: foreseeable harm in the practice of psychiatry. Book review. *American Journal of Psychiatry, 7149:9*, 1270–1271.

Taylor, S., Brownlee, K., and Mauro-Hopkins, K. (1996). Confidentiality versus the duty to protect: an ethical dilemma with HIV/AIDS clients. *The Social Worker, 64*(4), 9–17.

Thompson, G. (1996). Presentation at Canada's children conference. Ottawa: Child Welfare League of Canada.

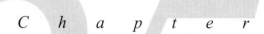

C   h   a   p   t   e   r

POVERTY

ISSUES

Peter Dunn

INTRODUCTION

Canada began the United Nations-declared Decade for the Eradication of Poverty (1997–2006) with roughly one in five of its citizens living in poverty (Cohen & Petten, 1997). The majority are women, children, and minorities. This chapter will provide information about those who are at highest risk of being poor in Canada, the impact of the concentration of power and wealth, the role of globalization, theories about the causes of poverty, and examples of innovative social intervention strategies.

It is first necessary to consider how poverty is defined and measured, for this can have a considerable effect on calculations about the extent of poverty, its characteristics, and trends. Recent attempts to develop new ways of calculating the federal government's poverty lines may significantly reduce the official number of individuals living in poverty in Canada. Rose, Scott, and Smith (2000) describe two basic methods of measuring poverty. The first is an absolute measure of poverty determined by a basket of goods and services necessary for physical and medical survival. The Montreal Diet Dispensary (MDD) and the Fraser Institute, for example, have developed absolute measures of poverty for basic physical functioning. The Metropolitan Toronto Social Planning Council (MTSPC) has gone beyond basic physical survival, determining a shopping basket of 13 categories of goods that will allow individuals to function at a minimum social standard in Toronto. The cost of these goods and services provides a dollar measurement of poverty.

While the absolute definition emphasizes that everyone should have some minimum income for the basics of life, a second method measures poverty as relative to the circumstances of the whole population (Ross et al., 2000). The Canadian Council on Social Development (CCSD) has established a relative measure of poverty in which one half of the average Canadian income is set as the poverty line for a family of three. This poverty line is adjusted for other household sizes.

Statistics Canada's measure of poverty is perhaps the most widely used. It provides a series of low-income cut-offs below which people live in "straightened circumstances" (Ross et al., 2000). In 1959, Statistics Canada determined that the average Canadian family spent about one-half of its income on food, clothing, and shelter. If a family spent significantly more (20% more) on basic essentials, they were considered to be living in "straightened circumstances." The cut-off point of 70% changed with new surveys of expenditures. The present cut-off is 54.7%. Statistics Canada adjusts its low-income cut-offs according to the size of family and community and whether the community is urban or rural. Ross et al. (2000) point out that people at Statistics Canada's level of poverty were left with only $2.22 per day in the late 1990s for all their daily expenses, including personal care, transportation, and household goods.

In Canada, the poorest one-fifth of the population receive about five percent of the total income per year and the top one-fifth receive about 44%. This relationship has not changed significantly over the past 50 years (Ross et al., 2000). In fact, Ternowetsky (1993) has found that the poor and middle class have been losing ground to the rich. Without government transfer payments and tax policies, this situation would be even worse (Ross et al., 2000).

An interesting alternative approach to measuring poverty is the relative deprivation index developed by Townsend (1979, 1993). He defines poverty as a point in the scale of the distribution of resources below which families find it difficult to share in the customs, activities, and diets comprising their society's style of living. Townsend developed a 60-item indicator of the common styles of living in Britain, based on a national survey. He then developed an index of deprivation by weighting these items. He found there was a level of income at which people withdrew sharply from common societal patterns of living. This level he designated as the poverty line.

THE POOR IN CANADA

Groups at Risk

Certain groups of people have a much greater risk of being marginalized and oppressed in Canada. Multiple structural factors create barriers for women, children, and minorities (Carniol, 2000).

According to the National Council of Welfare (2000a), women face a high risk of poverty. The poverty rate for unattached women who are seniors was 39.4% in 1998 compared to 28.9% for men. Single-parent mothers had a poverty rate of 54.2%; their families are four times more likely to be poor than male-led families. Eichler (1997) explains that women's poverty is a result of built-in labour-market injustices and discrimination, including the fact that women are paid significantly less than men. Evans (1996) further explains that the feminization of poverty is the result of inadequate policies and funding for programs such as child care, public assistance, and pensions.

Many of the poor in Canada are children and youth less than 18 years of age (Kitchen, 1991). In 1989 the Canadian Parliament declared war on child poverty and targeted the year 2000 to eliminate it. Since then the number of poor children has increased by 43%. This increase is partly due to a rise in unemployment in the early 1990s and the increasingly inadequate support of public assistance. Now roughly 20% of children in Canada are poor. Almost half live in families in which one parent has some work. Many of these parents are in low-paying part-time jobs without benefits (Campaign 2000, 2000). In addition, a very high proportion of young adults are living in poverty, especially those without high school diplomas.

The poverty rate among seniors has dropped dramatically since the 1960s—to about 18%—with the development of improved public and private pensions (National Council of Welfare, 2000a). Still, many seniors, especially women, live significantly below the poverty line. Leonard and Nichols (1994) argue that this inequality is partly due to the inequities of the pension system and to women being out of the labour force for long periods of time. The approximately 45% of seniors who are disabled face further barriers in transportation, home supports, and housing (Dunn, 1990). Roughly 60% of Canadians with disabilities live below the poverty line (Cohen & Petten, 1997).

People from the First Nations have incomes equal to about 60% of other Canadians. The portion of First Nations peoples falling below the poverty line is about 20% more than that of the Canadian population in general. On-reserve unemployment often exceeds 30% (Cohen & Petten, 1997). People from the First Nations have significantly higher rates of unemployment, school drop-out, incarceration, and suicide. The root causes of many of these problems can be traced to colonization, exploitation, and discrimination (Morrisette, McKenzie, & Morrissette, 1993).

Roughly 42% of those who immigrated to Canada after 1989—many of whom are from Third World countries—are living in poverty (National Council of Welfare, 2000a) . The poverty rate of visible minorities in Canada is approximately 36% (Ross et al., 2000). Many people who are visible minorities face discriminatory policies and practices in Canada.

The vast majority of people receiving some form of social assistance are living well below Statistics Canada's low-income cut-offs. The National Council of Welfare (2000b) found that social assistance rates throughout Canada varied from 9% to 70% of the poverty line depending on province, size of household, and type of benefit. According to Riches (1997), recent reductions in social assistance benefits have resulted in the dramatic increase in homelessness and food bank use.

Surprisingly, almost half of the poor below the age of 65 are working. Canadians are increasingly forced to rely on jobs which pay minimum wage, the value of which has fallen over the last 25 years with increased globalization of the economy. Many can obtain only short-term or seasonal employment. Real family incomes have decreased for the last 15 years despite the fact that most families have dual incomes and both earners are working more hours (Cohen & Petten, 1997).

Poverty in Canada is characterized by regional disparities. On the east coast, for example, fishing jobs are often seasonal, resulting in high rates of seasonal unemployment. Lower levels of education are also a factor in poverty (National Council of Welfare, 2000a). Many of the poor are tenants with inadequate and unstable housing environments. The problems of tenants have been exacerbated by a weakening of rent controls and tenants' rights in many parts of Canada. Women and visible minorities face additional barriers in the housing market (Hulchanski, 1993).

The Extent of Poverty in Canada

It is important to consider not only the level, but the depth or extent of poverty and the length of time people are poor. Single-parent mothers less than 65 years of age have the highest depth of poverty. In 1997 their average income was about $7,160 below the poverty line. Counter to stereotypes, most people did not stay on general welfare or family benefits for long. In the late 1980s the average single recipient of social assistance in Ontario remained on welfare for seven months, while the average lone-parent mother remained for about two to four years (Ross et al., 2000). Data from the National Council of Welfare (2000a) indicate that rates of poverty and the number of people receiving social assistance are closely tied to the rate of unemployment. However, jobs do not guarantee freedom from poverty. A sizeable portion of the working poor remained poor after five years because of inadequate pay (Ross et al., 2000).

THE CONCENTRATION OF POWER AND RESOURCES

Wealth and power are becoming increasingly concentrated in the hands of a few in Canada (McQuaig, 1998). There are now over 300 billionaires in North America, including about 30 in Canada (Newcomb & Kafka, 2000).

Clement (1975) concluded in his research that despite increasing social programs, the elite in Canada in the 1960s and 1970s were more exclusive in social origin, more upper class, and had closer family ties than those in the 1950s. He found that a small corporate elite made up primarily of white males of British origin dominates the Canadian economy and political decisions. Interlocking directorships have given this group control over corporations, banks, and insurance companies. In the 1970s, 100 people controlled 28% of directorships in the "big five" banks and 28% in insurance companies. By the 1980s, Canada's 32 wealthiest families and five conglomerates controlled half the country's financial assets.

Not only are wealth and power concentrated in the hands of a few, but the rich are getting richer (Moscovitch & Albert, 1987; Francis, 1996; Newman, 1997). Starting in the 1970s there was growing concern about foreign control of corporations and natural resources in Canada. The Special Senate Committee on Poverty (1971) concluded in its research that the nature of the market economy was the greatest contributor to poverty in Canada.

According to Hurtig (1991) and Barlow (1995), Canada's free trade deals with the United States and Mexico ushered in a new era. The Free Trade Agreement between Canada and the United States reduced or eliminated duties on imports and exports over a 10-year period. It did not mention social services, but allowed for the free movement of the companies that managed them. Neither agreement had social justice provisions similar to those in the European Common Market and both took place between countries with great differences in the size of their economies and levels of social programs.

Classical economists predicted that the price of goods would drop in Canada as a result of the free trade deals. There would be a short-term increase in unemployment followed by a period of economic growth and lower unemployment as Canada increasingly developed its economic advantage in the world marketplace. Social activists predicted that there would be a massive recession, a move away from corporate taxes to regressive taxation, and a "harmonization" of labour laws and social services between countries. Social activists felt that there would be increased pressure from corporations to make the national debt a priority and reduce government expenditures in order to lower corporate taxes. With less corporate tax, Canadian companies could be more competitive with U.S. firms (Drover, 1988).

McQuaig (1998) documents the impact of the free trade deal in Canada. In the early 1990s, a recession developed as industries moved south to take advantage of lower taxes and wages. While part of this recession was the result of a North American downturn, its extent was dramatic. Large numbers of people lost their jobs, corporations amalgamated and concentrated resources, the federal government reduced unemployment benefits and dramatically shifted from corporate taxes to sales tax and income taxes, and the political agenda focused on cutting the debt by slashing government jobs and transfer payments (Ralph, 1994).

The federal government stressed that human service expenditures were out of control and had to be reduced to deal with the growing deficit. Interestingly, a study by Minto and Cross (1991), economists at Statistics Canada, found that federal expenditures on social programs had remained stable at about 9% of GNP since the early 1970s. What had changed was corporate taxes, which dropped from 25% of all federal revenue in 1955 to 7% in 1992, the lowest rate of all G-7 nations. The federal government also gave additional tax points to the provinces and pursued a higher than necessary interest rate policy to keep inflation down.

Capitalism is undergoing change throughout the world, but the severity of changes in Canada can be explained by the specifics of the free trade deals with the U.S. and Mexico. The speed of global change has intensified with the break-up of the communist bloc and developments in technology and communications. Multinationals have grown to a point where some have revenues in excess of many Western nations. These mega-organizations operate transnationally beyond the control of individual governments. They control 70% of world trade. Industrial countries have drastically cut government expenditures, while businesses downsized their companies to be more competitive in the world marketplace. In turn, many Third World countries have turned to children for labour and used military force to crush unions (Teeple, 2000). Many of the cutbacks in Canada have especially affected women, children, and minorities. Despite improvements in the Canadian economy and growing government surpluses in the late 1990s, governments stressed tax cuts for the wealthy, rather than rebuilding the human service system.

THE IMPACT OF POVERTY

Poverty has debilitating effects on children and adults (Campaign 2000, 2000). Ross et al. (2000) found that the high school drop-out rate for children from poor families was 2.5 times higher than for children from other families. Child mortality is twice as high among children from the bottom 20% of the population as among those from the top 20%. Teens from poor families in Ontario were 1.8 times more likely to smoke than better-off teens, 1.8 times more likely to have alcohol problems, and 1.4 times more likely to use drugs (Bell-Rowbotham, 1996).

Offord, Boyle, and Racine (1989) undertook one of the most extensive studies on the impact of poverty on children in Canada. In their province-wide survey of school children in Ontario in 1983, and in a 1987 follow-up study, they found poor children to be 1.7 times more likely than children from other families to have psychiatric disorders, 1.8 times more likely to perform poorly in school, and 2.1 times more likely to develop destructive behaviour disorders.

The federal government initiated the National Longitudinal Survey of Children and Youth (NLSCY) to study factors affecting child development. Data from this representative sample of children across Canada indicate that differences in household income are closely associated with school readiness, parental depression, and family functioning (Ross, Scott, & Kelly, 1997).

In her summary of research on the relationship of poverty to physical growth and health, cognitive and socio-emotional development, and the concept of self, Bell-Rowbotham (1996) concludes that poverty is a strong predictor of a child's future. In contrast, wealth or power can insulate children from the ravages of many social problems. According to Hamburg (1985): "Poverty does not harm all children, but it does put them at greater developmental risk, through the direct physical consequences of deprivation, the indirect consequences of severe stress on the parent-child relationship and the overhanging pall of having a deprivated status in the social environment" (4).

Adults, too, are affected by poverty. Those who are poor are more likely to have poor mental health and to be in trouble with the law (Ross et al., 2000). There is also a close correlation between poverty and child neglect, physical abuse, and to a lesser extent sexual abuse (Drake & Pendey, 1996). Carniol (2000) gives voice to the impact of poverty on families. A mother states: "As a single parent on welfare, you feel so vulnerable, so unprotected. You're game for the weirdos on the streets. I've got a double lock on my door, but that doesn't stop the strain—the strain is financial and emotional and it can get to your health too" (94).

THEORIES ABOUT THE CAUSES OF AND SOLUTIONS TO POVERTY

Theories about the causes of poverty and its solutions affect how practitioners view poverty and the types of interventions they use. Townsend (1979) summarizes three approaches to poverty: (1) conditional welfare for the poor, (2) minimum rights for the many, and (3) distributional justice for all. He outlines a spectrum of sociological, economic, and political theories of poverty (Townsend, 1979, 1993). These concepts are supplemented in this chapter with theories about individual interventions, postmodernism, and theories emphasizing gender and responses to minorities in Canada.

Conservative social functionalists suggest that in order to ensure that all positions in society are filled, differential rewards must be given to each of these positions. Greater rewards motivate people to strive for certain positions. Inequality is thus necessary for all positions to be filled. Trickle down economic theory is closely connected to this idea. A certain amount of poverty is necessary for the smooth operation of society. Social interventions might include providing charity for a small number of deserving poor and introducing sanctions such as workfare to motivate people not to remain on welfare (Townsend, 1979; 1993).

Gans (1994) takes a more tongue-in-cheek approach to explain why poverty persists. He says the poor buy shoddy, stale, and damaged goods; undertake dirty, dangerous, and menial jobs; and subsidize the affluent by providing them with cheap domestic labour. They create jobs in social work, policing, and legal aid, thus creating groups with a vested interest in keeping things as they are.

Minority theory emphasizes the impact of poverty on certain groups. The earliest empirical studies of poverty identified characteristics of groups at higher risk of being poor (Townsend, 1979; 1993). They include people who are unemployed, single-parent families, people with disabilities, and seniors. Interventions include identifying the trends in poverty and directing better income-maintenance programs and other supports toward vulnerable groups.

Popular among the Canadian public is the concept of a subculture of poverty (Townsend, 1979; 1993). Poverty is seen as a way of life passed on from one generation to another. The poor have similar values, spending patterns, and time orientations. They buy as their needs arise, are heavy drinkers, and live in crowded quarters. The solution to these problems is to have social workers change the values and patterns of the poor and break their cycle of poverty.

Minuchin, Colapinto, and Minuchin (1998) theorize that many families who have been chronically poor are disorganized and stuck. Social workers must help them deal with problem interactions, communication patterns, and boundaries within families.

Rothery (1990) emphasizes ecological theory, including the notion that multi-problem poor families experience a chronic imbalance of stress over resources, which has a disorganizing effect. These families experience chronicity of crises and have inadequate help-seeking methods. Fragmented and dysfunctional human services fail them, often providing inappropriate interventions. Cameron, Vanderwood, Peirson, and Cheung (1994) propose solutions including dealing with clients' survival needs before developmental needs, stressing family-centred services that deal with the whole family, using social supports including informal networks, and coordinating services in packages that include multiple interventions. The role of the social worker is to develop a positive working relationship with the family, to advocate on their behalf, and to coordinate formal and informal services.

The classical economic theory of human capital views poverty as the result of a lack of "human capital," including education, skills, ability, and experience. It states that differences in levels of human capital create differences in wages and earnings. It does not deal with the impact of prejudice on income, but focuses on individual characteristics and proposes as solutions more education, skills, and training (Townsend, 1979; 1993).

The dual labour market theory points to forces other than individual characteristics that produce unequal wages and poverty among certain groups. It emphasizes that the labour market is segmented into primary and secondary sectors. The primary sector has stable employment, adequate pay, strong unions, and good career advancement, and the secondary sector has unstable, often contract or part-time jobs, low pay, no unions, and poor promotional opportunities. The latter is composed primarily of women and minorities. Poverty is caused by the disadvantages of the secondary labour market. Proposed solutions include adequate minimum wages, pro-union legislation, pay equity, and affirmative action hiring practices (Townsend, 1979; 1993).

Radical economists point out that capitalism, by its very nature, promotes inequalities. According to Marxist analysis, under capitalism the ownership of the means of production is vested with one set of individuals, while work is performed by another. A small economic elite controls both the means of production and political decisions. Capitalism is a system of class relationships of production that allows owners and controllers of the system to escape democratic accountability. Methods of control include coercion, economic dependency, raising aspirations, and the provision of social services. Class conflict, which will bring about economic changes as workers gain control over the means of production and abolish private ownership, is seen as natural and inevitable. Theories vary on how capitalism can be transformed, from a violent revolutionary overthrow to one of concerted peaceful reform (Mishra, 1990).

Feminist theories see poverty as a result of patriarchy and the unequal distribution of rights, wealth, and privileges. Work in the home is not valued or rewarded (Eichler, 1997). There are many feminist theories that deal with individual, community, and policy responses to poverty. Feminism does not offer one theory of women's oppression or a correct set of beliefs or values, but offers a wide spectrum of theories including liberal, Marxist, socialist, and radical feminism that may vary according to race, ability, or sexual orientation (Gilroy, 1990). All emphasize systemic inequalities in wealth and power between women and men. Smith (1999) points out that gender permeates all aspects of social, political, and economic organization. Solutions stress understanding patriarchy, empowering women, and creating a more just society. At an individual level feminist therapists emphasize making gender issues explicit, using collaborative strategies, and challenging traditional views of society (Cohen, 1993). Community work emphasizes collective interventions which stress women's empowerment. Social policies are proposed which assign domestic labour a real value, establish effective pay laws, and deal with oppressive welfare practices in order to respond effectively to the feminization of poverty (Gilroy, 1990).

Postmodernism questions the idea of progress and grand theories. According to Lessa (1998), the modern era, which encompassed a period from the eighteenth century to the 1970s, is now over. It was a period of faith in stable universal truths, including a belief that science and rationality would create progress for everyone. Theorists point out that poverty and inequalities have actually been increasing in many areas of the world as globalization increases. Welfare institutions often do not respond to the needs of consumers. Power in the hands of an economic elite has shaped and socially constructed our view of issues related to poverty. Postmodernists say that poverty must instead be understood in terms of how different individuals and groups are affected by it. Postmodernist theory stresses the importance of understanding and responding to the diversity of needs and claims arising from people living in poverty. It suggests a need for multiple solutions to poverty at different points in time. For example, narrative therapy is used to help individuals understand and reclaim their own stories. The actual practices of governments and agencies are critically analysed and deconstructed. New policies must be developed which challenge traditional power structures and respond to a diversity of human needs.

Townsend (1979, 1993) proposes a class structural theory of poverty with a social-democratic focus. He believes capitalism can be transformed through regulations, public control of the means of production, and more equitable distribution of income and opportunities. Mullaly (1997) expands structural theory by emphasizing diversity and how different people and groups are oppressed. He proposes changing a society characterized by exploitation, inequality, and oppression to one of emancipation and equality. Oppressions are often interlocking whether they are based on classism, sexism, colonization, racism, ableism, heterosexism, or ageism. Howse and Stalwick (1990) discuss how people from the First Nations have been oppressed through industrialization, assimilation, and detribalization. Land was stolen, traditional resources destroyed, families disrupted, and genocide promoted by sending children to boarding schools. Poverty is caused by unjust economic, political, and social forces. At an individual level, just therapists stress clients' strengths, identify oppressive policies, help reduce self-blame, and involve consumers in advocacy groups (Waldegrave, 1990). Mullaly (1997) calls for anti-oppressive practice which will promote social justice by stressing that the personal is political; by redefining problems; and through consciousness raising, empowerment, collectivization, and creating just and democratic institutions. Townsend (1979, 1993) proposes abolishing excessive wealth through changes to the tax system, eliminating unemployment, emphasizing human rights, changing hierarchical work situations, and providing more adequate community services which are controlled by consumers.

THE IMPLICATIONS FOR SOCIAL WORK PRACTICE IN CANADA

Theories of poverty have direct implications for social work practice. Some promising interventions at the individual, community, and policy levels are described in the following pages. Many blend various levels of intervention. They have been selected to illustrate a variety of theoretical perspectives and to provide information about interventions for a range of marginalized populations.

Individual Interventions

An example of an ecological approach is the Better Beginnings Better Futures program in Ontario. Initiated in 1991 by the Ontario government, it is a 25-year longitudinal research and primary prevention demonstration project for children and their families in 11 socioe-conomically disadvantaged communities. Community groups are funded to provide locally developed and innovative responses for children primarily up to the age of eight. These programs focus on multiple risk factors; they are comprehensive, flexible, and coordinated; and they deal with the discrete stages of child development, involve parents as lay helpers, and teach parenting skills. The projects stress adult education, social supports, social competency, and community development concepts (Lessa, 1996).

Independent Living and Resource Centres (ILRCs) stress a just therapy approach in their services to people with disabilities. Consumers usually provide the services and comprise at least 50% of board members. ILRCs provide information and referral, advocacy, research, service development, and peer support. While they do not use the term *just therapy*, they emphasize the principles of consumer control and self-direction, choice and options, freedom and flexibility. Staff from the centres help consumers to recognize that the problems associated with disability include over-dependence on professionals, inadequate support services, and architectural, economic, and attitudinal barriers. Peer support programs are operated by consumers who provide the advice and support needed to deal with individual issues, disabling environments, and restrictive social attitudes (Hutchison, Dunn, Pedlar, & Lord, 1996).

Morrissette, McKenzie, and Morrissette (1993) describe ethnically-sensitive structural social work interventions with poor Native youth in Manitoba. The *Ma Mawi Wi Chi Itala Centre* in Winnipeg, a nonmandated family and community services agency, is staffed and controlled by Aboriginal people. The youth program introduces youth to their ancestral culture, heals and empowers them through Native practices such as the use of the medicine wheel and talking circles, advocates social issues, assists in obtaining basic resources, and actively involves youth in all phases of the program. Individual interventions stress holism, emergence of a positive cultural identity, and balanced relationships between mind, body, and spirit. Traditional elders serve as teachers and healers and emphasize cultural teaching as a central aspect of helping. Cultural knowledge includes an understanding of colonization and the promotion of community activism. Balance is stressed through commitment to sustainable development, culture, and traditions. This service emphasizes structural theory. It is in contrast to interventions that have focused on a culture-of-poverty theory and stress changing Native value systems and promoting assimilation.

A number of lessons can be learned from these and other individual interventions. Postmodernist researchers point out that individuals who are poor have diverse needs and confront multiple oppressions. They may simply need a decent-paying job or may require brief counselling or more long-term professional assistance. Lightman (1997) notes that the traditional functionalist approach of workfare is one which does not work. Research from the United States and Canada indicates that workfare is costly, often destructive, and not very effective in helping people to obtain jobs, especially in times of high unemployment (Shragge, 1997).

Schorr (1997) found the following to be the most effective interventions for very poor families with multiple problems: (1) offer a broad spectrum of flexible and coherent services, (2) cross traditional professional and bureaucratic boundaries, (3) remove barriers to services, and (4) develop trust with consumers. Rothery (1990), in his review of the effectiveness of therapy with "multi-problem" families, discovered that coordinated service packages were most effective when they included a range of formal and informal supports that focus upon competence rather than pathology. These interventions should provide in-home services, use nonprofessional staff, and focus on survival needs before developmental ones. In their assessment of child welfare research, Cameron, Vanderwoerd, Peirson, and Cheung (1994) emphasize the use of social supports to address a range of stressors. Interventions should employ rapid and intensive responses to crisis with high levels of direct contact, offer effective follow-up strategies, combine comprehensive formal services with mutual-aid organizations and informal networks, and use primary workers for coordination. Carniol (2000), in working with oppressed people, advocated the use of narrative therapy, which involves listening to people's stories; feminist therapy; breaking down barriers between workers and consumers; replacing self-blame with a broader social analysis; empowerment; and collaborative action. Mullaly (1997) documents the importance of anti-oppressive practice and making agencies more responsive and democratic. Lee (1992) emphasizes the role of alternative types of interventions which are ethnically sensitive, such as the use of the Native medicine wheel. These practices can help transform human service organizations.

Community Work

One recent trend in reducing poverty in Canada involves alternative economies and sustainable growth. Galaway and Hudson (1994) provide examples of community economic development (CED) such as community development corporations, community employment and training, cooperatives, local enterprise agencies, community loan funds, loan circles, and collective kitchens and gardens. Another example is the Local Exchange Trading System (LETS) where goods and skills are exchanged between members (Shragge, 1993). While these projects are based on structural theory, the focus is less on redistributing resources than on developing sustainable economic development controlled by the community with social development as a primary goal. For example, the CDEC in Grand Plateau, Quebec has brought together local groups of single parents, immigrants, and unemployed youth to discuss how to deal with poverty in their area. A coalition was formed to provide community education about the causes of poverty and to assist in developing new businesses focusing on local social needs such as adequate housing. One initiative included the development of community loan funds to support new local enterprises (Mendell & Evoy, 1993).

Programs that provide English as a Second Language classes, skills upgrading, and education offering Canadian experience to refugees and immigrants to Canada are based in human capital theory. One innovative approach that incorporates CED principles is the work of the South Asian Women's Community Centre in Montreal. This centre brought together poor women from a diversity of South Asian backgrounds to form community enterprises. It offered skills training, Canadian work experience, education about Canadian laws and worker rights, and forums to discuss racism and sexism (Norton, 1993).

Recent cutbacks in human services and the growing disparity between the rich and poor are increasingly leading to interventions based on Marxist and structural theories with a feminist perspective. For example, the Mother Led Union in Ontario was formed to deal with inadequate income maintenance and reductions in part-time pay and to advocate for housework to be recognized as real work. The Newfoundland Day Care Advocacy Association was organized to advocate for adequate affordable day care, the Women's Network in PEI has lobbied for affordable and safe housing, and the Sitka housing cooperative has established affordable supportive homes for women in Vancouver (Cohen, 1993).

With the withdrawal of the welfare state and increased emphasis on self-reliance, there has been a resurgence of community work in Canada. There is less state intervention and more spontaneous grassroots initiatives, a move from a focus upon physical communities to communities of interest, an emphasis on diversity, and stress on mutual aid and social supports (Campfens, 1997). With the impact of globalization, community economic development has been important in developing sustainable resources that build connectedness and are responsive to local community needs (Shragge, 1993). Effective programs often stress sustainability, participation, respect for culture, and leadership by women. Consciousness-raising and social action have been critical in dealing with the changing economic, political, and social dynamics of Canada. Mass movements are required to counter reduction in human services. New partnerships that cut across public, private, and nonprofit sectors are needed (Campfens, 1997). Prilleltensky and Nelson (1997) advocate for a social justice agenda in community work, including: (1) connecting the personal and political, (2) involving constituents who are affected by social change, and (3) combining interventions at the micro, messo, and macro levels.

Social Policy

A number of social policy approaches have been used to tackle poverty in Canada. Minority group theory has been adopted in income maintenance polices that target high-risk groups such as seniors, women, and children. For example, the federal government initiated the Old Age Security Act in 1952 to provide monthly pensions to all people 65 years and older. In 1966, the Canada/Quebec Pension Plans were introduced to give pensions to retired workers and persons with disabilities based on contributions from employers, employees, and the self-employed. In 1967, a Guaranteed Income Supplement was paid to seniors who had little or no income. These and other income maintenance programs have lifted many seniors out of poverty (Guest, 1997). However, Leonard and Nichols (1994) point out that less than half of all seniors qualify for the Guaranteed Income Supplement and experiences vary between men and women. Women receive 65% of the average OAS-GIS income of men, less than 50% of men's CPP/QPP benefits, and 31% of men's occupational pension sources.

Policies dealing with the dual labour markets in Canada include minimum wage laws developed in the 1920s (National Council of Welfare, 1990). These laws are important to increasing pay in areas such as the service sector where women and visible minorities dominate. Employment training and laws obliging employers to evaluate their jobs in a nondiscriminatory manner and to ensure that women receive equal pay for work of equal value are vital to ensuring that women have an equal opportunity in the labour market. Future policies to address the dual labour market must ensure that part-time workers are treated with the same protection as full-time workers, minimum wages are indexed, and pay equity and affirmative action programs have sanctions and are implemented for all sectors (National Council of Welfare, 1990).

Interventions based on structural theory include policies to ensure greater consumer control of community services and the workplace. A series of social policies that have been proposed but not yet adopted in Canada are contained in the Alternative Federal Budget

(AFB). The AFB has been proposed annually by a broad coalition of social organizations and unions under the direction of the Canadian Centre for Policy Alternatives. It proposes alternatives to cutting unemployment insurance and social transfers, including job creation, strengthening social programs, equity legislation, a fair tax policy, and responsible targets for managing the debt. It recommends an Emergency Employment Investment Program to fund public transit, social housing, environmental programs, and infrastructure initiatives to reduce unemployment. Seven National Social Investment Funds would replace transfer programs and establish national standards for human services, and the debt would be reduced by raising taxes for corporations and the wealthy, and by eliminating tax loopholes (Canadian Centre for Policy Alternatives, 2000).

Social policies have been partially effective in targeting minority groups in need. Dual labour market policies such as higher minimum wages and better labour protection have been instrumental in assisting women and minorities in Canada. However, both the primary and secondary labour market sectors are now being dramatically affected by globalization. Ross et al. (2000) report that income maintenance policies have significantly reduced the poverty rate of seniors. But these policies do not deal with the fundamental power structure and are often limited to a few groups high on the political agenda. The Federal Alternative Budget provides a more comprehensive approach to changing the tax structure, establishing national standards for policies, emphasizing sustainability, and systematically addressing poverty in Canada. The National Council of Welfare (2000) points out that winning the war on poverty is not unrealistic. It estimates that the cost of bringing all people out of poverty in Canada is $17.9 billion more per year; a very sizeable amount, but achievable in a country where the federal, provincial, and territorial governments spent $361 billion in 1998.

Postmodern theorists stress the importance of critically analysing and deconstructing government policies, challenging those that are oppressive, and bringing together diverse groups in collective action (Lessa, 1998). Coalitions provide another way to spearhead common goals and take action against inequality and poverty. Wharf (1990) recommends that groups form more effective coalitions and social movements to mobilize for social justice and the reduction of poverty. Mullaly (1997) emphasizes the importance of building shared ideological positions among oppressed groups to create social change.

CONCLUSIONS

Further research is required to ascertain which interventions or combinations of interventions are most effective in different circumstances. With the growth of free trade, multinationals, globalization, and rapid changes in technology, the issues surrounding poverty have changed. Governments in Canada have slashed human services and increasingly blame individuals for poverty. There is growing disparity between the rich and poor and increased class polarization. Many of the solutions to poverty in Canada will need to respond to the international dynamics of capitalism through individual consciousness raising, social action, and redistributed social policies. A new vision is required which emphasizes equality and liberation. As the issues become more international in scope, the solutions will increasingly require the collaboration of people who are oppressed throughout Canada and around the world.

REFERENCES

Barlow, M. (1995). *Straight through the heart: how the Liberals abandoned Canada*. Toronto: Harper Collins.

Bell-Rowbotham, B. (1996). *Poverty and human growth and development*. Unpublished paper, Wilfrid Laurier University, Waterloo, ON.

Bourne, P. & P. Masters (Ed.), *Canadian women's issues, 1*, pp. 264–320. Toronto: James Lorimer & Company.

Cameron, G., Vanderwoerd, J., Peirson, L., & Cheung, M. (1994). *Promising programs and organizational realities: protecting children and supporting families*. Waterloo, ON: Centre for Social Welfare Studies.

Campaign 2000. (2000). *Child poverty in Canada: report card 2000.* Toronto: Campaign 2000.

Campfens, H. (Ed.). (1997). *Community development around the world: practice, theory, research and training*. Toronto: University of Toronto Press.

Canadian Centre for Policy Alternatives and Choices. (2000). *Alternative federal budget 2000.* Ottawa: Author.

Carniol, B. (2000). *Case critical: challenging social services in Canada*. Toronto: Between the Lines.

Clement, W. (1975). *The Canadian corporate elite: an analysis of economic power*. Toronto: McClelland and Stewart Limited.

Cohen, E.J. & Petten, A. (1997). *Sounding the alarm: poverty in Canada*. Ottawa: Senate.

Cohen, G.C. (1993). Social policy and social services. In R.R. Pierson, M.G. Cohen,

Drake, B. & Pandey, S. (1996). Understanding the relationship between neighbourhood poverty and specific types of child maltreatment. *Child Abuse and Neglect, 20*(11), 1003–1018.

Drover, G. (Ed.). (1988). *Free trade and social policy*. Ottawa: Canadian Council on Social Development.

Dunn, P. (1990). *Barriers confronting seniors with disabilities*. Ottawa: Statistics Canada.

Eichler, M. (1997). *Family shifts: families, policies, and gender equality*. Toronto: Oxford University Press.

Evans, P. (1996). Single mothers and Ontario's welfare policy: restructuring the debates. In J. Brodie (Ed.), *Women and Canadian public policy* (pp. 151–171). Toronto: Harcourt Brace.

Francis, D. (1996). *Fighting for Canada*. Toronto: Key Porter Books.

Galaway, B., & Hudson, J. (Eds.). (1994). *Community economic development: perspectives on research and policy*. Toronto: Thompson Educational Publishing.

Gans, H. (1994). The positive functions of the undeserving poor: uses of the underclass in America. *Politics and Society, 22,* 269–283.

Gilroy, J. (1990). Social work and the women's movement. In B. Wharf (Ed.), *Social work and social change in Canada* (pp. 52–78). Toronto: McClelland & Stewart.

Guest, D. (1997). *The emergence of social security in Canada*. Vancouver: University of British Columbia Press.

Hamburg, D. (1985). Reducing the casualties of early life: a preventive orientation. In *Annual Report* (p.4). New York: Carnegie Corporation.

Howse, Y. & Stalwick, H. (1990). Social work and the First Nation's movement. In B. Wharf (Ed.), *Social work and social change in Canada* (pp. 79–113). Toronto: McClelland & Stewart.

Hulchanski, D. (1993). *Barriers to equal access in the housing market: the role of discrimination on the basis of race and gender.* Toronto: Centre for Urban and Community Studies, University of Toronto.

Hurtig, M. (1991). *The betrayal of Canada.* Toronto: Stoddart.

Hutchison, P., Dunn, P., Pedlar, A., & Lord, J. (1996). *The impact of Independent Living Resource Centres in Canada.* Ottawa: Canadian Association of Independent Living Centres.

Kitchen, B. (1991). *Unequal features: the legacies of child poverty in Canada.* Toronto: Child Poverty Action Group.

Lee, B. (1992). Colonization and community: implications for First Nations development. *Community Development Journal, 27*(3), 211–219.

Leonard, P. & Nichols, B. (1994). *Gender, aging and the state.* Montreal: Black Rose Books.

Lessa, I. (1996). An atmosphere of action and change. *Canadian Social Work Review, 13*(1), pp. 109–124.

Lessa, I. (1998). *Restaging the welfare Diva: case studies on single motherhood and social policy.* Unpublished doctoral dissertation, Wilfrid Laurier University, Waterloo, ON.

Lightman, E. (1997). It's not a walk in the park: workfare in Ontario. In E. Shragge (Ed.), *Workfare: ideology for a new under-class* (pp. 85–107). Toronto: Garamond Press.

McQuaig, L. (1998). *The cult of impotence: selling the myth of powerlessness in the global economy.* Toronto: Viking.

Mendell, M. & Evoy, L. (1993). Democratizing capital: alternative investment strategies. In E. Shragge (Ed.), *Community economic development* (pp. 44–59). Toronto: Black Rose Books.

Minuchin, P., Colapinto, J., & Minuchin, S. (1998). *Working with families of the poor.* New York: Guilford Press.

Minto, H. & Cross, P. (1991). Growth of the federal debt. *Canadian Economic Observer*, 3.1–3.18.

Mishra, R. (1990). *The welfare state in capitalist society.* Toronto: University of Toronto Press.

Morrissette, V., McKenzie, B., & Morrisette, L. (1993). Towards an Aboriginal model of social work practice. *Canadian Social Work Review, 10*(1), 91–109.

Moscovitch, A. & Albert, J. (Eds.). (1987). *The benevolent state: the growth of welfare in Canada.* Toronto: Garamond Press.

Mullaly, R. (1997). *Structural social work.* Toronto: McClelland & Stewart.

National Council of Welfare. (1990). *Women and poverty revised.* Ottawa: Minister of Supply and Services Canada.

National Council of Welfare. (2000a). *Poverty profile 1998.*Ottawa: Minister of Supply and Services Canada.

National Council of Welfare. (2000b). *Welfare incomes 1999*. Ottawa: Minister of Supply and Services Canada.

Newcomb, P. & Kafka, P. (Eds.). (2000). The 400 richest people in America. *Forbes.* 166(10), 117–367.

Newman, P. (1997). *Defining moments: dispatches from an unfinished revolution*. Toronto: Viking.

Norton, J. (1993). Women, economic ideology and the struggle to build alternatives. In E. Shragge (Ed.), *Community economic development* (pp. 113–128). Toronto: Black Rose Books.

Offord, D., Boyle, M., & Racine, Y. (1989). *Ontario child health study: children at risk*. Toronto: Queen's Printer.

Prilleltensky, I., & Nelson, G. (1997). Community psychology: reclaiming social justice. In D. Fox & I. Prilleltensky (Eds.), *Critical psychology: an introduction* (pp. 166–184). London: Sage.

Ralph, D. (1994). Fighting for Canada's social programs. *Canadian Review of Social Policy, 34,* 91–108.

Riches, G. (1997). *First world hunger: food security and welfare politics*. New York: St. Martin's Press.

Ross, D., Scott, K., & Kelly, M. (1997). Overview: children in Canada in the 1990s. In Statistics Canada (Ed.), *National longitudinal survey of children and youth* (pp. 15–45). Ottawa: Industry Canada.

Ross, D., Scott, K., & Smith, P. (2000). *The Canadian fact book on poverty*. Ottawa: Canadian Council on Social Development.

Rothery, M. (1990). Family therapy with multiproblem families. In M. Rothery & G. Cameron (Eds.), *Child maltreatment: Expanding our concept of helping* (pp. 13–22). Hillsdale, NJ: Lawrence Erlbaum Associate Publishers.

Schorr, L. (1997). *Common purpose: strengthening families and neighborhoods to rebuild America*. New York: Anchor Books.

Shragge, E. (Ed.). (1993). *Community economic development: in search of empowerment*. Toronto: Black Rose Books.

Shragge, E. (Ed.). (1997). *Workfare: ideology for a new under-class*. Toronto: Garamond Press.

Smith, D. (1999). *Writing the social: critique, theory and investigations*. Toronto: University of Toronto Press.

Special Senate Committee on Poverty. (1971). *Poverty in Canada: report of the special senate committee on poverty*. Ottawa: Author.

Teeple, G. (2000). *The globalization and the decline of social reform*. Toronto: Garamond Press.

Ternowetsky, G. (1993). *Hunger in Regina: where do we go from here? Address to the World Food Day Hunger Symposium*, Regina, 1–6.

Townsend, P. (1979). *Poverty in the United Kingdom*. Markham, ON: Penguin.

Townsend, P. (1993). *The international analysis of poverty*. Toronto: Harvester Wheatsheaf.

Waldegrave, C. (1990). Just therapy. *Dulwish Centre Newsletter (New Zealand), 1,* 1–47.

Wharf, B. (1990). *Social work and social change in Canada*. Toronto: McClelland and Stewart.

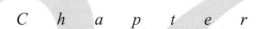

RESOURCE ISSUES

Malcolm J. Stewart

INTRODUCTION

The role of the state in ensuring that all citizens in need receive sufficient resources for food, clothing, shelter, and other necessities of life is central to social work practice. Beyond these basic necessities, the Canadian state provides a range of health care services to all citizens without charge, basic income security in old age for all citizens who meet minimal residency requirements, and a wide range of cash benefits and services directed towards various groups of citizens deemed to require special assistance. These include unemployed workers, persons with disabilities, First Nations people, immigrants and refugees, low income families with young children, battered women, abused and neglected children, low-income elderly, and students. While most of these benefits and services continue to be available in some form, most social workers are acutely aware of the overall decline in the direct provision of services by senior governments and in government funding for income security and human service programs of all kinds. They are also acutely aware of the negative impact this is having on families and individuals in need and on the social work profession itself. It is also generally recognized that as federal and provincial government funding and service provision have declined, increased responsibility has fallen to local governments, charitable organizations, and businesses.

During the first three quarters of the twentieth century, government cash transfers to individuals and public social insurance against sickness, unemployment, and old age evolved into important sources of income security for Canadian families and individuals, supplementing or replacing employment income, private insurance, and savings in times of need. In addition, public financial support in the forms of intergovernmental transfers, grants, and fees-for-service also made possible the development of a broad range of social services, from universal education and health care to personal social services. Taken as a whole, these tax-funded initiatives and programs have come to be referred to as the 'welfare state.' As an expression of collective responsibility for the well-being of all citizens, the welfare state may be regarded as one of the crowning achievements of Canadian democracy. However, as the twenty-first century begins, the political consensus and complex agreements under which our federal, provincial, and territorial governments have in the past made resources available for various social purposes are crumbling or have already been replaced. It can no longer be assumed that achieving the goals of the welfare state, which were once considered essential to ensuring fairness and equality of opportunity, are among the primary preoccupations of Canadian governments.

Diminishing governmental commitment to social security and the welfare state is not recent. This chapter will show that beginning in the 1970s, before Canada's welfare state was as fully developed as those of many other nations in the developed world, political strategies of retrenchment, dismantlement, and "reform," driven by neo-conservative economics and ideology, were introduced. These strategies were applied throughout the 1980s and 1990s. Fundamental changes to the public funding of social services were made, and governments reconceptualized the role of the state in providing income security, social services, and social amenities. Indeed, the very existence of the "welfare state" as it developed over the last half century has been under intensive review. Some critics predict dire consequences for the quality of life in this country if present trends continue, arguing that Canada is rapidly losing its reputation as a generous and caring nation. Welfare state detractors, on the other hand, contend that Canadians had become too dependent on state assistance in its various forms. They call for a return to individual, family, and local community responsibility for social welfare, arguing that the population will ultimately benefit from greater emphasis on personal and local self-sufficiency.

Past gains in Canadian social policy were hard-won, often entailing a tediously slow-moving and sometimes contentious process. Several reasons for this "incrementalist" tendency in Canadian social policy making have been offered. One reason is the dominance of liberal, individualist values in Canada (Esping-Andersen, 1989), which have prevailed despite the collectivist influences of toryism and social democracy on political thought and public policy. A second is the federal form of government, which requires a high level of consensus among the national, ten provincial, and three territorial governments, with their widely varied interests (Banting, 1987b). Canada's constitutional arrangements present obstacles to the exercise of strong central government leadership in the area of social policy, even at times when political consensus may be present (Pal, 1985). In addition, the diversity of cultural traditions and regional interests in the Canadian population have produced differing perceptions of human nature and the appropriate roles of the state, religion, the family, and other institutions in people's lives. It may be argued that these differences have mediated against a strong sense of national unity and common purpose necessary to support and sustain welfare state development.

This chapter will review the early development, expansion, and decline of the Canadian welfare state, compare it with welfare states in other developed countries, examine some explanations for its current decline and consider some alternative responses to the decline by social workers and others.

THE DEVELOPMENT AND DECLINE OF CANADA'S WELFARE STATE

Experimentation, consolidation, and expansion

Although industrialization and urbanization were slower in coming to Canada than to Europe and the United States (Guest, 1985; Banting, 1987b), by the end of the nineteenth century the problems generated by these transformative processes were increasingly difficult for governments to ignore. In an economy that relied predominantly on agriculture and the extraction of raw materials, the traditional, multi-generational family farm had provided social care for dependent children, the disabled, and infirm elderly; but these arrangements were rapidly breaking down and pressures were building for government action to relieve need (Burbidge, 1987). Early legislative initiatives included Mothers' Allowances, introduced by the provinces with federal funding assistance between 1916 and 1920 and Old Age Pensions, the first truly national social welfare program, introduced in 1927.

During the Great Depression of 1929–1939 the misery of unemployed and poverty-stricken Canadians was compounded by the unpreparedness of governments to relieve need on a major scale. After a decade of suffering, the outbreak of the Second World War in 1939 accomplished what had eluded politicians: full employment and an improved standard of living. The War also accelerated the processes of industrialization and urbanization, advanced science and technology, and created a strong sense of national unity and purpose among Canadians (Guest, 1985). During the post-War reconstruction period there was a surge of enthusiasm for state-led Keynesian economic management which promised to prevent the extremes of insecurity that were endemic to free market economies. A trained social scientist, Leonard Marsh, was invited to prepare a "blueprint" for Canadian social security, and over the next twenty years Parliament passed a wide variety of legislation that defined the new welfare state. Universal Family and Youth Allowances and Old Age Security benefits, the National Housing Act, Blind and Disabled Persons Allowances, the Canada Assistance Plan, the Canada/Quebec Pension Plans, and the Medical Services Act were among the highlights. But the expansion phase of the Canadian welfare state came to an abrupt halt with the oil crisis of 1973. Escalating oil prices led to stagflation—the concurrence of inflation and unemployment—and sudden loss of confidence in the Keynesian formula for economic stability. Efforts in the late 1970s to reduce the costs of the burgeoning welfare state through streamlining and rationalization—notably the federal-provincial Social Security Review—were largely ineffective, and by the early 1980s the stage was set for a major political attack on social spending.

Erosion and dismantlement

Following the 1984 election, the new Progressive Conservative government led by Brian Mulroney and his Minister of Finance, Michael Wilson, argued that reducing taxes on income and wealth would stimulate investment. To make up for reduced income tax revenue they introduced a comprehensive tax on consumption (the Goods and Services Tax). These actions, combined with negotiation of a free trade agreement with the United States and the Bank of Canada's anti-inflation policies, were almost guaranteed to bring about high rates of unemployment and poverty among the more vulnerable members of society

(McQuaig, 1995). The ideological pendulum had swung away from interventionist, Keynesian-style strategies for maintaining economic equilibrium and protecting the vulnerable, toward neo-conservatism, which defined increasing welfare state expenditures as the cause rather than merely a symptom of economic malaise. The proponents of neo-conservatism justified the reduction of social spending by emphasizing the need for Canadian businesses to become more competitive in the expanding, global marketplace, and the need to reduce public deficits and debt or face a down-grading of Canada's credit ratings, which would lead to even higher interest rates on government borrowing (McQuaig, 1995).

During the 1980s, reductions in social spending were accomplished through a variety of strategies, dubbed "social policy by stealth" (Gray, 1990), which included surreptitious changes to the rules and regulations governing taxation and unilateral changes to federal-provincial cost-sharing agreements. As well, the devolution of service delivery and funding responsibility from senior to lower levels of government continued throughout this period in a "cascading" effect, spilling over from the federal to the provincial to the municipal level, and from there to the non-profit, community service level (Freiler, 1986; McKenzie, 1994). This shift from public to private responsibility for social welfare during the 1980s has been described as a major structural transformation of the welfare state (Freiler, 1986). While more responsibility for service delivery fell to lower levels of government and non-government organizations, government grants that sustained voluntary, national research, and advocacy organizations concerned with social welfare were all but eliminated, severely limiting their ability to develop and advocate national positions on social issues. In the words of James Torczyner (1987),

> The voluntary sector, which once spearheaded movements for reform, financed a vast array of innovative services and occupied a central position in the formulation of social policy, found itself relegated to a marginal role in Canada. (280)

Universal social programs, a hallmark of advanced welfare states, ended in 1989 when income tax rules were modified to convert the Family Allowances for all families with young children to a selective Child Benefit for low-income families. In the same year, universal Old Age Security benefits were incrementally "clawed back" through the tax system from recipients with incomes over $50,000, until all OAS benefits were clawed back from those with incomes over $76,333. Moreover, partial indexation was adopted for all federal government benefits. This meant that the first three percentage points of inflation were omitted when calculating annual benefit increases, a change that produced long-term savings for the government and had subtle implications for recipients. Because of partial indexation, it has been calculated that by 2020 the clawback of OAS benefits could begin at incomes as low as $23,000 (in constant, 1989 dollars), and all benefits could be clawed back from those with incomes as low as $49,000 (Gee & McDaniel, 1991).

In 1990, the federal government unilaterally reduced its share of funding under the *Established Programs Financing Act*, with dire consequences for the provinces (Graham & Lightman, 1992). The EPFA was initiated in 1977 to regularize the payments to provinces for "established" cost-shared programs including health care and education. Similarly, annual increases in federal contributions under the *Canada Assistance Plan*, which had been introduced in 1966 to ensure equal federal-provincial sharing of the costs of programs for "persons in need," were unilaterally "capped" at five per cent for Ontario, British Columbia, and Alberta (ibid.). Unemployment Insurance premiums were increased and benefits reduced, the waiting period to qualify was lengthened, and benefits were eliminated for those who voluntarily quit their jobs (Gray, 1990). A net reduction of child-related benefits was introduced under the guise of targeting benefits to needier families, and child benefits became work-tested (Kitchen, 1984).

Concurrent with reduced spending on social programs, a number of changes were made to income tax rules to encourage investment and stimulate business. These included allowing certain business expenses to be deducted from personal and corporate taxable income; introducing a $500,000 life-time capital gains deduction; reducing taxes on corporate income; introducing a comprehensive tax on consumption—the Goods and Services Tax—which imposes a greater burden on lower and middle income earners than on higher income earners; and increasing the annual limits of tax-deductible contributions to Registered Pension Plan and Registered Retirement Savings Plans, which primarily benefit well-off taxpayers.

Thus, after nearly a decade of neo-conservative retrenchment, Canada entered the 1990s with its welfare state severely damaged, with diminished federal funding and with social welfare largely in the hands of the beleaguered provinces, some of which were bent on implementing their own neo-conservative agendas. To make matters worse, the economy entered the most serious and sustained downturn since the Great Depression of the 1930s.

Reforming the welfare state: The Social Security Review

Following the resignation of Brian Mulroney as Prime Minister in 1993, the Progressive Conservative government was soundly defeated, reduced from majority status to only two seats in Parliament. During its first term in office, the Liberal government headed by Prime Minister Jean Chrétien, while promoting itself as the party of fairness and social concern, essentially continued the previous government's neo-conservative policy of reducing the size of the federal government and attacking the national deficit through a process of "reform"—a euphemism for further social spending cuts. This policy direction met little political resistance. In Parliament, the Opposition was divided between the Reform Party of Canada, which espoused an even more extreme neo-conservative agenda than that of the Mulroney government, and the Bloc Québecois, whose primary agenda of separation of Quebec from Canada rendered it somewhat indifferent to national social policy. In such a political climate, defenders of welfare state policies were reduced to focusing on how to preserve some vestige of policies and programs built up over the past seventy-five years, and how to "do more with less."

Shortly after winning the 1993 election, the new Liberal government announced the Social Security Review, which would take place in stages. The first programs to be reviewed for their relevance to the current needs of Canadians would be Unemployment Insurance and Social Assistance, then income security for the aged—Old Age Security, Guaranteed Income Supplement, Spouses' Allowances, and the Canada Pension Plan—followed by health care. In the February 1995 budget the Minister of Finance, Paul Martin Jr., announced plans to reduce overall government expenditures by $25.3 billion, or 19 per cent over 3 years, $7.5 billion of which would be realized from reductions in social spending (Martin, 1995). Part of the latter reductions would be achieved through the Canada Health and Social Transfer (CHST), a block funding method of transferring federal funds to the provinces for health, education, and social services, which would take effect in the 1996–97 fiscal year. Other reductions would be realized by removing 45,000 positions from the federal civil service through attrition and layoffs. It was estimated that, when combined with reductions in funding for the health care system, about one quarter of social program spending would be lost by the turn of the century (Wiseman, 1996). While the budget included nominal increases in corporate taxes, reductions in subsidies to business, and a few minor reductions in tax expenditures that had benefitted primarily wealthy taxpayers and corporations, there were no proposals to rectify inequities or combat the national deficit through tax reform, debt repatriation, alternative fiscal policy, or means other than cuts in departmental spending and transfer payments.

CANADA'S WELFARE STATE IN INTERNATIONAL PERSPECTIVE

Despite official pronouncements of its superiority, Canada's welfare state is not and never has been as well developed as those of many other Western, industrialized nations, particularly those in Northern and Western Europe (Valpy, 1993). Evidence for this assertion will now be reviewed, with reference to both government revenues and social spending.

Government revenues

Given the frequently heard claim that Canada's levels of taxation are excessive, it is instructive to compare our overall tax burden with those of other developed countries. Figure 36.1 shows total taxes collected in 1997 by several countries belonging to the Organization for Economic Co-operation and Development (OECD) as proportions of their Gross Domestic Products (GDPs). Among these countries, taxes collected by Japan, the United States, and Great Britain were the smallest proportions of GDP, while those collected by France, Belgium, and Germany were the highest. Canada's taxes, at 36.8 of GDP, are in the lower half, just below the average for all OECD countries.

Social expenditures

It is also instructive to compare the levels of social spending of several OECD countries as a percent of GDP. Figure 36.2 indicates that in 1995 Canada was among those countries that spent the lowest proportions of their GDP on social programs. Canada's total spending on social programs is the fourth lowest among the fifteen countries included here, ahead of only Australia, the United States, and Japan.

Not surprisingly, there appears to be a fairly direct relationship between levels of social spending and national rates of poverty. Figure 36.3 indicates that, consistent with its relatively modest level of spending on income security, Canada ranks fifth among the eight developed nations shown in its national rate of child poverty after tax transfers. In marked contrast, countries like Sweden, Norway, Finland and the Netherlands have made significant progress towards alleviating child poverty through tax transfers.

While levels of social spending are an imperfect means of comparing the success of countries in alleviating poverty, Canada's relatively low level of spending may also help to account for its limited success in alleviating poverty among single mother-led families through tax and transfer policies. In this respect, Canada ranks with Australia and the United States in achieving far less positive results than many other countries (Hunsley, 1997).

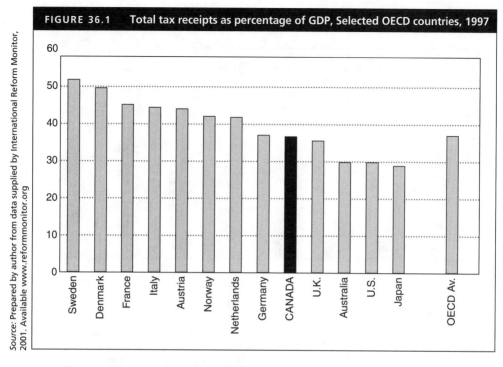

FIGURE 36.1   Total tax receipts as percentage of GDP, Selected OECD countries, 1997

Source: Prepared by author from data supplied by International Reform Monitor, 2001. Available www.reformmonitor.org

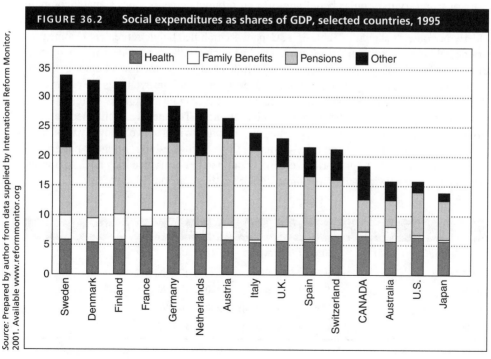

FIGURE 36.2   Social expenditures as shares of GDP, selected countries, 1995

Source: Prepared by author from data supplied by International Reform Monitor, 2001. Available www.reformmonitor.org

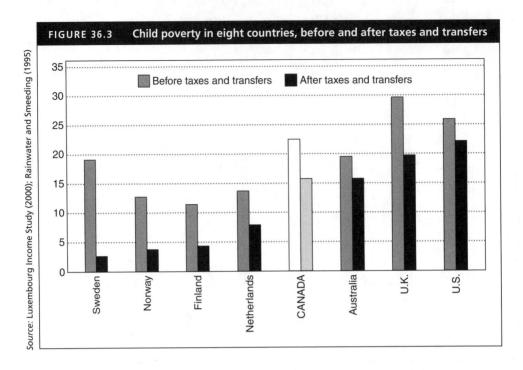

FIGURE 36.3   Child poverty in eight countries, before and after taxes and transfers

Source: Luxembourg Income Study (2000); Rainwater and Smeeding (1995)

Nor, contrary to popular belief and official pronouncements, does Canada compare favourably with other developed countries in its level of income support for low-income, elderly persons. As shown in Table 36.1, Canada's combined public retirement income programs (Old Age Security and the Canada/Quebec Pension Plans) provide a *maximum* benefit equal to only 40 percent of the Average Industrial Wage, the lowest among several other countries, including the United States. Despite overall improvements over the years, the inequalities of income found among men and women, public and private sector workers, and salaried and waged workers continue into retirement. The meagre public income security system forces workers to rely on private pensions and savings to avoid poverty in old age. Consequently, a significant minority—notably those with life-long, irregular patterns of work force participation (primarily women)—continue to experience high rates of impoverishment (National Council of Welfare, 1999; Statistics Canada, 1996).

Table 36.1	Public Pension Plan Income Replacement - Selected Countries
CANADA (C/QPP + OAS)	40% of Average Industrial Wage
France	50% of earnings up to 150% of AIW
Japan	75% of earnings up to 150% of AIW
United Kingdom	40% of earnings up to 200% of AIW
United States	41% of earnings up to 250% of AIW

Source: Ontario (1988). Task Force on Inflation Protection. Toronto: Queen's Printer.

FISCAL CRISIS AND WELFARE STATE DECLINE

Social spending

Despite the evidence that Canada's social spending is not excessive when compared with many other developed nations, a growing chorus of politicians claimed during the 1980s and 1990s that social spending was a major, if not the main, cause of public debt. As the government's total debt load approached 75 percent of Gross Domestic Product in the mid-1990s, politicians of all ideological persuasions seemed to reach an implicit agreement that social spending must be curtailed in order to avoid fiscal catastrophe. Alternative explanations for rising government deficits and debts included declining tax revenues due to deliberate tax policy changes introduced in the 1970s and 1980s (Mimoto & Cross, 1991); the imposition of high real interest rates by the Bank of Canada, which exacerbated the costs of government borrowing (McQuaig, 1995; Fortin, 1996); and persistent, high unemployment (Bellemare, 1993). However, alternative explanations which suggested approaches other than drastic government spending cuts, received scant attention.

It is true that social spending increased steadily in absolute terms, reaching an estimated total of $58.4 billion, or 49 per cent of total program spending in 1995–96. (Department of Finance, 1994a). This can be attributed to population growth, doubt that the addition of several new programs, periodic improvements of benefit levels, and the increasing needs of an aging population. There is, however, considerable social spending *caused* the national debt. Respected government officials Mimoto and Cross documented that social spending, as a percent of GDP, increased moderately during the twenty-five year period from 1960 until 1985, while Canada's welfare state was being constructed. But subsequently the proportion of GDP devoted to social spending began to fall, as did those of other government expenditures from 1980 on. Mimoto and Cross (1991) stated, "Generally, from the mid-1970s, social programs and other government spending have had a flat trend relative to GDP, after leading growth in the previous decade." They concluded that social spending did *not* contribute significantly to the growth of government spending relative to GDP after 1975. Rather, debt charges continued to grow steadily during this 25 year period (especially after 1975), while federal government revenues declined as a proportion of GDP. This can be attributed to sluggish economic growth, which resulted in reduced revenues from corporate income, personal income, and consumption taxes; and the transfer of tax points to the provinces (ibid., p. 3.1). On the other hand, social spending by provincial and local governments during this period rose as a result of high health, welfare, and social service expenditures during hard economic times (Battle and Torjman, 1993, p. 9).

Canada's tax system

In addition to direct spending on social and other government programs, tax expenditures—monies that are intentionally *not* collected by taxing authorities in order to provide assistance to certain groups or to encourage certain types of investment activity—have been estimated to cost the federal and provincial governments in excess of $90 billion annually (Department of Finance, 1994b). While some of these tax expenditures primarily benefit lower income Canadians, most disproportionately benefit corporations and higher income taxpayers, adding to the overall lack of progressivity in the Canadian tax system (Shillington, 1996).

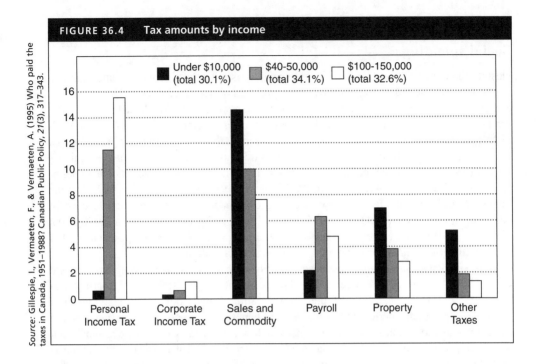

Source: Gillespie, I., Vermaeten, F., & Vermaeten, A. (1995) Who paid the taxes in Canada, 1951–1988? Canadian Public Policy, 21(3), 317–343.

FIGURE 36.4   Tax amounts by income

Contrary to popular belief, Canada's tax system is not progressive, that is, it is not based on the principle of "ability to pay" so that tax rates increase with income. Instead, as shown in Figure 36.4, the progressivity of income tax is offset by the regressivity of sales and property taxes, so that in the end everyone—rich and poor—pays between 30 and 34 percent of their total annual income in taxes. This is why our tax system is appropriately described as "neutral" rather than progressive in terms of income redistribution (Banting, 1987a; Gillespie, Vermaeten, & Vermaeten, 1995).

Monetarism

Monetarism—the theory that the problem of inflation (which is anathema to investors) is caused by excessive real wages and an over-supply of money—is a key element of neo-conservative fiscal policy. Monetarists would allow the "inherently efficient" free market to solve these problems by controlling the supply of money, thereby inducing price stability. The imposition of high interest rates on an economy is the method favoured by monetarists to control inflation. Unfortunately, high interest rates, by increasing the cost of borrowing and dampening the economy, also tend to produce high levels of unemployment. Monetarist thinking appears to have strongly influenced the policies of the former Progressive Conservative government and to a lesser extent those of the current Liberal government. Despite this political support for monetarism, the necessity and desirability of maintaining excessively low inflation in Canada's economy is hotly debated among economists and policy critics (Osberg & Fortin, 1996). Monetarism is, however, consistent with the requirements of global capitalism, discussed in more detail below. Moreover, it is a form of economic control which is exercised outside politics, since the supply of money and its value on world markets is controlled by increasingly autonomous central banks (like the Bank of Canada), and by autonomous international institutions of the global economy, such as bond rating services (McQuaig, 1995).

GLOBAL COMPETITION, MOBILE CAPITAL, FLEXIBLE LABOUR

Increasingly, commentators are directing attention toward globalization as the root cause of contemporary economic change. From this perspective, welfare state decline is seen as only one symptom.

Globalization has been defined as a complex set of political and economic trends which includes the expansion of trade, investment, production, and financial flows on an international scale; increased mobility of capital; the emergence of regional trading blocs and international economic agreements, leading to increased interdependence of national economies; and greater influence of international financial institutions and transnational corporations over national economies and trade relations (Wiseman, 1996). Broad (1995) argues that what we now call globalization is really the culmination of the development of international commerce that began over 500 years ago. According to Broad, the current situation reflects a "…deepening of the global economic structure" which has been applied for decades in the developing world and is now being applied to labour forces in the developed world, including North America. This "new international division of labour" began in the 1970s when the technologies of advanced capitalist production were introduced in Third World countries, enabling low labour costs to undercut First World workers. Labour flexibility—the willingness of workers to accept non-standard, low wage work with minimal employment security or rights—complements capital flexibility, which has been described as the capacity of business firms to respond quickly to new opportunities in "niche" markets, engage in "just-in-time" production, and relocate operations to the most unregulated countries (Harvey, 1990).

Teeple (1995) argues that this state of affairs is a consequence of the "victory of capitalism" over the widespread social democratic reforms which occurred in the post-war period in tandem with the expansion of welfare states. Indeed, the "victory of capitalism" renders national sovereignty secondary to international trade and calls the continuing viability of nation states into question.

RESPONDING TO DECLINING RESOURCES

Under conditions of declining government commitment to social welfare, social workers face difficult ethical and practical choices. Should one attempt to maintain a positive outlook while continuing to practice in the shrinking welfare state bureaucracy? Should one invest one's energies in struggling to find new resources and new ways of meeting urgent needs through non-profit agencies? Should one hone one's entrepreneurial skills and seize the business opportunities presented by the privatization of social services? Should one resist at all costs the retrenchment and reform of the welfare state? Canadian social workers and other social welfare advocates have typically responded to government abandonment of the welfare state in two ways: adaptation and resistance.

Adaptation

A common response to reduced government resources for social services is to seek creative ways to continue providing services and even "prosper in adversity." For non-profit social service agencies this may involve engaging in strategic planning to sharpen organizational focus; finding new sources of funding to replace lost government grants and fee-for-service contracts; developing and marketing profitable products or services to offset the costs of profit-neutral or subsidized programs; forming partnerships with other community agencies, corporations, or governments to leverage resources; amalgamating organizations or programs to improve co-ordination of service delivery; and developing quality control and outcome evaluation systems to enhance accountability. In a similar adaptive mode, individual social work practitioners may establish innovative direct practice and consultation businesses to complement or replace traditional employment.

The adaptive response suggests that we may be moving toward a new equilibrium in the provision of social services, captured in the concept of "welfare pluralism," a term used to describe the mix of auspices under which social welfare is provided in modern societies. In this conception, the total amount of welfare provision in a given society does not change appreciably with changing social, economic, and political circumstances. Rather, the proportions of resources and types of services provided by governmental, non-profit, commercial, and informal auspices are continually being altered or "re-balanced." Thus, when economic imperatives cause governments to reduce their level of resource provision, the other auspices under which social welfare is provided maintain the balance by taking on increased responsibility (Johnson, 1987).

However, uncritical acceptance of the welfare pluralism argument overlooks a number of important issues. For one, the sector comprised of non-profit, charitable, and religious service organizations is by nature highly diverse. It does not—and some would argue should not—have central leadership and direction. Even if this sector were willing to assume greater responsibility, it is unlikely that it could achieve a level of service accessibility or adequacy approaching that of government. For all the excellent and necessary work they do, non-profit organizations by definition are not accountable through statute to the public, nor do they have powers to tax or to enforce standards. Moreover, they cannot be expected to replace more than a small fraction of the resources provided by governments, especially the large amounts required for income security programs. Even if the effectiveness of charitable fund-raising were increased tenfold, and service provision were enhanced by a dramatic increase in the use of volunteers, there would likely be a serious shortfall of resources (Sharpe, 1994).

The willingness and capacity of the for-profit social services sector to expand its role may be less open to question, since the demand for social services generates a sizeable and growing market. However, increased reliance on this sector raises many of the issues of accountability noted above, and accentuates concerns related to access and standards of service.

Finally, increased reliance on informal sources of income security and social services really means increasing the burden of financial support and care giving on families, especially the taken-for-granted and unpaid care provided by women. This could prove to be an increasingly divisive political issue as our population ages, as well as having significant economic implications, given the growing importance of women in the emerging, knowledge-intensive economy.

Resistance

Another response to welfare state restructuring and cuts in welfare spending is resistance. During the 1980s and '90s many social workers joined with other advocates and consumers of health, education, and welfare services across Canada to convey, through peaceful protest, mass disapproval of government spending cuts. Complementary strategies include the development and dissemination of alternative, research-based policy options to inform public debate, garner political support, and counter the arguments advanced by neo-conservative think-tanks.

These strategies appeared to have little effect on the direction of either federal or provincial government policy. However, with the improvement of economic conditions and generation of budget surpluses in the late 1990s, advocates of renewed social spending have begun to attract public and political attention.

Institutional change

A third, more holistic and longer-term response to the shifting ground of social security and social welfare—one that builds on resistance—is to promote institutional change at the international level. From a global perspective, economists Goudzwaard and de Lange (1994) refer to the glaring contradiction of our times, in which worldwide unemployment and underemployment are spiralling out of control while environmental degradation rapidly pushes ecology to its limits; yet as a whole, corporations are more productive and are enjoying the highest levels of profit in history. Teeple (1995) argues that traditional forms of social and political resistance to the excesses and inequities of capitalism are failing because the conditions necessary for their existence are dissolving: the sovereignty of nation states is waning, but there is no universally recognized authority at the global level to take their place. A popular resistance movement must therefore seek to develop a new consensus between capital and labour, predicated on the assumption that social and environmental standards are ultimately in the interests of global capital as well as labour. There is a growing awareness that governments and transnational corporations must alleviate social need and injustice or face political, economic, and social instability, which are not conducive to global competitiveness (Wiseman, 1996). In the final analysis, corporations that wish to preserve their markets must heed the combined demands of consumers and labour for social and economic justice.

SUMMARY AND CONCLUSIONS

As we begin the new millennium, welfare state principles of universality, citizenship rights, and collective responsibility for social security and well-being, never fully developed in Canada, are being supplanted by values of the free market and individualism. The federal government continues to restrain spending by "reforming" income security programs while devolving increased control over the provision of social services to the provinces. The human costs and consequences of these radical departures—a growing gap between rich and poor, increasing poverty among young families with children, alarming rates of homelessness, burgeoning demand for food banks—are steadily mounting.

Alternative approaches to resolving the fiscal problems of Canadian governments, which are unjustly attributed to escalating welfare state costs are given little or no attention in public fora. In the absence of national leadership, some ideologically driven provincial governments choose to systematically privatize services that were once public and target vulnerable populations for punitive treatment. The pressures on non-government service providers and families to fill the gaping hole left by government withdrawal of resources are intensifying.

While adaptation and resistance are appropriate and necessary short-term responses to social security "reform" and the de-funding of social services in Canada, it is imperative that social workers join with other progressive forces to develop a politically and economically viable, as well as environmentally sustainable, alternative to the neo-conservative formula for global capitalism. This is a formidable challenge, which calls for co-ordination across national and cultural boundaries to advance a new, democratic vision for the future.

REFERENCES

Banting, K. (1987a). The welfare state and inequality in the 1980s. *Canadian Review of Sociology and Anthropology, 24*(3), 309–337.

Banting, K.G. (1987b). *The welfare state and Canadian federalism.* (2nd ed.). Kingston and Montreal: McGill-Queen's University Press.

Battle, K., & Torjman, S. (1993). *Opening the books on social spending.* Ottawa: Caledon Institute of Social Policy.

Bellemare, D. (1993). The history of economic insecurity. In D.P. Ross (Ed.), *Family security in insecure times* (Vol. 1, pp. 57–86). Ottawa: National Forum on Family Security.

Broad, D. (1995). Globalization versus labour. *Canadian Review of Social Policy, 36*(Winter), 75–85.

Burbidge, J. (1987). *Social security in Canada: an economic appraisal.* Toronto, Ontario: Canadian Tax Foundation.

Department of Finance. (1994a). *Agenda: jobs and growth.* Ottawa: Government of Canada.

Department of Finance. (1994b). *Government of Canada tax expenditures.* Ottawa: Government of Canada.

Esping-Andersen, G. (1989). The three political economies of the welfare state. *Canadian Review of Sociology and Anthropology, 26*(1), 10–36.

Fortin, P. (1996). Raise the inflation target and let Canada recover. *The Globe and Mail*, 26 September.

Freiler, C. (1986). *Privatization by design and default: a new era for volunteerism.* Toronto: United Way of Greater Toronto.

Gee, E.M. & McDaniel, S. (1991). Pension politics and challenges: retirement policy implications. *Canadian Public Policy, 17*(4), 456–72.

Gillespie, I., Vermaeten, F., & Vermaeten, A. (1995). Who paid the taxes in Canada, 1951–1988? *Canadian Public Policy, 21*(3), 317–43.

Goudzwaard, B. & Lange, H.D. (1994). *Beyond poverty and affluence: towards a Canadian economy of care* (Mark R. Vander Vennen, Trans.). Toronto: University of Toronto Press.

Graham, B. & Lightman, E. (1992). The crunch: financing Ontario's social programs. In T.M. Hunsley (Ed.), *Social policy in the global economy* . Kingston: School of Policy Studies, Queen's University.

Gray, G. (1990). Social policy by stealth. *Policy Options* (March), 17–29.

Guest, D. (1985). *The emergence of social security in Canada*. (2nd ed.). Vancouver: University of British Columbia Press.

Harvey, D. (1990). *The condition of postmodernity: an inquiry into the origins of cultural change*. Oxford: Basil Blackwell, Ltd.

Heclo, H. (1981). Toward a new welfare state? In P. Flora & A.J. Heidenheimer (Eds.), *The development of welfare states in Europe and America* . New Brunswick, NJ: Transaction Books.

Hunsley, T, (1997). *Lone Parent Incomes and Social Policy Outcomes: Canada in International Perspective*. Kingston: School of Policy Studies, Queen's University.

Johnson, N. (1987). *The welfare state in transition: theory and practice of welfare pluralism*. Brighton: Wheatsheaf.

Kitchen, B. (1984). The family and social policy. In M. Baker (Ed.), *The family: changing trends in Canada* (pp. 178–197). Toronto: McGraw-Hill-Ryerson.

Luxembourg Income Study (LIS) Key Figures. (2000). Relative Poverty Rates for the Total Population, Children and the Elderly. Available at http://lisweb.ceps.lu/keyfigures/povertytable.htm

McKenzie, B. (1994). Decentralized social services: a critique of models of service delivery. In A.F. Johnson, S. McBride, & P.J. Smith (Eds.), *Continuities and discontinuities: the political economy of social welfare and labour market policy in Canada* (pp. 97–109). Toronto: University of Toronto Press.

McQuaig, L. (1995). *Shooting the hippo: death by deficit and other Canadian myths*. Toronto: Viking.

Mimoto, H. & Cross, P. (1991). The growth of the federal debt. *Canadian Economic Observer* (June), 3.1–3.18.

National Council of Welfare (1999). *A Pension Primer*. Ottawa, National Council of Welfare.

Osberg, L. & Fortin., P. (Eds.). (1996). *Unnecessary Debts*. Toronto: James Lorimer & Co.

Pal, L.A. (1985). Federalism, social policy and the constitution. In J.Ismael (Ed.), *Canadian Social Welfare Policy* (pp. 1–20). Kingston and Montreal: McGill-Queen's University Press.

Martin, P., Jr. (1995). *1995 Budget Speech*. Ottawa: Department of Supply and Services.

Rainwater, L. & Smeeding, T. (1995). Doing poorly: the real income of American children in a comparative perspective. LIS Working Paper No. 127, Appendix A2. Available at http://lisweb.ceps.lu/publications/wpapersentire.htm

Ralph, D. (1994). Fighting for Canada's social programs. *Canadian Review of Social Policy, 34*(Winter), 75–85.

Sharpe, D. (1994). *A portrait of Canada's charities: the size, scope and financing of registered charities*. Toronto: Canadian Centre for Philanthropy.

Shillington, R. (1996). The tax system and social policy reform. In J. Pulkingham & G. Ternowetski (Eds.), *Remaking canadian social policy: social security in the late 1990s* (pp. 100–111). Halifax: Fernwood.

Statistics Canada. (1996). *Growing old in Canada*. Ottawa: Minister of Supply and Services.

Teeple, G. (1995). *Globalization and the decline of social reform*. Atlantic Highlands, NJ: Humanities Press.

Torczyner, J. (1987). The Canadian welfare state: retrenchment and change. In R.R. Friedman, N. Gilbert, & M. Sherer (Eds.), *Modern welfare states: a comparative view of trends and prospects.* Worcester: Billings & Sons Ltd.

Valpy, M. (1993). The myth of the myth of Canadian compassion. In D.P. Ross (Ed.), *Family security in insecure times* (Vol. 1, pp. 181–205). Ottawa: National Forum on Family Security.

Wiseman, J. (1996). National social policy in an age of global power: lessons from Canada and Australia. In J. Pulkingham & G. Ternowetski (Eds.), *Remaking Canadian social policy* (pp. 114–129). Halifax: Fernwood.

LEGAL

ISSUES

David Turner

INTRODUCTION

Law is a crystalline form of social policy that attempts to reflect the changing Canadian social context. Unlike most other helping professions, social work's mission and ethical obligation target the interaction between individuals or groups and their social environment. This focus on human beings as essentially social beings means that law and social policy, which express the formal nature of that interaction, have to be a major concern of social work. Law both shapes the context of much social work intervention and can be a vehicle for or an obstacle impeding progressive social change.

This chapter will explore the interface of social work practice and legal issues from three perspectives:

1. The key legal knowledge and understanding that social workers require in order to practice effectively.

2. The legal skills necessary for social workers to protect client rights and bring about structural change in the Canadian community.

3. The dilemmas that the law and legal system pose for social workers and how far they hinder or enable effective practice. It will also suggest a few strategies when engaging the legal system.

I will use a critical perspective in exploring the uneven distribution of power, authority, privilege, and resources that is often perpetuated by law despite its proclaimed goal of seeking justice. This analysis denies the notion of absolute justice, and assumes that "justice" is a situational value determined by the ideology of lawmakers (politicians) and adjudicators (judges).

KEY LEGAL KNOWLEDGE AND UNDERSTANDING

Understanding the following aspects of legal knowledge is essential for effective social work practice.

The Nature of Law

Turner and Uhlemann (1991) define law as

> ... a system of rules which orders society, defining a code of behaviour and establishing a framework of social institutions within which certain freedoms may be exercised. Law is the crystallized expression of Canadian public and social policy which, in turn, reflects the values of members of society. The elected officials in government who create laws are responding to their perception of public demands. These demands may reflect the values and interests of the majority in society (the consensual model of lawmaking), or the values of the powerful minority (the conflictual model), or they can reflect the interests of the group able to exert the most influence on a particular situation (the competitive model).

At first glance, laws such as the Criminal Code may be viewed as the consensual expression of social policy. But some aspects, such as the criminalization of certain behaviours, the imposition of serious penalties, and the selectivity of enforcement, often reflect the values of powerful sectors in society. Use of certain prohibited drugs carries serious penalties, yet corporations continue to put addictive substances in cigarettes, causing death or pollution in the environment, with minimal prosecution. Welfare fraud seems to merit inordinate criminal attention compared with tax evasion and the underground economy. Family law reflects white, male, mainstream values to the disadvantage of women, First Nations, and cultural minorities as evidenced by often token child maintenance payments for single-parent women or the still greatly disproportionate numbers of Aboriginal children and youth in care or correctional institutions.

These raise fundamental issues of democracy, equity, and fairness, which must be engaged by social workers on an individual and public level. Social work needs to expose the ideology and values behind laws and court decisions. As feminists rightly point out, "Law is not a free-floating entity, it is grounded in patriarchy, as well as class and ethnic divisions." It operates as if it incorporated "truth," but only from certain standpoints. Much of female and minority experience is denied. The power, self-righteousness, and exclusiveness of legal thought, legal tradition, and the legal profession need to be challenged. Social work must unveil these limitations and join the struggle for social justice and inclusiveness in the law and legal system.

The Function of Law in Society

The four major functions of law are to regulate, to empower and obligate, to resolve conflicts, and to enforce adherence. These functions, because of the interests law is designed to protect, operate differentially, as mentioned above.

A basic principle of our legal system is that a person may do anything that is not expressly prohibited by law. A complex set of laws, however, does regulate the behaviour of individuals and organizations. The most obvious example is the Criminal Code (GOC, 1970), which sets standards of behaviour and provides penalties for deviation. However, inequality of protection or freedom exists, such as in the minimal age for having vaginal (heterosexual) intercourse being 14 and for anal (primarily homosexual) being 18. Social workers may need to argue for greater protection for certain vulnerable groups (neglect and abuse of seniors, for instance) through legal regulation, and also for decriminalization of other behaviours such as soft drug use, where intrusive enforcement can create further suffering and profiteering.

Law can also be empowering and obligating. It may give powers for individuals to exercise their rights, as evidenced by the recent rise in civil suits for damages against perpetrators of sexual and physical assaults. Sometimes the law gives special powers to agencies, such as the Office of the Ombudsman, or to individuals such as police officers. Special obligations (duties) may be imposed on individuals or on governmental agencies, such as occurs with investigation of child abuse complaints or provision of income assistance to eligible persons. These same laws (statutes and regulations) provide recipients of service with avenues of complaint or appeal and ways to hold powerful agencies accountable.

The law provides dispute resolution mechanisms and processes (courts, tribunals) that administer remedies enforced by a legally mandated system (police, corrections). Having a system in place for resolving disputes discourages people from settling conflicts by themselves in unlawful ways. However, the system of litigation and costly access precludes certain groups from appropriate use. Alternatives such as mediation and Aboriginal justice systems are only gaining some recognition slowly. This is crucial to social work, since one of the field's obligations is to create institutions and processes which empower all peoples, not just the wealthy or mainstream.

Understanding these functions is very important for social workers, especially in assisting groups to become empowered in dealing with powerful agencies. Statutory authorities, such as Social Services in most provinces, carry within their enabling legislation all four functions: regulatory (administering eligibility criteria for income assistance), empowering and obligating (empowering their workers with limited discretion and obligations to disperse public monies under certain conditions), dispute-resolving (providing the welfare appeal system), and enforcing (investigating welfare abuse). Social workers administering the income assistance provisions need to clearly distinguish for themselves and their clients which functions are discretionary powers and which are obligatory duties, and how certain provisions and regulations are needlessly intrusive and socially repressive.

The Characteristics of the Legal System

The adversarial, hierarchical, dynamic, and remedial nature of law has implications for social work.

An adversarial system The adversarial style of the legal and court system, focusing on individual rights and pitting parties against each other, can often seem antithetical to the collaborative, reconciliatory nature of social work. Consumers of the system, particularly younger clients, can often experience dissonance between legal truth and moral justification. This is particularly so in young offenders hearings when procedural violations can be grounds for acquittal. The social worker will need to explain the distinction between legal and moral veracity, and that strict adherence to process is intended to protect individual freedom.

As Vayda and Satterfield explain, "The rationale of this system is that the rigour and zeal of each side to present the most compelling case in its favour and the most damaging case against the opposition will ensure that the truth of any given situation will be revealed in the balance" (1989). There are several problems for social workers inherent in this assumption. First, the law's presumption that it has a secure hold on "truth" is fallible, linear, causal, dogmatic, and patriarchal. Ways to acknowledge differing perceptions of truth and incorporate experience into the system need to be found. The acceptance of victim impact statements and victim-offender reconciliation in criminal law are two contributions of the social work field that serve to offset the partisan contest and include the participants and their experience in the process.

Social workers should work with lawmakers to encourage alternate dispute resolution methods, such as mediation and arbitration in legislation, and with lawyers to develop their dispute resolution skills without recourse to courts where possible. Alternative and less adversarial justice systems such as Aboriginal sentencing circles, neighbourhood accountability boards, and community panels that reflect ethnic and other diversity, need to be promoted.

Social workers may need to strengthen clients through coaching and other empowering strategies to withstand the stress of litigation or testifying, and to demystify the system. Social workers also need to prepare themselves in the skills of evidence-giving and court protocol to enhance their credibility should they also be required to testify.

Finally, because of differential access to power and resources, the adversarial system is usually a battle of unequals. Legal Aid is being seriously restricted across Canada, with preference to indigent persons charged with serious crimes. These are primarily males. So-called "women's concerns" around custody and maintenance, welfare appeals, income/property/pension issues and gender discrimination usually do not receive legal assistance, unless violence is involved. Advocating for a fairer, more comprehensive legal coverage—perhaps through Judicare (an insurance scheme akin to medical coverage)— should be a social justice target for social workers.

A hierarchical system Lawmaking by legislatures (federal, provincial, municipal, school board), adjudication by levels of courts with differing and occasionally overlapping jurisdictions,[1] coupled with enforcement arms (police, sheriffs, and corrections)—all make for a complex system. Space does not allow for extensive elaboration but the system and the concept of jurisdiction must be understood for several reasons: so that it can be used appropriately by social worker and client as a resource; so that workers can understand its limitations as decisions slowly progress through levels of appeal; and so that it can be appropriately targetted for change efforts. The interconnectedness of the system gives clues for intervention. If youth workers (probation officers with young offenders) wish to reduce youth crime, they need to reserve time for community prevention. Diversion of young people from the court system has been drastically reduced under the Young Offenders Act, preoccupying workers with court reports, supervision, correctional release planning, and dealing with recidivism. The professed right in the Act to "the least possible interference with freedom that is consistent with the protection of society" (GOC, 1985) seems in practice ignored and is having a drastic effect on the youth justice system (Corrado, 1988).

Laws that either exceed the authority of the parent legislation or are outside the jurisdiction of the level of government can be declared *ultra vires* (beyond the power of) and invalid. For instance, welfare regulations must operate within the scope and intent of the provincial income assistance act. Municipalities cannot pass by-laws that intrude into areas of the Criminal Code. A provincial health order issued for the detention of an HIV-positive prostitute could be challenged because of its intrusion into areas of federal power by applying criminal sanctions to behaviour that does not violate a federal criminal statute. Provinces have no jurisdiction on First Nations reserves, which leaves the issue of child welfare services (a provincial matter) inoperative on reserves unless there are special agreements.

---

[1] For instance, in British Columbia, Family Courts and the Supreme Court have similar jurisdictions in family matters except that division of property and dissolution of marriage are reserved to the Supreme Court.

The Constitution, which includes the Charter of Rights and Freedoms, is the supreme law and the template for all legislation and policy. Laws or provisions in statute that violate the Charter without an explicit exemption may be invalidated. These are some legal avenues for challenging repressive laws.

A dynamic system   The law is always changing as new legislative enactments are incorporated and new interpretations in daily decisions are handed down by our courts. In this sense, the legal system is dynamic. Decisions are also affected by such things as the physical structure of courts, the degree of procedural formality, and the place of the court in the court hierarchy. But most importantly, its progressive or traditional stance is determined by the participants, primarily the judge. Judges are appointed provincially to the provincial courts or federally at other court levels on the recommendation of judicial councils. This is still a classist, privileged, and gender-biased profession (Hughes, 1993) and presumably many prominent lawyers appointed by mainly conservative governments in Canada retain traditional values.

Judges do have a role in shaping legal interpretations of statutes and in developing common law (or judge-made case law), especially on the Supreme Court of Canada, which has split along gender lines. A recent decision[2] to allow defendants, if they can establish that it is relevant to their defence, to have access to the private counselling records (including health and student records) of victims of sexual assault must be acknowledged as affirming the priority of the rights of accused assaulters over the rights of sexual victims. Traditional legal scholars would view this decision as the correct assertion of the rights of individual liberty over rights to privacy. Others would argue it asserts the rights of powerful males over disempowered females, revictimizing them and undermining the importance of confidentiality in the counselling relationship. However, most legal change derives from the actions of legislators, not the courts, and this demands that social workers engage in the electoral and political process.

A remedial system   The legal system provides remedies (a legal recourse or solution) to correct a violation or settle a conflict. The law provides a framework for behaviour that seems to be honoured by most people most of the time. By setting out rules in advance, which most people obey, conflicts are avoided and problems can be resolved without the need to resort to the courts. A simple example would be cases dealing with the division of family assets. Because the Family Relations Act in British Columbia sets out basic rules for dividing assets, most divorcing couples can resolve their problems by following those existing rules. It is only when the meaning of those rules are obscure or a client is obstinate or claims unfairness that a case comes to court.

However, the courts themselves are primarily reactive, only rarely preventive. Some of the few preventive remedies available to the courts include: injunctions or restraining orders (preventing further action by one party), peace bonds (requiring the keeping of the peace and other conditions to prevent violations such as injury to a spouse), and sentencing powers over offences of conspiracy to commit crimes which have not yet occurred. (Since conspiracy is itself a crime, this is not truly preventive.)

Court decisions at best are restorative, rather than transformative. Courts do not generally exercise a redistributive function, leaving that up to political lawmakers. The social worker

---

[2] R. v. Bishop O'Connor (1996) 4.S.C.R.411. The federal government has announced that they intend to introduce legislation to more clearly define the issue of relevance that the courts must use as a criterion.

should be aware that courts are limited in the remedies they may grant. However, they may intervene where human rights have been violated or where principles of fairness and natural justice have been clearly ignored. A critique of the rights-based approach to remedies suggests that rights arguments, such as free speech, are more often used by the already powerful in society.

Key Legal Concepts

There are several other concepts that merit a social worker's understanding, including the civil and criminal process and remedies, evidence, and procedural fairness.

Criminal vs. civil process and remedies   Understanding the fundamental differences in process and outcomes between criminal and civil law is essential for social workers who may need to testify or empower their clients by demystifying the system. The specific details can be obtained elsewhere (Turner and Uhlemann, 1998, 11–16) but some key differences will be mentioned. In criminal process a consistent party is the Crown (the state as represented by the province through the role of prosecutor or Crown counsel) taking action against an individual or corporation, based on information from a police investigation. Crown counsel has the ultimate authority whether or not to prosecute, and may decide to divert or warn. Crown counsel is a key decision-maker and, especially with youth through a process of pre-trial inquiry, is open to social work input (probation officer/youth worker) in determining whether prosecution or diversion is appropriate. When proceeding to court, the onus of proof is on the Crown to show guilt beyond a reasonable doubt. The outcomes are acquittal or criminal penalties upon conviction imposed by the judge.

The control of civil process is in the hands of the individual who sues another for a civil wrong (tort). One party has to show the evidence is in his or her favour on the balance of probabilities. This is a less stringent standard of proof; it means, for example, that a victim of an assault can successfully sue for damages despite the accused's acquittal in criminal proceedings. This personalized action can be very empowering for such victims. Outcomes include financial compensation and court orders including prohibiting further injury.

For social workers involved with court systems such as family court, these distinctions become important. Youth court is criminal, the Crown is a crucial player, and a more formal process often applies there, especially since penalties can be severe given the life experience of the young people involved. Child welfare and family matters are civil. Contested family issues such as custody disputes can be adversarial but are driven by the individual parties and their counsel. They may consent to mediation or other resolution not involving the court. Child welfare is also civil, and though the Crown is not represented, action is taken on behalf of a child for its protection by a state office (superintendent or director) or contracted child welfare agency (Children's Aid Society). Removal of the child or extinction of parental rights are possible drastic consequences. Civil doctrines such as *res ipsa loquitor,* which allows the court to draw inferences of abuse when no other plausible explanation such as accident is evident for the injury, can be applied to assist in deciding on the balance of probabilities. This is not allowed in any criminal proceeding.

Laws Directly Relevant to Social Work Practice

Building on knowledge of the nature, function, characteristics, and concepts of law, this section will explore briefly the substantive law, legal skills, and values relevant to social work.

Substantive law Front-line social work deals primarily with disempowered individuals and groups, many of whom do not have adequate access to society's resources because their rights are not honoured by other individuals or institutions. Therefore knowledge of and the ability to apply the legal rights and concepts of equality dealt with in the Charter and the human rights provisions of the provincial and federal acts (Turner and Uhlemann, 1998, 36–59) is crucial. This means, for instance, not only recognizing potential rights violations or discrimination, but having a working familiarity with actionable grounds and the processes of complaint to seek a remedy. Complaint mechanisms and appeal processes in a variety of areas such as child welfare, tenant rights, income assistance, mental health, employment, and education should be known, or at least what advocacy agencies in the community can support such actions.

While a thorough knowledge of human rights is relevant for all social workers in whatever field of practice, a familiarity with the general principles of the substantive law in many areas is also required. Legislation of particular relevance to social work includes income assistance, mental health, child welfare, education, family law, young offenders, relevant criminal law such as abuse or family violence, and civil law such as professional liability. However, the legal mandate of a social worker's field must be understood in depth, especially the worker's authority, clients' rights, and power to challenge.

Social workers need to pay special attention to the rights of disempowered and vulnerable groups such as children and youth, women, First Nations, racial minorities, the mentally and physically challenged, older people, gays and lesbians. Social workers need to understand both generic human rights and those specific to persons affected by particular legislation, such as, for example, mental patients governed by a province's mental health act.

Procedural law Social workers who are in a service delivery role need to understand notions of fairness and equality. Since many clients are dependent on services from governments and contracted agencies, the principles of due process and administrative fairness (Turner and Uhlemann, 1998, 16–18), often referred to as the rules of natural justice, should be clearly understood.

Social work ethics demands maximizing partnership with the client. Thus, discussion with the social worker of a refusal to provide a service should take place, giving reasons for the decision and identifying any avenues of appeal. The more dire the consequences of an adverse decision, the greater the need for the opportunity to be heard and the greater the need for full adherence to the rules of due process. Decisions that violate a required standard of procedural fairness risk being set aside by the courts or other review bodies.

Good faith and an open mind are decision-maker qualities that are essential to maintaining the integrity of public administration. Social work ethics also demands such integrity to avoid (or to declare if unavoidable) any conflict or personal interest in the outcome of the decision.

In particular, social workers need to be familiar with those mechanisms that can be used to hold them and other governmental agencies accountable in this way, such as the Ombudsman, the Privacy Commissioner, the Child Advocate, the Police Complaints branch or the Inspector of Correctional Standards.

Professional law The third area of law that a social worker needs to understand is that directly related to the social work profession. This is the law concerned with the regulation of practice, with issues of professional liability and specific legal/ethical areas such as informed consent, confidentiality, and access to information. Other chapters deal with most of this. A very brief summary is given here.

Social workers like all other individuals are not immune from criminal or civil liability in the exercise of their role and duties. Although some functions such as child welfare interventions (GOC, 1996) have statutory immunity from personal liability in civil law, the worker's actions must be in good faith. This may not cover an action alleging negligence.

LEGAL SKILLS AND THE PROMOTION OF STRUCTURAL SOCIAL CHANGE

Along with knowledge of substantive and procedural law, social workers need special skills to practise effectively when legal issues are involved. These include skills of identifying legal issues, of advocacy and legal empowerment, conflict resolution, and statutory function skills such as investigation for courts, evidence-giving, and court order supervision. These skills are also necessary for empowering clients and community groups to deal with legal issues, and for helping to bring about constructive legal change.

Recognizing Legal Issues

While lawyers alone have the authority to give legal advice, social workers need to recognize when client or community issues have legal aspects and require legal advice. This is not always easy to determine and legal advice may be sought as a consultative, precautionary measure. Legal advice is usually essential where disputes or situations are likely to have an impact on a person's individual or family status (parental, marital), on financial status (e.g., property disputes or civil liability), or on legal rights, freedoms, or livelihood (e.g., threat of criminal conviction, change in income, or dismissal from employment). Knowing how lawyers function and how to access lawyers publicly (through Legal Aid) or privately is also important (Turner and Uhlemann, 1998, 27–28).

It is also useful to know where to find law, how to read a statute or regulation, and how to follow legal rules of due process, especially if the worker needs to advocate at a board meeting, council, government body, or tribunal of review.

Advocacy and Legal Empowerment[3]

The skills of advocacy and empowerment in the legal or quasi-legal arena (complaint mechanisms) are essential tools in the effective social worker's repertoire. Advocacy literally means "speaking to" an authority (such as a court, tribunal, committee, or an official) usually on behalf of another person or of a cause. Advocacy is the partisan representation of the interests of a client (individual or group). Like lawyers, advocates have the role and ethical obligation to represent to the best of their ability those interests. The advocate is clearly in his/her client's camp and not neutral, though will use mediation or facilitative skills if it will further the interests of the client. Case (individual) and cause (class or systemic) advocacy share some common skill components.

Class, cause, or systemic advocacy   This has been defined as action "to advance the cause of a group in order to establish a right or entitlement to an opportunity" (Sheafor, 542).

---

[3] For details on stages and skills involved in these activities and the strengths and limitations of advocacy and empowerment, see Chap 14 of second edition of Turner and Uhlemann, 1998: "Advocacy and Empowerment: Uses, Strengths, and Limitations".

Such advocacy focuses on changing law, policy, or practice for the betterment of a group or sector in society. While it can involve case advocacy, skills to bring about community change such as social and political action, and a public educational strategy are usually required to influence decision-makers and distributors of resources. Class advocacy often begins by empowering individuals, politicizing their concerns, and organizing coalitions as a basis of power, solidarity, and support before taking action in the public arena (Bishop, 1994; Mondros & Wilson, 1994, 233–236).

Mullaly (1993, 153–181) describes some skills for advocating from within the system and maintaining credibility. It is more difficult to obtain a mandate, clear instructions, and common interests from a larger number of people or groups. Causes may compete for priority. Sensitive, collaborative leadership and skills of conflict resolution and consensus-building (Shields, 1994) are invaluable to the advocate working with large groups or coalitions. For example, in the local anti-poverty coalition, conflict was heightened between the confrontational activists who wished to defy authority through civil disobedience and others who wanted to avoid police intervention and challenge repressive welfare regulations through legal means. A focus workshop for the coalition helped to define the common interests and shared goals, allowing for greater tolerance of the diverse means of achieving them. The advocate must develop mechanisms for effective relating to a group or coalition. Frequent reporting-back sessions may be required.

Lobbying for Legal Change

A planned public campaign of lobbying may be necessary to influence lawmakers. Penney Kome (1989) suggests that advocacy groups should develop action lists identifying targets such as politicians and key civil servants, media outlets, supporters' names, and other organizations that are allies in the cause. Using official channels such as presentations to elected bodies during public question period or submissions to legislative committees needs to be complemented by personal lobbying through letters and phone calls and by a diverse media campaign of news releases, conferences, talk shows, and demonstrations. The process whereby legislation and policy is approved and implemented should be known in order to shape an effective strategy. A planned public campaign should elicit support from beyond the converted. It might be necessary to make the cause an election issue through media exposure and persistent questionning at all-candidate meetings. The campaign needs to be monitored, fine-tuned, and evaluated. This may not be enough to get the attention of the people in power and legal action may be required.

In face-to-face discussions with politicians, the social worker as lobbyist should be as factual as possible, prepared to answer questions relating to the costs or social impacts of implementing changes or failure to do so. Straightforward presentations backed by data need some research capabilities within the lobbying group. As mentioned, an awareness of the values and interests of the person being lobbied can be useful in framing the approach so as to have an impact at both a rational and emotional level. Pressure from constituents may need to be applied. However, social workers must not forget the importance of relationship-building and friendly communication in their lobbying efforts. Making useful contacts and building friendships can sometimes influence the decisions of legislators and policy-makers.

To bring about substantial change in the legal and political arena, an integrated strategy of advocacy and lobbying, including a media campaign, may be required. Coalitions for support and action are required, especially for groups of marginalized persons (Bishop, 1994).

Conflict Resolution

The importance of the skills of conflict resolution (Turner and Uhlemann, 1997) is most apparent in the legal area of dispute resolution. Negotiation between the parties, mediation with the aid of a neutral third party, and arbitration in a less formal setting are seen as alternatives to court-based litigation. Mediation is becoming an essential social work skill and is recognized legally in several statutes in areas such as divorce (directing lawyers to point out mediation services to couples considering divorce) (GOC, 1985, *Divorce Act*), separation and child custody disputes (providing family court counsellors with limited legal privilege not to be compelled to testify when acting as mediators) (GOC, 1979), and in child protection (promoting the use of mediation in disputes between the family and the child welfare ministry) (GOC, 1996, s.22). Mediation is defined as a structured process of dispute resolution which assists the parties to come to their own agreement facilitated by a neutral third party, the mediator. It is a collaborative, interest-based process intended to empower the disputants to find their own solutions. However, mediation is open to a serious critique, especially where there is differential power between the parties (Turner and Cheboud, 2000).

Statutory Function Skills

Many social work roles, especially in governmental institutions, involve functions where the authority is derived from statute. For instance, all provinces have statutes that allow for the provision of income assistance by financial assistance workers or social workers. The criteria for eligibility to receive assistance are found in regulations pursuant to that statute.

But it is the court-based arena where law and social work can directly intersect. For example, the Young Offenders Act (GOC, 1985) describes the duties of a youth worker (a probation officer dealing with young offenders aged 12 to 17) as supervising young persons bound by probation, assisting them prior to sentence, attending court as required, preparing a pre-disposition (sentence) or progress report, and performing such other duties and functions as the provincial director requires. Even the components of a pre-disposition report are delineated in statute, including results in writing of interviews with the young person and the victim, and including information such as the young person's "age, maturity, character, behaviour and attitude ... and willingness to make amends" (GOC, 1985).

Other examples of statutory roles include child welfare worker, family court counsellor, and parole officer. All these have some common key skills such as working with a legal mandate, which raises issues of authority and often involuntariness and resistance in dealings with clients, investigating and reporting to court, evidence-giving, court order supervision, and enforcement. Certain roles such as probation officer, youth worker, or family court counsellor have an additional duty as court officer, which means that they must follow the judge's directions in carrying out their functions. This can sometimes result in conflicts between the court and the social worker's employing ministry or agency.

Social workers in these positions will be expected to have these skills (Turner, 1998) for operating in the legal setting, in dealing with their legal mandate.

DILEMMAS FACED BY SOCIAL WORKERS

Some authors have argued that there are perspectives that unify the disciplines of law and social work. Albert (1986) states that socio-legal problems are addressed most effectively when the social work profession appreciates:

- that there are legal boundaries for service delivery and for social worker–client problems,
- that a problem may provide a legal basis for intervention and/or may suggest a strategy for law reform,
- that interprofessional collaboration can be productive, if occasionally frustrating, and
- that certain legal concepts and skills are essential supplements to an intervention strategy.

These are valid comments and, as mentioned earlier, understanding of legal concepts and skills can improve practice. However, in my view, there are some fundamental contradictions between law and social work that render them not unifying and that can lead to ethical dilemmas for social workers. First, while the goals of law and social work may overlap, there is a distinction in emphasis. Both may share a vision of a socially just society but law is primarily conforming (the ordering and regulating of society) and social work is transforming (the progressive changing of society). Obviously both disciplines are affected by the political perspective of the lawyer or social work practitioner. A progressive lawyer may focus more on transformative legal interventions such as fighting for financial benefits for same-sex couples. A conservative social worker may advocate for traditional family values or utilize fairly repressive social control interventions. But the roots of each discipline differ. Law arose as the mechanism for control by the powerful and subsequently the state. Eventually law reform, rights, and justice movements arose to temper the excesses and injustices of the law. Social work began as a charitable voluntary movement with a vision of a better society, often advocating for the casualties of the legal, correctional, and welfare systems.

A resulting dilemma is how far social workers should carry out a legally obligated function of their employer which violates the vision and purpose of their discipline as contained in codes of ethics. An example is the expressed belief in "the obligation of all people, individually and collectively, to provide resources, services and opportunities for the overall benefit of humanity.... Functions of social work include ... advocating, promoting and acting to obtain a socially just distribution of societal resources" (BCASW, 1984). Social workers and financial assistance workers in British Columbia are currently compelled under welfare regulations to refuse income assistance to youth regardless of need. For most, this law violates their ethical standards. The Code of Ethics (BCASW, 18) speaks to this conflict and suggests strategies ranging from enlisting support of professional colleagues and associations, to subordinating the employer's interests, to resigning from that employment in extreme circumstances. Again Mullaly's comments for advocating within the system are instructive. However, there are limits on social action, political lobbying, or civil disobedience for social workers operating within the system who choose not to jeopardize their employment. Legal obligations may constrain effective practice for change.

Second, there is the issue arising from the feminist critique of law (Comack, 1993). Law, especially criminal law, in its struggle to deal with all individuals, usually denies individual, subjective experience, except when it can reframe it as that of the "reasonable person." The example given is of female "victims" responding in self defence to an attack from their battering partner and whether their response in repelling the assault and causing death or grievous bodily harm is justified. The criteria (GOC, Criminal Code, c-45, s.34(2)) are that it must be done under "reasonable apprehension of death or grievous bodily harm" and that the accused believes "on reasonable and probable grounds" that he or she (note the law only says "he") cannot preserve self from death or such harm. This objectifying is seen as arising primarily from male and often elitist perspectives. Although the Supreme Court

(GOC, 1990) recognized the unique experience and perception of battered females in these circumstances, the question raised is why this challenge needs to be mounted in the first place and why the law fails to embrace other diverse perceptions. The law's assumption of and monopoly on the "truth" of experience as it frames it is its limitation. This artificial authority is incorporated through archaic language and substantive and procedural laws into a mystical, often alien system which does not give validity or credibility to the diversity and uniqueness of human experience. This and the other characteristics of law mentioned earlier create obstacles of mystification, intimidation, and irrelevance for the social worker and consumers of legal services.

Social work is viewed as honouring and working with subjective experience, in validating individuals, and transforming society to respect the diversity of all. The partnership promoted between social worker and client contrasts with the authoritarian approach of law and the courts.

Third, the specific goals of the law to assign responsibility (guilt or liability as a process of dispute resolution) and legal accountability through court orders (of penal sentence or for damages) are different from social work's emphasis on collaborative problem-solving. Legal "truth" assumes the mantle of righteousness but is often very different from moral veracity. This is confusing to many non-lawyers who assume that the law has an exclusive claim on moral justice. Children and youth with a developing personal value system may be more confused and disillusioned. Social work usually avoids making moral judgments or attempts to engage self-responsibility through actualizing personal values and moral codes in its quest for change. The power and assumption of moral authority by the law can be disempowering for recipients. This may be appropriate in curbing the powers of the tyrannical, but many consumers that social workers engage are already disadvantaged, victimized, and powerless. The challenge for social work is to gain acknowledgment from the legal system of these serious limitations, to promote substantial reform, and to create alternatives to offset these negative aspects.

Other dilemmas for social workers using the legal system are the unpredictability of "justice," the time and cost involved, and the slow pace of legal change. Currently in British Columbia, human rights violations can take up to two years to reach a decision as to whether a hearing is merited. Indigent complainants are denied the benefit of legal advice during this time. Such structural inequities are common within the system. It is questionable how far some clients with deserving cases should be encouraged to run the gauntlet and engage the system. Ideally their rights should be protected and enforced, yet the reality falls short of this goal.

IMPORTANT STRATEGIES FOR ENGAGING THE LEGAL SYSTEM

Social workers need to be skilful in their interactions with and reforming of the legal system. Effectiveness can be enhanced by the following strategies.

1. *Work in partnership with lawyers.* Much has been written about the competing perceptions of lawyers and social workers and negative stereotypes of each other (Smith, 1970). Many lawyers perceive the courtroom as their "ballpark," where they retain control and play by their rules. Their focus on the individual and his or her partisan rights can often conflict with the more holistic perception of the social worker, especially when the

social worker represents a powerful statutory authority such as a child welfare agency. Such lawyers may see themselves as the last bastion of protection for the client from the leviathan of an oppressive government.

However, other research has identified more productive ground for collaboration (Weil, 1982), which can be promoted by more joint training, shared curriculum in law schools and social work schools, and discussions of the respective roles. Pre-court case conferencing, working groups in court settings to air concerns, and interprofessional public fora can all assist in improving relationships and enhancing working partnerships for the benefit of clients.

2. *Enhance own legal competence.* The legal arena is the working environment for lawyers. The professional credibility of social workers will be promoted by competence in the areas of legal knowledge, protocols, and skills whenever they are involved here. An opposing lawyer may take a less adversarial approach to questionning a social worker witness who displays such competence.

3. *Promote client choice in use of the system by realistically identifying the advantages and disadvantages of engagement.* It is well known how courts can revictimize victims, humiliate complainants, and shelter some offenders from responsibility. Legal representation in court, though necessary, can sometimes be disempowering for the client through limiting participation. Wherever possible, clients need to be able to make informed choices about engaging with the legal system. This means identifying the realistic advantages and disadvantages of engagement with the system. With those who have no choice, such as compellable witnesses and alleged offenders, the inappropriate negative outcomes need to be minimized. Social workers might act as support persons for disempowered clients in giving instructions to lawyers, for witnesses in testifying and debriefing courtroom experiences, and for promoting alternatives such as diversion from court.

4. *Explore both law and social work with a critical lens.* Without a critical analysis (Comack, 1999), social workers may become unwitting pawns in or apologists for an unjust system. Courts are essentially arenas for power plays. Mechanisms to equalize power and access to resources need to be developed. One example is the support that is being given to some groups of victims of abuse during their residential school or orphanage experience, who are now testifying against or suing the perpetrators. Connecting victims with each other is often necessary to boost their readiness to give evidence, although the law may not welcome this if it contaminates that evidence. More class actions could also be empowering.

5. *Be involved politically in reforming the legal system.* Finally, change in the legal system will come about only through political action. A critical analysis will identify areas for reform but only public pressure will demand that effective change be implemented. Social workers with their egalitarian values should seek political office as a way of changing laws, bylaws, and policies to truly reflect principles of social justice. Social work skills can have a significantly positive impact in the political arena (Turner, 1994; Cameron and Kerans, 1985). Social workers should be centrally involved in organizing groups and coalitions in challenging repressive laws and practices.

CONCLUSION

This chapter has discussed some of the important legal knowledge and skills that social workers require. Dilemmas and strategies for engaging the legal system have also been suggested.

All this needs to be incorporated into practice for the benefit of consumers and the community as a whole. As social workers endeavour to make the legal system more relevant and friendly to its consumers, the law and legal system may gradually become a more realistic instrument for bringing about the goals of social work: positive social change and justice for all.

REFERENCES

Albert, R. (1986). *Law and social work practice.* New York: Springer Publishing Co.

Bishop, A. (1994). *Becoming an ally: breaking the cycle of oppression.* Halifax: Fernwood Publishing.

British Columbia Association of Social Workers. (1984). Code of ethics.

Cameron, J.G., and Kerans, P. (1985). Social and political action. In Yelaja, S.A. (Ed.). *An introduction to social work practice in Canada.* Scarborough: Prentice-Hall.

Comack, E. (1993). *Feminist engagement with the law: the legal recognition of the battered woman syndrome.* Ottawa. Canadian Institute for the Advancement of Women.

Comack, E. (Ed.). (1999). *Locating Law: Race/Class/Gender Connections.* Halifax: Fernwood Publishing.

Corrado, R., and Markwart, A. (1988). The prices of rights and responsibilities: an examination of the impacts of the young offenders act in British Columbia. *Canadian Journal of Family Law,* 7(94).

Government of Canada. (1970). *Criminal Code, R.S.C.* c. C-34.

Government of Canada. (1979). *Family Relations Act, R.S.B.C.,* c.121, s.3.

Government of Canada. (1985). *Divorce Act, R.S.C.* c.3.s.10.

Government of Canada. (1985). *Young Offenders Act, R.S.C.* c.Y-1. s 3(f).

Government of Canada. (1990). R. v. Lavallee, SCC. Canadian Criminal Cases, vol 55. Canadian Law Book Inc.

Government of Canada. (1996). *Child, Family and Community Service Act, S.B.C.*

Hughes Commission on Gender Equality. (1993). Vancouver: Law Society of British Columbia.

Kome, P. (1989). *Every voice counts: a guide to personal and political action.* Ottawa: Canadian Council on Status of Women.

Mondros, J., and Wilson, S. (1994). *Organizing for power and empowerment.* New York, Columbia University Press.

Mullaly, R. (1993). *Structural social work: ideology, theory and practice.* Toronto. McLelland and Stewart.

Sheafor, B., Horesji, C., and Horesji, G. (1994). *Techniques and guidelines for social work practice* (3rd ed.). Massachusetts: Allyn and Bacon.

Shields, K. (1994). *In the tiger's mouth: an empowerment guide for social action.* Gabriola Island: New Society Publishers.

Smart, C. (1989). *Feminism and the power of law.* London: Rutledge.

Smith, A. (1970). The social worker in the legal aid setting: a study of interprofessional relationships. *Social Service Review.* June, *44*(2).

Turner, D. (1994). Social work skills in the political sphere: a case study of community empowerment, advocacy and conflict resolution. (Unpublished paper presented to Social Workers World Conference. Colombo, Sri Lanka). Victoria. School of Social Work.

Turner, D. and Cheboud, E. (2000). Advocacy and conflict resolution in social work: can they really promote justice? An Anti-Oppressive Approach. (Unpublished paper presented to International Federation of Social Workers Conference: Montreal.) School of Social Work, University of Victoria.

Turner, D., and Uhlemann, M.R. (Eds.). (1998). *A legal handbook for the helping professional.* (2nd ed.). Victoria, British Columbia: The Sedgewick Society for Consumer and Public Education. School of Social Work, University of Victoria.

Vayda, E.J., and Satterfield, M.T. (1989). *Law for social workers: a Canadian edition.* Toronto: Carswell.

Weil, M. (1982). Research in issues in collaboration between social workers and lawyers. *Social Service Review.* September, *56*(3).

PROFESSIONAL ASSOCIATIONS IN CANADA

Julie M. Foley

One measure of a profession is the strength of affiliation among its members; the best indicator of this is the professional association. It represents both the profession itself and its members. This chapter will chart a short history of social work professional associations in Canada. It will cover the structure of these organizations, their recent initiatives, and the critical issues they face in the present and in the near future. The chapter will underline the importance of membership in the professional association. It will conclude by drawing links to the international community of social workers.

Professional associations mobilize the collective efforts of a profession toward several ends. Some of those serve the general public, while others focus on meeting the needs of members. For social work, service to the public is inextricably woven with the interests of the profession and the latter often contribute to the former. In general, professional social work associations provide the following:

1. A valuable source of information to the general public about the profession, about specific services, and about social policy;

2. An avenue for collective advocacy and social policy development;

3. A sense of identification for and connection among members of the profession;

4. Enhancement of professional knowledge;

5. A variety of member services such as job search and liability insurance;

6. Development and promotion of high quality standards of practice;

7. Consultation to governments on services and matters of social and health policy;

8. Monitoring the practice of social work and its emerging trends.

All of the above result in visibility for the profession. Involvement in the associations provides valuable learning, networking, and leadership opportunities for individual social workers. Often these opportunities are not readily available otherwise. The associations support the mentoring of new graduates and allow all members to influence the ongoing development of the profession. A great deal of the work of associations is done by members who volunteer their time on committees or on the boards of directors that govern each organization.

In addition to the above, the social work associations in seven provinces have the responsibility for regulation of the profession. This means that the association oversees the applicable provincial social work legislation. The associations and their respective responsibilities across Canada are listed in Table 38.1.

In British Columbia, Prince Edward Island, and Ontario, where the regulatory body is separate from the associations, the latter were highly instrumental in establishing the former. In Ontario, membership in the regulatory body required membership in the association up to 1992. In British Columbia, the same applied until 1996. Membership in the Board of Registration in P.E.I. was always separate from the provincial association.

CASW: THE NATIONAL ASSOCIATION
History and Structure

The Canadian Association of Social Workers (CASW) was founded in 1926 as a membership organization for individual social workers. The purpose was: "To bring together professional social workers for such co-operative effort as may enable them more effectively to carry out their ideals of service to the community. To this end the Association shall seek to promote professional standards, encourage proper and adequate preparation and training, cultivate an informed public opinion which will recognize the professional and technical nature of social work, issue an official organ, maintain a professional employment service, conduct research and carry on such other activities as it may deem possible" (Mains, 1960, 2).

Given the number of members and the difficulties in communicating, never mind travelling across Canada in 1926, these aims were lofty indeed, and indicative of the tremendous commitment on the part of those involved. Services consisted of a placement service providing consultation to employers as well as information on employment opportunities for members,

---

TABLE 38.1 Provincial/Territorial Associations and Responsibility for the Regulation of Social Work Practice

British Columbia: British Columbia Association of Social Workers

Alberta: Alberta College of Social Workers*

Saskatchewan: Saskatchewan Association of Social Workers*

Manitoba: Manitoba Association of Social Workers/Manitoba Institute of Registered Social Workers*

Ontario: Ontario Association of Social Workers

Quebec: l'Ordre professionnel des travailleurs sociaux du Québec*

New Brunswick: New Brunswick Association of Social Workers*

Nova Scotia: Nova Scotia Association of Social Workers*

Prince Edward Island: Prince Edward Island Association of Social Workers

Newfoundland and Labrador: Newfoundland and Labrador Association for Social Workers*

Northwest Territories, Nunavut, Yukon: The Association of Social Workers of Northern Canada

---

*These associations have the responsibility to oversee regulatory functions.

the development of standards for both the delivery of service and for the employment of social workers and, from 1932 onwards, a focus on ethics.

By 1938, total membership was 540 and branches had been established in cities in British Columbia, Manitoba, and Ontario (Mains, 1960). As branches became active, association activities expanded to address the responsibility of social workers within the wider community. Membership increased and branches grew in number. Because of the uniqueness of each province, advocacy and organizational issues varied from one province to the next. It was not possible for a national organization to be appropriately responsive to all of these. It became apparent that a differential structure for the organization of the professional association in Canada was in order.

In 1975, CASW adopted a federated structure which was a reflection of the constitutional make-up of Canada, but also respected the manner in which social services were organized and delivered across the country. Several of what had originally been provincial branches of CASW had gradually become autonomous provincial organizations; each of those became a member of the CASW, which now became a national association of provincial organizations. Individual social workers would hold direct membership only in their provincial association: by virtue of the federated nature of CASW, they were automatically affiliated with the national association. Each provincial organization appointed directors to the CASW Board proportional to the number of provincial association members. The result was an unwieldy 33-member Board; the costs of gathering 33 members from across the country for a meeting were astronomical and meant that the Board could meet only once a year. This was not conducive to good governance. In addition, because the CASW Board members were usually the executive members of provincial associations, it was difficult for CASW to operate as a separate entity from the provincial organizations. This was often described as CASW needing to "have a life of its own."

In 1985, the structure for the CASW Board was streamlined. Henceforth, it was composed of only one director from each province, appointed by the provincial organization. Each director had a dual role: to represent the perspective of the province and to act in the interests of the profession nationally. Although not frequent, occasions arise when this duality poses a conflict for a Board member; it results in considerable soul searching and usually a collective struggle to find answers that respect the needs of both entities. This mirrors the same dichotomy faced at times by a social worker on the Board of a provincial association: she or he may represent one area of the province but is also expected to act in the best interests of the profession across the entire province.

With the new structure in 1985, whereby there was only one director from each province, the usual clout wielded by the large provinces was considerably diminished. The balance for this arrangement was to be vested in a tri-annual Delegate Assembly, a body that would be constituted in numbers directly proportional to the membership strength of each provincial organization. The Delegate Assembly would furnish CASW with periodic input and advice from a broadened cross section of the national membership base, and also provide the opportunity for provincial representatives to come together for the purpose of information and exchange.

Under the new arrangement there were three Delegate Assemblies: in 1989, in 1992, and in 1995. The Assemblies debated policy options and strategic priorities. They supplied advice to the CASW Board of Directors, which was invaluable in determining the short- and long-term priorities for the organization. However, the Assemblies were expensive gatherings for a limited number of social workers. A review of their purpose was undertaken.

By 1996, it was no longer considered necessary to balance the "one province-one director" constellation of the Board of Directors with a Delegate Assembly. The CASW Board functioned with a well-developed respect for all of its member organizations as well as a mature sense that the needs of its provincial organizations varied substantially and changed frequently. In addition, a new custom had developed: the provincial presidents met annually with the CASW Board, an event that not only yielded broad input to the national organization, but also provided the provincial organizations with the opportunity to meet and exchange experiences. It was decided that the Delegate Assembly would be replaced by a National Conference every two years, sponsored jointly with a provincial member organization. Such a gathering would benefit many more members of the profession than did the Delegate Assembly, which was limited to a small number of participants. The first National Conference was held in Edmonton in June 1998 and the second will be in Moncton in 2002. The Conference in 2000 was replaced by the International Conference in Montreal.

Up until 2000, there were no formal associations in the Northwest Territories, Nunavut, or the Yukon. For a brief period in the 1980s there was an association in N.W.T., but the limited number of social workers and the sheer expanse of geography made it difficult to sustain. In spite of these obstacles, social workers in the three Territories have recently established the Association of Social Workers of Northern Canada; this organization was welcomed as a formal member of CASW in March 2001.

Mandate

The CASW purposes, as summarized from its constitution, are:

1. To provide national leadership and to collaborate with member organizations to promote activities aimed at strengthening and unifying the social work profession in Canada;

2. To provide support to member organizations and to serve as a source of information and consultation on social work practice;

3. To encourage and assist in the development of high professional standards;

4. To study social problems and to take appropriate action to influence national social policy and legislation in order to promote the well-being of all people who live in Canada;

5. To encourage and/or undertake specialized studies and research in social work;

6. To publish and disseminate pertinent information to members of the Association and to the public at large;

7. To represent Canadian social workers and to advance the interests of the member organizations at the national and international levels.

Publications

One of the challenges faced by professional associations is the maintenance of meaningful communication with individual social workers. The written word is a principal avenue for such communication, both on paper and increasingly on the Internet. The CASW Web site can be found at www.casw-acts.ca.

The major publication of CASW is *The Social Worker*, which dates in one form or another to 1932. Currently, it is circulated once annually in journal format and twice in newsletter format. Articles for the journal edition are refereed by a volunteer editorial board comprising experienced social workers from a variety of practice areas across the country. Periodically, there are special journal editions such as the one on International Social Work in 2000 and a 2001 edition on HIV/AIDS.

A variety of material dealing with various fields of practice and/or standards of practice have been produced by CASW. Recent examples include:

Principles on Euthanasia and Assisted Suicide (1994)

Social Work Practice Guidelines in Dealing with Child Sexual Abuse (1994)

Elder Abuse in Ethnocultural Communities (1995)

Social Work Practice with Abused Women and Their Families (1995)

Standards of Practice in Social Work (1995)

Social Workers and HIV/AIDS (1996)

Comprehensive Guide for the Care of Persons with HIV Disease (1997)

Scope of Practice (2000)

Registry of Social Workers in Private Practice (annual)

Current Initiatives

Bilingualism: Since the mid-1940s CASW has provided some of its material in French. However, in 1991, the limited capacity of the association to operate in French was deemed to be insufficient and CASW committed itself to becoming a bilingual organization. For the previous several years it had been able to offer minimal services in both French and English, some documentation had been in both languages, and usually one staff person at the CASW office spoke both languages. Now, several staff members are bilingual and all staff have considerable capacity in both languages; all external communication and all important documents are in French and English.

National Social Work Week: National Social Work Week was initiated in 1991. It has come to be a significant event in many parts of the country, uniting social workers in a celebration of the profession. Events include public displays, contests, continuing education, and hospitality gatherings.

HIV/AIDS: CASW has produced several documents designed to enhance the expertise of its members about issues related to HIV/AIDS. These projects funded by Health Canada were started in 1989 and continued into 2001. Apart from the opportunity for many social workers working with HIV/AIDS to contribute, the tangible products of these initiatives have been two special volumes of the journal edition of *The Social Worker*, a training module on the psychosocial dimensions of HIV/AIDS, the CASW policy statement on the impact of HIV/AIDS, and increased visibility for the profession in the field of HIV/AIDS.

Child Welfare Project: In 2001, CASW launched this project aimed at developing strategies to support good practice in this critical area of social work. The project will report at the National Conference in 2002 with continued action thereafter.

G.S.T. Exemption: Since 1990, CASW has persistently lobbied the Federal Government to exempt social workers in private practice from charging the G.S.T. (psychologists are exempt). While the effort has still not produced the desired effect, CASW is cautiously optimistic that success may be on the horizon.

H.R.D.C. Sector Study: CASW, together with the Canadian Association of Schools of Social Work, the Committee of Deans & Directors (of Canadian Schools) and RUFUTS (the association of schools in Quebec) partnered with Human Resources Development Canada on an employment and human resources study of the social services sector. The study, completed in 2001, provides an important foundation for strategies the sector will have to develop in order to meet the substantial challenges of a weakened societal commitment to support the most vulnerable among us.

Coalitions: CASW participates in many coalitions. These include Campaign 2000, aimed at eliminating child poverty; HEAL, which is committed to preserving the best features of the national health care system; the Canadian Coalition on the Rights of Children, emanating from the UN Convention on the Rights of the Child; the National Coalition on Housing and Homelessness, which advocates significant federal reinvestment in housing; and others related to literacy, criminal justice, volunteerism, and preventative practices.

Social Work 2000: Together with the Canadian Association of Schools of Social Work and their two respective international associations, CASW organized the Joint (biannual) International Conference in Montreal in 2000. More than 1700 participants from 80 countries gathered to explore new developments and to share experiences of social work around the world.

Agreement on Internal Trade: This major agreement between the federal and provincial governments, signed in the mid-'90s, is intended to facilitate the movement of workers between provinces. The profession has been informed that its current varied requirements for practice across the country do not meet the criteria of the legislation. Thus, CASW is actively engaged with several other interest groups, including the schools and regulatory bodies, to build a consensus for national professional requirements.

Code of Ethics: There was a major revision of the Code in 1991 and the same is on the agenda for 2002. The work on A.I.T. may assist the next revision of the Code as the provincial/territorial organizations and regulatory bodies work out what is in the best interest of the profession nationally.

Promoting the Profession: CASW has established a National Committee with members from each member organization to coordinate, encourage, and share strategies on promotion of the profession. This followed substantial work by CASW on identifying national perceptions and obstacles.

Benefits for individual social workers: Although CASW does not have individual members, it has negotiated benefits that individual members of provincial organizations may utilize. This makes maximum use of the number of members across Canada, thus lowering the cost. The benefits include life insurance, liability insurance, legal consultation, insurance for disciplinary costs, and long-term disability coverage. These have been increasingly important as more social workers enter private practice or have only contract employment without benefits. An affinity card is also available and CASW provides assessment of foreign credentials.

PROVINCIAL/TERRITORIAL ASSOCIATIONS/ORGANIZATIONS[1]
History and Structure

During the 1930s, some provinces, regions, and large cities initiated branches of CASW. Those evolved over time in order to meet the needs of local members. By 1975, eight independent provincial organizations had been formed, some of them with responsibility to oversee provincial legislation, notably Quebec in the early 1960s and Alberta in 1967. Organizations in other provinces had been formed as follows: Manitoba in 1961, Ontario in 1962, Nova Scotia in 1963, New Brunswick in 1965, Saskatchewan in 1967, and Newfoundland in 1970. By the time that CASW moved to a federated structure in 1975, each province had its own organization.

Provincial associations are each governed by a board of directors, the members of which are chosen by the membership. Executive officer positions are usually elected by the entire membership, while other board members usually represent an area of the province or a specific constituency. In larger provinces, the membership is frequently divided into chapters or branches which cover a specific geographical area. This provides a vehicle for local affiliation and for local action.

It is interesting at this point to note the differences in membership structure between the professional social work associations in Canada and those in the United States. In the U.S., individual social workers are members of the National Association of Social Workers (NASW) and then, by virtue of that, divided into state chapters, with a few large cities such as New York being a separate chapter. However, although individual membership is directly in NASW, licensing is a state matter and varies considerably from one state to another.

Provincial/Territorial Mandates

All eleven provincial organizations share similar mandates, with seven having additional responsibility for the regulation of practice (all except B.C., Northern Canada, Ontario, and P.E.I.). Those with regulatory responsibility have first and foremost the obligation to serve and protect the public interest. Thereafter, all provincial associations are committed to a range of objectives encompassing social action, service to the public, support to members, continuing education, standards of practice, promoting the profession, pursuit of social justice, and services for individual members.

Provincial Publications

All provincial organizations except P.E.I.'s have a newsletter publication. These are important vehicles for visibility and communication. Quebec has a highly respected journal, *l'Intervention,* which is published several times yearly. Many provinces have additional publications that promote the profession or promulgate standards.

---

[1] OPTSQ, the Quebec organization, does not use the term "association" as it suggests a voluntary affiliation serving member interests. While OPTSQ does fulfill some of these functions, its primary mandate is protection of the public, and thus it uses as its main descriptive word "corporation" or "l'Ordre," the latter being the generic legislative word applied to all professional regulatory bodies in Quebec. Thus I have minimized use of the word "association," and utilized the word "organization" in its place as much as possible. Similarly, the same applies to Alberta, where the member organization is now called the College.

Recent Provincial Initiatives

The provincial organizations have devoted considerable resources to obtaining initial or enhanced legislation for social workers. The results are chequered across the country: Quebec has had legislation for nearly 40 years, the Atlantic provinces have been most successful in achieving control of both title and practice, while Ontario achieved first legislation in 1998. Alberta recently passed a new Health Professions Act which provides control of title to the College of Social Workers; the act is scheduled for proclamation in late 2001. Related issues involve "restricted acts" whereby the social work profession may be limited in its scope of practice if certain professional activities, such as diagnosis or psychotherapy, are confined by legislation to other professional activities such as medicine or psychology. These issues of overlap with other professions may occupy considerable energy on the part of the provincial organizations.

Several of the provincial organizations have had to battle recent incursions into job arenas customarily reserved for social workers. Many public and quasi-public employers have attempted to reclassify what had been social work positions into more generic positions. Often, the purpose is to allow the hiring of less qualified (community college instead of a BSW/MSW) or differently qualified (e.g., nurses) personnel. These issues require immediate response; often after impassioned and articulate presentations, the original requirements are upheld. This phenomenon of reclassification is also being experienced in the United States.

Most of the provincial organizations must pay considerable attention to membership recruitment and retention. Even with legislation, membership in many of the provincial associations is by and large voluntary. All provincial organizations have well-developed individual member services. Among others, these may include job postings, private practice registries, discounts on auto club or other memberships, standing or ad hoc committees on areas of practice, and discounts on hotel and car rentals.

Continuing education and advocacy are major priorities for most provincial organizations. Advocacy has encompassed consultation on proposed legislation, public support for or opposition to a provincial or local government initiative, and preparation of an Election Readiness Guide (Ontario 1995). There is one set of circumstances when provincial organizations must walk a fine line in their advocacy efforts: they may be working with a provincial government toward the establishment of or revision of social work legislation, and yet the association is also challenging that same government on issues of social justice. There have been instances where a politician or a senior civil servant has suggested that what the organization is seeking from the government could be jeopardized by vehement criticism of the same government on another front. It can be very difficult to ensure that fundamental principles are not compromised, and yet competing demands in the real world require skill and savvy to negotiate.

Membership in Provincial/Territorial Organizations

All but two provincial organizations require that members obtain a degree from an accredited school of social work, or a degree from a foreign university with the degree deemed to be equivalent to a BSW. or an MSW. The first exception is Alberta which, because of legislative requirements, grants membership to people with a community college diploma. The second is the Northern association, in which the traditions vary greatly from those in southern Canada.

NATIONAL VS. PROVINCIAL JURISDICTIONS

As the provincial associations evolved, so too did the requirement to differentiate the relative jurisdictions of the national and provincial bodies. Until the 1980s, there was a need for national material that could be used in all provinces: a code of ethics, standards of practice, personnel policies, etc. However, as some provinces assumed increased responsibility for public regulation of the profession, they sometimes had to develop new or related documents uniquely applicable to their jurisdiction; this requirement usually occurred in conjunction with the development of provincial social work legislation. Some provinces continue to rely upon CASW to fill these needs because their own resources are limited, or because the national documents are sufficient for their needs.

The 1985 restructuring of CASW delineated the differential jurisdictions of the national and the provincial bodies; it also recognized that there would be instances where jurisdictions might overlap, or where either body might wish to be active in an area ordinarily reserved for the other. The membership agreement between CASW and the provincial organizations includes a specific section on jurisdictional guidelines and procedures to handle matters of shared interest. One example was the introduction of the Canada Health and Social Transfer whereby the federal government was divesting itself of responsibility for social and health programs by eliminating cash transfers to the provinces. Although this was an action on the part of the federal government, the most direct impact was on provincial spending for health and social services. Because of the almost inevitable negative effect on services to vulnerable populations, CASW collaborated with several provincial organizations in vociferously opposing the downloading of these responsibilities.

The mandate of CASW requires that it provide independent national leadership, but also that it be responsive to its member organizations. At times, there is a dynamic tension to these two kinds of responsibilities. The national organization has taken action on issues that may not have been established priorities for all of its member organizations, as well as on items of importance to all of them. It does both with a view of what will benefit the profession as a whole. Thus its current activity related to the agreement on Internal Trade where failure to act as a whole will jeopardize the profession.

RELATIONSHIPS WITH REGULATORY BODIES

A debate surfaces periodically about whether the regulatory responsibilities to protect the public and the promotion of the profession represent an inherent conflict of interest. Some claim that, in principle, it is impossible to meet both purposes simultaneously and equally well. On the other hand, a strong professional association committed to high standards of practice is one of the best means of protecting the public.

A variety of models exist across the country, suggesting that like many other facets of the larger Canadian community there is not a single answer to the issue. In Quebec, l'Ordre professionnel des travailleurs sociaux du Québec (OPTSQ) has the longest-standing experience in regulating the profession. OPTSQ has very clear demarcations between protection of the public and services to its members or promotion of the profession: if there is a complaint against any of its members, protection of the public is the first responsibility. In Manitoba, the two functions were previously met by two separate bodies, which formed a parallel affiliation in the early 1990s, sharing one board of directors and one office. In Prince Edward Island, British Columbia, and Ontario there is a complete separation of the two bodies.

This separation can at times produce tension as each organization strives independently to fulfill its unique responsibilities; this tension can obscure the fact that both the association and the regulatory body are in positions to strengthen each other. It is quite possible for each body to contribute to the promotion of the other, directly or indirectly, without compromising the fundamental mandate of either. At the same time, it is important to keep the two distinct purposes in focus for two reasons: they are on occasion required to play very different roles with an individual member who is facing a charge of incompetent or unethical practice, and it is critical that both the public and the members know what to expect from each body. It is also essential that we respect the varying traditions or practices in different provinces. Above all, it is imperative that the need to maintain the distinctions not be so rigidly codified that the profession becomes in effect two solitudes. Neither the public nor the profession is thus well served.

FEES

The fees paid by individual members sustain the operation of a professional association. It is costly to support a presence in the form of an office and staff; advocacy and services to a small number of members or to members dispersed over vast distances in many areas of practice are expensive to maintain. CASW is financed through a formula based largely on a per capita levy, currently about $35, collected as part of the provincial membership dues. Membership fees for the provincial organizations vary considerably across the country as follows: just over $100 in Prince Edward Island; $250–300 in most provinces, and $421 in Quebec.

All fees except those listed for P.E.I., Ontario, and British Columbia include the regulatory functions; membership in the regulatory bodies in the provinces where that body is separate carries an additional fee of $100 in P.E.I., under $200 in British Columbia, and $370 in Ontario.

There are many reasons for the considerable differences in fees. Inevitably it costs more to operate two organizations than it does to cover both the regulatory and association functions in one body. This explains the relatively high (combined) fees in Ontario and British Columbia. It also costs more to service members who are spread across a large province; this helps to explain the low fees in P.E.I., which also does not maintain a staffed office as do the other provincial organizations. In some provinces the costs of ensuring representation from outside the capital city means that the provincial board of directors is able to meet only three or four times a year because the travel and accommodation costs rise quickly. And finally, expectations on the part of members vary considerably about the services and responsiveness that should be available from the provincial body.

THE QUESTION OF BELONGING: ETHICAL RESPONSIBILITY OR INDIVIDUAL INCLINATION?

Every professional has the ethical obligation to contribute to the ongoing development of the profession—all the more so when that profession is about service to vulnerable persons. A fundamental means of doing so is through membership in the professional association. Given basic social work principles about the connection between the individual and the wider systems within which a person lives, collective action is an imperative. There are times when an individual social worker is constrained by the rules or expectations of the workplace; their voices can then only be heard within the collective. Often in the course of public consultation governments and other public bodies seek the official voice of the profession, which can be expressed best and perhaps only through the professional association.

The proportion of social workers who belong to the professional association ranges from virtually 100% in Newfoundland, Nova Scotia, and New Brunswick, where the association has responsibility for the regulation of practice, to only 25% in Ontario, where the association and regulatory bodies are entirely separate entities. It is estimated that the proportion in Alberta will be close to 100% once the new legislation there is fully enacted. Such vast differences relate to several factors: the presence or absence of mandatory regulatory requirements, the connection if any between membership in the regulatory body and membership in the association, commitment to the profession, and for some, the costs of membership. In the Atlantic provinces, which enjoy strict regulation, if an individual is to be employed as a social worker or is to use the title of social worker, then that person must be a member of the social work regulatory body. This is equally the case whether the regulatory body is separate, as in P.E.I., or synonymous with the association as in the other three Atlantic provinces. Differences in association membership then show up in the provinces where there is a separation of the bodies: in P.E.I., membership in the regulatory body is 100% for practising social workers, but the association's membership rate is only one-third of those eligible.

PROFESSIONAL ASSOCIATIONS AND UNIONS

The culture in North America is such that professional associations and unions are usually two distinct and separate types of organizations: associations are based on professional affiliation, with membership cutting across all places of employment and including the front line as well as middle and senior managers. In contrast, unions are customarily composed of front-line individuals with a variety of work responsibilities, e.g., social worker, janitor, and secretary, who all work for the same employer. This dichotomy is quite different from the traditions in Europe where many of the professional associations are also unions. In Canada, only teachers and physicians use a similar model as in Europe, although many physicians and some teachers are uncomfortable with references to their associations as unions in spite of the collective bargaining responsibility carried by those associations.

In 1979–80 it was estimated that more that 50% (Todres & Lightman, 1979) or as much as 85% (Levine, 1980) of eligible social workers, i.e., those not in management, were members of a collective bargaining unit. Although these numbers were significantly higher than for the labour force as a whole, the reason was that so many social workers were employed in the public or quasi-public sectors where unionization was more prevalent than it was in the private sector. Social workers had been unionized as far back as 1930 at the Jewish Family and Child Service in Toronto, or 1943 in Saskatchewan (Levine, 1980), although most organizing occurred in the early 1970s. It is noteworthy that the experience of unionization for the profession is different in the United States, where relatively few social workers are members of a collective bargaining unit; this difference parallels the differences in organized labour generally in the two countries.

Most social workers in Canada who are unionized are members of a public sector union such as CUPE (Canadian Union of Public Employees), PSAC (Public Sector Alliance of Canada), or one of the provincial government employees' unions. With the dramatic layoffs in the public sector during the mid-1990s and the entry of many social workers into private practice, the 50–85% figures have undoubtedly decreased, but the extent of that decrease has not to the author's knowledge been charted.

Periodically, social workers struggle with the occasionally competing interests of their professional association and the directions pursued by the unions to which they belong. This occurs because the responsibility of the unions is to protect the rights of the social workers as employees, whereas professional ethics would focus on the impact of policy or action as it affects clients. While these two perspectives are often in tandem, there are times when they are not. This may occur in relation to the development of social work legislation that unions may view as elitist, or if there is a consideration to withdraw services in a strike. In the author's experience, the few occasions that find social workers on a picket line usually have developed after protracted negotiations, when there is a great deal of angst about the decision to strike, and when the social workers believe that the existing working conditions do not contribute to the best interests of the clients. The professional associations have by and large quietly supported their members who are on strike by discouraging the use of strike breakers; for example, the Ontario Association has a policy to refuse space in its positions publication for employment that serves to replace striking social workers.

OTHER AFFILIATIONS

Apart from the social work associations, many social workers are active in or belong to other organizations that further their work. Some of these are related to place of employment, others to specific fields of practice. Examples of the former include Family Service Canada, an association of family serving agencies. Affiliations related to a specific field of social work practice include the Canadian Association of Social Workers in Health Administration (CASWHA) or Social Workers in Nephrology. Other organizations such as the Association of Marriage and Family Therapy or the Canadian Association on Gerontology are not confined to one discipline, but rather focus on one area of practice.

CASWHA is an organization of social workers who are employed in an administrative capacity in health. In the past, it was composed mostly of social workers who were directors of social work in hospitals; more recently it has expanded its membership to other areas of health and to social workers who have any administrative or leadership responsibilities. During the mid-1990s CASWHA experienced a decline in membership as the move to program management in hospitals wiped out many director of social work positions; CASWHA is in the process of discussing closer affiliation with CASW in an effort to maintain a formalized focus on health issues from the perspective of social work.

CANADIAN ASSOCIATION OF SCHOOLS OF SOCIAL WORK (CASSW)

The Canadian Association of Schools of Social Work (CASSW) is a non-profit, voluntary association of university faculties, schools, and departments that offer professional education in social work. Its purpose is to advance the standards, effectiveness, and relevance of social work education and scholarship. CASSW has existed since 1967; its forerunner was the National Committee of Schools of Social Work, dating to 1948 (James & Gero, 1983). CASSW provides a vehicle for exchange among educators, and is responsible for the body that accredits the educational institutions. Although it has not always been the case, all faculties, schools, and departments in the country are currently members (1997). Membership in CASSW is available to the educational institutions but also to individual educators, alumni, and field instructors. From time to time, CASW and CASSW have worked collaboratively on projects of mutual interest such as the International Conference in 2000 and the Sector Study in 2001. CASW appoints one of its members to the accreditation arm of CASSW.

INTERNATIONAL ASSOCIATIONS
International Federation of Social Workers

The International Federation of Social Workers (IFSW) is a federated organization comprising national associations of social work from nearly 60 countries. IFSW is the successor to the International Permanent Secretariat of Social Workers, which was founded in Paris in 1928 and was active until the outbreak of World War II. The International Conference of Social Work in Paris in 1950 saw the birth of the IFSW. The organization operates in three official languages: English, French, and Spanish. Its goals are:

1. To promote social work as a profession through international cooperation, especially regarding professional values, standards, ethics, human rights, recognition, training, and working conditions;

2. To promote the establishment of national associations of social work or professional unions of social work;

3. To support the participation of social workers in social planning and the formulation of social policies nationally and internationally;

4. To encourage contacts among social workers of all countries;

5. To provide means for the discussion and exchange of ideas and experience through meetings, study visits, research projects, exchanges, publications, and other methods of communication;

6. To establish and maintain relations with international organizations relevant to social development and welfare;

7. To present and promote the point of view of the social work profession to international and national organizations carrying out social planning, social development, social action, and social welfare programs;

8. To maintain, promote, and amend if necessary the document Ethics of Social Work, Principles and Standards.

Special consultative status has been granted to IFSW by the Economic and Social Council of the United Nations and by UNICEF. As such there is official IFSW representation in New York, Vienna, and Geneva. IFSW sends representatives to United Nations NGO (Non-Government Organization) Forums such as the UN World Summit for Social Development, in Copenhagen in March 1995, and the 4th World Conference on Women, in Beijing in September 1995. At the regional level IFSW is linked to the Council of Europe, WHO Europe, and the European Union through a formal Liaison Committee. Such recognition provides the means of expressing the perspective of social workers at the world and regional levels on matters of concern to the profession and the clients it serves.

In partnership with the International Association of Schools of Social Work and the International Council on Social Welfare, IFSW publishes a quarterly journal, *International Social Work*. Its editor-in-chief is a well-known and respected Canadian, Dr. Frank Turner.

Formal membership in IFSW is granted only to national associations of social work, one per country. The Canadian Association of Social Workers has been an active member of the International Federation of Social Workers (IFSW) since 1952. In some European countries there is more than one national association, organized at times according to field of practice; in those cases, all of the national organizations must collaborate on a "co-ordinating committee," which acts as the single voice and single vote at IFSW meetings. Member organizations then are grouped into regions, roughly corresponding to continents. The exception is North America, which includes only Canada, the United States, and Mexico, with the latter not yet being a member of IFSW. CASW and NASW (the U.S. counterpart of CASW) have worked hard to encourage Mexico to become a member of IFSW, but thus far the issue is not a pressing one for our Mexican colleagues, particularly as they are not organized into one national association. CASW continues to facilitate greater activity in the Latin America and Caribbean region, which has difficulty securing the resources to maintain linkages and activity.

Each region has a vice-president who serves a two-year term. Since 1990, there has been an agreement between CASW and NASW to alternate the position of vice-president for North America between an American and a Canadian. Many Canadian social workers have served in positions of senior responsibility with IFSW: president (Gail Gilchrist James, Alberta), treasurer (Dick Ramsay and Margaret Dewhurst, both from Alberta), vice-president for North America (Gail MacDougall, Nova Scotia; Julie Foley, Ontario; and John Mould, Alberta), and elections officer (Eugenia Moreno, CASW Executive Director).

IFSW holds membership meetings biannually in conjunction with its International Conference. CASW undertook the huge task of sponsoring the bi-annual conference of IFSW in 1984 and in 2000, both in Montreal.

Although membership in IFSW is limited to national associations, the organization has developed a creative option for individuals who may wish to be involved with or support international social work. Individuals and organizations may take out a "Friends of IFSW" nominal membership, which entitles them to the newsletters, policy papers, and other publications and discounts on registration at world and regional IFSW conferences.

Sometimes the relevance of an international association may appear very remote to a frontline social worker in a small, relatively homogenous community in Canada. In some manner this is true, except that professionally we understand that political and economic activity in one part of the world may bring a dramatic impact elsewhere. Apart from that, we in the West have an obligation to link with and share resources with social activists elsewhere. Those who are involved internationally find that they learn a great deal more than could have been anticipated, as exchanges are far from one-sided. Listening to a social worker from Sri Lanka telling of his work in a refugee camp brings a new perspective to our work in Canada: it reminds us of our community development roots and it brings a humbling recognition that counselling and therapy are luxuries known only in the Western world.

CHALLENGES

Professional social work organizations face significant challenges now and in the near future. Precarious or non-existent job security and the whirlwind changes and overwhelming demands of the workplace often sap energy that might be otherwise committed to involvement in the professional association. Yet, more than ever, the professional organizations must have a strong voice to address deprofessionalization, multi-skilling, and the compelling political issues concerning social work legislation and advocacy about the vastly diminishing social safety net. Although most associations except for P.E.I. have full- or part-time staff, the work of the professional member organizations is driven by volunteers. The maintenance of an active coterie of volunteers is a daunting task, especially in provinces/territories with a relatively small number of social workers.

The Alberta organization led the way with the inaugural biannual National Conference in 1998. The hiatus of the International Conference in 2000 leaves New Brunswick with a challenge in 2002 to build on the commitment demonstrated in Edmonton to provide a conference of substance to social workers in many fields of practice. The anticipated success rests on the interest and energy of individual social workers who wish to create a truly national gathering.

The Agreement on Internal Trade provides a challenge the proportions of which the profession has, to date, rarely faced. The federated constitution of Canada has led to natural differences that reflect provincial history and tradition. While other professions technically face the same challenges, their differences in terms of basic requirements and public accountability are not nearly as wide as in social work.

The National Promotions Committee has important work to do if we are to maintain or strengthen our roles in traditional workplaces such as hospitals, but perhaps more importantly, if we are to assist in the pioneering of new venues for the profession.

The future of the profession is linked to the vitality of the professional association. It is not necessary that all of us agree on all of the priorities or all of the decisions of our association. But it is important that we belong and that we contribute, although the intensity of that will vary from time to time. Individual social workers may flourish regardless of the association, but selfhood loses some of its value without a professional community within which it is nurtured.

REFERENCES

Canadian Association of Social Workers (2001). Web site: www.casw-acts.ca.

International Association of Social Workers (1997). IFSW General Information [Online]. Available: webmaster@ifsw.org.

James, G.G. and Gero, B.M. (1983). Social work in rehabilitation teams: action and interaction, pp. 85–95. Ottawa: Department of National Health and Welfare.

Levine, G. (1980). Unionizing the professionals. *Perception.* July/August.

Mains, J.A. (1960 approximately). Through the years in CASW. Ottawa, CASW Archives.

Todres, R. and Lightman, E. (1979). Social work unions—options for the future. *The Social Worker,* *47*(2–3), 66–69.

HISTORICAL OVERVIEW AND CURRENT ISSUES IN SOCIAL WORK REGULATION[1]

Mary MacKenzie

Almost certainly, if one were to ask a person on the street what the role of the New Brunswick Association of Social Workers or the P.E.I. Social Work Registration Board is, the answer would be, "Isn't that where social workers get together to discuss common interests and concerns?" There would be few who would connect these bodies with their primary role of protecting the public interest—the body one can complain to, if as a consumer of social work service, you think you have been wronged through misconduct, negligence, or incompetence on the part of the professional. Indeed, many practising social workers do not understand the primary role of a professional regulatory body. Because there are different regulatory requirements in each province of the country, and because the issue has not always been addressed when training students, social workers as professionals have not been clear about what licensing, certification, or registration is about. Depending upon the jurisdiction in which the social worker is practising, any one of these terms may be used. So what do these terms mean? Basically, they each represent a document that signifies that the social worker has acquired specific knowledge, skills, and abilities, and has achieved a level of competence in his or her profession. Licensing, certification, or registration signifies to the public that they are protected from obtaining services from an unqualified person. It also signifies that the professional is required to abide by a code of ethics and standards of practice and that he or she may be disciplined for non-adherence to these or for other professional misconduct. Within the professions, these terms also imply a requirement for ongoing upgrading of educational qualifications to ensure the continuing competency of the professional.

[1] The author would like to thank the following individuals who, through long telephone conversations, contributed greatly to the development of this chapter: Bruce Cooper, Harold Beals, Karen Blakely, Clark Brownlee, Frank Bulger, Gayle Gilchrist James, Josette Losier, Shannon McCorquodale, Suzanne McKenna, Bruce MacPherson, René Pagé, Geoff Pawson, Gael Storey, and Bernie Zaharik.

ORIGIN OF REGULATION

From discussion with representatives of the profession from across the country, it would appear that self-regulation has evolved as the profession has evolved. The Canadian Association of Social Workers has provided a presence for social workers for many years at both the national and international level. In its early years the CASW was represented in several provinces through local chapters. These chapters eventually developed into provincial associations and it is from these associations that the need for regulation was identified and promoted. It was seen as necessary to outline the specific criteria for entrance into the profession and for ensuring ongoing training, and to develop a process for investigating complaints and imposing discipline. Social work as a self-regulating profession is still in its infancy. Legislation, where it exists, is unique to each province. There is much diversity across the country. A review of the situation in each province will indicate this more clearly.

The Newfoundland Association of Social Workers was formed in 1969. A small group of concerned and dedicated social workers worked for several years with the goal of obtaining a social work act. At least three attempts during the 1970s resulted in no legislation until 1979, when a Registration Act was passed (Gowanlock, 1986). However, this Act did not come into effect as the government did not appoint the members of the Board of Registration as required. Also, government appeared to be questioning the need for regulation (could employers not control the practice and standards of their employees?) and suspected that the profession was interested more in elitism than in regulating its members. As well, the Newfoundland Association of Social Workers, who until this time had accepted only BSWs or MSWs into their association, decided to allow others without credentials but who were practising in the field, to become members. This gave little credence to the title "social worker." This action angered and created division among members of NASW. As a result of these divisions and also because of lack of agreement between government social workers and labour unions, the act was never fully implemented (Gowanlock, 1996).

The revelation from the Mount Cashel Orphanage, where young boys were abused by their caregivers, was the crisis that created an awareness among government, social workers, and the public of the need for accountability for those providing service to some of our most vulnerable members of society. The NASW and the government jointly formed a Board of Registration to oversee the drafting of a new Act. A few years later, in 1992, the Social Workers Association Act was passed, granting control of title and practice to the profession. The Newfoundland-Labrador Association of Social Workers was established to implement and carry out the provisions of the Act (Cooper, 1996).

The Nova Scotia Association of Social Workers began in the 1940s with a small group of five members. At that time they were a branch of the Canadian Association of Social Workers. The N.S. Association of Social Workers became an incorporated body when the Social Workers' Act was passed in 1963. This Act provided for a voluntary registration of social workers, a governing body to investigate complaints and impose sanctions on those who were registered, and a process for appeal to a County Court Judge.

The N.S. Social Workers' Act of 1963 provided the beginnings of self-regulation. It remained virtually unchanged until 1993. However, as early as 1972, the Association began to see the need for more accountability within the profession and in 1974 brought to the membership the idea of licensing. Licensing of social workers under the umbrella of health professions was considered in the late 1970s, but was dropped when the government abandoned the concept as a possibility for self-regulating professions. In 1983, and again in 1986, the membership endorsed the concept of strengthening the Act "to reflect greater protection to the public" and to establish "mandatory registration as the first goal" (Nova Scotia Association of Social Workers, 1993, 7). Draft legislation was worked on in 1987 and amendments submitted to government in 1988; however, these were not brought forward to the legislature. At this point, there was recognition that both Nova Scotia's neighbouring provinces, New Brunswick and Prince Edward Island, had passed acts requiring mandatory registration and control of the title "social worker" and "registered social worker." The Association proceeded in this direction as well, confident that the government would support the move. Strategizing and drafting new legislation began in earnest and in 1993 the Social Workers' Act was passed. This Act provided a definition of social work practice and control of the title social worker, made clear the educational qualifications and professional experience required to register, established a process for handling complaints and imposing discipline, and established a process for "grandfathering in" those in social work practice who did not have a social work degree. An unusual provision, compared to other provinces, was the establishment in the legislation of a "registered social work candidate"—that is, a person who has acquired a professional social work degree but who has not yet had two years experience under the supervision of a registered social worker. The proclamation of this Act gives "the profession ... the statutory provisions that will hold it responsible and accountable for its standards of practice" in Nova Scotia and ensures that "the public at all times receives the services of ... competent, licensed social workers of high ethical standards" (NSASW, 1993, 12).

The Prince Edward Island Association of Social Workers began discussing the need for a social work act in the early 1980s. The concern arose out of Association members in various workplaces seeing untrained people providing social work services, as well as untrained people calling themselves social workers. It is not clear whether the concern was over the status of the profession being eroded or a concern that the public might be receiving substandard service. There was debate over whether such a small group of professionals could sustain a regulatory function and still have a stable base for an association. At one point, there was a recommendation that a voluntary college be formed that would carry the regulatory function but come under the auspices of the Association, similar to what had happened in Ontario a few years before. At the time, the general membership of the Association did not recognize the need for protection of the public. Despite this, a small committed group continued to work toward the goal of a Social Work Act. In 1985 the Leader of the Opposition stated that, if elected, his government would support legislation to regulate the profession of social work. This was confirmed when the government was elected and, two years later, in 1988, the Social Work Act was proclaimed. This Act granted control of title, control of practice, a mandatory registration in order to practice, a process for investigating complaints and imposing discipline, and an obligation on employers to employ only registered social workers in social work positions. The legislation also provided for two separate and distinct bodies—the Registration Board to regulate the profession and the Association to promote the interests of the profession.

A private members' bill in 1965 in New Brunswick, entitled An Act to Incorporate the New Brunswick Association of Social Workers, was the first serious attempt to have a registration process, and control of the title "Registered Social Worker/Travailleur Social Enregistré." This Act provided for voluntary registration, gave a committee of examiners the right to set up membership criteria—including the right to develop entrance examinations—and required proof of a social work degree and references. Initially only MSWs were admitted as members, but in 1977 a by-law change allowed BSWs or an approved equivalent (dependent upon courses taken and social work experience gained) to be admitted. Few members registered; also, it became evident that although the title "registered social worker" was protected, people employed in this area were using the unprotected title of social worker (Gowanlock, 1986). Much work was done on reviewing the licensing issue in the early 1980s, and changes to the Act received second reading in the Legislative Assembly. However, strong opposition from the union, which had as its members untrained persons working in social work positions, caused the amendments to go on hold.

The opposition was based on the fact that there was no grandfathering clause in the Act. The idea of including a grandfathering clause was later supported by the membership of the Association in New Brunswick. Lobbying for new legislation continued at the political level by the members, potential members, and educators in social work programs. The government at the time seemed to support the idea of regulation and even considered omnibus legislation ("A Health Discipline Act"), which would include the profession of social work. This omnibus legislation did not proceed, but in 1988 new legislation, An Act to Incorporate the New Brunswick Association of Social Workers, was passed. This Act incorporated a number of changes: control of practice and control of title were gained, registration became mandatory, and the N.B. Association of Social Work became responsible for the regulatory function. As well, a clause in the Act allowed for "grandfathering" into the Association those working in social work positions, provided they met established criteria. The Act was proclaimed in January of 1989 and the New Brunswick Association of Social Workers began the work of implementing the Act.

The history of organized social work in Quebec goes back to the 1920s, with an English chapter of CASW formed as early as 1927. By the mid-1950s, Quebec social workers were affiliated into three chapters of the Canadian Association of Social Workers. Shortly thereafter, these chapters became a provincial association. In 1960, a private members' bill created a professional corporation. The goals of the corporation included initiating a regulatory function, maintaining high professional standards, and developing and unifying the profession (Desautels, 1984).

In 1973, the National Assembly of Quebec passed a law called "Code des Professions" (Professional Code), which set up a process for regulating professions in Quebec. It came into effect in February of 1974. Under this legislation some professions, including social work, received "reserved title" status (previously referred to as "control of title"); other professions gained "reserved title and a reserved field of practice." The "Code des Professions" details the role and responsibilities of the Ordre professionnel des travailleurs sociaux du Québec and other professional bodies, the primary role being that of "protecting individual clients' interests and the public welfare" (Gowanlock, 1986). A government-appointed Professions' Board oversees the work and functioning of each professional order, ensuring that each has a code of ethics, a process for handling complaints and discipline, and an inspection committee for random reviews of the practice of its members. Registration is not mandatory and will likely continue to be this way until there are changes made to all the professions in Quebec who have "reserved title" status. The Ordre professionnel des travailleurs sociaux du Québec, with four thousand members, currently has the largest number of registered social workers of any province.

In Ontario, as elsewhere in Canada, the idea for social work to become a self-regulating profession arose out of the Ontario Association of Social Workers, beginning in the 1960s. It was recognized that there was a need for legislation to control the title "registered social worker" (Mertins-Kirkwood, 1991). Over the next several years, attempts were made to work with the ministries of social and family services to develop legislation that was consistent with the goal of protecting the public. This was a prerequisite. If the public was not protected nor had its interest served then there was no need for the legislation. Other points to be addressed were: Who should be included under the title "social worker"? What would be the impact of legislation on those who were already practising in the field without the required qualifications? Could people be registered without belonging to a professional association? How specifically would an act control and hold accountable those who were guilty of malpractice or misconduct? (Mertins-Kirkwood, 1991). Strategies to deal with issues were developed, but no legislation for regulating social work was forthcoming. Despite the lack of legislation, in 1982, the Ontario Association of Social Workers passed a by-law that formed the Ontario College of Certified Social Workers. This body initiated voluntary certification among social workers. The mandate of the Ontario College of Certified Social Workers is to "provide a forum for public complaints against certified social workers, provide for and enforce disciplinary actions against the social worker, develop standards of practice for the profession and ensure ongoing competence of social workers" (Mertins-Kirkwood, 1991).

Throughout 1985 and onwards, the Ontario College of Certified Social Workers and the Ontario Association of Professional Social Workers developed a joint initiative, called Project Legislation, to pursue a strategy for developing legislation to make social work a self-governing profession in that province. Despite this strategy, successive governments have continued to turn down requests for legislation. The Ontario College continues to govern those who voluntarily register, while still pursuing the legislation which would enable them to extend their mandate to all those practising social work in Ontario.

The Province of Manitoba was one of the first provinces to obtain legislation. In 1966, the Manitoba Association of Social Workers contacted a member of the legislature to introduce to the House a private members' bill—an Act to Incorporate the Manitoba Institute of Registered Social Workers. This Act provided for two separate bodies: the Institute and the Association. The Act gave to social workers the right to protect the title "registered social worker." Control of practice was not included, nor was registration made compulsory. For those who voluntarily registered, they were able to use the title "registered social worker," and the Institute was given the power to discipline those professionals who were found to be in violation of the Code of Ethics or guilty of unprofessional conduct. No amendments have been made to the legislation since 1966. Those involved in the administration of the Act have attempted to have changes incorporated into the legislation, including mandatory registration, changes to the complaint and discipline procedures, and the ability to set a baseline standard of practice for all those employed in social work practice. The government ministry responsible for the regulation of social work has requested that the Institute and the Association come together as one organization, that this body ensure that the majority of practising social workers become members, and that steps be taken to ensure that those untrained people currently practising social work become trained (Brownlee C., telephone interview November 22, 1996).

The Manitoba Law Reform Commission's Report (MLRC) on Regulating Professions and Occupations (1994) has affected the request for changes to the 1966 Act. Recommendation 9 in this Report says, "The traditional occupation-based approach to delineating scopes of practice should be replaced by a task-based model of occupational regulation in which tasks and services are regulated, rather than practitioners or occupations"

(MLRC, 31). This recommendation, if carried out, would divide the profession into two or more groups according to the task performed, with the idea that some tasks might require licensing/certification and other tasks might not. For the social work community, it is hard to imagine an area of social work practice that would not need to be regulated. Indeed, there is an acknowledgement among those practising that the vast majority of social work service is provided to vulnerable people who deserve protection and the right to have their complaints about incompetent or unethical practice heard and acted upon if valid. Another concern arising from this recommendation is this: Could a social worker who was found guilty of unethical behaviour while working in a regulated area of practice then move to an unregulated area of practice and continue to deal with clientele who, although less vulnerable than the first group, are still vulnerable? As a result of this and other issues, the government has essentially put on hold any changes to the Act that governs social work practice in Manitoba. The Institute and the Association have been functioning and are continuing to function as one body. This will likely remain the case until the government makes a commitment to major changes in the regulation of all professions in Manitoba.

Saskatchewan's first organized social workers came together as a branch of CASW in the 1950s. The Registered Social Workers' Act, passed in 1967, gave the Saskatchewan Association of Social Workers the mandate to administer the legislation. This Act provided for voluntary registration and initially only permitted those with MSWs to register. A few years later, BSWs were permitted to register as well as those organizations whose employees were practising social work. The latter component proved very difficult to monitor and was withdrawn after a three-year period. However, those with a B.A. degree who were supervised by a social worker were being registered, provided they satisfied the Board of Examiners that they were doing social work or that a combination of work and related educational experience enabled the person to be competent to perform social work. This was in part an attempt to get more members in the Association and through that process to educate members to the importance of regulation of practice and continuing competence. Over the years, there was discussion on issues related to licensing, such as whether there should be one Association or an Association of Social Workers and an Institute of Social Workers (the latter to carry the regulatory function); how to define social work practice; how to develop standards of practice for each field; and how to convince practitioners, employers, unions, and politicians of the value and importance of mandatory registration and regulation (Gowanlock, 1986).

In May of 1993, new legislation, The Social Workers' Act, was passed. It was proclaimed in April 1995. Registration continues to be voluntary. There is a "grandfathering in" period, until 1998, of those who have a B.A. and are working in the field under the supervision of a social worker. The ongoing minimum qualification for entry to SASW will be a Certificate of Social Work, which is granted after completing two years of a social work program at the university level. These certificates are offered by universities with the aim of upgrading the qualifications of practitioners in the rural areas of the province. It is expected that the CSW will eventually be replaced with the BSW as the minimum requirement for registration. Saskatchewan's Association of Social Workers continues to implement the provisions of the Social Workers' Act, including the processing of complaints and imposition of discipline as required.

The Alberta Association of Social Workers began in the 1960s to look at the issue of self-regulation. In 1969, the Social Workers' Act was brought into effect, which gave the Association control of the title "registered social worker." Registration was voluntary and was targeted at those who had a social work degree and those who had no social work degree but had gained social work experience through their workplaces. Social work practice was not specifically defined at that time (Gowanlock, 1986). Through the 1970s and 1980s, there were studies within the Alberta government regarding the regulation of other professions as well as social work. A draft of the Health Occupations Act was considered but rejected by government. Revisions to the Social Workers' Act were proposed but not implemented. In 1991 a new statute, The Social Work Profession Act, was passed; it was proclaimed in September of 1995.

The Social Work Profession Act has defined "registered social worker" and provides for the restricted use of this title as well as the abbreviation of such title. Scope of practice is not defined. This Act provides for a more detailed application process to become registered, updates the complaint and discipline process, and creates a Practice Review Board, which may, on its own initiative, review the practice of any registered social worker. The Practice Review Board also may advise Council regarding standards, competence, and general practice issues arising from its review. Registration, currently voluntary, is expected to become mandatory in Alberta in 1998.

The Social Workers' Act in British Columbia was passed in 1968 and proclaimed in 1969. Two separate bodies were created—The Board of Registration for Social Workers and the British Columbia Association of Social Workers. Membership in the Association was required to become a registered social worker, and administratively the two were together. The law provided for voluntary registration and a degree in social work to become registered. A provision for "grandfathering" was also included whereby those without degrees had their experience and training evaluated, took additional social work courses, and/or were supervised by a registered social worker and through this process were granted use of the title "registered social worker." As in many of the provinces, there were significant exemptions to the restricted use of the title "social worker"; for example, a person whose job title was "social worker" and who worked for the federal or provincial government could use the title "social worker," not have a degree, nor be required to be a member of the Board of Registration for Social Workers in B.C.

Since the mid-1970s, there have been attempts to have changes made to the Social Workers' Act —specifically to have control of the title "social worker" clearly established and to have a new designation of "registered social service worker", also established. Those proposals were rejected by the government in 1980. By 1989 some amendments to the Act were made that protected the use of the title "social worker" in the private practice of social work. Control of scope of practice continued to be an issue.

Over the years, the Association and the Board of Registration have continuously moved toward more separate identities for each body—first with separate employees, then separate budgets (1980), separate offices (mid-1980s), and a separation of files (early 1990s). In 1996, the requirement to be an association member in order to be registered was dropped, making the Association and the Board of Registration completely separate entities. The Board of Registration continues to be responsible for regulating the profession.

The Social Workers' Act in B.C. is seen as an out-of-date piece of legislation. The Board of Registration has asked the B.C. government to repeal the Social Work Act and to have social workers governed under the Health Professions Act. This omnibus legislation would provide for the regulation of all the health professions under separate colleges. It is likely that a College of Social Workers will soon be formed to replace the existing Board of Registration.

This brief historical overview of each of the provinces in relationship to the regulatory function of social work shows that self-regulation as a component of the profession is evolving in much the same way that practice and professional issues have evolved. The regulatory bodies are going through growing pains, learning from one another, but beginning to show the public and government that, as a profession, we are serious about regulating ourselves. The idea of standards, accountability, and professional judgment are coming to the forefront (McCorquodale, telephone interview, February 14, 1997). There is diversity across the country and with each regulatory body being at a different stage of development there is still much work to do.

CURRENT TRENDS AND ISSUES IN REGULATION

- There is a difficulty in applying an exclusive scope of practice in social work, as social work is broad-based and shares its knowledge, skills, and areas of expertise with related disciplines. The legislation in the Atlantic provinces defines scope of practice and grants control of practice as well as control of title to the profession (Regulatory Bodies Newsletter, 1996). Experience shows that control of title is more easily regulated than control of practice. More work needs to be done in each province to assist the profession and the public in understanding scope of practice and what it is that a social worker does.

- There is discussion in some provinces about certain specific tasks being regulated, i.e., those tasks that are at most risk of causing harm to the public: for example, "marriage therapist" could become a task that is governed by regulation. The person doing marital therapy would be regulated by a specific act no matter what their professional affiliation was. The same person could work in a related area that might not be regulated. Under this model, the goal would be to regulate only those tasks that pose a high level of risk to the public. This, it is argued, is more cost-effective and efficient and has more guarantee of ensuring protection for the public than the present system (MLRC, 1994). However, the Gove Inquiry (1995) states that "the professional body must have the power to define a scope of practice and to permit only those who are qualified to engage in that practice" (Gove, 1995, vol. 2, 124). In reality, there may evolve a combination of systems; for example, in Ontario, the government requires that only certified social workers complete assessments of individuals in long-term care despite the fact that there is no legislation regulating other practice areas of social work in that province.

- Members of the profession need to become more aware of their responsibility for their practice—their accountability to the public. Going hand in hand with this are requests from members for standards of practice. The regulatory bodies have work to do in this area, i.e., to define the standards that are expected in particular areas of social work without being too limiting. Recent research suggests that the issue of professional judgment is key in being responsible for your practice and accountable to the public, and that social workers have not paid enough attention to this. "There is no comprehensive set of practice standards in place that encourage professional judgment across all program areas. The standards that do exist may be too prescriptive and undermine the move toward improving professional social work judgement" (Bryce, 1995, 49).

- With the proclamation of the Internal Trade Agreement in 1995, there is an emphasis on reducing the barriers to the mobility of social workers between provinces. Each province has to work toward reducing the factors that impede mobility and put in place policies that will facilitate the social worker who wishes to move to another jurisdiction. This has raised fears that the standard for registering/licensing social workers will be reduced in some provinces. There are two provinces who register a person as a social worker after a two-year diploma program; other provinces require a social work degree in order to be registered. Government officials maintain that the intent of the Internal Trade Agreement (AIT) was never to lower qualifications to the lowest common denominator (AIT Guidelines for meeting the obligations of the labour mobility chapter, 1996). Currently, each of the regulatory bodies across the country is exchanging information with the aim of developing consensus on this issue. However, there are many differences provincially and it will take some time to develop unity on this topic.

- There is concern that the curriculum in some schools of social work does not meet the basic standard expected of an entry-level practitioner in social work. This may indicate that the profession, through its role of regulating members, needs to work more closely with schools of social work on this issue, or it may mean that provincial or national standard exams may be set either at the entry level or if a social worker intends to establish a private practice. Ontario requires standard examinations be passed in order to become certified, and Newfoundland is proposing a similar model.

- There is ongoing tension between the regulatory arm of the profession and the academic arm. Many professors in schools of social work are not members of their regulatory body. The debate seems to centre on a couple of areas: that regulation is an attempt to control, and as such it could limit the academic freedom of professors; and that regulation is not particularly relevant to professors as students are not clients. Regulators would argue that students receive a service that is of benefit and are entitled to know that their professors are required to adhere to a code of ethics and standards (Gilchirst-James, G. telephone interview, August 19, 1997). An argument has been made that academic freedom is not limited through regulation and that academics should not use this as an excuse to avoid being accountable.

- There is a variation across the country regarding continuing education requirements for the practising social worker. This provincial variation ranges from a standard of fifteen hours over a three-year period to a higher standard of forty hours of continuing education annually. The following question arises: If I complete the minimum requirement for continuing education in a province with a low standard, am I less competent than my counterpart in a neighbouring province? Within professions there is debate about the effectiveness of continuing education as a means to ensure competency (Ehri, 1994). Would regular or random reviews of practice such as Alberta and Quebec have established, be more effective? What about peer evaluation, or interviews with clients? Although it is generally accepted that continuing education is important and necessary in any profession, there will need to be ongoing discussion and research about the positive correlation between continuing education and competency.

- There is a lack of experience in several provinces in the processing and handling of complaints. Quebec and Ontario have the most experience in this regard and have systems in place to efficiently and effectively handle complaints. In the other provinces, there are varying degrees of experience. Processes may be developed and refined as complaints come in; many complaints are not being dealt with expediently enough for all parties involved. There may be no paid staff, volunteers get weary, and experience gained is not necessarily passed on to those new to the complaints committee or council. Much of the recent regulatory legislation has not been challenged legally, so it is unknown which laws will stand up to the scrutiny of the courts. More experience in this area will lead to amendments of both legislation and processes for handling complaints.

- Traditionally, self-governing bodies have held closed or "in camera" discipline hearings. The public has criticized this, saying the profession is more concerned with protecting its own members than protecting the public. There is a movement across the country to hold open hearings and several of the provinces have already established this as standard procedure. However, there may be instances where the self-regulating body may decide it is in the public interest to maintain a closed hearing—for example, if a criminal trial is proceeding concurrently with the discipline hearing.

- Those who are in the regulatory role agree that boards and committees need to have both members of the profession and members of the public. "The use of public members is fundamental in keeping government responsible to the needs of its citizens ... citizens can help create effective and equitable regulation and influence the formation of policies from a public interest perspective" (Ehri, 1994, 6). This is also consistent with the recommendations of the report "Regulating Professions and Occupations" (1994) by the Manitoba Law Reform Commission and with recommendation 45 of the Report of the Gove Inquiry (Gove, 1995 vol. 12, 124). Boards or councils have had public representation; the move now is to have that representation increased to at least one-third of the members of discipline committees and governing bodies.

- Mediation has been introduced in the legislation of several provinces as an option in resolving a dispute between a consumer of social work service and a practitioner. Mediation is a very useful tool and can be quite effective in satisfying all parties as well as protecting the public from possible further harm. It reduces both time and cost for the parties involved. The facts of the matter can be made available to the public, thus ensuring full accountability.

- Whether the quality of social work service to the public has improved as a result of regulation has yet to be studied. The four provinces where registration is mandatory might be an area to begin this study. Research also needs to be done on how regulation affects social workers; for example, has regulation limited social workers in their role as advocates and agents of social change? Certainly, regulation should not excuse us from remaining true to our holistic approach, from continuing to strive for social change and equality and promoting the best interests of the client, whether the client is an individual or a community. Regulatory bodies would agree that these ideals are consistent with their goals, but further discussion and analysis needs to occur. Until research is done, we are not able to say specifically how regulation has influenced social work practice and whether there are other unintended results of regulation, either positive or negative.

- The impact of legislation on Native Canadians practising social work has been raised as an issue in several provinces. Some provincial governments, before they will pass legislation requiring mandatory registration, want assurance that Aboriginal workers have had appropriate opportunity to be trained. Schools of social work have been grappling with training for Native people for several years now—how to adapt social work education to suit the needs and culture of the Native student. Social work education is evolving in this area, with some failures and some successes. With regard to registration, some Native social workers regard this process as "white man's rules," as elitist and not relevant to their issues. The authority of the governing body is questioned—can they be denied the right to practice based on methods and ideology of a white culture which is not necessarily responsive to Native culture? These and other questions will need to be addressed as the process of self-regulation evolves in these provinces.

• As mentioned in the historical overview, several provinces combine the role of regulating the profession with the role of promotion and enhancement of the profession in one body, usually referred to as the association. Three provinces operate with two distinct bodies carrying out each of these functions. Those who have separate entities state that this system creates less confusion for consumers and clarifies for the public that their welfare and protection is primary. Of equal importance, though, is whether the profession can maintain these two roles in two distinct entities. Social work in itself is a demanding profession and it is difficult to recruit the many volunteers needed in order to run two organizations. Where there are paid staff, it is often financially difficult to maintain the infrastructure of two offices. As a result, some provinces are feeling the pressure of not being able to support the function generally carried by the association. This could have grave consequences for the profession. However, studies such as the Manitoba Law Reform Commission Report (1994) state clearly that it is in the public's interest that the two functions remain separate.

IMPACT OF REGULATION ON THE PROFESSION

• Where there is legislated regulation, social workers appear to have more awareness and understanding of the need for accountability in their practice. This would also apply to those workers who have voluntarily joined a regulatory body in provinces where there is not a mandatory registration requirement. Social workers have become more vigilant about adherence to standards of practice and to a code of ethics. In practice areas where there are no standards of practice, social workers are asking for guidelines to assist them in knowing they are doing what is expected of them, to assist them in being clear to their clients about process and expected outcome, and to ensure for themselves that their practice is defensible in the case of a complaint being lodged.

• Scope of practice is being examined and defined and redefined. There continues to be a dialogue about what kind of a profession social work is and what it should be. Most social workers and most schools of social work define the scope of social work in a broad-based manner to include a social reform approach to solving problems as well as the more traditional casework approach. The public's view of social work is not as all-encompassing, and many citizens are probably more familiar with the traditional casework approach. In addition, social work shares some of its areas of expertise with related disciplines, so regulating a scope of practice can be threatening to others working in human services. This aspect has created tension between some provincial governments and the profession. Some regulatory bodies have stated that they do not want an exclusive definition of social work practice.

- For the most part, employers want members to be regulated. Employers support standards of practice as they can look to standards and a code of ethics to provide guidance in social work practice areas. The individual, as well as the profession and the employer, becomes accountable. Also, during a complaint process, the employer is more willing to support those social workers who are able to demonstrate that they have adhered to standards of practice in their work.

- A Bachelor of Social Work degree from an accredited school of social work is the basic requirement for entry into the profession in the majority of provinces. It is expected that the two other provinces will eventually adopt this as a standard.

- There is a growing awareness, especially among those who are practising privately, of the connection between accountability and liability. Knowing one is liable to sanctions for violation of a code of ethics or non-adherence to professional standards, makes one scrutinize one's practice more closely. Carrying liability insurance is now more common among all practitioners; indeed, in any province where the CASW Code of Ethics (1994) has been adopted, all private practitioners are required to carry liability insurance.

- Where there is regulation of social workers, there is a social, legal, and political recognition of the profession. Other professional bodies and governments are more eager to listen to and work with social workers on a number of issues ranging from the amount of health care services needed to standards that should be sought. This enhancement of the profession is seen by some as a positive by-product of regulation.

- Continuing education is a cornerstone of regulatory legislation. This fact has helped social workers to become aware of their obligation to update their skills. Continuing education is now seen as necessary. As the information age explodes, keeping current with new ideas, therapies, practice areas, and skills in delivery is essential. Competence in social work also requires review and reflection on what one has learned; these two points together (acquiring new knowledge and reflecting on experience through reading and consultation) are key to developing an attitude of lifelong learning, an attitude which all professionals must acquire.

- Despite the provincial differences and limitations, the public is now better protected because there is, in each province, an avenue for people to complain about inadequate or inappropriate service, unethical behaviour, negligence, or professional misconduct. The awareness of the right to make a complaint has increased in part because of complaints regarding other professionals being openly discussed in the media and other public forums. The complaints against social workers' practice have increased as well and are being handled by the respective regulatory bodies. Regulators need to review and critique their work, but the profession is demonstrating to government and to the public that social work is serious about regulating itself and is committed to doing this in a fair, impartial manner.

CONCLUSION

Regulation is necessary and is consistent with where we have come from as a profession. The profession has always advocated for the right of clients to be heard, to complain and address injustices whether at a policy or a personal level. What better way to ensure standards of practice and ethical behaviour than to let clients know from the moment the provision of service has begun that they have a right to lodge a complaint (Pagé, R., telephone interview, February 12, 1997)? This is consistent with how we would advise clients to handle issues in other areas of their lives. There is a reluctance among some in the profession to accept the concept of accountability in this manner, yet it is fundamental to the core of our profession. We must practise what we preach and model the behaviour we expect of others.

REFERENCES

British Columbia Association of Social Workers (1991). Professional regulation of social work in British Columbia: the issues and options. Vancouver: unpublished.

Bryce, K. (1995). The regulation of social work services in B.C.—research project for the Gove Inquiry into child protection. British Columbia: unpublished.

Cooper, B. (1996). *Newfoundland Labrador association of social workers exam implementation paper*. Newfoundland: Newfoundland Labrador Association of Social Workers.

Desautels, M. (1984). La Corporation au fils des ans. *Intervention, 69*, 31–42.

Ehri, D. (1994). *Regulating health care professionals: an overview* (Resource briefs 94-4). Council on licensure, enforcement and regulation.

Gove, T.J. (1995). *Report of the Gove Inquiry into child protection—Matthew's Legacy, Vol. 2.* British Columbia Ministry of Social Services.

Government of Canada (1995). *Agreement on internal trade: meeting the obligations of the labour mobility chapter*. Ottawa: Queen's Printer.

Gowanlock, G.J. (1986). *Social work regulation in Canada: 1926–1982*. Ontario: Canadian Association of Social Workers.

MacDonald, J.B. and Millar H. (1994). A background report on membership in BCASW and its relationship to registration. Vancouver: unpublished.

Manitoba Law Reform Commission (1994). *Regulating professions and occupations*. Winnipeg: Office of the Queen's Printer.

Mertins-Kirkwood, B. (1991). *An overview of the historical development of project legislation and a brief analysis*. (BSW student practicum, York University, 1991).

National Association of Social Workers (1973). *Encyclopedia of social work*. Washington: Boyd Printing Co. Inc.

Nova Scotia Association of Social Workers: licensure committee (1993). *Background paper proposed social workers' act*: Halifax: unpublished.

Saskatchewan Association of Social Workers (1996). SASW: the long road to the social workers' act. *The Social Worker, 64*, Ottawa. Myropen Publications Ltd.

Social Work Regulatory Bodies (1996). *The regulation of social work in Canada—an information sharing newsletter*. Newfoundland: Newfoundland Labrador Association of Social Workers.

Toth, S.A. (1994). Regulatory guidelines and principles for protecting the public interest. Speaking notes to C.L.E.A.R. Conference, April 30, 1994: unpublished.

Trebilcock, M.J. (1994). Critical issues in the design of governance regimes for the professions. Toronto: unpublished.

MEDIATION IN SOCIAL WORK PRACTICE

Luke J. Fusco

INTRODUCTION

Disagreements, disputes, and conflicts are present in all human lives. Most of these are interpersonal. The social systems involved can be as basic as parent-child, intimate partners, other family members, or as large as nations, cultural groups, or ethnic communities. Social workers may be involved in all of these situations.

Conflict is part of human experience. Professional social workers see these disputes in agencies, ministries, and other organizations where they are employed. Wherever and whenever disagreements arise, they will have an effect on both the working of the system and the relationship between or among the individuals in the system.

It is unrealistic to expect to eliminate disagreement from human relationships. A more productive focus is on how these disputes are addressed and resolved. People often say they will agree to disagree. This outcome recognizes differences, makes no judgment, permits the individuals to move on, and preserves their relationship. It provides an ending to the dispute without deciding the issue itself. People have different views on many things but continue to work together effectively and live together happily.

Unresolved conflict can also lead to disruptive, sometimes tragic, and even fatal consequences. Violence in families and communities, between individuals and nations, is reported daily in the media. Less dramatically, the consequences of festering conflict can make family life, professional endeavours, and organizational efforts unpleasant and unproductive. Conflict requires the investment of energy, energy which could be better utilized in supporting personal, professional, or organizational development.

The ability to assist others who are involved in a dispute is a valuable skill for a social worker. William Schwartz (1961) wrote about the mediating function of social group work. The aim was to assist people in managing the tension between their individual needs and the expectations of the group and rules of society. Schwartz and later Shulman (1999) described the mediating role as a core social work intervention.

Within the profession, mediation is often associated with separation and divorce (Irving & Benjamin, 1987, 1995; Landau et al., 2000). Indeed social workers do mediate in circumstances when couples separate, especially when minor children are involved. Mediation can also be utilized in other family situations. For example, in adolescent-parental conflicts a social worker employing mediation principles can help the family to more successfully include the growing teenager's demand for independence and autonomy with the continuous parental requirement of involvement and authority.

Decisions about living arrangements for elderly grandparents or parents also revolve around the issues of autonomy, safety, and control. A skilled social work mediator can work with elders and their families as they make these important decisions (Parsons & Cox, 1997).

Mediation is used in child protection (Barsky & Trocmé, 1998), adoption (Etter, 1997) and in other fields of social work micro-system practice. Some of the disputes are within families, others can be between clients or their care-givers and the agencies attempting to provide services. Usually there are no rights or wrongs in these conflicts. There is, however, an impasse. People are stuck, decisions are postponed, and often there appears to be no resolution possible. The intervention of an impartial third party can be of assistance, especially when decisions must be made.

Community mediation includes a broad range of differences and conflicts which arise at the community level. Barking dogs and loud music are common factors in neighbourhood arguments and tensions. Some community disputes are more related to community development issues. Differences within a community and conflicts between a community and local government over schools, law enforcement, recreational facilities, bus service, garbage collection, and other social or physical environment issues can be addressed and resolved through mediation (Kaminsky and Yellott, 1997).

Victim-offender mediation (Umbreit, 1995), social policy mediation (Stamato and Jaffe, 1991), and cultural or ethnic conflict mediation (Duryea and Grundison, 1993) are other arenas where social workers are able to apply mediation principles and skills.

In the rest of this chapter, the terms *negotiation* and *mediation* are described. Three models of mediation also are presented. Examples from social work practice are used to show how the models can be applied by professional social workers. Included in the descriptions and discussions are basic mediation interventions.

NEGOTIATION AND MEDIATION

Negotiation is part of almost all relationships. Most of our daily negotiations are informal, including, for example, who is going to do which tasks at home or at work. People compromise, go along, insist, trade off, and engage in other activities all designed to reach an agreement. We expect those we live or work with to be reasonable and fair and we reciprocate with a similar attitude. Pineapple on your half of the pizza, not on mine; at work we each do the cleaning up on a weekly rotating basis. Life goes smoothly.

In commercial situations prices for goods and services are negotiated at car dealers, flea markets, garage sales, banks, and over the phone or Internet. What characterizes all these transactions, whether they are about pizzas, a used car, or an interest rate is that the people who are involved speak for themselves directly. Sometimes representatives such as lawyers or agents do the actual negotiating. In those cases, the representatives speak as if they were the person they represent. No other roles are identified and no other people are present in these kinds of negotiations. In labour-management collective bargaining, teams of negotiators meet with legal counsel and other experts if needed. Teams of people are also part of the process during business, financial, international, and other complex negotiations. But normally only one person on each side conducts his or her part of the negotiation.

Mediation is a facilitation of a negotiation process. Usually the parties to the negotiation have been unsuccessful in their efforts to reach an agreement. They seek the assistance of an impartial third party, a mediator, to assist them in settling their outstanding issues. In its purest, most benign form, mediation is unintrusive and suggestive but not directive. However, there is a continuum along which a mediator may become increasingly active in the negotiation process if the parties are unable to make progress. Sometimes the mediator has been hired as a mediator-arbitrator. If mediation does not lead to an agreement after an agreed-upon time period, the mediator arbitrates and renders a judgment. Social workers rarely do this kind of mediation.

Barsky (2000) describes four approaches to negotiation: power-based, rights-based, interest-based, and transformative. The first two are not concerned with the relationship between the parties in dispute. Focusing on interests—yours and the other person's or group's—supports an empathic view of the differences. A transformative approach stresses the promotion of empowerment and recognition between the parties. Increased recognition and greater control over one's life will enable the parties to negotiate more successfully.

INTEREST-BASED NEGOTIATION

In their classic work, *Getting to Yes* (first published in 1981 and now in its third edition), Fisher, Ury, and Patton (1997) present the principles of interest-based negotiation. They provide an approach to negotiation which is useful to social workers, is practical, and is informed by values consistent with those of the social work profession.

Within the range of social work practice at the micro, mezzo, and macro levels it is almost always the case that the continuing functional relationship of the people involved is an important goal. A social worker may be negotiating directly with a client, colleague, agency, or ministry. It is also likely that a worker will assist others in negotiating. In these circumstances, the application of mediation skills and the education of the parties about an interest-based approach to their negotiations can be of assistance in reaching an agreement.

Interest-based (or principled) negotiation is built on a sequence of fundamental parts:

1. Focus on Interests, Not Positions,
2. Invent Options for Mutual Gain,
3. Use Objective Criteria,
4. Improve Communications and the Negotiating Relationship,
5. Consider Alternatives, and
6. Obtain Commitments.

1. Focus on Interests, Not Positions

Positions are inflexible demands. A person insisting on maintaining a position defines that outcome as the only acceptable one. Obviously, if someone else holds a different, perhaps even contradictory position, the result is an apparent impasse. If the positions are defined in quantifiable terms, the individuals may bargain or compromise until they reach a number which is mutually acceptable. Neither side has achieved its original position.

In social work, elderly family members may state they will never move from their own home while the adult children insist that their parents need to be in a nursing home. A community group states that they will never allow a group home for young offenders to be established in their neighbourhood even though an agency has announced an opening date. During separation agreement negotiations, both parents may demand sole custody of their children. These positions are mutually exclusive.

In examining interests, you look beyond the position. The parties explore their needs, desires, concerns, and fears. Why does the elderly parent insist on residing at home; why do the children insist on a nursing home? The interests involve autonomy, independence, and self-determination on the one side, and safety, security, and assurance on the other. The community group is worried about safety, noise, and neighbourhood image. Both parents want to make sure they maintain an active role in their children's lives. They may also be trying to deprive their estranged partner of the same role mainly because they want nothing more to do with that person.

Interests are the answers to the questions: Why do you want that and what scares you? Examining interests broadens the arena within which people can find outcomes which meet everyone's needs sufficiently. The result is that none of the parties obtains exactly what they wanted but everyone is satisfied and believes the outcome is fair. During the process, each person must also consider the other person's interests.

2. Invent Options for Mutual Gain

It is precisely at this point that the negotiations can focus on options which provide mutual gain. Be creative. At this stage no one is making a specific proposal. People are brainstorming. No idea is eliminated. Which options allow for everyone's interests to be included? How can the more promising options be modified to make them acceptable? Keeping the other party's interests in mind as well as your own helps to fashion options which might work.

In the case of the elderly parent, adequate home supports might allow for a continuation of the current living arrangements. The family could also begin planning for a time when a move will be required. They can begin looking now instead of waiting for a crisis. The people in the neighbourhood where the announced group home will be located can meet with the staff and the residents to address their concerns. A number of positive changes on both sides might result from these meetings. Recognizing that your partner's need to be a parent is essentially the same as your need can lead to a mutually satisfactory separation agreement where both parents remain actively involved in their children's lives. The importance of cooperative parenting becomes apparent during the negotiations.

Few ideas are totally outrageous. The community group representative may say in frustration that the neighbourhood will accept the group home if they can have final approval on who resides there. The agency would not agree to that but might respond with ideas for involving people in the community on a group home advisory board or as volunteers. Faced with an elderly parent or grandparent's insistence on remaining in his or her own house, the adult child or grandchild may suggest in exasperation that the whole family could move into the house. That seemingly facetious comment could lead to a discussion of options which provide security and autonomy for the family elder. Examples could be community supports, a separate apartment within the child's home, or a retirement home nearby.

Once interests are identified, there are many more options available with almost infinite variations. The list of interests becomes the point of reference against which options are considered. The negotiations become a process of refining various options to see if a plan can be devised which satisfies all of the interests of the parties, or at least the most important ones. The initial positions provide only two outcomes, neither being acceptable to both sides, people, or groups.

3. Use Objective Criteria

We are familiar with objective criteria when property values must be determined. How much is a car, house, computer, or dining room set worth? If the potential buyer and seller cannot agree they can ask for an independent expert to assess the value. During marital break-ups, houses, furnishings, possessions, and pensions must be valued in order to divide property fairly and equitably. In making decisions involving people where precise values are either inappropriate or impossible it is still possible to use objective or relatively objective criteria. For example, in the situation with the elderly family member who is adamant about remaining in his or her home, a gerontologist could be asked to evaluate the circumstances and provide an opinion. Similarly, courts often utilize the services of an expert on child development to advise them on issues of custody when the parents cannot agree.

When the outcome of the application of objective criteria is an exact figure (or an average of two or three appraisals) the parties can agree in advance to accept that result. If an expert opinion is sought, one of several situations could develop. The family or court could simply follow the advice. Often, however, one person or side will feel disgruntled with this third-party decision. Another use of this opinion is to incorporate it into the negotiations from that point on. If a mediator is involved, he or she would use that opinion as a point of reference. The gerontologist might say that the elder is quite capable of some life tasks but beginning to have difficulty with others. This professional opinion assists the family in adjusting their options to fit the assessed needs.

Similarly, if a child expert notes the importance of young children having frequent contact with both parents, a modified parenting plan can emerge. Neither parent is yielding to the other; both are acting in their children's best interest.

Neighbourhood groups frequently resist the incorporation of group homes or low rent housing in their community. Objections are expressed in predictions of doom for the area and its residents. Examining the experiences of other neighbourhoods in similar circumstances will provide information to the local people and the agency about outcome and process. How have things turned out in reality? What steps were taken which assisted everyone involved with the necessary transitions and adjustments? This information will also contain guidance about what actions to avoid. Objective criteria then can facilitate the negotiations or mediation process as well as being the basis for a final determination.

4. Improve Communications and the Negotiating Relationship

The intervention of social workers as facilitators or mediators almost always means that the clients will continue to have some kind of relationship after the issues are settled. It is fair to say then that the quality of that ongoing relationship is as important as any agreement the parties may reach. The social worker's role is to assist with communication and help to improve the negotiating relationship. Under these circumstances, our professional interventions should seek to enhance the individuals' ability to interact and resolve differences. No agreement will last very long if the parties to the agreement are actively hostile to each other or cannot communicate in a constructive manner.

Barsky (2000) identifies listening, questioning, and making statements as fundamental communication skills (45). Social work mediators can conceptualize a concurrent process of helping the individuals, families, groups, communities, or organizations to resolve their outstanding disagreements, conflicts, or disputes, and learn how to communicate more effectively as they work through the issues. Good social work intervention results in the worker becoming redundant. The clients gain the necessary skills and resources to manage future difficulties.

Enhancing the clients' negotiating relationship builds on their improved communication skills and helps them to develop probably the most important skills they will need in the future: problem-solving and conflict resolution. Ideally, people like each other and get along. Social workers work with people who must interact but may not particularly like each other. If separated parents, competing agencies, unfriendly co-workers, and antagonistic community groups have a process they can use when they are required to meet, they can achieve a successful outcome in their negotiations. Fisher and Brown (1988) suggest building the negotiating relationship on six principles:

1. Remain rational in the face of others' emotions,

2. Always try to understand the other party's ideas and feelings,

3. Ask both parties' opinions before making any decision that affects them,

4. Be honest; don't try to deceive,

5. Use persuasion, not coercion, and

6. Accept the other people and their concerns. (38)

5. Consider Alternatives

In interest-based negotiation, it is important for the people involved to keep alternatives in mind. Negotiation in the first place and continuing to negotiate at any time are alternatives. Not negotiating or stopping the process are also alternatives. Negotiators can identify what they will do if the other side won't negotiate or if they are unable to reach agreement. Each side should consider its best alternative to a negotiated agreement (BATNA) and calculate the other side's BATNA as well.

Going to court, quitting, moving away, civil disobedience, calling the media, and striking or locking out are examples of alternatives to negotiation. If you have a better alternative and the others do not then you might not want to negotiate. In evaluating either party's BATNA you need to consider the consequences of using that alternative. There is usually a cost; monetary, personal, and relational. Are these acceptable costs? When the other people say they are going to employ an alternative it may assist if you point out the consequences of doing so.

6. Obtain Commitments

Obtaining commitments appears straightforward. Everyone has agreed on the issues that were in dispute. You have settled; it's over. Well, not quite. Reaching agreement while sitting in a room has to translate into an implementation plan. Commitment must include a detailed discussion about what steps each person or group will take within an explicit time period. Who will pick up and transport the children on which days at what time? How often will the nurse visit and who will communicate to whom? Who will convey information to the neighbourhood organization by what date? Can the opening of the group home be postponed until there is another meeting?

Commitments are about effectively carrying out the terms of the agreement. It is good negotiation practice not to rush into an agreement and its requisite promises. This is especially true when the ability of the people to relate effectively in the future is at least as important as the agreement, if not actually more important.

TRANSFORMATIVE NEGOTIATION

Bush and Folger (1994) describe what they term *transformative mediation*. Barsky (2000) adapts their approach to negotiation (85–90). In either situation, the process is based on promoting empowerment of and recognition by each person or group. A social worker working with a client, especially when there are issues in dispute, may help the client to negotiate more effectively using a transformative approach. This model can be useful in agencies where the worker has legal power. (Fusco, 1983)

Individuals, families, groups, and communities seeking service or mandated under court or regulatory orders often find themselves at odds with their worker and the agency. A power-based response by the social worker is one approach. Another is to help clients to increase their ability to make their case and achieve their goals (empowerment), and to demonstrate empathy and understanding (recognition) during the process.

Clearly, there are times when directives must be given. Child protection and safety are the obvious examples. However, often there is time. Nothing must be decided immediately. Helping clients to describe their goals, become aware of all the options they control, and realize the internal and external resources available to them are ways that workers can promote empowerment in those clients. Assisting clients to negotiate more effectively is another aspect of empowerment.

Recognition is based on empathy and understanding. It is a basic tenet of social work practice. Conveying regard and respect for those with whom we relate creates an atmosphere where problems can be addressed and more likely be resolved. There is an idealistic tone in this discussion of transformative negotiation, which is consistent with good social work practice. This model, more than others, is far less interested in the agreement and much more focused on the enhancement of the people involved in the negotiation. It is not appropriate in all situations. Whenever building strength is one of the intervention goals, transformative negotiation may apply.

MEDIATION

It is not possible to understand mediation without first understanding negotiation. The preceding section has included a description of two approaches to negotiation. When the parties cannot proceed on their own, when they are at an impasse, they may ask for the assistance of an impartial third party, a mediator. I am less concerned about writing definitions of mediation, and more interested in describing activities, roles, and objectives that pertain to it.

Self-determination informs good mediation as it does most good social work practice. The parties to the negotiation are the important actors, not the mediator. Social work mediators help by assisting the clients to reach an agreement which will work and by focusing throughout the process on what kind of relationship they want in the future. Mediation can be done quite well without prior social work training. However, when the parties' ongoing relationship is important, social work mediators have the skills and knowledge to balance substantive issues with working relationships.

In formal mediation, a social worker will be labelled as a mediator and employed as one in a particular situation. Family and community mediation are the two most common areas for a social work mediator to be employed. But any social worker or other helping professional will find that generic mediation skills can be useful in a variety of professional contexts.

Three models of mediation are described below. Formal mediation may follow a particular model more rigorously than when social workers use mediation techniques in their practice.

INTEREST-BASED MEDIATION

The mediator helps the parties to use interest-based negotiation. Following the six sequential parts of negotiations focusing on interests, described above, the mediator asks the parties to list the interests which underlie their positions. It is useful to write these in such a way that they can be displayed during the subsequent sessions. Either party or the mediator can more easily make reference to the lists of interests.

Initially, people can see where there is either a convergence or overlapping of interests. "You both want the same thing" or "I see similarities in the two lists." People begin to explore possibilities because they are not defending a position. It is a more cooperative process which allows gains for everyone.

The mediator does as little as possible. The more the parties do on their own, the better. Mediators can guide, remind, suggest, and point out. The process should be moving back to the clients. Once interests are explored, refined, and possibly put in priority order, the participants can begin to create options.

Another key role for a mediator following the interest-based model is to get the parties to examine their alternatives to negotiating, especially their BATNAs. These provide a structure of reality around the process.

THERAPEUTIC MEDIATION

This model combines a kind of family therapy approach with mediation. (Irving & Benjamin, 1987; 1995). Therapy is not an objective. In the case of child custody negotiations the process is intended to assist the family as it makes the transition from being together to existing apart while retaining aspects of a family. There is a balance between reaching an agreement, ultimately a legal document which defines rights and obligations, and supporting the family, especially the parents, in thinking about and planning how they will carry on the family business of nurturing the children.

The agreement itself becomes the first written statement about the times the children will be with each parent. Events may occur almost immediately, which will require changes in the plan for a week, a month, or permanently. The family may return to mediation to re-negotiate the plan. They should do so if they are unable to agree on their own. Hopefully, they can.

The therapeutic portion of this model envisions a growth process focusing on the parents as managers of the child-rearing function of their family. The adults have decided to resolve their personal differences by ending their intimate relationship. Therapeutic mediation helps these same people to retain or form an effective parental relationship. A flexible agreement comes from such a relationship.

Therapeutic Family Mediation (TFM) has four phases: assessment, pre-mediation, mediation, and follow-up. During assessment, the mother and father are seen separately. They are assessed for their readiness to begin mediation. Some people enter mediation immediately.

Others begin the process after a period of pre-mediation. In some situations, there are clear contraindications for mediation: overwhelming stress, rage, and uncontrolled conflict; ongoing family violence; and other evidence of extreme dysfunction (Irving & Benjamin, 1995, 172–173).

Pre-mediation is basically a treatment phase. During the assessment, the client and mediator have determined that while they eventually will be able to negotiate, the current state of their relationship makes success unlikely. They may work with the mediator, other counsellors, or both until they are ready to negotiate directly.

The mediation or facilitated negotiation, if successful, will result in an agreement. A social work mediator may assist only with matters involving the parenting plan (custody and access) or may be involved in a more comprehensive mediation including spousal support, child support, and division of property. The wishes of the clients, the complexity of the issues, and the mediator's training will determine that decision. Follow-up occurs approximately six weeks after the agreement is reached. It is intended as a check on how the plan is working. Subsequent contact will vary according to the family's functioning.

While primarily a model applied to separation and divorce mediation, therapeutic mediation can be adapted to any system where the conflictual parties need to maintain a positive working relationship in the future. A creative mediator may use the principles of this model with communities and organizations.

TRANSFORMATIVE MEDIATION

By now, you may have noted a continuum among these three approaches, as they have been presented. Transformative mediation is the model least concerned with the actual agreement (Lang, 1996). Instead, the emphasis is on individual empowerment and recognition, and social harmony and understanding. The assumption underlying the approach is that if people gain greater self-esteem, an enhanced sense of their own strengths, and more acknowledgment of their abilities, they will have the capacities to negotiate a favourable outcome on their own. The focus of the mediator is on a humanistic change process. The agreement then will take care of itself.

MEDIATION PRINCIPLES AND INTERVENTIONS

Forms of mediated dispute resolution have been practised in all parts of the world for thousands of years (Moore, 1996, 20–40). It is not a new or even a recent idea. Generally, humans have been guided by a desire to preserve family, tribal, or community harmony while attempting to settle disputes. The higher ground was enduring relationships, social stability, and a relatively peaceful environment. The substantive resolution of the specific disagreement was usually less important than the quality of the relationships between or among the disputants and within the broader community.

Professional social workers working from a traditional value base and code of ethics are compatible with these ancient tenets. The attitudes and intervention of a social work mediator must always remain consistent with the profession's values and ethics. A client-centred approached based on self-determination is always appropriate. This means that sometimes negotiation, even with a competent mediator, is not the best approach. Mediation is voluntary, meaning that either party may stop the process and withdraw at any time.

Power imbalances, caused by many different factors, must be of concern to the mediator. Mediators can use a variety of methods for dealing with power inequalities. (Landau et al., 2000, 104–105). They can control the process through clear rules and procedures. Outside experts brought in to advise the clients and indirectly inform the mediation also help to balance the power differences. (In separation and divorce mediation, I always urge each partner to retain an attorney.) However, power is never equal despite our best efforts. If the situation results in an evidently unfair process, the mediator should stop the mediation.

Neutrality would appear to be an important characteristic of an ethical mediator. In reality, however, we can never be completely neutral. Professionals are human beings. They have opinions, feelings, and biases. What is expected and required of a social work mediator is impartiality in managing the process through which clients decide on their own outcomes. (Beer & Steif, 1997, 77–79). Fairness and balance are essential; true neutrality is probably impossible.

Generally, it is beneficial for the mediator to see each person or side in the conflict separately before attempting to begin mediation. A confidential interview allows the clients to state their case, express their emotions, and examine what they hope to gain. The mediator can assess the clients' readiness to negotiate, and also determine which issues will create the most difficulties. These sessions can be used to begin shaping the possible framework of an agreement. Impartiality dictates that each party be seen for about the same amount of time.

During the negotiations, it is useful to get an early agreement on some point, however small. Momentum can build from that. Writing down points of agreement in a manner that is constantly visible to everyone reminds people how much they have accomplished and what stands to be lost later, if things get more difficult. An example from marital mediation is each parent acknowledging the other's competence as a parent and the children's love and need for both parents (even allowing that they have not been successful marital partners).

Reframing positions into statements which attempt to capture both parties' interests helps to see impasses in a different way. Even after agreement is reached, mediators may predict that problems will arise in the future and ask the clients to think about how they will manage those difficulties. Pre-empting potential breakdowns and problem-solving in advance reinforces the individuals' abilities to manage their agreement themselves.

Once interests are established, the focus of the options under discussion should be meeting those interests. If the children's healthy development, a peaceful neighbourhood, or co-operative agency teamwork is the mutual interest, then the mediator can always go back to that if the participants begin to regress to rigid positions, arguing, or general chaos. A calm, "How does that help the kids, community, or agency?" brings people back to the high ground. It also makes it easier to compromise and move away from an inflexible stance. One agrees because it helps the children, not because one is yielding to an estranged ex-spouse.

CONCLUSIONS

Mediation knowledge and skills can be included in most social work practice. Whether the worker is doing formal mediation or not, principles and interventions of mediation are useful. But mediation cannot be learned by reading a chapter or a book. Training and practical experience are necessary, as they are in BSW and MSW programs. Many universities and colleges offer mediation training through continuing education, institutes, and workshops. Private firms of mediators also provide training in the field. Most of these programs include simulations and role plays. Later, newly trained mediators can work with an experienced practitioner, perhaps in a co-mediation role, to refine their skills.

Family service agencies and community organizations offer mediation services to their clients. There is a growing need and expanded opportunity for social workers to be part of this approach to alternative dispute resolution.

REFERENCES

Barsky, A.E. (2000).*Conflict resolution for the helping professions*. Belmont, CA: Wadsworth.

Barsky, A.E., and Trocmé, N. (1998). Essential aspects of mediation in child protection cases. *Child and Youth Services Review, 20*, 629–656.

Beer, J.E. and Stief, E. (1997). *The mediator's handbook.* (3rd ed.). Gabriola Island, BC: New Society Publishers.

Bush, R.A.B. and Folger, J.P. (1994). *The promise of mediation: responding to conflict through empowerment and recognition*. San Francisco: Jossey-Bass.

Duryea, M.L. and Grundison, B. (1993). *Conflict and culture: research in five communities in Vancouver, British Columbia*. Victoria, BC: University of Victoria Institute of Dispute Resolution, Multiculturalism and Dispute Resolution Project.

Etter, J. (1997). Applying mediation to the field of adoption. In E. Kruk (Ed.). *Mediation and conflict resolution in social work and the human services*. Chicago, IL: Nelson-Hall Publishers.

Fisher, R. and Brown, S. (1988). *Getting together: building relationships as we negotiate*. New York: Penguin.

Fisher, R., Ury, W., and Patton, B. (1997). *Getting to yes: negotiating agreement without giving in.* (3rd ed.). New York: Penguin.

Irving, H. and Benjamin, M.. (1995). *Family mediation: contemporary issues*. Thousand Oaks, CA: Sage.

Irving, H. and Benjamin, M.. (1987). *Family mediation: theory & practice of dispute resolution*. Toronto, ON: Carswell.

Kaminsky, H. and Yellott, A. (1997). Community mediation: the grassroots of alternative dispute resolution. In E. Kruk (Ed.). *Mediation and conflict resolution in social work and the human services*. Chicago, IL: Nelson-Hall Publishers.

Landau, B., Wolfson, L., Landau, N., Bartoletti, M., and Mesbur, Hon. R. (2000). *Family mediation handbook.* (3rd ed.). Toronto: Butterworths.

Lang, M. (Ed.). (1996). Transformative approaches to mediation (Special Issue). *Mediation Quarterly, 13*(4).

Moore, C.W. (1996). *The mediation process: practical strategies for resolving conflict.* (2nd ed.). San Francisco: Jossey-Bass Publishers.

Parsons, R. and Cox, E.O. (1997). Mediation in the aging field. In E. Kruk (Ed.). *Mediation and conflict resolution in social work and the human services*. Chicago, IL: Nelson-Hall Publishers, pp. 163–178.

Schwartz, W. (1961). The social worker in the group. In *New perspectives on services to groups: theory, organization, practice*. New York: National Association of Social Workers, pp. 7–34.

Shulman, L. (1999). The skills of helping individuals, family and groups. (4th ed.). Itasca, IL: F.E. Peacock Publishers, Inc.

Stamato, L. and Jaffe, S. (1991). Mediation and public policies: variations on a consensus theme. *Mediation Quarterly, 9*(2), pp. 165–178.

Umbreit, M. (1995). *Mediating interpersonal conflicts: a pathway to peace*. Concord, MN: CPI Publishing.

INFORMATION TECHNOLOGY IN SOCIAL WORK PRACTICE

Robert J. MacFadden

THE CONTEXT AND THE CHALLENGE

As the new millennium dawns, social workers are increasingly being challenged by the accelerating use of information technology in human services. As knowledge workers in information intensive organizations, social workers require both knowledge and skill in information technology (IT) and an awareness of how IT enables them to perform their professional tasks and responsibilities.

The goal of this chapter is to raise the awareness of social workers concerning the opportunities and issues presented by IT and to challenge social workers to identify how IT can enhance their personal practice and respond to the demands for practice effectiveness and accountability. The term "information technology" is defined broadly to include computer hardware, software, and other forms of technology (e.g., phones, faxes, scanners) involved in the creation, management, use, and transmission of information.

Given the growing significance, relevance, and utility of IT, it is becoming increasingly difficult for a social worker to justify not being knowledgeable and competent in information technology. The growing amount of relevant social work resources and information on the Internet alone would warrant professional use. As professionals, our ethical framework requires that we provide the best possible service to clients, which includes having knowledge and expertise in areas that would enhance this service. Competence in IT is clearly becoming a requirement of ethical social work practice at the beginning of the twenty-first century.

CHANGING REALITIES

Social work is essentially an organizationally-based profession and has formulated its identity, in part, in association with these organizations. Current economic and political realities have shaken the foundation of the profession.

Administrative support positions are being significantly reduced in numbers and some are being transformed into other administrative positions. More social work professionals are being required to use computers through being responsible for their own keyboarding and case recording or data entry. These formerly administrative support tasks are increasingly being absorbed by social work professionals and added as new responsibilities, reducing the amount of time available for direct client contact and substantially transforming the nature of professional social work tasks, skills, and duties.

In some areas, such as child protection intake, many social workers are performing direct data entry. They are recording information directly into the computer as they discuss the client's situation over the telephone or shortly thereafter.

The reduction in full-time social work positions has placed an emphasis on contract, full-time, or part-time services. This may increase the numbers and type of jobs held by social workers and the necessity for a broad range of knowledge and skills, particularly in IT. Indeed, knowledge and skill in IT is becoming an important distinguishing criterion for some social work employers as they try to select from a large range of employment applications.

ACCOUNTABILITY

Related to the changing social, economic, and political context is a growing emphasis on accountability. Social work services have to be shown to be effective. The belief is that the public cannot afford to spend scarce money on resources or services that cannot provide evidence of their worth. It is no longer enough to be merely providing social work services. These services must now be shown to yield some useful benefit to clients and society.

IT has a long association with an emphasis on effectiveness and accountability. The very use of IT is often believed to convey an increased accuracy and validity to any process. In a study of the computerization of eight social welfare organizations in Canada, Gandy and Tepperman (1990) note that despite the many assumptions within the professional literature that social workers feel negative towards computers, their study found that most staff were favourably inclined towards using computer technology within their organizations. This positive attitude existed even though specific problems with computerization were identified by workers, such as inaccurate data, failure to increase productivity, and an increase in paperwork associated with computerization. Gandy and Tepperman observed that staff in these agencies, even though they experienced some of these difficulties, still held the widely accepted view that computerization will benefit the organization through improved efficiency

Agencies which employ IT in a substantial manner are often viewed as being more cutting-edge and well managed than agencies which have not invested in this area. In reality, IT itself does not ensure better systems. There still needs to be a solid accountability framework in place that may be assisted through the power and flexibility of the technology. IT does not make a bad system better and indeed may amplify the difficulties. Solid planning, design, pilot testing, and refinement is required for IT to enhance an information system. A well-designed accountability framework, enhanced by IT, can provide funders and others with targeted information presented in a flexible and rapid manner.

Coping with these changing realities and demands for accountability requires social workers who are knowledgeable and skilful in the use of IT to ensure that the technology is employed to meet professional social work needs. Such knowledge and skill enables social workers to be proactive rather than reactive. It ensures that social workers have an influence on their world rather than being faced with adapting to systems that have been designed by others who may not share the same value base or experience. How is IT employed in a variety of social work settings and functions?

IT AND HUMAN SERVICE APPLICATIONS

Recent texts present the state of IT development within human services across the world (Steyaert, Columbi, & Rafferty, 1996), and specifically within Canada (MacFadden, Carlson, Firbank, & Sieppert, 1996) and the U.S. (Schoech, 1996).

Traditionally, in North America, social work has used IT for basic functions such as word processing, spreadsheet analysis, and statistical and database applications. Given that IT has evolved within social agencies through the administrative area, it is understandable that these functions would be emphasized first. Indeed, most of the early use of IT has largely been through administration. Activities related to budgeting, case recording, service analysis, and reporting are typical social work IT applications (MacFadden, 1991).

Social work information systems which are designed to track services and more recently, resources, personnel, and other areas are now mostly computerized. These systems have been critiqued as being designed by non-social workers and directed largely at administrative needs.

CONVERGENCE OF TECHNOLOGIES

There is a growing convergence in technologies that social workers will need to utilize. A single machine can now incorporate faxing, scanning (i.e., making images of pictures, text, figures), copying, telephoning, and printing. A fully featured social worker's computer can now be used to telephone a client; receive and store telephone messages, faxes, graphical and sound files, and e-mail; view an animation or television broadcast; listen to radio; and connect with the World Wide Web (WWW). This computer system can be controlled by voice commands and read a document aloud. It can also control the climate of a room, turn on the lights, power up appliances at a preset time, and alert a distant source to an intrusion. Cellular telephone technology has become ubiquitous and is converging with other technologies. With the appropriate equipment, social workers can now use a cell phone to connect their notebook computer to the agency's computers remotely. Cell phones, themselves, are capable of accessing the WWW and sending and receiving information directly. Increased technological convergence will both simplify the operation and increase the power, reach, and utility of these technologies.

EMERGING APPLICATIONS

Newer applications include presentation software, networking, and Internet browsing software. Presentation software involves designing professional presentations such as electronic slides which often includes graphics, text, and special effects. A set of these electronic slides are combined and may be presented via computer, overhead projectors, digital projectors, and/or hardcopy (on paper) using black and white or colour. The use of such software promotes clarity and focus and generally enhances the impact of the information. Some of the existing software in this area has been made more intuitive (i.e., you can frequently guess how to use the program without reading a manual) and can be learned quickly.

Networking refers to the ability to connect and communicate with others via computer. Social workers within an agency can send textual files, graphical images, and other data to various people within and outside the organization. This can promote the development and operation of work groups or committees using this technology. A classification of software known as groupware has been designed specifically for facilitating group interaction and activities. These activities would include, as examples: working on a common document, automatically scheduling group activities through networked appointment schedules, participating in on-line conferences, and maintaining minutes from meetings.

THE INTERNET OR INFORMATION SUPERHIGHWAY

The Internet is also known as the Information Superhighway and consists of a global network of computers connected in such a way that the network can still function if particular computers are inoperative. The Internet is an unregulated network of computers and users which comprise various commercial, personal, governmental and other groups that provide information, services, products, and other resources and features. The Internet provides electronic mail (e-mail) and listservs, which are a type of automated e-mail, to facilitate discussion among groups of people who are interested in similar topics. The Internet also provides for file transfers through the use of File Transfer Protocol (FTP) capabilities. Other Internet capabilities include Telnet which permits the user to control a remote computer as though the user was connected directly to it. Gopher is a type of software that permits users with very little technical expertise to access information stored on computers on the Internet. Material can be published on gopher sites which can be accessed from anywhere on the Internet using gopher software.

THE GRAPHICAL INTERNET: THE WORLD WIDE WEB

Perhaps one of the most significant innovations related to the Internet is the World Wide Web (WWW). The WWW is a component of the Internet which is characterized by its graphical and multimedia capabilities. Unlike pure text or numbers, the colours, sounds, animations, graphics, and pictures found on the WWW are engaging and appealing to many people.

Using the WWW, social workers can obtain information on many different subjects and connect with various organizations and groups. They can "chat" by written word or by voice directly with others across the world, or participate in special interest groups on specific topics. Social workers can also conduct research on a range of topics utilizing the WWW (Kardas and Milford, 1996).

The software used to travel the WWW is called a browser and the two most common ones are Netscape's Navigator and Microsoft's Internet Explorer. These browsers are constantly innovating and becoming more powerful. Many current browsers have incorporated FTP functions, e-mail, animation, sound, and voice transmission. These browsers can store bookmarks or WWW addresses of homepages which the user values and saves through navigating the Internet. One of the exciting aspects of this technology is that it makes written material more dynamic. Using a browser such as one of those described above, readers of this chapter can type in the WWW addresses cited throughout the text below and visit the actual sites or homepages described in this text. This can be done from anywhere in the world and at any time of the day or night.

SOCIAL AGENCIES AND THE WWW

Human service agencies are starting to place themselves on the WWW (e.g., www.peelcas.org for the Children's Aid Society of the Region of Peel, Ontario, Canada). Using a markup language called HTML, the agency creates a program that offers information that can be obtained by anyone in the world with access to the Internet and a browser. Users connect up to the agency site via an address or URL (Universal Resource Locator). Typically, the user types in an address such as www.utoronto.ca (The University of Toronto, Ontario, Canada). These addresses are usually but not always prefixed with www to indicate that they are WWW sites.

Social work agencies are creating homepages at these sites to provide information such as mission, mandate, location, maps, hours, e-mail to agency staff and administration, and frequently asked questions (FAQs) about the organization and services. A homepage is another name for the agency's HTML program which is contained on a site accessed through typing the agency's address into a browser. Such basic, preliminary homepages represent a type of first stage applications as described by Schoech (1999), which largely reflect traditional ways of thinking (e.g., an electronic agency brochure). The WWW technology offers new opportunities for innovative functions and resources or second/third stage applications. Some examples of these more advanced applications might include increasing the functionality of these sites to incorporate accessible databases, direct client feedback, educational and preventive materials, and computer-assisted educational programs. Social workers are challenged to think of other innovative applications that can emerge from the new possibilities associated with this WWW technology.

SOCIAL WORK PROFESSIONALS AND THE WWW

Besides agency sites or homepages on the WWW, individual practitioners are also establishing themselves on homepages. While these may be strictly personal sites with family pictures and personal messages, sometimes these sites are more professional, providing resumes, publications of the individual social work professional, and containing links to valued resources elsewhere on the WWW (e.g., www.cpieterson.ca, www.robertmacfadden.com, and www.clinicalsocialwork.com). Such personal-professional sites contain marketing opportunities which may become even more appropriate as social work moves to incorporate more private practice, independent contractor roles.

SPECIALIZED SOCIAL WORK SITES

Large social work sites are appearing on the WWW, featuring a wide range of information and resources relevant to social workers (e.g., www.nyu.edu/socialwork/wwwrsw/ and www.cahs.colostate.edu/sw/web%20links.html). There are several social work home pages that are a series of links to other information and sources such as sites of schools of social work, self-help groups, medical and psychiatric services (e.g., www.health.searchbeat.com/social-work.htm), and political and social advocacy homepages (e.g., www.community.web.ca/). There are also specific homepages associated with groups interested in IT in social work (e.g., www.uta.edu/cussn/cussn.html and www.fz.hse.nl/enith), an IT in social work index and abstracting site (www.fz.hse.nl/causa/swbib/), and journals focusing on IT in human services (e.g., www.chst.soton.ac.uk/nths/).

LIMITATIONS OF THE WWW

The rapid development of the Internet has placed an enormous range of information in the hands of both social workers and some of their clients. This information is extensive but of varying quality and professionals need to be cautious about relying on it. The Latin term *caveat emptor* or "buyer beware" is extremely appropriate at this stage in the development of the Internet. The Internet is one of the newest frontiers, uncharted and unregulated, resembling a type of an electronic Wild Wild West. With this complete lack of regulation, no clear way has yet been developed or agreed upon to establish the identity and affiliation of persons and organizations on the Internet. Any information and source needs to be checked for validity, accuracy, and ownership.

THE PROMISE OF THE WWW FOR SOCIAL WORKERS

Nevertheless, the WWW offers social workers unprecedented opportunities. Professionals can become more connected with a broader range of sources and persons. Social workers can connect with distant colleagues and exchange files, recent research and practice findings, new practice models, social work citations, and in some cases journals and journal articles. They can visit specialized medical sites to find out the latest information about a disease or visit a government site to read recent publications. Three-dimensional capabilities are developing where users can chat online with a virtual corporal existence (i.e., a 3-D body) (e.g., www.worlds.net) or employ a video camera to create a picture phone.

Virtual agencies may emerge on the WWW, paralleling the development of virtual universities. Social agencies based solely on the WWW might be formed to offer e-services such as specialized information and databases, connections with needed resources and forms of e-therapy (i.e., counselling delivered solely over the WWW). Social workers are now able to tour nursing homes on the WWW together, with their clients, to narrow down placement decisions and make these decisions more well informed. Clients who also have access to the technology can visit the site on their own. Professional conferences are establishing themselves early on the WWW to build up interest and promote activity associated with the event.

SOCIAL WORK SCHOOL SITES

Schools of social work are viewing the WWW as a significant opportunity to connect with their alumni across the lifespan. Social work school sites can provide information to many constituencies including: young students who want to know about social work and/or who are interested in doing school projects; students wishing to enrol in the faculty; students registering on-line; students in courses; graduates and alumni. These sites can provide a lifelong connection and assist social work professionals with many needs they will experience throughout their career and possibly retirement.

As examples, school sites can provide information about the profession, course requirements, admission processes, faculty resources, schedules, courses, professors, research, and professional activities. They can be a focus for research, social action, political change, and educational activities. Such sites can provide papers, research reports, statistics, graphs, databases, and ongoing conferences or special interest groups on certain topics. These school sites can be enriched with hypertext links, which are highlighted texts that contain addresses embedded within. When the cursor is placed on the link or button and clicked, the user is taken directly to related information either within the site or to another site. The increasing need for schools of social work to be connected to their graduates or alumni can be addressed through increased use of the WWW. Alumni can reach the school via their computers and participate in online discussions, conferences, and projects, and can contribute to fundraising and development initiatives within the school. Thus the WWW presents the opportunity for each school to become a more significant lifelong presence in the life of a social work professional. This has enormous implications for Continuing Education, fundraising, special projects, and the connectedness of all school constituencies, including students, administration, faculty, alumni, field practitioners, field instructors, field agencies, and others. This reality will take some time to be fully realized, given that individuals, groups, and organizations will vary in the speed at which they adopt this technology and the availability of resources to make this possible. As examples of school sites, one can visit the University of Southern California School of Social Work (www.usc.edu/dept/socialwork) or the University of Windsor, Canada (www.uwindsor.ca/faculty/socsci/socwk/) or the Faculty of Social Work at the University of Toronto (www.utoronto.ca/facsocwk).

SOCIAL AGENCIES AND THE INTRANET

Development of the WWW has occurred at an unprecedented rate and promises to have significance for social work agencies. Major software developers are constructing most of their products to interact with the WWW and sometimes directly through the WWW through a browser program. The browsers and WWW use is becoming increasingly popular and powerful. Some social work organizations are setting up their internal computer networks to use this browser format. Using this Internet browser interface and structure within an organization is termed an *Intranet*. Current development and direction suggests that future workers will turn their computers on and be immediately connected to the WWW and the browser may function as the computer's operating system (e.g., Windows). Using the resources on one's own computer will be only one choice of many. Thus the depth and breadth of the WWW will be integrated with the power of one's own computer to form a package of extensive resources and capabilities that will be both locally and globally oriented for the social worker.

Social workers will be able to sign on, connect with the agency's site, receive e-mail, check agency records and documents, receive training, conference with colleagues in real time (i.e., all are communicating during the same time period), review the minutes of committees, respond to inquiries from clients and other agencies, attend a virtual conference anchored within a distant country, and check on each colleague's availability to attend a meeting at a certain time.

THE CONNECTED SOCIAL WORKER

IT promises to affect social work practice in many unique and unknown ways. In child protection, as one example, there is considerable travel involved and need for quick, reliable information. IT is starting to change the way child protection practice occurs.

A front-line social worker in child protection frequently works out of his or her car. IT enables this car to become a mobile office. A notebook computer is used to record case information, to access local databases on the machine, to hook up through telephone line or cellular waves to the agency's computers, to send and receive alerts reports, and to query the agency's extensive database (MacFadden, 1989). Cellular phones can provide direct field contact with supervisors, supported by faxed documents to both locations. Global positioning technology through a small, handheld unit employs orbiting satellites to assist social workers in identifying their exact geographical locations. This could be very useful in large rural practices, as one example, where well-known landmarks may not be available.

The central office location of the child protection worker may not need to be as physically extensive. This computer-mediated communication and practice offers advantages and disadvantages. Currently, social work colleagues in child protection are important sources of social support through direct contact and close physical proximity with each other. How might this change with less direct and less physical contact through more communication using computers? How much of this direct, face-to-face contact should be maintained to ensure quality service and a satisfying working climate? Are the resource gains from reducing physical space requirements and providing maximum flexibility to workers offset by the lack of direct and close contact by colleagues? These are questions that will increasingly need to be answered as IT pervades our social work settings. With less space required, more resources may be saved, although this is not necessarily clear. It is important to note that IT usually requires up-front costs and needs to be upgraded fairly frequently. It should not be automatically assumed that there will be cost-savings involved in using IT. Actual costs may increase, depending on the application and context.

SPECIAL APPLICATIONS

Single System Evaluation

IT can be employed in all areas of social work. From a clinical perspective, computer technology is being used to assess and evaluate practice. As an illustration, there is a Windows-based program developed to assess, compute, monitor, and graph client scores in common problem areas (Hudson, 1996). This program is based on a single system approach to evaluation which involves establishing clear goals, measures, and baseline data and then comparing changes to the baseline scores as intervention progresses. The program includes standardized rapid assessment instruments which focus on common clinical targets such as self-esteem, depression, and couple satisfaction, as illustrations. Clients can complete the scales directly on the computer, using a paper and pencil format. The responses are scored and a graph produced to reflect changes in the goal from the baseline period. Typically, each scale has a clinical cutting score that is useful in determining the seriousness of a client's situation. Use of these scales in combination with a computer adds a level of rigour and systematization which is generally not common in social work practice. With support, some clients can operate the computer themselves, including producing a graph which illustrates their progress. This visual, graphical output can be powerful in showing clients how they are progressing, in relation to where they began. It also assists the practitioner in knowing when an intervention is working and when to alter a practice approach (see www.syspac.com/~walmyr/).

While a single system evaluation can be completed without a computer, the addition of this technology ensures more efficient, accurate processing and display, and may add more impact to the analysis itself. Clients may value computer generated information more than information produced by other means, given the reputation of the computer for providing precise, accurate, and reliable information.

E-Therapy

Online therapy or e-therapy is establishing itself on the WWW in various forms. Therap-e-mail (Murphy and Mitchell, 1998) and distance art therapy (Collie and Cubranic, 1999) are two examples. Some of these new e-therapies are exceedingly creative approaches designed for an online environment. Murphy and Mitchell discuss the use of "presence" techniques in their e-mail therapy or "Therap-e-mail," techniques which create a warm, accepting environment through strategies such as *emotional bracketing"* e.g., [feeling worried you might take my comments negatively] and *descriptive immediacy*, e.g., ["In my mind's eye, I'm stretching out my hand to you right now with a welcoming smile on my face saying, 'I am very pleased to meet you'. If I could, I'd offer you a nice cup of tea as well..."] (Collie, Mitchell and Murphy, 2000, 227). E-clients are encouraged to use these strategies to become more aware of their experiences and feelings and to communicate them in a rich, personal, and engaging way. Therap-e-mail is asynchronous, which means, like standard e-mail, the communication is delayed (i.e., the therapist and client are not exchanging messages in "real time"). There is synchronous e-therapy which involves communicating online, in real time, and this can be through a "chat session" format that involves typing short messages back and forth, videoconferencing with a Web cam (i.e., voice and picture) and Internet telephone (i.e., voice over the WWW). Some sites exist which provide a consumers' review of available e-therapists and a discussion of the benefits and drawbacks of this new approach (www.metanoia.org/imhs/index.html). While the online environment presents significantly new opportunities for the provision of therapy, it raises some fundamental questions about the nature of therapy and whether therapy can be provided over this medium in an effective and ethical manner. Indeed, social workers contemplating becoming e-therapists need to carefully review the issues associated with providing online therapy (e.g., online disclosure of child abuse and where this should be reported) and examine some existing ethical frameworks for the provision of e-therapy, such as the American Counseling Association's "Ethical Standards for Internet On-Line Counseling" at www.counseling.org/gc/cybertx.htm.

Self-Help Software

A category of software termed self-help software is also available to assist social workers and clients. Self-help software has been developed to assess and promote change in a range of dimensions including assertiveness, depression and anxiety. Many of these programs are cognitively based and identify faulty cognitions, and assist the user to substitute more realistic beliefs and thoughts. Some programs track change in these dimensions from an initial baseline to the end of the program. Social workers may wish to use some of these programs to support ongoing counselling. The self-help programs have advantages such as privacy and flexibility of use in time and location. Since this is a new category of software, minimal research exists as to the utility of such programs, but they are suggestive of new types of therapy that are emerging as the result of the availability of IT. Disadvantages of such software are related to their difficulty in individualizing each client, and in the manner in which they are used. If this type of program is used without professional support, there may be difficulties related to appropriateness and impact. As an example, it is possible to misinterpret the assessments given by these programs and to overestimate the importance of the assessments.

Computer-Assisted Instruction

Since a considerable part of social work practice involves educational processes, computer assisted instruction (CAI) can be a useful supplement to practice. CAI refers to the use of computer hardware and software to provide instruction. Programs are developed which provide content in some fashion and typically the learners are engaged in viewing the content and sometimes responding to questions and other requests. CAI can be used to build skills, acquire knowledge, challenge attitudes and perceptions, and simulate aspects of practice.

As an illustration, one CAI program was developed to teach new child protection workers some fundamentals of child sexual abuse assessment (MacFadden, 1988, 1989). Any CAI development involves the use of at least three technologies: the content area (e.g., child sexual abuse assessment); instructional (e.g., how to construct educational material); and computer (i.e., hardware and software). In the case of this example, a well-accepted model of child sexual abuse was selected. Content was presented in various modules and followed by a series of questions to test comprehension. Responses to incorrect choices added further clues, and users would make selections until the most correct response was identified. Users could choose the order of the modules selected and where they wished to use this CAI program. The program was available on disk and could be loaded into the learner's home or work computer.

A second example of CAI is called Keisha (Satterwhite & Schoech, 1995) and reflects a multimedia approach to training child protection professionals. Keisha is built around typical work dimensions, which include reports of abuse, agency files and records, telephone contacts, home visits, and supervisors, as examples. The learner utilizes this work simulation to assess a case and complete a risk assessment at the end. This CAI system incorporates graphics and sound and provides pictures of the abused child, her living environment and other resources such as case information and reactions from experts. Keisha permits learning in a simulated environment without risk to an actual client. It is being used in several U.S. states to supplement existing training approaches.

CAI has the potential to individualize instruction in a flexible and timely manner and in a safe context. The computer does not chastise or berate the user and permits no-risk exploration and learning. Limitations of CAI include the expense of creating quality courseware, the need for considerable expertise in the three technologies, the structured, programmed nature of the learning, and the necessity to have appropriate and sometimes costly hardware to use with these programs. One additional difficulty is that it is sometimes difficult for social work trainers to agree on what constitutes a good curriculum and learning materials. Thus considerable resources might be spent on constructing a CAI program and yet the nature of the content might not be appealing or accepted by many users.

Web-Based Education

With the growing popularity, convenience and availability of the WWW, social work education is increasingly being made available via the Internet. This is happening in various ways, from Web sites that support traditional, onground courses to totally Web-based courses to complete degree program offerings over the WWW.

Universities are beginning to provide Web sites where course instructors can develop basic course homepages with minimal expertise. Such homepages involve functions such as course registration and password access, course content in various forms and media, chat or discussion areas, hot links to related materials, and a section for bibliographies. These bibliographies can include direct links to electronic journals and materials that can be read online or printed off, if the user is a registered student. Social work courses are now being offered which require no text or package of course readings. All readings are accessible in digital form directly from the libraries via the Internet. One university indicates it offers approximately 13,000 full-text electronic journals, 450 indexes and abstracts, and 200 online newspapers (University of Toronto Libraries, 2000).

Individual, Web-based courses are available in several areas, including social work research with Dr. Tim Stocks from the School of Social Work, Michigan State University (www.msu.edu/user/sswwebed/), a social work ethics seminar with Dr. Frederic G. Reamer from the Tulane School of Social Work, Center for Lifelong Learning at www.tulane.edu/~tssw/CLL/Certificates/ethics_seminar_2000.htm, and social work and social welfare with Dr. Steve Hick, Carleton University, School of Social Work, Ottawa, Ontario, Canada at http://ia1.carleton.ca/52100/home.html.

At the social work program level, some examples include: The Maritime School of Social Work in Canada, which will initiate BSW and MSW Distance Education Programs commencing in September 2001 (www.dal.ca/~schsw/distance/); and The University of Utah, School of Social Work's "Technology-Enhanced Doctorate" which commenced in 2000 (www.socwk.utah.edu/phd/ted.html).

With the emerging nature of social work education on the WWW, other schools of social work are exploring various forms of cyber-education. One such experience involved the implementation and evaluation of a Web-based course on enhancing cultural competency of human service providers (MacFadden, Dumbrill, and Maiter, 2000; MacFadden, Maiter, and Dumbrill, in press).

In summary, Web-based education has been characterized as offering many advantages, including: high interactivity; multimedia capabilities; access to the vast resources of the WWW; time, distance, and place independence; global accessibility; learner centredness; convenience, ease of use, and cost-effectiveness (Khan, 1997). Yet many issues remain to be addressed, such as the costs and complexity in creating quality courseware, the effectiveness with various types of content and educational objectives, unequal access to the technology by various groups, differing technical competency levels and hardware capabilities of social workers, problems with acceptance for academic credit by some universities, particularly graduate schools, and appropriateness for learning in specific areas such as developing helping skills with clients.

Just-In-Time Training

A recent and related innovation in this area is termed, "just-in-time" training. This involves delivering the training to users exactly when they need it. An example would be when a social worker wishes to create a graph for displaying client progress. If the worker encounters difficulty in doing this, the program could be set up to provide immediate and basic, focused information about this process and perhaps even assist the worker with each step in creating the graph and viewing the results. Rather than creating a separate tutorial on graph creation, the system embeds some of this information as a "Help" feature right at the time the worker is experiencing difficulties.

Given the importance of education in social work practice and the specialized knowledge base that social workers have, they are in an ideal position to produce high quality, focused, and very useful CAI programs. While this would usually require collaboration with other professionals, this is part of the challenge that IT offers social workers. Becoming computer competent would enable social workers to lead the development and testing of such programs to meet important client and professional needs.

Advocacy and the WWW

Social action is another important role for social workers and IT is assisting with this. As a communication network through the Internet and WWW, social workers can connect with others who are promoting a particular cause or attempting to achieve particular goals. Online databases, research publications, and hypertext links with related resources can facilitate social action goals. Some groups have established WWW sites to promote particular causes such as the effects of government cutbacks on their communities. Singly, agencies may not be able to afford to do this, but by collaborating with other agencies through the medium of the Internet, these agencies can provide important, current information, resources, and connections to achieve their goals. Special cyber-communities of non-profit organizations that promote social action exist on the WWW (e.g., community.web.ca/).

FOCUS ON THE FRONT-LINE SOCIAL WORKER

The largest group within the social agency, front-line workers, have had minimal input into the design and use of IT systems within agencies. Some workers have viewed these social work information systems as large, mindless, data-feeding creatures (termed "Jaws" by one student), which constantly demand feeding from front-line social workers, yet offer minimal direct benefits to these same workers.

Given the historical emphasis on administrative tasks of IT in social work, front-line workers have been largely disenfranchised within the agencies. There have been few direct uses for front-line workers, yet these same workers spend a significant amount of their time in preparing and inputting data into these systems. Indeed, it is only recently that front-line social workers have become important considerations in the development of this IT.

The movement towards the use of more user-friendly operating systems reflects this new direction. Part of this change towards more use of IT by front-line workers is also related to the financial situations. These workers are increasingly being asked to do more tasks, and computers are viewed as assisting them in doing this. The belief that IT enables social workers to do more work is commonly held but generally has not been tested. Indeed, the promise that IT will reduce work and paperwork has generally not been supported. Yet new applications are changing the face of the agency.

ASSISTIVE TECHNOLOGIES

Besides the impact on the social work role, IT itself provides important resources for many social work clients and as such social workers need to be familiar with these resource opportunities. Advances in assistive technologies are enabling variously challenged clients to perform common daily functions that were previously difficult or impossible (www.nal.usda.gov/ttic/assist/asstbib.htm). Helping clients gain access to the many technologies is becoming a common social work strategy for professionals who are interested in client empowerment.

DOCUMENT MANAGEMENT

Document management is a more recent innovation that will have a significant impact on the everyday working life of a social worker. The term "document management" refers to the increasing computerization and management of all types of documentation and is designed to streamline the development, storage, and retrieval of information based on a set of rules that are created by an organization. Currently, many documents are paper-based and stored in filing cabinets. Frequently considerable time, effort and money are spent on developing, storing, transporting, retrieving, and destroying this documentation. In some social work settings, it is not unusual for some documentation to be difficult to access and sometimes read. This can affect whether a social worker uses this information, even though it may be critical to understanding or working with a case.

Advancements in various technologies and document management is permitting more effective management and access of these records. Large-scale storage and quick retrieval using optical disk technology are now available. Pictures of paper documents or electronic documents can be stored, ordered, retrieved, and transmitted quickly. The text of many of these documents can be scanned for words or phrases or other content that can be used for assessment, monitoring, and research.

ETHICAL ISSUES AND IT

The ongoing introduction and use of IT in social agencies has raised many important ethical issues. A prime dilemma relates to the spending of scarce resources on computer equipment when needed services are continually being cut back. Some agencies have taken a hard stance and resisted spending this money on IT. Some of these agencies have experienced considerable problems in being able to respond quickly and accurately to the demands of funders who are increasing their reporting expectations. Other agencies that are investing heavily in IT can be more responsive, flexible, and detailed to funders in their documentation. However, these agencies may also be subject to internal and external criticism regarding the appropriateness of substantial IT spending when client services are being cut.

Indeed, some social work agencies have not resolved this issue and continue to view IT in an ambivalent or mildly supportive manner. They may become caught in expensive cycles whereby some purchases are made and the equipment remains the same for years, which leads to low utilization and frustration for social work staff. Other social work agencies have recognized the importance of IT in attaining their organizational mission and have instituted a range of policies such as: senior positions for social worker responsible for IT functioning and development; a budget specifically for IT; a strategic plan for IT development with the agency linked to the agency's mission; ongoing upgrading, training, and support; a standing committee comprised of a range of staff to ensure ongoing development and refinement of the IT systems.

Other ethical issues are evident. How secure are the data? Who has access to them? Who owns them? How confidential are they? Can workers and clients say no to providing data? Is the burden placed on workers and clients to provide the data worth it? Is this information used to the benefit of the client and agency?

Other concerns include: What about clients who do not have access to these technologies (i.e., the Digital Divide)? Is this another type of systemic discrimination? How will this affect their welfare? Besides helping clients and social workers, how does the technology create barriers, support inequities, and lessen the quality of life for our clients and citizens? What are the dangers inherent in these emerging innovations?

These are serious issues that need to be addressed, and many reflect their own dilemmas. As one example, electronic data can be collected and stored in such a way that it is extremely difficult to read. Certainly this encrypted data is far more difficult to read than paper files. Yet security that can be developed can also be compromised. Once these electronic data are accessed and read, they can be removed in large amounts, hidden, and transferred at great distances easily and at a very low cost. Great innovations and capabilities usually come with considerable risk. The new technologies are creating situations that we have not encountered before and have not anticipated and that challenge our basic ethical systems.

AN IT BILL OF RIGHTS

Two social work authors have proposed a Bill of Rights for the Information Age (Glastonbury & LaMendola, 1992, 192–194).They argue that:

> Human rights … should be reasonably and prudently considered in all processes of IT development, use, and application. The consideration should take place in the widest public forum feasible, and involve representatives of all of those who will be affected, as well as appropriate expert, legally mandated, and ethical authorities;

> Decisions which directly affect a human being may not be made by an IT device alone. IT systems can be used as an aid to decision making, but only in circumstances where a designated person is accountable for the decision;

> Humans affected by device-aided decisions should be fully informed at all times, and have an incontrovertible right to appeal all such decisions through the courts or through formal appeal processes;

> Personal data is the property of the person who is the subject of the data …;

> Unintended or unrecognized consequences of any type resulting from the application of computer technologies are the responsibility of those who have implemented the application, and subject to remedy and compensation for actual or perceived damages;

> All IT applications should conform to best equal opportunity standards, as should the IT industry;

> Information technologies should be confined to developments for peaceful purposes and should be freely transferable to all countries. An international aid fund should be established to assist in technology transfer to poor communities, with an expert sub-committee charged with responsibility for establishing sensitive processes for cross-cultural transfers.

IT AND KNOWLEDGE DEVELOPMENT

Information technology is both a tool and a significant force in society and our profession. Most discussion focuses on the power of information technology as a tool, including its vast storage capacity, multimedia capabilities, computational abilities, and connectivity. Information technology, however, exerts an influence on how we generate knowledge.

As a tool, the computer is without precedence, continually transforming to meet current and future knowledge needs. As a paradigm, the computer will support the positivistic development of knowledge, emphasizing structure, taxonomies, and operational definitions. Computers, however, also offer the potential to develop knowledge through other, more exploratory, creative, and intuitive ways. In summary, computers will respond to meet the challenge of pluralism in knowledge development and our *many ways of knowing* (MacFadden, 1995, p.419*).*

THE CHALLENGE

In conclusion, information technology is increasingly becoming a significant feature of a social worker's environment. Competency in information technology is quickly becoming a prerequisite for social work positions. There are many challenges that face social workers, including: how to use the technology to enhance professional skill and knowledge; how the technology can assist social work clients directly and indirectly; how IT can make practice more effective; and how the technology can be used to further professional goals and to ensure ethical and responsible practice.

While the responses to these questions need to be made both collectively and at the level of each individual social work professional, it is clear that information technology is transforming both society and social work practice. It is hoped that some of the information, examples, and challenges described within this chapter will enable individual social workers to consider how they can best make use of technology to enhance and strengthen their practice.

REFERENCES

Bloom, J. and Walz, G. (2000). *Cybercounseling and cyberlearning: strategies and resources for the millennium*. Alexandria, VA: American Counseling Association.

Collie, K., Mitchell, D., and Murphy, L. (2000). Skills for online counseling: maximum impact at minimum bandwidth. In J. Bloom & G. Walz (Eds.). *Cybercounseling and cyberlearning: strategies and resources for the millennium*. Alexandria, VA: American Counseling Association.

Collie, K. and Cubranic, D. (1999). An art therapy solution to a telehealth problem. *Art Therapy: The Journal of the American Art Therapy Association, 16*(4), 186–193.

Gandy, J. and Tepperman, L. (1990*). False alarm: the computerization of eight social welfare organizations*. Waterloo, ON: Wilfrid Laurier Press.

Glastonbury, B. and LaMendola, W. (1992*). The integrity of intelligence: a bill of rights for the information age*. NY: St. Martin's Press.

Hudson, W. (1996). Professional practice for the 21st century: information implications. In J. Steyaert (Ed.). *Information technology and human services: more than computers?* Utrecht: NIZW.

Kardas, E. and Milford, T. (1996). *Using the internet for social science research and practice*. Belmont, CA: Wadsworth Publishing Company.

MacFadden, R. (1988). The electronic Aristotle: computer assisted instruction in the human services. In B. Glastonbury, W. LaMendola & S. Toole (Eds.). *Information technology and the human services*. (pp.168–174).Chichester, UK: John Wiley & Sons.

MacFadden, R. (1989). Microcomputers in child welfare: a day in the life of Chip Henry protection worker. *Ontario Association of Children's Aid Societies Journal, 33*(7), September, 6–10.

MacFadden, R. (1989). Sexual abuse assessment training: developing CAI in child welfare. *Computers in Human Services, 5*(3/4), 29–41.

MacFadden, R. (1991). The technological challenge: computers and social work administrators in health care. In P. Taylor & J. Devereux (Eds.). *Social work administrative practice in health care settings* (pp.193–202). Toronto, CA: Canadian Scholars' Press.

MacFadden, R. (1995). IT and knowledge development in human services: tool paradigm and promise. In J. Rafferty, J. Steyaert, & D. Columbi (Eds.). *Human services in the information age.* (pp.419–430). NY: Haworth Press.

MacFadden, R., Carlson, R., Firbank, O., and Sieppert, J. (1996). Canada. In J. Steyaert, D. Columbi & J. Rafferty (Eds.). *Human services and information technology: an international perspective* (pp.71–82). Brookfield, VT: Ashgate Publishing Company.

MacFadden, R., Dumbrill, G., and Maiter, S. (2000). Web-based education in a graduate faculty of social work: Crossing the new frontier. *New Technology in the Human Services, 13*(1/2), 27–38.

MacFadden, R., Maiter, S., and Dumbrill, G. (in press). High tech and high touch: The human face of online education. In H. Resnick & P. Anderson, (Eds.*). Innovations in technology and human services: practice and education*. NY: Haworth Press.

Murphy, L., and Mitchell, D. (1998). When writing helps to heal: e-mail as therapy. *British Journal of Guidance and Counselling, 26*, 21–31.

Satterwhite, R. and Schoech, D. (1995). Multimedia training for child protective service workers: initial test results. In J. Rafferty, J. Steyaert, and D. Columbi (Eds.). *Human services in the information age.* (pp. 81–97). NY: Haworth Press.

Schoech, D. (1999). *Human services technology*. NY: Haworth Press.

Schoech, D. (1996). America (USA). In J. Steyaert, D. Columbi, and J. Rafferty (Eds.). *Human services and information technology: an international perspective.* (pp.71–82). Brookfield, VT: Ashgate Publishing Company.

Steyaert, J., Columbi, D., and Rafferty, J. (Eds.) , (1996). *Human services and information technology: an international perspective*. Brookfield, VT: Ashgate Publishing Company.

University of Toronto Libraries, (2000*). Resource guide for faculty, 2000–2001*. Toronto, CA: University of Toronto Libraries.

THE SOCIAL WORKER AS EXPERT WITNESS Barbara A. Chisholm

The historic role of social workers as facilitators, enablers, and where possible, reconcilers, has included participation in legal (court) proceedings on a very limited scale. The most familiar activity has been support for a Protection Application to a court on behalf of children believed to be in need of protection, or for direction from the court concerning formal planning for such children's care.

The past decade has witnessed a significant increase in court attendance by social workers, particularly in matters of the custody of and access to children involved in separation/divorce disputes about them. As well, social workers have been involved in litigation in areas such as trauma-impact assessment, sexual abuse allegations, and capacity evaluations.

Attendance at court can be an intimidating experience for those unfamiliar with its rules and procedures, and a trying one even for those social workers more acquainted with the process. Cross-examination can, indeed, seem to be just that, cross, and the pressure brought to bear by a lawyer may be distressing, irritating, and/or confusing. Even so, the experience can be met effectively, with understanding of the process, and with preparation. The court is entitled to see and hear a professional whose comments and/or recommendations in the disputed matter are being presented and challenged. The judge is free, of course, to accept or not accept such comments or recommendations in whole or in part. A reasoned, contained, fair, and firm presentation of evidence will assist in that choice. A halting, confused, contradictory or weak presentation, a willingness to back away from or even change one or more earlier statements under the pressure of cross-examination, will diminish the court's reliance on the social worker's assistance.

Instead of avoiding the court experience, the competent social worker prepares for it, cooperates willingly, and participates politely in the process. The judge may or may not agree with the recommendations or point of view of the social worker/witness, but nevertheless will have formed some opinion about the social worker and the usefulness of professional social work. Handling oneself well in court, therefore, makes a three-part contribution: to the resolution of the matter in dispute, to the individual social worker's professional reputation, and to the image of social work and social workers generally.

THE EXPERT WITNESS DESIGNATION

There is a significant difference between an "ordinary" witness and an "expert" witness. The former may comment only on what he or she did, said, or saw. There are no expectations or requirements for the use of an ordinary witness; such use is the responsibility of a lawyer who must determine in shaping the presentation of his or her client's case that that person's evidence will be of value at a practical fact-establishing level. Such witnesses may not express any opinion at all.

To be classified as an *expert* witness, the individual must satisfy the court that he or she meets the minimal legal requirements of specialized knowledge, skill, experience, training, or education *in relation to the matter at hand*. This will be presented by the lawyer who has called the social worker, and a decision that the social worker is to be accepted as an expert in the pertinent area(s) of the case must be made by the judge before any questions may be put to him or her. The "expert" witness is distinct from an "ordinary" witness in that an expert may give opinion evidence in one or more aspects of the case. Such opinions, of course, must be limited to those areas of professional competence that the qualifying lawyer specifically indicated during the presentation of the social worker's training, background, etc., as mentioned above. Professional opinion outside of these designated and accepted areas of competence will not be allowed.

Not every social worker may be accepted as an expert witness. A social worker may be rejected if the presiding judge determines that either the training or the experience of the proposed witness is insufficient to assist the judge or a jury, if there is one, to understand the evidence or to determine a fact in issue. If that occurs, the social worker/witness will retain the status of an ordinary, or lay, witness, and may not express professional opinions in the matter.

THE COURT CONTEXT

Sometimes the court experience is very trying. Occasionally, a lawyer may become more than assertive in cross-examination. The social worker, whose task is to be helpful to the court, may feel harassed, irritated, and bewildered, confused as to why the judge is allowing such behaviour to continue or why the lawyer on the other side is not objecting. The social worker at such moments may feel alone, attacked, and abandoned. Some awareness of the background of court process will be helpful, as well as an understanding of the "rules of the game," to facilitate managing and getting through such moments.

Our North American court system shares a common basis—the Socratic notion that the truth of a matter is to be found in a forceful and earnest contest between adversaries. Evidence that might mislead (such as hearsay) is generally excluded, even if it is true, because it cannot be tested under cross-examination. Over time, many exceptions to the so-called Hearsay Rule have been allowed (such as, for example, the information given to a social worker about past events, which is contained in a report).

A trial or hearing is composed of many parts: admissible evidence, questioning and challenge of the other side's evidence, legal argument concerning the relevant portion of the pertinent law, and perhaps reference to previous judgments which have come down on the same or a similar fact situation. At the conclusion, a judgment or decision will be delivered by the judge. Reasons for judgment will be prepared, setting out the judge's conclusions, the facts accepted as established (or rejected), the relevant law, the applicability (or otherwise) of other precedent judgments to the matter at hand, and finally, the reasoning that has led to the judge's conclusions and orders.

It is useful to recall that the purpose of a trial or hearing is not to arrive at "the whole truth," even if there could be agreement as to what that is. It is to arrive at a decision. In a civil proceeding (which is what family law matters are, as contrasted to criminal proceedings), the test that must be met is "a balance of probabilities," (as contrasted with "proof beyond a reasonable doubt," on the criminal side). The judge, as a trier of fact, ultimately decides what has been established, what has not, who was credible as a witness, who was (perhaps) not, what evidence has led to a certain conclusion, a decision, and an order.

It is also useful to recognize that the right (and responsibility) for the decision and the order that follows is a prerogative of the judge only. It is inappropriate for a social worker to "tell" the judge what he or she should do, or worse, must do. One must avoid any suggestion of making "findings"; that is the sole entitlement of the judge. Some judges welcome advice and information from mental health professionals. Some judges are sensitive to any suggestion (real or perceived) that their role as Decider is being usurped, and are more resistant to such assistance. Respect for this prerogative of the court will help the social worker to remain calm and to reply to interjected comments or questions from the judge with care and respect.

The role and function of a lawyer is defined in the rules of practice. Lawyers must be loyal to their client. They may not undertake to deceive or mislead the court, but they are under no obligation to betray their own client. Lawyers may not "lead" their own witnesses (that is, ask questions in such a way as to signal the wanted reply), although they may certainly ask leading questions of the other side's witnesses during cross-examination. The social worker as expert witness is loyal only to his or her professional standards and ethics. He or she is not "on side," even though called as a witness by one side. In that sense, the expert witness/social worker (and other professionals qualified as experts) may be looked upon as the court's witness.

It helps to visualize the court process as a medieval jousting match: thrust and parry, with each knight (the lawyer) trying to knock the opposing knight (the other side's lawyer) off his or her horse, to penetrate the armour, and to strike the telling blow that will be fatal to the other side's case.

As in all wars, skirmishes take place, various manoeuvres are tried, actual battles are joined. In court, there are rules to govern the encounter, and one of the functions of the judge is to ensure that the rules are observed. Some judges give lawyers a lot of leeway in their styles of examination and cross-examination. This may appear to the social worker/witness as unfair, but the judge may have a reason—perhaps to see how a witness's evidence holds up; perhaps to see if the lawyer will contain the behaviour or go too far.

Very aggressive, harassing behaviour by the cross-examining lawyer may in fact suggest to the social worker/witness that the lawyer does not have a strong case, or is not certain where to go next in the cross-examination. Rather than being "in charge" as a lawyer's behaviour is supposed to suggest, the lawyer may be on what is commonly referred to as a "fishing expedition," running the line here and there, hoping for a catch. By letting the behaviour go on for a while, the judge may be waiting to see if that is so. By remaining outwardly calm and consistent (regardless of inner reaction), the social worker/witness counters the strategy. Eventually, the judge either suggests that the lawyer move on, or the lawyer retreats voluntarily from that particular jousting effort.

PREPARATION FOR ATTENDANCE AT COURT

"Be prepared" is a motto for others than just the Scouts. No matter how familiar with court and legal procedures a social worker considers himself/herself to be, each court appearance is a new and sometimes quite unique experience. Nothing equips the social worker to be a useful and competent witness so much as adequate preparation.

Preparation has two parts: the structural, physical part (curriculum vitae, your file), and the professional performance part (review of the process of the social work contact, the content of any report, and the basis for any conclusions and recommendations).

Structural Preparation

1. *Curriculum Vitae:* An up-to-date, cleanly typed copy of the social worker's c.v. should be made available to all lawyers attending in the matter. Bring one or two extra copies to court, in case they are needed. The c.v. forms the basis for the request for the social worker/witness to be qualified as an expert witness in the matter. A copy will be filed with the court.

   The c.v. should be clearly organized and set out, so the necessary aspects of education, training, professional experience, and relevant professional activity may be readily noted.

2. *The Case File:* Prior to the court date, the case file should be organized so that the needed information can be readily located. Entries should be up-to-date; dates and lengths of time of case activities should be listed. The file should be brought to court and made available graciously if you are directed to do so by the judge. Professional ethical guidelines concerning confidentiality are not the same as lawyer/client privilege and may be overridden by the court's direction that both sides have access to the notes, or to any part of the file. Disclosure of information is a necessary part of a trial. This is a difficult area; mental health professionals generally resist open scrutiny of their case files, finding that it assails their concept of confidentiality and places them at risk of damaging their relationship with the client(s). While there has been some recognition by the courts that revelation of certain information may be or could be damaging and therefore may be withheld (no guarantee), generally the position remains that pertinent information contained in professional files must be shared with the lawyers for both sides.

Professional Performance Preparation

Close to the actual court appearance date, the file should be re-read, in particular the interview notes with the parties and any collateral sources. Such re-familiarizing oneself with the file facilitates not only recall of the matter and the people involved, but allows clarification of the following points, which may be raised in court:

1. *The five W's: who, what, where, when, and why:* Who was interviewed, with what response, where and on what date, and for what purposes? The answers to these questions speak to thoroughness, fairness, and balance in the conduct of the social worker service.

2. *The social worker's position and why he/she holds it:* The social worker/witness will be required to clarify the basis of any opinions and conclusions. Credibility will be associated with a capacity to explain clearly and coherently how a professional opinion/conclu-

sion was arrived at, and why that opinion/conclusion was more persuasive than another. This may involve describing the steps undertaken in the social work process, the data obtained, and the professional theories or body of knowledge relied upon in formulating opinion and conclusions. A careful think-through a day or so ahead of court will focus the mind and help to recapture the thinking and weighting of information that was part of the social work process. Although a particular case may be recalled, it is surprising how quickly some detail begins to fade, especially as one is involved in new undertakings. Do the review, don't rely on memory to provide the details.

3. *Familiarity with the professional sources relied upon (and not relied upon):* The study of human behaviour and relationships is not an exact science. We know a great deal about human behaviour and relationships and child development. There is much more yet to learn. In the meantime, responsible social work practitioners acquaint themselves with the relevant literature and research findings, and keep up-to-date as knowledge and theory emerge.

Points of view and philosophy differ. Recognized authorities may advocate one position, one process, over another. Earlier literature, long honoured as near "dogma," may find challenge in the work of current professionals. Old "givens" give way to new formulations.

The opinions and conclusions stated by a social worker/witness will have added impact if reference can be made to recognized literature in the field of expertise under examination. It will help to be able to explain why one point of view is preferred over another. So, review the relevant citations a day or two ahead, including those whose points of view are less appealing. Writing the citations and authors' names on a small filing card to have on the witness stand may assist in accurate reference to the works. Such references suggest that the social worker/witness is aware of currently held professional thinking in the statements made on the witness stand, and that he or she is part of a recognized professional group, not simply one individual expressing personal opinions.

4. *Having a preparatory session with the lawyer calling the social worker:* The lawyer seeking the assistance of an expert professional witness has a responsibility to prepare that witness for the focus of the anticipated examination-in-chief. That preparation should take place a few days before the actual court appearance, to allow the social worker to complete his or her familiarization with the case file. In the event that the lawyer does not undertake this preparation, the social worker is entitled to request it, and should do so. This is of particular value if opinion evidence is going to be sought by the lawyer.

GUIDELINES FOR DIRECT EXAMINATION

At the court house, waiting to be called is often a boring time. The tendency is for the assembled people to visit and chat. It is advisable not to become too involved in discussion with either of the parties, their friends, or relatives. Be courteous and pleasant, and discreet. Do not discuss the pending testimony with anyone except the lawyer for the side that has called you. Prior discussions should already have been held with that lawyer, as indicated, reviewing the areas most likely to be explored. Last-minute briefings may be useful, but cannot replace good preparation.

Apart from having prepared as indicated above, the following guidelines will assist the social worker in the first phase on the witness stand, called direct examination, or sometimes examination-in-chief. There are undoubtedly more aspects that could be included. An experienced social worker/witness will develop his or her own style and approach. The following, however, have proven useful over time.

- *Dress comfortably yet professionally in clothes that are comfortable for usual professional work.* This does *not* mean slacks or T-shirts. The purpose is twofold: to convey a professional image and respect to the court, and to help the social worker/witness feel comfortable. The more the latter is the case, the more likelihood the former will be the case. As the TV ad says: there's never a second chance to make a first impression.

- *Speak up in a clear, firm voice that conveys to the court confidence and knowledgeability.* The judge, the court reporter, and the lawyers are all trying to follow each reply word for word. It is annoying for any one of them to have to keep requesting the witness to repeat, and to speak up. If nervous about being on the witness stand, the social worker should practise in advance, reciting information such as name, address, and the local weather conditions, for example, until the recitation comes easily. Speak out toward the lawyer asking the questions, with head up rather than gazing down in the witness box. *Speak slowly*, as people are writing down the answers. *Spell proper names or technical terms* for the court reporter, slowly.

  The social worker/witness's testimony is important. Supportive, explanatory information from the person who knows the parties/children in a professional way is of interest. Presenting that information clearly facilitates possible acceptance.

- *Listen carefully to the wording of each question.* Sometimes lawyers ask convoluted questions. Sometimes it appears that their head is moving faster than their mouth, and they jumble one question with another dealing with another point. Even the "friendly" lawyer from the party calling the social worker as their witness may seek agreement with a fact or an assumption that is not seen by the social worker/witness as correct.

  In any of these circumstances, *do not answer a question that was not understood.* Pause and consider. If necessary, request that the question be repeated, even more than once. Better to be slow and accurate than quick and appear glib.

- *Ask permission to refer to notes in the file.* Do not rely just on memory when asked about dates, times, frequency of contacts, and so forth. It is appropriate to check the activity sheet in the file. But because checking the file means looking at materials, copies of which may not be in the possession of all the lawyers, there may be a challenge from the opposite side.

  To address that issue, if you wish to check the file in order to obtain accurate information, the correct procedure is to ask permission of the court (the judge) to do so, and then wait a moment. There may be a challenge from the other lawyer, who may just wish to ensure later access to the file if needed prior to cross-examination. That acknowledged, the court will grant permission for the file to be consulted. Having the file there to be referred to demonstrates, among other things, the wish of the social worker/witness to be accurate in all information given. Having organized the file beforehand pays off here, as the required data can be readily accessed.

- *Take the time needed to answer a question.* It is most important that the testimony presented by the social worker/witness be accurate, that it is indeed what was meant to be said. If a question has been confusing or complicated, too quick a reply, given before there has been time for thought, could see the social worker/witness agreeing to a position not intended, or even contradicting earlier statements. That development will not be missed by the other side, and may be used in cross-examination later.

Taking the time needed does not mean inordinate delay, while wishing the lawyer would ask something else. It means being careful and thoughtful, clear as to the question asked and the reply presented.

- *Always reply to a question.* The question may be awkward, the reply embarrassing. Nevertheless, the social worker/witness is not in a position to decline to answer. An answer of some sort must be given. To refuse to reply is a serious mistake and can have a fatal impact on the social worker/witness's credit and credibility before the court.

  This issue is more commonly seen in cross-examination, where the social worker/witness may be feeling pressured. But it may also arise in direct examination, when a zealous lawyer asks an awkward question. Head into it, answer as frankly and clearly as possible, and leave it to counsel to attempt to do "damage control" if necessary. No social work process is absolutely perfect; more could always have been done or attempted. Be ready to explain what was done or not done. Acknowledging the limitations in a given situation actually improves the impression the social worker is creating, as reasonable, forthright, and appropriately modest about what social work and he or she as a social worker can try to accomplish. Arrogance on the witness stand does not go down well and weakens the value of the social worker/witness's evidence.

- *Remember: giving evidence is not the same as having a conversation or participating in a meeting.* The social worker/witness is on the stand in his or her capacity as a professional. The purpose is serious, the outcome is serious. Examination-in-chief and cross-examination are the established methods for eliciting the information pertinent to the dispute which each side wants the court to hear. The lawyer asking the questions has boundaries that must be observed in the way the questions may be framed. The point-by-point approach, which may seem tedious at times, reflects the system available to the lawyer to use in eliciting wanted replies. During the question/answer process, the asking lawyer is, so to speak, "in charge" of the exchange. The relationship with the social worker/witness is vertical, as opposed to the horizontal context of personal conversations or case conferences.

  A social worker/witness, while being alert and attentive, must cooperate with the process. If there are problems, the judge or the opposing lawyer may intervene, and either direct the asking lawyer to another question or challenge the acceptance of the way the pending question was worded.

  It is not the prerogative of the social worker/witness to attempt to change the way questions are asked. It is not proper to make "editorial comments," to interrupt the lawyer mid-question, or to try to be amusing. Do not "visit" with the lawyer. Court testimony is not a personal conversation. Stick to the questions asked, reply, and wait patiently for the next question. *Avoid using body language as a communication device*: moving about in exasperation, raising eyes to heaven, sighing audibly, hitting the stand for emphasis, shaking one's head (more in sorrow than in anger, and all that) while a question is being put. While this may be especially tempting during the cross-examination, the attitudes such behaviour suggest may also be present during direct examination. Perhaps the lawyer is not asking the one question wanted, which would "clinch" the social work position on the issues. No matter. It is up to the lawyer to seek the information wanted, and to frame the questions appropriately. It is the role of the social worker/witness to remain cool, courteous, careful, and cooperative.

- *Admit that you do not know the answer to a question, if that is the case.* It is not really expected that social workers have all the answers to the issues in family or other relationships. As acknowledged earlier, the science of human behaviour is not exact. There may be areas of professional research one is not familiar with, books advocating a position contrary to that being put forward that one has not heard of or read, a piece of information brought forward after the social work service completed, and so forth. That is all right; no social worker can know everything about his or her practice area.

- *Never try to invent a reply.* There is nothing wrong or damaging in stating a lack of knowledge of or about an item raised by the lawyer. In point of fact, it strengthens the social worker/witness's credibility to indicate an inability to answer the question, either because the answer is not known or the necessary information is lacking. An up-front, direct admission that the question can't be answered ("I'm sorry, I don't know the answer to that question," or "I'm sorry, I don't have that information and don't know how to reply to that particular question") is responsible and professional and suggests security with one's unavoidable limitations. Even experts have limitations. No one responds well to a "know-it-all." There is always more to learn.

  "Winging" an answer is very risky business. A social worker/witness may appear to be avoiding an area, and that will invite pursuit in cross-examination. Or it may be seen as sort of "showing off" (the I-can-handle-anything attitude). This may have the effect of putting people off, and weakening rather than strengthening the social worker/witness's credibility. If you did not undertake a certain task when conducting the casework, admit it, and be prepared to explain why.

- *Be humble, even while appearing confident.* The social worker/witness's manner on the stand is noted by the judge, and forms part of the impression being gained about him or her, and the testimony being presented. Low-key self-confidence as a practising professional is appropriate. Don't try to show off or be arrogant—it's off-putting. On the other hand, one need not be apologetic for one's professional choice, about limited experience in a certain area, or for belonging to a profession that has few, if any, absolutes within its body of knowledge.

GUIDELINES FOR COPING WITH CROSS-EXAMINATION

Cross-examination has acquired something of a bad reputation. It can be a difficult and trying experience, although in fairness, that is not always the case. Many lawyers conduct the cross-examination cordially and courteously, trying neither to confuse nor to badger, harass or intimidate. It is always a pleasure to meet these lawyers across the witness stand: their manner allows the social worker/witness to put full energy and attention into understanding their questions, assessing where they are heading, and formulating appropriate replies. (One should not be led astray by a quiet approach, however, and be lulled into believing that the cross-examination will be easy. It is never easy.)

It is useful here to recall the image of the medieval jousting match. One knight has already ridden the course (examination-in-chief). Now comes the adversary: the opposing knight, bent on unseating his opponent, or failing that, to weaken his position enough to undo the points he scored. As applied to the social worker/witness, this means a determined effort to challenge and undo as many as possible of the points that were scored in examination-in-chief, and to make points for the challenging side instead.

Competent lawyers prepare carefully for cross-examination. They study any social work report and discuss its content, conclusions, and any recommendations with their client. They may have sought outside professional opinion about the social work service. They have identified areas that may suggest vulnerability of the social worker/witness to questions of thoroughness, fairness, bias, or unprofessional action of some kind. Other questions may have emerged from the questions and answers presented in examination-in-chief.

Although they may act surprised or chagrined or disbelieving during the course of the cross-examination, don't be diverted by these histrionics. The competent cross-examining lawyer has a very clear view of the desired goal. As indicated earlier, a "fishing expedition," usually accompanied with some pressure and increased emotional temperature, almost always suggests that the lawyer has a weak case and knows it, yet persists in asking questions. The hope is to catch a contradiction, an evasion, a retreat from a position, an admission of error or failure, to bolster the cause. Competent social workers/witnesses learn to recognize these signs, and not to be carried away into making comments later regretted.

As with examination-in-chief, good preparation is the best tool with which to meet cross-examination. Knowing the case, the process relied upon, the bases for any conclusions and recommendations, the reasons for choices made or discarded, and the professional basis for theory, will equip the social worker/witness more than adequately. With these tools and attention to handling oneself, the social worker/witness will come through just fine.

But it is necessary to be alert to cross-examination strategies, to be aware of where the questions seem to be leading, and to be prepared to withstand the challenges with some counter-strategies. The lawyer may seem to be behaving outrageously; do not respond in kind. Cross-examination is even less of a conversation than examination-in-chief. So be aware, pay attention, and consider the following:

- *Wherever possible, avoid simple "yes" or "no" answers to questions in cross-examination.* Many questions posed in cross-examination are anything but straightforward. The lawyer may frame them in such a way as to lead toward a certain answer. A common device, for example, is to begin a question with "Would you agree with me that such and such is a fact?" or "Wouldn't you agree that such and such is a preferred way of doing this or that?" The question may be followed directly with the directive, "Please answer yes or no."

    If the social worker/witness begins the reply with something like "Well, yes, but ....," the lawyer will very likely stop any qualifying statements, not wanting to weaken the impact of the "yes."

    It is more useful, if a qualification is indicated in the social worker/witness's professional opinion, to begin the reply with that qualification, and end with the direct or possible "yes." This may be expressed as follows: "There are differing opinions still on that particular issue and there is more for us yet to learn, but in my own professional opinion I lean more to the such and such position. I could elaborate more on that if you wish, but in answer to your question, I would reply with a qualified but not full "yes." This approach allows the qualification to be expressed, while still replying to the question, and protects the social worker/witness from being caught in apparently agreeing with a complex statement or proposition without reservation, which is not in fact a true reflection of his or her view.

- *Use pauses in giving answers.* Sometimes the rhythm of the question-answer exchange takes on almost a metronomic quality. Both lawyers and the social worker/witness can get caught up in this. This lawyer knows what goal is intended, what strong "real" question will "force" the social worker/witness into a concession, an admission, a change in position, and so forth. Every competent lawyer knows or assumes what the answer to each question will be, so the next one flows logically from that point. The questions and their anticipated answers have already been written down.

Sometimes the lawyer becomes so engrossed in following his or her notes, as the question-answer rhythm proceeds, that not enough attention is paid to the social worker/witness. The momentum is beginning to carry the process toward the conclusion wanted by the cross-examining lawyer. Breaking that metronomic effect can be helpful in ensuring that the social worker/witness does not get swept along to "suddenly" apparently agreeing to a conclusion unacceptable to him or her. If one is aware that the rhythm effect is building, take longer between some answers, change the tempo. This changes the atmosphere, and keeps the social worker/witness alert at the same time.

- *Ask to have questions repeated.* This is, of course, necessary if the social worker/witness did not hear the question, did not understand the question, or if the lawyer has rolled two or three or more questions into one, and the social worker/witness doesn't know where to start by way of reply. It is quite appropriate to indicate that one didn't hear or understand, or know which of the four questions the lawyer wants answered first. A repeat will readily follow.

  But it is in another area that the request for a repeat of the questions is also useful: when the lawyer is pressing, crowding, pushing, perhaps even with a voice raised a bit. Politely asking to have a question repeated interrupts that pressure, even for a moment. That may be enough for the social worker/witness to pull his or her thoughts together, to regain control of any slipping emotions, to recognize the strategy at play, but to continue to be a cooperative witness. Sometimes, too, the interruption serves to slow down the lawyer who was in too much of a hurry to get to the "important" questions.

- *What to do when the question is personal, rather than directed at the professional self.* Sometimes the focus of the questions in cross-examination shifts from the social work service to the social worker. Although not always easy to deal with, this tactic, like the "fishing expedition," signals the lawyer's frustration in finding more vulnerable points of attack. In a sense, it is an echo of the familiar adage from other trial situations: "If you can't attack the evidence, attack the witness." That means, of course, the witness's credibility.

  It is usually useful to go along with one or two more personal questions. The change in tactic should be reassuring, not distressing. It is a sign that the social worker/witness's evidence so far has been strong, consistent, and difficult to assail. The marital status of the social worker/witness may be replied to. However, if the social worker/witness is unmarried, a question as to how many children he or she has is not a question to reply to. One can see the direction about to be followed: if not married, and/or without children, how can the social worker/witness comment, for example, on his or her client's parenting capacity?

  At that point, asking to have the particular question repeated, once or even twice, helps to alert the other lawyer, and the judge, to what is going on, and invites them to intervene. Pause after the second request, and see if that happens.

  If that result does not ensue, the social worker/witness may ask permission to address the court (the judge) and with that permission ask for the court's assistance.

"The social worker/witness is there in his or her professional capacity, therefore could the judge please help by directing whether to reply to personal questions, since they are confusing, and one is not certain whether to respond, etc."

Judges are, of course, well aware of the games of the joust. They were formerly in the arena, too. At that point the judge may suggest that the lawyer/warrior-knight seek another target, and either ask other questions or end the cross-examination.

- *Ask assistance from the judge as you feel the need of it.* Other pressure may develop during a long or protracted cross-examination. It is quite permissible to make certain requests from the judge. Ask politely if you may address the Bench; permission will always be readily forthcoming.

Requests may include a comfort break, a chair if standing for a long time, a glass of water or a refill. The court will always be considerate of an expert witness. The interruption may be all that is needed for the social worker/witness to take a deep breath, cool down any growing irritation, regroup concerning the professional point of view being challenged, shake the fatigue out a bit. Fatigue and anger interfere with focused attention to what is going on.

- *Don't allow eye contact by a harassing cross-examining lawyer.* Eye contact is almost an essential ingredient of meaningful human conversation or interaction. Whether through love, anger, or sincerity, people look directly at another person when trying to ensure an important message is "getting through."

Sometimes the cross-examining lawyer tries to "hold" the social worker/witness "in place" so to speak, as the crunch questions loom up. The lawyer may move physically much closer to the social worker/witness and try to establish direct, intense eye contact. In this context, such eye contact is a power behaviour, seeming to convey the message that the social worker/witness must now answer this next question (in a way that is wanted).

The most effective way to neutralize this power behaviour is simply to deny the lawyer the connection. The social worker/witness does not allow the eye contact to remain in place, glances down at the floor of the witness box, or at the far wall in the courtroom. Or the social worker/witness may stand with head bowed slightly and eyes shut, suggesting that he/she is listening very carefully indeed to the question (as is very important to do), in order to answer it correctly.

Breaking the "control connection" in this power play by not allowing sustained up-close eye contact frees the social worker/witness to pay attention, and listen very carefully to the wording of the next questions, in order to avoid unwanted, impulsive, or incorrect answers.

- *Take something to drop in the witness box.* In spite of experience, and all advice, it is difficult sometimes not to get rattled and/or irritated by a cross-examination. At such a moment it is wonderfully useful to have something to drop: a paper clip, a pen, a small elastic band, a small-hand size notebook, for example. Dropping something on the floor of the witness box, apologizing to the court for the interruption, bending down to retrieve the lost object, and then replacing it somewhere will buy precious seconds to allow the social worker/witness to take a couple of deep breaths (literally), which will help settle the emotions down. Apologize again to the judge for the interruption and politely ask the lawyer to repeat the last question. A fail-safe strategy.

- *Keep your temper*. Even very experienced social workers/witnesses can become stretched and testy in a long and aggressive cross-examination. Points repeated over and over, probing "fishing expeditions," lawyer behaviour that has been unpleasant but not checked by the judge, personal questions—all can bring a very tired social worker/witness to the edge of anger. It is then that the something-to-drop tactic is so vital; regaining poise and control is essential.

  Along with that regained control comes the recognition that, unpleasant though it may sometimes be, the pressure of cross-examination is not personal. The task is directed at the work and professional opinions of the social worker/witness, even if personal questions were introduced. In 99 percent of the cases, tough cross-examination is no more than a lawyer serving his or her client's position as well as possible. In the occasional 1 percent situation, where cross-examination becomes too intense, the social worker/witness will recognize that the experience is similar to dealing with a very difficult, resistive, or even hostile client: manageable, but tiring, a real challenge to maintaining professional control.

QUESTIONS TO ANTICIPATE

The following list sets out the areas most likely to be canvassed in either examination-in-chief or cross-examination. Working through the list, prior to court attendance, will put the social worker/witness in a good position to answer most questions. This list is by no means exhaustive, nor does it purport to address all aspects of social work function. The first questions put to the social worker/witness, of course, will be those directed at qualifying him or her as an expert witness. The following list now begins to address areas that may be touched on in the body of the testimony.

Elements That Will Be Covered in Direct Examination

1. When and how you became involved as a social worker in the matter.
2. Your method—generally and in this particular matter.
3. Sources of information—who, what, and how obtained.
4. Where, when, and under what circumstances you met each of the parties and/or the children.
5. What tests, if any, were administered. (Be careful here: if you are not a qualified psychologist or psychiatrist, what basis did you have to conduct any tests?)
6. What those tests purport to measure.
7. How the reliability of the tests is gauged.
8. The wishes of the children, if any, and how those were obtained and taken into account.
9. Strengths and weaknesses of each party.
10. Whether you were able to reach definite conclusions regarding, for example, custody of and access to children, as a result of an assessment.
11. What those conclusions were.
12. How the conclusions connect to the data in a report.
13. The theoretical basis for the professional conclusions and opinions, and why that theory and not another applies.

14. Which other contemporary authorities would hold the same viewpoint and who would not.

15. How your opinion might be modified if any of the disputed facts were other than you believed them to be.

16. Which aspects of your social work practice in the matter might have been extended or altered, in retrospect.

17. Why the arrangement proposed by you would meet the needs of the family better than other proposed arrangements.

Elements That Will Be Covered in Cross-Examination

1. Was the social work undertaken thorough—are there gaps in the data?

2. Was any assessment fair? Is there bias in method, conclusion, or expression?

3. Do the data support any recommendations? Are other recommendations equally supportable by the data?

4. Was any report balanced? Why were certain items (not) included?

5. How were culture, religion, lifestyle differences handled? What consideration was given to an individual's right to be different?

6. If there are other possible resolutions to this matter, why did you not use one of them?

7. Could you be wrong?

Final Points to Remember

1. A court hearing is not a case conference or a conversation.

2. The lawyers are doing their job. It is a different approach to problem-solving than that used by social workers. That does not make either one wrong.

3. The purpose of a hearing/trial is to arrive at a decision in a matter, not the "whole" (elusive, subjective) truth. The decision about the dispute is entirely the prerogative of the judge (or judge and jury).

4. The social worker/witness's role is to be of assistance to the court, not to tell the court what to do.

5. Lawyers' challenges are not directed at you personally, even if personal questions are included.

6. The testimony is but one piece of evidence to be taken into consideration by the judge. Other opinions may prevail. The judge may not agree with the social worker/witness's professional opinion.

7. The best way to give your evidence and your professional opinions the greatest weight is to present them professionally.

CONCLUSION

Social work is not an exact science. While there is an identifiable body of knowledge and an extensive collection of professional skills, social work practice addresses an elusive and variable target: human nature and the human condition. While much has been learned, much is yet to be understood. And all perceived understanding or new insight is subject to the variables of culture, geography, religion, and convention. Notions of morality, duty, gender roles, and intergenerational obligation dominate and influence behaviour, judgment, and decision-making.

Within the broad context of what is Canadian, or seen to be Canadian, professional social work practice seeks to enhance and facilitate positive functioning of individuals, families, groups, and communities in a mingling of those variables. It is not an easy task. But social work's particular focus on the nature and dynamics of interactive relationships can provide aspects of society such as our legal system with valuable insights. These insights flesh out and give specific life to the "skeleton" of a fact-situation, assisting those charged with the responsibility of decision-making to render judgments that are at once considered and informed. One significant forum for such a contribution is the courtroom.

The professional social worker, functioning as a recognized and accepted expert witness, is in a position to make a unique addition to the legal system's grasp of the issues in a dispute. As such, in spite of the sometimes trying aspects of court attendance, the expert social worker may welcome the request to participate in a hearing. A well-prepared social worker who is clear as to professional practice and opinion will make a genuine contribution to all concerned.

REFERENCES

Bell, E.F. (1976). How to be an expert witness. *The Journal of Legal Medicine.* October, 1976.

Brodsky, S.W. (1991). *Testifying in court: guidelines and maxims for the expert witness.* Washington, D.C.: American Psychological Association.

Buckhout, R. (1976). Nobody likes a smartass: expert testimony by psychologists. Presentation to the Symposium on Accuracy of Eyewitness Testimony: The Psychologist As An Expert Witness. American Psychological Association Convention, Washington, D.C., September 6, 1976.

Chisholm, B.A. and MacNaughton, H.C. (1990). *Custody/access assessments: a practical guide for lawyers and assessors.* Toronto, Canada. Carswell.

DeBoo, R. (1982). Preparation of a witness: the expert. *Advocacy.* 150th Anniversary Symposium. The Canadian Bar Association / The Law Society of Upper Canada (Ontario). And "Commentary" by Sir David Napley, 1982.

Duquette, D.N. (1981). The expert witness in child abuse and neglect: an interdisciplinary process. *Child Abuse and Neglect, 5,* 325–334.

Levine, S.V. The role of the mental health expert witness in family law disputes. Dept. of Psychiatry, University of Toronto, undated.

Schultz, R. (1995). Evaluating the expert witness: the mental health expert in child sexual abuse cases. *American Journal of Family Law, 9,* 1–9. (St. Louis, Mo. Bar Journal, 1995).

INTERPRETERS IN SOCIAL WORK PRACTICE

Francis J. Turner

One of the exciting realities of our Canadian multicultural mosaic is the diversity of lifestyles of which our country is composed. In a few moments on a downtown corner of any Canadian city or town one can see in the passing parade a rich array of the world's cultures. Included, of course, in this amalgam is a diversity of spoken languages. At this time there are probably in Canada well over a hundred different languages used by Canadians, many by persons who are monolingual and not able to communicate in either French or English.

As we know from our practices, regardless of background, culture, ethnic group, and language, many people will need the services of a social worker. Thus the only way most social workers will be able to communicate with them is through the medium of an interpreter. That we do and will have social workers who are fluent in other languages is of course a given. Indeed the day may come soon when a requirement for entry into a school of social work in Canada will be fluency in at least two languages. But for at least the next three decades, few agencies or services will be able to interview across the broad spectrum of languages spoken by our clients and we will either not serve such people or will serve them through an interpreter (Mirdal, 1988).

Since social work is a profession where communication is our essential medium, ours should be the one that leads the way in this form of communication. Unfortunately, although most social workers at one time or another have needed to make use of this type of interview, there is little written in the literature of the helping professions about this aspect of practice and even less research related to the differential use of this professional adjunct. It is urgent that this soon change.

In the meantime we need to make use of what knowledge and experience there is and as rapidly as possible build up a cadre of practice wisdom. Simultaneously, we must test this accumulated experience by means of well-designed research.

The following material starts from three assumptions. First, that interpreters are highly skilled professionals requiring training as intensive as that which we impose upon ourselves. Second, that it is possible to conduct in-depth interviews with the collaboration of a professional interpreter. Third, that serious misunderstanding and indeed harm can result when persons are placed in the role of the interpreter without understanding their function or who lack the requisite skill to carry out this role effectively. Thus there are serious ethical challenges and issues related to this component of Canadian social work practice.

THE INTERPRETER ROLE

One of the difficulties involved in discussing the use of interpreters is that there is far from total unanimity on what is the proper role of the interpreter in social work practice. A discussion of the topic among social workers usually divides into two positions. The one holds that the role of the interpreter is to transmit between and among the participants in a conversation as exact a rendition of the spoken word of each speaker as is possible with no added explanations or commentary on what either the client or worker mean.

The second position is that as well as serving as a language transmitter the interpreter needs also to function as a cultural or ethnic interpreter. That is, in addition to conveying between the client and myself the words each of us is speaking, the interpreter will also explain to the client some phrase or some aspect of my communication that may not be understood by the client because of cultural differences. As well, the interpreter will inform me during the process of the interview that some phraseology of the client may also have a cultural significance that I may fail to comprehend if I only have the literal interpretation of the words.

This difference in the perceived role of the interpreter implies two different styles of interpreting. If the interpreter is viewed only as a transmitter of language, then he or she will only speak in the first person of both the client and the social worker and will never elaborate on what is being said or engage in a side discussion with either the client or the worker during the process of the interview. In the second instance, where a broader role of the interpreter is the perceived preferred one, it frequently will happen during the interview that the interpreter will have a direct conversation with the social worker or client as an aside to the process of the interview. This could happen for a variety of reasons; for example, to clarify some meaning, to explain some particular aspect of the client's life situation, or the cultural significance of some content, or to explain to the client some aspect of the social worker's role or content of the interview. Hence in this style of interpreting, there can be exchanges between worker and client through the interpreter, exchanges between client and interpreter, and exchanges between interpreter and social worker. In each of the two latter situations either the worker or the client is excluded from the primary interchange of content. Most of us have had experiences where these side discussions become quite involved and can totally exclude either the client or the interviewer. At times, such discussions can last several minutes. This in turn can result in serious challenges to the development and maintenance of a therapeutic milieu (Parks, 1982).

In addition to the two different perceptions of the interpreter role, there is a further difference in interpreting style that needs to be considered. The distinction is between the interpreter functioning in a simultaneous mode and in a consecutive mode. In the first, the interpreter functions in a manner in which she or he interprets to each party what is being said, while it is being spoken. This particular format requires high-level language fluency and skill in both of the interview languages. When this format is used skilled interpreters can function in a manner in which they are only five or six words behind the flow of the conversation. With very little practice a client and social worker can quickly become accustomed to this mode and very soon the interchange becomes one of direct exchange between client and social worker with only the slight delay caused by the interpretative process. This is not unlike getting used to the delay that takes place between verbal exchanges on some international phone calls.

Another format of interpreting is one which might be called consecutive interpreting. In this format the interpreter functions by breaking the conversation of each party into discrete sections so that there are breaks in the conversation. In these instances, the worker speaks for a few moments, stops, and then lets the interpreter convey these words in the first person to the client. The client then responds, at which point they pause again while the interpreter conveys this material to the worker. This makes for a much more disjointed interview-conversation than when the simultaneous mode is used.

In the above and following discussions we are presuming that the format of the interview is one client with one worker. Clearly, in our practice there will be occasions when more than one client is present, such as in couple, family, or group work. In these latter instances the role of the interpreter, or indeed interpreters, becomes even more complex; however, the same issues that will be discussed here will apply.

The remainder of this chapter will be divided into two parts, the first dealing with situations where we are collaborating with professional interpreters and the second with persons gifted with competence in two or more languages but who are not trained in the interpreter role.

In making this distinction it is important to keep in mind that it is not a fully dichotomous one but ought to be viewed as a continuum ranging from persons with no experience in this role to those who are fully trained and experienced. That is, we frequently find in agencies persons who have long functioned as volunteer interpreters and in so doing have developed a high level of competence. It would be wrong to imply in any way that such persons are not and cannot be highly facilitative in the interpreting role.

WORKING WITH THE TRAINED INTERPRETER

There are several factors to keep in mind in working with the professional interpreter (Freed, 1988). If it is not someone you know, or if it is someone not acquainted with our professional vocabulary, it is useful to review with them any of the technical terms that might come up in an interview prior to the interview. If there is sufficient time, an interpreter might look through a basic social work text or journal to get a sense of our technical language.

As well, there should be a discussion of roles prior to the interview to ensure that there is a communality of perception, and if one does not exist, then differences can be worked out. This should not take place in the presence of the client. Frequently, persons who have not worked with interpreters focus the preparation on the function of the agency and the anticipated nature of the interview rather than on the much more important aspect of mutual roles and expectations.

As well, it is important to review with the interpreter your expectations in general and any specific details of the process in which you are about to engage. For example, the question of where you want the interviewer to sit is important and thus prior to the interview you need to establish that there is consensus on such technical aspects of the process. As will be mentioned later, you may wish that the interpreter not be present in the room but function instead from behind a one-way mirror or even through a speaker phone connection only.

If the interpreter is to be present in the interview, then where possible the client should be made aware before the interview as to who the interpreter will be. There are times when the name, gender, age, class, place of origin, occupation, or religion of the interpreter may create high stress levels for the client or indeed be totally unacceptable to them. This is one of the reasons why some colleagues have found it more helpful not to have the interpreter in the interviewing room so that he or she is only a voice to the client and the worker and truly functions as a voice conduit only (Baker, 1981).

Some professional interpreters like to have an opportunity to meet or speak to the client prior to the interview to ensure that the necessary and expected language competence is present. This is most important since in many countries there are several languages spoken as well as distinct dialects within languages, requiring highly specific language abilities.

For the most part, once we become comfortable in the role of working with an interpreter present, and are aware of the potential effectiveness of quality interpreting, the process of interviewing with the assistance of a trained interpreter is not difficult. Only in rare instances of clashes of personality or serious disagreements of role do problems arise. Indeed, after a little experience the presence of a skilled interpreter becomes less and less evident to both client and worker. I remember clearly an instance in which I was interviewing a senior government official from China, an elderly man with a deep voice. The interpreter was a young woman with a high-pitched voice who sat behind the man, speaking over his shoulder. After a very few minutes, I was only aware of his voice, with her voice almost unheard yet giving me the required interpretation.

THE UNTRAINED INTERPRETER

A much more common situation for us in social work practice in Canada is one in which the interpreter is functioning on a voluntary ad hoc basis. For example, we suddenly find ourselves in a situation where an interpreter is required and scurry to find someone who speaks the language of the client. This can vary from a one-time-only use of someone who is available and possesses the language competence, to use on a more regular basis of colleagues and staff members with such competencies, to pools of volunteers with a combined range of language skills who are frequently available in many large agencies or communities. Often it happens that a person will bring a friend or relative along to the agency to function in this role. This, of course, can be very helpful but it is also a situation that can be fraught with difficulty from the perspective of the relationship, confidentiality, and objectivity of the interpreter and the content of the interview.

An even more complex situation arises when the only person available is a member of the immediate family. In our research we have found that in first generation immigrant families it is often the children who have developed a competence in French or English beyond that of the parents. When this happens the children are expected to assume the role of the interpreter in many day-to-day situations. This too has very serious implications in a therapeutic situation and in this author's view should be strenuously avoided and only used when there is no other alternative and then only for the gathering of basic information. But even in these apparently neutral information-content instances one can quickly get into sensitive material that creates very complex psycho-dynamic challenges for both the interpreter, the interviewee, and the social worker.

Another situation that can create difficulties in the interviewing process is when we use a colleague from our own profession who is able to speak the desired language. Of course, this situation has much to recommend it over using a friend or family member but it also can create other kinds of role stresses on the interview. If our colleague does not fully understand the interpreter role and is not able to fully function as interpreter only, we can quickly create a situation in which there are two social workers interviewing the client. When this happens the client can quickly become confused and uncertain as to who to speak to and who is in charge of the interview. These situations can also develop into complex relationship situations that at times can become subtle power struggles between the two workers as to who is the primary professional in the situation.

A further difficulty that can occur with the untrained interpreter is one of over-identification with either the client or the worker. Thus we can have situations where the interpreting person begins to over-identify with the client and his or her difficulties, or be overwhelmed by them and unwittingly understate or distort their seriousness in the process of interpreting. This process can range along a continuum of deliberate misrepresentation to unconscious distortions for self-protection. In the same way an interpreter can over-identify with the worker and become angry, shocked, or disappointed in the client and subtly let the interpreting process take on a moralistic tone that does not reflect the social worker's treatment thrust. This can become even more complex when the client realizes through tonality and body language that different messages are being transmitted by each of the parties.

Nevertheless, it would be wrong to take too pessimistic an attitude about the use of the volunteer interpreter. Most are very desirous of doing a good job. I am increasingly convinced that many of the difficulties that arise stem from our uncertainty about their expected role and our failure to help them understand how they can be most helpful. Since it is certain that we are going to have to make use of volunteer interpreters in our practice, with some assistance from us, a very helpful and effective collegial relationship can be developed (Knapp-Potthoff, & Knapp, 1986).

What follows are some suggestions built on our experience to date and suggestions gained from colleagues experienced in working with volunteer interpreters. As mentioned earlier, it is critical that we give consideration to what we ourselves consider the role of the interpreter to be. That is, do we want the interpreter to interpret not only the literal meaning of words but also the possible cultural significance of the material? Or do we want the interpreter to function as a voice conduit as discussed above. It is my position that it is our task to learn about the client's culture and that it greatly complicates the interpreter's task to give it this dual function (Glasser, 1983).

Following from this it is critical that we should give special attention to orienting the interpreter to our expectations and as far as possible reach consensus on this question. If we decide that the interpreter's role is one of conveying language only then is it important to encourage the volunteer to learn to speak in the first person. That is, they are to speak as if they were the client when the client speaks and the social worker when the social worker is talking. Thus we do not want the interpreter to say, "She says she is feeling upset." Rather we want them to say, "I am feeling upset." This same strategy applies equally to our comments to the client. Thus we must avoid saying to the interpreter, "Ask her how she and her husband are getting along." Rather we want to say directly to the client, "How are you and your husband getting along," which the interpreter will then render into the other language.

Where we have a particular problem with this use of the first person is in situations where the person functioning as interpreter is not fully fluent in one, or indeed at times either, of the languages and frequently needs to have side discussions with the client or with us as to what it is we are trying to say. Because of this it is important for the interpreter to speak with the client before an interview begins, to ascertain if there is sufficient fluency between the client and interpreter to function in the complex process of a professional interview (Segalowitz, 1976). But in so doing we and the interpreter have to be careful that the interpreter and the client do not begin the interviewing process. Because of this risk, it is useful for ourselves or another person to be present to ensure that the social work process does not begin and that the exchange is around language implications only. Hence this preparatory contact should be very brief and its purpose well understood by both client and interpreter. In this regard one of the difficulties of volunteer interpreters is that at times their own reputations and self-image are involved. It is frequently difficult for some people to say they do not have the requisite fluency to function in a particular situation when they have volunteered to do so. In as far as possible the person, origins, and history of the interpreter should be minimized. We want them to be as neutral a resource as possible in the interviewing and relationship-building process.

If the situation permits, it is helpful to orient a volunteer not so much to the services and policies of our setting but rather to the type of vocabulary that we might be using that he or she may not be able to interpret without some advance thinking. It is not the interpreter's task to understand the agency, its services, its eligibility requirements, etc. The interpreter's role is to find the best and clearest way to convey ideas in a second language.

As suggested earlier, in the actual interview some prior thought needs to be put into where the volunteer is to sit. As far as possible we should avoid situations, such as having him or her sit either close to us or close to the client, where the position conveys a message as to who owns the interpreter. My own preference is that we structure the interview so our direct contact both physically and visually is with the client, with the interpreter sitting off to one side, equi-distant from both of us. Sometimes the way we arrange lighting can also aid in playing down the interpreter and promoting contact between us and the client.

As mentioned earlier, one strategy in the use of interpreters is to not have the interpreter present in the interviewing room but either in another location connected by microphones or behind a one-way mirror. It is my view that this aids considerably in avoiding the potential power and relationship struggles that can emerge in a three-way interview situation and strengthens the desired neutrality of the interpreter. Others argue that if the interpreter cannot see the body language of the client and the worker the possibility of understanding the meanings being conveyed is greatly reduced. Some limited research using this method has shown that at least some clients very much prefer not having the interpreter present, and that not knowing who he or she is has no detrimental impact on the interviewing process.

From another perspective, by making use of distant interpreters through speaker telephones it is possible to provide a much greater choice of interpreters at a minimum cost. Australia has developed a very elaborate system whereby social workers and other professionals have twenty-four hour access to a broad range of language experts by means of telephones. Considerably more research is needed to further our knowledge of the advantages and possible disadvantages of this type of interviewing procedure (MacKinon & Michels, 1971).

One other very important factor in relation to the use of interpreters relates to the question of resources. As mentioned earlier, interpreting is a profession requiring a high level of training. Hence interpreters are expensive. As yet, except in some limited situations, we have not faced the question of who is going to pay for these costs. This is a complex question and touches on issues of human rights. In what circumstances does a Canadian have the right to have interpreting services available to them? Clearly each agency is not going to be able to have professional staff able to respond to all languages. Thus we are either going to have to be ready to make use of commercial interpreting services or continue to use volunteers. In the latter instance, I suggest that much more attention needs be given to the training of such volunteers in the skills of effective interpreting. It may be that some of our larger agencies should consider having on staff a professional interpreter whose task will be not to function in the direct interpreting role but rather to give in-service training to both volunteers and practitioners as to how to best make use of this role and this needed resource.

In addition, as a profession we need to spend much more time, effort, and resources on research into how, when, and where to use interpreters and how to use their skills differentially. Again, the literature and research on this topic is sparse. With the complex and varying cultures with which we interact it may well be that how we use interpreters, and who we use as interpreters, will vary considerably across cultures and across value-orientation differences within cultures. If so, a critical diagnostic factor may well become the best way to involve an interpreter when needed in particular cases. To make these decisions responsibly and ethically requires that we study this component of practice much more thoroughly than we have done thus far (Klufert & Koolage, 1984).

We cannot argue that interpreters can be dispensed with on grounds that our work is so special that, apart from some factual material, it is not possible to establish a therapeutic relationship and deal with highly complex and sensitive material through an interpreter. Throughout history, interpreters have been used to settle wars, to transact huge international pacts, to negotiate mammoth financial projects, and to assist in critical life-and-death judicial cases. Thus it would appear possible that with more experience and study we should be able to provide a rich and intense range of psycho-social services to a broad spectrum of clients who speak any of the world's languages through this medium.

If this is not possible then the reality of the next couple of decades in this country is that many persons will be deprived of needed services and assistance. The development of skill in this area is a most fitting one for social work and if we seize the opportunity, as we must, not only can we better serve clients but we can also take a leadership role to help teach other colleagues in other professions how to make use of this resource so as to better serve the multi-lingual population of which our country is so proudly composed (Turner, 1990).

REFERENCES

Baker, N.G. (1981). Social work through an interpreter. *Social Work, 26*(5), September.

Freed, A. (1988). Interviewing through an interpreter. *Social Work, 33*(4), July–August, 315–319.

Glasser, I. (1983). Guidelines for using an interpreter in social work. *Child Welfare, 62*(9), 468–470.

Klufert, J.M. & Koolage, W.W. (1984). Role conflict among "culture brokers": the experience of native Canadian medical interpreters. *Social Science and Medicine, 18*(3), 283–286.

Knapp-Potthoff, A. & Knapp, K. (1986). Interviewing two discourses: the difficult task of the non-professional interpreter. In House, J. & Blum-Kulka, S. (Eds.). *Interlingual and intercultural communication: discourse and cognition in translation and second language acquisition studies.* Tubingen: Narr, 151–168.

MacKinnon, R.A. & Michels, R. (1971). Interviewing through an interpreter. *The psychiatric interview in clinical practice.* Philadelphia: W.B. Saunders Company.

Marcos, L.R. (1979). Effects of interpreters on the evaluation of psychopathology in non-English-speaking patients. *American Journal of Psychiatry, 136*(2), February, 171–174.

Mirdal, G.M. (1988). The interpreter in cross-cultural therapy. *International Migration, 26*(3), 327–334.

Parks, G.B. (1982). What language do interpreters speak? *Rassegna Italiana di Linguistica Applicata, 14*(1), Jan–April, 121–135.

Sagalowitz, N. (1976) Communicative incompetence and the non-fluent bilingual. *Canadian Journal of Behavioural Science, 8*(2), 122–131.

Turner, F.J. (1990). Interpreters and social workers: contemporary professional challenges. Bowen, D. & Bowen, M. (Eds.). *Interpreting—yesterday, today, and tomorrow.* New York: American Translators Association. (Vol. 4).

ENHANCING PRACTICE KNOWLEDGE THROUGH SUPERVISION AND CONSULTATION

Barbara Thomlison

With the increased emphasis on a scientific orientation to social work practice, supervision has also needed to readjust to the new practice realities. Acquiring evidence-supported knowledge for practice is a complicated task involving many related activities for practitioners. Various practising social workers were not educated in social work programs where scientific and evidence-based practice interventions were part of the curriculum. Theory and knowledge about human functioning has increased substantially and models of practice accountability and critical thinking are now emphasized.

While supervision has always been an important aspect of learning about practice processes in social work, the role and focus of supervision needs to be different now. Social workers will have to seek consultation from colleagues who have demonstrated knowledge and competence in matters related to evidenced-based interventions, which reduce the risks in practice resulting from errors of decision-making by practitioners. Supervision plays a role of critical appraisal and provides the competency-based and criterion-referenced ongoing training required to attain specific practice outcomes. To meet the needs of evidence-based practice realities, supervision practice must focus on promoting the progression of practice knowledge that is effective, culturally relevant, and ethical, while meeting standards for the specific intervention. In order to carry out effective supervision practice, supervisors need to be highly informed, knowledgeable about the scientific basis of practice interventions, and able to use advanced technology and the Internet. Despite significant changes in social work practice and agency settings, the role of supervision and consultation in many organizations has not been adequately addressed or restructured for changing service mandates, population shifts, and the required evidence-based practice environments.

This chapter highlights the development and role of supervision, practice guidelines for supervision and consultation, and supervision content and approaches.

DEVELOPMENT AND ROLE OF SUPERVISION

Supervision serves as the primary method and process for developing ongoing expertise and skills for practice at both the pre- and post-education service level as well as providing an important ongoing function for socialization to the profession of social work (Kadushin, 1992). The role of the supervisor is to assist social workers in developing practice skills, learning job functions, and increasing self-awareness and change. In addition, evaluation, ethical practice, and knowledge acquisition are features of supervision. Supervision and consultation take many different forms, but first it is essential to understand the importance of supervision, what it is, and how to learn from it.

Historically, practitioners came to the service setting with little formal or academic social work preparation and therefore had to be educated about the practice of social work "on the job." Almost all social workers now start employment with at least a BSW degree and most have a MSW degree if they are in a clinical setting. Supervisors can assume that a novice practitioner has an orientation to the profession of social work and the various fields of practice, as well as some supervised field-based learning experiences. For the most part, post-professional education supervision is essentially focused on the complex task of helping social workers advance their knowledge and skills to help people enhance the quality of their lives and to ensure job functions are competently fulfilled.

As well, there is a substantial theoretical and evidence-supported literature base for effective supervisory and learning approaches. Kadushin (1992) identified the main tasks and responsibilities of supervisors as teaching, supporting, educating, and administrating. Shulman (1983, 1993) recognized the skills and behaviours of effective supervisors, which has continued to receive attention. These authors found that the specific tasks of supervision proceeded within a framework consisting of beginning, middle, and end phases of a dynamic supervisory relationship. Munson (1989, 1993, 2000) and others contributed to the understanding of differential techniques by studying specific interactional models, supervisory styles, systematic tasks, and evidence-based supervision (Grossman & Perry, 1995; Schneck, 1995; Shulman, 1993; Thomlison, et al., 1996). Recent increases in violations of the power, authority, and trust components of supervisory and staff relationships are examined for their ethical and legal issue implications (CASW, 1996; Munson, 2000; NASW 1996; 1999).

The relationship of learning activities to quality of field instruction and performance among students found variations in learning preferences and outcomes of practice (Fortune, McCarthy, & Abramson, 2001; Rogers & Thomlison, 2000). Sowers-Hoag and Thyer (1985) found that students who were taught specific skills in a structured and systematic competency-based approach functioned in the field at a higher level than students who were not taught using this approach. Platt (1992) found that clinical understanding and technical competence proceeded along a developmental continuum from global to concrete to more differentiated and integrated levels, indicating that practice learning processes progress over time when reflective activities are engaged in. Supervision is oriented to addressing educational and administrative functions related to specific cases, and to addressing practice concerns and quality assurance to clients. The collective view of supervision is that it is an important element in achieving client-targeted outcomes and the delivery of quality services.

WHAT IS SUPERVISION?

Supervision is a complex, dynamic process occurring within a specific context for a specific purpose and can take many forms. As it involves reflecting critically on performance activities, supervision is where the being, knowing, thinking, and doing parts of social work practice are explored, developed, and enhanced through the supervisor-supervisee relationship (Thomlison, Rogers, Collins, & Grinnell, 1996). Supervision should offer the social worker helpful views of practice and administrative activities toward the development of expertise. It is usual for a supervisor to set learning objectives to facilitate the development of a worker's competence within professional practice, rather than focusing on personal issues and growth, and this distinguishes supervision from therapy. Although working with people evokes personal issues for social workers, it is necessary to keep personal issues separate from professional work decisions. While this may be difficult at times, supervision is different from therapy by both choice and purpose. The role of the social worker is not one of a client, and the role of the supervisor is not one of a therapist. Supervision as discussed here is related to the demands of the practice situation. Therefore, social work supervision serves the purpose of providing useful observations, suggestions, ideas, reflections, and directions for social workers learning about the context of working with people and the systems that have an impact on them.

WHAT IS CONSULTATION?

Consultation is also an important process in acquiring professional competence. Consultation has been defined (Barker, 1995, 33) as a problem-solving process in which the consultant gives specifically focused advice to the social worker, the group or staff, or setting. The relationship between supervisor and social worker is often involuntary and is an ongoing one. The relationship between consultant and social worker is voluntary and usually time-limited for specific content, expertise, or the development of special skills (Kaiser, 1997). For example, a social worker may go outside the setting to receive consultation for accreditation or other requirements such as the American Association of Marriage and Family Therapy.

In the supervisor-supervisee relationship, power is derived from the authority inherent in the structure of the setting. Social workers are accountable to their supervisors. In the consultant-consultee relationship, power flows from the consultant's expertise and skills. Consultants do not normally evaluate performance, progress, learning, or other aspects of social workers' jobs and tasks. The consultant is usually a professional peer who offers advice regarding specific case- or practice-skill problems, and this advice may or may not be followed. Peer and team conferences are examples of consultation approaches that are more collaborative in nature. Other peers may also be identified as experts, and consult or offer advice about cases and practice issues, special content, training, or knowledge in a subject area. Although the power and level of accountability distinguishes the differences between supervision and consultation, a collaborative relationship is ideally involved in both.

Use of a supervisor is ongoing and occurs on a regular basis for matters such as aspects of practice, tasks, agency administrative information, and the general appraisal of one's social work performance. Social workers are usually bound to carry out the suggestions and directions determined by the supervisor. The use of a consultant, by contrast, may be associated with either a regularly scheduled time or an informal opportunity to seek assistance.

More often, a consultant is helpful when social workers need technical assistance or specialized training and information. An external consultant is considered when curricula, or specific practice knowledge and training content, are required to meet identified learning needs.

If a consulting relationship is to be helpful, it is important for the worker to examine his or her reasons for wanting to engage the consultant. Knowledge and practice needs must be connected and the potential benefits of the relationship must be clearly identified. When the consultant is an existing individual in the practitioner's organization, then the relationship is less formal and consultation may often be on an ad hoc or as-needed basis. Another supervisor may also be used as a consultant on practice or case issues.

Preparation for both supervision or consultation meetings is desirable. Consider the following:

1. What will be the focus of the meeting?
2. What questions do I need to ask?
3. What do I hope to achieve by the consultation or case conference?
4. What materials do I have to prepare for the meeting?

Included, for example, may be basic work requirements, knowledge about the population served, treatment approaches, the treatment setting, presentation of aspects of your work from such products as case notes, reviews, records, reports, and finally a discussion of your personal impressions, reactions, and experiences.

Furthermore, there are specific practice indications for supervision use that a social worker needs to know about. Immediate supervision or consultation should be obtained when there are sudden unexpected changes in those being served. This may include deterioration in behaviours or mental status, problems that emerge after a contact that were not apparent initially, or when there is danger or issues of safety and protection, particularly in cases of family violence and child maltreatment. Certain other conflicts or stressful situations for individuals or families may also precipitate requesting immediate guidance from supervisors or consultants. Social workers need to realize that such situations require early or even immediate attention. Specific issues should not be reserved until the next scheduled supervision or consultation conference in such instances.

ETHICS AND STANDARDS

Supervision and consultation practices are guided by a strong emphasis on ethics and integrity. The power influences of these relationships places special emphasis on the character and integrity of supervisors and consultants for assuring fairness and confidentiality, and acting in accordance with the highest standards of professional integrity and impartiality (CASW Code of Ethics, 1996; NASW Code of Ethics, 1999). Most settings have established general policies and protocols to address ethical and integrity issues; these are intended to protect the well-being of those persons receiving services, of social workers, and of the profession.

Professional relationships are not to be exploited for personal gain. Examples of malpractice which constitute violations of a professional, ethical, and legal nature include, but are not limited to, the following: issues of personal boundaries, discrimination, harassment, confidentiality with minors, and sexual relationships with clients and supervisors. Unwanted contacts, actions, comments, and behaviours may potentially come not only from supervisors, but also from peers, colleagues, and others. If such problems or issues arise for you or someone who is receiving services, recognize that these are contrary to the social work profession and codes of ethics in work places. You have a right to file a complaint or grievance and demand that the behaviour be stopped. Most agencies have guidelines for this procedure. It is necessary that the tasks and processes or context of supervision follow ethical as well as common-sense practices.

SUPERVISION CONTENT

Teaching, learning, and the process of change occur through the supervisory system or relationship. It is a particular type of alliance with goals specific to practice experiences of the social worker and conceptual orientation of the supervisor. Supervisors ask probing questions to encourage the worker to think conceptually, explore alternatives, and jointly seek solutions for client outcomes. Research suggests that social workers tend to practice with individuals and families by replicating the supervisory system. Kniskern and Gurman (1979) note "trainees learn by what they live in the immediacy of their interaction with their supervisors" (87). Thus the influence and role assumed by the supervisor and social worker is primary in shaping practice outcomes at multiple levels. Similarly, the social worker's ability to parallel the supervisory system and conceptualize the problem-solving process with client systems leads to the acquisition of professional competence.

Supervisor characteristics, including their theoretical practice frameworks, are factors that further influence the qualities of the supervisory system. It is critical that supervisors model impeccable professional behaviours through teaching, supporting, and modelling examples of behaviours. Supervisors using a structured competency-based approach to the acquisition of professional behaviours are more likely to have social workers function at a higher practice level than those workers not exposed to this supervisory format (Kadushin, 1992; Sowers-Hoag & Thyer, 1985; Tourse, McInnes-Dittrich, & Platt, 1999). Other factors affecting the quality of the supervisor-supervisee alliance include managing the elements of authority, trust, and sharing (Kaiser, 1997). Supervisory systems are more likely to be useful if they take advantage of what is known about factors related to the practice situation from the supervisor's own practice, if they consider the best interests and needs of the supervisee, and if they focus on the accuracy of different kinds of data needed for competent service to clients.

GUIDELINES FOR THE SUPERVISORY SYSTEM

Guidelines for the essential supervisory system, derived from key authors (Baird, 1996; Kaiser, 1997; Munson, 1989, 2000; Rogers & Thomlison, 2000; Schulman, 1993; Thomlison, et al., 1996), establish the following criteria:

1. **Good supervisors are good role models.** Supervisors must be approachable, accessible, and model qualities of genuineness and congruence for social workers. Social work supervisors should have social work credentials. Learning from other disciplines is valuable, but it is not the same as learning from another social worker. Regular planned supervision is desirable, and missed conferences or meetings are rescheduled.

2. **Supervisors balance assignments or workload.** Workload should be manageable, providing a balance of difficult and familiar assignments, combining challenge (in terms of learning new skills) with relevancy for the supervisee's level of competence.

3. **Supervisors are knowledgeable.** Supervisors must demonstrate mastery of knowledge and practice and the ability to manage learner requirements. At the same time, supervisors must be confident enough to be open to questioning and display a preference for testing inferences. Supervisors assist in helping social workers view alternative thinking about practice cases, projects, or other assignments. The practice context today requires supervisors to impart evidence-supported practice knowledge for minimizing risks in decision-making. This occurs when supervisors model respect and fairness as part of the context of learning, and at the same time follow through with joint decision-making processes and back-up of supervisee actions. Access to the Internet and other research sources is very important. Many agencies develop a partnership with a university school of social work to enhance practice knowledge and evidence-based interventions needed for ongoing staff development.

4. **Supervisors provide balanced feedback.** Supervisors provide clear, frequent, timely, and relevant feedback about performance that balances supervisee strengths and vulnerabilities. Feedback on performance is most useful when it occurs as soon as possible after the practice situation because it sets the stage for change opportunities. Feedback needs to be stated clearly, in a language easily understood. It also requires receiving information that is balanced—focused on both the strengths and issues, *but* providing suggestions or alternatives to a specific event, incident, or action for practice. Feedback also needs to be reciprocal, providing opportunities for the supervisee to comment and to contribute varying perspectives (Thomlison, et al., 1996). Confident supervisors also ask for feedback and comments.

    Feedback during supervision typically elicits a range of feelings, emotions, and value conflicts for social workers. It is an opportunity to discuss and understand the impact of practice dynamics and how these elements affect the responses of social workers. Feedback from all supervision approaches should convey a positive can-do attitude to supervisees and should focus on the present.

5. **Supervisors build competencies.** Supervisors identify supervisees' assets rather than their deficiencies. Identifying strengths builds competencies and encourages social workers to search for positive alternatives to unwanted practice behaviours. Social workers need to focus on their clients' strengths and identify their own practice and knowledge strengths.

6. **Supervisors tend to practical matters**. The frequency and amount of supervision, the context of supervisory conferences, the objectives of supervision and how these are to be demonstrated and evaluated, and the extent that personal issues of concern to practice are to be addressed should all be defined. When and how often will supervision occur? What needs to be prepared in advance for supervision? What portion of supervision time is to be spent on case discussion, specific topics, specific skills, review of cases, issues, personal concerns etc? What activities are most/least helpful in supervision? Tending to practical matters captures and supports a supervisee's readiness to learn.

7. **Supervisors focus on how things work.** Supervisors need to explore ways to assess supervisees' approach to practice. Many social workers like to experience an event before they can understand it. Others like to think it through first before setting out to see a client. Each social worker will have a unique learning style and each supervisor will

have a unique teaching style for approaching practice. Practice patterns and themes are identified and then discussion moves to the conceptual or abstract aspects of the practice situation. Practice exemplars illustrate theory, and, through reflection, understanding emerges for the social worker.

When a narrative account of a practice situation is shared and examined in supervision, social workers can discover the assumptions and exceptions underlying the assessment and interventions in the practice situation. Testing for inferences raises new questions and generates new understandings. Reflecting on and discussing in the course of an interview many similar and dissimilar client situations, social workers may learn to expect a certain course of events without ever formally stating those expectations. Learning is a unique mixture of personal knowledge, past concrete situations, individual preferences and cognitive characteristics, and paradigms. Certain patterns, themes, and sets are developed through this approach to learning.

Social workers share belief systems about self, cases, and assignments. Often these matters will centre on worries stated as, "I don't know what to do with this person," or "How do I go about doing it?" and "I am afraid my client will know I don't know what to do" or "I don't like my client." This also translates into "I don't know what to do if my supervisor realizes I am not helping this person" or "I am afraid my supervisor will know I don't know what to do with my client." Novice social workers are concerned about competence or poor evaluations. From the outset, the creation of a safe, accepting supervisory system is necessary (Thomlison et al., 1996).

Supervision activities vary, but supervision is essentially the place for social workers to tell their story, which includes explanations and reactions to practice. Different supervision activities promote cognitive, affective, and operative learning. Content is presented in written and verbal formats. Tapes, didactic discussion, role-plays, journals or logs, simulations, case discussion of reports, process recordings, direct observations of casework, and working jointly are also activities that may form the content of supervision. These activities, experiences, and expectations are clarified as a shared meaning of practice develops between supervisor and social worker. For a more complete discussion of documentation, clinical notes, and records see Rogers and Thomlison (2000) and Baird (1996).

DIVERSITY

The supervisory system assumes a commitment to learning in an environment of caring, cooperation, and collaboration, and a sensitivity to and respect for the importance of the social worker's cultural context and life experiences. Demographics in Canada suggest that social workers and supervisors are working with and are themselves diverse groups of people. Learning about diversity is about understanding the influences of our backgrounds and belief systems, and how others influence and shape us. Some of the diverse professional issues supervisors and social workers are required to understand include those of Aboriginal peoples, ethnic and religious minority groups, older persons, women, and diverse socioeconomic groups. Diversity issues should take a central role in the supervisory system. Teaching and learning about the history, lifestyles, and experiences of diverse groups assists both supervisor and social worker to understand and identify the systemic and structural causes of racism, sexism, discrimination, and oppression.

Culture is a developmental force that shapes early experiences for each of us and provides us with the sense of being different (Thomlison & Rogers, 1995). Self-understanding and communication must go beyond simple descriptions of cultural differences to incorporating culturally sensitive thinking and practice methods. This assumes that supervisors are able to identify and engage in discourse about negative stereotypes. Understanding the sources of our own assumptions and belief systems opens the way to developing awareness, knowledge, and skills related to diversity issues.

The first step is to unlearn many things. Canadian social work education tends to be highly ethnocentric, often disregarding the diversity of the population and exposing students to theory and concepts that may perpetuate policy, practice, and economic inequities and social injustice in the delivery of Canadian social services. The ability of supervisors to acknowledge the factors of difference in the supervisory system involves recognizing the impact of culture, gender, economics, and language as dimensions of personal identity and cultural competence (Thomlison & Rogers, 1995). Self-awareness develops the potential for confronting negative stereotypes, myths, and assumptions. The ability to practice and establish effective relationships across differences is then possible (Thomlison & Rogers, 1995). A social worker needs a supervisor who is able to recognize and be sensitive to the fact that the supervisee may in fact be an individual who has experienced various forms of discrimination. In addition, supervisors must be open to exploring agency policies, practices, and personal attitudes to pinpoint areas of racism, prejudice, and cultural vulnerability. Supervisors have two key tasks: (1) to encourage the development of the cultural competence of social workers; and (2) to promote ethnic and cultural diversity and competence at the organizational level so that multiracial and multicultural discussions are systemically reinforced and supported. Five principles of diversity-centred supervision are summarized below:

- *Principle one* – Provide a safe environment to explore diversity dilemmas. The supervisor needs to raise and sustain discourse on taboo topics—directly addressing the dilemma and the power differential.

- *Principle two* – Increase awareness and gain insight regarding the sources or causes of dilemmas. Supervisors need to unwrap their own theoretical thinking about certain persons or groups and avoid being defensive and needing to be right.

- *Principle three* – Identify challenging practice issues and situations. Supervisors need to realize that many of the common assessment and intervention tools are limited when applied to non-mainstream cultures.

- *Principle four* – Explore alternatives. Supervisors must be aware of any cultural explanations of a response to someone in authority and differences in communication patterns, and must not assume the meaning of these events, circumstances, and relationships.

- *Principle five* – Acquire new ways of thinking and acting in response to practice dilemmas. Supervisors must raise awareness of discriminatory and oppressive practices and institutionalized forms of racism, sexism, ageism, ableism, and homophobia that create barriers. (Thomlison & Rogers, 1995).

Supervisors need to first demonstrate their own willingness to take risks and, through the process of the supervisory system, model ways to address cross-cultural issues. As supervisors develop strategies for dealing openly with social workers, social workers in turn develop the ability to deal openly with the possible challenges and resources of persons receiving services and the social contexts that pertain to their backgrounds.

SUPERVISION APPROACHES

Supervision can take many different forms, but in general the social worker tends to be supervised in a tutorial model, that is, one-on-one. The more experienced and advanced social worker will have a consultative or more ad hoc model for supervision. Depending on the type of setting, more than one approach may be used, for example, such as peer supervision, group supervision, live supervision, or team supervision. The major approaches are summarized briefly here.

Individual Tutor Model

In this model, one social worker and one supervisor meet regularly for a planned collaborative conference. The tasks of the social work supervisor are to model critical thinking skills and examine the supervisee's work, encouraging openness and honesty about practice, through the sharing of feelings, thoughts, and struggles. The most typical activity in one-to-one supervision is case discussion. Responses to authority, power, and relationship issues are all important aspects for discussion. Case discussions involve describing the social worker's experience with the person, problem, and situation. Usually the social worker identifies the elements of the case experience and analyzes why things happened as they did, to discover causes, usefulness, and applicability of what was learned from the contact. Through discussion, the supervisor teaches the supervisee concepts of the case for generalizing knowledge and skills acquired in specific situations so that they can be applied in other practice situations.

Team or Peer Supervision

Team or peer supervision brings together individuals with the same or different professional orientation, to provide specific assistance related to case or practice issues. Teams provide exposure to a wide range of problem-solving techniques and the opportunity to compare practice experiences and generate different observations and suggestions among the team members (Thomlison, 1995). For example, team members may observe a practice case directly ("reflecting team" supervision), through the one-way observation mirror or indirectly through a team/peer conference after the fact, to provide feedback to other team members on performance, practice issues, and interventions. Team discussion develops a menu of different perspectives and understandings of the case. Case presentations and role-plays may also occur among the team members in an effort to assist. The impact of differences such as professional socialization, age, gender, ethnicity, race, and ability is not only more evident in supervision teams, it is also easier to discuss within the group.

Group Supervision

Group supervision is another approach through which social workers can develop practice expertise and skills, and obtain moral support, self-confidence, and awareness. Some supervisees may prefer the peer group context to the individual model, while others may need or prefer using both supervision approaches. Social workers will differ in their learning preferences, but most will benefit from alternate perspectives. Within the setting of the group, members share conflicts, problems, and dilemmas related to their practice and receive assistance from their peers. Although group supervision has not received a great deal of attention in the literature, the focus is similar to individual supervision, but sufficient empirical literature is not yet available to know how effective it is. Many social work settings provide for teaching, learning, and supporting practice processes, balanced in both individual and group structures. Supervision groups must, however, assist social workers in addressing individual client needs and interventions.

Live Supervision

Live supervision is most often used in interdisciplinary and family therapy settings as a technique for training or developing clinical skills. In this approach, the supervisor or team of colleagues observes the supervisee through a one-way mirror or closed-circuit taping, or sit in with the social worker during an actual interview. This form of supervision involves co-working, monitoring, or suggesting various interventions about dynamics during the actual interview, usually with a family. The supervisor and other team members watch and listen from behind the observation window. Direct or immediate feedback is given to the social worker in the interviewing room through a variety of communication devices, such as telephone, ear microphone, notes, or other interventions. The benefits of live supervision to the teaching and learning process are substantial. Immediate corrective feedback is the strongest advantage of this method. Case dynamics are immediately apparent and prompt feedback on performance is available. Live supervision also brings a multidimensional perspective to the case analysis. This method provides a greater opportunity for enhancing competence and personal development. From this supervision approach, supervisees are more likely to integrate new learning in the practice context (Thomlison et al., 1996).

Coaches and Mentors

Another form of learning practice gaining prominence is the use of coaching and mentor relationships. Social workers may acquire coaches or mentors to assist them in learning from on-the-job activities by having someone co-work with them. In this way, social workers can acquire on-the-job and on-the-spot practice skills and receive first-hand advice, instruction, and direction. Coaches and mentors are considered to have special wisdom, expertise, or ability, and serve as expert role models. The use of these collaborative learning and teaching roles has evolved particularly in child welfare settings and organizations serving diverse populations.

SUMMARY

The topic of supervision and consultation deserves considerably more space than one chapter, and the overview provided here is intended only to help you begin to discover the joys of learning through supervision. Supervision continues to be a primary forum for learning and maintaining practice skills and competencies. I encourage both supervisors and social workers to be open to learning, and to seek consultation and collaborations regularly. There is a wide range of supervisors and supervisory styles just as there is a wide range of supervisees. The suggestions presented here are intended to highlight the key elements in a systematic and collaborative strategy to consultation and supervisory systems. My hope is that both supervisors and supervisees will experience a special shared meaning within the supervisory system. Learning to practice social work is a decision to accept and seek ongoing supervision as an essential part of learning for the entirety of your professional career. Today's practice environment requires both practitioners and supervisors to acquire more sophisticated knowledge as clients have the right to receive the best practice interventions available. The need for ongoing development through supervision is paramount. New tools such as computer supervision are being used to enhance practice knowledge, and they present new opportunities for learning. This may prove to be helpful for those practising in northern communities as well as those needing immediate feedback in home visitation interventions. Experience in telemedicine and recent social work technology in education indicate that this is a promising tool for social workers as well.

REFERENCES

Barker, R.L. (1995). *The social work dictionary* (3rd Edition). Washington, DC: NASW Press.

Baird, B. (1996). *The internship, practicum, and field placement handbook. A guide for the helping professions.* Upper Saddle River, NJ: Prentice Hall.

CASW (1996). *Code of Ethics.* Canadian Association of Social Workers.

Grossman, B. & Perry, R. (1995) Reengaging social work education with the public social services: the California experience and its relevance to Canada. In G. Rogers (Ed.). *Social work field education: views and visions*, 251–271. Dubuque, IA: Kendall Hunt.

Kaiser, T.L. (1997). *Supervisory relationships. exploring the human element.* Pacific Grove, CA: Brooks/Cole.

Kaiser, T.L. & Barretta-Herman, A. (1999). The Supervision Institute: a model for supervisory training. *The Clinical Supervisor, 18*(1), 33–46.

Kadushin, A. (1992). *Supervision in social work.* (3rd ed.), New York: Columbia University Press.

Kniskern, D. & Gurman, A. (1979). Research on training in marriage and family therapy: status, issues and directions. *Journal of Marital and Family Therapy, 5*, 93–94.

Martin, G.E. & McBride, M.C. (1987). The results of implementation of a professional supervision model on counsellor trainee behavior. *Counselor Education and Supervision, 27*, 155–167.

Fortune, A.E., McCarthy, M., & Abramson, J. (2001). Student Learning Processes in field education: Relationship of learning activities to quality of field instruction, satisfaction, and performance among MSW students. *Journal of Social Work Education, 37*(1), 111–127.

Munson, B. (2000). Supervision standards of practice. In P. Allen-Meares and C. Garvin (Eds.), *The Handbook of social work practice,* 611–632. Thousand Oaks, CA: Sage.

Munson, C. (1993). *Clinical social work supervision* (2nd ed.). New York: Haworth Press.

Munson, C. (1989). Editorial. *The Clinical Supervisor, 7*(1), 1–4.

NASW (1996). National Association of Social Workers Code of Ethics (revised 1999). Silver Spring, MD: Author.

Platt, S. (1992). *The process of learning in clinical social work students.* Unpublished doctoral dissertation, Smith College School of Social Work, Northampton, MA.

Sowers-Hoag, K. & Thyer, B. (1995). Teaching social work practice: a review and analysis of empirical research. *Journal of Social Work Education, 21*(3), 5–15.

Rogers, G. & Thomlison, B. (2000). The write stuff: documenting learning in the practicum. In R. Power and G. Kenyon (Eds.) *No magic: readings in social work education*. Toronto, ON: Canadian Scholars' Press.

Rogers, G. & Thomlison, B. (1996). *Learning styles and structured exercises: enhancing field-based learning.* Final research report for The University of Calgary Teaching Development Office & Faculty of Social Work, December 1996.

Schneck, D. (1995). The promise of field education in social work. In G. Rogers (Ed.). *Social work field education: views and visions*, 3–14. Dubuque, IA: Kendall Hunt.

Shulman, L. (1993). *Interactional supervision*. Washington, DC: NASW Press.

Shulman, L. (1982). *Skills of supervision and staff management*. Itasca, IL: F.E. Peacock.

Thomlison, B. (1995). Student perceptions of reflective team supervision. In G. Rogers (Ed.). *Social work field education: views and visions*, 234–244. Dubuque, IA: Kendall Hunt.

Thomlison, B. & Rogers, G. (1995). *Guidelines for developing cultural competence in field education.* Juried paper presentation at the Fieldwork Symposium, Annual Program Meeting of the Council on Social Work Education, March 03, 1995, San Diego, CA.

Thomlison, B., Rogers, G., Collins, D., & Grinnell, Jr., R.M. (1996). *The social work practicum: an access guide (*2nd Edition). Itasca, Ill: F. E. Peacock.

Tourse, R.W., McInnis-Dittrich, K., & Platt, S. (1999). The road to autonomous practice: a practice competency teaching approach for supervision. *Journal of Teaching in Social Work, 19*(1/2), 3–19.

ONGOING PROFESSIONAL EDUCATION

Roberta M. Roberts

INTRODUCTION

What is ongoing professional education and where does it fit within the field of education? "Education has traditionally been seen as a means of preparing youth for life. The skills and knowledge acquired in school were believed to be all that was needed to serve them in their future careers and in any other undertakings that they encountered throughout their lives" (Couillard, 1995, 47). However, a major shift has occurred that requires a very different conceptualization of what is needed in a global economic world and one in which there has been an information explosion, both of these facts having an impact on the workplace.

Social services are not exempt from these newly emerging realities. Restructuring, downsizing, and the subsequent new patterns of service delivery have challenged the very values and applications inherent in social work practice. The repercussions of massive cuts in major areas of employment and the changes in how we do business are having effects on the social workers' own employment situations and career paths.

Lifelong learning is now both a necessity and a reality of one's professional life. Adult education has become an essential element in the context of lifelong learning. "It is no longer considered a second or last chance education but a normal and necessary ongoing activity" (Couillard, 1995, 48).

Necessity is driving change and refocusing the way we do things. The clientele has been modified; the resources, the time frames, the context are drastically altered. Consequently, social workers are faced with the demand to review and revise their practice framework and activities, to upgrade their skills in order to survive, and to provide services to their clients in a meaningful and relevant manner.

This is where ongoing professional education or continuing education finds its place. However, in examining this subject, the definitional boundaries of professional learning are blurred. Professional education broadly covers community college and diploma courses, undergraduate and graduate degrees, post-graduate degrees, diplomas, distance learning, in-service staff training, staff development, seminars, workshops, and lectures. There is no inclusive definition that is accepted even within the social work community in Canada. For the Canadian Association of Social Workers (CASW), continuing education is "the life-long process of engaging in activities to learn new knowledge and skills and deepen professional competency" (CASW, March 1994). In reviewing the definition of lifelong learning, Roberge (1987) commented on the abundance of new terminology in education about which consensus had not been reached, with terms including *lifelong, recurrent, lifespan, continuing, permanent, distance,* and *adult.*

Definitions, policies, and the provision of continuing education programs appear to be based on the assumption that education results in competency. More precisely, the goal appears to be for "continuing competency," as will be deduced from the statements and activities of professional associations and regulatory bodies. This is supported by CASW's belief "in the importance of continuing education to ethical, well-regulated and competent practice" (CASW, March 1994). The CASW Code of Ethics is the basis for each of the provincial codes of ethics. Its "standard of practice" (the standard of care ordinarily expected of a competent social worker) means that the public is assured that a social worker has the training, skill, and the diligence to provide them with professional social work services. One of the ethical duties and obligations is that "a social worker shall have and maintain competence in the provision of social work service to a client" (CASW #3, March 1994); and in the chapter relating to competence, "a social worker shall have, maintain and endeavour periodically to update an acceptable level of knowledge and skills to meet the standards of practice of the profession" (CASW, #3.6, March 1994).

There is an increasing trend toward the regulation of the profession of social work throughout North America. This has been driven by the technological developments in the workplace and the demand for accountability by the public, reflecting the power of the consumer movement.

THE CHANGING NATURE OF PRACTICE

The latter part of the 1990s has been characterized by upheaval, and experienced as a period of transition to a new order (Bridges, 1994). No longer is there a system of permanent positions where jobs are predictable and where it is common for people to transfer within an organization or to move to another agency as a promotion or to broaden their experience. Changing jobs every two to three years in early professional life was formerly both usual and even recommended in order to progress and build a career. As fiscal constraints began to impact on organizations, however, a reduction in job mobility was seen: hiring freezes precluded the advent of new employees and fewer supervisory and middle management positions became available. Those in supervisory positions were reluctant to risk the security of seniority and positioning in an organization as opportunities elsewhere diminished. This has been followed by a growth in contract rather than permanent positions, sometimes on a part-time and time-limited basis. Practice has become more focused, with short-term interventions. Along with the expectation to do "more with less" comes a reformulation of the task and a demand to provide a briefer and hence different service in the continuum of care. In many situations, staff members may be dealing not only with the impact of cutbacks, but also with the spectre of the closing of the organization itself or the merging of two or more organizations and the resultant reverberations.

The move to eliminate in-house employees and replace them through "out-sourcing" has created an acceleration of private practice. Some social workers have responded to these changing employment patterns by constructing their work from a combination of part-time positions and/or contract projects. As MacKenzie Davies (1996) aptly observes, "Social workers no longer have the option of continuing along the familiar well-travelled path. We cannot go back but instead must move forward, despite the fact that we may not know the route," adding a fitting quote from Yogi Berra, "The future ain't what it used to be."

With this change in organizational and agency structures has come a radical alteration in the views about ongoing professional education. The traditional staff training and development function is being removed from the employer to the individual worker. The reduction or elimination of middle managers has erased the historic role of clinical supervision and on-the-job training. This role has been eroded during recent years as administrative accountability remains without the other functions of education and support. In addition, in secondary settings, the manager is likely not to be a social worker as departments of social work are gradually subsumed under functional-service programs. Competence in the use of technology will be required rather than just computer literacy. Attention to political issues as they emerge may determine mandated training—for example, harassment in the workplace and multiculturalism.

On-the-job training may become much more narrowly focused on specifically assigned tasks required to meet the needs of the targeted populations, and on an orientation to new systems and procedures rather than on professional growth and development of the employee as a professional. A previous philosophy was that a professionally growing and developing employee made a richer contribution to the organization. Is this now a luxury which is no longer either affordable or relevant? Will employers seek only those who already have the knowledge and skills and experience? A new trend is beginning to emerge where some organizations are requiring new employees to complete their orientation program at their own expense. Such ventures provide a clear example of the shifting of responsibility for staff training from the employer to the employee.

With the redesign of the service delivery systems, is this only the beginning in a continual cycle of change? The emerging scenarios seem to be totally different from what has been known in the past, although human distress and need are ongoing (Bridges, 1980; Egan, 1988).

RESPONSIBILITY FOR LEARNING

These challenges are not unique to social work, but are part of a larger scene in the field of lifelong learning as reflected in the Ontario Premier's Council (1994) report on lifelong learning. "Learning (is) ... the process by which we will cope with the overwhelming changes our society is undergoing" (Summary Report, 2). Because of the unpredictable nature of a person's work life, education and training will need to be "customized" accordingly. The report identified that in addition to knowledge and skills, self-esteem and a positive attitude toward change will be needed (Summary Report, 4). Flexible movement between a broad variety of educational formats will be required, together with new linkages between educational institutions, workplaces, and community (Report, 11,15).

These current changes relocate the responsibility for professional continuing education on to the employee: "Individuals will have to reshape their aspirations and take more responsibility for managing their own education and training over a larger part of their life" (Report, 8). Further evidence of this change in expectation is illustrated by the CEO of a large hospital who suggests that "if employees are not spending at least one night a week learning, they will get behind. Employees have a responsibility to keep up .... People who cannot achieve, who don't keep learning, cannot stay" (Hudson, 1996).

CASW agrees that primary responsibility for engaging in continuing education rests with the individual social worker, but the ability to engage in continuing education requires mutually shared responsibilities for support, access, and availability (CASW, March 1994). Other professions, of course, have similar expectations of their members (Canadian Association of Occupational Therapists, 1992; Canadian Nurses Association, 1992).

In addition, there has been a growing number of social workers engaging in private practice which, until a decade or so ago, was perceived as being outside the culture of the profession (Levin & Rasmussen, 1991). With the radical reduction in traditional institutionally-based service delivery and the trend to privatization of services, a greater number have moved into this area, either on a full-time basis or part-time as a supplement to current agency employment or in anticipation of job loss. Private practice is now a more accepted endeavour. Clearly, in this case the initiative for continuing education comes from the individual practitioner. In 1995, the Canadian Association of Social Workers published the first *National Registry of Social Workers in Private Practice*. A requirement to be listed in this registry includes a minimum of 40 hours of continuing education annually.

CONTINUING EDUCATION REQUIREMENTS IN THE PROVINCES

In the mid-1980s, interest in what was happening in continuing education across Canada led to a national project on continuing education for social workers in Canada being carried out between 1986 and 1990, co-sponsored by the Canadian Association of Social Workers and the Canadian Association of Schools of Social Work, with funding by the National Welfare Grants of Health and Welfare Canada. In 1992, a second phase was initiated to consult further, specifically with the professional associations, to consider CASW's role in relation to continuing professional education for Canadian social workers. One of the recommendations arising out of this consultation was to establish a CASW Education Subcommittee to develop a continuing education policy statement.

Subsequently, a policy was approved in March 1994, providing a general framework within which provincial organizations could develop necessary procedures and designed to be general enough to meet the needs of social workers in geographically isolated areas and in a wide range of practice settings. This document supported mandatory continuing education for social workers throughout Canada and recommended a minimum of 40 hours of continuing education activities per annum. It was the provincial organizations' responsibility to monitor adherence to their own policy.

In Canada, the legislation of the professions is under provincial jurisdiction and so there is variation across the country, with each of the ten provinces specifying requirements for its members; as a result, policies for continuing education/professional development activities are not consistent across the country.

Currently, some provincial organizations, either through the provincial association itself or through their provincial model for accountability for practice, have been engaged in requiring continuing education activities as part of membership and/or certification or registration. The format differs in each province, depending on its particular legislative regulation. See Chapter 38 for further discussion.

Four provinces have licensing and title protection (Newfoundland and Labrador, PEI, Nova Scotia, and New Brunswick), and six have title protection. In Newfoundland and Labrador, registration requires 40 hours per annum with a completed form for each activity.

In Prince Edward Island, registration is mandatory under legislation amended in 1999 and includes requirement of forty hours of continuing education. Location on a small island without a university brings its own unique challenges in accessing learning opportunities and there are links with Memorial University in Newfoundland.

In Nova Scotia, professional development is a condition of regulation. The program of 40 hours annually is self-directed and self-accountable. The association has links with the Continuing Education program at Dalhousie University which also is now offering courses at the City University of Hong Kong.

In New Brunswick, membership in the association is mandatory for registration as a social worker, with continuing education requirements of 40 hours on a self-report basis.

The legislation in Quebec does not include continuing education as a condition of regulation. However, if a member does not have some activities reported during the inspection, a recommendation would be made. In addition, if there is no involvement in continuing education and the worker is found to be incompetent, then the Board could impose participation in some programs

In Ontario, registration is mandatory under the Ontario College of Social Workers and Social Service Workers, created under the Social Work and Social Service Work Act 1998 (proclaimed in 1999), which also provides title protection. As yet, no requirements have been defined. As in past years, the provincial association continues to encourage and develop accessible and affordable programs through local branch initiatives.

In Manitoba, the Manitoba Institute of Registered Social Workers requires a minimum of 40 hours annually, and requires evidence to be submitted with membership fees.

Saskatchewan has control of title so that to use the title of "social worker" in that province, membership in the professional association is required. The voluntary regulatory function has been part of the association's role since 1995. Forty hours of continuing education activities are expected annually on a voluntary basis. However, there is a proposal to move to a mandatory basis.

At present in Alberta there is no requirement for continuing education activities. The Alberta College of Social Workers is developing policies for a new Act. There is a proposal for continuing competence requirements.

In British Columbia, there are no continuing education requirements for registration, but members of the Board of Registration with private practitioner status have a review of practice every four years and at that time must submit their records of continuing education activities. No minimum is specified, but there is a proposal to require 40 hours.

As previously mentioned, at the national level, the requirements for listing in the *CASW National Registry of Social Workers in Private Practice* include a minimum of 40 hours of continuing education.

Those provinces that do not have specific requirements are discussing or considering engagement in continuing education as mandatory for membership. Such decisions will have an impact on existing resources, stimulating new growth in the provision of educational services to accommodate the changing demand.

SOURCES FOR CONTINUING EDUCATION

Where do social workers find activities both for their own professional development and to meet this growing expectation from regulatory bodies? Walmsley (June 1992) reported that, as expected, opportunities varied tremendously across the country, from one province to another but also within each province, with huge differences between north and south; urban and rural; populated and isolated communities; proximity to agencies, colleges, and universities. More than two-thirds of all activities were found in the major metropolitan areas. A wide range of activities were identified, including both formal activities such as conferences, certificate programs, and courses, and informal ones such as study tours, job exchanges, and professional reading and writing.

Sponsors of events tended to focus on specialized areas of practice. Joint sponsorship was common across the country, with three major forms predominating, particularly in the provision of conferences and workshops, but also, though relatively uncommon, in the provision of certificate programs: the professional association and a university; a university and a social service organization; and joint social services agencies or interagency committees. All provincial associations had at least one organizational format to respond to members' needs and demands, and included various continuing education or conference committees at the provincial or branch level.

Walmsley (September 1992) identified the major barriers as the absence of the following things: political commitment to continuing education as signalled by employers cutting back on funding and allowing time off; a professional culture promoting and encouraging continuing education; commitment to the principle of lifelong learning; equitable geographical distribution of social work educational activities outside urban centres; and co-ordination of programs and exchange of information.

Although this survey was done in 1992, there is little reason to expect that there has been significant improvement in these areas. In fact, it is clear that the expectation of support from employers is much more limited than in the past. Even more, anxiety is expressed that even if time could be found to attend, any absence from the workplace, even for laudable educational purposes, may put employment in jeopardy.

The providers of learning experiences are changing. "The most effective approaches to helping people get these skills quicker are based on new linkages between institutions and organizations which have traditionally operated in isolation from one another" (Ontario Premier's Council, Report, 1994, 15).

To address the perplexity of the assortment of educational endeavours, a useful classification is offered by UNESCO (1976), which defines education as any organized and sustained communication that brings about learning. It distinguishes between three levels of education and/or learning: formal and non-formal structured education, informal learning, and random learning. *Formal education* is institutionalized, graded, and hierarchically structured, spanning primary school to university. It includes regular, post-compulsory education taken on a full-time or part-time basis leading to formal qualifications such as a certificate, a diploma, or a degree. This would cover all social work studies for BSW, MSW, DSW/PhD, and various formal certificates, in specific subjects such as addictions and gerontology or in methods such as administration and research. *Non-formal education* refers to intentionally organized learning events that are taken outside the formal system and, as a consequence, are not graded. This arrangement comprises a large variety of activities such as structured training, various courses, seminars, tutorials, or workshops offered on a full-time or part-time basis by an institution or other agency. Here it would apply to professional associations and independent educators. *Informal learning* is intentional but unorganized and unstructured. These kinds of learning events may occur in the family, the workplace, or in normal daily life. They may include self-learning, on-the-job training, or may be the result of the educational influences of parents, friends, the media, etc. *Random learning* is unintentional learning, occurring at any time and in any place throughout everyday life.

These definitions can provide the underpinnings for the designation and planning of continuing education activities. In the provinces, originality and flexibility have been introduced in an effort to provide relevant learning opportunities that are both available and accessible to all members. The growth of technology augurs well, but there exists the myth of the existence of extensive relevant continuing education content for social workers, as well as that of accessibility. The Francophone community is not well served by a predominantly Anglophone Internet. The challenge is to create and make available opportunities beyond the conventional way. Walmsley observed the inequity of access to programs outside urban areas. A new phenomenon that is developing is that, as the pressure builds in the diminishing employment situation, professionals, even in some urban areas, are finding it difficult to allocate time for participation. With the increased number of single-parent households or with the necessity of both parents working for extended hours if they are fortunate enough to be employed, new barriers are mounting. While undoubtedly geography and winter weather in Canada create huge barriers to participating in continuing education, efforts must be directed to address these in some more equitable way. Will the increase of mandatory education requirements inspire and motivate members of the profession to maintain their credibility and competence? Where does motivation come from and what barriers diminish its realization?

MOTIVATION FOR CONTINUING EDUCATION

Doubt has been raised about the efficacy of mandatory continuing education as a guarantor of competency. Edward & Green (1983) state that, in the United States, the mandatory status was instituted as a response to the concerns raised by consumer groups, government agencies, state legislatures and, to some extent, the professions themselves. In the past, once a social worker had graduated or was licensed, competence was assured evermore and competency was increased by doing the work. Whether or not that was ever really so, the explosion of knowledge and changing societal structures has threatened to make those workers obsolete who do not keep their knowledge and skills up-to-date; and indeed, without strenuous effort, competence will actually wane. It is Edward & Green's contention that evidence of continuing education does not give evidence or a measure of competency, but is only a means of gaining competence.

The National Association of Social Workers (NASW) in the United States established a voluntary certification body, the Academy of Certified Social Workers (ACSW), and included a policy of mandatory recertification through continuing education. This policy was never implemented and was rescinded in 1981 because of the cost and complexity in implementation. Currently, NASW has standards for continuing professional education that expect social workers to complete 90 hours every three years, and to contribute to the development and improvement of continuing education. NASW also includes responsibilities for providers of such education, and for administrators. Responsibility for meeting these expectations is on the individual social workers and does not require accounting to the national body. All but seventeen of the states have continuing education as part of licensing requirements (American State Social Work Boards, 1996).

Taylor (1987) provides an in-depth review of the issue of mandatory continuing education for professionals and documents the various experiences and arguments both for and against it. She observes that a major drawback is that mandatory education in any form is not congruent with adult-education learning principles, that the quality of the learning is reduced when attendance is only to obtain credit. Arguments (Griffith, 1988) supporting the mandatory position include the protection of the public, the removal of those who are not interested in keeping up-to-date, the increase of professional exchange, the maintenance and improvement of public confidence, and educational activities being less threatening than examinations for relicensing. Arguments against having mandatory education include the problems with accessibility, affordability, consistency in criteria for credits and in quality, reciprocity across the country, and evaluation.

There are also concerns that people will avoid addressing the weaknesses and gaps in their practice skills unless these are identified by a regulatory body and education is prescribed as a remedy for reinstatement. A review of the literature on this matter shows no consensus about how to ensure and maintain competence and whether making such activities mandatory is more effective. However, in practice, the trend toward the adoption of mandatory requirements for social workers has taken hold in Canada. It would seem that participation in continuing education is perceived by the public-at-large as a measure of professional competence, as indeed generally is the completion of formal professional courses and examinations throughout the educational system on all levels. Research is needed to support this perception and to indicate ways in which competence can be enhanced by engagement in learning activities.

Professionals will be influenced by their own life and educational and work experiences, which may create or reinforce a commitment to lifelong learning. Schools and faculties are challenged to create a culture wherein students are imbued with valuing and implementing this commitment as a professional practitioner. The University of Victoria initiated a required core course on educational strategies in social work to teach graduating social workers how to assess their learning styles and needs, and to plan continuing education after graduation (Browning, 27).

A study in Israel (Laufer & Sharon, 1987) found that social workers who are most satisfied with their jobs tend to participate more in continuing education and that continuing education is not an escape route for unsatisfied workers. Roat (1988) reviewed 14 studies dealing with the effects of continuing education on staff performance in human service organizations and reported that participants in continuing education perceived improvement in skills and knowledge, increased confidence and job satisfaction, and improved staff-agency performance.

STAGES IN CAREER AND DEVELOPMENT

The major shifts in the workplace are affecting social workers at different stages in their careers. It seems no one is immune to change or even job loss (Bridges, 1994). In some sectors, there has been a cessation of hiring new workers, a practice which severely challenges new graduates looking for work. At the same time, unless the service is being eliminated altogether, openings may arise albeit on a short-term or contract basis. These new graduates need to develop and expand their knowledge and skills to broaden the net of

possible realms of practice. Also, additional professional expertise can enrich their curricula vitae, so they should be focusing on areas that will enhance their marketability both
for the short- and the long-term.

On the other end of the career spectrum are those in the latter years anticipating retirement or eligibility for severance packages. Unless they have had access to additional financial means or have decided to make a profound career shift away from the field of social work,
most practitioners have planned retirement for their sixties, depending on the retirement
policies of their organizations. In fact, there have been instances of appeals of mandatory
retirement age policies by those who wished to prolong active work. Nowadays in many
of the large institutional settings, workers are faced with the uncertainty of whether their positions will exist or what the work will consist of, or deciding about a "package" if they are fortunate to be eligible for such compensation. For them, the needs for continuing education will
depend on how they foresee their professional activities in the short term.

Then there is the group of those who are midway in their professional lives, who may or
may not have confronted the changes of recent years. With many years of employment still
ahead, a considerable attitude adjustment has been needed. They entered the workforce
when there was still choice and mobility and probably have specialized in a particular field
of service. They may be in middle management positions, more frequently now the target of
elimination, or their responsibilities may have shifted with administrative promotion out
of the social work milieu. Access to continuing education geared to information and skill
development in newly emerging employment opportunities is critical.

For all these groups, continuing education offers the possibility to develop and hone
their knowledge and experience accumulated and refined over many years of service. It is
wise for the profession not to lose these hard-won human resources and it must strive creatively to assure the continuing contribution of practitioners, in part by offering opportunities to assist them in redirecting and redesigning their professional practice.

Another factor that relates to the vagaries of present times is described by Karpiak
(1992), who refers to crisis events and moments of turbulence in people's lives as "teachable moments." She suggests that social workers should not be viewed as static and homo-
geneous and that there are important differences in the ages and developmental stages of the
newly graduated group of workers and those of the mid-life and pre-retirement group. The
content and focus of learning contains inherent distinctions. New graduates need to test
their competence by doing the work. The "teachable moment" for them is when things do
not work and this jumpstarts the first phase of continuing education, the technical, skills-
building, "how-to" of practice. Sources of knowledge are the agency manuals, understanding procedures, in-service training, and how-to questions to supervisors and colleagues.
The next phase is primarily rational, conceptual, and conscious, coming from the desire to
be aware of what one is doing or not doing. Formal courses, conferences, reading, and
collegial exchange respond to this quest. Not unexpectedly the third "teachable moment"
arrives during the early mid-life period when deeper questions emerge concerning the
meaning of the work. Competence may not be the issue but a feeling that something is
missing. Personal life crisis may precipitate this stage or a crisis in the workplace affecting
job prospects. There is less concern with acquiring new knowledge and skills and more
searching for improving the quality of life, a major shift in the direction of learning. The
fourth "teachable moment" is likely precipitated by a crisis of a personal or professional
nature. The goal at this time is based on concern for wider societal well-being and may
be directed through social responsibility and social action. Continuing education needs to

respond to both the "expanding" phase of the novice and the "contracting" phase of the seasoned worker.

How can these two streams, the upheaval in the workplace and the inherent developmental process, be reconciled within continuing education programs? Maybe they cannot, but a broad range of responses to these divergent needs should be recognized.

DELIVERY OF PROGRAMS

For social work, "partnerships" have always been there in some form. Cultivation of more intentional collaboration will enhance the networking that is part of the intrinsic connectedness avowed by the profession. More active links among individuals, agencies, professional associations, and the established seats of learning, the faculties and schools of social work, will thereby be strengthened. Some graduates never return to the university for learning. Others connect again as they engage in field education responsibilities and a learning component is usually a part of this experience. Another advantage of such partnerships with the schools is the renewing of the links between the educational process and current practice, illustrating the integrative nature of continuing education.

Continuing education programs may be mounted by the faculty or school alone, but a fruitful collaboration can be cultivated with professional associations; this ensures members' access to relevant educational events to meet ongoing demands for specialization and maintaining competence, as well as to fulfill their continuing education requirements. Drover (1989) anticipated that because degree programs are subject to increasing pressures to emphasize research and knowledge construction, continuing education could provide a way to accommodate demands for practice specialization. One operational model might involve the associations as administrators and certifiers, the universities as educators, and the employers as supporters. Even with the decline in agency funding for education, this possibility should not be discarded.

The Post-Graduate Certificate Course in Discharge Planning for Social Workers was developed in 1990 in Newfoundland through seed money from the National Consultation Project. This successful program has been presented in British Columbia, Manitoba, Ontario, Quebec, Nova Scotia, and Newfoundland, and continues as an active continuing education program. An Instructor's Training Handbook was later produced so that trainers could be trained to provide the course in their local areas. Another example from the same project, *The Practice of Field Instruction in Social Work: A Teaching Guide*, prepared in 1990 by M. Bogo and E. Vayda, continues as a resource in field education.

Co-sponsorship on an inter-agency basis can provide joint events, maximizing limited staff development resources. Again, for settings with common interests and mandates, these may afford opportunities for staff members to collaborate and network as a secondary benefit to the training component. With increasing caseloads, such activities have been seriously curtailed but are an essential link in service delivery.

Doctoral studies are at the top end of the continuum in formal social work education. Are these perceived as continuing education endeavours? At least one professional association, Newfoundland and Labrador, includes this in the criteria for continuing education credit; others do not. It is specifically excluded in the NASW (U.S.) standards. The interpretation will depend on the philosophy of the faculty offering the program and the goals and motivation of the post-graduate students themselves. For some, it is an essential shift from practice in the field to an academic career involving research and teaching and, therefore, not categorized as a continuing education activity. For others, probably fewer in number, it is a time-limited stepping-out to examine critically an aspect of practice and to develop a theoretical perspective which can be added to the published literature and enhance their own expertise. This would then be discerned as part of ongoing professional development.

RESOURCES FOR FRANCOPHONES

Special issues arise for Francophone members of the profession concerning the resources in French for their continuing education. Again the terminology needs to be clarified, both for its meaning in university-based programs and in distance learning programs. For some, there are programs providing credit toward a social work degree; for others, for credit or non-credit following graduation. For example, Laurentian University in Sudbury, Ontario, offers both on-site and distance education in French at the BSW level. The distance education program is currently available in printed form, and work toward including an Internet delivery mode is being planned. The challenge is how to serve a limited number of students balancing the on-site and distance programs.

While distance from educational institutions is a problem for all social workers in Canada outside the urban areas, and especially so in more remote geographical locations, for Francophones, barriers to access to learning opportunities in French exist even in some cities with large concentrations of Francophones. In Ottawa, with a population of 200,000 Francophones, there is no social work undergraduate degree program in French and it is only in recent years that there has been a graduate degree available. Outside of Quebec, Ontario, and New Brunswick there are only three universities offering degree programs in French for Bachelor of Arts, located in Nova Scotia, Manitoba, and Alberta. Therefore, there are barriers for these graduates to access a French social work degree program and for the recruitment of potential students for the profession. Indeed the University of Laval may be the only university in the world offering a doctorate in social work in French. While there are a few schools offering undergraduate social work studies in French, outside of Quebec and Ontario (at the University of Ottawa), only the University of Moncton provides this in a totally Francophone milieu.

Outside of Quebec and New Brunswick, Francophone social workers are located in clusters and are widely dispersed. With the paucity of degree programs in French and the lack of accessibility in most provinces, the viability of distance learning is timely. Laurentian University offers the BSW program in French through this medium and there may be similar arrangements in other provinces to capitalize on this methodology. Certainly, for provincial associations and other providers of continuing education, the potential for distance learning is propitious, and access to programs in French is vital for Francophone members.

RESOURCES FOR FIRST NATIONS SOCIAL WORKERS

Another whole field has been developing for First Nations social workers. In Ontario, the Laurentian University program at the BSW level is offered both on-site and through distance learning. Other programs are provided in Canada, for example, in Saskatchewan and British Columbia. It is important for providers of continuing education to consult with First Nations social workers regarding the inclusion of their needs as programs are developed. Content on practice with First Nations peoples should also be integrated into ongoing educational schedules.

THE GROWTH OF DISTANCE EDUCATION

Distance learning is not a new invention (MacFadden, 1996). Correspondence courses have existed for over 75 years in North America. Educational radio programs, for credit and non-credit, have been part of the alternative programs for decades. At its most basic level, distance education takes place when a teacher and students are separated by physical distance, and technology (i.e., voice, video, data, and print), often in concert with face-to-face communication, is used to bridge the instructional gap. These types of programs can provide adults with a second chance at a college/university education; can reach those disadvantaged by limited time, distance, or physical disability; and can update the knowledge base of workers at their places of employment.

Research comparing distance education to traditional face-to-face instruction indicates that teaching and studying at a distance can be as effective as traditional instruction when the method and technologies used are appropriate to the instructional tasks, when there is student-to-student interaction, and when there is timely teacher-to-student feedback. Expertise is being developed in this area and feasibility for continuing education is being explored and evaluated (Faria, 2000). In her study, Herie (2000) asked health care and counselling practitioners (including social workers) in Ontario about their participation in education and training activities, preferences with respect to educational format, and attitudes towards computers and online learning. She concluded that Web-based instruction (WBI) can be regarded as an extension of the independent study in which practitioners are already engaged. Her findings that individuals find it difficult to access continuing professional education for a variety of reasons related to travel, work, and home constraints supports the research that online learning is well-positioned to provide an alternative education and training modality. It is not surprising that Herie found that as the Internet grows, institutions of higher learning have also expanded online distance education offerings.

Many schools of social work across Canada provide online information about their programs, including undergraduate, graduate, and continuing education. In addition, some offer online courses as well. At the University of Victoria, the Distance BSW Program is offered in all regions of the province of British Columbia as well as in Alberta, the Yukon and the North West Territories. The Maritime University School of Social Work offers its MSW Program through the Internet and teleconferencing.

Through the "World Lecture Hall" in the United States, courses related to social work are available, and the "World Wide Web Resources for Social Work" in New York presents a wide range of information for social workers. The National Association of Social Workers is offering a World Wide Web-based continuing education curriculum on ethics and HIV in March 2001.

For Francophones, Le réseau d'enseignement francophone à distance du Canada (REFAD), can be used to access educational and training resources in French.

As mentioned in the previous section, First Nations degree programs at the BSW level are provided through distance education, for example, from Laurentian University in Sudbury, Ontario.

CONCLUSION

Everyone agrees that there has to be ongoing educational activity as a means to ensure and maintain professional competency. The debate is how best to achieve this goal. The standards of the profession make it clear that it is the responsibility of each social worker to develop and maintain competency. While national guidelines have been accepted, the various jurisdictions have developed their own benchmarks to measure competency and the means of maintaining this as locally appropriate. As conventional service delivery is transformed from the welfare state paradigm, the profession is charged with challenging its members to confront the emerging demands as an invitation to engage in new learning and practice, and to be imaginative, inventive, and resourceful, not only to stimulate professional growth, but also to create and implement continuing educational opportunities for fellow professionals. Mandatory requirements are only part of the process; a culture of lifelong learning needs to be instilled and fostered as part of the professional equipment. The expectation for continuing education has always been there, but with increasing regulation and changing trends in practice, it has become more explicit.

Clearly, the roles of professional associations are: to be the lead players in collaborative ventures with others, be they university or agency, allied professionals or governments; to maximize the potential of technology for providing access and availability for all members in all areas of the country; to advocate for the removal of barriers including those related to language, ability, financial need, and geography; and to facilitate the realization of ongoing social work practice competence.

REFERENCES

American State Social Work Boards. (1996). Social work laws and board regulations.

Bridges, W. (1980). *Transitions: making sense of life's changes*. Reading, Massachusetts: Addison-Wesley Publishing Company.

Bridges, W. (1994). *Jobshift: how to prosper in a workplace without jobs*. Reading, Massachusetts: Addison-Wesley Publishing Company.

Browning, R. (1988). *National Consultation Workshop on Continuing Education in Social Work: Summary Report*.

Canadian Association of Occupational Therapists. (1992). *Continuing Education Committee*.

Canadian Association of Social Workers. (January 1994). *Social Work Code of Ethics*.

Canadian Association of Social Workers. (March 1994). *Policy Statement on Continuing Education*.

Canadian Nurses Association. (1992). *Position statement, continuing nursing education*.

Carrière, R. (1996). Francophone issues in distance education. Presentation to Professional Development Training Day. Ontario Association of Social Workers.

Carrière, R. (2001). Personal communication.

Couillard, R. (1995). Adult education: a practical definition. *Education Quarterly Review 2*(1) 47–57.

Drover, G. (1989). Continuing education and voluntary certification: notes on identity. Speech to Consultation Workshop of CASW/CASSW. Continuing Education for Social Workers Project.

Edward, R.L. and Green, R.K. (1983). Mandatory continuing education: time for reevaluation. *Social Work 28*(1), 43–48.

Egan, G. (1988). *Change-Agent Skills B: managing innovation & change*. University Associates: San Diego, CA.

Faria, G. (2000) Distance Education: 21st Century Madness or Miracle? Paper presented at Joint Conference of the International Federation of Social Workers and International Association of Schools of Social Work, Montreal, July 30, 2000.

Griffith, W. (1987). *Comments on the review of literature pertaining to adult education.* Continuing Professional Education for Social Workers Project.

Herie, M. (2000) 1999–2000 Internet Education and Training Feasibility Study. Toronto: Centre for Addiction and Mental Health.

Hudson, A. (1996). Presentation. *Journal of Ontario Association of Children's Aid Societies, 40*(2), 21.

Karpiak, I.E. (1992). Beyond competence: continuing education and the evolving self. *The Social Worker 60*(1), 53–57.

Laufer, Z. and Sharon, N. (1987). Social work job satisfaction and participation in continuing education; implication for administrators of social services. Journal abstract. *Journal of Continuing Social Work Education 3*(3), 3–7.

Lenin R. and Rasmussen, P. (1991). Is independent practice a legitimate form of social work? *The Social Worker 59*(4), 149–153.

Lowenthal, W. (1981). Continuing education for professionals. *Journal of Higher Education 52*(5), 519–538. As quoted by Taylor, L.

MacFadden, R. (1996). Distance education. Presentation to Professional Development Training Day, Ontario Association of Social Workers, from Distance Education at a Glance, Guide #1. Engineering Outreach, College of Engineering, University of Idaho.

MacKenzie Davies, J. (1996). [Editorial]. *Newsmagazine,* Ontario Association of Social Workers, *23* (3), 5.

National Association of Social Workers (US). (1992). *NASW standards for continuing education.*

Ontario Premier's Council on Economic Renewal. (1994). *Lifelong learning and the new economy.* Queen's Printer for Ontario.

Ontario Premier's Council on Economic Renewal. (1994). *Summary report. Lifelong learning and the new economy.* Queen's Printer for Ontario.

Roat, J. (1988). The effects of continuing education on staff performance. Journal abstract. *Journal of Continuing Social Work Education 4*(4), 26–30.

Roberge, P. (1987). Speech. National Consultation Workshop on Continuing Education in Social Work. Themes for learning in social work. November.

Taylor, L. (1987). Continuing education in social work: literature review. CASW/ CASSW. Continuing Education in Canadian Social Workers Project.

Unesco. (1976). International standard classification of education. Paris. Unesco/Office of Statistics. As quoted by Couillard.

Walmsley, C. (June 1992). *Provincial social work association survey.* CASW National Consultation on Continuing Professional Education.

Walmsley, C. (September 1992). *Report of the CASW National Consultation on Continuing Professional Education.*

THE PRACTITIONER

AS RESEARCHER Grant Macdonald

The current Canadian fiscal climate of economic retrenchment and social service cutbacks has increased the pressure on the social work service sector to demonstrate that public resources and professional services are allocated responsibly and that these activities lead to desired client outcomes. Public and private funders of Canadian social programs are making it increasingly clear that continued fiscal support is contingent on these programs and services providing evidence that they are effective in what they purport to do. From a social work perspective, the demand for public accountability is not only a current practice reality, it is also central to the notion of ethical social work practice. Ethical practitioners must commit themselves to evaluating the programs and services in which they participate and ensure that they are indeed helping and not hurting the clients they serve.

As a profession, social work can no longer rely simply on personal values, beliefs, and subjective claims of effectiveness for its credibility. The current reality in Canada demands that social work, like other professions, must rest its credibility on demonstrative evidence of effectiveness. Social workers must pay as much attention to results and outcomes as they do to process.

This dual emphasis on process and outcome offers some interesting challenges for someone just entering the profession. Many beginning social work students have negative feelings about research and the role that science might play in their work. Some have trouble seeing how their clients might benefit from research and sometimes are apprehensive or even doubt their own abilities to do research. Students often think research is dry, mechanistic, and mathematical. These are certainly not the qualities that attracted them to social work in the first place. It is hoped that this chapter will challenge these ideas and demonstrate that research has a critical role to play in Canadian social work practice.

Many social work students find that certain types of interventions they learn about seem to fit better with their ideas, personal styles, and beliefs than others. Similarly, they may find that of the wide range of research methods available to them, some seem to fit better with their own interests, beliefs, and research questions. In short, just as there are many ways one can practise social work, there are many ways of conducting research to generate practice knowledge. Each method has its own supporters, values, strengths, and limitations. Each method has a part to play in social work.

Before examining the dominant research paradigms—qualitative and quantitative approaches—it is helpful to define what we mean by social work research and look at the general kinds of questions it helps us answer. *Social work research* can be defined broadly as the systematic procedures employed for the purpose of developing knowledge that informs and guides social work practice. What makes social work research different from other social scientific research is that it is conducted with specific ends in mind. It arises out of practice concerns of social workers and its outcome is designed to inform and guide the policy and planning or direct practice decisions of social workers. It is not research carried out simply to advance knowledge for knowledge's sake. Unlike "pure" research, if there is such a thing, social work research always has an applied component to it.

The questions social work research addresses arise from the people, problems, and interventions involved in social work practice. The type of questions addressed by research have been broadly categorized under three types (Schuerman, 1983).

1. What is the nature of the individuals, couples, families, groups, organizations, and communities with whom practitioners work? This research might include studies on such things as family and marital dynamics, specific ethnic or racial groups, organizational behaviour, or human growth and development.

2. What is the nature of the problems that confront practitioners in their practices? What are the dynamics of a problem, how does it develop, what kinds of things alleviate the problem and what things make it worse? How do global and economic influences impact on the problems?

3. Does social work intervention work? Are our efforts effective? How can they be improved? What interventions work with what type of person(s), in what types of circumstances, producing what types of outcome? What are the social impacts of new policies or legislation?

These three broad categories of questions help address issues that are central to social work practice. Researchers call these issues "research problems" and write about how they can be "formulated" or translated into research questions that can be answered. A research problem is simply a description (not a question) about what we would like to know about people, problems, and/or interventions central to our practice. Questions arising out of these problems are as diverse as the settings where social work is being done. What are the seriousness and extent of the social problems in the community? Are the services delivered by practitioners needed and used? Are the services and programs serving the intended clientele? Who needs services but is not accessing them and why? Are there important issues of accessibility that need to be addressed that may be based on race, gender, disability, age, ethnicity, sexual orientation, or socio-economic background? How well are social workers being trained or supervised? How do social workers use their time? Do they have problematic attitudes toward certain groups or sub-groups of clients? Are certain social policies detrimental to social welfare? How well are agencies being administered? Are programs being run efficiently? Do our interventions work? What are the issues related to accountability and how can we demonstrate to increasingly skeptical public and private funders that our services and programs are worth the cost? In short, social work research addresses virtually all of the issues that are important to social work practice.

The answers to these kinds of questions are of interest to a variety of groups within the community. Each group has its own stake or interest in the problems, services, or interventions being examined. Some of the "stakeholders" include social workers, clients, or potential clients, the general public, the media, policy-makers and planners, governments at all levels, and actual and potential funders. Each of these "stakeholders" have their own reasons for wanting to know about the social problems in their communities and how they are dealt with.

THE PRACTITIONER AS SCIENTIST

The title of this chapter, *The Practitioner as Researcher*, implies that social workers have a particular obligation, role, or responsibility related to research. The implication of the title is that social workers should somehow combine their role as practitioners with the role of scientist. Those who think of the terms *science* and *research* as words that emerge from the physical and biological world, might question what possible role science could play in their practice. The world of people is very different from the objects and processes that are studied by classical scientists. Human behaviour cannot be determined with certainty, and social work researchers can never hope to discover laws as a few fortunate classical scientists have. If social workers are to argue for the involvement of science in social work practice, they need to adopt a broad definition of the term *science*. Therefore, for the purposes of this chapter, science is viewed as a range of methods of inquiry that help us learn and understand the social world around us.

Before examining what these methods are, as they pertain to social work, it might be helpful to ask why social workers should concern themselves with research in the first place. More particularly, we might ask why social workers should conduct research themselves and not leave this role up to research specialists.

In most parts of Canada, the profession of social work is under attack as downsizing and cutbacks have ripped holes in Canada's social safety net. The profession is being asked to define what it does and to account for the public trust that has been placed in it. Governments and funders want to be assured that scarce resources are being allocated in ways that maximize the benefit to social welfare. Administrators of social services need to demonstrate not only that they are getting results, but that these results are being achieved at a low or at least reasonable cost. There was a time in the history of social work when administrators were simply asked to account for the work the programs did. How many clients were seen? What sorts or services and programs were being delivered? This has been gradually replaced by demands for proof that services and interventions are in fact effective, and that programs are achieving their stated objectives. More recently, the profession is being asked more difficult questions. Are our services and programs both effective and efficient? Are we achieving our desired outcomes at the lowest possible cost?

Part of this drive for demonstrated efficiency has, in many sectors, led to an analysis of what social workers actually do. What skills do they employ in their work? Do they have any unique competencies that others do not have? What types of professional activities should be done by MSW graduates and what activities can be done at lower cost by BSW graduates? Some question whether social workers have a unique set of skills. Can social service graduates, nurses, nursing assistants, volunteers, or others perform social work functions as effectively and perhaps with greater efficiency?

The future of social work as a profession rests on our ability to respond critically to the demands for accountability currently placed upon it. We need to participate in this movement toward accountable practice and help define ourselves and our roles or we will find that others will define them for us. The answer to these questions requires research, and social workers need to place themselves at the centre of this process. We have a unique perspective that gives us knowledge, experience, and insight into the problems faced by clients, service providers, and the social service delivery system in general, as well as an understanding of the structural influences that help generate and sustain these problems. We need to use this perspective to help define the problems that need to be addressed and shape the questions that are asked. We need to take control of our own research agenda. This does not necessarily mean that we must always do the research ourselves, but we should strive to always participate in the formulation of research questions that are relevant and important to our clients, our profession, and the broader social system.

APPROACHES TO SOCIAL WORK INQUIRY

It is beyond the scope of this chapter to discuss the full range of methods or techniques a practitioner might employ to generate social work knowledge. Those readers interested in exploring some of these methods in detail may want to read a textbook entitled *Research Methods for Social Work*, by Rubin and Babbie (2000).

For the purposes of this chapter, it will be helpful to explore the two dominant paradigms in social work inquiry—quantitative and qualitative approaches to knowledge-building. The term *paradigm*, made famous by Thomas Kuhn (1960), refers to an orientation or underlying perspective a person may have which organizes how one views the world, a problem or issue, or a research question. In a sense, Kuhn suggests that we view the world through our own particular conceptual "lenses"—lenses that are shaped and tinted by our own experiences, training, assumptions, and beliefs. Where we focus our attention and what we see is influenced by the lenses we wear. Where we look for answers influences to a great degree what we find.

In the social sciences, the two dominant research paradigms centre around *quantitative* and *qualitative* modes of inquiry. There has been much debate in the literature about the relative merits of each approach. Much of this debate in the past has been destructive, as each side critiqued and discredited the methods of the other. More recently, the debate has worn itself into a discussion about the qualities of each approach, and some now even argue that the best approaches should combine both methods. Tutty, Rothery, and Grinnell (1996), for example, assert that "both quantitative and qualitative research approaches contribute to our knowledge base, in different but competing ways. They are like two good wines, one red, the other white (white wine may go better with fish and red wine with lamb, for example)" (8). As we shall see, each mode of inquiry makes important but different kinds of contributions to the knowledge-base of social work, and social workers have an obligation to be familiar with and respectful of both. At the same time, just as one may prefer one type of wine over another, many social workers feel an attraction to one or other of the dominant research approaches. An individual's personal style, education, background, or beliefs may make him or her favour one approach over the other.

Quantitative methods include the more traditional methods of inquiry whose foundations lie in careful empirical observation. These methods are rooted in logical positivism, a philosophy of science that maintains that the scientific method of inquiry is the source of all true or certain knowledge. These approaches to knowledge-building in social work employ hypothesis testing and seek to examine the relationships between variables and to discover facts that are generalizable. Since much of the data analysis in this type of research requires the statistical manipulation of numbers, these approaches are commonly labelled quantitative methods. These methods are particularly useful when we want to determine whether or not a cause produces an effect. In social work, when we want to establish with a high degree of certainty that a particular social work intervention is effective in achieving a desired treatment outcome, a quantitative method is normally employed.

In contrast, *qualitative* research methods address the meaning of human experience and seek to generate an understanding of these experiences. As an approach to social work inquiry, its most important distinguishing feature from quantitative research is its commitment to the emic perspective (Morse, 1992). By emic perspective, we mean that the researcher seeks to discover the subject or participant's perspective on their experience, rather than the perspective of the researcher. Research of this kind involves the exploration of the participant's values and beliefs, and great effort is made in the design not to impose the researcher's beliefs and biases on the data (Morse, 1992).

A qualitative study that illustrates this effort was conducted by McKeever (1992) on mothering of chronically-ill children who are technology-dependent. These children were cared for by their mothers in their own homes and were dependent on some type of technological device to keep them alive. The researcher was interested in exploring and understanding the subjective personal experiences of the mothers and the nature of their relationships with significant others. Part of the method this researcher employed was to obtain unstructured narrative accounts from 25 of these caregiving mothers by way of a single in-depth interview. Each mother was asked one question and lengthy responses were typed, transcribed, and analyzed for themes. The single question was "what has your life been like since (child's name) was born/diagnosed/injured?" (107). This single question permitted the participant mothers to individually express their own thoughts and feelings about their lives and share with the researcher the things that had meaning to them.

Table 46.1 summarizes some of the important differences between the two dominant modes of inquiry. A reader who looks at the contents of the two columns in the table may find that one or other of the approaches seems to fit better with his or her own personality or beliefs. For example, those readers who think of themselves as imaginative, flexible, adventurous, egalitarian, and comfortable with intense interactions with others, may find themselves more attracted to qualitative approaches. Those who like structure, having a plan, knowing where they are going and how to get there, and who are comfortable with mathematical concepts, may find themselves more attracted to quantitative approaches.

Regardless of our preferences, choice of method largely rests with the questions to which we seek answers. When we are interested in examining a new phenomenon that has not been extensively researched, we likely would want to choose a qualitative design, which stresses in-depth analyses and discovery, and which is flexible enough to lead to a better understanding of the phenomenon. We might also want to select a qualitative design if we were interested in studying a highly complex phenomenon with the expectation that we might develop or refine concepts which might lead to the development of theory that could later be tested by further research.

In contrast, if we know a fair amount about a subject or problem, there is less need for discovery and an increased need for a carefully designed study that can describe the prob-

TABLE 46.1   Characteristics of Quantitative and Qualitative Modes of Social Work Inquiry

Quantitative	Qualitative
Primary Objectives of the Approach • testing theory or testing hypotheses • discovering generalizable facts • predicting • describing relationships among variables	**Primary Objectives of the Approach** • developing theory or refining concepts • developing an understanding • explaining • formulating or generating
Words Associated with the Approach • experimental • positivism • statistical • survey • variable • reliability and validity • hypotheses	**Words Associated with the Approach** • ethnography • naturalistic • descriptive/thematic • case study • meaning • understanding • exploration
Features of Research Designs • structured • predetermined • formal • specific • detailed plan	**Features of Research Designs** • evolving • flexible • informal • general • discovery
Research Proposals • extensive • detailed and specific method • hypotheses and/or research questions	**Research Proposals** • comparatively short • general statement of approach • broad areas of possible exploration specified
Forms of Data • quantitative and numerical • questionnaires, self-reports, scales, tests, inventories, and indexes	**Forms of Data** • descriptive and text-based • field notes, photographs, documents, tape-recordings, videotape
Sample • large—many subjects • representative • control groups and random selecting of subjects when feasible	**Sample** • small—few participants • non-representative • no control group
Common Techniques Employed • experiments • quasi-experimental designs • surveys • structured interviews	**Common Techniques Employed** • observation • document analyses • participant observation • open-ended interviews
Relationship of Researchers with Subjects • detached • short-term • subject–researcher	**Relationship of Researchers with Subjects** • intense, long-term • egalitarian
Instruments and Tools • questionnaires • indexes, scales, and test scores • computer programs (e.g., SPSS or SAS)	**Instruments and Tools** • tape recorder • transcriber • computer programs (e.g., Ethnograph or NUD*IST)
Data Analysis • occurs when all data collected • statistical data analysis • deductive	**Data Analysis** • ongoing • search for themes and concepts • inductive

Sources: Bogdan & Biklen (1982), Creswell (1994), and Neuman (2000).

lem accurately. A quantitative method, such as a survey, might be selected if, for example, we wanted to describe how a group of people think, what problems they have or what they report doing. We might select an experimental or quasi-experimental design, also quantitative approaches, if we want to establish whether or not a particular form of treatment is effective in helping individuals suffering from a specific problem. In this type of study, a researcher typically divides subjects into two or more groups. An attempt is made to treat the groups identically, except that one group receives the social work intervention. The researcher selects measures that assess the possible impact of treatment on the individuals. With these types of designs, the researcher hopes to conclude that differences observed between the groups are a result of the treatment. The better the controls for this type of treatment, the more confident the researcher can be in his or her conclusions about the effectiveness of treatment.

At the heart of the differences between the two modes of inquiry is the system of logic they employ. Quantitative methods, which have emerged out of traditional approaches to science, employ deductive logic. This method of logic, described by Creswell (1994), begins when the researcher wants to test a theory by way of a hypothesis or research question that was derived from the theory. The researcher then operationalizes the concepts or variables and uses specific measures or instruments as indicators of them. Finally, the hypotheses or questions are resolved through the quantitative analysis of empirical data. Deductive logic begins with an abstract theoretical notion and moves towards "hard" empirical evidence. Many students remember that deductive reasoning moves from the general to the particular.

In contrast, the system of logic that drives qualitative research is inductive reasoning, a way of reasoning which moves from the particular to the general. In this approach, the researcher pours over a large amount of data obtained from a comparatively small number of individuals or events. The data are meticulously examined, analyzed and interpreted, for relationships, patterns, similarities, and differences. Eventually the patterns may evolve into propositions and hopefully into theory (Creswell, 1994). Thus, inductive reasoning moves from specific detailed observations of a phenomenon toward more abstract generalizations and the development of theory.

ESTABLISHING EFFECTIVENESS IN SOCIAL WORK PRACTICE

While research contributes to social work knowledge in a number of different ways, perhaps the most important contribution it can make is establishing the effectiveness of social work interventions. Both qualitative and quantitative approaches can contribute to our evolving knowledge around questions of effectiveness. When it comes to claims of effectiveness of a new intervention, there are a number of levels of certainty from claim to proof (Curtis, 1996). These levels are illustrated in Table 46.2.

At the early stages, new treatments or therapies are evaluated by way of single case reports or anecdotal observations. A researcher typically describes the cases where the new therapeutic approach is being tried and discusses the apparent benefits that result. These types of case studies, common in the social work literature, often involve only a few cases and typically rely on fairly subjective and anecdotal observations. While producing only "tentative" evidence of effectiveness (see Table 46.2), these studies and reports are important because they expose treatment ideas to others and invite further research to help establish stronger evidence of effectiveness.

The next level of research typically involves more subjects and greater care is taken in describing the subjects and measuring the changes. These types of studies are helpful in estab-

TABLE 46.2 Evaluating Research Claims of Effective Treatment		
Tentative Evidence of Effectiveness		
Subjects/Sample • typically about 1–10 subjects	Intervention(s) • single intervention	Outcome Measures • anecdotal • self-reports • reports of others
Common Criticisms • subjects not typical • subjects treated previously • subject knows researcher	Common Criticisms • lots of other things happening that could influence outcome	Common Criticisms • largely subjective • limited reliability and validity of measures
Promising Evidence of Effectiveness		
Subjects/Sample • typically about 10–50 subjects (sometimes in the 100s)	Intervention(s) • single intervention	Outcome Measures • largely objective measures —but subjective findings and observations often included • often no before-treatment measures
Common Criticisms • subject treated previously • treatment begins at time of crisis. Natural improvement often occurs without treatment	Common Criticisms • other helping efforts underway • does treatment cause the result or does something else?	Common Criticisms • other factors might account for the improvement observed
Strong Evidence of Effectiveness		
Subjects/Sample • typically 30+ subjects in two or more groups	Intervention(s) • new treatment compared with no treatment control or a traditional treatment method	Outcome Measures • largely objective, reliable, and valid measures • standardized rating scales —before and after measurement
Common Criticisms • sample limited in many ways • not enough subjects	Common Criticisms • two groups not really comparable	Common Criticisms • measures not sensitive enough to detect differences • other important measures not assessed in study

lishing that treated individuals do indeed improve or change in a desired way. The major shortfall is that one cannot say with certainty that the changes observed and measured are a result of treatment. Most clients seek help at a time of personal crisis. Natural improvement may well occur, even if no treatment is sought. These types of studies do not have comparison or control groups and therefore do not eliminate other possible explanations for the improvements observed in the clients. Although these types of studies do have their limitations, they can produce what has been described as "promising" evidence of effectiveness (Curtis, 1996).

Strong evidence of effectiveness of treatment can be obtained from research designs where comparison or control groups are used, and the researcher tries to limit the possibility that other factors are responsible for the changes observed and measured. The designs that are generally considered to have the greatest credibility are ones in which there is random assignment to a treatment group and to a non-treatment control. Random assignment is one way of assuring that equally difficult cases are found in each group. If the treatment group fairs much better than the control group, and maximum effort has been made to limit the possibility of confounding influences, then strong evidence of effectiveness can be demonstrated.

For practice interventions to reach the level of "established" effectiveness, controlled studies need to be replicated or repeated with the same or slightly different conditions. The question of effectiveness does not end here. Further studies need to be conducted to determine whether the results are also positive for different groups of clients, based perhaps on race, ethnicity, gender, or other client characteristics.

CONCLUSION

The social work profession in Canada is increasingly being challenged to demonstrate that it is accountable for the services it provides and that these efforts are worth the cost. Cutbacks in the social service sector have left many social workers struggling to find new, creative methods to protect the disadvantaged and those in need. The Canadian *Social Work Code of Ethics* (CASW, 1994) states that the best interests of the client require "that all actions and interventions of the social worker are taken subject to the reasonable belief that the client will benefit from the action" (4). The current fiscal reality, combined with our ethical obligation to carry out our work for the benefit of our clients, forces social workers across the country to try new and innovative ways of helping and to evaluate the results of these efforts. This chapter has reviewed some of the ways social workers might employ research methods to address the enormous problems and challenges of Canadian social work practice.

REFERENCES

Bogdan, R.C. and Biklen, S.K. (1982). *Qualitative research for education: an introduction to theory and methods.* Toronto, ON: Allyn and Bacon.

CASW (Canadian Association of Social Workers) (1994), *Social work code of ethics*, Ottawa.

Creswell, J.W. (1994). *Research designs: qualitative and quantitative approaches.* Thousand Oaks: Sage Publications.

Curtis, G.C. (1996). The scientific evaluation of new claims. *Research on Social Work Practice, 6,* 117–121.

Kuhn, T.S. (1962). *The structure of scientific revolutions.* Chicago, IL: University of Chicago Press.

McKeever, P. (1992). *Mothering chronically-ill technology-dependent children: an analysis using critical theory.* Unpublished doctoral dissertation, York University, North York.

Morse, J.M. (Ed.). (1992). *Qualitative health research.* Newbury Park, CA: Sage Publications.

Neuman, W.L. (2000). *Social research methods: qualitative and quantitative approaches* (4th ed.). Toronto, ON: Allyn and Bacon.

Rubin, A. & Babbie, E., (2000). *Research methods for social workers.* Pacific Grove, CA.: Brooks/Cole Publishing Company.

Schuerman, J.R. (1983). *Research and evaluation in the human services.* New York, NY: The Free Press.

Tutty, L.M., Rothery, M.A., and Grinnell, R.M., Jr. (1996). *Qualitative research for social workers.* Toronto, ON: Allyn and Bacon.

EPILOGUE

Francis J. Turner

As stated in the preface, this work originally began from the premise that there is a cluster of values and practices that are sufficiently idiosyncratic to deserve the title of "*Canadian Social Work Practice.*" Such a conviction arose from a long acquaintance with colleagues in several countries and a growing awareness that as I looked at practice in these countries there was something unique about the way our profession is practised here in Canada. Indeed, I have found that when teaching or lecturing in other countries some of the concepts and suggestions from Canadian practice, which I presumed I shared with the audience, were viewed as different and indeed at times innovative.

The impetus to address this perception in a concrete fashion was further reinforced by feedback and suggestions from teaching colleagues in various regions of our country who reported an ongoing wish from their students for texts that were "more Canadian." This appeared to reflect a more profound desire than merely to have more Canadian case examples and vignettes and more "pictures from home" in those few social work books that have illustrations. Rather it seemed to reflect a sense on the part of both professors and students that, as excellent as many of the texts used in Canadian schools and faculties of social work may be, they were just not hitting the mark of where both the students and contemporary practice are in this country.

Thus the process out of which this book emerged began first with a query, and then with a conviction that certain observations were valid. But it also began with an awareness that these observations, or rather, this proposition, was untested and could well be only the fantasizing of an over-enthusiastic Canadian. Indeed, when the project was taking shape and being appraised by colleagues invited by the publishers to assess the idea, it was suggested by some that it was a project without merit, since "there was no such thing as a distinctive entity that could be called Canadian social work practice."

However, now that the work has withstood the test of a first edition, we remain convinced of its necessity for Canadian social work practice and are committed to a process of continuing review and improvement. As in the first edition, considerable effort was put into the new table of contents, based on my own reconceptualizing and assisted by the comments of reviewers and users of the first edition. As stated in the first edition, as a researcher I am well aware of the probable bias in the assembly of authors who are the participants. In selecting these authors, there was no effort on my part to work from a process that could be called random. Rather, we sought to build a group of highly experienced persons who represented the country and as well included a mixture of both practitioners and teachers. The selection process was essentially built on a networking strategy and hence may well reflect some particular groupings. If so, we live with this limitation!

As mentioned in the Preface, I remain aware of at least one glaring omission, one which is a keen disappointment to me. This volume as it now stands is essentially one written from an English language perspective and will probably only be published in English, and this in spite of the fact that we practise in a country that is officially bilingual, and in practice multilingual. It is my earnest hope that if this volume moves into further editions it will be possible to publish it in both of the country's official languages, a goal to which I have long aspired.

Now that we have reached the end of the process, several things are evident to me that indeed reinforce my early assumptions. Clearly, there is something that rightly can be called social work practice in Canada. But rather than being a clear-cut entity, as was predicted in the first chapter, it has a highly divergent profile, one that reflects our history, our openness to diversity, our highly varied and extreme geography, our unique political structure, and the multifaceted influences that shaped the mosaic-like emergence of our social safety net. A comparison of the table of contents of this volume to practice books from other countries reflects this diversity. Indeed we have been challenged by some who maintain that the work tries to do too much in covering such a broad spectrum of topics; in so doing, some allege it may be unsuitable for first-level students. Only the test of time will answer this concern.

In spite of some of these concerns, we make no apology for the wide range of topics addressed in these chapters. Indeed, we may well be challenged that other topics should also have been addressed, such as "practice in remote areas," or "social work's role in disaster situations." What has long been evident to me and to many of my colleagues is that one of the challenges for new social work graduates in Canada today is the high probability of finding themselves practising in small communities with few formal resources and hence expected to be competent in the entire scope of situations and skills addressed in these pages. Very early in their post-graduation practices new social workers here in Canada may well find themselves interviewing through the medium of an interpreter, being called to court as a witness, being involved in complex political issues, or interviewing clients hundreds of miles away through a radio or telephone hook-up, and all of this with a minimum of supervision or collegial consultation. Too often our teaching reflects the outlines of many of the texts we currently use. In so doing, professional practice is presented as taking place only in large metropolitan areas with rich networks of services, in settings where beginning practitioners are provided with ongoing in-service training and supervisions. Desirable as this might be, it is not what happens to many, indeed to most, of our new graduates. Hence it is critical that we build into our teaching both a readiness and respect for diversity, and a comprehension that it is an exciting resource that needs to be tapped and utilized rather than feared or criticized.

Understandably, one of the results of a project that seeks to spin such a rich purview of practice in Canada is that there is not full consensus among the various authors. Some emphasize different aspects of practice more than others. There remain vestiges of the macro-micro dichotomy, in which one end of the spectrum is viewed as being of more importance than another. There are still some ambiguities about terminology in regard to such concepts as treatment, counselling, intervention service, etc. Do these various usages mean the same thing? In either case, how does such terminological imprecision affect practice and policy? These are questions yet to be decided. Nevertheless, throughout there is a strong consensus about the critical need for responsible, accountable, and ethical practice, and hence a concomitant stress on the important role that supervision and consultation, professional associations, continuing education colleges, ethics committees, registration, certification, and licensing play in achieving these goals. In a similar way there is a pervasive commitment to the need for, and the responsibility to strengthen, an ongoing and active commitment to the process of evaluating our interventions through a never-ending program of research.

Although throughout there has been a focus on diversity as a part of the Canadian social work identity, as a closing note we need to emphasize that these must not be overstated. Yes, there are aspects of Canadian social work practice that are sufficiently unique to permit us to claim for it a unique identity. However, we are still talking about a process that has much about it that is universal. Social work is social work is social work the world 'round.

Hence there is much in these chapters that can and will be of use to colleagues in other countries. As has already been mentioned in this book, for decades we have relied on texts from other countries as our sources for teaching and reference. In spite of the Canadian tendency to diffidence, we are now learning that much of what is essential to our own format of practice can be of use in other parts of the world.

Thus it is hoped that, as useful as this text will be in meeting the needs of our students who are seeking more Canadian content, it will also serve a broader constituency. Hence I envisage that the work of my much-respected colleagues who participated in this project will be recognized, appreciated, and applied in parts of the world where snow plows are unknown, where there are more than three downs in football, and where freedom is a much desired luxury.

Index